Fodor's

New
SIXTH EDITION

Healthy Escapes

Fodor's Travel Publications, Inc.
New York • Toronto • London • Sydney • Auckland
www.fodors.com

Fodor's Healthy Escapes

EDITOR: Amy McConnell

Editorial Contributors: Bernard Burt, with Stephanie Adler, Jennifer Bartlett, Eve Becker, Miriam Carey, Paula Consolo, Heather Elton, Julie Fay, Alicia Fedorczak, Paula Flanders, Mary Gillespie, Marilyn Haddrill, Kimberly Harwell, Pamela Lechtman, Andrea Lehman, Irvina Lew, Sue Kernaghan, Daniel Mangin, Jane McConnell, Hilary Nangle, Anne Peracca, Helayne Schiff, Elizabeth Thompson, Kay Winzenried, Nancy Zimmerman
Design: Fabrizio La Rocca, *creative director*
Production/Manufacturing: Robert B. Shields
Cover Design: Tigist Getachew
Cover Photograph: Ken Scott/TSW

Original edition written by Bernard Burt.

Copyright

Sixth Edition

ISBN 0–679–00188–3

Special Sales

Fodor's Travel Publications are available at special discounts for bulk purchases for sales promotions or premiums. Special editions, including personalized covers, excerpts of existing guides, and corporate imprints, can be created in large quantities for special needs. For more information contact your local bookseller or write to Special Markets, Fodor's Travel Publications, 201 East 50th Street, New York, NY 10022. Inquiries from Canada should be directed to your local Canadian bookseller or sent to Random House of Canada, Ltd., Marketing Department, 2775 Matheson Boulevard East, Mississauga, Ontario L4W 4P7. Inquiries from the United Kingdom should be sent to Fodor's Travel Publications, 20 Vauxhall Bridge Road, London, England SW1V 2SA.

PRINTED IN THE UNITED STATES OF AMERICA

10 9 8 7 6 5 4 3 2 1

CONTENTS

HOW TO USE THIS BOOK

FODOR'S HEALTHY ESCAPES surveys the entire range of fitness holiday opportunities in North America. In the pages of this guide, the in-depth profiles of more than 240 spas, fitness resorts, and cruise ships provide the detailed information anyone needs to begin to plan a vacation with a purpose.

In the **Introduction,** we explain why more and more people are taking wellness-oriented vacations, with a brief synopsis of recent trends in the industry. This is followed by practical information on how to plan your spa vacation, including descriptions of the various types of fitness vacations from which you can choose.

Spa reviews are organized by region: Each chapter covers a particular region or, in the case of large states with an inordinate number of spas—California, for example—a particular state. In each **chapter introduction** we give you the lowdown on what the spas of that region are known for, be it fitness programs in spectacular desert landscapes, grand old resorts with historic hot springs, or all-inclusive resorts in the tropics. Within each chapter, spas are organized alphabetically by state (or, in the case of California, by geography within the state). If you wish to look up all the spas that share a particular designation, consult the **directories** in the back of the book: Directory 1 gives the complete list of each type of resort and indicates the page on which each review appears; Directory 2 lists all the resorts alphabetically. For those unfamiliar with spa terminology, we've defined commonly used terms such as "Trager massage" and "kur" in the **Glossary** that appears after the last spa review.

For each of the spas and fitness resorts profiled in this book, we have used boldface type to indicate the particular focus of the program (*see* "Planning Your Escape," *below,* for an explanation of the six different designations we use). Following the overall description of each spa, resort, or fitness cruise is practical information covering facilities and services, accommodations, dining (including sample meals), rates and packages, and directions.

Because most spas constantly update their equipment, under **Exercise Equipment** we list the generic names for machines such as treadmills and stair climbers. In addition to exercise equipment, almost all full-scale spas have steam baths, saunas, and whirlpools, usually with separate facilities for women and men.

Under **Services,** we provide a representative sampling of the types of spa treatments offered, including various kinds of massage, body treatments, water treatments, and facials. In addition to standard spa services, most full-service spas have salons that provide hair, nail, and skin care. Reservations for spa and beauty services are always a good idea, as appointments generally get booked quickly. If the service you request is unavailable, many spas will let you leave your name on a waiting list; same-day cancellations are also worth checking into. Tipping is expected for all services at most spas. A 15%–20% tip is the norm, though you may tip as little or as much as you feel is appropriate.

Children's Programs are sometimes available for younger children; these are noted when applicable. Many spas have a minimum age requirement of 16 or 18; always call ahead if you're planning on bringing a child.

Under **Rates and Packages,** rates listed are for double-occupancy accommodations in the high season. Except in those reviews where we've noted that tax and tip are included, you must add both. Some states levy a hotel tax in addition to a sales tax; at establishments where a service charge (usually 15%) is also applied, the additional cost can be as much as 30%. In many reviews, we've also listed rates for one or more spa packages: These usually include accommodations, meals, and selected spa services for one or more days. Deposits usually must be received in advance of the guest's arrival, and a cancellation charge applies to most bookings. Each resort makes its own policy with respect to accepting payment by personal check, traveler's check, money order, or credit card. The following abbreviations are used to indicate the types of credit cards accepted: AE, American Express; D, Discover; DC, Diners Club; MC, MasterCard; V, Visa.

Acknowledgments

Recognized internationally as an authority on the spa experience, **Bernard Burt** wrote the original edition of this book in 1987 and has updated six editions in the decade since. A travel industry consultant based in Washington, D.C., Burt has written two guidebooks to that city and contributed articles to *American Health, The Washington Flyer, Potomac Life, Spa,* and *Spa Management Magazine*. He was founding director of The International Spa & Fitness Association and publishes *SpaGoer* newsletter. Burt was honored by the State of Maryland as Travel Writer of the Year in 1985.

As the former editor-in-chief and publisher of *Women's Sports & Fitness,* **Jane McConnell** has covered health and fitness trends for more than a decade. She has written about sports, fitness, and travel for *Shape, Self,* and *Outside* magazines and has covered her home state of Colorado for Fodor's in the *Rockies, Colorado, USA,* and *Skiing USA* guides. The mother of three young children, she is currently writing a book on natural parenting.

We are grateful for the assistance of the contributing reviewers and Jeanne Jones, author of *Light Cuisine,* Jenni Lippa of Spa Trek, Mike Nelson of Roads Scholar Press, and T George Harris, founding editor of *American Health* magazine.

Travel was facilitated by Air Canada, American Airlines, Midway Airlines, Aeromexico, Air Jamaica, Aspen Mountain Air, and Taka Airlines.

Additional information on programs and therapies is available from the International Spa and Fitness Association (✉ 546 E. Main St., Lexington, KY 40508, ☎ 606/226–4260 or 888/651–4772, FAX 606/226–4445).

Don't Forget to Write

You can use this book in the confidence that all prices and opening times are based on information supplied to us at press time; Fodor's cannot accept responsibility for any errors. Time inevitably brings changes, so always confirm information when it matters. In addition, when making reservations be sure to speak up if you have a disability or are traveling with children, if you prefer a private bath or a certain type of bed, or if you have specific dietary needs or other concerns.

Were the spas we recommended as described? Did they exceed your expectations? If you have complaints, we'll look into them and revise our entries when the facts warrant it. If you've discovered a special resort that we haven't included, we'll pass the information along to our correspondents and have them check it out. So send us your feedback, positive or negative: e-mail us at editors@fodors.com (specifying Healthy Escapes on the subject line) or write the Healthy Escapes editor at Fodor's, 201 East 50th Street, New York, New York 10022. Enjoy your journey toward wellness!

Karen Cure

Karen Cure
Editorial Director

INTRODUCTION

ONCE CONSIDERED fat farms or pampering palaces for self-indulgent women of leisure, today's spas are more like universities of well-being, where you can pick and choose from classes focusing on everything from rock-climbing to spiritual healing. In today's sped-up, information-glutted world, healthy vacations are no longer regarded as an indulgence, and physical and emotional nurturing are recognized as beneficial, even essential. With programs in stress management and classes that teach self-awareness, spas offer their guests the tools to learn to repair their mind and spirit as well as their physical health.

More and more Americans are recognizing that they can take their health into their own hands. With studies showing that one in three Americans will contract some form of cancer and that 75 percent of all diseases are lifestyle-related, a behavior-changing spa vacation begins to sound like a worthwhile investment in one's health. At the same time, alternative medicine is becoming more mainstream. According to Andrew Weil, M.D., author of the best-selling book *Spontaneous Healing,* one out of three Americans is using alternatives to traditional medicine. Treatments like massage and acupuncture no longer seem like extravagances, and are even covered by some insurance companies. Many cutting-edge spas now offer alternative medicine along with traditional medical evaluations. At the Aspen Club in Colorado, the staff at the Center for Well-Being can perform a Chinese herbal remedy, lymphatic drainage, or sound therapy.

Along with a more holistic approach to health, spas have begun placing an increasing emphasis on spirituality. Although many spa-goers are mainly interested in stress reduction or weight loss, and at best are closet spiritualists, nearly everyone is looking for that "aha," or epiphany, says Mel Zuckerman, owner of Canyon Ranch, one of the first destination spas in the country. The result has been a rekindled interest in the ancient arts of yoga, tai chi, and meditation. At Canyon Ranch, guests are advised to take at least one class a day in "spiritual fitness," and Zuckerman estimates that attendance in breathing and relaxation classes is ten times what it was five years ago. At Miraval spa, in Tucson, Arizona, whether guests are hiking, taking a Spinning class, or eating breakfast, they are encouraged to adopt a zenlike, mindful approach, paying full attention to the present moment.

This increased emphasis on the health of body, mind, and spirit has transformed the spa experience. "Visiting a spa used to mean jumping around in an aerobics class under fluorescent lights, eating a diet lunch, and then sitting in the Jacuzzi and talking about food," says Spa-Finders president Frank Van Putten. "Now instead of going to a spa to lose weight and get beautiful, people go to increase their health and vitality—a huge shift." Accordingly, the top spas are providing more and more classes beyond the standard ABCs of nutrition and fitness. Canyon Ranch's program guide lists more than 125 different classes and workshops, ranging from consultations in Life Transitions to workshops in Exceptional Sex.

Recognizing that most spa-goers already work out regularly and want to try something new on vacation, spas are including in their fitness options everything from line dancing to kick-boxing. A number of years ago spas opened their doors to the outside, embracing outdoor activities such as hiking and mountain biking. Now some spas have taken the "soft adventure" concept a step further: Miraval offers outdoor challenge activities with a mental component, including a rock-climbing wall, a ropes course, and an equine experience that guides guests toward self-discovery through interaction with horses.

As spas are broadening their offerings, they are also softening their approach. Nowadays, it's not unusual to find spas serving a glass of wine with dinner, or reserving tee times at a nearby golf course. "In the '80s, spas were defined by all the things you *couldn't* do there. Now the opposite is true," says Van Putten. Pampering treatments are still a cornerstone of the spa experience, but even they are designed to work on several different levels. The Nature, Body, Spirit treatment at the Vail Athletic Club in Colorado, for example, uses six different aromatherapy scents in one massage, including stimulating rosemary oil on the legs, calming lavender oil on the back, and refreshing lemon oil at the end of the massage. Green Valley Spa in St. George, Utah, employs color therapy with bath salts and candles in the treatment rooms to evoke different moods each day of the week.

Just as Americans are buying more organic food than ever, clients are demanding pure oils and extracts in their spa treatments. The Dr. Hauschka and Jurlique skin care lines, for example, used in many top spas, are manufactured from hand-harvested organic herbs. And just as regional cuisine that relies on fresh, local produce is all the rage, spas are beginning to look close to home for indigenous ingredients to use in their treatments. Green Valley, in Utah's Mojave desert, formulates its own skin-care line out of desert botanicals such as sage and juniper, and uses salt from the red cliffs and desert sand in spa treatments. Hawaiian spas offer seaweed body wraps and papaya-enzyme scrubs. At The Raj in Iowa, milk for the milk baths is delivered still warm from a dairy down the road.

As spas have changed, so has their clientele: Spas today attract people of all ages and income levels, from all across the country. The biggest change in the market in the last few years has been the number of men taking spa vacations. At the same time that spas have started to offer a broader range of outdoor activities, men have begun to discover the benefits of taking care of themselves with massage and facials. As a result, men, who used to account for less than 10 percent of all spa visits, now make up over a quarter of the clientele, according to Spa-Finders, the world's largest spa travel and reservation company. Now that there are spas close to home all over the country, the idea is catching on in small towns as well as cities, from the Northwest to the Midwest to the South. In 1991, 81 percent of spa-goers came from major urban areas, according to Spa-Finders Research; today the figure is less than 60 percent. Spa-goers today represent both ends of the age spectrum: In 1987 less than a quarter of spa visits were by those age 35 and under; 10 years later, more than half of all spa-goers were between 30 and 55. In 1998, 22 percent of spa visitors made less than $50,000 a year, up from 8 percent in 1992.

If you want to come back from your next vacation with more than just a tan, look through this book and find a resort tailored to your needs. A spa vacation may or may not change your life, but it's bound to give you more than just an enjoyable break from your daily routine—chances are, you'll come away with new ideas about what makes you feel healthy and whole.

— Jane McConnell

Planning Your Escape

In addition to self-contained destination spas such as Canyon Ranch, there are an increasing number of resort spas where exercise facilities and spa services are an added amenity. If you're looking to start a weight-management program, embark on a fitness regimen, or make other lifestyle changes, a destination spa is your best bet: You'll be totally immersed in an atmosphere of wellness along with other like-minded people, away from the temptations found at most resorts. If, on the other hand, you want to be with your family on vacation, mix golf or sightseeing with a spa visit, or simply indulge in a little pampering, a resort spa is a better choice. Some spas offer a blend of both approaches: The Pritikin Center at Loews Santa Monica Beach Hotel is a one- to three-week medically supervised program that takes place at a glamorous beachfront resort; the Peaks Resort & Spa's "Next Level Spa" is a four- or seven-night package where participants have 24-hour access to the spa, and dine from a Next Level spa menu.

While destination spas number only about 30 in the United States, resort spas have grown to more than 250—in fact, nearly every luxury hotel these days lists a spa among its amenities. Most of the resort spas in this book have full-scale fitness facilities with regularly scheduled classes, body- and skin-care treatments beyond standard massages and facials, and some kind of spa cuisine or heart-healthy menu options. Those that do not fit these criteria have been included in this book because of other exceptional features.

Another kind of healthy escape is less obvious but no less worthwhile: health-and-fitness cruises. An increasing number of luxury liners have full-scale spas that combine abundant fresh air and sunshine, seawater-fed pools, and aerobics classes on deck. Some cruise lines even have special fitness and beauty cruises, with lectures on subjects such as nutrition and sports medicine, and shore excursions to local golf courses and fitness centers.

Yet another health-and-fitness phenomenon that has exploded in recent years is the day spa. Filling the need for rejuvenating quick fixes closer to home, these urban retreats combine elements of beauty salons, health clubs, and destination spas. At most day spas you'll find pampering treatments, yoga or meditation classes, and possibly a café serving spa cuisine. At press time, a new chain of Golden Door day spas was scheduled to open within several Grand Bay hotels and resorts, including the Boulders in Carefree, Arizona, and the Peaks Hotel & Resort in Telluride, Colorado. At the same time, Canyon Ranch was planning to open a chain of day spas called the Canyon Ranch Spa Clubs, each with up to 30 massage rooms and 15 facial rooms, in New York City, Boston, Atlanta, Las Vegas, Orlando, and various parts of the Caribbean. Because there are so many day spas in the United States, more than 800 at last count, they are not covered in this guide. If you are interested in finding the ones nearest you, look in city hotels, and even in major airports; check with your local health club or salon; or consult the Yellow Pages (under S for spas).

Once you decide on a destination- or resort-spa vacation or a health-and-fitness cruise, consider what you're hoping to get out of your spa visit. Some pleasure seekers may prefer to relax and enjoy the amenities of a posh resort; others will find gratification in adhering to a rigorous schedule. If you're interested in learning how ancient therapies are combined with the latest concepts in behavior modification, consider a New Age retreat, a yoga ashram, or a natural-healing center. Some establishments preach preventive medicine, taking a holistic approach toward strengthening the body against illness through improved nutrition and an understanding of the relationship between

mind and body. Others address problems such as the need to lose weight, stop smoking, or deal with stress. These programs educate participants, reinforce motivation, and promote effective long-term improvement and well-being.

The cost of a spa vacation can vary widely. For luxury and personal attention, expect to pay premium prices. Budget-conscious travelers can find options for less than $100 a day, including meals, and most resort facilities can be used for a small daily fee, even if you are not participating in the spa program. (These fees are often waived when you book spa treatments.) In some areas the off-season brings markedly reduced rates and bargain packages; always call ahead to find out about the latest deals. At most resorts, spa treatments cost extra; packages are often available including one or more treatments a day. Fees for medical services may be covered by your health insurance and under some circumstances may be tax deductible; consult the resort's program director and/or your tax advisor for further information.

To make your selection easier, we've categorized the resorts in this book under six headings that reflect the various emphases discussed above. Many spas fit more than one category.

Luxury Pampering

Staff members often outnumber guests at resorts where luxury pampering is the focus. Therapeutic, rejuvenating services usually include exotic body and skin-care treatments and the latest image-enhancers at the beauty salon, among them glycolic-acid complexion peels, loofah body scrubs with sea salts and almond oil, aromatherapy massage, and paraffin facial masks for dehydrated skin. European hydrotherapy treatments, or kurs, include underwater massage, thalassotherapy with seaweed products and seawater, and traditional herbal baths. In recent years, luxury pampering has also begun to incorporate Ayurvedic treatments based on the 5,000-year-old traditional medicine of India—particularly the Shirodhara, in which warm oil is dripped onto the forehead, or "third eye." Spa meals are light but gourmet; exercise classes and a weight-loss diet can be part of the program but are usually optional.

Deluxe accommodations and amenities are basic to this type of resort.

Nutrition and Diet

Learning how to lose weight properly and to maintain a healthy balance in body mass is the basis of programs that deal with nutrition and diet or weight management. These are not courses for dramatic weight loss; rather, they teach proper eating habits. Participants gain a new perspective on nutrition through lectures and first-hand experience in food preparation. How foods affect your health, how to shop for groceries, how to choose from restaurant menus, and how to plan and prepare meals are among the subjects covered. Students attend courses in which menus and recipes for nutritious dining are generated and given out for take-home use. Along with these courses, resorts often integrate motivational sessions with exercise, sports and outdoor activities, and pampering treatments—education with recreation. Some programs involve supervised juice fasts. Some have residential retreats for people struggling with obesity.

Carefully controlled and supervised, the typical nutrition-and-diet regimen is tailored to the individual's fitness level and health needs. A team of specialists—therapists and nutritionists—coaches you on the basics of beginning and maintaining a personal program. Additional motivation and support arise in the camaraderie of being with a group of like-minded dieters.

Sports Conditioning

Active vacationers and athletes seeking new challenges can learn how to stretch their endurance limits with sports-conditioning programs, which usually involve advanced training in various sports, workouts with experts, and high-tech training with the latest in exercise equipment. Most sports-focused programs are based in areas that lend themselves to outdoor pursuits, such as Colorado or Utah; seasonal activities often include mountain biking and vigorous hikes in summer and cross-country skiing or snowshoeing in winter.

Mental training techniques are often incorporated into sports-conditioning programs. Following the lead of Olympic athletes and professional golfers, trainers give courses in guided relaxation, affirmations (positive statements), and visualization to improve the competitive edge. These practices are more than morale boosters; the visualization of successful performance may create neural patterns that the brain will use in telling the muscles what to do.

Therapy for sports-related injuries is a feature of some resorts. Others specialize in the mind-body relationship, incorporating disciplines such as martial arts, yoga, and tai chi, to promote both physical and spiritual development.

Holistic Health

The premise of holistic health programs is that true fitness and health depends on emotional, intellectual, and spiritual wholeness, not just physical well-being. Followers of this philosophy believe that illness results from a lack of balance within the body, whether caused by stress or physical conditions, and that balance can be restored without the use of medicine. Accordingly, holistic health programs foster personal growth and transformation through workouts that synchronize mind and body to make one aware of one's inner resources. Nontraditional therapies, alternative education, and cleansing or vegetarian diets are used to achieve a sense of wholeness with the world and oneself. The experience may draw on any number of Eastern and Western philosophies, incorporating yogic training or sensory awareness. Private counseling and group sessions are usually available for both beginning and advanced meditators. Retreats rather than resorts, these centers for spiritual training are usually found in secluded areas of natural beauty, where distractions and externally induced tensions are minimal.

Medical Wellness

Medical wellness centers take a scientific approach to health and fitness by combining traditional medical services with advanced concepts for the prevention or treatment of illness. Programs are designed for people who want to learn how to maintain their good health, as well as for those dealing with serious medical concerns, from cardiovascular disease to obesity. Medical and fitness testing, counseling on nutrition and stress control, and exercise activities are usually available, along with massage and bodywork.

Often developed in consultation with patrons' personal physicians, medical wellness programs are carefully structured, supervised at all times, and require complete commitment. Participants work with a team of physiotherapists and doctors to learn how to eliminate negative habits and modify a lifestyle for survival. One-on-one training with fitness instructors, nutritionists, and psychologists becomes a blueprint for accomplishing personal goals.

Along with hospital-related programs, specialized centers for preventive medicine can now be found at leading fitness resorts and at retreats under the auspices of medical-service organizations. They bring together specialists in all fields of health and nutrition to provide a comprehensive prescription for healthy living.

Mineral Springs

The word *spa* is borrowed from the Belgian town of Spa, where cure-takers have bathed since the time of the Romans. Some say the town's name is an acronym for the Latin *salus per aqua*, which means "health by water." Today, taking the waters—which may involve drinking six to eight glasses of mineral water daily—is practiced for health and relaxation at fashionable spas around the world.

The popularity of water-based therapies and mud baths at American fitness resorts is a recent phenomenon. The integration of European and American approaches to maintaining a healthy body and a glowing complexion has revived interest in bathing at grand old resorts where natural waters are available free for the asking. Related treatments that involve seaweed, algae, and seawater are offered at spas that specialize in thalassotherapy.

For the purist, a secluded hot spring promises the best kind of stress-reduction therapy. Others need the added stimulation of body scrubs with sea salts by a masseur, or a whirlpool bath bubbling with herbal essences.

1 California

*Northern California,
Southern California*

THE BIRTHPLACE OF THE CONTEMPORARY AMERICAN spa, California has been luring health-conscious visitors since the Spanish explorers first landed in San Diego in the 16th century. In Southern California, 150 miles of coastline between Los Angeles and Mexico boast more varieties of health spa than any other part of the nation: mud treatments, mineral waters, vegetarian diets, luxury pampering, and spiritual retreats are widespread. Northern Californians consider themselves residents of a different state. For them the Wine Country north of San Francisco is a principal attraction, and taking mud baths at Calistoga ranks with visiting the vineyards of Napa and Sonoma counties.

Prevention of illness, rather than pampering, now keynotes California spa life. New emphasis comes from the Pritikin Longevity Center at Loews Santa Monica Beach Hotel, a spa and fitness facility open to the public. At the Claremont Resort near San Francisco, distinguished cardiologist and diet innovator Dr. Dean Ornish continues to lead weeklong retreats sponsored by the Preventive Medicine Research Institute. In La Jolla, the Chopra Center for Well Being has a full-time medical director. It's a telling sign of the times that California Blue Shield now reimburses members for partial cost of treatments at 12 spa resorts; perhaps others will follow its lead.

NORTHERN CALIFORNIA

CALISTOGA SPA HOT SPRINGS

Mineral springs

Dozens of spas have tapped the thermal spring mineral waters and mud that spurts forth from the ground in Calistoga, a tiny town tucked into the vineyards of the Napa Valley. The geysers, which were considered sacred to the Wappo tribe of northern California, also attracted 17th-century Spanish explorers, who named them *agua caliente,* or hot springs. Later, in 1859, San Franciscan developer Sam Brannan coined the name Calistoga, a contraction of California and Saratoga Springs (the then-fashionable New York spa). Today the town has a mellow, laid-back look that's part Victorian restoration (no building over two stories) and part low-cost housing for workers in the nearby wineries.

The mud baths that draw people from all over the world to Calistoga are generally a mixture of volcanic ash and peat. The ensemble—which has a slightly sulphuric odor (but that's part of the charm)—is heated to a little over 100°F. You lie down in a tub, an attendant covers you with mud, and you let the heat penetrate your muscles and joints for 10 minutes. Following this you soak for 10 or 15 minutes in a mineral bath (spring water from the town's geysers), sit in the steam room for a spell, and then relax with a cotton blanket wrapped around you for 15 minutes, a gentle way to cool down.

German tourists and families from California are much in evidence at Calistoga Spa and Hot Springs, the best of the town's more utilitarian establishments. The spa's no-nonsense approach puts less emphasis on pampering and luxury touches than is the case at other spas in town, but the mud still works its magic, and the resort's pluses include a health club, three outdoor pools with naturally heated mineral water of varying temperatures, and a hot tub. Aerobics classes and use of exercise equipment are complimentary for guests. The pools, mud bath, and massage are available to the public and can be booked by the day if you are not staying on the premises.

The no-frills motel-style guest rooms, which are arranged around the pools, are modern and well maintained, with fully stocked kitchenettes (there's a grocery store a block away).

FACILITIES
Exercise Equipment: Rowing machines, stair climbers, stationary bikes, treadmills, weight-training circuits, free weights. **Services:** Massage, blanket wrap, mud bath. **Swimming:** 3 pools. **Classes and Programs:** Aerobics.

ACCOMMODATIONS
57 rooms.

DINING
No meals served, but many restaurants within walking distance.

RATES AND PACKAGES
Mud bath (includes mineral bath, time in steam room, and blanket wrap) $44. Mud bath plus massage $69–$88. Massage $35–$60. Rates for a double room $87–$132. 2-night minimum on weekends (3-night minimum on holiday weekends). MC, V.

DIRECTIONS
✉ *1006 Washington St., 94515,* ☎ *707/942–6269.*

From San Francisco: Cross the Golden Gate Bridge, go north on U.S. 101, east on Highway 37, north and east on Highway 121, northwest on Highway 29 to Calistoga; turn right (east) on Lincoln Avenue and right (south) on Washington Avenue.

THE CLAREMONT RESORT, SPA, & TENNIS CLUB

Luxury pampering

This grand, white-turreted resort hotel presides over 22 acres of landscaped grounds in the hills of Oakland and Berkeley, beckoning frazzled city dwellers with its excellent spa facilities and programs. Most guests come for à la carte services combined with a night or two at the hotel, but there's also a periodically scheduled Weekend Adventure package, as well as several week-long retreats sponsored by the Preventive Medicine Research Institute.

Though the spa building feels small by today's standards, the menu of services is extensive. Among the relaxation therapies available is a one-hour restorative yoga session in which a trainer positions you so that gravity will work to help rejuvenate your whole body. Personal trainers will help you restyle your workout routine, and more than 20 different scheduled aerobics classes provide variety. Also on the property are 10 tennis courts (all lit for night play), two lap pools (one Olympic size), a full-service salon, and a bay-view café with a low-calorie menu.

In true grand resort tradition, the Claremont stands out for its cuisine and accommodations. The main restaurant, Jordan's, combines Pacific Rim influence with the freshest ideas in spa cuisine, complemented by California wines. Beyond the tall windows of the elegant dining room stretches a panorama of San Francisco Bay. Choice rooms in the sprawling, Victorian mansion are in the spa wing, which connects to the fitness center, and in the original towers, where art deco minisuites have views of the bay. In summer, a kids' camp adds to the country-club mood. Another advantage: You can stroll to Berkeley's galleries and museums within minutes, and San Francisco is only 20 minutes away.

FACILITIES
Exercise Equipment: Rowing machines, stair climbers, stationary bikes, treadmills, weight-training circuit, free weights. **Services:** Aromatherapy massage, deep-tissue massage, pressure-point massage; herbal wrap, loofah scrub; facial. **Swimming:** 2 pools. **Classes and Programs:** Tennis and swimming lessons, one-on-one training, nutritional counseling. **Recreation:** Tennis, hiking, jogging; golf and horseback riding nearby. **Children's Programs:** Adventure Day Camp (ages 4–10), summer swimming and tennis clinics (ages 6–16).

ACCOMMODATIONS
279 rooms.

DINING
Spa cuisine available at Jordan's. A la carte or prix-fixe 4-course menu options. **Sample Meals:** Lettuce-wrapped halibut with ginger-soy marinade and Asian greens (lunch); mesquite-grilled swordfish with papaya chutney, or rack of lamb with preserved lemon, sautéed spinach, and roasted tomatoes (dinner).

RATES AND PACKAGES
Daily room rate $199–$315 single or double; suites $289–$1,000 for 2. Spa Retreat and overnight accommodations for 2 nights: $550 single, $390 per person double. Day packages, $100–$350. 1-night deposit required. AE, D, DC, MC, V.

DIRECTIONS
✉ *41 Tunnel Rd., Berkeley, CA 94705,* ☎ *510/843–3000 or 800/551–7266,* FAX *510/843–6239.*

From San Francisco: Bay Bridge to Highway 580 East to Highway 24 East, Claremont Avenue exit to Ashby Avenue. Continue 2 blocks to Tunnel Road (30 mins).

ESALEN INSTITUTE

Holistic health
Mineral springs

Letting it all hang out is the order of the day at the hilltop campus of the Esalen Institute. Soaking in clifftop hot springs where clothing is optional, immersing yourself in seminars on everything from esoteric religions to Gestalt therapy, you'll relive a bit of the "human potential" movement that was nurtured here more than 35 years ago.

Once considered a hippie haven, the Esalen Institute is now known across the country. Michael Murphy and the late Richard Price, who founded the institute in 1962, are credited with having invented the Esalen style of sensuous massage that turned encounter therapy into an art form. As in the beginning, Esalen remains focused on personal and social transformation. Seminars and workshops on such topics as psychosynthesis, shamanic healing, and neurolinguistics draw an eclectic group of scholars and New Age seekers of a healthy lifestyle. Ever popular are the Esalen massage workshops that embody the institute's core concepts.

Many who come here simply want to unwind in what easily ranks as one of California's most beautiful settings. Overnight guests (accommodated only when space permits) can book a massage, soak in natural rock pools filled by hot mineral springs, or hike in the Ventana Wilderness. (The institute also offers a hiking trip to Tassajara Zen Monastery (*see below*). A few exercise classes are available, including tai chi and a morning exercise routine.

Guests double up in simple, rustic lodge rooms with no TVs, phones, air-conditioning, or maid service. A beautiful setting compensates for the spartan surroundings: You'll be treated to ocean views by day, and the sound of the surf by night. The buffet-style meals are just as casual as the accommodations, but the food is wonderfully wholesome, including produce grown organically on the property.

FACILITIES
Services: Craniosacral massage, deep-tissue massage, Esalen massage, Hellerwork, Feldenkrais Method, Rolfing. **Swimming:** Pool. **Classes and Programs:** Morning exercise class, tai chi, lectures. **Recreation:** Hiking, mineral baths. **Children's Programs:** Special activities and dining plan; limited child-care facilities.

ACCOMMODATIONS
110 dormitory beds.

3 buffet-style meals daily. Meat, fish, and poultry, organic produce, salad bar. **Sample Meals:** Pasta salad with potato-leek soup (lunch); spinach lasagna (dinner).

RATES AND PACKAGES
Tuition plus standard accommodations: weekend $425, 5-day $795, 7-day $1,220. Daily rate with meals $80–$125; bunk bed daily $80–$85, weekend $325. $150 deposit required for weekends, $200–$300 for longer programs. AE, MC, V.

DIRECTIONS
✉ Hwy. 1, Big Sur, CA 93920, ☎ 408/667–3000 or 408/667–3005 for reservations, ℻ 408/667–2724.

From San Francisco: Highway 101 south to Monterey, west to Coastal marker 156, Highway 1 south to Esalen road marker (3½ hrs).

HEALTH SPA NAPA VALLEY

Luxury pampering

The Napa Valley is known for upscale dining and lodging, but many of the region's spas lean toward the utilitarian. That something more elaborate would be required of the first full-service spa and fitness center to open in tony St. Helena was clear to the proprietors of Health Spa Napa Valley, who blended the best elements of Mediterranean design and Wine Country style to fashion a complex that includes the day spa and the affiliated Inn at Southbridge. Luxury pampering—herbal and other wraps, aromatherapy, reflexology, indoor and outdoor massage—is the order of the day, but this being California, New Age notions lightly influence some of the proceedings. Two attendants, for instance, perform the Panchakarma massage, an Ayurvedic-inspired treatment that involves a veritable geyser of warm sesame oil.

Grapeseed-mud wraps and grapeseed-oil massages are the spa's trademarks. Unlike the mudbaths offered in the nearby town of Calistoga, which entail immersion in a vat of gooey volcanic ash, the mudwrap process is more dignified: The attendant slathers you with a mixture of French clay, lavender, and crushed grape seeds (it smells great, almost like a rustic zinfandel) and wraps you up. The clay helps draw out impurities, and the grape seeds are said to contain antioxidants to help rejuvenate the skin. After 20 minutes or so, you rinse off the mud and proceed to the massage table. You can also opt for a grapeseed body polish, an exfoliating treatment.

Before or after your massage you can work out at a compact but well-equipped fitness center, whose glass doors open out onto the pool area; swim laps or sunbathe by the 25-meter pool; or take a yoga or Spinning class. The changing areas, which have spacious steam rooms and great-smelling shampoos, skin creams, and other amenities, receive constant attention from the spa's staff. Within the complex is a lively, postmodern pizzeria, Tomatina's, whose menu also includes Mediterranean fare; Tra Vigne and other stellar Napa Valley restaurants are nearby.

FACILITIES
Exercise Equipment: Oscillating stair climbers, standard stair climbers, stationary bikes, treadmills, weight-training circuit, free weights. **Services:** Ayurvedic massage, deep tissue massage, grapeseed oil massage, reflexology, shiatsu; grapeseed mud wrap, grapeseed body polish, herbal wrap, salt glow, seaweed wrap; facial. **Swimming:** Pool. **Classes and Programs:** Spinning and yoga classes. Fitness, body-composition, stress evaluations.

20 rooms and 1 suite at affiliated Inn at Southbridge.

DINING
No meals provided at spa. Restaurants within walking distance. Continental breakfast served at Inn at Southbridge.

RATES AND PACKAGES
Spa: Massage therapies, $40–$135; body/skin-care treatments, $40–$115; treatment packages, $135–$200. Fitness center and pool: $15 weekdays, $20 weekends. Inn: $205 (winter weekdays; standard double room)–$450 (summer weekends; suite), plus 12% tax.

DIRECTIONS
✉ *1030 Main St., St. Helena, CA 94576,* ☎ *707/967–8800,* ℻ *707/967–8801.*

From San Francisco: North from Golden Gate Bridge on U.S. 101, east on Highway 37, north and east on Highway 121, and northwest on Highway 29.

HEARTWOOD INSTITUTE

Holistic health
Medical wellness

This budget-priced country retreat north of San Francisco has a 240-acre campus in the mountains of California's north coast. The institute's credo is that illness results from imbalances in the body's normal states, and that this balance can be restored by therapies such as acupuncture, modified nutrition, herbal preparations, and homeopathy. Experts in Hatha Iyengar yoga, transcendental meditation, and nutrition teach regularly scheduled classes, and weekend-long wellness workshops, held about once a month, draw about 20 participants each.

The wilderness setting is ideal for walking in the woods, mountain biking, or participating in group meditation under a wooden dome in the forest. Housed in a picturesque log lodge, classrooms and private treatment rooms are rustic but pleasant. Guests either camp outside (bring your own gear) or sleep in small, simple dormitory rooms. Also on campus are an outdoor hot tub, a wood-fired sauna, and an unheated swimming pool. Spa services are not available, unless requested in advance. Three daily vegetarian meals, included in the tuition, are served buffet-style in the cozy dining room or on a spacious deck in nice weather.

FACILITIES
Services: Acupressure, deep-tissue massage, Esalen massage, shiatsu; breathwork, hypnotherapy, jin shin jyutsu, polarity therapy, transformational therapy. **Swimming:** Pool. **Classes and Programs:** Yoga, nutritional counseling. Lectures on massage and nutrition, dances.

ACCOMMODATIONS
15 dormitory rooms, all with shared bath; 36 campsites.

DINING
3 buffet-style meals daily, primarily vegetarian. Organic vegetables, grains, fruits, nuts, dairy products, eggs; fish served once a week. **Sample Meals:** Organic Indian dal, coconut rice, apple-raisin chutney, Indian breads (lunch); breaded baked fish filet with spicy lemon glaze, baked potato, vegetable medley (dinner).

RATES AND PACKAGES
$90 per night single, $150 2 persons per night, $65 for campsite. 3 daily meals included. Weekend retreat available with $50 deposit. Men's, Women's and Yoga weekend retreats with varying fees.

DIRECTIONS
✉ *220 Harmony La., Garberville, CA 95542,* ☎ *707/923–5000,* FAX *707/923–5010.*

From San Francisco: Highway 101 north to first Garberville exit (3 hrs)

INDIAN SPRINGS RESORT

Mineral springs

Mud baths at most resorts are a mixture of volcanic ash and peat, but Indian Springs, which has a cache of ash right on its property, uses 100% volcanic ash—you'll feel like a bug suspended in amber after the attendant heaps several handfuls on you. The regimen here includes a 10-minute session in the mud followed by a 15-minute soak in a mineral tub (during which you rehydrate by sipping the house cooler, spring water flavored with orange and cucumber slices). Then comes a respite in the steam room, and a blanket wrap. After your mud bath, you can have a massage (from 30 to 90 minutes), get a facial, or have a manicure or pedicure. If sitting in mud doesn't appeal to you, you can opt for a mineral bath, followed by a visit to the steam room and a blanket wrap.

The spa, which has operated under various names since the late 1800s, was renamed Indian Springs in the mid-1980s. Major renovations to the 1913 Arts and Crafts–style bathhouse preserved its character; the 1940s-era duplex cottages, which hold studio and one-bedroom units, have been modernized but maintain a retro charm. There's also a one-bedroom cottage with a full kitchen and a three-bedroom house. All the accommodations have kitchenettes, gas fireplaces, and TVs. A big plus if you're a swimmer is the naturally heated outdoor Olympic-size mineral-water pool, which has a garden of succulents at one end.

The service at Indian Springs, which has separate facilities for men and women, has slipped a tad in recent years—the attendants aren't as quick to daub the sweat off your forehead while you're lying in the mud and sometimes chatter among themselves, breaking the meditative calm a mud-bath session can provide. But the pure volcanic ash will make your skin silky smooth, and the skill of the massage technicians is generally quite high.

FACILITIES
Services: Swedish massage, body scrub, mud bath, facial. **Swimming:** Pool. **Recreation:** Biking, tennis.

ACCOMMODATIONS
16 rooms, 1 1-bedroom house, 1 3-bedroom house.

DINING
No meals served, but many restaurants within walking distance.

RATES AND PACKAGES
Mineral bath $55, mud bath $65, massage $45–$120, body scrub $75, facial $45–$75. Mineral bath with massage $95–$120. Mud bath with massage $105–$130. Rates for cottages $150–$180; 3-bedroom house $450. Nov.–mid-March package: two free mud baths with Sun.–Thurs. stay. MC, V.

DIRECTIONS
1712 Lincoln Ave., Calistoga, 94515, ☎ *707/942–4913,* FAX *707/942–4919.*

From San Francisco: Cross the Golden Gate Bridge, go north on U.S. 101, east on Highway 37, north and east on Highway 121, northwest on Highway 29 to Calistoga; turn right (east) on Lincoln Avenue

THE LODGE AT SKYLONDA

Luxury pampering

Combine an idyllic mountain lodge with top-notch massage therapists and exercise instructors, an enticing indoor swimming pool with a view of the redwoods, and gourmet meals so good that it's hard to believe they contain less than 15% fat, and you have the makings of a romantic retreat for fitness buffs. Anyone who's intimidated by the idea of working out and dieting at a spa will feel at home here, where hard-core exercise is out and pampering is in. Even if you don't take advantage of the myriad hiking trails and fitness classes available, you're bound to feel rejuvenated after a couple of nights in the quiet calm of this elegant log-and-stone lodge.

The daily schedule at Skylonda is exceedingly civilized. After an optional morning stretch class that incorporates yoga techniques, and a hearty but healthy self-serve breakfast of fresh-baked muffins and homemade granola plus a hearty hot entrée, you'll be given a water bottle and ushered out for a guided hike along trails through deep redwood canyons and grassy meadows, sudden ravines, and silent hollows. Though the spa occupies 16 forested acres of coastal hills near Silicon Valley, hikes often venture even farther afield to various parks within the Santa Cruz Mountains. Choices range from 6 to 9 miles, or 3 to 5 miles; along the way you'll learn about the area's ecosystem as well as bits of folklore. At the end of the trail, a van will meet your group, so no backtracking is necessary.

For those with more energy to burn, Cybex circuit training, tai chi, restorative yoga, and aqua aerobics are all optional midday activities. After lunch, you're on your own to indulge in top-notch spa treatments; set off on a solo hike; or enjoy the gorgeous, glassed-in pool or the adjoining outdoor whirlpool—on a deck surrounded by redwoods, it's the ultimate California perch. At 5 PM there's more yoga and stretching (strictly optional). At six, hors d'oeuvres are served in the high-ceiling Great Room, where overstuffed sofas, a fireplace, games like backgammon and chess, a lending library, and a grand piano make guests feel right at home.

Dinner, served from 7 to 8:30, is worth waiting for. Candles dress up the rustic dining room, where picture windows look out on the redwoods. Menus on every table announce the two entrée choices of the day, always featuring fresh local produce supplied by organic farmers, and the day's catch from the Pacific, with calories and fat grams noted for each. Meals are so tasty that chef Sue Chapman gives evening cooking classes, by popular demand, twice a week.

Because every day begins early, nighttime activities are scarce—all the better to enjoy the huge, ecosavvy rooms, so quiet you can hear yourself think. There are no TVs, radios, or even alarm clocks; instead you have a private deck, comforter-covered bed with fluffy, white-cotton reading pillows, and full bathroom with a deep soaking tub (rubber duckie included).Choice top-floor rooms have 12-foot vaulted ceilings.

A small caveat: Because hiking is the focus here, cardiovascular equipment is limited to a few stationary bikes, one treadmill, and a mountain climber. The gym doubles as the exercise studio, so you'll be ousted from the machines when classes are in session. With so many other exercise options, however, this is hardly a concern.

FACILITIES

Exercise Equipment: Stair climber, stationary bikes, vertical ladder climber, weight-training circuit, free weights. **Services:** Aromatherapy massage, jin shin jyutsu, reflexology, shiatsu, Swedish massage; body wrap; facial. **Swimming:** Indoor pool. **Classes and Programs:** Aquaerobics, one-on-one circuit training, tai chi, yoga, private guided hikes, cooking classes.

ACCOMMODATIONS

16 rooms.

DINING

3 meals daily, averaging about 1,400 calories. **Sample Meals:** Sweet-potato-and-apple bisque with fresh thyme, quinoa salad with chicken and pumpkin (lunch); baby-arugula salad with marmalade-mustard dressing, seared swordfish with sugar-snap peas and tangerine-dill "beurre blanc," or New Mexican stuffed potato with black beans, goat cheese, and chipotle pepper on wilted kale (dinner).

RATES AND PACKAGES

Nightly package rates $350–$450 single, $222–$288 per person, double. 50% deposit required. AE, MC, V.

DIRECTIONS

⊠ *16350 Skyline Blvd., Woodside, CA 94062,* ☎ *650/851–4500 or 800/ 851–2222,* ℻ *650/851–5504.*

From San Francisco: I–380 west to I–280 south, Highway 92W to Scenic Highway 35 (Skyline Boulevard), follow 10½ miles past Bear Gulch Road; look for lodge on the right (45 mins).

MEADOWOOD RESORT

Luxury pampering

The chic town of St. Helena has a reputation for fine wineries and restaurants, and high-style boutiques and galleries. It's no surprise, then, that the town is also home to one of the state's most elegant spas. Nestled among the oaks 65 miles north of San Francisco, Meadowood recalls the grand old resorts of the early 1900s with its gabled lodges overlooking the manicured croquet lawn and golf course—but remarkably, most of its buildings are of recent vintage. The health spa was added in 1993 and epitomizes the Napa Valley lifestyle: easy informality and superb taste.

Epicurean pleasures are a major part of the Meadowood experience. Many of the area's best wineries are within spitting distance, as are fine restaurants such as Tra Vigne and the Culinary Institute of America, housed in the century-old Greystone Winery. Vineyard tours begin right outside the resort; for groups of four or more, the resident wine tutor, John Thoreen, sets up guided tours and tastings. Meals in the main dining room and the more casual café are first-rate, with chef Roy Breiman's Provençal-inspired seasonal menu drawing on local produce. Though vegetarian and heart-healthy meals are available, this is not the place to diet, especially if you are intent on sampling some of the area's finest vintages, served by the glass or the bottle in both restaurants.

The airy spa building is rarely crowded, and guests are treated like VIP club members. Scheduled classes open to all guests include an early-morning stretch session followed by a 90-minute total-body workout. Other daily group exercise sessions include aquaerobics, yoga, and step classes; there's also a line-dancing choreographed to country music—a creative way to get a workout while making new friends. An extensive selection of massage therapies, body and facial treatments, and fitness classes is available at à la carte prices or as part of a personalized renewal program. In addition, there are guided walks within Meadowood's 250 acres, and mountain bike rides through St. Helena and the surrounding countryside.

Creature comforts count for a lot in this sybaritic corner of the world, and accommodations are predictably up to par. Terraced up the hillside along a 9-hole golf course, most guest units have a French country style, with fieldstone fireplaces, high ceilings, and gabled roofs. You can opt for seclusion (involving a hike up the hill if you don't have a car), or select a terrace unit facing the croquet green.

FACILITIES

Exercise Equipment: Stair climbers, stationary bikes, treadmills, weight-training circuit, free weights. **Services:** Aromatherapy massage, deep-tissue massage, reflexology, Swedish massage; salt glow; facial. **Swimming:** 2 pools. **Classes and Programs:** Exercise consultation, personal training, body-composition test, nutrition analysis. **Recreation:** Biking, hiking, golf, tennis, guided winery tours.

ACCOMMODATIONS

38 rooms, 47 suites.

DINING

Vegetarian and heart-healthy options available in both restaurants. **Sample Meals:** Grilled salmon with arugula, fennel, and orange reduction, or fettuccine with mushrooms, tomatoes, basil, and garlic (lunch); sea scallops steamed in corn husks with vanilla-bean butter and corn-shiitake ragout (dinner).

RATES AND PACKAGES

$310–$675 per night for 2; suites $515–$2,630. AE, D, DC, MC, V.

DIRECTIONS

✉ *900 Meadowood La., St. Helena, CA 94574,* ☎ *707/963–3646 or 800/458–8080,* FAX *707/963–3532.*

From San Francisco: Highway 101 via Golden Gate Bridge to Highway 37 to Napa. Take Highway 121 to Highway 29 North, continue 25 min to Zinfandel Lane, turn left on Silverado Trail, right on Howell Mountain Road, left on Meadowood Lane (2 hrs).

MOUNT VIEW HOTEL

Mineral springs

Calistoga's classiest spa is inside the Mount View Hotel, a restored 1930s Art Deco structure that's been designated a National Historic Landmark. The hotel's typical California casual-but-elegant ambience continues in the spa, which offers a full complement of services, from mud baths to body wraps to massages and facials. Luxury pampering is the goal here, and by and large the spa succeeds.

Fango mud is used at this spa—it's a blend of volcanic ash, pine oil, and salicyl. (The latter is the base of aspirin, and has anti-inflammatory properties.) The effect is relaxing and analgesic, and the mud does not cling to the skin. Private treatment rooms with double-size whirlpools are ideal for couples. Near the spa is a quiet courtyard with an outdoor heated pool and a whirlpool filled with mineral water from the inn's hot spring well.

Like the spa itself, the hotel is romantic and classy. Enter the lobby and you'll find potted palms, sky-lit ceilings, and overstuffed couches. Cottages have secluded patios with hot tubs, and wet bars stocked with sparkling beverages from local springs. Many of the standard rooms overlook the hotel's palm-shaded courtyard, and eight pricier accommodations include the art deco Jean Harlow suite and the Victorian-style Robert Louis Stevenson suite.

Come mealtime, the acclaimed Catahoula Restaurant and Saloon will tempt you with its California-Cajun cuisine prepared in a wood-burning oven. You can dine in the funky restaurant, gazing at a giant avant-garde mural and photos of the Catahoula hound for which the restaurant is named, or take your meal by the pool in the courtyard.

FACILITIES
Services: Aromatherapy massage, reflexology, shiatsu, sports massage, Swedish massage; Dead Sea mud wrap, herbal linen wrap, stress relief hydro wrap; customized whirlpool bath, hydro-active mineral bath, milk-whey bath; facial. **Swimming:** Pool.

ACCOMMODATIONS
22 rooms, 8 suites, 3 cottages.

DINING
California-Cajun cuisine at Catahoula Restaurant and Saloon. **Sample Meals:** Caesar salad with spicy rock shrimp, or pizza pie with andouille sausage, onion confit, and oven-roasted tomatoes (lunch); oven-roasted bone marrow with tomato-mushroom jam, spicy paella with mussels, clams, rock shrimp, and homemade chorizo, or Southern-fried rabbit with dirty rice and collard greens (dinner).

RATES AND PACKAGES
$85–$130 standard double occupancy; suites, $145–$190; cottages $194. Mount View Sampler (mineral bath and massage), $85; Calistoga Splurge (choice of water treatment, plus massage and body wrap), $145; Napa Sparkler (choice of water treatment, plus massage, herbal wrap, and facial), $170. Advance deposit required. AE, MC, V.

DIRECTIONS
✉ *1457 Lincoln Ave., Calistoga, CA 94515,* ☎ *707/942–5789 (spa) or 800/772–8838,* ⨎ *707/942–9165.*

From San Francisco: Cross the Golden Gate Bridge, take Route 101 to Novato, Routes 37, 121 to Napa, Route 29/128 to Calistoga (1½ hr).

OSMOSIS ENZYME BATH & MASSAGE

Luxury pampering

One good reason to visit this unusual day spa in the tiny town of Freestone is to be able to boast that you've spent the day fermenting. The process is as bizarre as it sounds: After drinking a pot of herbal tea mixed with digestive enzymes from Japan, you'll be shepherded to a bath area and into a big, sand-box-like tub containing a fragrant mixture of organic plant enzymes, cedar fibers, and rice bran that's naturally heated up to 135°F. After an attendant digs a hole for you and then covers you up to the chin, you'll be left to, well, ferment (and perspire), for 20 minutes or so. After you've brushed off the wood chips and showered, you can opt for a 75-minute massage in one of the freestanding Japanese-style pagodas near the creek that runs through the property, or conclude instead with a half-hour "blanket wrap" meant to help you relax as the heat and energy of the enzymes continue flowing through your body.

Though Osmosis is the first and, as yet, only spa to offer this form of heat treatment in the U.S., enzyme baths are ubiquitous in Japan, especially within the past 25 years. Proponents claim that the fermentation process of the enzyme baths gives a natural boost to the internal organs, promoting a natural cleansing process that helps the body break down toxins and wastes, as well as improving circulation and metabolism. Whatever the claims, the treatment does feel quite calming, especially when followed by the 75-minute massage.

Part of the experience of Osmosis is the serene, Japanese-inspired setting. The spa is in a two-story clapboard house that occupies extensive grounds. The meditative Japanese tea garden is a perfect place to begin your treatment, with a softly gurgling fountain and intricately planted bonsai trees and plants. To reach the pagodas where massages take place, you'll hike along a secluded trail where all you can hear is the sound of the wind in the trees, and maybe a chirping bird.

Make a day of your visit to Osmosis by setting aside some time afterwards to explore the tiny town of Freestone, and nearby Occidental, where the elegant Inn at Occidental (⊠ 3657 Church St., Box 857, Occidental 95465, ☎ 707/874–1047 or 800/522–6324) makes a great base for exploring the area.

FACILITIES
Services: Massage (Esalen, Swedish), enzyme bath and blanket wrap.

ACCOMMODATIONS
No lodging at spa. Referrals available at front desk.

DINING
No meals provided at spa. Restaurants within easy driving distance.

RATES AND PACKAGES
Bath and blanket wrap, $60 ($50 for two guests or more). Bath and massage, $125 ($115 for two guests or more). Massage only, $65 (pagoda massage $15 extra). AE, MC, V.

DIRECTIONS
⊠ 209 Bohemian Hwy., Freestone, CA 95472, ☎ 707/823–8231.

From San Francisco: Highway 101 North to Washington Street/Petaluma exit, 25 miles west to Valley Ford, right on Freestone/Valley Ford Road, right on Bodega Highway, left on Bohemian Highway.

POST RANCH INN

Luxury pampering

Sensuous and spiritual, the road along the Pacific Coast has a heart-stopping grandeur that inspires naturalists to fight to protect this place of outstanding natural beauty. Novelist Henry Miller heard Big Sur's siren call in the 1940s, writing after his first visit, "If the soul were to choose an arena in which to stage its agonies, this would be the place for it." He might have added that if the body were to choose a beautiful setting in which to be pampered, the Post Ranch Inn would be a great choice.

Geographically, Big Sur consists of about 90 miles of jagged central California coastline. Carmel anchors the northern end, about 130 miles south of San Francisco. At the southern limit are San Simeon and Hearst Castle, approximately 240 miles north of Los Angeles. The name derives from "El Sur Grande" (the big South), an appellation given by Spanish settlers who lived near Monterey. Protected by several outstanding state parks, the area has few overnight lodgings, one of which is the luxurious Post Ranch Inn.

Blending in with the redwoods are 30 suites in secluded wooden houses with glass, marble, slate, and granite interiors. Some guest units are built on stilts or hidden under sod roofs. Interiors feature redwood beams and natural materials. Each unit has a wood-burning fireplace, stereo system, whirlpool tub, and massage table in case you should want to book a massage or facial in the privacy of your room. Electric vans provide transport within the 98-acre compound; guests are asked to leave their cars in the parking lot upon arrival.

The ranch's spa is housed in a small cottage scented by sea air and refreshing pines. Don't worry about rushing through your day to fit in your spa treatments: Appointments are scheduled until midnight. Depending on weather, some sessions of yoga and star-gazing take place outdoors, taking advantage of the smashing views of the Pacific Ocean and Ventana Peak. Invigorating sessions of aerobic speed walking, yoga, and guided nature and wilderness hikes are scheduled regularly.

Dining at the Inn's Sierra Mar Restaurant, you'll have a vantage point 1,200 feet above the Pacific Ocean. The daily-changing menu is based largely on fresh seafood and local produce; gourmet picnics are provided on request. For more epicurean pleasures, stick around on a Saturday for a wine tasting.

FACILITIES
Exercise Equipment: Stair climber, stationary bikes, weight-training circuit, free weights. **Services**: Esalen massage, sports massage; herbal wrap; facial. **Swimming**: Pool. **Classes and Programs**: One-on-one training, guided hikes. **Recreation**: Horseback riding and scuba diving nearby.

ACCOMMODATIONS
30 suites.

DINING
Continental breakfast buffet included in room rates. Dining room with prix-fixe or à la carte menu. Spa selections low in fat, salt, and calories. **Sample Meals**: Grilled portabello mushroom with tomato and basil on a roll, cold rosemary-lemon roast chicken (lunch); fennel-crusted halibut with chive-mashed potatoes and red wine; grilled mahi mahi with saffron pearl couscous and lobster jus (dinner).

RATES AND PACKAGES
$285–$545 daily. AE, MC, V.

DIRECTIONS
✉ *Hwy. 1, Box 219, Big Sur, CA 93920,* ☎ *408/667–2200 or 800/527–2200,* FAX *408/667–2824.*

From Carmel: Highway 1 south 26 miles to Big Sur. Continue 1.5 miles past Pfeiffer State Park, look for Post Ranch Inn sign on west side of Highway 1 (40 mins).

PREVENTIVE MEDICINE RESEARCH INSTITUTE

Medical wellness
Nutrition and diet

Changing your lifestyle to reverse the progression of cardiovascular disease is the focus of the four week-long retreats held at the Claremont Resort (*see above*), under the auspices of the Preventive Medicine Research Institute. Directed by Dean Ornish, M.D., and led by health professionals from the institute, this highly structured program includes lectures and experiential sessions, as well as cooking instruction by celebrity chefs. Stress management techniques, exercise in the resort's well-equipped fitness center, and group support help you discover how understanding your physical and emotional states can improve your mental health.

Participation in the retreat is limited to 100 and includes all meals, professional staff time, classes, and take-home material. Part of the fee contributes to ongoing programs at the Preventive Medicine Research Institute, a nonprofit public institute associated with the University of California, San Francisco.

Lodging at The Claremont Resort is arranged separately, allowing you to choose the type of room or suite that fits your budget. Specially-prepared meals for program participants are served in a private dining room in the hotel. Services in the Claremont spa and salon (not included in the price of programs) add a welcome bit of pampering to this educational, perhaps life-changing experience.

FACILITIES
See Claremont Resort, *above*.

ACCOMMODATIONS
Call The Claremont Resort (*see above*) to arrange lodging during one of the institute's 4 week-long retreats.

DINING
3 meals daily, all low-fat, low-cholesterol, and mainly vegetarian. **Sample Meals:** Lentil soup and garden salad, or pasta salad (lunch); vegetarian lasagna, or stir-fry vegetables and brown rice (dinner).

RATES AND PACKAGES
$2,900 single, $2,200 for spouse or companion sharing room. Includes meals, professional staff time, classes, and take-home materials. Lodging not included.

DIRECTIONS
✉ *Mailing address: 900 Bridgeway, Suite 2, Sausalito, CA 94965,* ☎ *415/ 332–2525 or 800/775–7674,* FAX *415/332–5730.*

See The Claremont Resort, *above*, for driving directions.

ST. HELENA HOSPITAL HEALTH CENTER

Medical wellness
Nutrition and diet

Taking charge of your health requires a commitment to lifestyle changes, and this program provides the tools. Seventy miles north of San Francisco in the beautiful town of St. Helena, the health center feels more like a hotel than a clinic, with vineyards spreading for miles below its hillside perch. Though it's part of a hospital complex run by the Seventh-Day Adventists, programs are nondenominational and nonsectarian, structured to provide complete medical and lifestyle evaluations.

Self-management and disease prevention are the goals. Following a physical examination and diet analysis that takes into account your physical condition, nutritional requirements, and weight-loss goals, doctors and health professionals prescribe a course of action intended to help you achieve a healthier lifestyle. The health center's association with St. Helena Hospital enables it to draw on sophisticated medical facilities, biofeedback, and medical consultants appropriate to your special problems. You can choose to focus on smoking cessation, lifestyle change through nutrition, alcohol and chemical recovery, pulmonary rehabilitation, pain rehabilitation, personalized health, or prime-of-life fitness. Hydrotherapy treatments, massage, and medical tests are available at an additional charge.

The 12-day McDougall Program, dealing with diet and nutrition, includes group therapy and relaxation techniques, vegetarian cooking classes in a teaching kitchen, and massages, plus use of the steam baths, sauna, and whirlpool. Consultation with Dr. John McDougall, author of four books on the prevention and treatment of disease, focuses on lifestyle changes to lower cholesterol and improve personal health and well-being. The program is scheduled once a month.

Participants have full use of a gymnasium, running track, and an indoor-outdoor swimming pool. You can also opt for a rest and relaxation program, designed for stress management, or a personalized health program (weekdays only), including massages. A special combination rate is available for those accompanied by a spouse or family member.

FACILITIES
Exercise Equipment: Rowing machines, stair climbers, stationary bikes, treadmill. **Services:** Massage. **Swimming:** Pool. **Classes and Programs:** Exercise instruction, private medical counseling, group discussions, group relaxation, informal lectures on health-related topics, cooking classes. **Recreation:** Biking, hiking; golf, tennis, and glider rides nearby.

ACCOMMODATIONS
24 rooms.

DINING
3 vegetarian meals daily, buffet style. No caffeinated beverages, no condiments. Cooking without butter and oil; vegetables sautéed in water. Fresh fruit at all meals. **Sample Meals:** Bean enchiladas with verde sauce and two vegetables, or Chinese noodles, oriental soup, and two vegetables (lunch); split-pea soup and polenta with marinara sauce, or green-pepper-and-tomato teriyaki with brown rice (dinner).

RATES AND PACKAGES
4-day/3-night Personalized Health Program $1,551; 7-day smoking cessation program $2,860 single, $2,685 double; 12-day McDougall program $4,710 single, $4,410 double. Meals included. (Medical insurance may cover part of cost.) Deposit required for some programs. AE, D, MC, V.

DIRECTIONS
✉ *Box 250, Deer Park, CA 94576,* ☎ *707/963–6207 or 800/358–9195,* FAX *707/967–5618.*

From San Francisco: I–80 north past Vallejo to Highway 37 going west, Highway 29 through St. Helena to Deer Park Road, across Silverado Trail, left on Sanitarium Road (90 mins).

SIVANANDA ASHRAM YOGA FARM

Holistic health

At a simple farmhouse in a valley north of Sacramento, you can spend a few days studying the practice and principles of yoga. Two daily sessions of traditional postures (asanas), breathing techniques, and meditation are intended to foster a better understanding of the mind-body connection.

The program is based on the yogic principles of Swami Devananda, whose followers and new students join in practicing the 12 asana positions, from a headstand to a spinal twist, each believed to have specific benefits for the body. Participants learn that the proper breathing (*pranayama*) in each position is essential for energy control.

Meditation at 6 AM begins the morning session. A buffet-style brunch is served at 10, and then your schedule is open until 4 PM, when a second session of yoga is held. Attendance at classes and meditations is mandatory.

The 80-acre farm attracts a diverse group, families as well as senior citizens. Guests are asked to share bedrooms and to contribute time to communal activities. You may arrive on any day and stay as long as you wish.

FACILITIES
Swimming: Pool. **Classes and Programs:** Yoga, meditation; lectures on Hindu philosophy. **Recreation:** Skiing at nearby resorts.

ACCOMMODATIONS
18 dormitory beds in 4 dorms, 1 double room, 1 single room, 10 new cabins, all with shared bath. Campsites available.

DINING
2 vegeterian meals daily. **Sample Meals:** Home-made granola with yogurt, home-made breads, hot grain cereal, fruit (brunch); rice with potato-carrot curry, fresh steamed greens, ginger–soy broth soup, dal, and salad, or steamed vegetables, rice, and scrambled tofu (dinner).

RATES AND PACKAGES
$35 per person per day (includes dormitory lodging, program, meals). Double room $45 per person, single room $55, cabins $75 per person single or double; campers pay $25. Prices increase $5 on weekends. Supplemental charges for special programs. 1-night deposit required. MC, V.

DIRECTIONS
✉ *14651 Ballantree La., Grass Valley, CA 95949,* ☎ *530/272–9322 or 800/469–9642,* ℻ *530/477–6054.*

From Sacramento: I–80 to Auburn, Highway 49 (1½ hrs).

SONOMA MISSION INN & SPA

Luxury pampering
Mineral springs

Since the turn of the century, San Franciscans have been "taking the cure" at the Sonoma Mission Inn, perhaps the best-known spa in Sonoma County. Despite its unlikely location off the main street of tiny, down-home Boyes Hot Springs, guests continue to come from afar to enjoy the extensive spa facilities and treatments—including a pool that's heated by warm mineral water pumped from underground wells—and also for the classic spa cuisine. A few days spent on these 10 eucalyptus-shaded acres can do wonders for your spirits, which might explain why it's a frequent stopover on Wine Country tours.

Soaking in the natural, hot artesian mineral water remains one of the most popular activities at the spa. A spring funnels 135°F mineral-rich spring water into the exercise and swimming pools, whose temperatures are regulated and adjusted to achieve maximum therapeutic benefits. (A brochure about the inn's history documents examples of the miraculous health benefits of these waters.) Among the standout treatments is the 105-minute "Rejuvenator," which combines a scalp massage using warm aromatic oil with a 30-minute facial using nourishing botanicals, followed by a body massage and a stint in the steam room.

A big part of the inn's allure is its classy 1920s style: Behind the pale pink facade, Mediterranean meets California mission for a look that's early Hollywood. The baronial reception hall, with its huge stone fireplace and cool tile floors, sets the mood of casual elegance. The cavernous guest rooms, awash in terra-cotta and soft salmon shades, invite indolence with plush robes, canopied beds with billowy pillows, marble bathrooms, and a complimentary bottle of wine. In the main building, 100 of the inn's original rooms have a historic flavor. There are also 70 Wine Country–theme rooms, and luxury suites with private garden units.

Gardens scented by camellia and jasmine surround the fitness pavilion, whose airy, two-story atrium belies the building's origins as a Quonset hut. Glass-walled exercise rooms face a sunlit marble fountain; upstairs are treatment rooms where you can watch TV and sip herbal tea as you wait to be summoned. Classes are scheduled in the aerobics studio throughout the day, beginning at 7 AM with tai chi and yoga attracting a regular group of 10 or so local members. Hikers can sign up for 90-minute morning excursions, which depart from the inn by van at 7 AM, and a Wine Country picnic on Saturday. (These activities entail additional fees.)

As expected in this part of the world, the dining is sublime: Even non-spa guests often make reservations to dine here. The fashionable Grille and more casual café feel far removed from the rigors of calorie counting, even though a spa menu is available. Complementing the healthy but sophisticated cuisine is a wine list with more than 200 selections.

FACILITIES
Exercise Equipment: Stair climbers, stationary bikes, treadmills, weight-training gym, free weights. **Services:** Esalen massage, shiatsu, Swedish massage; citrus scrub, herbal wrap, mud wrap, seaweed wrap; facial. **Swimming:** 2 pools. **Classes and Programs:** Image consultation, personalized meditation, tarot-card reading. **Recreation:** Biking, hiking, tennis; horseback riding and golf nearby.

ACCOMMODATIONS
168 rooms, 30 suites.

DINING
Spa menu totaling 1,000–1,200 calories per day available at Grille; healthy options available at Café. **Sample Meals:** Roasted pepper omelette with potatoes, or vegetarian pizza (lunch); broiled swordfish in charred tomato broth with risotto, or sautéed prawns with shiitake mushrooms, Roma tomatoes, and spinach (dinner).

RATES AND PACKAGES
Hotel tariff $145–$795 per room. Basic Spa package per night $235–$475, $159–$279 double; Spa Sampler package with 2 meals daily $315–$550, $240–$359 double; Deluxe spa package $410–$659, $340–$410 double per night, including 3 meals. (More for 1-bedroom suites). Packages, available Sun.–Thurs. only, including classes, gratuities, and tax. Day Spa package $190–$395. 1-night deposit required, $500 for package. AE, DC, MC, V.

DIRECTIONS
✉ *18140 Sonoma Hwy. 12, Boyes Hot Springs, CA 95416, or Box 1447, Sonoma, CA 95476 (reservations),* ☎ *707/938–9000 or 800/358–9022; 800/862–4945 in CA.*

From San Francisco: Golden Gate Bridge, Highway 101, Highway 37 to Sonoma, Highway 12 (45 mins).

TASSAJARA ZEN MONASTERY

Holistic health
Mineral springs
Nutrition and diet

Big Sur and Zen meditation are a natural combination at this legendary retreat in the mountains, where resident monks lead daily sessions of meditation and basic Zen philosophy, as well as workshops in yoga, poetry, and sensory awareness. The site, surrounded by formidable mountains and overlooking the Pacific Ocean, has been a place of healing and purification for centuries. Native Americans used the hot springs, and Spanish hunters gathered here. Now, among other activities, Tassajara guests bathe in the slightly sulfurous water (clothing optional) until parboiled, then stretch out on the rocks to contemplate nature.

Your day begins at 5:40 AM when a bell ringer awakens you for meditation in the Japanese-style hall, or Zendo, which is the center of the Zen monastery at Tassajara. Students in black garb and with shaved heads join visitors seeking to become familiar with Buddhist practices. This is an excellent place to learn about Zen and meditation: Participation in all activities is optional, and the atmosphere is non-threatening.

Among the retreat's most popular traditions is its Zen cuisine. Those who know Tassajara primarily through its cookbooks on vegetarian meals and bread baking can begin to experience Zen cooking in a one-week workshop dubbed "Cooking as Meditation," led by Ed Brown, former head chef here and author of *The Tassajara Bread Book*. In addition to preparing food, guests learn about the spiritual aspects of cooking.

The Zen ideal of simplicity is apparent in guest quarters, which have kerosene lamps for lighting and foam cushions (in most rooms) for bedding. All rooms open onto a sundeck, with access to spring-fed pools and a stream.There are no housekeeping services.

Programs take place only from May through August. Those who wish to participate in the Practice Retreat—the main program, based on the study of Buddhist meditation—are required to perform about a half day of work on the buildings and farm.

FACILITIES
Services: Meditation retreats, workshops in yoga, cooking, Japanese arts. **Swimming:** 2 pools, creek. **Classes and Programs:** Lectures, meditation. **Recreation:** Thermal springs (clothing optional).

ACCOMMODATIONS
36 rooms, 1 2-room suite for 4–6 persons, dormitory room with 4 beds.

DINING
3 vegetarian meals, family-style. Different breads baked daily. **Sample Meals:** Lentil loaf, or steamed vegetables with tofu and brown rice (lunch); Japanese udon, or pasta primavera (dinner).

RATES AND PACKAGES
$130–$216 single, $80–$144 double, including 3 meals. Dormitory $70–$84 per night; 2-room suite $120–$144 per person (4–6 beds). Practice Retreat (3-night min.) $125–$250. 50% deposit required. No credit cards.

DIRECTIONS

✉ *Carmel Valley, CA 93924 (reservations); Zen Center, 300 Page St., San Francisco, CA 94102,* ☎ *415/431–3771,* FAX *408/659–2229.*

From San Francisco: I–280 south to Highway 17 via Monterey to Carmel, Route G16 (Carmel Valley Road) for 23.2 miles, right on Tassajara Road to Jamesburg (3 hrs).

SOUTHERN CALIFORNIA

THE ASHRAM HEALTH RETREAT

Holistic health
Nutrition and diet

Challenging yourself to achieve a higher level of holistic fitness may be the best reason for spending a week at this Los Angeles area retreat. Barbra Streisand called the Ashram "a boot camp without food." Others have found it a rite of passage to a new self-image. Shirley MacLaine described it in *Out on a Limb* as "a spiritually involved health camp." In fact, The Ashram displaces old stresses with new ones. Most of the fairly affluent achievers who come here have high-pressure jobs, and by challenging themselves to a week of enormous physical exertion and minimal meals, they can experience what some speak of as a transcendent, positive change in attitude.

Guests live together in close quarters in groups of only 10 to 12. Everyone follows the same routine of mountain hikes, exercise, and yoga. A daily massage and a few hours of relaxation are the only respite. Group togetherness is emphasized in this intimate setting, and participation in every activity is required.

Turning the concept of a retreat (the original meaning of ashram) into the ultimate challenge was the brainchild of Dr. Anne-Marie Bennstrom, now the Ashram's owner and chiropractor. A cross-country skiing champion in her native Sweden, Bennstrom tested her personal limits by spending five months alone in a Guatemalan jungle—an experience that inspired her to help others discover their own inner power. The Ashram has operated at this site since 1975, accepting men and women between the ages of 20 and 70.

Each day begins at 6:30 AM with yoga, stretching, and breathing exercises that help take the kinks out of sore muscles and build energy for a strenuous hike into the hills. Breakfast is a glass of orange juice. The morning schedule usually includes an hour of weight lifting followed by an hour of exercise in the pool and winds down with a game of water volleyball. Calisthenics and at least a two-hour walk complete the day. Bennstrom sets the pace for the hike, so the distance varies daily, but some groups have walked more than 90 miles in a week. In the afternoon each guest has a one-hour massage (five massages are included in the week-long rate).

Spartan accommodations fit right in with the boot-camp theme. Guests double up in five bedrooms in a plain, two-story stucco ranch house, with shared bathroom facilities, library, lounge, and weights room. Outside is a garden surrounded by towering eucalyptus trees, with a small swimming pool, a solarium for sunbathing, and a geodesic dome where yoga and meditation sessions take place.

FACILITIES
Exercise Equipment: Free weights. **Services:** Massage. **Swimming:** Pool. **Classes and Programs:** Meditation and yoga, nutritional counseling, lectures on health and spirituality. **Recreation:** Hiking, water volleyball.

ACCOMMODATIONS
5 rooms (roommates matched upon registration), all with shared bath.

DINING

3 lacto-vegetarian meals daily, based largely on fruit, vegetables, sprouts, seeds, and nuts. Snacks of raw vegetables and juices throughout the day. **Sample Meals:** Yogurt-and-cottage-cheese blend with fruit slices (lunch); black-bean soup, baked potato, green salad (dinner).

RATES AND PACKAGES

$2,500 per week, all-inclusive. MC, V.

DIRECTIONS

✉ *Box 8009, Calabasas, CA 91372,* ☎ *818/222–6900,* FAX *818/222–7393.*

From Los Angeles: 1 hr by complimentary shuttle; not accessible by private car. All guests picked up by van at specified locations in the area.

CAL-A-VIE SPA AND HEALTH RESORT

Luxury pampering

Terraced into a hillside, the 24 country villas of Cal-a-Vie look more like Provence than Southern California. This is one of the best destination spas in the nation, attracting a sophisticated clientele from many parts of the world. Because the guest capacity is limited to 48, you get lots of personal attention, and the intimacy is intensified by the cozy setting. The dining room resembles a private residence in the rambling style of Spanish haciendas. Guests gather for pre-dinner social hour in front of the fireplace in the living room, as if attending a private dinner party. Accommodations are in rustically elegant villa suites with French country furniture, carved wood armoires, and private garden entrances.

You'll hear the words "detoxify" and "cleanse" frequently, since European hydrotherapy and beauty treatments are the specialty of the house. Seaweed wraps to cleanse the pores, lymphatic massage for detoxification, and underwater-massage tubs are designed to heal the body by restoring the balance of mind, body, and spirit. These treatments, together with a weeklong regimen of hikes, aerobics classes, and calorie-controlled meals, form the core of the program.

Upon arrival you'll be given a computerized fitness evaluation to determine flexibility, cardiovascular capability, and upper and lower body strength; your personal diet and exercise regimen are based on the printout. Each morning the group, usually coed, meets for coffee or tea and a stretch prior to a pre-breakfast hike—long or short depending on your preference—on trails through the property and an adjoining golf course. After breakfast there are group workouts in the swimming pool, or in the gym with a personal trainer. Yoga, tai chi, and aerobics classes are scheduled regularly. Sparring in the "Boxercise" class helps build finesse and stamina.

FACILITIES

Exercise Equipment: Stair climbers, stationary bikes, weight-training circuit, free weights. **Services:** Aromatherapy massage, reflexology, shiatsu, Swedish massage; hydrotherapy, thalassotherapy; facial. **Swimming:** Pool. **Classes and Programs:** Aquaerobics, step aerobics; lectures on fitness and nutrition; cooking demonstrations. **Recreation:** Tennis, volleyball. Golf nearby.

ACCOMMODATIONS

24 villas.

DINING
3 meals daily, based on suggested calorie intake. 1,200–1,400-calorie diet program optional. **Sample Meals:** Whole-wheat pizza with roasted and grilled vegetables, or sautéed tofu and lentils (lunch); sautéed free-range chicken with rosemary and roasted garlic, or rice paper–wrapped salmon with ginger sauce, steamed vegetables, and brown rice (dinner).

RATES AND PACKAGES
All-inclusive European Plan $4,550; California Plan with limited treatments $4,150; summer weeks, European plan $4,150; California Plan, $3,850. $500 nonrefundable deposit required. AE, MC, V.

DIRECTIONS
✉ 2249 Somerset Rd., Vista, CA 92084, ☎ 760/945–2055, FAX 760/630–0074.

From San Diego: Route 163 to I–15 North to Canyon Road, turn left and go 2½ miles past golf course to Kilbirnie Road, turn left on Kilbirnie, which turns into Somerset Road (1 hr).

THE CHOPRA CENTER FOR WELL BEING

Holistic health

Learning the precepts in Deepak Chopra's best-selling book, *The Seven Laws of Spiritual Success,* may be the best reason to enroll in a workshop at the Chopra Center. Inspired by the 5,000-year-old Hindu system of natural medicine known as Ayurveda, the center was founded in 1996 by Chopra himself, the India-born and Harvard-educated endocrinologist credited with reviving this ancient science. Beautifully situated in the seaside town of La Jolla, the center welcomes guests for one-day services or three- to seven-day programs oriented towards natural health, spirituality, and inner growth. Meals are included with each workshop, but lodging is arranged separately—either at a nearby hotel or in modestly priced rooms in private homes.

For the non-initiated, the program may feel almost too cosmic, despite a sincere openness to strangers on the part of the leaders. Beyond meditation, the focus is on education in ancient philosophies. After an introductory briefing, an examination by a staff of MDs decides which of three *doshas* or body-mind types you belong to: *kapha* (solid, stable, earthy), *vatta* (quick changeable, airy), or *pitta* (intense, sharp, fiery). Based on a detailed questionnaire about your lifestyle, the doctors recommend certain foods and activities. Serious medical issues are treated with a combination of Western medicine and Eastern healing principles.

Bodywork treatments are based on Panchakarma. *Pizichilli* is a purifying experience in which a continuous stream of warm, herbalized oil is poured over the body as two therapists perform a gentle massage. Equally soothing is an herbal body wrap in which specially blended oils are applied to stress points. In *Shirodhara* (a treatment for madness in India), warm sesame oil drips over your forehead for a half-hour, inducing a state of mental calm. *Abhyanga* massage entails five successive kneadings of oil on every muscle from head to toe. Vital Touch enlivens "marma points," which follow the basic map of Chinese acupuncture points. Also available are facials and deep-tissue massage. Exercise consists mainly of yoga, practiced in guided sessions.

Chopra and his associates lead some of the workshops. The most basic of these is a three-day overview program that includes private counseling. The most advanced is a seven-day Ayurvedic purification program, which includes two physician consultations, six Panchakarma treatments, nutritional counseling, three daily meals, prepared Ayurvedically, daily group meditation, two consultations with an Ayurvedic nurse-educator, instruction in primordial sound meditation, and six yoga sessions. There's also a five-day "Magic of Healing" program.

The center's two-story building includes treatment rooms, a yoga studio, and a sun-dappled vegetarian café called Quantum Soup, open to the public. Upstairs are various function rooms, including the hushed Meditation Room, padded with gold brocade velvet pillows, where guests practice "primordial sounds." Also upstairs is the Food Court, where diners are seated around a long oak table evocative of the court of King Arthur—a theme inspired by Chopra's novel, *The Return of Merlin*. The richness of the food can be surprising, but servers explain how each dish is meant to promote balance and harmony. Kept in easy reach to accompany the cosmic curries are glass jars of three types of mixed teas, meant to complement the three types of beings: Kapha (invigorating peppermint), Vatta (spicy cinnamon), and Pitta (mellow chamomile).

FACILITIES

Services: Abhayanga, deep-tissue massage, full-body massage, pizichilli, reflexology, shirodhara, vishesh, vital-touch massage; Ayurvedic body scrub, Ayurvedic herbal wrap, Swedana, Shiroabhyanganasyh; Ayurvedic facial, deep-cleansing facial. **Classes and Programs:** Corporate training courses, creating health classes, natural cooking class, natural skin care, prenatal course, primordial sound meditation, yoga and breathing techniques; seven spiritual laws study group; mind-body medical consultation.

ACCOMMODATIONS

Lodging arranged separately (contacts provided on request).

DINING

Vegetarian and traditional Ayurvedic cuisine served at Quantum Soup café. 3 meals daily included in multi-day programs; lunch included in half-day and full-day programs. **Sample Meals:** Red- or green-lentil dal, tofu burgers in leek sauce, green salad and bread (lunch); Italian white-bean soup, or curried vegetables with carrot soup (dinner).

RATES AND PACKAGES

1-day programs including yoga, meditation, spa treatments, lunch, and educational class, from $335–$520; half-day program $195. 3-day programs including meals but no lodging, $1,250–$1,750; 7-day programs $2,750–$3,450. À la carte treatments, $65–$180. AE, MC, V.

DIRECTIONS

✉ *7630 Fay Ave., La Jolla, CA 92037,* ☎ *619/551–7788 or 888/424–6772,* ℻ *619/551–7811.*

From San Diego: I-5 north to Ardath Road exit, Torrey Pines Road to Girard Road (20 mins).

GIVENCHY SPA & HOTEL

Luxury pampering

In early 1998, Merv Griffin bought this high-profile spa designed by the Hubert de Givenchy, by far the most expensive and glamorous in the area. Celebrities and luxury-seekers come here to indulge in pricey treatments (a single service can cost up to $175), and to enjoy an atmosphere of exclusivity and monied tradition. The mood is formal and traditional, with more emphasis on luxury pampering than on fitness and lifestyle change. Though the sophisticated level of service might be intimidating for those seeking a more down-two-earth venue in which to recharge, it also makes this the ultimate sybaritic retreat.

Aside from its utterly anachronistic formality, the most striking feature of this Givenchy-designed Versailles of the West is its extraordinary design. Formal French gardens resplendent with roses separate the Palladian-windowed spa complex from the dazzlingly white, contemporary French Renaissance–style hotel buildings (appropriately named Le Pavilion, Le Grand Trianon, and Le Petit Trianon). Strolling the 14 lushly landscaped acres, you're bound to feel like Marie Antoinette or Louis XIV; were it not for the palm trees and views of the nearby San Jacinto Mountains, this could easily be France.

In keeping with the French spa philosophy that youth and wellness have more to do with beauty than fitness, the Givenchy Spa caters mainly to those who want to be primped and pampered. The beauty salon is under the direction of Gerard Alexandre, who loves to mingle with the stars. While you wait for a pricey haircut or pedicure, check out one of his scrapbooks documenting his career with hundreds of celebrities, from Paul Anka to Dr. Ruth Westheimer. If you are interested in working out, there's a good chance you'll have the pristinely maintained gym all to yourself.

The same soft approach applies to dining at Givenchy. Michelin two-star chef Gerard Vie obviously subscribes to the idea that food is meant to be enjoyed. Want caviar? Champagne? A chocolate soufflée? Chances are that you'll find all three at the two main restaurants: the formal Le Restaurant, where women wear Chanel and men wear jackets, and the Garden Terrace—both in the main pavilion. During the day, however, clad in your robe, you may prefer to dine between treatments at the charming Le Café, which looks like something out of a French Impressionist painting and serves guilt-free "cuisine légère."

As in the most elite European spas, the Givenchy Spa has separate facilities for men and women, including separate treatment rooms and even swimming pools. This traditional approach extends to the luxurious, ultra-classic guest rooms, all of which have separate his-and-hers bathrooms. Most guest rooms are in the châteaulike main building, although there are also 12 private single-floor villas idea for entertaining. High-rolling celebrities, politicians, and the occasional sheik opt to stay in Le Grand Suite, which has four bedrooms, a duplex living room with a grand piano, and a reception salon.

FACILITIES
Exercise Equipment: Cross-country ski track, rowing machines, stair climber, stationary bikes, treadmills. **Services:** Aromatherapy massage, deep-tissue massage, lymphatic massage, reflexology, sports massage, shiatsu; hydrotherapy, watsu; herbal wrap, mud wrap, seaweed wrap; facial. **Swimming:** 2 pools. **Classes and Programs:** Aquaerobics, Chi Kung, tai chi, yoga. **Recreation:** Biking, golf, tennis; hot-air ballooning, horseback riding nearby.

ACCOMMODATIONS
37 rooms, 50 suites, 12 villas.

DINING
3 meals daily (included in spa package only), served in Le Restaurant and in Garden Terrace; spa cuisine in The Café. À la carte and fixed menus available. **Sample Meals:** Romaine salad in a tulip of Parmesan cheese, fresh berries and crème brûlée (lunch); crispy sea bass wrapped in threads of potato with saffron sauce (dinner).

RATES AND PACKAGES
Daily rates for room, $175–$250 single, $250–$325 for double; 12 deluxe villas on request, $575. 6-night, 7-day spa package, including accommodations, 3 meals daily, treatments, and spa services $3,500. One-day Givenchy Beauté program, without accommodations, $275–$375. AE, D, MC, V.

DIRECTIONS
✉ *4200 East Palm Canyon Dr., Palm Springs, CA 92264-5291,* ☎ *619/ 770–5000 or 800/276–5000,* ℻ *619/324–6104.*

From Los Angeles: I–10 to Gene Autry off-ramp south, to East Palm Canyon Drive.

GLEN IVY HOT SPRINGS SPA

Mineral springs

Nestled in the foothills of the Santa Ana coastal range between Los Angeles and San Diego, halfway between the desert and the ocean, Glen Ivy Springs is a day spa with mud baths, rejuvenating mineral pools, concerts under the stars, and à la carte spa facilities. Bathers float in the pools on rented rafts, dozing, reading, meditating, as the warm desert sun, cool mountain breezes, and gardens provide the ambience for a relaxing, indulgent escape. For less than $20 a day, it's a virtual tropical paradise.

The white stucco buildings and clay-tile roofs counterpoint palm trees and bougainvillea. Hotel accommodations are not available at the springs, but those who stay at the nearby Mission Inn and Country Side Inn gain free admission to Glen Ivy Springs, which includes the pools, sauna, and mud baths. The mud baths are free, and so is membership into the famous "Club Mud," for those who take a dip in the vat of soft red clay that's been mined nearby. After you coat your body and hair, sit poolside and let the clay bake until it dries. Then rinse in the mineral water shower; your skin will feel satiny and healthy. The pools are drained and filled with fresh, chlorinated water every day.

Water temperatures vary between 90°F and 110°F at the two wells that supply a constant flow of mineral water to the pools. You'll be cautioned not to stay in the hot water too long, particularly if you're dieting or in poor health. The only organized activity is a 2 PM aquaerobics class held in the big swimming pool. Sign up for massage or salon services when you arrive, or call ahead for appointments. There are 16 massage rooms and well-equipped dressing areas for men and women, complete with dry saunas.

The waters here have been known for their healing powers ever since the Luiseno tribe first built mud saunas around the springs during the 14th century (No traces of these buildings remain.) The natives used an Aztec word imported by Franciscan missionaries, "temescal," meaning "sweathouse," to name the valley. In 1890, a 10-room adobe house opened as the first hotel to serve the orange ranchers from nearby towns. Artifacts and photos of these early days are on display in the Hot Springs Cafe. In 1912 the springs became popular with city dwellers who flocked from Los Angeles to the waters until 1969, when a flood wiped out the bathhouse and mud bath. With the rebirth of interest in natural therapies came new facilities and gardens. The homey country inn survived as a private residence, and the pools, sundecks, and landscaping were re-created in 1977 when the current management company was formed.

Although sun protection is provided at a covered hot pool, you'll need to bring sunscreen. An old swimsuit and towel are recommended for the mud bath. Food and drink are available at the Spa Cafe, or you can pack a picnic and use shaded tables in a designated area. Perhaps a jog down the road to shop at the farm market will feel invigorating after lazing in the primal ooze.

FACILITIES
Services: Aromatherapy massage; anticellulite treatment, body polish; facial. **Swimming:** Pool. **Recreation:** Mineral baths. Seasonal concerts (ticketed separately).

ACCOMMODATIONS
Free admission to Glen Ivy Springs included in rates at The Mission Inn (⊠ 3649 Mission Inn Ave., Riverside, CA 92501, ☎ 909/784–0300 or 800/843–7755; $170 for 2; AE, D, MC, V), and Country Side Inn (⊠ 2260 Griffin Way, Corona, CA 91719, ☎ 909/734–2140; $85 single, $115 double, including full breakfast; AE, MC, V).

DINING
Outdoor café with à la carte menu of soup, salad, sandwiches, snacks. **Sample Meals:** Chicken breast sandwich, veggie burger, or Caesar salad (lunch). No dinner (spa closes at 6 PM).

RATES AND PACKAGES
Daily admission to pools, sauna, mud bath: $19.50 weekdays, $25 Friday–Sunday. Children under 2 free. AE, MC, V.

DIRECTIONS
⊠ *25000 Glen Ivy Rd., Corona, CA 91719,* ☎ *909/277–3529 or 800/ 454–8772,* ℻ *909/277–1202.*

From Los Angeles: I–10, I–60, or Highway 91 eastbound to I–15 south, exit right onto Temescal Canyon Road, right on Glen Ivy Road (1 hr).

THE GOLDEN DOOR

Luxury pampering
Nutrition and diet

Imagine spending a week in the care of a full-time staff whose sole job is to customize a daily schedule of fitness and learning activities for you, and then to ensure that you follow the schedule religiously. Welcome to the Golden Door, trendsetter and long-time favorite of serious spa-goers since 1959. Secluded on 177 acres of canyon and orchards, "The Door" welcomes no more than 39 guests for a minimum one-week stay during which you're expected to follow the program. All decisions are made for you in advance, so all you can do is go with the flow. Miss an appointment and a staffer will come searching for you.

But the Golden Door is no boot camp; in fact, it's more like a summer camp with thoroughly enjoyable activities and a beautiful setting. Would you prefer to sign up for tennis, instruction in lap-swimming techniques, or a cooking class, you'll be asked when you arrive. And what time would you like your daily massage?

The same kind of individual attention goes into your dining plan. A nutritionist will help you determine your daily calorie needs, and the dining room will serve portions according to those guidelines. Meals are a celebration of California's freshest produce, most of it grown in the spa's organic gardens and orchards. Each day's menu presents three lunch and dinner options, and you can request extras or changes. On a designated evening each week, you can join the chefs for a cooking demonstration in the kitchen.

Each day begins at 5:45 AM with stretches and a brisk hike, sometimes even rock climbing, led by staff members who, Sherpa-like, supply flasks of cool water and fruit to sustain until breakfast time. On the breakfast tray that's delivered to your suite, you'll find a fan-shaped personal schedule for the day. A 45-minute exercise period takes up the rest of the morning; afternoons are for pampering and personal pursuits—perhaps a workout with the tennis pro, a few hours with a personal trainer, or a class in Pilates, yoga, or cardio-boxing. You can have lunch by the pool, in the dining room, or in the privacy of your room. Massages can be alfresco in the hillside solarium or in your room; you can even arrange for an evening mini-massage to prepare you for early bedtime.

Some activities have a spiritual bent. A stone mosaic pathway called the Labyrinth is used as a metaphor for one's journey through life. As you walk the path alone or in a group, accompanied by drumming or simply the sound of splashing fountains, you'll be advised to pause, take a deep breath, and slow down. You will then be instructed to focus on integrating the insights you have received in this peaceful place.

On the orientation tour for first-time guests, one can't help but be impressed by the attention to detail and devotion to comfort that have been incorporated into the spa's impressive design, a cross between a first-class resort and a Japanese country inn. Four spacious exercise studios have sliding glass walls that open to lush gardens. Guest suites, which are linked by elevated wooden walkways, have sitting areas that open onto garden courts; one has a koi fish pond, another is traditional sand sculpture. All rooms are single-occupancy, and their subdued Japanese design—woodblock prints, parquet floors with carpets, sliding shoji screens, and jalousie windows—promotes contemplation and serenity (no rooms have TVs). Welcome creature comforts include *yukata* robes, hats, gloves, and raingear for guest use, and complimentary daily laundry service.

Open year-round, the program varies only during theme weeks and just before year-end holidays, when a four-day package is offered. Five weeks throughout the year are designated for men, and four for couples; for the rest of the year, this is the private domain of women.

FACILITIES
Exercise Equipment: Rowing machines, stationary bikes, treadmills, weight-training circuit, free weights. **Services:** Aromatherapy massage, deep-tissue massage, hot-rock massage, shiatsu, Trager massage; body scrub, herbal wrap; facial. **Swimming:** 2 pools. **Classes and Programs:** Cardio-boxing, circuit training, tai chi, yoga, swimming instruction, fitness and stress evaluations, classes in crafts, flower arranging, and gardening. **Recreation:** Hiking, tennis. Lectures on nutrition, stress management, sports medicine, and other health-related topics; movies.

ACCOMMODATIONS
39 suites, 1 private cottage.

DINING
3 meals plus snacks served daily. High-energy meals, low in cholesterol, salt, sugar, and fat, rich in fiber and whole grains. **Sample Meals:** California rolls, chicken tostadas (lunch); chilled melon soup, wild-rice pilaf with pineapple and ginger, baked ham with steamed vegetables (dinner).

RATES AND PACKAGES
$5,000 weekly; $4,500 during July, Aug., Thanksgiving weekend, New Year's week. $500 deposit required with reservation. Gratuities included. MC, V.

DIRECTIONS

✉ *Deer Springs Rd., Box 463077, Escondido, CA 92046,* ☎ *760/744–5777 or 800/424–0777,* ⊠ *760/471–2393.*

From San Diego: Highway 163 to I–15, north to Deer Springs Road exit (40 mins).

LA COSTA RESORT & SPA

Luxury pampering
Nutrition and diet

A mega-resort for the fun and fitness crowd, La Costa Resort & Spa focuses more on recreation and pampering than on structured wellness programs. Tennis and golf are the resort's main attractions, and superb facilities are a short distance from the spa building. The Racquet Club has 21 tennis courts of various surfaces, and two PGA-rated championship golf courses spread over 400 acres in a gentle bowl of land that retains the sun's warmth all day while drawing a constant breeze off the ocean. Lawns and flower-filled gardens nestle at the foot of a quiet lagoon just off El Camino Real, the Royal Road of California's Spanish Colonial era.

Unfortunately, the spa building does not live up to this lovely setting: At press time (winter 1999), it was overcrowded and outdated, though renovation plans have long been in the works. Great service almost makes up for any flaws, however: Locker-room attendants remember your name and slipper size and hand out fresh towels and robes without being asked. Within the separate men's and women's locker rooms are eucalyptus-scented inhalation rooms, steam rooms, saunas, Swiss multihead showers, hot and cold plunge pools, and an outdoor whirlpool. Although treatment facilities are not mixed, you might be less than comfortable with the production-line look of massage tables separated only by curtains.

Various packages at La Costa range from simple to elaborate. The La Costa Spa Experience is the cheapest; it includes standard accommodations, use of the spa facilities, and one spa treatment. The four-night La Costa Fitness Getaway is more comprehensive, including various exercise classes, lectures, cooking classes and demonstrations, a body-composition analysis, fitness evaulation, and nutritional counseling, in addition to standard accommodations, use of spa facilities, and four one-hour spa treatments. The eight-night La Costa Healthy Lifestyles package is the most decadent, including deluxe accommodations, three meals daily, unlimited tennis-court time, 18 holes of golf daily, and seven spa treatments, in addition to the personal services and facilities included in the Getaway package.

Spanish Colonial influences prevail at La Costa: Lodgings are spread out in red-tile-roofed, pink-stucco buildings and a campus-style spa. Some of the largest guest rooms are among the oldest, but are closest to the spa building. Newer rooms overlook the golf course.

With acres of space to walk in, you can take an early morning hike on the golf course paths, or explore La Costa's residential areas. There are four restaurants on the property, most serving spa cuisine, though many guests seem to favor steak, fish, and pasta. Especially enjoyable is lunch at the Aquatic Center's swimming pool (one of five at the resort), where waterfalls and a pond filled with colorful koi fish provide a quintessentially Californian ambience.

FACILITIES

Exercise Equipment: Weight-training equipment, treadmills, stair climbers, rowing machines, stationary bikes, cross-country ski machines, free weights.

Services: Aromatherapy massage, reflexology, shiatsu, therapeutic massage; herbal wrap, loofah body scrub, thermal-mineral exfoliating scrub, Turkish scrub; aromatherapy bath, Hungarian kur bath, thalassobath; aloe-vital facial, elasto-firm facial, men's executive facial, optimal oxygenating facial. **Swimming:** 5 pools. **Classes and Programs:** Aerobics, aquaerobics, interval circuit classes, relaxation/visualization classes, water toning, yoga; body-composition analysis, fitness evaluation, golf and tennis instruction, personal training; nutrition counseling, restaurant dining strategies, supermarket survival skills; special programs in eating-behavior patterns, lifestyle evaluation, and positive self-imaging. **Recreation:** Biking, croquet, golf, tennis. On-site ballroom and theater; live entertainment for dancing. **Children's Programs:** Camp La Costa (ages 5–12).

ACCOMMODATIONS
397 rooms, 77 suites; 5 private residences.

DINING
Seafood at Pisces, contemporary cuisine at Ristorante Figaro, eclectic menu at Brasserie La Costa; casual dining and snacks at Center Court and Poolside Terrace. Spa cuisine served at 3 restaurants. **Sample Meals:** Shrimp cocktail, California burger with maple-wood-smoked bacon and Gruyere cheese, black pepper–seared tuna with papaya salsa and roasted vegetables (lunch), artichoke-leek lasagna with fresh vegetables, Moroccan couscous risotto with morel mushrooms, filet mignon with potato or grain and fresh vegetables (dinner).

RATES AND PACKAGES
Daily rate $275–$460 double. La Costa Experience weeknights, $180 per person per night, double occupancy, $225 weekends. 4-night La Costa Fitness Getaway $250 per person per night double occupancy, $370 per night single. 8-night La Costa Healthy Lifestyles $360 per person per night double occupancy, $500 per night single.

DIRECTIONS
✉ *Costa del Mar Rd., Carlsbad, CA 92009,* ☎ *760/438–9111 or 800/ 854–5000,* 𝔽𝔸𝕏 *760/931–7569.*

From San Diego: Take I–5 north to La Costa Ave. exit, take a right, turn left onto El Camino Real, hotel is ¼ mile on the right (40 min.).

MARRIOTT'S DESERT SPRINGS RESORT

Luxury pampering

A mega-resort oasis in the Coachella Valley, Desert Springs is the Marriott Corporation's most elaborate flagship: It's so large (400 acres) that a water taxi shuttles guests from the lobby to the 30,000-square-foot spa complex and surrounding lagoons and golf courses. It's no intimate getaway, but bigness has its own rewards.

At the 30,000-square-foot spa, the biggest in the Palm Springs area, you can join any one of six daily scheduled classes—among them yoga, step aerobics, and body sculpting—in expansive studios flooded with light. In the airy weight room, an unusual feature is the dry flotation unit, a space-age capsule appropriately named Superspace Relaxer, complete with its own audio, video, and sensory stimulation unit.

Water is involved in many of the treatments and services, from hot and cold plunge pools and a Turkish steam room to a vigorous aquaerobics class. Underwater massage in private tubs is enhanced with crystals from Hungarian mineral springs, combined with relaxing aromatherapy oils and spirulina algae or freeze-dried French seaweed.

Getting oriented to the hotel's multiple wings, you'll discover 10 restaurants (three of which serve spa cuisine), two huge swimming pools, and 20 tennis courts. There are almost 900 rooms and suites with minibars, refrigerators, and modern amenities; many have balconies with views of the Santa Rosa Mountains and the valley below. Golfers can book their own private villas near the course.

Full-day and half-day packages allow guests to use the spa without staying at the hotel. For a longer getaway, consider the European Thermal Mineral Kur Program, which combines a series of baths and bodywork; or the Spa Experience, which gives you a choice of one-hour services, unlimited aerobics classes, breakfast or lunch in the spa café, and a body composition test, plus hotel accommodations on a nightly basis. Kids can sign up for rock-climbing instruction or a round of golf on the 18-hole putting green, while parents pamper themselves desert-style.

FACILITIES
Exercise Equipment: Stair climbers, stationary bikes, weight-training circuit, free weights. **Services:** Aromatherapy massage, reflexology, shiatsu, sports massage; aloe wrap, Bindi, herbal wrap, loofah body scrub, mud wrap, spirulina wrap; facial. **Swimming:** Pool. **Classes and Programs:** Nutrition counseling, computerized fitness and body-composition analysis. Resort entertainment. **Recreation:** Croquet, golf, tennis, water volleyball. Biking, horseback riding, skiing nearby. **Children's Programs:** Kids Klub (ages 3–12).

ACCOMMODATIONS
833 rooms, 51 suites.

DINING
10 restaurants, 3 with spa cuisine. Meals served à la carte, or as part of Spa Experience package. **Sample Meals:** Spinach salad, cold poached salmon (lunch); grilled loin of veal, broiled chicken, or pasta primavera (dinner).

RATES AND PACKAGES
Daily room rates $169–$439 single or double; suites $435–$2,820. 3-night Spa Experience package priced by season, $219–$469 single, $299–$569 for 2. Day packages (no lodging) $85– $275. Packages include gratuities, tax. AE, DC, MC, V.

DIRECTIONS
✉ *74-855 Country Club Dr., Palm Desert, CA 92260,* ☎ *760/341–2211,* FAX *760/341–1872.*

From Los Angeles: Santa Monica Freeway (I-10) to Cook Street, turn right, 2 blocks, right again on Country Club Drive.

THE OAKS AT OJAI

Nutrition and diet

Fitness and weight-control programs are the raison d'être at this no-frills spa, whose clientele consists mainly of executive women and grandmothers, and a sprinkling of men, who come to burn calories, condition the heart and lungs, and tone the body. With its daily program of up to 17 exercise classes and activities, and a diet of fresh, natural foods totaling only 1,000 calories, this is the perfect setting for shaping up and slimming down. Sheila Cluff, a former professional ice skater and physical fitness instructor, developed the fitness facilities together with her husband Don, in the 1970s. Since then they have refined their staff of exercise physiologists, aestheticians, and nutritionists, and expanded their programs, adding theme packages focusing on mother-daughter bonding, spa cooking, stress management, and yoga.

Occupying a square block in the town of Ojai, just over an hour from Los Angeles in a fertile valley near Los Padres National Forest, the dignified wood-and-stone structure was built in 1918. Under the ownership of the Cluffs since the 1970s, the complex now includes coed saunas, an aerobics studio, a large swimming pool, and a cluster of guest bungalows, plus a main lodge with additional guest quarters. All rooms are simple but comfortable.

FACILITIES

Exercise Equipment: Stair climbers, stationary bikes, treadmills, weight-training circuit, free weights. **Services:** Aromatherapy massage, pregnancy massage, Reiki, reflexology; facials. **Swimming:** Pool. **Classes and Programs:** Lectures on health and fitness. **Recreation:** Hiking; biking, golf, tennis nearby.

ACCOMMODATIONS

27 rooms, 19 cottages.

DINING

3 meals daily. Natural foods, no additives, salt, white flour, or sugar. **Sample Meals:** Tostada with Mexican bean salad, gazpacho soup, or vegetable crêpes (lunch); lemon-broiled salmon with baby-green salad (dinner).

RATES AND PACKAGES

$200–$225 single, $135–$171 double, cottages $179–$283. 5-day program (Sun.–Fri. with 1 service) $1,000–$1,075 single, $675–$895 double; 7-day program with 2 services $1,400–$1,505 single, $945–$1,253 per person double. Spa Day (3 meals, classes; no lodging) $95. 1-night deposit required. D, MC, V.

DIRECTIONS

✉ *122 E. Ojai Ave., Ojai, CA 93023,* ☎ *805/646–5573 or 800/753–6257,* FAX *805/640–1504.*

From Los Angeles: Ventura Freeway (Highway 101) to Ventura, Highway 33 North to Ojai, Highway 150 to center of town (80 mins).

OJAI VALLEY INN & SPA

Luxury pampering

Anyone who remembers Frank Capra's 1937 epic *Lost Horizon* will recognize Ojai Valley's Topa Topa Mountains, which surround the Ojai Valley Inn & Spa. Like the mythical Shangri-La of Capra's movie, this Southern California newcomer (opened in 1998) strives to capture the carefree flavor of a place where people never grow old. To this end, every element of the experience here is shrouded in whimsical fancy: Guests enter the spa through the River of Life doors, and cross the village courtyard to the Fountain of the Sun, whose restorative waters are meant to wash away the cares of life.

Built around a golf resort dating from 1923, the spa is characterized by Moorish and Spanish Colonial architecture. Curving outdoor staircases, trickling fountains, terraces, and loggias surprise and delight at every turn. A bell tower rises 50 feet over the courtyard, where guests mingle as the chefs prepare meals on the outdoor grill. Surrounding this area are the art studio, the Acorn Cafe, and Yamaguchi at Ojai—a full-service hair and nail salon.

The inn, with its terra-cotta tile roofs, decorative ironwork and tiles, and flagstone terraces, feels like a Spanish estate, with 10 buildings occupying 220 tree-shaded acres. In the original Hacienda building, Spanish Colonial–style rooms have four-poster beds, carved furniture, and carefully restored floors and decorative tile from the 1920s. A few spa suites have private treatment rooms and whirlpools on the terrace. The ultra-private suites on the Alhambra-esque penthouse floor are decadently outfitted with carved chests, fringed ottomans, and oversize sofas, plus fireplaces and terraces with whirlpools. One has a meditation loft with expansive views of the mountains and golf course. In addition to the main inn, there are five cottages, each with a parlor, fireplace, and private terrace facing the golf course.

The spa itself carries on the Spanish Colonial theme, with plastered Andalusian ceilings, custom-designed tile floors, and mosaics of hand-painted tile. Each of the 28 treatment areas has hand-stenciled walls painted in warm shades, many with fireplaces.

Native American influences and local ingredients are easy to discern in many of the treatments here. To hydrate your skin, try an elderberry wrap, said to have originated with the Chumash Indians. The Ojai Honey Scrub uses local organic honey, and an exfoliation treatment called "Petals" uses fragrant crushed rose petals and rose powder to soothe the skin. The spa's signature treatment is the *Kuyam* (koo yahm), a Chumash word meaning "a place to rest together." The traditional healing treatment begins with the self-application of cleansing clays and homegrown herbs, which are baked into the skin by the heat of the Kuyam. Herb-infused steam then fills the domed room, softening the clay and providing inhalation therapy. A walk-through Swiss shower is used to remove the clays, and a second shower provides the final cleansing. After showering, you'll be wrapped in warm linen and left to relax on the outdoor loggia.

More than 50 classes are scheduled each week, including yoga and meditation at 7 AM daily. In addition to fitness-oriented courses, there are arts and crafts workshops, and seminars in calligraphy, painting, and wreath making with resident artists (for an additional fee). For those who prefer a less structured approach, the beautiful Ojai Valley—named the "nest" by the Chumash—is easily explorable on foot, bike, or horseback. The inn's 220 acres of softly rolling hills include a ranch with stables where you can get outfitted for a trail ride with naturalists through Los Padres National Forest. Guided hikes and birdwatching at Lake Casitas can be arranged by the spa concierge for an hourly fee; or you can borrow a bike and explore on your own.

With its par-70 golf course, three swimming pools, and first-rate fitness center—all complimentary and open to all guests—plus adults' workshops and children's programs, this is a great place for family vacations. Camp Ojai keeps kids busy learning ancient legends, visiting the animal petting farm, taking pony rides, and participating in sports.

FACILITIES

Exercise Equipment: Stationary bikes, stair climbers, treadmills, weight-training circuit, free weights. **Services:** Aromatherapy massage, deep-tissue massage, men's rubdown, pregnancy massage, reflexology, shiatsu, synchronized massage; Ayurvedic herbal detoxification wrap, elderberry herbal wrap, detoxifying spirulina wrap, Ojai honey scrub, Shirodhara; hydrotherapy massage, Ojai bath, Vichy shower; men's deep-cleansing facial, Ojai honey facial, spirulina facial. **Swimming:** 3 pools. **Classes and Programs:** Aerobics, aquaerobics, Spinning, tai chi, yoga; arts and crafts, batik, herb-wreath-making, hike-and-sketch class. **Recreation:** Biking, bird-watching, hiking, horseback riding, golf, tennis. **Children's Programs:** Camp Ojai (ages 3–12).

ACCOMMODATIONS
191 rooms, 11 suites, 4 cottages.

DINING
À la carte menus with spa cuisine choices at four dining locations. Options for vegetarian prix-fixe menu, spa menu, and six-course tasting menu at Maravilla restaurant, with daily changing selections. Organic produce grown in spa garden. **Sample Meals:** Roasted parsnip and Manilla clam chowder with herbs, organic greens with blood-orange–ginger dressing, broiled halibut with local vegetables and thyme (lunch); Dungeness crab cake with Fuji apple slaw and passionfruit dressing, warm arugula salad with sun-dried tomatoes and fennel, roast ostrich with banana-ginger compote and herb quinoa (dinner).

RATES AND PACKAGES
Rooms $210–$290 daily single or double, suites $345–$490, 2-bedroom cottages $750, 3-bedroom cottage $900. Discovery package (2-night minimum) $358 per night, $508 per night double. Day spa packages including lunch, $220 per person. AE, D, MC, V.

DIRECTIONS
⊠ *905 Country Club Rd., Ojai, CA 93023,* ☎ *805/646–5511 or 800/ 422–6524,* ℻ *805/6460–0305.*

From Los Angeles: Ventura Freeway (Highway 101) north to Highway 33, Highway 150 to Country Club Road.

THE PALMS

Nutrition and diet

Finding an informal and affordable place in which to exercise and diet among the many resorts of Palm Springs is a feat, which is why this relatively small, value-oriented spa is such a pleasant surprise. Modeled on The Oaks at Ojai (which is under the same ownership), the Palms attracts serious spa-goers, mostly women, in search of a serious weight-loss and fitness-oriented program. Devoted fans of Sheila Cluff come for her workouts and one-on-one fitness training, as well as her trademark 1,000-calorie daily diet, which insures successful weight loss.

With up to 16 activities offered daily, this is a "come as you are" place with plenty of options and no attendance requirements. Goal-oriented guests can have programs tailored to suit their abilities, interests, and needs. Activity centers on a large swimming pool, set amid bungalows and a lush garden. Classes are held indoors in a small aerobics studio, in the pool, or outside under the palms. Special weeks feature high-powered speakers on health, nutrition, and fitness; a seminar on women in management; a 21-day course on quitting smoking; and, in January and May, mother-daughter weeks. Although there is no hydrotherapy, a beauty salon, massage rooms, and a coed sauna and whirlpool are tucked into the complex. The converted manor house and cluster of private bungalows have a 1950s-style Spanish Colonial ambience, with motel-style furniture.

The program operates on an all-inclusive American Plan, regardless of how long you stay, and guests may arrive on any day, unless a workshop is scheduled. The flexibility allows you to enjoy the many attractions of the Palm Springs area, some within walking distance.

FACILITIES

Exercise Equipment: Stair climbers, stationary bikes, treadmills, weight-training circuit, free weights. **Services:** Massage, aloe body wrap. **Swimming:** Pool. **Classes and Programs:** Fitness consultation, body-composition analysis. Talks on dressing for success, the history of Palm Springs, and other subjects. **Recreation:** Biking, hiking, golf, horseback riding, and skiing nearby.

ACCOMMODATIONS

37 rooms, 8 bungalows.

DINING

3 meals daily, totaling 1,000 calories. No salt, sugar, or chemical additives. Mid-morning broth break, afternoon vegetable snack. **Sample Meals:** Vegetable burgers, stir-fry vegetables, or vegetable crepes (lunch); broiled red snapper in tomato sauce, turkey divan, or vegetarian lasagna (dinner).

RATES AND PACKAGES

$240–$271 single, $214–$226 double, on daily-program basis; $159–$171 with shared bath; 5-night midweek package with 1 treatment $1,075 single, $675–895 double; 7-night package with 2 treatments, $1,505, $1,253 double. 1-night deposit required. 2-day minimum stay. Day Spa package (classes, 3 meals; no lodging) $89. AE, D, MC, V.

DIRECTIONS

✉ *572 N. Indian Canyon Dr., Palm Springs, CA 92262,* ☎ *760/325–1111 or 800/753–7256,* ℻ *760/327–0867.*

From Los Angeles: I–10 to Highway 111, left at Alejo 1 block, left at N. Indian Canyon Drive (2½ hrs).

PRITIKIN LONGEVITY CENTER AT LOEWS SANTA MONICA BEACH HOTEL

Luxury pampering
Medical wellness
Nutrition and diet
Sports conditioning

Dedicated to the diet and exercise regimen espoused in the 1970s by the late Nathan Pritikin, the Pritikin Longevity Center has long been the development center for wellness programs offered around the country. Since 1978, guests have come to this beachfront facility to learn how to take charge of their health, prevent degenerative disease, and improve their quality of life. In 1998 the facility moved one block and a world away, to the Loews Santa Monica Beach Hotel; now guests can enjoy the glamor of a four-star hotel while undergoing the Pritikin's medically supervised program in one- to three-week packages available with hotel accommodations.

Learning to love the low-fat, largely vegetarian Pritikin diet is no hardship when you're ensconced in this airy beachfront hotel, with its eight-story atrium, private cooking classes, and ocean-view dining room. Meals are based on the Pritikin Eating Plan, which consists of 10% fat, 10–15% protein, 80% unrefined carbohydrates, all without sugar, salt, or butter. Special workshops with titles such as "Dining Out in the Real World," "Planning Your Eating Strategy," and "Supermarket Savvy" are designed to help you incorporate what you've learned into your everyday routine.

If the Pritikin's low-fat mantra fails to inspire you, the buffed bodies on nearby Venice Beach (a.k.a. Surfer's SoHo) should give you some impetus to pull in your waistline—and there are plenty of facilities to help you do just that. In addition to a glass-domed indoor–outdoor swimming pool with regularly scheduled aquaerobics classes, there's a full line of cardiovascular and strength-training equipment, including a cardio theater, plus a studio for aerobics, stretching and toning, and yoga classes. Physical therapy and orthopedic sports rehabilitation services are available, and training sessions can be arranged.

For all participants, the daily schedule includes three supervised exercise sessions (cardiovascular training on motorized treadmills, strength training, and elective exercise classes such as water aerobics), cooking classes, lifestyle counseling, and workshops that provide sound, practical strategies for healthy living. Graduates of the program receive a complimentary alumni newsletter and a telephone hotline providing free access to the Center's dieticians and exercise physiologists. If you're ever going to make a long-lasting lifestyle change, this is your chance.

FACILITIES
Exercise Equipment: Stair climbers, stationary bikes, treadmills, weight-training equipment, free weights. **Services:** Massage; aromatherapy wrap, mud bath; facial. **Swimming:** 2 pools, ocean beach. **Classes and Programs**: Fitness evaluation, one-on-one training. Live entertainment nightly. **Recreation**: Biking, in-line skating; golf and tennis nearby.

ACCOMMODATIONS
350 rooms.

DINING
3 meals plus 3 snacks daily included in program rates. Meals are mainly vegetarian; whole-grain dishes available buffet-style throughout the day. Breakfast, lunch, and snacks self-service; dinners served. **Sample Meals:** Full salad bar, plus vegetarian lasagna, tacos, or wraps, and fresh vegetable soups (lunch); spicy raspberry chicken, or paella with clams, lobster, and scallops (dinner).

RATES AND PACKAGES
One-week program (Sun.–Sat.) $3,036 single, $1,500 for second person sharing room; medical fees $522. 2-week program, $5,928 single, $2,600 for second person sharing room; medical fees $590. 3-week program $8,920, $3,600 for second person sharing room; medical fees up to $658. $500 deposit required. MC, V.

DIRECTIONS
✉ *1700 Ocean Ave., Santa Monica, CA 90401,* ☎ *310/829–6229 or 800/ 421–9911,* FAX *310/829–6440.*

From downtown Los Angeles: Santa Monica Freeway (Highway 10 West) to 4th Street exit, left on 4th Street, right on Pico Boulevard, right on Ocean Avenue (25 min.).

SPA HOTEL & CASINO

Mineral springs

The Spa Hotel & Casino is built on the site of hot mineral springs used by Native Americans for centuries. The Agua Caliente Band of the Cahuillia tribe owns the land and hotel, as well as the adjoining casino. Although this high-volume spa in the center of town is more utilitarian than chic, its therapeutic springs and extensive menu of spa services make it worthwhile, especially for those interested in visiting the casino and other attractions in Palm Springs. What's more, the Spa Hotel is a great value, with room rates dropping as low as $59 during the hottest part of the summer season.

The spa, which opened in 1963 and is a now a Palm Springs landmark, has been upgraded with Native American–influenced murals, clay-tile flooring, and meditative deep-blue lighting, emphasizing its unique cultural heritage. More than 50 body and facial services are now available, and there's also a fitness center with cardiovascular equipment. One-on-one training can be arranged for a fee, though there's no organized fitness program.

The best way to get a sense of the Spa Hotel is to indulge in the Spa Experience, a Native American–influenced mineral-water treatment. First you'll spend 15 minutes breathing eucalyptus-scented steam in the Inhalation Room. This is followed by a 20-minute soak in one of the spa's 34 ceramic-tiled whirlpool tubs whose 103°F mineral water is fed by two 50,000-gallon tanks. After your soak, you can treat yourself to a nap in the Tranquility Room, before proceeding to your private treatment room for a massage or other body-conditioning service.

Although there is no formal spa cuisine program and no nutritionist on staff, the Agua Grill & Dining Room has a well-balanced menu, and special requests are accommodated. The garden patio is the perfect place for lunch on mild days; you can also dine at the pool bar.

FACILITIES

Exercise Equipment: Stationary bikes, treadmill. **Services:** Aromatherapy massage, shiatsu, sports massage, Swedish massage; body scrub, herbal wrap, mud wrap; facial. **Swimming:** Pool. **Recreation:** Cross-country skiing, golf, hiking, horseback riding, tennis nearby.

ACCOMMODATIONS

210 rooms, 20 suites.

DINING

2 breakfasts and dinners included with Desert Escape package; otherwise, meals à la carte. **Sample Meals:** Cold salmon (lunch); lamb medallions, whole-wheat pasta, or grilled shrimp and vegetables (dinner).

RATES AND PACKAGES

Daily European plan per room: summer/fall $69–$179, winter $159–$229, suite $235. Desert Escape 2-night package with spa services $619.85 for 2 (Sun.–Thurs. only). 1-night deposit required. Packages include gratuities. AE, DC, MC, V.

DIRECTIONS

✉ *100 N. Indian Canyon Dr., Palm Springs, CA 92262,* ☎ *760/325–1461 or 800/854–1279,* ℻ *760/325–3344.*

From Los Angeles: I–10 to Highway 111 in Palm Canyon or to Tahquitz Way, turn left one block to hotel.

TWO BUNCH PALMS

Luxury pampering
Mineral springs

Remember the old song "Midnight at the Oasis"? If you've forgotten it, a good way to remember is to set out for Two Bunch Palms, an oasis if there ever was one. This desert hideaway was named by a survey team from the U.S. Camel Corps back in 1907 because of two groves of palm trees adjacent to artesian-fed springs. More than 90 years later, it's alive and well, with a clientele composed largely of Hollywood stars and writers who savor the privacy ensured by a guarded and gated entrance and isolated villas.

With no spa packages (but 26 à la carte services), no gym or golf course, and no organized social activities, Two Bunch Palms is best suited for those who prefer not to have a dawn-to-sunset schedule. Stationary bikes, yoga classes, and a jogging trail are available, but the main focus is on relaxing in a splendidly calming, almost spiritual environment. You can meditate alongside a flowing mineral creek, or soak in a warm, therapeutic pool fed by geothermal springs. The water, which comes out at 148°F (it's cooled a bit for comfort), splashes over a rock waterfall into a turquoise grotto framed by tropical shrubbery, under a canopy of fan palms and tamarisk trees. (Moviegoers might recognize the pool from Robert Altman's satirical film *The Player*.) For an especially magical treat, try an evening soak under the stars.

The dry heat of the desert induces a certain lethargy. To avoid the sun, guests indulge in the spa's extraordinary repertoire of bodywork and beauty treatments. One innovation is the esoteric massage, "designed to balance and harmonize the physical, emotional, and spiritual bodies." Another specialty is *watsu* massage in the pool: You float in the hot pool on six inner tubes while undergoing hand and foot massage. Another novelty is the mud bath in the palm-shaded Clay Cabana, which involves soaking in warm, green clay dug from mineral-water wells on the property. For total bliss follow this with a shower, a soak in the mineral pool, and a massage.

Near the pool are spacious villas and motel-like buildings. Many guests request number 14, a two-bedroom suite that goes for a whopping $480 a night; the big draws here, besides the private tanning deck, are a bullet hole in the mirror, and a desktop inscribed with the initials A.C. (The spa is said to have been a favorite hideaway of Al Capone.) Each of the villas has a private garden, whirlpool, and kitchen.

Some guests dine in the Casino Dining Room, a former casino whose walls are dedicated to movie memorabilia, but many order meals to be delivered to their villas: This is, after all, a bastion of privacy. If you're in the market to socialize, look elsewhere. If, on the other hand, you crave peace and the intoxicating effect of mineral healing water and healing hands, you've found your oasis.

FACILITIES
Services: Aromatherapy massage, deep-tissue massage, jin shin jyutsu, reflexology, shiatsu, Swedish massage, Trager massage; herbal wrap, mud wrap, salt glow; facial. **Swimming:** Pool. **Recreation:** Tennis, biking.

ACCOMMODATIONS
15 pool-side villas, 9 1-bedroom villas, 9 casitas, 6 deluxe studios, 6 2-bedroom apartments.

DINING
3 meals daily. No spa diet, but salads, grilled fish or chicken, and seasonal fresh fruit available. **Sample Meals:** Whole-wheat enchilada with Jack cheese and grilled vegetables, or Albacore tuna and sprouts on seven-grain bread (lunch); rosemary rack of lamb, grilled swordfish (dinner).

RATES AND PACKAGES
$175–$570 for 2 persons, including Continental breakfast. 2-night minimum. 1-night deposit required. AE, DC, MC, V.

DIRECTIONS
✉ *67425 Two Bunch Palms Trail, Desert Hot Springs, CA 92240,* ☎ *760/329–8791 or 800/472–4334,* FAX *760/329–1317.*

From Los Angeles: I–10 to Palm Drive exit, to Two Bunch Palms Trail (2 hrs).

2 The Southwest

Arizona, Colorado, Nevada, New Mexico, Utah

HEALTH RESORTS BECAME A NEW BONANZA in the Old West during the fitness fad of the 1980s, when ranches and lodges in the desert began offering the latest in diet, nutrition, and exercise programs, and fitness routines. Today your workouts can include meditation, thalassotherapy, and Ayurvedic treatments as well as skiing, mountain biking, and hiking. Spas in the Southwest are rediscovering their roots, using shamanistic healers, Native American–inspired treatments, and organic food in holistic programs designed to relieve stress and inspire well being.

The pioneer among fitness resorts in the Southwest is Canyon Ranch, near Tucson, Arizona. Nearby, the upscale Miraval resort artfully weaves exercises in mindfulness with luxury in the high desert. In the Rocky Mountain states, Colorado has the Peaks Resort & Spa for sports conditioning, the elegant spa at The Broadmoor in Colorado Springs, and a host of rustic, dress-down hot springs. With the 1998 opening of The Aspen Club, you can combine spa treatments, sports, and performing arts. Marriott's Camelback Inn, The Phoenician Centre for Well-Being, and the new Arizona Biltmore spa give you easy access to the major-league attractions of Phoenix and Scottsdale, Arizona. In "Utah's Banana Belt," a.k.a. southwestern Utah, the Franklin Quest Institute of Fitness now offers one of the best values in weight loss and wellness; and the nearby Green Valley Spa has extensive sports programs such as a tennis camp. The Winter Olympic Games of 2002, to be hosted by resorts near Salt Lake City, Utah, will undoubtedly bring new attractions and new facilities to the area, including a sports-medicine center at the Cliff Lodge at Snowbird.

ARIZONA

THE ARIZONA BILTMORE

Luxury pampering

Crowned "The Jewel of the Desert" when it first opened in 1929, the Frank Lloyd Wright–inspired Arizona Biltmore remains both an architectural landmark and an ultra-fashionable resort. Entering the grand hall of this storied palace is like stepping back to a time when movie stars and captains of industry gathered on the palm-fringed golf course to escape from the real world. With the addition of a spa linking the swimming pool and tennis complex, the Biltmore has an even broader appeal than before, for families on vacation, sophisticated travelers in search of privacy and attentive service, and business people who take advantage of the Biltmore's vast conference halls and meeting facilities.

The storied history of the Biltmore accounts for much of its allure. In order to produce the more than 250,000 indigenous concrete blocks needed for the signature "Biltmore block" (which features a geometric design inspired by the trunk of a palm tree), a temporary factory was established on site. When the estimated $1 million construction cost doubled, chewing-gum magnate William Wrigley, Jr. became the sole owner of the hotel and oversaw the installation of the legendary Catalina Pool, with its intricately tiled bottom, and the Aztec Room, with its gold-leaf domed ceiling supported by 40-ton copper filigreed beams. In the 1930s the hotel became famous as a luxury oasis where celebrities such as Carole Lombard and Clark Gable sought seclusion. Exceptional service became the Biltmore's hallmark, which might explain why every U.S. President since Herbert Hoover has stayed here.

In 1996, Sam and Peggy Grossman undertook a major enhancement project to bring the hotel into the 20th century, including additions such as the Paradise Pool with its 92-foot-long water slide, an 18-hole golf course, new luxury villas, and—to cap it all off—a 32,000-square foot spa, completed in January 1998. Despite cramped interiors, the spa building has 17 treatment rooms (three of them outdoor), three therapeutic pools with warm cascading water, a hydrotherapy tub, an aerobics room and fitness center with personal trainers, a full-service beauty salon, direct access to 8 tennis courts, and a boutique stocked with European and American skin care products. Nearby is the Paradise Pool, with indoor alcoves where you can escape from the heat with refreshing juice drinks, and private outdoor cabanas where you have a choice of manicure, pedicure, and massage.

On the residential side of the resort, covered garden promenades and flower-edged walkways meander to a variety of lodging annexes, where guest rooms and suites pay homage to Frank Lloyd Wright with mission-style furnishings, desert palettes of sand and ivory, and 1930s-style lamps. Most rooms have balconies or patios with views of Squaw Peak, the Paradise Pool, or various lawns, fountains, or gardens. The Paradise Wing is closest to the spa. A newer complex of villas is ideal for groups and those in search of seclusion; each has one or two bedrooms, two bathrooms, a kitchen, indoor and outdoor dining area, fireplace, and oversize patio or balcony with views of Squaw Peak, the Camelback Mountains, and the Catalina Pool, where Marilyn Monroe swam.

Relaxing in the open-air lounge, or over tea in the lobby, guests savor Biltmore traditions. Try a thirst-quenching Biltmore Breezes (raspberry tea with lemonade). For lunch, dinner, or Sunday brunch at Wright's, the hotel's Aztec mural–decorated restaurant featuring seasonal New American cuisine, reservations are essential. The informal Grill Room is a popular choice because of its 1930s ambience and outdoor dining patio with a selection of heart-healthy items.

It would be easy to spend several days exploring this grand resort; every time you feel oriented, some new feature of the resort comes into view: giant chess pieces on the lawn, a croquet green, and a putting course discretely worked into the landscape.

However, for those interested in exploring the Phoenix area, the Biltmore is also an ideal jumping-off point. You can take a brisk guided walk or bicycle through the estates that surround the resort (look for the Spanish-colonial mansion of William Wrigley, Jr., incongruously perched at the top of a desert hill.) Though the stables where Jean Harlow and Lee Tracy filmed *The Blonde Bombshell* in 1933 are gone, you can get a ride by hotel shuttle van to the Biltmore Fashion Park to shop and dine. Or rent a car or join a guided tour to the high-desert canyons and energy vortexes of Sedona, about 90 minutes from the Biltmore, the perfect antidote for the frenetic pace of Phoenix.

FACILITIES
Exercise Equipment: Rowing machines, stationary bikes, stair climbers, treadmills, weight-training circuit, free weights. **Services:** Aromatherapy massage, lymphatic drainage, reflexology, shiatsu, sports massage, Swedish massage; Bindi herbal body treatment, essential oil aroma wrap, desert body glow, hydrating body paraffin wrap, seaweed body mask; aromatherapy hydro-massage, Ayurvedic bath, balneotherapy, slimming hydrotherapy; Ayurvedic rejuvenating facial, deep-cleansing facial, gentleman facial, sensitive facial. **Swimming:** 6 pools. **Classes and Programs:** Aquaerobics, golf and tennis clinics, fitness evaluation; cooking class, wine tasting. **Recreation:** Biking, croquet, hiking, lawn chess, golf, tennis.

ACCOMMODATIONS
600 rooms, 50 villas.

DINING
New American cuisine at Wright's, American and regional favorites at the Biltmore Grill & Patio, poolside dining at Cabana Club Restaurant & Bar. À la carte menu selection. **Sample Meals:** Charred tuna with wasabi crème fraîche, peanut-crusted lobster cakes, ginger-miso poached salmon (lunch); grilled halibut with couscous and parsnip cakes, smoked venison loin with black-truffle spaetzle and garlic spinach, or grilled lamb chops with polenta and roasted fennel sauce (dinner).

RATES AND PACKAGES
Seasonal daily rate per room, $145–$495, suites $325–$620, villas $725–$1,745. Biltmore's Best package includes lodging plus one-hour massage, facial, fitness evaluation, and breakfast $505–$639 single, $840–$980 double. AE, D, DC, MC, V.

DIRECTIONS
✉ *24th St. and Missouri Ave., Phoenix, AZ 85016,* ☎ *602/955–6600 or 800/950–0086,* FAX *602/955–6013.*

From Sky Harbor Airport: Highway 51 (Squaw Peak Parkway) north to Highland Ave. exit, right to 24th Street, left to Missouri Avenue (15 mins).

CANYON RANCH

Holistic health
Luxury pampering
Medical wellness
Nutrition and diet

If you can only go to one spa in your life, Canyon Ranch is a logical choice. Since its opening in 1979, founders Mel and Enid Zuckerman have set the trends in the spa industry, developing many lifestyle programs that emphasize fitness of mind, body, and spirit. A staff-to-guest ratio of nearly three to one includes medical doctors, psychologists and counselors, exercise physiologists, nutritionists, movement therapists, acupuncturists, and tennis and racquetball pros. There are more than 40 fitness classes daily, plus tennis, hiking, and biking programs, and spiritual awareness classes such as yoga, tai chi, and meditation. Workshops in lifestyle change, stress management, disease prevention, smoking cessation, and weight loss appeal to those with serious issues, while rejuvenating spa treatments and a spectacular setting make for a health-oriented but thoroughly pleasant vacation.

Low-lying adobe-style cottages accommodate up to 200 guests at the sprawling ranch, which is set on 70 acres in the foothills of the Santa Catalina Mountains near Tucson. Walking trails weave through natural desert vegetation, and the interior grounds are landscaped with flowers, cactus gardens, tropical trees, streams, pools, and fountains. In the midst of all this are a 62,000-square-foot spa complex and an 8,000-square-foot Health and Healing Center. The spa complex has seven gyms, aerobics studios, strength and cardio machines, one squash and three racquetball courts; yoga dome; and men's and women's locker rooms with separate sauna, steam, and inhalation rooms, whirlpool baths, and private sunbathing areas. Also in the spa building are skin-care and beauty salons, and massage, herbal wrap, and hydrotherapy rooms.

A day at Canyon Ranch can be as busy or low-key as you like. Unlike more rigidly programmed resorts, the ranch allows you to select your own activities, and program coordinators are on hand to help you plan your days. Several prebreakfast hikes of various lengths begin at dawn, along paths through the desert landscape of cacti, mesquite, acacia, and palo verde trees. From 9 AM on, fitness classes are scheduled at every hour until 5 PM, with a lunch break at noon. The last class of the day is meditation in the yoga dome—a therapeutic way to wind down after a day of physical challenges.

Dining at the ranch is an integral part of the wellness experience. Here you'll learn that healthy eating does not require depriving yourself. You can choose from traditional dishes, regional specialities, vegetarian fare, daily chef's specials, and even dessert—all of it low in fat and nutritionally balanced. Information about the nutritional content of each item is provided so that you can learn about healthy eating as you enjoy it.

Periodically Canyon Ranch offers theme weeks: Adult Asthma Week, Executive Women's Week, Healthy Heart, Living with Arthritis, New Directions in Diabetes, and more. For men and women over 60, ElderCamp® weeks provide a friendly, supportive environment for exploration of positive approaches to aging. These tend to attract an interesting mix of singles and seniors from various parts of the world.

At the Life Enhancement Center, those committed to making serious lifestyle changes are teamed with specialists on physical and emotional problems. Workshops deal with everything from diet to healthy aging, with experts on health, nutrition, stress management, and prevention of illness conducting one-on-one sessions. A medical checkup is included in the program fee. Participants share meals in a private dining room and bunk in special living quarters, but also have access to the spa's facilities and services.

FACILITIES

Exercise Equipment: Cross-country ski track, rowing machines, stair climbers, stationary bikes, treadmills, vertical ladder climber, weight-training circuit, free weights. **Services:** Aromatherapy massage, craniosacral massage, head-neck-shoulder massage, lymphatic massage, reflexology, Reiki, shiatsu, Swedish massage; aloe glaze, aroma wrap, herbal wrap, mud wrap, Parisian body polish, salt scrub, seaweed body treatment; hydro-massage, watsu; aloe-algae mask, aromatherapy facial, European facial, freeze masque, in-depth facial. **Swimming:** 4 pools (1 indoor). **Classes and Programs:** Aerobics, aquaerobics, boxercise, breathing and relaxation, cardio-circuit training, chi gong, meditation, Spinning, stretch class, tai chi, yoga; jin shin jyutsu self-help workshop, Swedish massage workshop; consultation on nutrition and diet, holistic health, body composition, and fitness level. Biofeedback program, smoking cessation. Astrology, cooking class, handwriting analysis, tarot-card reading; talks by psychologists, authors, naturalists, and other specialists. **Recreation:** Basketball, golf, hiking, mountain biking, racquetball, squash, trail running, volleyball, wallyball.

ACCOMMODATIONS

180 rooms in casitas, suites, and private condominium cottages.

DINING

3 meals daily included in packages. Some vegetarian choices. **Sample Meals:** Chicken fajitas, Oriental noodle salad, pasta primavera, vegetarian bean chili (lunch); lobster with tarragon sauce, roast turkey with garlic-mashed potatoes, mustard-crusted rack of lamb (dinner).

RATES AND PACKAGES

5-day/4-night package, standard accommodation $1,750–$2,520. 8-day/7-night package, standard accommodation $3,480–$4,120 single, $2,870–$3,340 per person double occupancy. 8-day/7 night Life Enhancement program (Sun.–Sun.) $3,480–$4,120 single, $2,870–$3,340 per person double occupancy. 2-night deposit required. 4-night minimum stay (mid-Sept.–mid-June). AE, D, MC, V.

DIRECTIONS

✉ *8600 E. Rockcliff Rd., Tucson, AZ 85750,* ☎ *520/749–9000 or 800/726–9900,* ℻ *520/749–7755.*

From Tucson: Speedway Boulevard east to Kolb Road, Tanque Verde Road to Sabino Canyon Road, Snyder Road to Rockcliff (30 mins).

MARRIOTT'S SPA AT CAMELBACK INN

Luxury pampering

Within a spectacular hacienda-style structure in the foothills of Mummy Mountain, the Spa at Camelback Inn is both a bonus for guests of the hotel and a destination in itself. This 125-acre retreat surrounded by striking desert landscape combines the latest bodyworks technologies and Old World therapies with heart-healthy cuisine for a top-notch spa experience.

Discerning spa goers will not be disappointed here: Facilities are the most complete in the Phoenix–Scottsdale area. Many of the spa therapists have University of Arizona degrees in physiology, and some are trained in esoteric massage techniques at workshops in nearby Sedona or California. This may be one of the only spas to offer classes in Pilates, a highly specialized class designed to correct postural alignment and strengthen the back and abdomen. Other unusual programs include healing rituals inspired by the Native American culture, using indigenous desert plants and herbs. Skin-care treatments are the most complete in the Southwest, including sun protection, Bindi herbal body treatments, and aloe-vera rehydration after golf and tennis. Private massage rooms feature aromatherapy, reflexology, shiatsu, and jin shin jyutsu stress-reduction massage from Japan. The selection of group exercise sessions also is impressive, including yoga and aeroboxing as well as aerobics.

Advancing the art of fitness evaluations, Camelback has linked up with the Institute of Aerobic Research in Texas, where testing procedures are based on those of aerobics pioneer Dr. Kenneth R. Cooper. Fitcheck is a one-hour assessment of body composition, flexibility, cardiovascular endurance, and body strength. A computerized evaluation of your data provides individualized recommendations for improving fitness levels. For a more advanced look at your lifestyle, schedule a Personalized Aerobic Lifestyle System (PALS) evaluation, which includes follow-up material and guidelines from the Cooper Clinic.

Most guests begin the day with a four-mile power walk up the mountainside for grand views of the Phoenix valley and surrounding desert. The guided group walk at 6:30 AM is open to all resort guests without charge, and if you book at least an hour of services, the daily spa admission charge ($22) is waived. Use of the fitness facility costs $10 daily if you are not on a spa package, or plan a full day at the spa, so you can sample different physical activities and then indulge in a bodywork session and salon services. Workout clothes, robes, and slippers are provided; just bring exercise shoes.

Southwestern art and ceramics brighten the locker rooms and lounges, where bottles of water are always at hand to ward off dehydration in the dry Arizona climate. Specially equipped treatment rooms and the sauna and steam room are in an atrium, which has a cold plunge pool and hot whirlpool. Guests stay in Southwestern-style casitas, some with private sundecks. The most luxurious guest quarters have private pools.

FACILITIES
Exercise Equipment: Cross-country ski tracks, rowing machines, stationary bikes, stair climbers, treadmills, weight-training circuit, free weights. **Services:** Aromatherapy massage, shiatsu, sports massage, Swedish massage; aloe-vera rehydrating treatment, Bindi herbal body treatment, loofah body scrub; hydrotherapy, thalassotherapy; aromatherapy facial, collagen facial, European facial. **Swimming:** 3 pools. **Classes and Programs:** Aerobics, aerobox, aquaerobics, ballet stretch, body sculpting, meditation, tai chi, yoga; fitness and wellness evaluations, body-composition analysis, nutritional counseling, one-on-one training. **Recreation:** Basketball, golf, pitch-and-putt, Ping-Pong, shuffleboard, tennis. Horseback riding and hiking nearby. Resort entertainment.

ACCOMMODATIONS
420 casitas, 27 suites.

DINING
Continental cuisine at The Chapparal; Southwestern meals at The Navajo; heart-healthy spa cuisine at Sprouts Restaurant at the Spa casual dining and snacks at Kokopelli Café, Camelback Golf Club Restaurant, Oasis Lounge, and Hoppin' Jacks. **Sample Meals:** Grilled pompano stuffed with crabmeat, or cold skinless breast of chicken (lunch); poached lamb

loin, grilled ahi tuna with papaya relish, or roast breast of capon stuffed with ricotta cheese (dinner).

RATES AND PACKAGES
Spa Getaway with breakfast or lunch (per night) $188 single, $274 for 2; 3-night/4-day Revitalizer with meals, spa services $908 single, $1,505 for 2; 6-night/7-day Renewal package $1,741 single, $2,875 for 2; Stay & Play package with golf (per night) $138–$210 single, $169–$313 for 2; daily room, spa admission, and breakfast $139–$144 single or double. 1-night deposit required. Spa Day (lodging not included) $75–$235. AE, DC, MC, V.

DIRECTIONS
✉ *5402 E. Lincoln Dr., Scottsdale, AZ 85253,* ☎ *602/948–1700 or 800/ 242–2635,* FAX *602/596–7018.*

From Phoenix: By car, north on 44th Street, Tatum Boulevard to Lincoln Drive (30 min).

MIRAVAL

Holistic health
Luxury pampering

One experienced spa goer called it a cross between Outward Bound and New Age. Indeed, this desert resort near Tucson is more than a spa; part ranch, part self-discovery center, it's an upscale destination for achievers seeking new challenges or total relaxation. The motto is "Life in Balance." Accordingly, you may find yourself trying things you've never done before: jumping off a 25-foot pole (you'll be harnessed to ropes, of course), climbing a custom-designed rock wall, perhaps even taking a workshop in grooming horses who interact with you on an emotional level. The goal of most programs is to teach guests how to balance their lives, by learning to challenge themselves physically and spiritually.

Besides its innovative programs, the real joy of Miraval is its spectacular setting: Sprawling over 135 acres in the foothills of the Santa Catalina Mountains of southern Arizona, this resort enjoys the same beneficent climate as neighboring Canyon Ranch. Hikes and trail rides through the Sonoran desert are a favorite pastime; a cool, dry energy prevails, even in the heat of summer. Combined with the exercise classes that can be challenging or mood-enhancing, the effect is invigorating.

When the desert sun is too much, you can take shelter in the best-equipped fitness center this side of the Rio Grande. In addition to strength and cardiovascular training, there are two aerobics studios (one has a suspended hardwood floor), a six-lane lap pool (25 meters), and locker rooms. Personal trainers are on hand, and their services can be added to your package rate.

Miraval's all-inclusive package rates cover everything from morning tai chi and yoga to body treatments—massage, facial, scalp treatment, pedicure—and one-on-one training. One personal service per day is included; additional treatments or training can be scheduled for a fee. No tipping is allowed. Your choice of activities is planned in advance by a program counselor who arranges airport transfers and fitness evaluation.

The spa's specialty is LaStone Therapy, a form of massage using hot and cold lava rocks. These are placed on stress points across your back and stomach; their warmth penetrates your body during your massage, inducing relaxation, and in turn permitting deeper muscle penetration and quicker pain release. An added effect is the feeling of being connected to the desert.

Accommodations in spacious stucco-walled casitas are another part of the desert experience. One hundred and six adobe buildings accommodating up to 180 guests are amid palm trees, Zen-like meditation gardens, and meandering streams. Each room is equipped with minibar and coffeemaker; suites have fireplaces. Twenty-four-hour room service is available at no extra cost.; There are five outdoor swimming pools, including the spa lap pool. Water comes from the resort's own aquifer; fruit and bottles of mineral water are supplied in your room.

FACILITIES
Exercise Equipment: Stationary bikes, stair climbers, treadmills, weight training units, free weights. **Services**: Hot-rock or therapeutic massage; body wrap; hydrotherapy; facial. Fitness evaluation, one-on-one training. **Swimming**: 4 pools. **Classes and Programs**: Tennis instruction. Arts and crafts, and cooking classes. Music, entertainment. **Recreation**: Croquet, horseback riding, tennis. Golf nearby.

ACCOMMODATIONS
92 rooms, 14 suites.

DINING
3 meals daily included in package; complimentary in-room refreshments.
Sample Meals: Vegetarian corn crêpe, braised artichokes, grilled swordfish salad (lunch); braised cactus and baby vegetables with loin of venison, vegetable lasagna, grilled grouper, or grape leaves stuffed with grilled salmon and sea scallops (dinner).

RATES AND PACKAGES
Daily $200–$1,000 per person, single or double. 4-day/3-night package $950–$1,785 per person, single or double. Seasonal packages available. 1-night deposit required. AE, DC, MC, V.

DIRECTIONS
✉ 5000 E. Via Estancia Miraval, Catalina, AZ 85739, ☎ 520/825–4000 or 800/232–3969, 🖷 520/792–5870.

From Tucson: North on I-10, east on Tangerine Road, north on Oracle Road, east on Golder Ranch Road, north on Lago del Oro Parkway, right to resort (45 min).

THE PHOENICIAN CENTRE FOR WELL-BEING

Luxury pampering
Nutrition and diet

Nestled on 250 acres of manicured lawn and desert terrain at the base of Camelback Mountain, the Phoenician has lots of flash and splash. An excess of luxury—cascading waters, polished marble, crystal chandeliers, and candle-lit terraces—engulf you from the moment you arrive. The crowd here ranges from convention groups and corporate moguls to ladies taking tea. Somehow, it all works.

Exceptional service matches the grandeur of the public areas; oversize guest rooms are quiet retreats with all the amenities of a world-class resort. Similarly, the Centre for Well-Being is an oasis of pampering, where the goal is as often as not to get you in shape for the evening's big bash. Treatments here are largely inspired by Native American therapeutic traditions, using desert plants and minerals. Special programs are customized to fit the skin-care needs of men and women: Herbal wraps with muslin sheets soaked in a fragrant blend of sage, juniper, and rosemary are offered as a calming treatment prior to massage, for example.

The two-level Centre rises from a verdant lawn surrounded by casitas, separated from the resort's main building by a series of swimming pools and water slides. Past the reception area and boutique are a meditation atrium, water bar, and 24 treatment rooms. Upstairs is the fitness center, with Cybex strength-training and cardiovascular equipment, a glass-walled aerobics studio equipped with a sprung-wood floor, and beauty salon and barber shop, all with beautiful desert views.

Accommodations are spread around in the main hotel, the canyon wing, and separate casitas; some of the nicest are close to the spa. Golfers may want to opt for a suite in the Canyon Building, which is close to the course. Most accommodations have oversize bathrooms in Italian marble. Suites have hand-carved travertine fireplaces.

FACILITIES

Exercise Equipment: Rowing machines, stationary bikes, stair climbers, treadmills, weight-training circuit, free weights. **Services:** Aromatherapy massage, jin shin jyutsu, lymphatic drainage, reflexology, shiatsu, sports massage, Swedish massage; aloe-vera wrap, body scrub, desert clay wrap, herbal wrap, Moor mud wrap, shirodhara; facial. **Swimming:** 9 pools. **Classes and Programs:** Aerobics, self-defense, tai chi, yoga. Fitness consultation, body-composition analysis, cholesterol testing. Astrology, herbology, tarot-card reading. **Recreation:** Archery, badminton, biking, croquet, golf, lawn bowling, tennis, volleyball, water basketball and volleyball.

ACCOMMODATIONS
654 rooms.

DINING
Spa cuisine available at Mary Elaine's (formal, French), Windows on the Green (casual Southwestern), and the Terrace (favored for brunch). **Sample Meals:** Grilled-vegetable sandwich, grilled portabello taco with roasted peppers, avocado, and cheese (lunch); grilled salmon with gazpacho relish, penne with grilled chicken, roasted peppers, and eggplant (dinner).

RATES AND PACKAGES
Summer: $190–$310, suites $500–$750; winter: $410–$565, suites 1,075–$1,725. 4-day/3-night Turnaround $1,320–$1,995 single, $1,995–$2,775 per couple. 8-day/7-night Quest Choice package $3,010–$4,830 single, $4,610–$6,425 per couple. Twice-as-Nice 4-day/3-night golf/spa package $1,510–$2,485 per couple. 1-day Retreat (no lodging or meals) $95–$190. Daily spa admission ($16; $6 after 5 PM) waived in conjunction with treatments or program. AE, DC, MC, V.

DIRECTIONS
✉ *6000 E. Camelback Rd., Scottsdale, AZ 85251,* ☎ *602/941–8200 or 800/888–8234,* FAX *602/947–4311.*

From Phoenix: North on 44th Street to Camelback Road, right to Jokake Road, left into resort (20 mins).

SCOTTSDALE PRINCESS

Luxury pampering

The towers of the Scottsdale Princess rise from the Sonoran Desert like a mirage surrounded by a velvet green golf course. True to its name, the 450-acre oasis has a king-size spa and fitness center offering packages of royal indulgence for a day, or use of the exercise equipment and participation in the five daily aerobics classes. Other day spa packages combine sports and relaxation.

A fitness staff member sets the pace on a 45-minute morning walk in the crisp desert air along the grounds and golf course. The rest of the day is your own to schedule with bodywork and a bit of luxury pampering. Participating in a wide range of outdoor sports is the major attraction for most guests: wallyball, Ping-Pong, a fun run, and desert biking are scheduled daily, in addition to tennis, golf, and water aerobics. Golfers have direct access to 36 holes within the resort, including a top-rated TPC stadium course, par 72.

The fitness center is top of the line. There's a mirrored aerobics studio with a suspended hardwood floor ideal for step, low-impact, stretch, yoga, and body-sculpture classes. Encompassing 10,000 square feet of workout space, the Fitness Center has an array of exercise equipment, and separate men's and women's locker rooms with eucalyptus steam, 16-jet Swiss shower, sauna, and whirlpools. The daily admission fee is waived when you schedule a massage or any spa treatment. Other options include nearby hiking trails in the McDowell Mountains, renting a mountain bike, and horseback riding at the nearby 400-acre equestrian park.

Surrounded by waterscapes, rustling palm trees, purple jacaranda, and giant red hibiscus, the hotel complex evokes the feeling of a Spanish-colonial city, with shady arcades for strolling. Standard rooms are done in Mexican-colonial style, with terraces, wet bars, and separate living and work areas, and the sunbleached color scheme is relaxing even if the furniture is showing its age. For extra luxury and privacy, the casitas are choice accommodations. If you want to swim laps, head for the quiet East Pool; the South Pool, a 12-sided extravaganza with a hot tub, gets lots of play from families and conventioneers.

FACILITIES
Exercise Equipment: Cross-country ski track, rowing machine, stair climbers, stationary bikes, weight-training circuit, free weights. **Services:** Aromatherapy massage, hot-rock massage reflexology, shiatsu, Swedish massage; aloe or algae body mask, loofah body scrub, mud wrap, salt glow. **Swimming:** 3 pools. **Recreation:** Basketball, biking, croquet, fishing, golf, racquetball, squash, tennis, volleyball, wallyball. Nearby equestrian center with riding, shows, and polo. Resort entertainment. **Children's Programs:** Kids Klub (ages 5–12).

ACCOMMODATIONS
429 rooms, 21 suites, 125 casitas, 75 villas.

DINING
The Grill (golf clubhouse) offers steaks and grilled seafood; Las Ventanas (pool view) features Southwestern-style seafood, chicken, and salads. La Hacienda serves Mexican specialties, and the Marquesa features Catalan cuisine. **Sample Meals:** Grilled salmon with spicy couscous and lemonade vinaigrette, gazpacho, wood-roast pizza of braised vegetables and dry Jack cheese, mango quesadilla with prickly-pear vinaigrette (lunch); paella, "ceviche-style" scallops with cilantro-pesto vinaigrette, jalapeño-glazed mahi mahi (dinner).

RATES AND PACKAGES
Standard rooms $155–$430 single or double, suites $470–$2,750. 2-night Royal Indulgence spa package $295–$904 per person, includes Continental breakfast, services. AE, DC, MC, V.

DIRECTIONS
✉ 7575 E. Princess Dr., Scottsdale, AZ 85255, ☎ 602/585–4848 or 800/344–4758, FAX 602/585–0086.

From Phoenix: Highway 51 north to Shea Boulevard, east to Scottsdale Road, north to Princess Drive (30 min).

COLORADO

THE ASPEN CLUB

Luxury pampering
Medical wellness
Nutrition and diet
Sports conditioning

A holistic approach to health care is the philosophy of the Aspen Club, whose 28-year-old owner, Michael D. Fox, has transformed this former tennis and racquet club into one of the country's premier sports destinations. Following a major renovation in 1998, the club now consists of four centers under one roof—a state-of-the-art fitness club, a full-service spa, a sports-medicine institute, and the Center for Well Being. The latter provides the cornerstone to Fox's approach toward medicine: It's a complementary medical center counting chiropractors, acupuncturists, and sports psychologists among its staff. Here you can try sessions in biofeedback or sound therapy, get a metabolic test, or even take home a customized Chinese herbal medicine prescription or a personalized blend of aromatherapy oils.

A 3,500-square-foot, two-story workout facility, capped by a 50-by-28-foot skylight, forms the core of the remodeled club. The architecture communicates vitality and energy, through a vibrant red, green, and gold color scheme and an abundance of natural light. You can challenge yourself with classes in Spinning, kickboxing, salsaerobics, Chi Kung, Pilates, and four kinds of yoga. The Club can also arrange snowshoeing and hiking excursions right from the property, and cross-country skiing and bicycling outings nearby. There's even an indoor simulated ski- and snowboard-training studio where an instructor helps first-timers learn the skills by using a harness on a treadmill ramp; afterwards, you can head to the mountain to try the real thing. The Club counts Martina Navratilova among its members, and about half of the US Ski Team trains here. Visitors can drop in to use the fitness facilities or get spa treatments, or you can meet with a Vitality Guide to design a multi-day package around your goals.

At Spa Aspen, traditional European treatments range from a detoxifying thermal mineral kur to therapeutic bath and massage. Guests can relax between treatments in a lounge overlooking a meditation garden, lulled by the sound of a waterfall. The Sports Medicine Center treats injuries as well as providing preventive treatments like sports-specific training and orthotics design. An evening lecture series includes two to three talks a week on various health and fitness topics.

The Aspen Club does not have its own lodging, but works with hotels throughout the area to arrange accommodations. (Most rentals have sundecks and Jacuzzis.) Other nearby accommodations are the St. Regis, the Jerome, and the Gant. Continental breakfast, lunch, and health-club facilities are included in the rates at the Aspen Club Lodge; for dinner, Aspen's many restaurants are within easy driving distance.

FACILITIES

Exercise Equipment: Rowing machines, stationary bikes, stair climbers, treadmills, weight-training circuit, free weights. **Services:** Alpine body wrap, aromatherapy massage, sports massage; Ayurvedic services, Feldenkrais, thermal mineral kur, thermal scrub; hydrotherapy. **Swimming:** Indoor pool. **Classes and Programs:** Chi Kung, kickboxing, Pilates, salsaerobics, Spinning, yoga; biomechanical examination, blood-profile analysis, body-composition analysis, maximal stress test, nutritional and food-allergy evaluation, one-on-one training, post-injury therapy, strength and flexibility test; sports-performance seminars, fitness and nutrition seminars. **Recreation:** Aikido, basketball, cycling, fencing, hiking, racquetball, skiing, squash, tennis, volleyball, wallyball; golf and horseback riding nearby. **Children's Programs:** Nursery and toddler swim classes, children's athletic programs in racquetball, squash, swimming, tennis, and dance.

ACCOMMODATIONS

Club can arrange accommodations at nearby hotels, condominiums, and private homes.

DINING

Heart-healthy breakfast and lunch (with organic juice bar) included in spa packages, and served in Club dining room. **Sample Meals:** Linguini with wild mushrooms, smoked salmon sandwich, Asian noodle bowl and spring rolls, grilled vegetable sandwich (lunch).

RATES AND PACKAGES

3-day Vitality Tune-Up $670 per person (not including lodging), 1-night Spa Package $300 (with lodging) per 2 persons. AE, D, MC, V.

DIRECTIONS

✉ *1450 Crystal Lake Rd., Aspen, CO 81611,* ☎ *970/925–8900; 800/ 554–2773, or Aspen Central Reservations 800/554–2773,* 🖷 *970/925– 9543.*

From Denver: I-70 to Glenwood Springs, Route 82 to Aspen.

THE BROADMOOR

Luxury pampering

Since 1918, The Broadmoor has been a Colorado classic. Visiting this mountain resort is like taking a step back to the golden era when Colorado Springs attracted health seekers from around the world. Set on 3,000 well-groomed acres with a private lake and five swimming pools, it's a grand Italian Renaissance–style palace flanked by nine hotel buildings. With the addition of a two-level lakefront spa-and-fitness complex (opened in 1994), the Broadmoor is now considered the premier health and sports resort in the Rocky Mountain region.

A major part of the draw here is the dramatic mountain setting. Within a few miles are the red-rock canyons of the Garden of the Gods, the mineral waters of Manitou Springs, and the training center for Olympic athletes. You can ride the original cog railway on Pikes Peak, tour the US Air Force Academy, go hot-air ballooning or boating, hike or ride horseback into the foothills. At night, you can drive into town for a trip to the movies or the local nightclub, or dine at one of nine fine restaurants.

Instead, though, you might choose to spend all your time enjoying the facilities at the spa, which overlooks 12 tennis courts and three championship golf courses. Also housed here are the golf clubhouse and three restaurants. There is an aerobics studio for scheduled classes in step, slide, body sculpting, and box aerobics, a complete Cybex weight room, and cardiovascular equipment. Families can splash in the huge indoor swimming pool under a soaring, skylit ceiling; adults swim in a two-lane outdoor lap pool. Alongside the pool is a juice bar for lunch and snacks, with tables on a sunny terrace overlooking the first tee. The fitness facilities are available to all resort guests for a daily fee or as part of spa packages.

The spa offers an exclusive line of body treatments using native Colorado ingredients. The Broadmoor Falls water massage is a surprisingly invigorating experience: In a shower with heated granite walls, your scalp and body are massaged by 17 hot and cold jets of pure mountain water. Seven different kinds of therapeutic baths are used to soothe sore muscles, smooth the skin, and encourage the circulation. The spa lounge is an inner sanctum for relaxation, warmed by a log fire, where you sip tea or lemonade while absorbing the changing moods of the mountains from the veranda. A visit to the spa is a pure Colorado experience, infused with scents of spruce and cedar, decorated with the state flower (columbine), and invigorated by mountain air.

Against a backdrop of nearby mountain ranges, black swans swim in the lake, watched over by the resident canine whose job it is to chase them back in the water to keep the walkways free of droppings. It's a minor detail, but typical of the level of care that makes the Broadmoor unique.

FACILITIES
Exercise Equipment: Rowing machines, stationary bikes, stair climbers, weight-training circuit, free weights. **Services:** Aromatherapy massage, shiatsu, Swedish massage; aromabath, herbal wrap, milk-whey bath, mud bath, salt glow; hydrotherapy; facial. **Swimming:** 4 pools (1 indoor). **Recreation**: Biking, golf, horseback riding, hot-air ballooning, ice skating, paddleboats, shuffleboard, skeet- and trap-shooting. Downhill skiing nearby.

ACCOMMODATIONS
591 rooms, 109 suites.

DINING
Cuisine Vivant items on all menus (marked CV) are 20%–25% fat, 50%–55% carbohydrates, 15%–20% protein. Selections are à la carte. **Sample Meals:** Grilled swordfish steak with Mediterranean sauce, sautéed Colorado red trout fillet (lunch); broiled red snapper and halibut, vegetable ravioli with shiitake mushrooms (dinner).

RATES AND PACKAGES
Daily rates per room $294–$394 peak season, $190–$290 off-season, suites $390–$2,200. Spa packages including accommodation and spa gratuity Apr. 1–Nov. 1: 1-night Spa Splurge from $192.50 per person, double; 3-night Spa Spectacular from $938–$1183 per person, double. AE, D, MC, V.

DIRECTIONS
✉ *Box 1439, Colorado Springs, CO 80901,* ☎ *719/634–7711 or 800/ 634–7711, ext. 5770,* FAX *719/577–5700.*

From Denver: 2 mi west of I–25 at corner of Lake Avenue and Lake Circle (90 min).

GLENWOOD HOT SPRINGS LODGE & POOL

Mineral springs

Join the crowd soaking in the steaming waters of the Rockies' largest natural thermal-springs pool. Open year-round, even in subfreezing temperatures, the mineral water flows constantly at 130°F. Dashing into the pool on a winter day is a bracing experience. Shrouded in mist, nearby trees become covered with ice. Skiers and hunters drop by to relax, and families come for fun.

In summer, though, the springs really come alive. A 405-foot-long swimming pool that's usually filled with families and teenagers is cooled for comfortable swimming, and a smaller, 104-degree therapy pool is equipped with underwater jets for massage. Together, the pools contain 1.1 million gallons of mineral water (it's changed three times daily). The entire complex, with a 3-story lodge and athletic club, is two blocks long.

If you opt to stay at the geothermally heated lodge, you'll have direct, complimentary access to the outdoor pools and the Hot Springs Athletic Club fitness facility, including coed saunas and whirlpools. There are scheduled fitness classes in aquaerobics, low-impact aerobics, and Jazzercise. Guests also have access to racquetball, handball, and walleyball courts, for a small fee.

For a real sweat, walk over to the vapor caves, where the hot springs can be as hot as 115°F. Cold-water hoses are available, but there is no soaking pool. Day visitors are welcome both at the caves and at the pools; lodge guests pay a nominal admission fee.

FACILITIES
Exercise Equipment: Stationary bikes, stair climbers, weight-training circuit. **Services:** Massage, chiropractic adjustment, facial. **Swimming:** 2 pools. **Recreation:** Handball, hiking, racquetball, trout fishing, water.

ACCOMMODATIONS
107 rooms.

DINING
No meal plan. Meals served at lodge café.

RATES AND PACKAGES
$56–$95 per day single, $63–$102 double. Daily pool admission $7.25 adults, $4.75 children. Discount on admission to pools and athletic club for lodge guests. 1-night deposit required. AE, DC, MC, V.

DIRECTIONS
✉ *Box 308, 415 E. 6th St. Glenwood Springs, CO 81601,* ☎ *970/945–6571,* FAX *970/947–2950.*

From Denver: I–70 (3 hrs).

GLOBAL FITNESS ADVENTURES

Holistic health
Nutrition and diet
Sports conditioning

Inspired by the majesty and splendor of the Rockies, former fashion model Kristina Hurrell and her husband, Dr. Rob Krakovitz—author and holistic health authority—designed a life-energizing program focused around hiking in some of the world's most beautiful places. Though based in Aspen, this is a traveling spa, with week-long programs in eight locations around the world, including Sedona, Arizona, and Santa Barbara, California, as well as Kauai, Island of Dominica, Bali, Kenya, and Lake Como.

The program is limited to 12 participants. Hikes of 6 to 18 miles geared to individual fitness levels fill most mornings; afterward, guests can challenge themselves with sports unique to each location, such as horseback riding, scuba diving, and kayaking. Days begin with yoga and meditation—in Sedona, these activities take place on a rock vortex with incredible views—and end with dinner by candlelight. Regular massages and cultural outings, such as hikes to ancient settlements near Sedona, are included in the program rate. Optional cooking classes, Indian sweat lodges, and drumming experiences are often available.

Each retreat is structured around the same basic program, but draws its inspiration from the beauty of its locale. Accommodations, always upscale, range from country inns to villas to jungle lodges. The Aspen Adventure takes place on a picturesque 1500-acre ranch, 45 miles from Aspen, surrounded by 2 million acres of the White River National Forest. Guests stay in private cabins or rooms in the main lodge, with all the amenities of a full-service hotel, and congregate around a huge rock fireplace at night. In Sedona, Southwestern-style houses in Oak Creek Canyon have fireplaces, kitchens, and wooden decks.

The combination of healthy eating and extensive daily exercise forms a basis for weight loss. Spa-cuisine meals are mostly vegetarian, with some organic chicken or freshly caught fish as part of the fare. Supervised juice or water regimens are also available. By adhering to a course of exercise and attending classes on topics ranging from improving communication skills and personal relations to enhancing mental, emotional, and physical energies, you'll achieve a sense of well-being in a magical place that will put you on the road to peak vitality.

FACILITIES

Facilities vary according to locale. Below are facilities offered in Aspen program:

Services: Massage, natural-healing bodywork. **Swimming:** Nearby lake. **Classes and Programs:** Yoga and meditation training, horseback-riding instruction, informal workshops on health and nutrition; personal consultation on medical and health problems, with holistic therapies (fee). Dance and drumming workshops. **Recreation:** Canoeing, horseback riding, rowing, snowshoeing, trout fishing, mountain biking; golf and tennis nearby.

ACCOMMODATIONS

Accommodations vary by locale, from private mountain cabins to country inns, Italian villas, and jungle lodges.

DINING

3 vegetarian meals daily served family style, plus snacks. Meals vary according to locale. **Sample Meals:** Salad with tofu, lemon-garlic, and tempeh, sprout sandwich (lunch); steamed squash, steamed brown rice with vegetables, grilled trout (dinner).

RATES AND PACKAGES

Rates and packages vary for each program. Below are rates for Aspen property:

$2,275 per person, double occupancy for 1 week, includes all meals, massages. $500 deposit due 30 days prior to arrival. No credit cards.

DIRECTIONS

✉ *Headquarters: Box 1390, Aspen, CO 81612,* ☎ *970/927–9593 or 800/488–8747,* ℻ *970/927–4793.*

GOLD LAKE MOUNTAIN RESORT & SPA

Luxury pampering
Sports conditioning

In the mountains west of Boulder, this turn-of-the-century fishing resort and girls' camp is now an unusual small spa. Inspired by the environmentally correct Post Ranch Inn in Big Sur, California, owners Alice and Karel Starek set out to create a high-end resort high in the mountains where manmade art and natural beauty would blend harmoniously—an eclectic blend of rusticity and luxury.

Gold Lake itself is the focal point for most of the resort's activities: hiking its perimeter, paddling around it in a canoe or kayak, ice skating in winter, or simply luxuriating in one of four hot pools built into the rocks above the lake. There are purposely no indoor fitness facilities or classes here—the intent is for guests to be outdoors, soaking in the splendor of the Rockies.

The indoor environment is, however, carefully crafted. Guests stay in log cabins with exquisite slate-and-copper bathrooms and log beds with raw silk and hemp duvets. Alice's Restaurant is a rough-hewn beauty, with unpeeled birch-log furniture and a copper fireplace. And it's all the more enjoyable thanks to the "mountain spa cuisine" menu developed by chef Ron Pickarski, the first vegetarian chef to be certified by the American Culinary Federation. He uses organically grown vegetables and grains to create richness and texture, but also incorporates wild game and fresh fish. About half the menu is vegetarian.

Spa treatments such as radiance technique and polarity therapy are designed to work on a spiritual as well as physical level. The dual massage, however, is just plain decadent: Two masseurs or masseuses work in tandem, synchronizing their strokes. Imagine having your scalp and feet massaged at the same time.

FACILITIES
Exercise Equipment: None. **Services:** Massage, clay body treatments, salt glow, thalassotherapy, aromatherapy facial. **Recreation:** Canoeing, fly-fishing, horseback riding, ice skating, kayaking, mountain biking; cross-country skiing, snowshoeing.

ACCOMMODATIONS
17 single- or double-bedroom log cabins; 1 3-bedroom house.

DINING
Complimentary full breakfast. À la carte lunch at Karel's Bad Tavern; 3-course prix-fixe dinner at Alice's Restaurant. **Sample Meals:** Black-bean-and-corn-squash stew on roast garlic-mashed potatoes, or Asian salmon burger with pickled cucumbers (lunch); Portabello mushrooms stuffed with Italian sausage, red peppers, and asiago cheese, or baked salmon with roast carrot sauce and potato-spinach-gorgonzola soufflée (dinner).

RATES AND PACKAGES
$195–$315 ($495 for 3-bedroom Lake House) in summer, $140–$280 ($395 for Lake House) spring, fall, and winter. AE, DC, MC, V.

DIRECTIONS
✉ *3371 Gold Lake Rd., Ward, CO 80481,* ☎ *303/459–3544 or 800/450–3544,* ℻ *303/459–3541.*

From Denver: U.S. 36 to Boulder, Route 119 to Ward.

INDIAN SPRINGS RESORT

Mineral springs

At the historic Indian Springs Resort you can swim in mineral water surrounded by tropical foliage beneath an arched glass roof. And here's the kicker: You can do it *sans* swimsuit, as this resort caters to nude bathers (there are separate pools for men and women). For those who are sheepish about this stipulation, private tubs can be booked by the hour—a popular alternative for couples and families.

Sacred to Native Americans, the hot springs were first developed for prospectors during the local gold rush, and devotees have traveled from around the world to bathe in them ever since. The water flows from three springs, at temperatures ranging from 104°F to 112°F. The pools are entered via caves, which adds to the mystical mood of the whole affair.

Chemical analysis of the water has found that it contains trace minerals essential to good health. While no conclusive scientific claims have been made for the waters, experts cite the benefits of bathing for those who suffer from arthritis and rheumatism. Unlike most hot springs, the waters here do not smell of sulfur.

Though the historic resort is beginning to show its age, it's still a bargain getaway. Both day visitors and overnight guests are welcome; the latter stay at an atmospheric Victorian hotel, built in 1869, where the ornate dining room is still intact. Rooms in the original building have half baths and few modern conveniences; those in the newer adjoining inn are more modern.

FACILITIES
Services: Massage. **Swimming:** Pool, geo-thermal cave baths. **Recreation:** Hiking, horseback riding, fishing.

ACCOMMODATIONS
68 rooms, some with half bath.

DINING
No meal plan, but dining room serves 3 meals daily.

RATES AND PACKAGES
Rooms and suites $44–$71 for 1 or 2 persons; campsite $15. Bathhouse admission $10. 1-night credit card deposit required. MC, V.

DIRECTIONS
✉ *Box 1990, Idaho Springs, CO 80452,* ☎ *303/989–6666,* 🖷 *303/567–9304.*

From Denver: I–70 west to Idaho Springs exit, Highway 241A; left on Soda Creek Road.

THE LODGE & SPA AT CORDILLERA

Luxury pampering
Sports conditioning

Imagine spending the morning fly-and-float fishing on a private three-mile stretch of the Eagle River, or working out in a glass-walled fitness center with expansive Rocky Mountain views, then indulging in the afternoon with a Decleor-product facial. To follow the reverie to its completion, picture yourself dining on healthful but sophisticated cuisine prepared by a renowned French chef, and then retiring to your own private estate, where a butler has turned down your bed and fluffed your pillows. At Cordillera, this perfect dream can come true.

Set on 2,500 acres of its own mountaintop between the resorts of Vail and Beaver Creek, the lodge is secluded and intimate, with stone and stucco walls and deeply sloping roofs of Chinese slate (it was built to resemble a Pyrenées manor house). Most of its 56 spacious rooms have fireplaces and glass doors opening onto terraces with sweeping views of the mountains. For those who wish to indulge in the lifestyle of the rich and famous for an interlude, private luxury estates in the Cordillera residential community can be rented, complete with a personal butler who will serve cocktails, schedule tee times, and perform just about any task to make your vacation more enjoyable.

With a 10-hole short course and a Hale Irwin 18-hole Mountain Course, Cordillera is one of the country's top golf destinations. Outdoorspeople can also take advantage of 12 miles of privately maintained trails for hiking, biking, or cross-country skiing, as well as tennis courts and sporting clays. The glass-walled fitness center has the latest equipment, including Keiser Cam III weights and an AquaCiser underwater treadmill. Adjoining it are an indoor lap pool and an aerobics studio with a floating wooden floor. Programs are available for two to seven days, or you can drop in for an afternoon or full-day escape.

After a day on the slopes or in the spa, you'll be ready for an epicurean performance in the Picasso restaurant, named for its original Picasso lithographs. Chef Fabrice Beaudoin uses vegetable and fruit reductions and herbs from the Cordillera kitchen garden in the place of butter and cream to create a lighter style of French cuisine. Afterwards, retire to the lobby to sink into a plush sofa in front of a carved limestone fireplace. This is getting away in style.

FACILITIES

Exercise Equipment: Rowing machine, stationary bikes, stair climbers, treadmills, weight-training circuit. **Services:** Swedish massage; aromatherapy or sea-algae body wrap, body polish; hydrotherapy; facial. **Swimming:** 2 pools (1 indoor). **Classes and Programs:** Aerobics; endurance testing, fitness assessment, personal training. **Recreation:** Badminton, biking, croquet, golf, hiking, tennis, trout fishing, volleyball. Cross-country skiing, dog-sled rides, ice skating, snowmobiling; nearby downhill skiing.

ACCOMMODATIONS

48 rooms, 3 suites, 5 lofts; home rentals also available.

DINING

Breakfast buffet included in room rate. Nutritionally balanced menus for guests on fitness program. À la carte menu at Restaurant Picasso. **Sample Meals:** Chicken breast marinated in sherry vinaigrette, salmon fillet wrapped in grape leaves (lunch); veal loin Provençale, or fish of the day steamed with vegetable julienne (dinner).

RATES AND PACKAGES

$150–$460 per night, single or double for standard room; with fireplace, $195–$425. Suites $320–$750 for 2. 2-night Getaway with spa services and meals, $622–$1,525 for 2. 1-night deposit required. AE, D, DC, MC, V.

DIRECTIONS

✉ *Box 1110, Edwards, CO 81632,* ☎ *970/926–2200 or 800/877–3529,* ℻ *970/926–2486.*

From Denver: I–70 to Exit 163 at Edwards, Route 6 to Squaw Creek Road, Cordillera Way (2½ hrs).

THE PEAKS RESORT & GOLDEN DOOR SPA

Luxury pampering
Nutrition and diet
Sports conditioning

Scenic splendor, the best spa facilities this side of the Rockies, and family programs make the Peaks an all-seasons destination for kids and adults of all ages. Set amid the ski slopes in Southwest Colorado, the 10-story hotel is surrounded by majestic views of the Rocky Mountains. Diversity distinguishes the daily spa program: Choices range from sunrise yoga in a window-walled studio to a guided vision quest to a group-exercise class called "Yoga for Golf," said to help control the golfing mind while stretching the golfing muscles. Outdoor enthusiasts can go hiking, horseback riding, mountain biking, rock climbing, and skiing. In addition, a free gondola lift links the resort to the historic silver mining town of Telluride, so guests can take advantage of the many activities in town.

The spa program, which capitalizes on Southwestern traditions and Native American lore, offers the Rockies' widest range of skin-care treatments and bodywork, day and night. Try a soak in a Kivah whirlpool—a treatment inspired by a cleansing ritual that's part Native American sweat lodge, part Scandinavian sauna and steam—or an Alpine Aromatherapy massage with custom-blended oils of geranium, sage, tangerine, sandalwood, cardamom, and frankincense. Specialized spa treatments incorporate advanced concepts. One of the most unusual is "Cardio Coaching," where an exercise physiologist interprets sensors on your body while you work out, in order to give you guidance on how to maximize your exercise. Another program prepares you for activity at altitude (the resort is at about 10,000 feet).

Family-friendly activities are a specialty at The Peaks. Entertaining and educational programs combine with exercise and healthy meals at the resort's KidSpa, a day camp that allows parents to pursue activities without worrying about childcare. Depending on the weather, kids go on guided hikes, take swimming lessons, practice yoga, or pan for gold in nearby streams. For budding athletes, junior ski and snowboarding lessons are available.

Next Level Spa, a new program of indoor–outdoor adventure quests, is designed for active vacationers, featuring excursions as well as special accommodations in the hotel. Warm-weather options include mountain biking, whitewater rafting, fly-fishing, horseback riding, rock climbing, golf, and tennis. Next Level Spa guests have separate accommodations in 16 deluxe guest rooms with extra amenities such as a foot massager, scent diffuser, and bath salts. Next Level Spa packages, four or seven nights, include complimentary use of the facilities, plus selected treatments, three meals daily, and surprise gifts each night. A concierge will confirm your spa appointments for you.

Skiers will be in business here. The Peaks' location provides ski-in, ski-out access to the Telluride Ski Area for enthusiasts of every experience level. Overnight servicing of your equipment is an added cost. After a day on the slopes, you can indulge in moisturizing treatments such as a soothing thermal mud wrap, or a therapeutic sports massage.

FACILITIES
Exercise Equipment: Cross-country ski track, rowing machines, stationary bikes, stair climbers, treadmills, vertical ladder climber, weight-training system, free weights. **Services:** Aromatherapy massage, shiatsu, shirodhara, sports massage; body facial, cellulite treatment, fango wrap, hydrotherapy bath with seaweed, purification bath. **Swimming:** 2 pools. **Classes and Programs:** Pilates; fitness evaluation, nutritition consultation, personal training, stress management using biofeedback, Ultratone body shaping. **Recreation:** Badminton, climbing (indoor wall), fly-fishing, golf, mountain biking, paddle tennis, racquetball, squash, tennis; cross-country and downhill skiing. **Children's Programs:** KidSpa (2-1/2–11).

ACCOMMODATIONS
116 rooms, 29 suites.

DINING
À la carte meals prepared under specific nutritional guidelines for minimal sodium, fat, and caloric content. **Sample Meals:** Bow-tie pasta with scallops in tomato-saffron broth, pizza made with tomatoes, fresh moz-

zarella, and basil (lunch); hearty lobster stew, grilled sea bass with chickpea-mashed potatoes (dinner).

RATES AND PACKAGES

Daily rate $150–$595 per person single or double. Call for packages, which vary seasonally. Deposit of first and last night by credit card. AE, DC, MC, V.

DIRECTIONS

✉ *136 A Top Country Club Drive, Box 2702, Telluride, CO 81435,* ☎ *970/728–6800 or 800/789–2220,* FAX *970/728–6567.*

From Denver: I–70 west to Grand Junction, south on Highway 50, west on Highway 62, south on Highway 145 (7 hrs).

SONNENALP RESORT

Luxury pampering

In the faux-Tyrolean village of Vail, the Sonnenalp stands out as the real thing, run with *Gemütlichkeit* (warmth) by the Bavarian Fassler family, fourth-generation hoteliers. The sprawling resort in the heart of Vail is as luxurious and service-oriented as any four-star resort in the Alps; the staff will even ship your skis to and from your home for you, or lend you a cellular phone to take with you on the mountain.

An open fireplace is the centerpiece of the sunny Bavaria Haus spa, where picture windows frame views of the woods and Gore Creek. The glassed-in fitness room has a few carefully chosen pieces of equipment, and the indoor-outdoor pool is capped by a waterfall at one end. Treatments use body-firming seaweed, salt scrubs, and moor mud. The smaller Swiss Haus spa offers facials, manicures, and pedicures as well as body treatments.

Three different guest houses all have distinct flavors: The all-suite Bavaria Haus is the most elegant building, with gas fireplaces and mammoth bathrooms that have heated marble floors. Here the staff dress in dirndls and lederhosen. Swiss Haus rooms have down comforters and pine armoires. Barnwood and open brick walls lend a more rustic feel to the Austria Haus.

Do not plan on dieting here: Each day begins with a full European breakfast of muesli, pastries, cold cuts, fruit, and a hot entrée of eggs or pancakes, topped off by an oversized china cup of the richest hot chocolate in the Vail Valley. Ludwig's, the most elegant of the resort's three restaurants, serves sophisticated Bavarian fare. The Swiss Chalet serves calorie-laden fondue and raclette, and at Bully Ranch you can partake of ribs.

FACILITIES

Exercise Equipment: Rowing machine, stair climbers, stationary bikes, treadmills, free weights. **Services:** Massage, hydrotherapy, facial. **Swimming:** Pool. **Recreation:** Golf, tennis, skiing.

ACCOMMODATIONS

174 rooms.

DINING

Full European breakfast included in packages. Bavarian specialties at Ludwig's, fondue at Swiss Chalet, ribs at Bully Ranch. **Sample Meals:** Cheese fondue (lunch); veal medallions with chanterelle mushrooms and potato gnocchi (dinner).

RATES AND PACKAGES

Daily per room, single or double: $150–$415 summer, $260–$675 winter. AE, DC, MC, V.

DIRECTIONS

⊠ *Sonnenalp Resort, 20 Vail Road, Vail, CO 81657,* ☎ *970/476–5656 or 800/654–8312,* FAX *970/476–1639.*

THE VAIL ATHLETIC CLUB

Luxury pampering
Sports conditioning

Vail is Valhalla for skiers in winter, and for golfers, mountain bikers, and hikers in summer. In the midst of the bustling village, the Vail Athletic Club Hotel and Spa is an ideal home base for a sports-centered getaway. You can use the health club and spa on a daily basis, or stay in one of the 38 hotel rooms and take advantage of the facilities for free.

The athletic club and spa have a sleek, modern look, with gray slate tiles and polished chrome fixtures. A 20-meter indoor lap pool and outdoor hot tub overlook Gore Creek and the Vail Mountain ski slopes. The two-story rock-climbing wall is the most dramatic feature of the club (lessons are offered for the uninitiated). Equally impressive is the list of classes, including Pilates, several different forms of yoga, and Spinning. Ballroom dancing and fencing round out the option.

Spa treatments with Dr. Hauschka's botanical oils and lotions from Germany use aromatherapy to balance and harmonize the senses. The signature treatment, "Nature, Body, and Spirit," incorporates sage, rosemary, lavender, rose, and lemon oil on different parts of the body to alternately stimulate, calm, and refresh.

Terra Bistro, the hotel restaurant, relies on organic produce whenever possible, and caters to the meat-and-potatoes eaters as well as vegetarians. Terra Bistro also claims to offer the most affordably-priced bubblies of any restaurant in the United States. Hotel rooms are basic, but include such amenities as ski boot warmers, refrigerators, coffee makers, and private balconies.

FACILITIES
Exercise Equipment: Cross-country ski track, rowing machine, stair climbers, stationary bikes, treadmill, vertical ladder climber, weight-training circuit, free weights. **Services:** Reflexology, sports massage; mud bath, shirodhara; hydrotherapy, Swiss shower; facial. **Swimming:** Indoor pool. **Classes and Programs:** Boxing aerobics, fencing, Pilates, Spinning, yoga; personal training. **Recreation:** Climbing (indoor wall), skiing.

ACCOMMODATIONS
38 rooms.

DINING
No spa menu. Complimentary Continental breakfast buffet. À la carte specialties served at Terra Bistro. **Sample Meals:** Coriander-rubbed tuna with tamari vinaigrette, sesame-crusted salmon (lunch); rum-soaked drunken pork chop, grilled portobello mushroom with wild-rice pilaf and miso gravy (dinner).

RATES AND PACKAGES
Daily tariff per room, single or double $175–$1,100 winter, $125–$375 spring–fall. Day use fee for spa $15–$28. AE, D, MC, V.

DIRECTIONS

⊠ *352 E. Meadow Dr., Vail, CO 81657,* ☎ *970/476–0700 or 800/822–4754,* FAX *970/476–6451.*

From Denver: I–70 to Vail (2 hrs).

VAIL CASCADE HOTEL & CLUB

Sports conditioning

A ski vacation at the Vail Cascade Hotel & Club is pretty near hassle-free: The ski concierge has your equipment warmed and waiting for you in the morning, and the resort's own chairlift whisks you up the mountain right from the hotel. Non-skiers, too, will find plenty to keep them busy at this 17-acre resort. The 78,000-square-foot Cascade Club has an aerobics studio with mountain views, full-court basketball, four tennis courts, squash, racquetball, a running track, and a golf simulator—all indoors, for year-round use. When summer rolls around, rates drop, and guests can practice their swings on the golf course or go swimming in three outdoor pools, mountain biking or in-line skating on the bike path into Vail Village (rentals are available from the resort), hiking on Vail Mountain, horseback riding, rafting, or fly-fishing.

Spa treatments are as broad in scope as the range of sports activities: A dynamic sports massage, along with assisted stretches, prepares you for a day of skiing or biking; the Rejuvenating Foot Treatment is a great après-hike pick-me-up. Locally gathered ingredients are used in treatments such as the Wildflower Honey Scrub.

The hotel's four-story wings are designed to look like a European chateau. Rooms are decorated in jewel tones, and have courtyard or mountain views, some with back doors opening right onto Gore Creek. Some suites and deluxe mountain-view rooms have fireplaces and whirlpools or saunas.

FACILITIES
Exercise Equipment: Cardio theater, ergometer, rowing machines, stair climbers, stationary bikes, treadmills, weight-training circuit, free weights. **Services**: Sports massage, Swedish massage; body polish, body wrap; facial. **Swimming**: Pool. **Recreation**: Biking, racquetball, squash, tennis. Golf and white-water rafting nearby.

ACCOMMODATIONS
201 rooms, 28 suites.

DINING
No meal plan. Heart-healthy fare in The Cafe, including vegetable juice squeezed to order; regional American cuisine at Alfredo's. **Sample Meals:** Caesar salad, Thai chicken salad, vegetable sandwich (lunch); grilled mushrooms and spring asparagus, sesame-cured pork loin with salad roll (dinner).

RATES AND PACKAGES
Daily per room: $200–$500 double, suites $300–$1,000. Cascade Club $12. Summer spa packages $165–$240 single, $225–$340 double. Confirmation by credit card. AE, DC, MC, V.

DIRECTIONS
✉ 1300 Westhaven Dr., Cascade Village, Vail, CO 81657, ☎ 970/476-7111 or 800/420-2424, Inter-Continental Hotels 800/327-0200, ℻ 970/479-7025.

From Denver: I–70 to west Vail, turn on Westhaven Drive (2 hr).

WIESBADEN HOT SPRINGS SPA & LODGINGS

Mineral springs

On a starlit night, soaking in the outdoor thermal-water pool at this mountainside resort can be an uplifting experience—especially after a steam bath in a natural, rock-walled vapor cave. You can indulge in this relaxing ritual at Wiesbaden Hot Springs Lodge, a family-owned-and-operated mountainside resort that began as a motel and morphed, over the years, into a well-established, full-fledged health resort.

The resort's facilities include a lodge, an exercise room with video monitors but no instructors, a weights room, and a sauna. A massage therapist is on staff, and you can also sign up for facials with Aveda skin care products, aromatherapy wraps, and acupressure treatments to achieve deep relaxation. As in the past, however, the main attraction is the series of naturally heated outdoor pools and rock-walled vapor caves, which are open to the public for day use for a $10 fee, and are free to lodge guests. One private soaking pool has a clothing-optional policy.

The spiritual quality of the cave was recognized by the Ute Indians and other Native American tribes who traveled for days to reach the curative waters. The original bathhouse, built in 1879, was replaced by a medical clinic in the 1920s, then a guest lodge. Rooms are decorated with antiques, some have a wood stove. A glass-walled lounge overlooks the swimming pool and sundeck.

At an altitude of 7,700 feet, the picturesque old mountain town of Ouray is sheltered from winds by the surrounding forest. Few roads traverse these mountains, which are the source of the Rio Grande and several hot springs. The geothermal water that heats the motel and swimming pool flows from two springs at temperatures of 111°F–134°F. The mineral water is also circulated through soaking pools, avoiding the need for chemical purification.

Scenic canyons in the national forest are a major attraction for hikers. The makings for a picnic can be found in town, a few blocks away (the lodge has no dining room). Dinner at the Bon Ton Restaurant in the nearby St. Elmo Hotel is recommended for a taste of the town's Victorian gold-rush days.

FACILITIES
Exercise Equipment: Stair climber, stationary bike, free weights. **Services:** Acupressure, reflexology, Swedish massage; body mask, mud wrap; facial. **Swimming:** Pool. **Recreation:** Biking, hiking.

ACCOMMODATIONS
20 rooms, 2 private apartments, 1 house.

RATES AND PACKAGES
Daily rate per room for 2 persons $90–$145. Private house for 2, $145. 1-night deposit required. D, MC, V.

DIRECTIONS
✉ 625 5th St., Box 349, Ouray, CO 81427, ☎ 970/325–4347, FAX 970/325–4358.

From Denver: I–70 to Grand Junction, Highway 550 (5 1/2 hrs).

WOMEN'S QUEST FITNESS RETREATS

Holistic health
Sports conditioning

"Let go, play hard, and be free" is the mantra at these five-day fitness retreats designed to build confidence and empower women of all ages and athletic abilities. Founded in 1992 by Colleen Cannon, a former world-champion triathlete, and staffed by nationally ranked athletes including seven-time Ironman winner Ray Browning and four-time marathon Olympian and bronze medalist Lorraine Moller, this unique program is built on the philosophy that physical activity is one of the most powerful and, perhaps, most under-used tool for personal discovery, balance, and transformation.

Programs take place either at the rustic Woodspur Lodge in the ski-resort town of Winter Park, Colorado, in late June, mid-July, and early August; at the Franklin Quest Institute of Fitness in St. George, Utah (*see* Franklin Quest review, *below*), in late April and early November; and in Vermont (location to be determined) in early February. Though the focus of the summer programs is on instruction in trail running, mountain biking, and swimming (or, for winter programs, cross-country skiing, snowshoeing, and swimming), participants are taught to combine these activities with yoga, meditation, and journal writing to create inner balance. The staff takes a playful, unintimidating approach toward encouraging participants to stretch their limits, and cooperation rather than competition is encouraged.

A typical day at the Colorado Women's Quest retreat begins with pre-breakfast yoga and meditation in the Great Room of the Woodspur Lodge, where glass doors look out on the snow-capped Rockies. After breakfast there's a group mountain-bike ride. Swimming instruction, yoga, and free time for journal writing and relaxing follow lunchtime. After dinner there are lectures on subjects such as heart-rate monitor training, herbs and the female athlete, or nutrition and body image; toward the end of the session, a traditional sweat-lodge ceremony promotes group bonding under the stars. On the final day, when the group has become acclimated and fit, there's an all-day hike to the top of the Continental Divide, where the positive discoveries made at this retreat are bound to come into focus.

The 35 women who attend these retreats may be as young as 17 or as old as 65, as fit as a competitive triathlete or as new to sports as someone who has never ridden a bicycle, and yet by the end of each session lasting friendships have inevitably formed. Camaraderie and mutual support are emphasized; all activities are done as a group, including sports outings, discussions, and meals. On the first day of camp, each participant is paired with a roommate, although you can opt to pay extra for a single room. The lodge is rustic and homey; some rooms have bunk beds, and all have log-hewn walls. Meals are served at big common tables, giving participants a chance to make new friends every evening.

FACILITIES

Services: Massage. **Classes and Programs:** Guided visualization and imagery, meditation, yoga. Instruction in mountain biking, trail running, and swimming. Lectures and inspirational talks on topics ranging from nutrition and diet to high-performance training to self-esteem and goal-setting. **Recreation:** Mountain biking, trail running and hiking, swimming, cross-country skiing, snowshoeing.

ACCOMMODATIONS

Accommodations vary by program (*see above*).

DINING

3 meals included in rates. Salad bar available at lunch and dinner, home-made bread with all meals. **Sample Meals:** Tofu eggless salad, tuna salad, garden burgers (lunch); stir-fried vegetables with chicken or fish, fajitas, pasta with meat sauce or marinara sauce, and steamed vegetables (dinner).

RATES AND PACKAGES

$1,150 for 5-day Winter Park and St. George programs, including double-occupancy lodging, meals, sports instruction, and bike rental. $200 deposit required. No credit cards.

DIRECTIONS

✉ *Headquarters: 2525 Arapahoe Ave., Suite E4-181, Boulder, CO 80302,* ☎ *303/443–5930,* FAX *303/443–3620.*

Call for directions.

NEVADA

THE DESERT INN RESORT & CASINO

Luxury pampering

The Desert Inn is a one-stop shop: A health and fitness club within a country club and casino. A daily facilities charge and several packages allow guests to enjoy its well-equipped exercise facility without entering the casino. It's the ideal place for couples who want to spend their vacations together, each pursuing his or her own activities.

Italian marble statues and Greek columns create the effect of an ancient spa, but the recently expanded facilities are state-of-the-art. Gambling $200 million on The Sands renovation, ITT Sheraton Corporation gave the spa building a new look in 1997. A stunning glass-walled, floor-to-ceiling rotunda in the men's and women's pavilions leads to therapy pools, hot- and cold- water plunges, and a big central Jacuzzi. The steam rooms, saunas, and hydrotherapy room are a few steps away. There's also a 14,500-foot free-form, lagoon-style swimming pool, and the only championship golf course in this part of town.

Luxurious guest quarters are spread among four different towers and a complex of villas. Minisuites in the Palm tower have oversize Jacuzzi tubs, some with views of the hotel grounds, lagoon, and golf course. Three bi-level suites have private swimming pool and patio, and up to four bedrooms overlooking the lagoon. For the biggest splurge of all, opt for a villa in the Villas del Lago complex. Nine of these are three-bedroom suites, each with swimming pools and hot tubs on private patios, workout rooms, entertainment rooms, dining rooms, and butler service.

As a result of the current building boom along The Strip, there are larger and glitzier spas at The Mirage and MGM Grand resorts. However, the country-club atmosphere at Desert Inn will appeal to those who prefer to work out in style.

FACILITIES
Exercise Equipment: Ergometer, rowing machine, stair climber, stationary bikes, treadmills, vertical ladder climber, weight-training circuit, free weights. **Services:** Aromatherapy massage, reflexology, shiatsu, sports massage, Swedish massage; aloe-vera revitalizer, aromatherapy salt glow, herbal body wrap, desert-clay body wrap, seaweed or sea-clay body wrap; balneotherapy with moor mud, thalassotherapy with micronized seaweed or sea salts; aromatherapy facial, collagen facial, enzyme facial, paraffin facial. **Swimming:** Pool. **Classes and Programs:** Nightly lounge entertainment. **Recreation:** Golf, tennis; gambling.

ACCOMMODATIONS
608 rooms, 107 suites.

DINING
À la carte dining at four on-site restaurants: Ho Wan (Asian), Portofino (Mediterranean-influenced), Monte Carlo (French), Terrace Pointe (American and Continental). **Sample Meals:** Mixed-vegetable fried rice, cashew chicken, spaghetti carbonara (lunch), tomato soup with roasted pumpkin oil, wild greens with balsamic vinaigrette, grilled veal medallions with niçoise olives and tomato-basil coulis, steamed or grilled vegetable plate (dinner).

$215–$275 a day, single or double; minisuites $350–$390. Spa packages $145–$315 a day, plus lodging. Daily facility charge $20 for guests;
$25 for non-guests. 1-night deposit required. AE, DC, MC, V.

DIRECTIONS
✉ *3145 Las Vegas Blvd. S, Las Vegas, NV 89109,* ☎ *702/733–4444,
800/634–6906, or 800/634–6906 for room reservations,* FAX *702/733–
4437.*

From Los Angeles: I–15 north to Spring Mountain exit east to Las Vegas
Boulevard (4½ hrs).

WALLEY'S HOT SPRINGS RESORT

Luxury pampering
Mineral springs

Established in 1862, Walley's Hot Springs is scheduled to reopen after a
management change in 1999. At press time, plans called for 150 two-
bedroom vacation-ownership townhouses that would include a modern
spa facility with 13 treatment rooms. Just 25 minutes from South Lake
Tahoe, 50 minutes from Reno, the resort provides a rejuvenating experience after days on the slopes and nights in the casinos.

Early pioneers of the West discovered the soothing thermal waters here.
An artesian well supplies six mineral pools with water that ranges from
96°F–104°F. There's also fresh-water swimming, a steam room and
sauna with separate men's and women's shower areas, and a small exercise room. Massages can be scheduled, and tennis courts are available
(call ahead to reserve court space).

FACILITIES
Exercise Equipment: Cross-country ski machine, stair climber, stationary
bikes, treadmill, weight-training circuit, free weights. **Services:** Massage.
Swimming: Pool. **Classes and Programs:** Aquaerobics. **Recreation:** Tennis; downhill and cross-country skiing nearby.

ACCOMMODATIONS
150 suites.

DINING
Lunch served at café.

RATES AND PACKAGES
Undetermined at press time; call for details.

DIRECTIONS
✉ *2001 Foothill La., Box 26, Genoa, NV 89411,* ☎ *702/782–8155 or
800/628–7831,* FAX *702/782–2103.*

From Reno: Highway 395 south to Genoa, Genoa Lane to Foothill Lane
(60 min).

NEW MEXICO

OJO CALIENTE MINERAL SPRINGS

Mineral springs

Ojo Caliente calls itself "the oldest spa in North America," and the claim would be hard to dispute. As far back as AD 1200, the ancestors of today's Pueblo Indians built their pueblos on a mesa overlooking the mineral-rich waters of the natural hot springs hidden here in a secluded valley. Fifty-five miles north of Santa Fe, Ojo is the only place in the world where five different types of mineral water—soda, arsenic, lithia, iron, and sodium—bubble to the surface (more than 100,000 gallons per day).

In Spanish, *ojo caliente* means "hot eye" for the eye of the spring, and was so dubbed when the Spanish explorer Cabeza de Vaca visited here in 1535 and assumed he had stumbled upon the Fountain of Youth. He recorded his excitement in his journal: "The greatest treasure I have found these strange people to possess are some hot springs which burst out of the foot of a mountain that gives evidence of being an active volcano. So powerful are the chemicals contained in this water that the inhabitants have a belief that the waters were given to them by their gods after weeping many tears. From the effect of the waters upon my remaining men, I am inclined to believe that the waters will do many things that our doctors are not capable of doing...I believe I have found the Fountain of Youth."

Modern-day visitors draw similar conclusions about the restorative powers of the springs, and they find little changed since those early days. The spa itself, built in the 1920s (no one knows the exact date), is a funky, no-frills establishment that includes a hotel, cottages, a restaurant, a gift shop, massage rooms, men's and women's bathhouses, a chlorine-free swimming pool, and indoor and outdoor mineral tubs. Accommodations are decidedly spartan but clean and comfortable, with cozy down comforters on the beds and rudimentary bathrooms *sans* showers or tubs—you've come for the mineral springs, after all. (The bathhouse is equipped with showers.) The hotel, one of the original bathhouses, and the springs themselves are all on the National Register of Historic Places, as is the adjacent Round Barn, from which visitors can take horseback tours and guided hikes to the ruins of the ancient pueblo dwellings and petroglyph-etched rocks.

With nary a celebrity in sight to trigger unwanted physical comparisons, Ojo Caliente is the kind of place where you needn't feel self-conscious about a protruding belly or cellulite-dappled thighs. Ensconced in a rock-lined iron-mineral pool at the base of a sandstone cliff, inhaling the clean, high-desert air as you contemplate the vivid-blue New Mexico sky, it's easy to imagine yourself one of the early pueblo-dwellers who soaked here centuries ago.

Concessions to the demands of 20th-century patrons allow for expanded amenities, and the spa has added herbal wraps, aromatherapy treatments, facials, mud wraps, and acupuncture to its menu. Included in the nightly lodging rates are use of the swimming pool, mineral spa, iron pool, and soda pool, as well as two "milagro wraps" (dry blanket wraps to induce the release of toxins), plus entry to three new outdoor mineral and mud pools. Other services can be added individually or as packages.

Just an hour and a quarter from Santa Fe, Ojo Caliente can be a restful day trip or a worthwhile overnight or multiple-night getaway. The remote rural setting enhances the sense of detachment and relaxation.

FACILITIES

Exercise Equipment: None. **Services:** Acupuncture, back of body massage, deep-tissue massage, honey-pat face and scalp massage, Swedish massage; herbal wrap, seaweed wrap, moor mud wrap, salt glow; aromatic facial, blue-cornmeal facial massage. **Swimming:** Pool. **Recreation:** Hiking, horseback riding, mountain biking; downhill skiing and rafting nearby; archaeological tours.

ACCOMMODATIONS

19 hotel rooms, 19 cottages.

DINING

3 meals served à la carte meals at Poppy's Café & Grill. **Sample Meals:** Chicken-mushroom melt sandwich, Ojo Club on a whole-wheat tortilla, red or green chili with beans (lunch); Chimayo chicken with charred-tomato salsa, pasta puttanesca, New York strip steak, vegetable stir fry (dinner).

RATES AND PACKAGES

Jan.–Feb. and Nov.–Dec., $60 single, $86 double for hotel rooms; $70–$80 single, $100–$110 double for cottages. Mar.–Oct. and during Christmas vacation, $70 single, $94 double for hotel rooms; $80–$90 single, $110–$130 double for cottages. AE, D, DC, MC, V.

DIRECTIONS

✉ *Box 68, Ojo Caliente, NM 87549,* ☎ *505/583–2233 or 800/222–9162,* FAX *505/583–2464.*

From Santa Fe: Take U.S. 84/285 through Española; follow U.S. 285 where it branches off at junction of U.S. 285 and U.S. 68 (1 hr).

TEN THOUSAND WAVES

Mineral springs

Perched on a hill overlooking Santa Fe and the spectacular Sangre de Cristo Mountains, Ten Thousand Waves brings a bit of Japan to the Southwest. From the corral-style parking lot you climb a steep path through fragrant cedars, piñon pines, and juniper bushes to the spa and 5-room guest lodge. Despite the dozens of people who often soak in the communal pool, a serene hush pervades the crisp desert air, especially at night.

Sybaritic rather than fitness-oriented, this resort has an esoteric menu of treatments: Massage choices include Ayurvedic (hot herbal oils and calamus root powder), deep-tissue, shiatsu, or watsu under a waterfall. Most bodywork takes place in breezy, cedar-paneled rooms; options include group sessions and rooms for couples. The open-air soaking tubs (which are refilled after every use) resemble authentic Japanese *onsen* baths (but without thermal mineral-spring water). The Japanese mood is further enhanced by the accommodations, which center around a lantern-lit garden.

Clad in a cotton kimono and sandals issued at check-in, you follow paths from the pools to your room at the Houses of the Moon. Furnished with futons and beds, most rooms accommodate up to 4 persons; one has tatami-mat floor in the style of a Japanese country inn. All are equipped with a fireplace for chilly nights.

Nine tubs are available by the hour; some are small and wooden, others accommodate groups. The tiled Imperial Ofuro holds 10 people and has private bathroom and changing area plus two balconies. The Waterfall has a natural rock deck, warm tub, and cold plunge pool, and holds up to 12 people. The new Kojiro has a pebble bottom. All have access to cold plunge pools and saunas or a steam room. A communal tub is reserved for women daily from noon until 8:30 PM, except on Tuesday, when it opens at 4:30 PM; there's also a coed communal tub open daily until 8:30, except Tuesday, when it's open from 4:30 PM until closing. Bathing suits are optional at all times.

Cleanliness of the bathhouse and baths is stressed, as the hot tubs are equipped with purification systems using ozone and ultraviolet light rather than chlorine. Forget inhibitions about nudity. The resort's laid-back atmosphere attracts a large number of gay patrons.

Twenty minutes from Santa Fe restaurants, museums, and seasonal attractions, this is a place to meditate and de-stress naturally.

FACILITIES
Services: Massage; herbal wrap, salt glow; watsu, facial. **Recreation:** Hiking, horseback riding; downhill skiing and rafting nearby.

ACCOMMODATIONS
3 rooms, 5 suites.

RATES AND PACKAGES
Accommodations without meals, single or double occupancy: $119–$204 per night; additional persons $10 each. 20% discount for locals at various times of year; 50% discount for seniors and kids year-round. Spa packages $98–$296. Bath-only $18–$25 per person per hour. Add tax, gratuities. D, MC, V.

DIRECTIONS
✉ *Hyde Park Rd., Box 10200, Santa Fe, NM 87504,* ☎ *505/982–9304,* FAX *505/989–5077.*

From Santa Fe: Washington Avenue to Artist Road to Hyde Park Road (20 min).

TRUTH OR CONSEQUENCES

Mineral springs

A series of independently operated hot-springs resorts in this funky, easy-going little town offer a taste of authentic New Mexico–style recreation, at bargain prices. Native Americans believed the hot mineral water from natural underground springs in this area had health-restoring properties long before modern settlements and bathhouses were built. Originally the town was called Hot Springs; the name Truth or Consequences came about when the 1950s TV game show of the same name offered a reward to any town in the country willing to name itself after the show. Classy it may not be, but the area does attract many artists and senior citizens in search of affordable alternatives to Santa Fe.

The downtown district is where the mineral water is easily tapped and available at bargain prices as low as $4 hourly for a good soak. There was talk of constructing a brand new, luxury resort motel in the hot springs district, but nothing had materialized as of 1998. For now, Truth or Consequences is still a down-home place with a low-key flavor and low prices to match.

Among Truth or Consequences' many resorts are **Spirit Place Adventures Spa** and **Hay-Yo-Kay Hot Springs** (✉ 300 Austin Ave., ☎ 505/894–2228), under the same ownership one block south of Broadway. The spa offers massages and weekend retreats for couples in a modern, two-bedroom condominium. The hot springs features a complex of five natural flowing pools.

At the **Hot Mineral Bathhouse & RV Parks** (✉ 312 Marr, ☎ 505/894–2684), camping is available for recreational vehicles. **The Charles Motel**

& Bath House (✉ 601 Broadway, ☎ 505/894–7154; $35–$45 double) has a motel with kitchenettes in rooms, along with hot mineral baths in individual, sanitized tubs. Massages, reflexology, holistic healing, tai chi, yoga, and Ayurvedic science also are among the services here.

Riverbend Hot Springs (✉ 100 Austin, ☎ 505/894–6183) is an extraordinarily user-friendly, ultra-casual facility with clean but slightly dilapidated hostel accommodations. Three outdoor tanks once used for growing minnows as fish bait have been converted into hot tubs, available free for lodgers twice daily. The tubs can be rented hourly for private use at other times of the day. You can soak in a hot "minnow bath" while being serenaded by the murmuring waters of the Rio Grande, and gazing out at the changing shadows of Turtleback Mountain. In the evenings, guests gather for conversation around a fire pit. There's also a meditation area.

An adobe villa undergoing renovation in 1998, **Firewater Lodge** (✉ 309 Broadway, ☎ 505/894–3405) offers lodging and mineral baths in large, private rooms. Holistic healing methods are practiced at this lodge, where plans included addition of a restaurant and an outdoor pool.

Ask for individual rooms with turtle, lizard, or Mimbres petroglyph themes at **The Marshall Hot Springs** (✉ 311 Marr, ☎ 505/894–9286). New Age music and incense enhance spiritual "good vibes" here.

FACILITIES
Services: *See* individual spa reviews, *above,* for services offered at each.
Swimming: Nearby lake. **Recreation:** Hiking, tubing.

ACCOMMODATIONS
See individual resort reviews, *above.*

DINING
No restaurants at bathhouse resorts. Dining options within walking distance.

RATES AND PACKAGES
For prices, *see* individual reviews, *above.* Most bathhouse resorts accept cash only.

DIRECTIONS
✉ *Chamber of Commerce, Drawer 31, Truth or Consequences, NM 87901,* ☎ *505/894–3536.*

From Albuquerque: I–25 south (2½ hrs).

VISTA CLARA RANCH RESORT AND SPA

Holistic health
Luxury pampering

An up-to-the-minute facility incorporating ancient Native American healing arts, Vista Clara occupies a former ranch in the Galisteo Basin amid soul-stirring mountains, rock formations carved with prehistoric petroglyphs, and inspiring high-desert vistas. The overall experience here is one of renewal and well-being tinged with a spirituality that seems to emanate from the land itself. Only 20 minutes from Santa Fe, Vista Clara's sense of detachment creates an environment conducive to the pursuit of health and peace of mind. The piñon-scented air is clean and crisp; the skyscrapers are an ever-changing panorama, and the serenity of the setting seems to penetrate bone-deep.

The contrast of old and new is a recurring theme here; guests can enjoy a state-of-the-art gym and the latest techniques in massage and beauty treatments while also participating in a cleansing sweat-lodge ceremony and "Ancestral Ways" program that explores Native American history, culture, and spirituality.

The setting is expansive, but the scale of the resort itself is intimate, almost cozy. Accommodations are spacious and decorated in Southwest style, with carved wooden furnishings and log-beamed ceilings; all have either a deck or patio. There's a chlorine-free ozone pool and an outdoor spa (also chlorine-free) with panoramic views of the basin.

In a dining room that's part of the original historic ranch house, you'll be treated to the "Southwest Spa Cuisine" of award-winning chefs Steve and Kristin Jarrett. Their use of fresh local ingredients, many from the spa's own organic garden, makes each dish come alive with flavor—you won't have to worry about a diet of raw vegetables and sprouts, and you'll find their reverence for high-quality, organic ingredients is contagious.

In addition to spa staples such as massage, beauty treatments (including organic hair coloring), and body masks and wraps, there are also horseback rides, daily guided hikes to historic sites, cooking classes, art classes, and art tours to Santa Fe's famous galleries. Other activities include personal training sessions, movement and dances classes, and evening lectures on a variety of topics. Also available are astrology readings and various holistic therapies—though the atmosphere remains down-to-earth, with none of the New Age ambience and attitude that pervade some spas.

A typical day at Vista Clara begins with a gourmet breakfast, followed by a hike and dance class. After a cooking class and demonstration by the resident chefs, a healthy lunch is served. The afternoon might include a massage (choose among Swedish, polarity, shiatsu, four-handed, or chair massage) and a body treatment (body mask, herbal wrap, salt glow, reflexology, facial, pedicure, or craniosacral therapy). Finish up with a beauty treatment such as a manicure with paraffin, shampoo with scalp massage and deep conditioning, or hair treatment with cut. The resort also is developing various programs to enhance its self-sufficiency and natural approach to health, among them permaculture, organic livestock, and water-use methods that preserve water without limiting its use.

Five- and seven-night packages include accommodations; three meals and two snacks daily; use of all resort facilities including Spa Therapy Center and gym; fitness, movement, cooking, and art classes; Ancestral Ways program; sweat lodge ceremony; daily guided hike; evening lectures and activities; and round-trip transportation from Santa Fe. Day-spa packages include a full-body massage, fitness classes, one body treatment, and lunch (Pamper Package), or a nature hike, breakfast, a full-body massage, one body treatment, one beauty treatment, lunch, fitness classes, and round-trip transportation from Santa Fe (Day at the Ranch Package). Overnight lodging rates include breakfast, use of facilities and gym, classes, lectures, and hikes.

FACILITIES

Exercise Equipment: Stair climbers, stationary bikes, treadmills, free weights. **Services:** Four-handed massage, polarity massage, reflexology, shiatsu, Swedish massage; aromatherapy wrap, moor mud wrap; Swiss showers. **Swimming:** Pool. **Classes and Programs:** Aerobics, aquaerobics; classes in breath and movement, hip-hop funk, dance, meditation, tai chi, yoga; art and cooking classes; personal training; sweat lodge; astrological services. **Recreation:** Hiking, horseback riding; downhill skiing nearby.

ACCOMMODATIONS
10 rooms.

RATES AND PACKAGES

$265 single, $165 per person double. Per-person fees for multi-day pack-ages, including double-occupancy room and spa treatments: 5 nights, $1,380. Pamper Package $145; Day at the Ranch package $225. Services also available à la carte. MC, V.

DIRECTIONS

⊠ *HC 75 Box 111, Galisteo, NM 87540, 505/466–4772,* ℻ *505/466–1942.*

From Santa Fe: Take I-25 north to Eldorado Exit/U.S. 285 exit, then fol-low U.S. 285 about 5 miles.

UTAH

CLIFF SPA AT SNOWBIRD

Luxury pampering
Sports conditioning

A penthouse spa with alpine views, 1,900 acres of groomed ski slopes, and a 23-court tennis club are a few of the attractions at the sports-oriented Cliff Lodge. Set in Utah's scenic Wasatch Mountains near Salt Lake City, the multistory lodge is every bit as enticing as the finest resorts in the Alps, with scenic tram rides and spectacular hiking and mountain biking in summer, and some of the country's best skiing and snowboarding in winter.

Sports enthusiasts will be in heaven here. In summer, there are rock-climbing classes, overnight backpacking trips, bike tours, and guided treks to the peaks of the Wasatch Cache National Forest. For golfers, there is helicopter service to the courses in nearby Wasatch National Park and at Jeremy Ranch. In winter, the same helicopters whisk skiers up to the powdery upper slopes. For an even greater challenge, you can enroll in one of several courses at Snowbird's new Adventure Park. The orienteering program is based on the European land-navigation sport that combines hiking with exploration aided by a map and compass.

Tennis players can take advantage of the 23 tennis courts (10 indoor) at the Canyon Raquet Club, 10 miles from the resort. The 11-acre club also has racquetball and squash courts, spa and fitness facilities, and an outdoor Olympic-size pool. Complimentary shuttle service is available.

The Cliff Spa itself is a two-story complex on the top floors of the hotel, with a 60-foot outdoor lap pool and a giant outdoor whirlpool with glorious mountain views. The same views can be enjoyed from the fitness center, which has an aerobics studio with a suspended wooden floor, as well as a full line of Keiser resistance equipment. There are 20 treatment rooms, separate women's and men's saunas, a steam room, solarium, salon, and a café with healthy snacks and drinks.

Several packages combine spa treatments with outdoor activities. The one-day Natural Woman package includes a two-hour guided nature hike, 30-minute salt glow, 50-minute mud bath, and 50-minute sports massage with natural oils, plus a spa meal. The four-night Mountain Experience includes spa treatments, a group tennis lesson and unlimited use of the Canyon Raquet Club, tram-served mountain biking, a guided mountain hike, an Adventure Park confidence course, fitness and health assessment, unlimited fitness classes and use of spa facilities, four nights accommodation, and three spa meals daily. These are ideal for those who want to combine challenging sports activities with pampering treatments.

There's plenty for children to do while their parents exercise or pamper themselves. The Chikadee program for ages 3–4 pairs two children with a ski instructor. For children ages 5–15, child/teen super classes include ski lessons, lunch, pizza parties, and adult supervision from 9 AM to 4 PM. Those who prefer to ski with their children 12 and under can enjoy a break on lift tickets: Children 12 and under ski free when accompanied by adults. The resort also has a children's day-care center, a nursery, and Kid Club evening parties, with ski movies, videos, and an electronic game room.

FACILITIES

Exercise Equipment: Rowing machines, stair climbers, stationary bikes, treadmills, training circuit. **Services:** Aromatherapy massage, high-altitude massage, massage therapy with acupressure and polarity therapy, maternity massage, shiatsu; alpine salt glow, body glow, herbal wrap, remineralizing body pack; aroma-hydro massage, balneotherapy, mud bath, thalassotherapy; hydrating facial, men's facial, sensitive facial, mini-facial. **Swimming:** 3 pools. **Classes and Programs:** Aerobics, aquaerobics, tai chi, stretching; guided nature hikes and mountain treks, personal fitness training; team-building exercises on ropes course. **Recreation:** Hiking, mountain biking, racquetball, rock climbing, skiing, squash, tennis; golf and horseback riding nearby. Cross-country and downhill skiing, snowboarding. **Children's Programs:** Day-care center, nursery, ski instruction (ages 3–15).

ACCOMMODATIONS

532 rooms and suites.

DINING

À la carte meals served at Wildflower Ristorante, Keyhole Junction (Southwestern cuisine), Lodge Club, and Summit Café (fruit smoothies, soups, salads, and vegetarian dishes). **Sample Meals:** Wild-mushroom enchiladas (lunch), vegetarian eggplant lasagna; duck ravioli, smoked-asparagus lasagna (dinner).

RATES AND PACKAGES

Standard rooms $145–$229 for 2 persons per day, deluxe bedroom $235–$389; suites $384–$943. 4-night Mountain Experience package $1,170 single, $1,462 per person double; Wasatch Winter Weekend $1,360 single, $1,971 double; half-day Refresher package, $185; 1-day packages $250–$480. 2-night deposit required in winter. AE, D, DC, MC, V.

DIRECTIONS

✉ *Little Cottonwood Canyon Rd., Snowbird, UT 84092,* ☎ *801/933-2222 or 800/453-3000,* FAX *801/947-3300.*

From Salt Lake City: I–75, I–80, Route 210 to Little Cottonwood Canyon (40 mins).

FRANKLIN QUEST INSTITUTE OF FITNESS

Nutrition and diet

A solid health-and-fitness program, good value, and spectacular desert scenery combine to make Franklin Quest a worthwhile fitness resort. Red sandstone towers and pink slickrock mounds near Snow Canyon State Park, near St. George, Utah, provide the setting for the institute, where guests come for intensive educational one-week programs that center around hiking, working out in the fitness center, and learning about time management as well as weight control. Founded in 1985 by physiologist Marc Sorenson and his wife Vicki as the National Institute of Fitness, the institute is now owned by the Franklin Quest Company, but the goal remains unchanged: providing motivational tools for a healthier lifestyle.

Classes in nutrition, movement, and stress management are combined with a take-home outline of your plan for health and fitness. But the prime attraction is exploring some of the most glorious canyon country in the West. Often called the "Walking Spa," the program allows you to train with certified coaches on hikes as well as in aerobics classes. The 150–200 participants are divided into groups classified C (most fit), B (average), A (moderate), and Special A (limited fitness). At daybreak, before breakfast, guided groups hike more than 30 trails in Snow Canyon State Park, just outside the Institute complex. Along the way are lava caves, ancient Indian petroglyphs, and a variety of desert plants. Mild in winter, the desert climate is dry and invigorating.

Vigorous exercise, rather than pampering or bodywork, is central here. On arrival participants are given a fitness evaluation that includes a cardiovascular endurance test. The results-oriented program is designed to get you off diets and drugs and to restore normal cholesterol and sugar levels. Guests with serious weight problems stay a month or more, often shedding 50 pounds. Bodywork and personal services are optional extras.

FACILITIES
Exercise Equipment: Cross-country ski track, stair climbers, stationary bikes, treadmills, weight-training circuit, free weights. **Services:** Aromatherapy massage, deep-tissue massage, foot massage, reflexology, Russian massage, Swedish massage; body wrap, body polish; facial. **Swimming:** 2 indoor pools. **Classes and Programs:** Tai chi, yoga; workshops on nutrition and health; cooking class. **Recreation:** Hiking, tennis; golf nearby.

ACCOMMODATIONS
112 rooms in 9 buildings.

DINING
3 meals daily, included in program fee. Low-fat, low-cholesterol, low-sodium in controlled portions; vegan and vegetarian options available. Salad bar daily. **Sample Meals:** Mexican hominy, split-pea soup (lunch); barbecued chicken, polenta with black-bean and red-pepper salsa (dinner).

RATES AND PACKAGES
1-week program $1,399–$1,559 single, $987–$1,147 per person double. $100 nonrefundable deposit. MC, V.

DIRECTIONS
✉ *202 N. Snow Canyon Rd., Box 938, Ivins, UT 84738,* ☎ *435/673–4905 or 800/447–3002,* ℻ *435/673–1363.*

From Las Vegas: I–15 to St. George, Bluff Street north to town of Santa Clara, Sunset Boulevard to Ivins, continue ½ mile, look for signs (2 hrs).

GREEN VALLEY SPA & TENNIS RESORT

Luxury pampering
Nutrition and diet

Discovering a full-service spa along with a concentrated weight-loss and fitness program in the dry desert of southern Utah is reason for many to spend a week or two at the Green Valley resort. Guests can also enjoy full resort facilities plus sophisticated bodywork with locally formulated herbal, mud, and mineral products used exclusively in the spa. A certain color will be used to activate the senses each day; for instance, a red day will surround you with red flowers, red-tinted baths, even red dishes. Native American healing traditions are integrated into treatments and services. The nutritious high-energy meals are a revelation, demonstrating the variety and quantity of food that one can enjoy while losing weight. Exchanging tips with the Green Valley cook in a dining room–cum-demo kitchen is encouraged.

Fitness training emphasizes correct posture and body movements, and shaping and contouring, as weight is lost. With a maximum of 60 participants per week, the staff physiologists and nutritionists can maintain personal interaction with guests. Begin your day with the 7 AM group hike, covering up to 8 miles over trails in nearby state parks; or choose exercise classes, scheduled all day 9:30 AM to 5:30 PM. Tennis and golf lessons can be scheduled instead of treatments; the resort is home to Vic Braden's Tennis College and the Golf Digest School.

Set amid palm trees, the modern spa building is an oasis of health and beauty. Filled with Native American and Southwestern art, the 25,000-square-foot spa draws on indigenous healing traditions and New Age experiences. Among specialties are treatments with volcanic clay and herbs.

Provided with a picnic lunch, you can join a small group guided by staffers and a naturalist for a hike through sandstone ravines and volcanic and red-rock canyons, where you come upon 1,000-year-old petroglyphs left by Anasazi Indians. Camaraderie develops quickly among hikers, some opting for a 12-mile challenge, others taking a beginners' course. You can also go on rock-climbing expeditions (from beginner to expert) or take a trip by van to Zion National Park, taking in vistas from atop cliffs, where the dry desert air is scented by fresh sage.

Featuring treatments with indigenous herbs and flowers, the spa provides an introduction to Native American cultures. But the facilities are solidly contemporary and comfortable. The Coyote Inn, which opened in 1998, contains rooms with either a king-size four-poster feather bed or two queen-size feather beds, plus three TVs (one to watch meditation videos while you're soaking in the tub), a microwave, a refrigerator, a private patio, a two-line direct-dial phone, and a fax machine. Amenities include terry robe, slippers, spa outfit, and Starbucks coffee.

FACILITIES
Exercise Equipment: Lifecycles, Lifesteppers, CamStar weight training studio, Trotter treadmills, Reebok Power Cycle, Reebok Studio Cycles, workout bags, free weights. **Services:** Massage (Swedish, shiatsu, aromatherapy, lymph), Reiki, stone therapy, acupuncture, reflexology, mud and herbal wraps, facials, powdered-pearl body rub; nail and skin care. **Swimming:** 5 outdoor pools, 1 enclosed heated pool, diving pool. **Classes and Programs:** Personal counseling on weight loss, coloring and makeup, skin care, talks on health and nutrition, stress management, bread baking, Native American culture. **Recreation:** 15 outdoor and 4 indoor tennis courts, volleyball, basketball, 2 racquetball courts; golf school with play at nearby courses. **Children's Programs:** Summer fitness/health and tennis camp for children, with Vic Braden Tennis College.

ACCOMMODATIONS
38 rooms.

DINING
3 meals daily plus snacks. Low-fat diet, no sugar or salt. **Sample Meals:** Turkey burger and french fries, pizza, chicken pita sandwich (lunch); salmon with seasonal vegetable, rice, and fat-free desserts with fresh fruit, yogurt, and other ingredients (dinner).

RATES AND PACKAGES
Daily rate begins at $395 single in off-season. All-inclusive Spa Vacation includes five prescheduled spa services (three massages, facial, reflexology/pedicure) $2,575–$2,925 single; $2,400–$2,750 double. AE, D, MC, V.

DIRECTIONS
✉ 1871 W. Canyon View Dr., St. George, UT 84770, ☎ 435/628–8060 or 800/237–1068, FAX 435/673–4084.

From Las Vegas. By car, I–15 to St. George (2 hrs). By plane, commuter flights on Skywest and Delta (40 mins). Free pickup from and return to St. George airport. Shuttle service from/to Las Vegas on St. George Shuttle (tel. 800/933–8320) costs $25 each way. Car rental, taxi available.

THE LAST RESORT

Holistic health
Nutrition and diet

Yoga studies, meditation, and a natural-foods diet are used as vehicles for rejuvenating the body and mind at the Last Resort, an informal mountain retreat that accommodates up to 10 guests. In southern Utah about 40 miles southwest of Bryce Canyon and 8,700 feet above sea level, the two-story log building enjoys spectacular mountain views: It's a suitably majestic environment for the spiritually oriented program.

Directors Pujari and Abhilasha offer a multidimensional experience, a seven-day retreat that includes two Iyengar yoga workouts and two meditation sessions daily, with free time for walking and reading. Every evening there are videos and discourses on yoga, nutrition, and related topics. Each session includes a full day of silence, plus a visit to the Pah Tempe Hot Springs and other spectacular canyons in the area. In addition, there's a natural-foods cooking course that teaches meal planning and preparation of tofu, tempeh, whole grains, beans, fresh vegetables, and other healthy ingredients; and a "spring cleaning of the body" retreat that includes four days of juice fasting and bowel cleansing, with meditation and light yoga. A relationship workshop teaches partners how to listen and communicate with each other.

Though there are no group exercise sessions besides yoga, marked trails attract hikers and backpackers in summer and autumn. In winter the light powder snow makes ideal conditions for cross-country skiing.

FACILITIES
Swimming: Nearby lakes. **Classes and Programs:** Meditation instruction, rebirthing, Iyengar yoga classes, cooking classes, lectures and videos on yoga and nutrition. **Recreation:** Hiking, cross-country skiing.

ACCOMMODATIONS
Dormitory beds and private rooms for couples, all with shared bath.

DINING
2 meals daily included with package. Vegetarian meals prepared by a nutritionist, tea, and juice come with retreats. Menus include steamed fresh vegetables, whole grains, rice, casseroles.

RATES AND PACKAGES
7-day yoga retreat $750 per person, 5-day cooking course $495, 8-day spring retreat $750; year-end Vipassana meditation, 5 days $425, 10 days $650. $200 deposit required.

DIRECTIONS
✉ Box 707, Cedar City, UT 84727, ☎ 435/682–2289 or 619/283–8663.

From Las Vegas: I–15 to Cedar City, Route 14 (3 hrs).

3 The Northwest

Alaska, Montana, Oregon, Washington, Wyoming

NATIVE AMERICANS BELIEVED long ago that the Great Spirit lived at the earth's center and that steaming hot springs produced "big medicine" waters. Rediscovered by a new generation, the hot springs of the Northwest can be enjoyed in settings of great natural beauty or at large new resort developments. One such sacred spot in Oregon is the resort Kah-Nee-Ta, owned and operated by the Confederated Tribes of the Warm Springs. Near Yellowstone National Park in Wyoming, Hot Springs State Park occupies land purchased from the Shoshone and Arapahoe tribes. Sol Duc Hot Springs Resort in Olympic National Park, Washington, is another warm watering spot.

Montana's "big sky" country is full of family-oriented fitness resorts, including Fairmont Hot Springs, the rustic Chico Hot Springs Lodge, and the Feathered Pipe Ranch, near Helana. Washington's resorts include the Skamania Lodge, whose fitness center overlooks the Columbia River Gorge, and the Salish Lodge, on the Pacific coast, where sybaritic soaks take place in an Oriental-style spa.

Alaskan hot springs are simply for soaking: In a verdant valley rich with Gold Rush lore outside Fairbanks the sulfur sprites of Chena Hot Springs have welcomed homesteaders and "cheechako" travelers since 1905.

ALASKA

CHENA HOT SPRINGS RESORT

Mineral springs

A soak at the historic Chena Hot Springs Resort near Fairbanks comes accompanied by reminders of pioneer days. Cabins and pools here were built in the early 1900s, when most visitors were gold miners who had traveled by dogsled and on horseback in search of relief from rheumatism and arthritis in the hot springs. Images of the miners still smile from the photographs of the Victorian era that decorate the dining room and lounge.

The old-time character of the resort has not changed, despite several renovations. The bathhouse has tile floors and showers in the locker rooms, and expansive use of glass walls in the pool area. The hot mineral water that bubbles to the surface at 156°F is cooled to a tolerable 110°F in the soaking pools, 90°F for swimming. Thermal water also heats the lodge rooms and three whirlpools.

The cluster of cabins around the main lodge has the general appearance of a mining camp. The machinery, carts, and tools that the miners once used now dot the gardens between the steaming ponds where the spring waters run into a creek. Moose have been spotted wandering the grounds, and antlers adorn some of the buildings. Adding to the rustic feel, seven Trapper Cabins have washbasins and chemical toilets (some also have wood-burning stoves). Campers have use of showers and laundry facilities.

A lively crowd from the university in Fairbanks 60 miles down the road comes to ski the slopes and well-marked trails. Local outfitters also provide snowmobiling and dogsledding in winter; in summer, you can take self-guided history and nature hikes, or sign up for horseback-riding excursions.

FACILITIES
Swimming: Pool. **Recreation:** Croquet, fishing, hiking, horseback riding, horseshoes, mountain climbing, volleyball; dogsled rides, downhill and cross-country skiing, ice skating, snowmobiling, sledding.

ACCOMMODATIONS
48 lodge rooms, some with shared bath, 7 cabins. Campsites with RV hookups available.

DINING
Full menu in historic lodge restaurant; no meal packages. **Sample Meals:** Roast beef, ham, roast turkey (lunch and dinner). Fresh produce in season.

RATES AND PACKAGES
Lodge rooms $70–$125 per day; cabins $50–$110 per day for 1–8 persons. AE, DC, MC, V.

DIRECTIONS
✉ *57 Chena Hot Springs Rd. Reservations: Box 73440, Fairbanks, AK 99707,* ☎ *907/452–7867 or 800/478–4681(in Alaska),* FAX *907/456–3122.*

From Fairbanks: Route 2 (Steese Highway) to Chena Springs Road (80 mins).

MCKINLEY CHALET RESORT

Luxury pampering
Sports conditioning

Overlooking majestic mountains at a scenic turn in the Nenana River, the McKinley Chalet Resort is a cluster of chalets, rustic cabins, and a modern mountain lodge in an accessible area of the wilderness of Denali National Park, open to guests from mid-May to mid-September. Guests enjoy free use of a swimming pool and indoor health club. For those who prefer to take their exercise in the great outdoors, the possibilities are limitless: You can challenge yourself on a rugged outdoor trek, guided by a ranger; or settle in for a guided bus tour along park roads that are closed to private cars in the summer. River rafting and a scenic float are additional options.

The long days of summer are an ideal time to take a wildlife tour. Departing from the resort's main lodge, the six- to eight-hour narrated tour usually includes sightings of moose, caribou, Dall sheep, foxes, birds, wolves, and grizzly bears. There are also three-hour natural-history tours of the taiga forest and rolling tundra. Guides explain the geological formations around Mt. McKinley, which the Athabasca called Denali, meaning "the high one."

Accommodations at the McKinley Chalet resort are on a terraced hillside with views of the mountains and wild river. Alpine-style chalets contain 345 suites with sitting rooms, bedrooms, and wooden balconies. Rustic elegance combines with wilderness cuisine served in the Nenana View Restaurant, where the menu features native salmon. The resort's dinner theater offers a taste of the Alaska Gold Rush.

FACILITIES

Exercise Equipment: Rowing machine, stair climber, stationary bikes, weight-training circuit, free weights. **Services:** Swedish massage. **Classes and Programs:** Dinner theater. **Recreation:** Backcountry hiking, river rafting. **Children's Programs:** Nature hikes.

ACCOMMODATIONS
345 suites in chalets, cabins, and lodge.

DINING
À la carte menu. **Sample Meals:** Shrimp caesar salad, Reuben sandwich (lunch); poached halibut, roast leg of lamb (dinner).

RATES AND PACKAGES
$189.39 for 2 persons, double occupancy. Daily 7-hour Tundra Wildlife bus tour, $58 per person; 3-hour Denali Natural History tour, $34 per person; rafting $50. 1-night deposit required. AE, D, MC, V.

DIRECTIONS
⊠ *Milepost 239 Parks Hwy. Denali Park, AK 99755,* ☎ *907/683–2215,* ℻ *907/683–2398. Reservations: Box 202516, Anchorage, AK 99520,* ☎ *907/279–2653 or 800/276–7234, ℻ 907/258–3668.*

From Anchorage: Route 3 (George Parks Highway) to National Park gateway (5 hrs).

MONTANA

BOULDER HOT SPRINGS

Mineral springs

Montana's Peace Valley is an idyllic and historic place in which to take the waters. Built in 1888, Boulder Hot Springs was the first permanent building in the area, and was host to various Presidents and wealthy ranchers. It occupies 274 acres bordering the Deerlodge National Forest. (The name Peace Valley derives from the Native Americans, who designated this area a sanctuary where no fighting was allowed.) These days you can still enjoy a peaceful getaway here, enjoying the healing properties of the mineral-spring baths and hikes in the surrounding mountains.

The geothermal water, which ranges in temperature from 140°F to 175°F, is piped to indoor pools, where it is mixed with cold spring water; new water flows in every four hours. No chemicals are added to the indoor pools. Men and women have separate bathhouse facilities, which also contain steam rooms and changing rooms. Bathing suits are optional. There's also an outdoor pool with a temperature of about 96 °F.

The grand old hotel at Boulder Hot Springs has seven bed-and-breakfast rooms done in Arts and Crafts style, plus 26 simpler rooms used to accommodate groups. Breakfast is served every morning, and there's also a Sunday brunch buffet.

FACILITIES
Services: Massage. **Swimming:** Pool. **Recreation:** Hiking, fishing; cross-country skiing.

ACCOMMODATIONS
33 rooms.

DINING
Breakfast included in lodging rate. Hotel restaurant open for pre-reserved groups only. **Sample Meals:** Banana-walnut pancakes and waffles, homemade biscuits and muffins, bacon, sausage, eggs, fresh fruit, dessert (brunch).

RATES AND PACKAGES
$45–$65 single, $70–$90 for 2 persons; other rooms available at a lower rate. MC, V.

DIRECTIONS
✉ *Box 930, Boulder, MT 59632,* ☎ *406/225–4339,* FAX *406/225–4345.*

From Helena: I–15 to Boulder, Highway 69 to Boulder Springs (40 mins).

CHICO HOT SPRINGS LODGE

Mineral springs

After a day in the saddle, the prospect of a hot soak makes sore muscles bearable. There's nothing glamorous about the Chico Hot Springs Lodge, but the two hot-springs pools on its 157-acre grounds encourage many visitors to Yellowstone Park to detour. About 30 miles from the park's northern gateway, the resort offers horseback riding and pack trips into the Gallatin National Forest and the Absaroka range of the Rockies.

Surrounded by spectacular mountain scenery, the open-air pools are fed by 110°F untreated mineral water from several springs. Four private areas in the bathhouse have redwood hot tubs large enough for a family of four. Rustic facilities are available for changing; bring a towel if you're not staying at the ranch. The pools are open to the public (for a fee) as well as to registered guests (for free), and as you soak you might even spot deer on the slopes.

Guests stay either in the cozy guest rooms of the turn-the-century Main Lodge, or in a newer lodge that maintains the western look. Also available are family-size suites and a 5-bedroom log house. Meals are appropriately Western style: There's homestyle cooking at the lodge (served family style), or you can opt for outdoor barbecue.

With resident wranglers and a 35-horse stable, Chico Hot Springs has year-round programs for outdoor adventure. In winter, there's cross-country skiing and dogsledding. Hikers and mountain bikers head up to the Absaroka Beartooth mountains right from the lodge, and Yellowstone is a 30-minute drive down the road. Staffers at the Activity Center map trails to suit your fitness level. Anglers can test their skills in Chico's hillside pond, and guides lead outings to the spring-fed creeks that run through the forest. A fitness center is a welcome addition to the resort.

FACILITIES
Services: Deep-tissue massage, reflexology, shiatsu, Swedish massage. **Swimming:** Pool. **Recreation:** Boating, hayrides, horseback riding, mountain biking, trout fishing; cross-country skiing, snowmobiling.

ACCOMMODATIONS
68 lodge rooms, some with shared bath; 2 suites; 1 5-bedroom log house.

DINING
À la carte lunch menu and dinner menus. **Sample Meals:** Grilled-beef sandwich with mushroom and bell peppers, topped with Swiss cheese (lunch); beef Wellington baked *en croute* with duck liver paté and Dutchess potatoes, roast venison, grilled trout (dinner).

RATES AND PACKAGES
Lodge rooms $45–$85 for 2 persons, double occupancy; lower lodge $95–$169 for 2 persons per day. 2-bedroom cabin $75–$94 per day. Condominium apartment with kitchen and bath, $125–$315 for 2. Confirmation by credit card. AE, D, MC, V.

DIRECTIONS
✉ *Pray, MT 59065*, ☎ *406/333–4933 or 800/468–9232*, ℻ *406/333–4694*.

From Bozeman: I–90 to Highway 89 (1 1/2 hrs).

FAIRMONT HOT SPRINGS RESORT

Mineral springs

Big Sky country and big springs come together here. Nestled near the Pintlar Wilderness in an area of boundless views and numerous springs, the Fairmont Hot Springs Resort combines striking modern architecture and Western hospitality. The range of amenities and activities—including horseback riding, fishing, golf, and more—makes it ideal for a family vacation in summer or a skiing holiday in winter.

Native Americans worshiped the "medicine water" of the natural hot springs. The mineral water, 160°F when it surfaces, is treated and cooled for the two Olympic-size swimming pools and the indoor and outdoor soaking pools. Resort facilities include men's and women's steam baths. There are many organized activities to keep children busy.

Accommodations range from rooms at the Fairmont Hot Springs Lodge to a fully furnished condominium apartment.

FACILITIES
Services: Massage. **Swimming:** 1 outdoor pool, 1 indoor pool. **Recreation:** Golf, hay rides, horseback riding, tennis, trout fishing; cross-country skiing. **Children's Programs:** Hay rides, sleigh rides.

ACCOMMODATIONS
152 rooms. Campsites available, with RV hookups.

DINING
Standard American fare for breakfast and dinner in the restaurant.

RATES AND PACKAGES
Rooms $89–$109, suites $229–$299; 1 night payable in advance. AE, D, MC, V.

DIRECTIONS
✉ *1500 Fairmont Rd., Anaconda, MT 59711,* ☎ *406/797–3241, 800/443–2381, or 800/332–3272 in MT.*

From Butte: I–90 (15 mins).

FEATHERED PIPE RANCH

Holistic health

Subjects as diverse as astrology, women's studies, shamanism, massage training, and Iyengar yoga are the focus of intensive programs from June through September at Feathered Pipe Ranch. Since 1975 people from many backgrounds, professionals in the healing arts, and novice students have been coming here to gain new ideas and experiences and to attend workshops taught by world-renowned teachers and practitioners. The number of participants ranges from 35 to 50, and some families attend with young children.

In the Montana Rockies close to the Continental Divide, the retreat sits on land that was once inhabited by a Native American tribe. Climbing to "sacred rocks" for meditation, you gain a panoramic view of the 110-acre ranch. Miles of hiking trails, a sparkling lake and stream, and the dry, clear air add to the experience.

Log and stone buildings give the impression of a frontier outpost. Beyond the main lodge are Native American teepees and a traditional sweat lodge. Lodging can be in a teepee, Mongolian yurts, cabins (some with bath), and basic tents. A cedar bathhouse holds huge hot tubs, a sauna, and a massage room staffed by professional therapists.

The search for insight is the ranch's principal attraction. Serious concentration is the norm here, with little of the fun-and-fitness holiday atmosphere.

FACILITIES
Services: Massage (shiatsu, Swedish, and many other styles). **Swimming:** Mountain lake. **Classes and Programs:** Talks related to study programs; entertainment. **Recreation:** Hiking, volleyball.

ACCOMMODATIONS
12–16 dorm beds, 6 cabins (3 with bath), plus tents and tepees.

DINING
3 vegetarian meals daily included in package rate, served cafeteria style. Organically grown produce. **Sample Meals:** Bean enchiladas, tuna-fish

salad with pita bread, pasta with vegetables (lunch); baked trout, egg-plant and cheese casserole, zucchini baked with tomatoes (dinner).

RATES AND PACKAGES
1-week program $1,195 in dormitory, $1,320–$1,445 per person in cabin. Lodging, meals, instruction included. $300 deposit required. MC, V.

DIRECTIONS
✉ *2409 Colorado Gulch, Helena, MT 59601,* ☎ *406/443–0430. Mailing address: Box 1682, Helena, MT 59624,* ☎ *406/442–8196.*

From Helena: Highway 12, Colorado Gulch Turn (20 mins).

LODGE AT POTOSI HOT SPRINGS

Mineral springs
Sports conditioning

Guided walks and hikes in the Tobacco Root Mountains are the basis of the affordable program at this ranch in a scenic canyon of southwest Montana. Daily outings are planned and escorted by the lodgekeeper, based on the fitness level of participants. A trek to Potosi Peak takes you through mountain meadows to subalpine lakes and rocky ridges over-looking pristine vistas.

Mountain biking is another option, with equipment provided if you sign up for the all-inclusive rate during summer months. And this being Montana, the fishing is great. The nearby Madison and Jefferson rivers are known for trout, but you may want to try one of the creeks and ponds where private access can be arranged.

After an active day, soaking in the thermal mineral water pools is restorative. At the end of the day, stroll a short distance up a side canyon behind the lodge and you come to natural soaking pools, one 90°F, another 102°F.

Guests sleep in four log cabins that front on South Willow Creek. Each can accommodate up to six people, with a sleeping loft, kitchen, and living room with a wood stove and river-rock fireplace. Cabins have no air-conditioning or phones. Most guests elect to have meals family-style in the main lodge, where meals are prepared by an award-winning chef.

FACILITIES
Services: Massage. **Swimming:** Pond, pool. **Recreation:** Hiking and moun-tain biking, horseback riding (fee).

ACCOMMODATIONS
4 cabins.

DINING
3 meals daily in optional package during summer months. Prepared to order, served family style. **Sample Meals:** Box lunch with gourmet sand-wich (lunch); broiled salmon, 5-onion soup, mesclun salad (dinner).

RATES AND PACKAGES
Lodging $250 daily for double (June–Oct.); lodging and breakfast (Oct.–May) $200 per person, double. Add $50 per additional person in cabin. With meals and program $200 per person. D, MC, V.

DIRECTIONS
✉ *Box 688, Pony, MT 59747,* ☎ *406/685–3594 or 800/770–0088,* FAX *406/685–3594 (call first).*

From Bozeman: I–90 west, Highway 287 south to Harrison, Pony Road (90 mins).

OREGON

BREITENBUSH HOT SPRINGS RETREAT

Holistic health
Mineral springs

The Esalen of the Northwest, Breitenbush Hot Springs and Retreat is a community of rustic cabins on the banks of the Breitenbush River, in the Willamette National Forest. Like its counterpart in California, Breitenbush is known for its workshops that focus on personal health and spiritual growth, and for its hot mineral springs, where a clothing-optional policy prevails.

The daily schedule begins at 7 AM meditation followed by stretching classes. Daily yoga sessions and therapeutic rituals and ceremonies take place in a pyramid-roofed sanctuary and a Native American sweat lodge. Workshops on topics ranging from breathing to botany are scheduled throughout the year. Participation is optional, and there's no charge beyond the lodging fee. (Bodywork services at the bathhouse are moderately priced.)

Natural springs and artesian wells supply 180°F mineral water for the steam sauna and outdoor pools. At an idyllic spot in the woods, the water flows through four tiled tubs of varying temperatures and a rock-lined pool in the meadow. Each of the colorfully tiled, geothermally heated bathhouses (one for men, one for women) has two stall showers, a tub with shower head, and a bench.

Cabins, which accommodate up to four people, are bare-bones, with only a sheet on the bed (no telephones or TVs), and are heated geothermally. Blankets, sheets, and towels can be rented from June through October. Nights can get cold during summer, so no air-conditioning is needed.

About 90 miles from Portland, Breitenbush is surrounded by tall forests on the western slopes of Oregon's Cascades. Expect to encounter the high-minded environmentalism and slightly eccentric idealism of the '70s.

FACILITIES
Services: Craniosacral therapy, Reiki, Thai massage; emotional-release bodywork, herbal wrap; hydrotherapy. **Swimming:** Pool, glacial river. **Classes and Programs:** Counseling on health and healing, weekly concerts, chanting, dances. **Recreation:** Hiking, cross-country skiing.

ACCOMMODATIONS
42 cabins, some with shared bath; 20 tents; campsites available.

DINING
Lodging includes 3 vegetarian meals. Wheat-free, egg-free, and dairy-free diets accommodated by prior request. **Sample Meals:** Vegetarian pizza, or rice and green salad with sprouts (lunch); vegetarian lasagna, spinach pie with Greek salad and home-baked bread (dinner).

RATES AND PACKAGES
$55–$75 per day in shared room. Private cabin with bathroom $85–$90. Tent $40–$45, campsite $40 per person. Meals included 1-night deposit required. MC, V.

DIRECTIONS
✉ Box 578, Detroit, OR 97342, ☎ 503/854–3314, FAX 503/854–3819.

From Portland: I–5 south to Salem, Highway 22 to Detroit, Highway 46 to Breitenbush (2 hrs).

KAH-NEE-TA RESORT

Mineral springs

The Kah-Nee-Ta Resort, owned and managed by a confederation of tribes whose ancestors once worshiped at the springs on their reservation, strikes a delicate balance between tradition and modernity. Guests are invited to tribal ceremonies and festivals and to a salmon-bake feast. Huge swimming pools attract families, and bathhouses offer private soaks and a massage.

The Dalles recreation area and Mt. Hood National Forest provide an ideal setting for this outdoors-oriented resort. The imposing guest lodge and conference center sit atop a rocky ridge overlooking the Warm Springs River and a recreation complex. The resort's Indian village, vacation villas, and hot springs bathhouse can be visited on a daily basis. The Lodge also has a casino, Indianhead, for adult gaming.

Trails for biking, hiking, and horseback riding fan out toward the distant Cascade Mountains on the 60,000-acre reservation. Activities such as horseback riding and soaking in the mineral pools are priced à la carte, and fees are modest. Arrangements can be made on short notice on any day of the week.

Village accommodations include a 30-unit motel, plus teepees and RV sites. In the lodge, cedar-paneled rooms have balconies with views; some suites have fireplaces and whirlpools.

FACILITIES
Services: Aromatherapy massage, reflexology, Reiki, sports massage; mud wrap; Vichy shower. **Swimming:** 2 pools. **Classes and Programs:** Drumming, ceremonies, rituals, salmon bake. **Recreation:** Golf, horseback riding, kayaking, mountain biking, tennis, trout fishing. **Children's Programs:** Day-care (ages 3–14).

ACCOMMODATIONS
139 rooms, 21 tepees.

DINING
À la carte meals served in lodge dining room. **Sample Meals:** Salad with field greens, huckleberry vinaigrette, Oregon blue cheese, and candied pecans (lunch); boned Cornish Game Hen with wild Juniper rice (dinner).

RATES AND PACKAGES
Lodge and Village rooms $120–$155 per day, single or double; suites (2 bedrooms) $165–$215. 1-night deposit required. AE, DC, MC, V.

DIRECTIONS
✉ *Box K, Warm Springs, OR 97761,* ☎ *541/553–1112 or 800/554–4786,* FAX *541/553–1071.*

From Portland: Highway 26 east to Warm Springs (2½ hrs).

WASHINGTON

CARSON HOT MINERAL SPRINGS RESORT

Mineral springs

The claw-foot enamel tubs are characteristic of the old-fashioned friendliness bathers enjoy at the Carson Hot Mineral Springs Resort. Proud of using "the same bath methods for over 100 years," the management strives to remain unpretentious and comfortable. The rustic cabins (no TVs or phones), a landmark hotel with nine simple rooms, and bathhouses on the banks of the Wind River near its junction with the mighty Columbia date from 1876. The oldest remaining structure, a three-story wood hotel, was built in 1897 to accommodate bathers who traveled by steamboat from Portland, Oregon. The cabins were built in the early 1920s.

Taking the waters is a simple, two-step procedure: A tub soak is followed by the traditional sweat wrap, in which an attendant wraps bathers in sheets and heavy blankets to induce a good sweat. The 126°F mineral water is piped directly into the tubs (eight for men, six for women), which are drained and refilled after each use. The water is not treated with chemicals; analysis shows it to be high in sodium and calcium, like springs at principal European spas. The crowning touch is the hour-long massage or herbal wrap.

FACILITIES
Services: Massage. **Recreation:** Fishing, golf, hiking.

ACCOMMODATIONS
9 rooms, 23 cabins.

DINING
3 hearty meals daily in hotel restaurant, served à la carte. **Sample Meals:** Club sandwich, pasta salad, beef lasagna (lunch); prime rib, vegetable burger, grilled salmon (dinner).

RATES AND PACKAGES
Rooms and cabins $35–$50 for 2 persons, $5 each additional person. Reservation guaranteed by credit card. MC, V.

DIRECTIONS
✉ *Box 1169, Carson, WA 98610,* ☎ *509/427–8292 or 800/607–3678,* 𝔽𝔸𝕏 *509/427–7242.*

From Portland: I–84 east to Bridge of the Gods, Route 14 to Carson (70 mins).

ROSARIO RESORT

Luxury pampering

The natural beauty of this peaceful cove in the San Juan Islands makes Rosario Resort an obvious choice for relaxation and renewal. Sea-inspired treatments for the body and a full complement of outdoor recreational activities are added attractions at this 1909 mansion-cum-resort spa, built around the former home of the shipbuilding magnate Robert Moran.

Arriving by ferry, yacht, or floatplane, one sees little sign of a hotel. Guest cottages cluster around the hillside and grounds surrounding the mansion. Some have fireplaces and whirlpool tubs, and most have views of Cascade Bay. From the cottages, it's a short walk to the spa and the mansion, where meals are served (there's no room service). Public rooms have a nautical look; portholes and other parts salvaged from old ships pop up in the indoor-swimming-pool room and other unexpected places. The mansion's centerpiece is an Aeolian pipe organ that sits in a spectacular music room with cathedral ceilings and stained-glass windows; here, daily concerts are held in the summer.

Extensive spa treatments are available at Rosario's Natural Wellness Center. In addition, there are swimming pools and whirlpools, a coed sauna, weights room, and aerobics studio where the daily schedule might consist of yoga, water aerobics, step aerobics, strengthening and conditioning classes. Outside the spa, simple pleasures include hunting for driftwood on the 2-mile long beach, hiking to the lookout over the San Juans from the top of Mt. Constitution, or exploring Orcas Island by mountain bike. Vancouver, B.C., and the Canadian Rockies are a few hours drive north, and charming Victoria is just seven miles away by water.

FACILITIES
Exercise Equipment: Cross-country ski machine, rowing machine, weight-training circuit, stair climbers, stationary bikes, free weights. **Services:** Aromatherapy massage, reflexology, shiatsu, Swedish massage; salt glow; facial. **Swimming:** 3 pools (1 indoor), ocean beach, mountain lake. **Recreation:** Boating, hiking, kayaking, tennis, whale watching; golf nearby.

ACCOMMODATIONS
127 rooms, 8 suites.

DINING
No meal plan. À la carte meals served in the Orcas Room and in the more upscale Compass Dining Room. **Sample Meals:** Green salad dressed with fruit juice and cayenne pepper, chicken baked in romaine lettuce, beer-steamed Lopez Island mussels (lunch); grilled salmon with peppercorn-basil-red-pepper sauce, veal topped with crab and asparagus, carpaccio of yellowfin tuna with baby greens and braised Washington lingcod (dinner).

RATES AND PACKAGES
Daily rate $108–$241 per person double, additional person $20; suites $185–$485. 1-night deposit required. AE, DC, MC, V.

DIRECTIONS
✉ *1 Rosario Way, Eastsound, Orcas Island, WA 98245,* ☎ *360/376–2222 or 800/562–8820.*

From Seattle: I–5 to Anacortes to Eastsound (½ hr), ferry to Orcas Island, ½ hr drive to resort (3½ hr).

THE SALISH LODGE

Luxury pampering

This Pacific Rim-style health retreat, a sister to the Skamania Lodge (*see below*), looks out on the magnificent scenery of the Cascade Mountains. Oriental touches enhance the airy, wood-and-glass pavilion, evoking the feeling of a bathhouse at a Japanese hot spring. Seaweed treatments, shiatsu massage, and an Asian-influenced spa-cuisine menu add to the cross-cultural experience.

Viewers of the TV series "Twin Peaks" might recognize the four-story lodge, which is perched at the crest of a waterfall taller than Niagara. It opened in 1988, re-creating an inn built on the site in 1916. The original dining room was restored, using indigenous stone, copper, and wood. Rooms all have a wood-burning stone fireplace, Northwest-designed furniture, and either a balcony or window seat. Large bathrooms have oversize whirlpool tubs. Those who prefer spending time in public spaces can sip complimentary morning coffee, tea, and mineral water by the fireplace in the lodge's library-lounge.

The facility's most spectacular features are two hydrotherapy pools (both coed) set in natural rock and joined by a waterfall. In addition, there are four private rooms for Swedish massage, shiatsu, and bodywork, plus a wet-treatment room with a Vichy shower, and a coed sauna and eucalyptus steam room. For privacy, you can arrange a fireside massage in your room. Treatments are available à la carte or in packages such as the Falls Refresher, which includes a 30-minute aromatherapy massage, a mini "Salish facial," a sea-salt deep-cleansing hand and foot polish, and a spa snack. Although there are no aerobics classes or organized exercise programs, a small fitness center has a good mix of equipment. For adventure-minded guests, there's hiking in Snoqualmie Falls Park, mountain-biking, white-water rafting, and horseback trail-riding; ask for details at the lodge.

FACILITIES

Exercise Equipment: Rowing machine, stair climber, stationary bike, treadmill, weight-training circuit, free weights. **Services:** Reflexology, shiatsu, sports massage, Swedish massage; body scrub, mud wrap, seaweed wrap; Vichy shower; facial. **Swimming:** None. **Classes and Programs:** Entertainment in Attic Lounge. **Recreation:** Sports court, mountain bikes.

ACCOMMODATIONS

91 rooms, 4 suites.

DINING

Calorie-counted spa cuisine served à la carte in The Dining Room. Seafood from local fisheries, wines from local vineyards. **Sample Meals:** Spinach fusilli, cashew-crusted sea bass with dried-current polenta and green-curry sauce (lunch); vegetable terrine with wild-rice crêpe, pan-seared ostrich with chanterelle-parsnip cake and sweet-potato flan in pinot noir sauce (dinner).

RATES AND PACKAGES

$275 per room for 2 people, suites $675 for 2. Additional person $25 per night. Spa packages, including accommodations: Fireside Massage $400 per couple; Salish Falls Refresher $200 single, Cascade Escape Spa Package $400 per person including lunch. 1-night deposit required. AE, DC, MC, V.

DIRECTIONS

✉ *U.S. Hwy. 202, Box 1109, Snoqualmie, WA 98065,* ☎ *425/831–6500 or 800/826–6124,* ℻ *425/888–2420.*

From Seattle: I–90 east, exit 27 to Snoqualmie (45 mins).

SKAMANIA LODGE

Luxury pampering

The panoramic sweep of the Cascade Mountains and the mighty Columbia River welcomes visitors to the Skamania Lodge, built on a ridge in the Gorge National Scenic Area 45 minutes from Portland. This is a dramatic area, great for hiking and well known for the blustery winds that blow through the Gorge and make it a thriving center for sailboarding. But the history of this region long predates the construction of the first Windsurfer: This is Chinook tribe territory, and Skamania Lodge's architecture reflects the past. Creating the casual, calming interior are Native American–style rugs, Pendleton fabrics, and mission-style wood furnishings. A stone fireplace dominates the three-story Great Room. While working out in the spa you enjoy views of the golf course and surrounding forest.

With the Cascade mountain range looming to the northeast, and lush botanical areas and waterfalls nearby, the Lodge is ideally situated for hikers. The Forest Service information center in the Lodge provides information on guided treks to the area devastated by the eruption of Mount St. Helens in 1980. Those who prefer to work out indoors can take advantage of the fitness center (there's a trainer on staff), and 60-foot lap pool complete with its own waterfall. The spa also includes indoor whirlpools and a Jacuzzi on a sundeck. A midweek spa package includes dinner and two treatments, as well as use of the sports facilities.

Also on the grounds is an 18-hole golf course that winds through the forest. Golfers warm up on a driving range, putting green, and practice bunker before tackling this challenging course. Guided trail rides on horseback are reserved through the lodge's guest services desk. In winter, trails are groomed for cross-country skiing.

FACILITIES
Exercise Equipment: Rowing machines, stair climbers, treadmills, weight-training circuit. **Services:** Massage. **Swimming:** Indoor pool. **Recreation:** Golf, hiking, mountain biking, tennis, volleyball.

ACCOMMODATIONS
195 rooms.

DINING
À la carte menu of Pacific Northwest cuisine. **Sample Meals:** Trail Wagon burger (lunch); plank-roasted salmon with chardonnay-butter sauce, roast leg of venison with wild-berry relish (dinner).

RATES AND PACKAGES
$125–$225 per day single or double occupancy; suites $225–$340. AE, DC, MC, V.

DIRECTIONS
⊠ *Box 189, Stevenson, WA 98648,* ☎ *509/427–7700 or 800/221–7117,* ℻ *509/427–2547.*

From Portland: I–84 east to Bridge of the Gods, or Highway 14 (45 mins).

SOL DUC HOT SPRINGS RESORT

Mineral springs

Here's the place to bring the family for a soak and a swim after a drive or a hike in Olympic National Park. Operating as a concession of the Department of the Interior within the park, the Sol Duc Hot Springs Resort is open from May through October, with 32 minimally outfitted cabins (six with kitchens and all with modern baths), 20 RV sites, a restaurant, and mineral spring-fed pools as well as a 30-lap freshwater swimming pool.

Park visitors can use the public and private pools for a fee; overnight guests use them for free. Piped into a heat exchanger at a temperature of 123°F, the mineral water is cooled for use in three large outdoor soaking pools. The water's continuous flow into the pools makes chlorination unnecessary.

FACILITIES
Swimming: Pool. **Classes and Programs:** Talks by park rangers. **Recreation:** Fishing, hiking. **Children's Programs:** Ranger-led nature walks for children (5–15).

ACCOMMODATIONS

32 cabins, 20 RV sites.

DINING

Vegetarian, fish, and chicken dishes at restaurant. **Sample Meals:** Vegetarian sandwich with roasted red peppers, cucumbers, tomatoes, sprouts, and cheddar cheese (lunch); baked cod with mushrooms, stuffed acorn squash with wild rice pilaf, mushrooms, and tarragon beurre blanc.

RATES AND PACKAGES

Cabin with kitchen $108.71–$164.74 per day, without kitchen $97.50–$153.54, for 2 persons. 1-night deposit required. AE, D, MC, V.

DIRECTIONS

✉ *Soleduc River Rd., Olympic National Park, WA. Reservations: Box 2169, Port Angeles, WA 98362, ☎ 360/327–3583.*

From Seattle: Highway 101 to Fairholm, Soleduc Road 11 mi to resort (4 hrs).

WYOMING

ANTELOPE RETREAT AND EDUCATION CENTER

Holistic health

An isolated ranch in the foothills of the Continental Divide, the Antelope Retreat Center puts you to work preparing meals, joining in ranch chores, and gardening. Guests are initiated at a sweat-lodge ceremony and taught personal awareness exercises. Some even get to help with lambing the small herd of sheep. Living like a rancher comes naturally here, with accommodations in an 1890s house or in outlying yurts built into earthen mounds.

John Boyer, who grew up on the ranch and founded the retreat center in 1986, says his goal was to share his love of nature and the inner quiet learned from neighboring Native Americans. To that end, he runs special weekly programs such as vision quests based on the Native American rite of passage, including a three-day wilderness fast; and a nature-awareness week devoted to learning survival skills while camping in the Red Desert and Medicine Bow National Forest. Focus programs include gender weeks, with a personal sojourn in the desert; and Sacred Hoop week, which involves exploring Dakota traditions.

FACILITIES
Swimming: Stream. **Classes and Programs:** Sweat lodge. **Recreation:** Hiking, skiing, outings to rodeos and nearby attractions, gardening, ranching.

ACCOMMODATIONS
4 rooms in ranch house, plus 2 4-bed yurts, all with shared bath.

DINING
3 meals daily included in rates, served family style. Vision Quest involves 3-day fast. **Sample Meals:** Soup and salad, sandwiches on homemade bread (lunch); barbecued chicken, grilled fish, spaghetti, tofu casserole, vegetable stir-fry (dinner).

RATES AND PACKAGES
Daily $60–$150 per person. Vacation week (no program) $400–$1,050. $500–$1,050 per week with program (Sat.–Sat.). 50% deposit required. No credit cards.

DIRECTIONS
✉ *Box 156, Savery, WY 82332,* ☎ *307/383–2625 or 888/268–2732.*

From Denver, CO: I–70 west, exit at Dillon, Route 9 to Kremmling, Route 40 west via Steamboat Springs to Craig, Highway 13/789 to Baggs, right on Route 70 via Dixon to Savery, left on Creek Road (5½ hr).

HOT SPRINGS STATE PARK

Mineral springs

Soak up some history and fun in a town devoted to taking the waters. Nestled among foothills of the Owl Creek Mountains, and resting beside Big Horn River, Thermopolis claims to have the world's largest mineral hot spring. Long before explorers discovered the Big Spring, it was a bathing place for the Shoshone and Arapahoe tribes. When the land was purchased by the federal government in 1896, the deed stipulated that the springs remain open and free to all. Accordingly, the State Bath

House is free to the public, with both private bathtubs and a public tiled pool.

The water here wells from the earth at a temperature of 135°F and spills down a series of mineral-glazed terraces on its way to the Big Horn River. Some of the flow is diverted to the state-run baths, as well as privately operated bathhouses and swimming pools, such as those at Tepee Spa, the Star Plunge, the Fountain of Youth RV Park, and the Holiday Inn of the Waters.

Facilities in the area are patronized by families en route to Yellowstone and by senior citizens from a nearby retirement home. Those who wish to spend the night have several options; the Holiday Inn on the bank of the Horn River has the most extensive facilities, including an athletic club and outdoor swimming pool, separate men's and women's bathhouses for private soaks, and an outdoor hydrojet pool filled with warm mineral water.

Surrounded by high buttes about 150 miles from the East Gate of Yellowstone National Park, the town of Thermopolis offers a taste of the Old West. Head to the park's 1000-acre preserve, where bison still roam. For family fun, there's melodrama on stage at the Little Broadway Theatre, and an 18-hole public miniature golf course.

FACILITIES
Exercise Equipment: Stationary bikes, weight-training circuit. **Services:** Massage. **Swimming:** Pool. **Recreation:** Biking, racquetball; golf, fishing, skiing, snowmobiling nearby.

ACCOMMODATIONS
80 rooms.

DINING
No meal plan. 3 à la carte meals served in hotel restaurant. **Sample Meals:** Western steaks, grilled fish, baked mountain trout, salads in season.

RATES AND PACKAGES
$55–$98 single, $61–$98 per day double. 1-night deposit required. AE, MC, V.

DIRECTIONS
✉ *Thermopolis Chamber of Commerce, 220 Park St., Thermopolis, WY 82443,* ☎ *307/864–2636.*

Holiday Inn of the Waters, 115 E. Park St., Box 1323, Thermopolis, WY 82443, ☎ 307/864–3131 or 800/465–4329, FAX 307/864–3131.

From Cheyenne: I–25 to Casper, Highway 20 via Moneta (3 hrs).

4 The Central States

Oklahoma, South Dakota, Texas

DALLAS HAS BEEN IN THE FOREFRONT of recent fitness developments in the Central States. Dr. Kenneth Cooper, who did pioneering research in exercise and nutrition in the U.S. Air Force and at the Cooper Clinic, is the guiding spirit for the residential program at the Aerobics Center. In the suburbs, the Greenhouse offers luxury pampering and body conditioning for women only. And for golfers or executives on the go, The Four Seasons Resort's full-service spa and health club provide a deluxe retreat for a day or a week.

Texans have taken to European hydrotherapy with the Kneipp herbal baths and Kur Program at the Alamo Plaza Spa in San Antonio and at the Lake Austin Spa Resort near Austin. An alternative holistic curriculum at the Optimum Health Institute in Austin includes wheatgrass juicing, daily exercise, and emotional detoxification in a structured residential program.

The combination of big-city attractions and secluded resorts may be just what you want for an active vacation. But outside Oklahoma City, the Akia retreat for women provides concentrated programs on weekends as well as extended workouts in a scenic mountain area. And at South Dakota's Black Hills Health and Education Center, a family-oriented spiritual retreat is operated by Seventh-Day Adventists.

OKLAHOMA

AKIA

Nutrition and diet

A weight-loss diet and plenty of exercise are the main ingredients of the no-frills weekends and five-day programs at Akia, a fitness retreat for a dozen women. Guests participate in full days of hiking, stretching, and body toning in a rigorous dawn-to-dusk schedule that takes advantage of the scenic Arbuckle Mountains and nearby lakes and forests. Programs take place during 13 spring and fall sessions.

The day begins with exercise on the redwood deck that surrounds the main building. The two-mile hike before breakfast is followed by more stretching and toning in a lakeside pavilion. Aerobics classes, relaxation exercises, and other activities begin the afternoon. Then participants have the option of soaking in the hot tub, getting a massage, walking, bicycling, or swimming in a nearby lake. Private consultation on nutrition with a registered dietitian and one-on-one training with the exercise instructor help you plan a personal fitness program.

Ninety miles south of Oklahoma City and 100 miles north of Dallas, the retreat has a compound ringed by rock cottages, each accommodating three women. Participants bring their own linens and towels and help with housekeeping. Gourmet meals are prepared by a spa-cuisine chef. A three-course dinner is served by candlelight and is followed by discussions on health and nutrition.

FACILITIES
Services: Massage, body-composition test, color analysis, nutritional counseling. **Swimming:** Nearby lake. **Classes and Programs:** Lectures on nutrition and body care; movies. **Recreation:** Bicycling.

ACCOMMODATIONS
All cottages share baths.

DINING
3 meals daily total 950–1,200 calories. **Sample Meals:** Vegetable–black-bean pasta salad, tuna salad on pita bread (lunch); spinach lasagna with green salad, peppers stuffed with lentils and brown rice (dinner).

RATES AND PACKAGES
$200 for 2-day weekend, $450 for 5-day session. $100 deposit required. No credit cards.

DIRECTIONS
✉ *Sulphur, OK. Office: 2316 N.W. 45th Place, Oklahoma City, OK 73112,* ☎ *405/842–6269.*

From Oklahoma City: I–35 south to Exit 55, Highway 7 to Sulphur (1½ hrs).

SOUTH DAKOTA

BLACK HILLS HEALTH AND EDUCATION CENTER

Holistic health

Learn how to take control of health problems and eliminate addictions as you find energy within at the Black Hills Health and Education Center. Set on a wooded campus close to Rapid City, these structured, highly regimented, 13- to 20-day programs attract people of all ages, though many of the participants are over 50. The mood is informal and down-to-business: Guests arrive in motor homes that can be hooked up outside, or stay in the lodge; some bring children and a baby-sitter.

Black Hills's medically supervised programs are designed to teach guests healthy habits, and to help those who suffer from diabetes, arthritis, hypertension, heart problems, and obesity. Each person's lifestyle is analyzed and a suitable regimen of exercise and diet prescribed. Rehabilitation therapy is provided for persons who have had cardiac surgery.

The program begins with a complete physical examination, blood tests, and medical counseling. Hydrotherapy (included in the program fee) and massage may be recommended; the lodge is equipped with a whirlpool, a steam cabinet, and a shower that alternates hot and cold water from six sprays. Once or twice a week an excursion takes participants to a fitness center and a swimming pool fed by warm springs.

Though lectures cover stress control and nutrition, the central philosophy is one of learning by doing. Everyone joins in bread-making and cooking classes, and outings to a supermarket and restaurant are led by staff members who demonstrate how to shop for and order nutritious foods.

Run by Seventh-Day Adventists as an affiliate of the Black Hills Missionary College, the Healing Center draws on the campus for services. On Friday evenings, students and guests traditionally gather around the big stone fireplace in the lounge and join in a music program. The campus is set in the scenic Banana Belt of the Black Hills, so named for the temperate climate and sunny days that prevail even in winter. Nearby, guests explore the canyons, cliffs, and farmlands on daily hikes.

FACILITIES
Exercise Equipment: Rowing machine, stationary bikes, treadmill, weight-training circuit. **Services:** Massage, hydrotherapy. **Swimming:** Pool nearby. **Classes and Programs:** Medical consultation, one-on-one training; informal talks and films on health-related topics, medical lectures. Music program Fri. **Recreation:** Mt. Rushmore and Crazy Horse Memorial day trips; gold panning, rock collecting; downhill skiing nearby.

ACCOMMODATIONS
12 rooms. Campground with RV hookups.

DINING
3 vegetarian meals daily, served buffet style. Fruits, vegetables, legumes, and natural fat sources such as nuts and avocados. Whole-grain bread baked daily. No dairy products, eggs, coffee, tea, condiments. **Sample Meals:** Salad bar, water-steamed vegetables, vegetarian lasagna with nondairy cheese (lunch); vegetarian taco salad, baked tofu, cashew chow mein.

RATES AND PACKAGES
Daily rate $45 per room. 5-day program $500; $450 per person for double; 13-day program $1,800 single, $1,620 per person doubles; 20-day

program $2,600 single, $4,630 per person double. $100–$200 reduction for motor home use. $100 per-person deposit required. D, MC, V

DIRECTIONS
✉ *Box 19, Hermosa, SD 57744,* ☎ *605/255–4101 or 800/658–5433,* FAX *605/255–4687.*

From Rapid City: Highway 79 south to Hermosa, Highway 40 west 4 miles to entrance road (30 mins).

TEXAS

ALAMO PLAZA SPA AT THE MENGER HOTEL

Luxury pampering
Mineral springs

Kneipp herbal baths are a standout feature of the historic Menger Hotel, which has a European hydrotherapy program at its Alamo Plaza Spa. Built on the site of a pioneer beer brewery and Russian-Turkish bathhouse, the hotel taps its own Edwards Aquifer for spring water to fill the big claw-footed Victorian bathtubs in its original 1859 building and the new spa beneath the fitness center. Directly across from the Alamo, the shrine of Texas independence, this is an urban retreat for body and mind.

Personalized regimens are set up for guests by advance reservation. The spa has five treatment rooms, sauna and steam rooms, and whirlpool. An aesthetician is available for facials and treatments on hands and feet. Using Kneipp herbal essences and aromatic oils made in Germany, your *kur* (treatment course) can include water applications, exercise, diet, and combinations of dry heat, wet massage, wet heat, and dry massage. Day spa packages are available as well as overnight programs.

Dr. Jonathan Paul de Vierville, who was trained at the Kneipp center in Bad Wörishofen, adapted these popular European traditions to American lifestyles, opening the Alamo Plaza Spa in 1993 while continuing his state-certified school for bodyworkers. In the tradition of the classic spas in Baden-Baden, Karlsbad, and Vichy, the Alamo Spa at the Menger Hotel capitalizes on the rich cultural resources and natural wonders of the area.

Many rooms and suites at the Menger Hotel have ornate balconies over-looking an interior garden that has tropical foliage and a swimming pool filled with heated mineral water. Near the hotel is the River Walk, lined with restaurants and strolling musicians. Tour buses and motorized trol-ley cars take you to museums, galleries, and a performing arts center, as well as to the Alamo Dome.

FACILITIES
Exercise Equipment: Stair climbers, stationary bikes, treadmill, free weights. **Services:** Reflexology, sports massage, Swedish massage; fango treatment, herbal body scrub, hot-linen herbal wrap; hydrotherapy, tha-lassotherapy; facial. **Swimming:** Pool.

ACCOMMODATIONS
295 rooms, 23 suites.

DINING
Breakfast, lunch, and beverage breaks included in spa packages; one din-ner only in American Kur Spa Classic. Kneipp Menu choices in hotel din-ing room include high-protein foods such as cottage cheese, fish, lean meat, whole-grain products, vegetables, fresh fruit.

RATES AND PACKAGES
Daily room rate for 2 persons $132–$142, double occupancy; suites $186–$598. San Antonio Kur Spa Full-Day Customized (no lodging; includes lunch) $215. $100 deposit required. AE, D, MC, V.

DIRECTIONS
✉ *204 Alamo Plaza, San Antonio, TX 78205,* ☎ *210/223–5772; hotel reservations 800/345–9285,* ℻ *210/228–0022.*

From San Antonio Airport: I–35 south, Commerce Street exit, right on Bowie Street, to Crockett Street, left to Lady Bird Fountain behind the Alamo (20 mins).

THE COOPER AEROBICS CENTER

Medical wellness
Nutrition and diet

A recognized leader in the study of the medical value of exercise, the Aerobics Center has a residential Cooper Wellness Program designed to help participants achieve permanent changes in lifestyle. Programs of 7–13 days and a 4-day wellness weekend teach the cultivation and adoption of healthy habits. Or you can schedule an intensive one-day workout, with optional workshop.

At first look, the guest lodge seems more like a country club than a health center; the stately redbrick mansion is for the exclusive use of guests, members, and visiting professionals. Visitors have meals in the private restaurant and full use of the Aerobics Center.

Four exercise sessions are part of each day's program. You can work out on a treadmill or walk and jog on paved and lighted trails that wind through the 30-acre wooded estate. A gymnasium has basketball and racquetball courts and a three-lane running track. Two heated outdoor lap pools are six lanes wide and 75 feet long. The four outdoor Laykold lighted tennis courts are equipped with automatic ball machines.

Your stay can begin with an optional ($1,100) physical examination. The first day's schedule includes a chest X-ray, a test for pulmonary function, and vision, hearing, and dental exams. A standard skinfold test and weigh-in on an underwater scale determine your ideal body weight. Blood pressure is measured during and after exercise, and an ECG treadmill test measures stress. Before and after the program, 24 blood tests, including HDL and LDL for cholesterol, are administered. (Your health insurance may cover this.) The comprehensive medical report determines the exercise program that will be recommended for you.

Lecture topics include nutrition and health, and you participate in cooking and bread-making demonstrations. Volleyball, aerobics in the swimming pool, and other forms of group exercise are scheduled. The whirlpool, sauna, and steam room are open every night; massage appointments cost extra.

The combination of a supportive environment, state-of-the-art equipment and facilities, and the professional staff creates a disciplined program, and many guests here see significant results in lowering cholesterol and triglyceride levels in only two weeks. Follow-up calls and return visits have confirmed participants' success in lowering blood pressure and increasing vitality and alertness. The center encourages friends and couples to work together on behavior modification, offering a choice of services and workshops in the standard package or more comprehensive premier package. Lodging and a medical evaluation are not included in the program prices, giving you the option of staying at a nearby hotel.

Limited to groups of no more than 20, the program appeals to high-powered executives who have lost control of their health. Here they work with a team of nine full-time physicians, a dentist, nutritionists, and exercise technologists. Guided by Dr. Kenneth H. Cooper, whose pioneering research on aerobics inspired the founding of the center in the 1970s, these professionals make wellness meaningful to everyday life.

FACILITIES
Exercise Equipment: Cardiovascular equipment, weight-training circuit.
Services: Swedish massage. **Swimming:** 2 pools. **Classes and Programs:**
Personal counseling on fitness, diet, and exercise; medical testing and eval-
uation; talks on nutrition and health; cooking school. **Recreation:** Bas-
ketball, handball, racquetball, tennis, volleyball; golf course nearby.

ACCOMMODATIONS
50 rooms, 12 suites.

DINING
3 calorie-controlled meals daily from planned menu, plus snacks. **Sample Meals:** Tossed salad with low-calorie dressing, Hawaiian chicken
with potatoes and baked tomato, fresh fruit (lunch); beef Burgundy on
a bed of pasta, with snap peas and spinach salad (dinner).

RATES AND PACKAGES
Rooms at Guest Lodge $110–$120, single or double, suites $160–$250.
4-day program $2,095; 7-day $2,695; 13-day $3,595. AE, MC, V.

DIRECTIONS
✉ *12230 Preston Rd., Dallas, TX 75230,* ☎ *972/386–4777 or 800/444–
5192,* FAX *972/386–0039.*

From Dallas: Highway 635 (LBJ Freeway), Preston Road (20 mins).

FOUR SEASONS RESORT AND CLUB

Luxury pampering
Sports conditioning

Big in every way, the Four Seasons Resort and Club is the best little spa
in Texas. The centerpiece of this 400-acre urban resort is the four-level
Sports Club, which is connected to the spa by underground tunnel. Two
golf courses, indoor and outdoor tennis, squash, and racquetball courts,
and jogging tracks complete the picture.

Eight daily exercise classes are among the options at the spa, plus weight
training, total fitness regimens, stretch groups, water works, and a range
of indoor sports and workout facilities. Sophisticated bodywork treatments use Phytomer seaweed and kelp products. Programs can be tailored
to suit your needs: You can work out on the advanced Nautilus equipment, do aerobics and body-building exercises, and play a round of golf
or team up for tennis. Personal trainers, nutritional counseling, and fitness evaluations are available at an hourly rate that can be combined with
any of the resort's special packages.

More than 25 spa treatments and beauty salon services can be booked à
la carte. Services range from massage to aromatherapy, herbal wraps, and
baths. There are two sets of Jacuzzis, saunas, steam rooms, hydrotherapy tubs, and hot/cold pools in separate wings for men and women. The
spa program assures personal attention from the staff and access to a private swimming pool and whirlpool.

Seven miles from Dallas/Fort Worth International Airport, the resort attracts golfers, corporate executives, and local families, who stay in either
a nine-story tower or in a handful of two-story golf villas, set between a
free-form swimming pool, the golf course, and the sports club. Most rooms
in the towers have a private balcony (ask for golf course view).

FACILITIES
Exercise Equipment: Cross-country ski machine, rowing machines, stair
climber, stationary bikes, treadmills, weight-training circuit, free weights.

Services: Aromatherapy massage, reflexology, shiatsu, sports massage, Swedish massage; heated mud pack, herbal wrap, sea-kelp bath, loofah body scrub; facial. **Swimming:** 4 pools. **Classes and Programs:** Tae kwon do; personal training, fitness evaluation. **Recreation:** Basketball, handball, racquetball, softball, tennis. **Children's Programs:** Child-care center (6 months–8 years).

ACCOMMODATIONS
331 rooms, 26 suites.

DINING
3 meals daily in 2–6 night spa packages. Four Seasons Alternative Cuisine low in cholesterol, fat, calories, sodium. Daily caloric intake under 1,000. **Sample Meals:** Broiled chicken, Mexican chicken enchilada (lunch); grilled salmon, roast quail with fresh berry sauce (dinner).

RATES AND PACKAGES
Rooms $140–$285. 1-day spa package $340–$410 weekdays, weekend $280–$360, suites to $1,000. Fresh Start spa package 2 nights/3 days $950–$1,080 single, $1,380–$1,620 per couple. AE, DC, MC, V.

DIRECTIONS
✉ *4150 N. MacArthur Blvd., Irving, TX 75038,* ☎ *972/717–0700 or 800/332–3442,* ⟨FAX⟩ *972/717–2550.*

From Dallas: Highway 35 to Highway 183 (Airport Freeway), MacArthur Boulevard exit (20 mins).

THE GREENHOUSE

Luxury pampering

Privacy and freedom from stress are precious commodities to the harried young career women, well-heeled society matrons, and spotlight-dodging celebrities who check into The Greenhouse for a week of physical and emotional rejuvenation. Completely self-contained, with a staff of more than 160 serving a maximum of 39 guests, this elegant enclave specializes in the classic spa tradition of total pampering. A special destination for the knowledgeable spa set since 1965, the Greenhouse has maintained its high standard of service and accommodations while expanding programs to appeal to the ever-changing needs and desires of guests. Repeat visitors make up 75-80% of the clientele.

Attention to detail distinguishes a stay here. From the airport, you'll be whisked in a chauffeured limousine to The Greenhouse, set amid gardens and fitness trails. Upon arrival you'll be assigned a personal aesthetician, hairdresser, manicurist, and masseuse for the week. A resident exercise physiologist, nurse, and other staff members will plan a schedule to accommodate you every need.

Meals are creative and, for the most part, low in calories and fat. One evening each week, the spa's executive chef plays host to an informal cooking class, preparing Greenhouse cuisine and providing recipes for dishes that can be made at home. Guests can opt to take all their meals in their room, though most choose to enjoy the refined elegance of the dining room, where the exquisite table settings change nightly.

Each day begins around 7 AM with breakfast in bed. Your daily schedule comes on the tray, and a fresh leotard and robe await you. A brisk guided walk through the garden is followed by exercise classes to energize and tone the body. Choices include aerobics (high- and low-impact), step classes, yogarobics, tai chi, strength training, aquatics (Hydratone, Splashdance, and step), relaxation and breathing, boxing, and Pilates. The

Greenhouse trainers study your fitness profile (prepared on your arrival) and work with you at your pace.

Lunch is served poolside, followed by a daily massage and serious pampering. Daily schedules are adhered to unless guests request otherwise. A once-a-week shopping excursion shuttles guests to the tony Stanley Korshak boutique; other off-premises excursions may be arranged individually. Evenings begin with hors d'oeuvre service in the drawing room, followed by dinner in the formal dining room and scheduled group programs. An in-room "tuck-in" foot or shoulder massage ends each day.

Airy, bright, and expensively furnished, The Greenhouse has the look of a semitropical sybaritic hideaway. The skylighted, marble-floor atrium for swimming and the luxuriously feminine bedrooms are very much a part of the therapy. The overall camaraderie of the women, particularly by the end of the week, is akin to the friendships and kinships found in a sorority house.

FACILITIES
Exercise Equipment: Cross-country ski machine, stair climbers, stationary bikes, treadmills, weight-training circuit, free weights. **Services**: Acupressure, craniosacral therapy, reflexology, shiatsu, sports massage, Swedish massage, watsu; salt scrub, loofah scrub, manual lymph drainage, Tibetan botanical skin treatments; thalassotherapy; facial. **Swimming**: Indoor and outdoor pools. **Classes and Programs**: Feature films, fashion shows, musical entertainment, discussions on stress, wellness, makeup, and cosmetic surgery. Personal fitness, nutrition, health, beauty, and relaxation programs. Cooking classes. **Recreation**: Tennis, jogging.

ACCOMMODATIONS
37 rooms, 2 suites.

DINING
Choice of weight loss or maintenance: 1,000–1,200 or 1,500 calories a day. 3 meals plus mid-morning snack and afternoon fruit frappe. **Sample Meals**: Vegetarian pizza with baby greens salad, grilled tuna steak with pineapple salsa, seafood-and-vegetable terrine (lunch); Cornish hens with ratatouille, broiled lobster tail with spaetzle and citrus sauce (dinner).

RATES AND PACKAGES
From $4,405 to $5,535 per week. Mini-week $2,892–$4,022. $1,000-deposit required. MC, V.

DIRECTIONS
✉ *Box 1144, Arlington, TX 76004,* ☎ *817/640–4000,* FAX *817/649–0422.*

From Dallas: I–30 to Arlington, Highway 360 to Avenue II, left to 107th Street (20 mins).

LAKE AUSTIN SPA RESORT

Luxury pampering
Nutrition and diet

Scenic rolling hills and placid lakes surround the Lake Austin Spa Resort, a laid-back retreat that's close to the city, yet secluded. Here you can view the nature and ecology of Texas Hill Country up close—white-tail deer, armadillos, rabbits, squirrels, raccoons, and red fox are frequently spotted by the lake—while enjoying Hill Country hikes and workouts out at the lakeside gym, plus pampering treatments and relaxation.

Although the program offers a wide range of activity choices, you pay a basic daily rate that includes fitness classes, meals, and guided hikes and canoe trips. Group walks at 7 AM range from 2 to 4 miles. One all-day outing combines a canoe trip with sightings of birds and other wildlife. Also available, for an additional fee, are European facials, mud masks, Ayurvedic treatments, and other personal services in the salon. Try the honey-mango scrub, a gentle body cleanser that incorporates applications of herbs and aloe vera, followed by a full-body massage.

Accommodations range from basic cottages to luxury suites. Antiques, fluffy comforters on the beds, and lots of pillows create a country B&B feeling; nightly turndown service adds an air of luxury. A roommate-matching service is available for single guests. Guests have access to an indoor lap pool with resistant jets, a coed Jacuzzi, sauna, steam room, and outdoor swimming pool. The glass-walled gym and aerobics studio, with suspended wooden floor, overlooks beautiful Lake Austin. Hiking and jogging trails extend into the woods.

Meals are designed to help you maintain a balanced diet, with natural meats, fresh fruit, vegetables, and herbs from an organic garden on the property, where a staff horticulturist is happy to answer questions. Snacks and energy drinks are available throughout the day, and you can request a brown-bag lunch for outings.

FACILITIES
Exercise Equipment: Rowing machine, stair climbers, stationary bikes, treadmill, weight-training circuit, free weights. **Services:** Aromatherapy massage, Swedish, massage, reflexology, shiatsu; body brushing, body polish, herbal wrap, moor-mud therapy, sea-salt body scrub, seaweed body masque; hydrotherapy; facial. **Swimming:** Indoor and outdoor pools. **Classes and Programs:** Personal consultation on fitness, nutrition, skin analysis, special dietary needs; talks on health and fitness. Music, comedy. **Recreation:** Badminton, mountain biking, tennis, volleyball; wildflower walks; canoeing, kayaking, paddleboating, sculling. Golf and horseback riding nearby.

ACCOMMODATIONS
40 rooms, 10 garden rooms.

DINING
3 meals daily, plus snacks, high in complex carbohydrates and fiber, low in fat, sugar, and salt, with organic, natural foods and vegetarian choices from menu. **Sample Meals:** Enchiladas; spinach lasagna; fajitas; vegetarian pizza, barbecued chicken (lunch); Thai noodle bowl; muffalettas; crawfish creole; pasta primavera (dinner).

RATES AND PACKAGES
Daily rate $345 single, $280 per person double. 3-night refresher package $1,090 single, $890 per person double occupancy; 4-night refresher package $1,290 single, $1,090 double; 7-night refresher package $1,990 single, $1,790 double. Living Well package (Sun.–Sun.) $2,290 single, $2,090 per person double occupancy. Add service charge, 17% gratuities, and 6% tax. Deposit: $500 per person. AE, D, MC, V.

DIRECTIONS
✉ *1705 South Quinlan Park Rd., Austin, TX 78732,* ☎ *512/372–7300 or 800/847–5637 (Canada 800/338–6651),* FAX *512/266–1572.*

From Austin. By car, Ranch Rd. 2222, FM 620 to Stone Ranch Road, Quinlan Park Road left to resort sign (45 mins).

5 The Middle West

Illinois, Indiana, Iowa, Minnesota, Missouri, Ohio, Wisconsin

MIDWEST WELLNESS TRADITIONS TRACE THEIR ROOTS to Native Americans who frequented healing springs and practiced invigorating rituals. Today, many Midwestern spas still practice ancient healing therapies with plants and flowers. It was in a Michigan sanitarium that Dr. Harvey Kellogg, M.D., declared, "Anything you can do to increase the amount of pure water consumed by the American people will be a blessing to the country." Remember this is as you sit down to your daily cereal bowl ritual of corn flakes and perhaps a can of La Croix water: It all began in the heartland.

Programs in this part of the country tend to be informal and outdoorsy, focusing on weight loss and general well-being. Wisconsin has the widest variety of choices, from the sports-oriented American Club to the sophisticated Fontana Spa at the Abbey Resort on Lake Geneva. In Ohio you can experience yoga at the Kerr House, a registered historic landmark, or revel in the Americana feel of Mario's International Spa near Cleveland. For another kind of spa experience, take the thermal waters at French Lick Springs in Indiana and the Elms in Missouri, both popular since the turn of the century with the famous and the infamous.

Destination spas such as Birdwing in Minnesota, and the Heartland Spa, near Chicago, are known for personal attention and group camaraderie. Perhaps the most unusual example is the Raj, in Fairfield, Iowa, devoted to the ancient system of preventive natural medicine known as Ayurvedic therapy. Near Minneapolis, The Marsh is another example of a dedicated wellness program for prevention of illness. At these country retreats you'll learn to handle stress, manage your diet, and balance mind, body, and spirit.

ILLINOIS

THE HEARTLAND SPA

Nutrition and diet

Like an adult camp in the country, the Heartland Spa reeks of hospitality. The charming lakefront mansion occupies a 30-acre estate, with a fitness center in the former barn, and a guest list limited to 28. Structured programs for a long weekend or full-week retreat, and easy access from Chicago are additional features that have made The Heartland Spa a repeat destination for Midwesterners.

There are no rules or restrictions here; your day can be as structured or unstructured as you please. High-tech workouts and circuit-training sessions are held in the barn, an impressive three-level fitness center, including an indoor pool and spa-treatment rooms, all reached through an underground passage from the house. Scheduled group exercise classes in the top-floor studio include aerobics, martial arts, and meditation.

Personal consultation with staff is included in the five-day and seven-day programs. They advise you to concentrate on activities you enjoy and to continue them when you return home. (Try yoga and race walking!) In addition to aquaerobics, step aerobics, martial arts, and self-awareness training, there's a challenging ropes course, and cross-country skiing. You don't need to sign up for scheduled exercise classes, but do make appointments for massage and facials. Bodywork and beauty treatments are included in package rates. Weekends are the busiest time; the best deal is a five-day stay, from Sunday to Friday noon. Longer, discounted stays can also be arranged to concentrate on weight loss or recuperation from illness.

FACILITIES
Exercise Equipment: Cross-country ski track, rowing machines, stair climbers, stationary bikes, weight-training units, free weights. **Services:** Foot massage, relaxation massage; facial. **Swimming:** Indoor pool, lake. **Classes and Programs:** Nutrition evaluation, underwater body-composition test. Informal discussions on health-related topics. Guest speakers on stress management, life enhancement, financial planning. **Recreation:** Hiking, mountain biking, tennis, cross-country skiing.

ACCOMMODATIONS
14 rooms.

DINING
3 meals daily. Snacks and fruit all day. Mostly vegetarian menu; dairy products, fish served occasionally. No salt, sugar, or added fats. 1,200 calories a day for women, 1,500 for men. **Sample Meals:** Portabello-mushroom sandwich, Japanese mushroom salad (lunch); home-made spinach ravioli with sage broth, grilled swordfish with rosemary, corn crêpes with spinach soufflé (dinner).

RATES AND PACKAGES
2-day weekend $720–$756 single, $500–$530 per person double; 5 days $1,615–$1,700 single, $1,131–$1190 double; 8 days/7 nights (Sun.–Sun.) $2,261–$2,380 single, $1,583–$1,666 double. Roommates matched on request. 50% deposit required. AE, D, DC, MC, V.

DIRECTIONS

✉ *1237 E. 1600 North Rd., Gilman, IL 60938*, ☎ *815/683–2182 or 800/545–4853*, ⅁ᴀ̲x̲ *815/683–2144*.

From Chicago: Dan Ryan Expressway south, I–57 to Kankakee Exit 308, Highway 52/45 (becomes Highway 49) to Route 24, west 2 miles. (90 mins).

INDIANA

FRENCH LICK SPRINGS RESORT

Luxury pampering
Mineral springs

French Lick Springs Resort's claim to fame is its so-called "Pluto Water"—
sulfurous spring water that attracted a wealthy elite as early as the 19th
century. "What Mother Nature doesn't do," the old ads say, "Pluto
water will." Modeled on the great spas of Europe, the French Lick Springs
Resort was built in the early 1840s and ideally positioned to take advantage
of the therapeutic mineral waters. Today, the famous Pluto Water is still
used in the Pluto Bath in the hotel health club, where relaxing soaks can
be complemented with exercise classes and a wide range of skin-care treatments.

Though it has been restored several times, the hotel retains its original
Victorian elegance, with high-ceilinged rooms, French doors, carved
woodwork, and verandas that overlook formal gardens. Its 2,600 acres
of lawns and rolling woodlands contain the most complete tennis complex in the Midwest (with 18 courts, eight of them indoors), and two championship golf courses; nearby are trails ideal for hiking and horseback
riding. With all these recreation facilities at hand, the mineral springs are
no longer the sole attraction; yet you can still have a sip from a well beneath a gazebo or take a bath in spring water piped into a claw-foot tub.

The spa can be enjoyed on a daily-rate basis or with baths and beauty
services included in packages. No formal program of activities is offered;
you set your own schedule. The spa director will consult with you on a
meal plan, exercise classes, and bodywork.

FACILITIES
Exercise Equipment: Rowing machines, stair climbers, stationary bikes,
weight-training circuit. **Services:** Reflexology, Swedish massage; loofah
body scrub, salt rub; facial. **Swimming:** Indoor and outdoor pools. **Classes
and Programs:** Personal consultation on exercise. **Recreation:** Biking,
billiards, bowling, fishing, hiking, horseback riding, sailing, skiing. Resort entertainment. **Children's Programs:** Supervised day camp for children during summer; playground, miniature train ride, wading pool.

ACCOMMODATIONS
500 rooms and suites.

DINING
3 meals daily with spa packages. Low-calorie selections. Vegetarian meals
on request. **Sample Meals:** Shrimp shish kebab and teriyaki chicken
(lunch); poached salmon (dinner).

RATES AND PACKAGES
2-night midweek package $384 single, $299 per person double. 5-night
spa program $860 single, $662 per person double. $149 day-spa pack-
age with lunch. Credit card confirmation or $100 per person deposit re-
quired for spa packages. AE, DC, MC, V.

DIRECTIONS
✉ *French Lick, IN 47432,* ☎ *812/936–9300 or 800/457–4042,* ℻
812/936–2100.

From Louisville: I–64 west, Highway 150 to Paoli, Route 56 west (1 hr).

INDIAN OAK RESORT

Luxury pampering

Hidden behind a shopping mall, the Indian Oak Resort doesn't look like much from the outside. But once guests enter the property, they are set at ease by its tranquil setting overlooking 100 acres of lush, well-maintained grounds, including woods and a private lake full of wildlife and waterfowl. This nonstructured resort offers a variety of services, many of which are aimed at those new to the spa experience. Spa director Katie Gaffney is incorporating holistic programs and has added leading-edge therapeutic spa treatments, such as seaweed rejuvenating facials, detoxifying lymphatic drainage massage, hydrotherapy cellulite treatments, and energy-based La Stone therapy massage. The emphasis is on refreshing the mind, body, and spirit with spa services that detoxify, exfoliate, hydrate, nourish, and relax.

Spa packages include a selection of personal services such as massages, facials, and herbal body wraps, as well as meals. There are nine rooms for massage, facials, and reflexology, and a room for wet treatments with mud and seaweed. All guests can use the facilities and participate in exercise classes, such as aquacize and Step Reebok. Start the morning with meditation classes, yoga, or tai chi on the deck overlooking Lake Chubb. Or enjoy the indoor lap pool and whirlpool, as well as the steam room and sauna. Wingfield's restaurant and pub offers Midwestern fare with some health-oriented spa dishes. The resort is also a good getaway spot for corporate strategy meetings, offering aromatherapy pick me-ups, onsite chair massages, and personal wellness workshops on topics such as tai chi, magnetic acupuncture, Chinese herbal medicine, vegetarian cooking, and relaxation techniques.

FACILITIES
Exercise Equipment: Cross-country ski track, stair climbers, stationary bikes, treadmills, weight-training circuit, free weights. **Services:** Esalen massage, La Stone therapy massage, lymphatic drainage massage, polarity therapy, shiatsu; herbal wrap; hydrotherapy cellulite treatment, seaweed treatment; facial. **Swimming:** Indoor pool, lake. **Recreation:** Biking, boating, fishing, hiking; cross-country skiing.

ACCOMMODATIONS
100 rooms.

DINING
Continental breakfast included in all room rates. 2-night spa package includes 2 meals daily. Meals low in fat, salt, and calories.

RATES AND PACKAGES
$120–$190 single, $130–$190 for 2 persons double occupancy; suites $130–$175. 1-night spa package $235–$268 single, $245–$278 per person double; 2-night spa package $385–$451 single, $395–$461 per person double. Credit-card deposit required for first night. AE, D, DC, MC, V.

DIRECTIONS
⊠ *558 Indian Boundry, Chesterton, IN 46304,* ☎ *219/926–2200 or 800/ 552–4232,* ℻ *219/929–4285.*

From Chicago: I–80/90 to I–94 (1 hr).

IOWA

THE RAJ

Holistic health
Medical wellness

Learn the secrets of Ayurveda under supervision of Western medical doctors and Indian experts in a structured program designed to stimulate health and vitality. Set amid farmland, The Raj is a self-contained world of quiet elegance, dedicated to holistic philosophies of health and healing that have been practiced in India for centuries.

Treatment begins with an assessment of your physiological makeup by a physician concerned with both physical and spiritual health. Maharishi therapies, designed to restore balance in your body, are deeply relaxing. Traditionally known as *panchakarma*, treatments include warm herbal-oil massages, herbal steam baths, and internal cleansing. Aromatic Ayurvedic oils are used to enliven energy points (*marmas*) to create a feeling of well-being. For stress reduction and to expand inner awareness, you are introduced to transcendental meditation and given a mantra.

Developed by Maharishi university professor Rodgers Badgett, Jr., and his wife Candace, the program includes luxurious accommodations in suites or villas, and three gourmet vegetarian meals a day. The facilities are limited, usually to groups of ten, and all treatments are in private suites. Informal discussion groups often form in the living room, and guest speakers cover everything from attitudes toward beauty to prevention of chronic disorders. The daily session of yoga brings everyone together in a carpeted studio. Long walks in the rolling meadows and woodlands are a nice complement to the daily activities.

A three- to seven-day skin-rejuvenation program involves a medical consultation, followed by daily mud baths, milk baths, and massage. Called the Royal Beauty From Within program, it is a natural evolution of ancient and contemporary philosophies that exemplify the goals of The Raj.

FACILITIES
Exercise Equipment: Stair climbers, stationary bikes, treadmills, free weights. **Services:** Aromatherapy massage, Ayurvedic massage. **Classes and Programs:** Internal cleansing, nutrition and diet counseling, sound therapy, stress management, transcendental meditation, yoga. Videotapes and guest lectures on health-related topics.

ACCOMMODATIONS
16 suites in Raj Court Hotel.

DINING
3 gourmet organic vegetarian meals daily, prepared according to Ayurvedic standards. **Sample Meals:** Dal with basmati rice and cilantro sauce, organic lemon broccoli or dilled green beans (lunch); jade soup, fresh green peas in coconut milk, and summer squash sauté, or couscous pilaf and asparagus phyllo rolls (dinner).

RATES AND PACKAGES
Lodging per night $85 single, $120 for 2, double occupancy. Royal Beauty From Within program per day $597; Rejuvenation program 3-day $1611, 5-day $2,685, 7-day $3,760. TM training not included in program fee. 50% deposit required. AE, D, MC, V.

DIRECTIONS

✉ *1734 Jasmine Ave., Fairfield, IA 52556,* ☎ *515/472–9580 or 800/248–9050,* 🖷 *515/472–2496.*

From Cedar Rapids: I–380 south, Route 1 south to Airport Road, right on Jasmine Avenue, right turn on Rural Road 8 (1¼ hrs).

MINNESOTA

BIRDWING SPA

Luxury pampering
Nutrition and diet

Birdwing Spa blends European therapy and Minnesota traditions. Once a working farm, this 300-acre country estate has a Tudor-style mansion, outdoor swimming pool, and 12 miles of groomed walking and cross-country ski trails. What really sets this spa apart, though, is the personalized attention lavished on guests by Elizabeth Carlson, a registered nurse, and her husband Richard, who tailor the program for each group (no more than 25 guests attend at a time). There are picnics in the country and visits to historic sites. Staff members mother you—most of the therapists have been here for years—and explain treatments for newcomers.

Oriented to outdoor activity, the spa provides equipment for skiing, canoeing, and biking, in addition to circuit weight training. In two daily "image sessions," guests have a choice of facial, massage, or manicure. Aerobic exercise or an hour of yoga completes the daily schedule.

In the chalet-like main building guests relax in a sauna and Jacuzzi, or talk to the chef in the kitchen. Rooms have Ethan Allen furnishings, draperies, shared baths. Five suites have private whirlpool baths; one also has a fireplace and steam bath. Beauty-treatment facilities are housed in an adjacent building.

FACILITIES
Exercise Equipment: Stair climbers, stationary bikes, treadmills, free weights. **Services:** Esalen massage, Swedish massage; back treatment, paraffin therapy, facial. **Swimming:** Outdoor pool. **Classes and Programs:** Cooking classes, nutritional counseling, fitness evaluation, exercise instruction. Guest speakers on stress control, nutrition, cardiac health, and problems of career women. **Recreation:** Bicycling, bird-watching, canoeing, cross-country skiing. Tennis and golf nearby. Special weeks for art and nature studies. Feature films.

ACCOMMODATIONS
4 rooms, 9 suites.

DINING
3 weight-loss meals daily included in program rates. **Sample Meals:** Fruit kebabs, chicken tacos with salsa, turkey pizza (lunch); chicken asparagus rolls (dinner).

RATES AND PACKAGES
1-day overnight package $275–$325; 2-day retreat $395–$450 standard rooms in main house, $475–$550 per person in suite; 5-day program standard rooms $1,175 single, $1,050 double, $1,350 single in suite, $1,250 per person double; 7-day program standard rooms $1,475 single, $1,259 double, suite accommodation $1,775 single, $1,500 per person double. $150 in advance for weekends, $300 for other programs. MC, V.

DIRECTIONS
✉ *21398 575th Ave., Litchfield, MN 55355,* ☎ *320/693–6064 or 800/ 644–5541 (central reservations).*

From Minneapolis: I–394, Highway 12 west to Litchfield, Routes 1 and 23 (90 mins).

THE MARSH—A CENTER FOR BALANCE AND FITNESS

Holistic health
Medical wellness

In her battle against crippling lupus, Ruth Stricker discovered the philosophy that now governs her wellness center: achieving the balance of mind and body to promote health. For Marsh guests, this means a holistic health center with hydrotherapy treatments, a meditation tower, treadmills, and tai chi classes all under one roof. Set at the edge of a marshland near Minneapolis, Stricker's center serves as both a fitness club for community members and a retreat for international visitors. A KidFitness center serves the community as well as visitors, inspiring teenagers to incorporate fitness regimens with an active lifestyle.

The most comprehensive wellness center in the Midwest, the 27,000-square-foot structure includes a climbing wall, a flotation tank, and a silo-shape meditation tower equipped with a computer-controlled "mind gym," with sounds that help guests to meditate. During the day you can sign up for tai chi, yoga, kickboxing, stretching, somatics (movements to help manage chronic back pain), centering (exercises for alignment and stretching), flo-motion in the pool, and back therapy with physio-gymnastic balls, among other workouts. Alternatively, you can swim laps in the 75-foot pool, or take a walk along the wetland. A full-service spa provides massage, skin care, and hydrotherapy treatments.

Educational programs, classes, and special services can be part of a treatment program. Arrangements can be made for a personalized fitness assessment including nutritional consultation and physical therapy. Or you can simply join the scheduled activities at the center, reserving time for spa services and meals.

The Marsh is fronted by an Asian-style portico leading into a tranquil wooden expanse. Such Eastern influences permeate the entire center, which was doubled to 67,000 square feet in 1993. The expansion also added the full-service spa and overnight accommodations for 12 guests in a private wing. Every inch of the Marsh is accessible to wheelchairs, and many programs cater to senior citizens and people living with illness or pain.

FACILITIES
Exercise Equipment: Cross-country ski machines, rowing machines, stair climbers, stationary bikes, treadmills, weight-training circuit. **Services**: Alexander technique, somatics, Swedish massage, Feldenkrais; herbal wrap. **Swimming**: Indoor pool. **Classes and Programs**: Pilates. **Recreation**: Golf, hiking, racquetball, rock climbing, squash. **Children's Programs**: Child care and developmental activities (ages 6 wks–6 yrs).

ACCOMMODATIONS
6 rooms.

DINING
Continental breakfast included with room; lunch and dinner à la carte. **Sample Meals**: Mango salad with home-made bread, chicken breast with wild mushrooms (lunch); poached salmon with cucumber-dill sauce, pork medallions with salsa (dinner).

RATES AND PACKAGES
$90–$100 single, $100–$120 for 2 persons double occupancy, per night. AE, MC, V.

DIRECTIONS
✉ *15000 Minnetonka Blvd., Minnetonka, MN 55345,* ☎ *612/935–2202,* FAX *612/935–9685.*

From Minneapolis: Highway 394 west to Carlson Parkway, Highway 494 south to Minnetonka Boulevard, right for ¼ mile (30 mins).

MISSOURI

THE ELMS RESORT

Luxury pampering
Mineral springs

In the 1800s high-living health seekers descended on this sleepy little Missouri town each season to take the mineral waters. The Elms, built to accommodate them in the grand manner, became a tradition that survived two devastating fires; the present limestone and concrete structure was built in 1912 and incorporates the New Leaf Spa.

Ten "environmental rooms" are programmed for jungle rain, wet steam, or dry sauna and equipped with a hot tub for two. The European swim track, which can be mildly claustrophobic, is a one-lane lap pool filled with tap water.

There's a lot of nostalgic charm about the Elms, complete with stories of Harry Truman's visits and all-night parties hosted by Al Capone. Croquet and badminton are played on the lawn, and the tennis court is free to guests. A quaint village of boutiques completes the resort. Popular for conventions and sales meetings, the 23-acre wooded resort is less than an hour from Kansas City.

FACILITIES
Exercise Equipment: Stair climber, stationary bike, weight-training circuit, free weights. Indoor running track. **Services:** Swedish massage, hydrotherapy, facial. **Swimming:** 2 pools (1 indoor). **Classes and Programs:** Nutrition programs, stress-reduction techniques. **Recreation:** Badminton, golf, horseshoes, horseback riding, mountain biking, tennis, volleyball. Resort entertainment

ACCOMMODATIONS
111 rooms, 42 suites.

DINING
American and European cuisine. Some meals included in packages. **Sample Meals:** Baked acorn squash with buckwheat soba noodles and ragout of organic vegetables in artichoke broth (lunch); seared yellowtail snapper on purple sticky rice with cranberry-mint reduction and baby organic vegetables (dinner).

RATES AND PACKAGES
$75–$105 per night double occupancy; suites $145–$345; $148.68 summer weekend package for 2; 2-night Escape package for 2 $239–$379. AE, D, DC, MC, V.

DIRECTIONS
✉ *401 Regent Ave., Excelsior Springs, MO 64024,* ☎ *816/630–5500 or 800/843–3567,* ℻ *816/630–5380.*

From Kansas City: I–35 north to Excelsior Springs, Highway 69 to Route 10 (30 mins).

TAN-TAR-A MARRIOTT RESORT, GOLF CLUB & SPA

Luxury pampering

Outdoor recreation is the principal attraction of Marriott's Tan-Tar-A Resort, surrounded by 420 acres in the Lake of the Ozarks region. Established in 1960 as a 12-cottage lakeside resort, Tan-Tar-A now includes more than 930 guest rooms, nine restaurants, a 27-hole championship golf course surrounded by oak trees and gnarled cedar, and the full-service Windjammer Spa.

The spa, which is connected to the resort's indoor swimming pool and fitness facility overlooking a sandy beach, has a hydrotherapy tub, coed steam room, and whirlpool. Massage and aromatherapy, as well as body scrubs, can be booked à la carte or as part of eight different packages. Programs are individually designed, from after-sports relaxation to pure luxury.

Tan-Tar-A is an ideal family destination, with supervised children's programs in summer, and countless sports options. The lake is great for boating and fishing, waterskiing, and parasailing; there are also tennis and racquetball courts and facilities for shooting sporting clays, horseback riding, miniature golf, and more. Bikes can be rented to explore the woodland trails, and there's a guided fishing excursion on the lake. In the vicinity are Harry Truman's home and library as well as Abraham Lincoln's boyhood home and burial place.

Marriott-style lodging and dining have predictably high standards. In addition to standard rooms, there are spacious suites with balconies, fireplaces, and barbecue grills—plus a limited number of Tan-Tar-A Estate guest homes with individually keyed guest rooms and suites for added privacy. Though there's no dining plan for spa-goers, nine restaurants and lounges serve everything from Ozarks favorites to seafood.

FACILITIES
Exercise Equipment: Rowing machines, stationary bikes, treadmills, weight-training circuit. **Services:** Swedish massage, reflexology; aromatherapy oil wrap, herbal linen wrap, paraffin body wrap, sea-salt glow; aromatherapy hydro-bath; facial. **Swimming:** 3 outdoor pools, 1 indoor pool, private beach on lake. **Classes and Programs:** Aerobics. **Recreation:** Billiards, bowling, golf, hiking, horseback riding, ice-skating, miniature golf, mountain biking, racquetball, sporting clays, tennis; boating, fishing, jet-skiing, parasailing. Resort entertainment. **Children's Programs:** Supervised morning play camp for youngsters, teenage games and indoor activity in summer.

ACCOMMODATIONS
930 rooms.

DINING
Windrose on the Water serves Southwestern/California cuisine and light fare. **Sample Meals:** Fish is cooked to order (broiled, baked, sautéed, blackened).

RATES AND PACKAGES
Double rooms $69–$169, 1-bedroom suites $196–$219, 2-bedroom suites $338. 2-night golf package for 2, $186–$255 including breakfast and unlimited golf. Day Getaway Spa packages (not including accommodations or meals) $65–$223. 1-night deposit required. AE, D, DC, MC, V.

DIRECTIONS
✉ *State Road KK, Osage Beach, MO 65065,* ☎ *573/348–3131, 800/826–8272, or 800/268–8181 in Canada; Windjammer Spa: 573/348–8433.*

From St. Louis: I–70 to Highway 54 to KK (2½ hrs).

OHIO

THE KERR HOUSE

Holistic health
Luxury pampering
Nutrition and diet

The Kerr House is an antiques-filled Victorian mansion that functions as a hideaway for men and women who seek privacy and quiet time devoted mainly to yoga and relaxation. With just five to seven guests in residence at a time, the facility takes on the atmosphere of a private club. Some weeks are reserved for men only, women only, or corporate groups.

Yoga, the specialty of the house, is taught in a carpeted exercise room on the top floor; guests usually practice three hours per day. As taught here, Hatha yoga consists of exercises for stretching and toning every part of your body, deep breathing, and total relaxation. Sessions are held twice a day, followed by discussion of how to adapt what you've learned in a program at home. Laurie Hostetler, the instructor, uses her own book of *asanas,* the exercise positions of Hatha yoga. Other exercise options include low-impact aerobics, walking, and working out in the small exercise room.

Personal counseling makes this spa experience attractive for those who want to learn healthy habits. A good deal of time is spent discussing ways to build self-esteem and deal with everyday stress. Many people choose to give up smoking here, often with success: During the initial chemical withdrawal, breathing exercises to cleanse the lungs and flush impurities from the body are prescribed. Whirlpool, sauna, and massage add a bit of welcome pampering.

Guests at Kerr House share bedrooms and bathrooms; private accommodations are available for a supplemental charge. Copiously draped in linens and velvet, the rooms exude a warm aura of security and old-fashioned living, enhanced by the absence of TVs. The handsome, authentic antiques, furniture, and memorabilia are appropriately high Victorian style, as the house dates from 1878. High-ceiling rooms accented by lace curtains, stained glass windows, and massive wood doors reflect Hostetler's love of antique furniture and manners. Breakfast and your daily schedule are delivered on a tray in your bedroom. In the candlelit dining room, a harpist plays as dinner is served. After dinner, there are often lectures by guest speakers.

An international roster of guests frequents the Kerr House, which has operated for more than 20 years. Usually women fill the guest list, though the coed and men's weeks have become increasingly popular. The schedule is relaxed; no one insists that you take part in anything, but the group spirit will encourage you to try.

If you're up for a little exploring, Grand Rapids is full of Americana. Near the Kerr House are hiking paths along the Maumee River, and the towpath of the historic Miami & Erie Canal. In the area, you can visit studios of crafts artists, as well as a water-powered grist mill. Hydroplane races are held here in September, and barge rides on the canal are a weekly feature of the Kerr House program.

FACILITIES
Exercise Equipment: Cross-country ski machine, treadmill. **Services:** Polarity therapy, reflexology, shiatsu; herbal wrap, mud bath; mineral baths. **Swimming:** Community pool nearby. **Classes and Programs:** Hatha yoga, speakers. **Recreation:** Boating, hiking.

ACCOMMODATIONS
5 rooms.

DINING
3 meals included in rates. Diet of 750–1,000 calories per day, mainly veg-etarian, with fish and chicken. Low in fat and cholesterol; no salt, sugar, refined flour, or additives. **Sample Meals:** Senegalese carrot soup, lettuce salad, pita bread with couscous stuffing (lunch); eggplant Parmesan with tomato sauce, baked chicken breast on wild rice, shrimp and baked potato (dinner).

RATES AND PACKAGES
Weekends $675 single, $575 double. 5-day program (Sun.–Fri.) $2,150 per person double, $2,550 single. Tax and services included. 50% deposit required. AE, D, MC, V.

DIRECTIONS
✉ *17777 Beaver St., Grand Rapids, OH 43551,* ☎ *419/832–1733,* FAX *419/832–4303.*

From Toledo: Ohio Turnpike (I–75) to Route 6, Route 65 to Route 24 (20 mins).

MARIO'S INTERNATIONAL SPA

Luxury pampering

Getting a new look can involve therapy as well as a makeover at Mario's International Spa, where beauty treatments and post-operative procedures attract a sophisticated crowd. Though this country inn-cum-spa a few miles from the Ohio Turnpike might seem rustic to big-city types, Mario's is perhaps the most serious spa in the area. Corporate facilities are first-rate here; it's easy to spot business executives squeezing in massage ap-pointments between meetings.

Beauty treatments at Mario's range from standard to advanced. A video scope is used to magnify images of skin, hair, and nails in order to iden-tify problem areas and track results of ongoing therapy. A new cooper-ative program between the spa and Akron General Hospital provides rehabilitation therapy after surgery or plastic surgery: Patients are instructed on proper nutrition after plastic surgery, and treated with oxygen facials to hasten recovery. Another course of treatments can be coordinated to address arthritis or tennis elbow; these can be undertaken in conjunction with medical doctors.

In addition to the spa building, which was being expanded in 1998, the complex has a conference center, and is headquarters for Mario's Inter-national, a line of beauty salons and spas owned and operated by Mario and Joanne Luizzo. Construction of new facilities and an indoor swim-ming pool are scheduled for completion in 1999. Meanwhile, the spa has installed Vichy showers and a hydrotherapy tub for underwater pressure massage with detoxifying volcanic mud, invigorating pine-needle ex-tract, milk-whey protein, or stimulating seaweed. The seaweed, called *dulse,* is harvested on Grand Manan Island in Canadian waters, where Mario's operates a bed-and-breakfast spa.

Outside the spa, the Victorian-style dining area is the hub for most guests. Couples enjoy formal dinners by candlelight, and spa guests in terry-cloth robes nibble on healthy gourmet pizzas. Elsewhere, the inn looks a bit run-down; if you're looking for modern chic, this is not the place for you. One of the buildings was a stagecoach inn more than 130 years ago, and the old-fashioned air remains.

Still, Mario's is an ideal destination for a luxurious day near Cleveland. (Beware: Many Clevelanders know this; the spa facilities and restaurant can be quite crowded on weekends.) Nearby are the Aurora Premium Outlet Mall, Sea World, and Geauga Lake Amusement Park. In summer, the Cleveland Symphony Orchestra performs at the Blossom Pavilion, also nearby. The surrounding scenery is an added attraction: Set atop a slight, rolling hill, the International Spa greets visitors with a cobblestone courtyard, complete with fountain. A great time to visit is autumn, when the brilliant colors of changing foliage surround the property.

FACILITIES
Services: Massage; body scrub, fango mud treatment; hydrotherapy, Vichy shower; facial. **Classes and Programs:** Makeup consultation; personalized exercise instruction in power walking, aquacise, and other activities; health and diet analysis; pre- and post-plastic surgery treatments. Lectures on health topics. **Recreation:** Bicycling; golf, tennis, horseback riding nearby; downhill and cross-country skiing.

ACCOMMODATIONS
13 rooms, 1 suite.

DINING
3 meals daily with Retreat packages. **Sample Meals:** Shrimp and vegetable kebab, grilled chicken salad (lunch); mesclun salad, choice of specialty pastas, sautéed shrimp, oven-roasted boneless chicken breast or beef tenderloin (dinner).

RATES AND PACKAGES
3-day/3-night Retreat package $1,225 single, $2,099 per couple. Day at the Spa package with treatments, lunch $250 per person. One-third of total payable on booking. AE, D, DC, MC, V.

DIRECTIONS
⊠ *35 E. Garfield Rd., Aurora, OH 44202,* ☎ *330/562–9171 or 888/ 464–7721,* FAX *330/562–2386.*

From Cleveland: I–480 to Route 91, Route 82 and 306; or the Ohio Turnpike (I–80) to Exit 13 (40 mins).

WISCONSIN

THE AMERICAN CLUB

Luxury pampering

Part company town, part sybaritic escape, the American Club is an unusual oasis in a town dominated by the nation's leading manufacturer of plumbing fixtures and bathtubs. When it was built in 1918 as a dormitory for immigrants working at the Kohler factory, the American Club symbolized a new way of life for the town's residents. These days the club is accessible to anyone seeking a luxurious and healthful escape in the heart of the Midwest.

Part of the charm of the American Club lies in being in a place that looks like a Hollywood vision of middle America yet functions with the precision of a posh resort. The original Tudor-style dormitory, reminiscent of a country inn, has been duplicated across a garden courtyard where a Victorian greenhouse serves as an ice-cream parlor. The building's red-brick Tudor-style exterior is capped by a steeply pitched roof of blue Vermont slate, just as it was originally. The resort occupies a 500-acre nature preserve where you can stroll among Scots pines, Japanese yews, and pear trees, all bordered by Wisconsin native flowers, ferns, and grasses. Country gourmet meals are served in a secluded log lodge.

Adjoining the club is an expansive fitness and spa facility known as the Sports Core, where you'll find six indoor tennis courts (available for an hourly fee) and six outdoor courts (free); racquetball courts that are also used for handball and wallyball; a 75-foot indoor lap pool and indoor jogging track, exercise rooms, an aerobics studio, and spa treatment rooms. Wellness programs here are tailored to the individual, for stress reduction as much as for aerobics or strength, and to lose weight. Tennis instruction is provided by the Peter Burwash International staff. All facilities are available to American Club guests free of charge, except for court fees and aerobics classes.

The resort itself is a showplace of traditional comfort. Guest rooms have wood paneling, carved oak doors, sitting areas, and four-poster brass beds with feather comforters. Suites have fireplaces and whirlpools for two set on glass-covered terraces and in mirrored baths. For the ultimate in hedonism, ask for a suite equipped with the Kohler Shower Tower (similar to Swiss shower) or the Habitat, a master bath with an hour's serenity programmed into it: The sounds of a rain forest, soft breezes, a gentle mist, a steam bath, even desert tanning are simulated. Rooms in the Carriage House are reached by crossing the parking lot or using an underground walkway.

The River Wildlife nature preserve is a place apart, one where the outdoors and good food are celebrated. Marksmen practice, hikers explore more than 30 miles of woodland trails, and canoeists and fishermen enjoy the winding Sheboygan River. Horseback rides can be solo or escorted. In winter the trails are groomed for cross-country skiing. Lunch is served daily in a rustic lodge, dinner on weekends in front of the huge fireplace. American Club guests pay a nominal fee for a pass to use the facilities; the trails are open to all.

FACILITIES

Exercise Equipment: Cross-country machine, rowing machines, stair climbers, stationary bikes, weight-training circuit, free weights. **Services:** Massage; body wrap, herbal wrap; hydrotherapy; facial. **Swimming:** Indoor lap pool, lake. **Classes and Programs:** Aerobics, clay marksmanship course, crazy-quail shooting, archery instruction, fitness consultation. **Recreation:** Biking, canoeing, fishing, golf, handball/racquetball courts, hiking; cross-country skiing.

ACCOMMODATIONS
223 rooms, 13 suites.

DINING
Breakfast buffet and Sunday brunch in the Wisconsin Room. Lunch at Lean Bean or the Horse & Plow pub restaurant. Dinner at the Immigrant and The River Wildlife. Meals included in some packages. **Sample Meals:** Salad of sprouts and seasonal greens, hamburgers (lunch); broiled fresh brook trout stuffed with vegetables, veal scallops with pesto and 5-cheese sauce (dinner).

RATES AND PACKAGES
$125–$635 single, $155–$635 for 2 double occupancy. 2-night escape packages for 2 persons, including a bubble massage at the Sports Core and some meals, $345–$580. For golfers, 2 rounds at Blackwolf Run, plus amenities, $830–$1,360 for 2 persons double occupancy. 1-day spa package with services and lunch $315; half-day $160. 1-night deposit required. AE, DC, MC, V.

DIRECTIONS
⊠ *Highland Dr., Kohler, WI 53044,* ☎ *920/457–8000 or 800/344–2838,* ℻ *920/457–0299.*

From Milwaukee: I–43 to Exit 126, Route 23 west to Kohler (about 1 hr).

THE FONTANA SPA AT THE ABBEY

Holistic health
Luxury pampering

The first thing you notice at the Fontana Spa is the friendly feel. Here's a getaway that delivers pure luxury and sophisticated technique without the elitist fuss of some facilities. Convivial chatter can be heard among the terry-robed patrons and the friendly staff between treatments (though the wishes of those who prefer soothing silence are fully respected).

From the glass-walled swimming pool and aerobics studio, you can see Lake Geneva and nearby woods. Though the Abbey resort, which adjoins the spa, has a country-lodge feel, the ambience at the 10-year-old spa is airy and modern. Director Vicky Lilla succeeds in providing treats for all the senses: The aroma of herbs and oils from the imported French Phytomer skin-care products wafts through the salon as skilled technicians soothe and stimulate patrons with more than 33 treatment options, including everything from loofah scrubs, thalassotherapy, and herbal wraps to European hand and foot treatments. In addition to the treatments, there's a full range of multilevel aerobic and aquatic fitness classes, as well as individualized fitness assessments and a gym full of workout equipment. Pitchers of fresh juice and baskets of fruit are laid out each morning for guests, who can later lunch comfortably by the pool in their robes, opting either for room service or the vast, low-fat midday buffet.

Popular with women and men—there's an equal-sized men's spa next door to the women's—Fontana works for all ages and fitness levels by offering programs that are carefully customized for every guest's needs and desires.

Exercise Equipment: Rowing machines, stair climbers, stationary bikes, treadmills, weight-training circuit, free weights. **Services:** Lymphatic drainage, reflexology, Reiki, shiatsu, Swedish massage; body polish, color therapy, fango, herbal wrap, loofah body scrub; hydrotherapy, mineral baths, thalassotherapy, Swiss shower; facial. **Swimming:** 3 pools (2 indoor), lake. **Classes and Programs:** Aerobics, aquaerobics; fitness evaluation, nutrition analysis. **Recreation:** Boating, golf, ice skating, racquetball, tennis, hiking, parasailing all nearby. Movie rentals, resort entertainment. **Children's Programs:** Kids Kapades (ages 5–12).

334 rooms in modern resort.

Spa choices low in calories, saturated fat, and cholesterol. Some packages include meals. **Sample Meals:** Open-faced vegetable melt (lunch); chargrilled swordfish with fruit salsa, spinach-wrapped sea bass with saffron couscous (dinner).

1-day Spa Spree (including overnight Sun.–Thurs.) $262.50–$291.25 single, $222.19–$236.56 per person double; 2-night spa escape package midweek $323.38–$402.94 single, $247.13–$286.91 per person double, weekends $345.48–$458.19 single, $258.18–$314.54 per person double; 5-night package $1,600.16–$1,771.44 single, $1,409.55–$1,495.19 per person double. Day-use spa facility fee $22.50. Spa packages include gratuities and taxes. 50% advance payment. AE, DC, MC, V.

⊠ *Hwy. 67/Fontana Blvd., Fontana, WI 53125,* ☎ *414/275–6811 or 800/772–1000, 414/275–5948.*

From Chicago: I–94, Routes 50 and 67 (1 1/2 hrs).

6 The South

Alabama, Arkansas, Florida, Georgia, Kentucky, North Carolina, South Carolina, Tennessee, Virginia

HISTORICALLY, THE FIRST AMERICAN SPAS were in the South. Searching for the legendary fountain of youth, 16th-century Spanish Conquistadors discovered hot springs in Florida and Arkansas. By the 19th and early 20th centuries, grand resorts such as The Homestead, in Virginia, and Arkansas's Hot Springs, now partly a national park, were attracting visitors eager to take the waters. Today southern spas go beyond hydrotherapy to incorporate spa and beauty treatments from around the world, cutting-edge concepts in nutrition and fitness, and a wide range of recreational opportunities that often take advantage of the region's generally warm climate. As a result, the South's spas are very popular, and new ones open every year.

Your spa experience can be as diverse or concentrated as you like. Enjoy pampering by the beach at such places as The Cloister, in Georgia, or Florida's Fisher Island, or combine a beach vacation with lifestyle enhancement and weight management at the Fit for Life resort, in Pompano Beach, or the Pritikin Longevity Center, in Miami Beach. Among medically managed programs, Duke University Medical Center in Durham, North Carolina, is a leader in nutrition research and offers residential programs that focus on diet, fitness, and lifestyle. Taking a holistic approach, Florida's Hippocrates Health Institute has a curriculum for vegetarians.

Because the South, and especially Florida, is a golf and tennis mecca, it's easy to find resorts offering these sports along with extensive spa services. PGA National Resort & Spa, Saddlebrook Resort, Ponte Vedra Inn & Club, and the Doral Golf Resort and Spa have been joined by spa newcomer Turnberry Isle, near Miami, and, soon, two venerable Florida hotels, The Breakers, in Palm Beach, and the Boca Raton Resort & Club. However, the movement to combine fun and fitness doesn't end with golf and tennis. You can sample vintage wines at the Atlanta area's Chateau Elan, a romantic hideaway with an equestrian center, summer concerts in the vineyards, and a full program of fitness and pampering in addition to golf and tennis. At Walt Disney World's Disney Institute, you can take courses in anything from animation to cooking or visit a theme park in between treatments. In Virginia, history buffs can combine walks in Colonial Williamsburg with workouts and golf at the Kingsmill Resort.

If all this sounds too expensive, relax. (That is the point of most spa vacations, after all.) Choices for budget-conscious vacationers do exist. You can try the Tennessee Fitness Spa, which features mountain lodges and down-home hospitality. Other options include day spa packages that offer service samplers without requiring an overnight stay. To learn about these special values, found at more and more resorts, call the spa reservations desk at the resort you're interested in. In Florida, for instance, you can spend a day at the Don CeSar, in St. Petersburg Beach; the Hyatt Regency Pier Sixty-Six, in Fort Lauderdale; the Pier House, in Key West; or the Saddlebrook Resort, near Tampa. Chances are there's a program where you can heal, rev up, or unwind to your heart's content.

ALABAMA

UCHEE PINES LIFESTYLE CENTER

Medical wellness
Nutrition and diet

Unlike facilities designed for stressed-out, fitness-obsessed yuppies, this homelike, conservative Christian retreat is for people over 50 with lifestyle problems who want to take control of habits affecting their health and well-being. Many have diseases, such as chronic fatigue or diabetes, that have not responded adequately to traditional medicine. Programs to lose weight and to stop smoking or drinking as well as medically directed programs treating most degenerative diseases are also offered.

The Health Conditioning Center expounds traditional Seventh-Day Adventist philosophies on nutrition and mental and spiritual health but is nondenominational and nonsectarian. Led by three physicians, the staff combines medical and natural healing. A nutritional analysis, aided by computers, provides specific dietary recommendations and takes into account your physical condition, nutritional needs, and weight-loss goals. Following a complete physical examination (some of which may be covered by medical insurance), a physician prescribes a personal schedule and continues to monitor your progress throughout the program.

The suggested stay is three weeks. Mornings are for education—perhaps a doctor's lecture on preventive medicine or nutrition or a class on cooking, simple home remedies, or relieving stress. On Monday, Wednesday, and Friday, this is followed by a doctor's visit. A hearty lunch—along with breakfast, one of the two vegetarian meals suggested per day—is served family-style around one or two tables in the dining room. The afternoon is reserved for a recommended walk; treatments, many of which involve hydrotherapy as well as herbal and spiritual treatments; and then rest. For those who cannot go without a third meal, a very light supper is served, followed by a health video and time in the evening to get together and share stories.

The health center is equipped with a heated, full-body whirlpool, steam bath, massage tables, and ultrasound therapy units. Special treatments include fomentation—application of moist heat to the body for relief from congestion or pain—and the use of ice packs to slow down circulation or arrest a physical reaction. Only limited exercise equipment is available, as walking is the exercise of choice.

Small groups—only 14 guests can be housed—make it easy for first-timers to get comfortable. The center's living accommodations, secluded in a 200-acre woodland preserve near the Chattahoochee River, consist of twin-bedded rooms with modern furniture, flowered bedspreads, ceiling fans, and reading lamps. Shared bathrooms don't detract too much from the feeling of privacy and comfort. The resulting low-stress atmosphere brings returnees back to reenergize.

FACILITIES
Exercise Equipment: Stationary bike. **Services:** Massage; fomentation hot-pack treatment; hydrotherapy. **Classes and Programs:** Classes, nutritional evaluation and consultation, informal discussions of health-related topics, lectures. **Recreation:** Biking, gardening, hiking.

ACCOMMODATIONS
7 rooms, all with shared bath.

DINING

2–3 meals daily. **Sample Meals:** Hot and cold cereal, fruit, blueberry millet pudding (breakfast); vegetarian lasagna, whole-wheat pizza (lunch); fruit, bread, popcorn (dinner).

RATES AND PACKAGES

$1,200 each for first and second weeks, $900 for third week, all-inclusive; $550 for first and second weeks, $295 for third week for companion with medical (includes physical and lab work); $350 per week for companion nonmedical. $500 deposit required; 5% discount for full payment. D, MC, V.

DIRECTIONS

✉ *30 Uchee Pines Rd., Seale, AL 36875,* ☎ *334/855–4764,* FAX *334/855–9014.*

From Atlanta: I–185 via Columbus, Route 80 to Route 431, south to Routes 24 and 39 (about 5 hrs).

ARKANSAS

HOT SPRINGS NATIONAL PARK

Mineral springs

Still drawing visitors to its public waters, the aptly named Hot Springs has a long and interesting history. Native Americans once dubbed the area the Valley of the Vapors because of the awe-inspiring clouds of steam that emanated from the 47 springs. Hernando de Soto and his fellow explorers relaxed here in 1541, and in 1832 the city partnered with the federal government to set aside four sections of the springs as a health reservation, the first in U.S. history. Throughout the 1800s and early 1900s, Hot Springs's therapeutic reputation grew, and its thermal waters lured fashionable visitors to take the cure, to be pampered, and to gamble at nearby casinos. In 1921, Hot Springs National Park was officially designated—the first and only national park devoted to taking the waters. Today private operators of a half-dozen bathhouses and hotels tap hot mineral water from National Park Service reservoirs and provide it—cooled to a balmy 100°F—for bathing. Though no medical claims are now made about the springs' miraculous powers, people still come to soak and relieve stress at the numerous public baths they also come to see the town itself, Bill Clinton's boyhood home.

One of the best ways to learn about Hot Springs is to join an introductory tour at the park's visitor center. Providing bits of local lore, park rangers concentrate on the spring water's 4,000-year journey from deep within the earth (where it's 143°F) to the surface. A stroll along Bathhouse Row gives a taste of spa life in the golden age. Lined with ancient magnolias, the promenade has several Art Deco buildings open to the public. The most splendid is The Fordyce, built in 1915 by a colonel of the same name, who credited the spring waters with saving his life. The interior has stained-glass windows and a skylight with scenes of water nymphs, appropriate for the Museum of Bathing, which was created as part of the building's restoration in 1989.

If you're not staying at a hotel with a bathhouse, the best place to sample the waters is at the Buckstaff, a stately three-story brick-and-marble edifice. Here bathers step into a private porcelain tub filled with mineral water heated to 103°F. Plan on about 1½ hours for a soak in the thermal waters, the whirlpools, and a massage. The entire treatment at Buckstaff, including hot packs on sore muscles and a multineedled shower, costs about $35. Reservations are essential (☎ 501/623–2308). Little has changed here since the building opened in 1912, with separate facilities for men and women and sundecks for bathing *au naturel*. Declared a National Historic Landmark in 1987, the Buckstaff bath is a revitalizing tradition.

Vacationing in today's Hot Springs is a far different experience from the hedonism of earlier times. Mansions built by wealthy families now offer bed-and-breakfast accommodations. In addition, many hotels have spring-fed bathing facilities, including the grand, 484-room Arlington Hotel (⊠ 239 Central Ave., ☎ 800/643–1502). Along historic Central Avenue, 18 art galleries host a Gallery Walk the first Thursday and Friday of each month. In the center of town, the recently opened Museum of Hot Springs documents resort life in the 1800s. Also available are self-guided walking tours of landmarks familiar to President Clinton when he was growing up, and the nearby Ouachita National Forest offers a wealth of recreational opportunities. Local eating options range from fine dining to deli food to down-home fare.

Hot Springs is also a center for the advanced therapy of degenerative diseases and rehabilitation treatments for postcardiac or surgery patients. For rehabilitation therapy, contact Hot Springs Health Spa (☎ 501/321–9664) or the Rehabilitation Center of Hot Springs (☎ 501/624–4411).

FACILITIES

Services: Massage; hot-pack treatment. **Swimming:** Pools at area hotels and at Hot Springs Health Spa (*see above*); 3 lakes in park. **Classes and Programs:** Slide show in park visitor center. **Recreation:** Biking, boating, fishing, hiking, horseback riding, cross-country skiing in Ouachita Mountains; golf and tennis at hotels.

ACCOMMODATIONS

Hotels, motels, cabins, bed-and-breakfast inns in town of Hot Springs; camping facilities in the park. Referrals available from Hot Springs Convention & Visitors Bureau (☎ 800/772–2489).

DINING

Restaurants in town.

DIRECTIONS

✉ *Hot Springs National Park, Box 1860, Hot Springs, AR 71902,* ☎ *501/624–3383 ext.640,* FAX *501/624–1536.*

From Little Rock: I–30 to Hot Springs exit, Route 70 West (1 hr).

FLORIDA

DISNEY INSTITUTE

Luxury pampering
Sports conditioning

A workout with Mickey and Minnie isn't on the agenda here, but virtually everything else can be found at this educational institute and spa that appeals to youngsters as well as adults. Learning, relaxation, and fitness can be combined with a visit to Disney theme parks and other Orlando attractions to create one of the most diverse spa vacations around. Any way you look at it, Disney's imagineers want to get you into the act.

Learning experiences are the foundation of the institute. Programmers on campus can help you sign up for workshops on sports, fitness, and the arts; the weekly schedule has more than 40 full- or half-day offerings. Course selections include Animation and Story Arts, Culinary Arts, Gardens and the Great Outdoors, Television and Film, and Behind the Scenes. Special events such as a photography workshop add to the curriculum. Family members can pursue hobbies, explore nature trails, or make a movie. Camp Disney involves kids between the ages of 7 and 15 in creative workshops, from drawing animated cartoons to producing a TV show in real studios, as well as golf and tennis clinics.

Sports are a major focus here. A golf pro provides one-on-one instruction using the tension-free system developed by Brian Roddy at the 18-hole golf course, where two-hour practice sessions can be scheduled most mornings. In the spacious fitness center, personal trainers introduce you to the latest Cybex interactive exercise equipment. Tennis courts and swimming pools are also on campus, and other sports opportunities, such as Harlem Globetrotter fantasy camps and Atlanta Braves spring training at the new Wide World of Sports complex, are elsewhere on Walt Disney World property.

And then there's the institute's spa—an oasis of calm in the midst of all these activities. Its 10 treatment rooms are used for massage, hydrotherapy, and skin care. Both men's and women's locker rooms have a large whirlpool, sauna, and steam room. Workout clothing and grooming supplies are provided, and you can order lunch from room service in the lounge. Making an appointment for treatments gets you free access to the spa facilities; charges are credited to your account.

You can choose to stay in one of the institute's accommodations—perhaps a small bungalow, a villa next to the golf course, a wooded villa on stilts, a luxurious condo, or a one- or two-bedroom town house— or participate in a program sampler with a $69 day pass. Institute accommodations sleep between four and eight people and vary not only in number and type of rooms but in luxury of furnishings and services. Though most units are not as plush as the resort hotels, they are more personal and homey than hotel rooms. And they're close to all the activities on campus as well as at the Downtown Disney dining and entertainment complex. A typical unit might have a bedroom, bathroom, sitting room with sofa bed, dining room with patio; some also have full kitchens. A laundry facility is in each cluster. The institute campus also contains a movie theater, concert hall, and Seasons restaurant, which features an à la carte menu of Floridian cuisine, freshly squeezed vegetable juice, and a special spa menu with calorie and cholesterol counts. Portions are large and prepared to order.

FACILITIES

Exercise Equipment: Rowing machines, stationary bikes, treadmills, weight-training units. **Services:** Massage; body scrub, herbal wrap; hydrotherapy; facial. **Swimming:** 6 pools (1 indoor). **Classes and Programs:** Golf and tennis clinics, cooking and gardening classes, animation art classes, naturalist-led canoe trips. **Recreation:** Basketball, climbing, golf, tennis. Movies, concerts.

ACCOMMODATIONS

572 units.

DINING

All meals à la carte. **Sample Meals:** Papaya, melon, and grapefruit salad, grilled lamb with couscous, stir fry of soba noodles with steamed vegetables (lunch). Ahi tuna layered with tomatoes, fava beans, asparagus, and black olives, stir-fried shrimp with artichoke hearts and barley, grilled sirloin with fingerling potatoes, chicken breast wrapped with pineapple and yucca (dinner).

RATES AND PACKAGES

3-night package in bungalow $529–$597 per person, double occupancy; townhouse $718–$777. Additional plans for dining, spa services, golf, tennis, recreation, admission to theme parks. AE, MC, V.

DIRECTIONS

✉ *1960 Magnolia Way, Lake Buena Vista, FL 32830,* ☎ *407/827–6971 or 800/282–9282,* FAX *407/939–4898.*

From Orlando: Beeline Expressway (Toll Road 528) to I–4 west, Exit 26 on Bonnet Creek Parkway to Community Drive (45 mins).

DON CESAR BEACH RESORT

Luxury pampering

This pink palace with an elegant European aura is a self-contained world of luxury. Laden with crystal chandeliers, marble floors, and elaborate architecture, the 10-story hotel opened in 1928, survived the Stock Market Crash, served as an Air Force convalescent center in the 1940s, and came through a succession of facelifts to emerge as a savvy resort for the '90s. A mix of Continental visitors and American families attests to its enduring popularity.

Secluded on the Gulf of Mexico, the spa complements a traditional beach holiday. The compact but complete spa gives you access to the beachfront swimming pools and whirlpool, garden terrace bar, and an informal restaurant. Rather than a fixed program, the spa offers services à la carte and is open to nonguests as well as hotel residents. Exercise equipment is top of the line and can be used for a small daily fee; if you sign up for a massage or facial, the fee is waived.

Selecting from a menu of eight sea-oriented body treatments, you can set a course to rejuvenate, relax, or restore. Scrubs and polishes are recommended to prepare your skin for the full benefits of body wraps and massage therapies. Seaweed body wraps, using Floraspa products imported from France, are said to revitalize. Most treatments are priced at $60–$70. Adjoining the spa is a beauty salon with services for men and women.

Apart from the spa, there is much to do and enjoy. Activities at the Don include water aerobics, shell-collecting walks on the beach, yoga aerobics; and ballroom dance instruction in a private studio. A supervised program for kids includes weekend movie parties with pizza; during the baseball season, a hotel van provides transportation to Tropicana Field. (A pregame meal package is available.) Biking, deep-sea fishing, and sailing excursions can also be arranged.

What's more, the Don is surrounded by areas of outstanding natural beauty. Barrier islands stretch southward, providing paved paths for in-line skating and jogging as well as ecology adventures. Fort DeSoto State Park—consisting of 900 unspoiled acres, 7 miles of beaches, and picnic and camping areas—is about 20 minutes away by car. The park is home to a historic fort built during the Spanish-American War as well as a vast variety of birds and aquatic life, including pelicans, herons, ibis, mullet, and conch. Manatees occasionally visit these warm waters during the winter months. Guided hiking and kayaking trips can be arranged, or you can pick up a self-guided hiking brochure at the park visitor center.

Guest rooms at the Don CeSar range from small standard rooms with single beds to spacious, high-ceiling suites with a small balcony facing the sea. Healthy selections appear on the menus of four restaurants. You can have dinner in the fashionable Maritana Grille, which features Floribbean fare, or the more casual Sea Porch Café, where spa cuisine is served at boardwalk tables. An old-fashioned ice cream parlor provides one final indulgence.

FACILITIES
Exercise Equipment: Stair climbers, stationary bikes, treadmills, weight-training circuit, free weights. **Services**: Aromatherapy, reflexology; sea scrub, spirulina body masque. **Swimming**: 2 pools, ocean beach. **Classes and Programs:** Personal training, fitness assessment. **Recreation**: Beachfront water sports, tennis; golf, deep-sea fishing, sailing nearby. **Children's Programs:** Day care (ages 5–12).

ACCOMMODATIONS
225 rooms, 50 suites, 2 penthouses.

DINING
Breakfast or lunch included in Pink Palace package. **Sample Meals:** Plain or fruit yogurt, homemade grain and nut cereal (breakfast); Caesar with roasted chicken salad, green-bean salad with roasted shallots and balsamic vinaigrette (lunch); fire-roasted gulf fish with warm potato-and-leek salad, pan-seared tuna with warm fennel, baby spinach, and gingered carrot broth.

RATES AND PACKAGES
Hotel rooms $184–$369 per person double occupancy. Pink Palace Refresher 3-night package for 2 persons $789–$1,214. Day spa package (no lodging) $100–$275. AE, D, MC, V.

DIRECTIONS
✉ *3400 Gulf Blvd., St. Petersburg Beach, FL 33706,* ☎ *813/360–1881, 800/282–1116, or 800/637–7200,* FAX *813/367–6952.*

From Tampa: I–275 (25 mins).

THE DORAL GOLF RESORT AND SPA

Luxury pampering
Sports conditioning

Create your own sport/spa package at this self-contained resort known for golf, tennis, and the largest spa facility in the South. In addition to stepping up their standards in spa treatments during the 1980s, the resort broadened its emphasis on wellness. Psychology lectures are out; cooking classes in the demonstration kitchen are in. And, with renovated spa villa suites, the resort and spa are as beautiful and luxurious as ever.

Personal services begin in the spa's locker room—lounges, where fresh work-out clothing is issued and where you'll find whirlpools, saunas (dry and steam), and a sundeck. A therapist then escorts you by elevator to private rooms around the lofty central dining atrium. In total there are 26 private massage rooms offering a selection of treatments, a coed beauty salon and skin-care treatment rooms, and a running track, as well as aerobics studios, a cardiovascular and weight-training room, and indoor and outdoor lap pools. The Doral's spa blends European and American health concepts but keeps daily regimens flexible. Classes tend to be jazzy, low-impact workouts that appeal to men as well as women. All spa facilities can be enjoyed by paying a daily fee, which is waived when you book a treatment. Day packages also are available, with or without accommodations.

Accommodations are fit for royalty. You can either enjoy the country club atmosphere of the main lodge or any of the other golf lodges, or use the spa villa as a luxurious hideaway. The villa looks Tuscan outside, Floridian inside. Rising above formal gardens, statuary, and cascading fountains, the orange tile—roofed building overlooks the challenging Blue Monster golf course, yet is a world apart. The mood inside is modern, without a trace of sweaty workouts to disturb the calm. The 48 extra-large suites are among the best accommodations at any American spas: Each has twin baths, Jacuzzi, wet bar and refrigerator, a VCR with access to a video library, and two dressing areas. Suites with private terrace or balcony overlook the golf course or garden. Guests in the golf lodges can work out with Cybex equipment in a new fitness center.

Of course, golf and tennis are major attractions at Doral, and a number of tournaments and group events are scheduled. Golfers can tee off on five championship courses, including the legendary Blue Monster, a favorite stop on the PGA tour, and the Gold Course, which has water hazards on every hole. Tennis instruction at the 15-court complex is furnished by professionals from Peter Burwash International. If you want a swim, you can opt for a pool with cascades, an Olympic-length lap pool, or an indoor pool for aquatics. With all these activities, you might decide to stay put at the 650-acre resort, 7 miles west of Miami International Airport. If not, you can explore South Beach and all that Miami has to offer.

FACILITIES

Exercise Equipment: Elliptical trainers, ladder steppers, rowing machines, stair climbers, stationary bikes, treadmills, weight-training circuit, free weights. **Services:** Aromatherapy massage, back-and-shoulder massage, deep-tissue massage, reflexology, Reiki, Swedish massage, Trager therapy; aloe-vera wrap, aromatherapy scrub and wrap, herbal wrap, fango, Turkish body scrub; hydrotherapy and sport fango, hydro-aromatherapy, marine therapy and massage; deep-pore cleansing facial, energy facial, European facial, revitalizing facial. **Swimming:** 3 pools. **Classes and Programs:** Aquaerobics, body awareness, boxaerobics, interval training, power walk, Spinning, step aerobics, stretch classes, tai chi, tap dancing, yoga; customized walking program, personal training, one-on-one golf workout; diet analysis, personal menu planning, spa-cooking instruction. Lecture and discussion group daily. **Recreation:** Basketball, biking, golf, hiking, horseback riding, softball, tennis, volleyball. **Children's Programs:** Camp Doral (ages 5–14).

ACCOMMODATIONS
646 rooms, 48 suites.

DINING
3 daily meals included in spa packages, plus snacks and fruit smoothies. Seafood served nightly. **Sample Meals:** Carrot-ginger soup, individual pizza

topped with turkey sausage (lunch); lobster tail Fra Diablo over capellini, grilled honey-basil chicken with rice and fresh vegetables, polenta lasagna with smoked chicken and spinach (dinner).

RATES AND PACKAGES

Spa suites $495–$1,375. 2-night Grande Getaway package $745–$1,170 single, $945–$1,820 double; 4-night Spa Renewal package $2,160–$3,050 single, $1,670–$2,410 per person double; 7-night Spa Renewal package $3,485–$5,885 single, $2,595–$3.985 per person double; 7-night weight management package $3,745–$5,830 single, $2,965–$4,150 per person double. $500 deposit required. Refundable up to 7 days prior to arrival date. AE, DC, MC, V.

DIRECTIONS

✉ *8755 N.W. 36th St., Miami, FL 33178,* ☎ *305/593–6030 or 800/331–7768,* FAX *305/591–8266.*

From Miami International Airport: State Road 836 West (Dolphin Expressway), Exit NW 87th Avenue North, left at stop sign to intersection of NW 36th Street.

EDEN ROC RESORT & SPA

Luxury pampering
Sports conditioning

Legendary as one of Miami Beach's grand 1950s hotels, the stylish art deco–style Eden Roc has a prime beachfront location within minutes of South Beach's discos, shops, and restaurants; the lively Lincoln Road Mall; and the new Convention Center. Though not far from the center of action, it rises above the crowds and noise. The hotel spared no expense in creating the Spa of Eden, whose best feature might be its air-conditioned cardiovascular and strength-training rooms complete with ocean view. As a result, the spa and sports complex are now the best value on the beach for fitness buffs.

The spa contains many of the facilities you'd expect. With a weight room full of Cybex equipment; a cardiovascular theater with computerized treadmills, cycles, and stair climbers plugged into an audiovisual system; and a variety of aerobics classes, the spa can keep you busy and out of the sun. More surprising is the indoor court complex on the beach terrace, featuring a regulation basketball court, squash and racquetball courts, and South Florida's only rock-climbing wall—all in air-conditioned comfort and available at no charge for spa plan guests.

Most rooms in the 14-story oceanfront hotel have a balcony, sitting area, and deco-style furniture. Corner suite balconies have drop-dead views of the ocean and yachts on the Intracoastal Waterway. Steps away, the boardwalk makes morning jogs and walks a good way to work off pounds. A slightly longer run gets you to South Beach to take in the latest in trendoid wear and food. Here buffed and waxed muscle boys in skintight shorts vie with fashion models doing publicity shoots. Cell phones are de rigueur among the pink and blue Deco hotels, and in-line skating is a major sport.

Though you might be tempted to sample from the many chic South Beach cafés and restaurants, spa packages include meals at two Eden Roc restaurants: Miami Dolphins coach Jimmy Johnson's sports bar and grill, overlooking the beach, and the Mediterranean-theme Fresco Cafe, which offers a choice of spa cuisine or traditional Florida favorites, with plenty of temptations on the menu. It's like stepping back to the 1950s with healthy options.

FACILITIES
Exercise Equipment: Stair climbers, stationary bikes, treadmills, weight-training circuit, free weights. **Services**: Aromatherapy, deep-tissue massage, reflexology, shiatsu, sports massage, Swedish massage; algae body masque, body polish, herbal or Dead Sea mud wrap. **Swimming**: Pool, ocean beach. **Classes and Programs**: Aerobics classes. **Recreation**: Basketball, kayaking, parasailing, racquetball, rock climbing, sailing, scuba, squash, yachting.

ACCOMMODATIONS
301 rooms, 49 suites.

DINING
3 meals daily with Week of Luxury package; breakfast and dinner daily with Escape to Eden. **Sample Meals**: Grilled chicken breast on spinach, vegetable lasagna, or couscous-stuffed grape leaves (lunch); stir-fried mahi mahi, steamed halibut in lettuce leaf, or pizza with vegetables (dinner).

RATES AND PACKAGES
3-night Escape to Eden package $1,090–$1,441 single, $1,809–$2,160 double. 7-night Week of Luxury $2,458–$3,370 single, $4,050–$5,055 double. Day spa package $205; half-day $120. AE, D, MC, V.

DIRECTIONS
⊠ *4525 Collins Ave., Miami Beach, FL 33140,* ☎ *305/531–0000 or 800/327–8337, spa reservations 305/674–5585,* fAX *305/531–6955.*

From Miami International Airport: MacArthur Causeway to Highway A1A, Collins Avenue (25 mins)

FISHER ISLAND CLUB SPA INTERNAZIONALE

Luxury pampering

Privacy is the primary focus on this secluded 216-acre island off the southern tip of Miami. Once a private hideaway for family and friends of William K. Vanderbilt, it's now a condominium community with golf course, beach club, marina, and a small spa. Boarding the island's exclusive ferry, you go through a security check before reaching registration. Then an escort welcomes you, and you hop aboard your own golf cart, which you use to get around during your stay.

The waterfront spa has an indoor swimming pool with retractable roof, 15 beautifully appointed treatment rooms, a VIP Suite for private services, a salon, two aerobics studios, and a cardio- and weight-training room. In a secluded garden, you discover a Roman whirlpool where a waterfall cascades refreshingly cool water as you await a massage in the open-air cabanas. Separate men's and women's saunas, steam rooms, and lounges stocked with fruit and juices add to the clublike atmosphere. Among your choices of treatments are Kerstin Florian's thermal mineral kur from Hungary, aromatherapy hydromassage in a French tub fitted with 47 underwater jets, and the Parisian hydradermie facial, which cleanses and moisturizes your face to combat Miami's subtropical climate.

Since there's a maximum of 20 guests padding about, the spa staff is available to lavish attention on you. For beginners, this eliminates problems during yoga and aerobics. The daily schedule lists six classes, from Reebok Bodywalk to step, waterworks, Spinning, boxing aerobics, and body toning. Cross-training is organized with a full line of Keiser equipment. Don't expect to interact with a group; programs are tailored to your time and needs. Club members who work out at the spa are a mix of hip

Europeans and island or Miami residents, and there isn't much socializing with outsiders, who are charged a daily membership fee, or a facility fee as part of spa packages.

Accommodations range from casitas to oceanfront condominium apartments to cottages, including three original Vanderbilt cottages fit for a millionaire's holiday. The Vanderbilt cottages and seaside contemporary suites have a kitchen, living room with period furniture, and up to three bedrooms, each with bathroom. Casitas have polished marble floors and large bathrooms with whirlpool tubs. Some suites, terraced for ocean views, have an outdoor whirlpool; cottages have a private patio and whirlpool.

The Vanderbilt mansion, now a restaurant, is not on the spa plan, but you can enjoy its big swimming pool set in a lush garden. Relaxation, rather than diet and exercise, distinguishes this island escape.

FACILITIES
Exercise Equipment: Rowing machines, stair climbers, stationary bikes, treadmills, weight-training circuit, free weights. **Services:** Aromatherapy, reflexology, shiatsu; algae body masque, body polish, herbal wrap; hydrotub; facial. **Swimming:** 16 pools (on island; 1 indoor); ocean beach. **Classes and Programs:** Aerobics, Spinning, yoga. **Recreation:** Biking, golf, tennis; deep-sea fishing, yachting.

ACCOMMODATIONS
60 suites.

DINING
3 meals daily with spa packages. **Sample Meals:** Grilled mahi mahi pita sandwich, or grilled shrimp with red-pepper relish (lunch); grilled fillet of salmon on spinach with sorrel sauce, whole-wheat pasta with fresh vegetables (dinner).

RATES AND PACKAGES
Guest rooms, villas, cottages, and suites $330–$1,400 daily for 2 persons. $25 daily club membership fee per couple. 3-night/4-day spa package $1,945–$2,365 single, $1,420–$1,655 per person double occupancy; 7-night/8-day spa package $4,175–$4,695 single, $3,020–$3,455 double. Perfect Spa Day package for island residents $195. AE, DC, MC, V.

DIRECTIONS
✉ *1 Fisher Island Dr., Fisher Island, FL 33109,* ☎ *305/535–6020 or 800/537–3708,* ℻ *305/535–6032.*

From Miami: MacArthur Causeway to Fisher Island ferry terminal.

FIT FOR LIFE HEALTH RESORT & SPA

Holistic health
Nutrition and diet

This three-story home-style, oceanfront motel turned spa is a simple, moderately priced place to relax, de-stress, and shed pounds. Guided by the resident health director, you learn to lose weight and cope with emotional problems through exercise, meditation, and nutritious meals. Friendly staff members encourage lifestyle changes, and participants, mostly women who range from teenagers to octogenarians, mingle like family. Designed as an eight-day shape-up (minimum stay is four days), the program includes all the basics and meals. Optional treatments can be scheduled at an additional cost.

The principles of the food program are based on *Fit for Life,* a book co-authored by Harvey Diamond and sold in the tiny boutique. The program was begun in 1995 at the former Royal Atlantic Spa. Essentially, it's a diet to detoxify your body and make you feel better from the inside out. The director, chef, and staff (many from Unicorn, a wonderful former restaurant in Aventura) are dedicated to preparing a variety of delicious and beautifully presented vegan dishes. Fresh, top-quality produce—better than what you'd find at many more expensive luxury resort spas—is served in abundance. There are self-service buffets for breakfast (unlimited fresh fruits) and lunch (vegetarian soup and a salad bar of raw vegetables, including a variety of sprouts and unusual greens). Dinner, which consists of a vegetarian entrée, is more formal, with servers and candlelit tables. No breads or baked goods are served. A juicing program, supervised by the health director and nurse and based on an evaluation of your physical and nutritional needs, is available as well. After three days of a liquid diet of fresh fruit or simply water, you should feel cleaner and more energetic.

Structured for group camaraderie, the daily schedule allows you to be as active or relaxed as you choose, though activities are scheduled from 7 AM to 7:30 PM. Each day begins with a walk along the beach right outside your door, or you can opt to walk on the sidewalks or go by van to a hard-surface route off-property. This is followed by stretching, step, and other low-impact classes. To improve body awareness and flexibility, you can join a session of yoga or tai chi held under the palm trees or aqua conditioning in the swimming pool. The spa treatment rooms, sauna, and beauty salon are in the U-shape hotel complex surrounding a private garden with an open-air pool and Jacuzzi. Indoor fitness activities take place in an exercise room off the poolside dining room or in a weight room. Tours to a health food store might also be included. Cooking classes in gourmet vegetarian cuisine are held most evenings, with lessons in how fruits, vegetables, and starches can eliminate cravings and reduce the fats and proteins that contribute to weight problems, heart disease, diabetes, cancer, and aging. Daily lectures cover all aspects of health and nutrition, with practical guidelines to take home.

Directly on the beach, this informal resort has simple but comfortable accommodations. Most are efficiencies with motel-style furnishings. All have some ocean view; garden-level rooms have private patios that open to the pool and beach, and oceanfront rooms have balconies. The new owners have planned renovations—and not merely to the facility itself. Services and programs are expected to expand as well.

FACILITIES
Exercise Equipment: Stationary bikes, treadmills, weight-training circuit, free weights. **Services:** Acupuncture, acupressure, aromatherapy massage, reflexology; anti-cellulite wrap, herbal, mud, or seaweed wrap; facial. **Swimming:** Pool, ocean beach. **Classes and Programs:** Behavioral change therapy, cooking classes, exercise and fitness classes, health and nutrition lectures, informal discussion groups. **Recreation:** Biking, tennis; fishing, snorkeling. Golf nearby. Scheduled trips to malls, Sunday flea-market outing.

ACCOMMODATIONS
70 rooms.

DINING
3 low-cal vegetarian meals daily. Juice and water diets optional. **Sample Meals:** Buffet of salads, soup, and fruit (lunch); grilled vegetable terrine, New Orleans gumbo wrap (dinner).

RATES AND PACKAGES
1-week program with meals and accommodations $1,178–$1,356 single, $943–$1,110 per person double. $100 deposit required. AE, MC, V.

✉ *1460 S. Ocean Blvd., Pompano Beach, FL 33062,* ☎ *954/941–6688 or 800/583–3500,* FAX *954/943–1219.*

From Fort Lauderdale International Airport: I–95 to Commercial Boulevard, east to Highway A1A (20 mins).

HIPPOCRATES HEALTH INSTITUTE

Holistic health
Nutrition and diet

Serious lifestyle change is the goal at this secluded retreat near Palm Beach. A holistic health center and learning institute, Hippocrates evolved from a Boston-based experiment in detoxification, cleansing, and revitalization of the body, mind, and spirit. Under the direction of Brian and Anna Maria Clement, the program now has a permanent home in woodlands close to Atlantic beaches and the West Palm Beach international airport.

The Hippocrates lifestyle involves learning to be self-sufficient in matters of food and medicine. A vegetarian diet, medical and psychological consultation, and chiropractic therapy are central to the highly structured but individually designed, three-week life-change program. Included are live-cell analysis, electromagnetic treatments, nutritional education, regular exercise, massage, and reflexology, as well as detoxification, brought about by consuming only "live foods"—unprocessed, organically grown fruits and vegetables, all eaten raw. Deep-relaxation techniques are taught to aid in prevention of illness and to enhance healing, creativity, and inspiration. A psychologist and M.D. work closely with the medical director to monitor your progress and advise you on personal problems. Focus programs provide intensive training in fitness and other health-related issues. For recreation there are excursions to the beach, shopping areas, museums, and parks. A typical day begins at 8 AM with light exercise before breakfast, then a blood-pressure check and discussion session on health and diet. One- and two-week programs are available, as are refresher courses.

The detox diet is a drastic change for the first few days. The institute's chefs prepare meals composed of 60% green vegetables and the sprouts of such plants as sunflower, buckwheat, alfalfa, clover, cress, dill, garlic, peas, radish, and spinach. Vegetables such as carrots, squash, radishes, and corn make up 15% of the diet, all eaten raw to preserve nutrients. Fruits, nuts, seeds, sea plants and algae, legumes, herbs, and juices are also served, and cooked foods are limited to no more than 20% of the diet. Presented at a sumptuous buffet, the organic, enzyme-rich food is a sequence of new tastes and textures, a natural part of lifestyle change advocated by the institute. Guests learn and practice how to sprout and grow greens and wheatgrass for home use.

Accommodations on the 30-acre wooded estate range from three luxury suites in a spacious Spanish-style hacienda to garden apartments to two cottages; some have a marble-walled bath and whirlpools. Off-premises accommodations are also available. Most rooms have Southwestern-style furnishings. A peaceful, healing serenity pervades the grounds, where walkways wind through tropical surroundings to a dry sauna and four ozonated swimming pools. Expansion in 1995 included a hydrotherapy building offering massage and an extensive selection of spa services. Colonic irrigation, Thai massage, acupuncture, polarity energy balancing, and watsu water-supported massage are available on request. An adjoining residential community is planned.

FACILITIES

Exercise Equipment: Cross-country ski track, stationary bikes, weight-training circuit. **Services:** Acupuncture, craniosacral massage, deep-tissue massage, neuromuscular massage, reflexology, shiatsu, Swedish massage, Thai massage; colon irrigation, energy work, lymphatic drainage, yoga therapy; hydrotherapy. **Swimming:** Pool, ocean beach nearby. **Classes and Programs:** Personal training, health consultations. Lectures and discussions nightly. **Recreation:** Golf, tennis, boating nearby.

ACCOMMODATIONS

25 rooms, some with shared bath.

DINING

3 meals daily, with days designated for juice fasting. **Sample Meals:** Red pepper stuffed with mix of nuts and seeds (lunch); sauerkraut-and-seed loaf (dinner).

RATES AND PACKAGES

1-week Health Encounter $1,650–$3,300 with private room, $1,650–$2,090 in shared accommodations with up to 2 persons. 2 weeks in private bedroom $3,850–$7,150, sharing $2,750-$3,850 per person; 3 weeks in private bedroom $4,950–$8,250, sharing $3,550–$4,950. 50% of room rate required as a nonrefundable deposit by certified check or major credit card. AE, D, DC, MC, V.

DIRECTIONS

✉ *1443 Palmdale Ct., West Palm Beach, FL 33411, 561/471–8876 or 800/842–2125,* FAX *561/471–9464.*

From Miami: Florida's Turnpike (I–95) to Palm Beach Exit 40, Okeechobee Boulevard to Skees Road (1 hr).

LIDO SPA HOTEL

Nutrition and diet

An all-inclusive daily rate that covers massage, exercise classes, meals, and nutritional guidance makes this hotel a good alternative to luxury spas. Actually, the Lido is more of a residential hotel, as many of the older guests who make up the majority of its regular clientele tend to stay for weeks or the entire season (October–May). And many among this friendly community of mature adults return year after year. They work out together in the swimming pool, play cards at night, and go shopping or to shows in the hotel van.

Under the same family management since it opened, the Lido is a survivor of the 1960s. It has a comfortable, lived-in look but shows its age. The main building, opened in 1962, is flanked by one- and two-story garden wings, which house motel-like accommodations. Fifteen fully equipped apartments are nearby. In keeping with the property's vintage, furniture has a plastic, 1960s look, but it's well maintained and serviced daily. TV, telephone, and air-conditioning are provided.

Occupying choice frontage on Biscayne Bay, the hotel offers easy access to Miami Beach via the scenic Venetian Causeway, a toll road for Miami commuters. You can walk or ride to the beaches and nearby museums or take the free hotel van anywhere in the immediate area as well as to the airport or train station on departure.

The daily schedule includes two low-impact exercise classes in the air-conditioned gym and occasional workouts in a pool. Otherwise you're on your own to schedule massage appointments, swim in the two outdoor pools (one contains filtered saltwater), sunbathe in private cabanas, or take advantage of the steam room, hot tub, or private whirlpools. The managers of the men's and women's spas provide limited guidance, but they are responsive to guests' personal needs and interests. If you are self-motivated and can set your own schedule, the Lido could offer a pleasant, relaxed vacation.

FACILITIES
Exercise Equipment: Stair climbers, stationary bikes, treadmills, free weights. **Services:** Swedish massage loofah body scrub, facial (for women only). **Swimming:** 2 pools. **Classes and Programs:** Live entertainment, lectures, bingo, movies.

ACCOMMODATIONS
106 rooms, 15 apartments.

DINING
3 meals a day included. Kosher and vegetarian food on request. **Sample Meals:** Chef salad, pasta salad (lunch); grilled snapper, broiled chicken with sweet potato (dinner).

RATES AND PACKAGES
Varies with season, $72–$130 single, $62–$101 double. Daily rate includes massage (30 min), 3 meals, exercise classes, outings. Deposit: $100 per room. AE, MC, V.

DIRECTIONS
✉ 40 Island Ave., Miami Beach, FL 33139, ☎ 305/538–4621 or 800/327–8363, ℻ 305/534–3680.

From Miami: Biscayne Boulevard to Venetian Causeway.

PALM-AIRE RESORT & SPA

Luxury pampering
Sports conditioning

The Palm-Aire that was, isn't. After five owners in nine years, Fairfield Communities, Inc., a time-share corporation, bought the spa and is making changes. It's building three 10-story towers, the first of which should be finished by August 1999, and has refurbished the well-designed and architecturally pleasing 40,000-square-foot spa building. Renovations include a new roof, new fitness equipment, and fresh new decor. This is primarily a day spa with fitness options—albeit in a large and very complete spa facility. The glamour days when Elizabeth Taylor reduced, relaxed, and reshaped here are gone, as are the spa meals, the structured program, the service-oriented attention, and the locker room attendants.

Today's clientele is composed of resident members (including many winter "snowbirds"), vacationing time-share owners, and guests on day packages. They mingle in robes and slippers in spacious, separate-but-equal spa pavilions. Large lounges have walls of glass overlooking big circular exercise pools set within a high-walled and flower-decked terrace. Each outdoor area offers private sunning space and a gazebo for outdoor massage. Within each pavilion are private sunken Roman baths, Swiss showers with 17 nozzles alternating warm and cold water, a sauna, and steam room. There's also a coed gym, racquetball courts, and a coed outdoor pool.

You can plan your own day at Palm-Aire. Start with a morning walk on a convenient ¾-mile track, and choose among fitness classes, scheduled between 9 AM and 2 PM, that include stretch, tone, aerobics, interval training, abs, water combo, and yoga. Outside are five 18-hole championship golf courses, 35 clay and hard-surface tennis courts, and condominium apartment buildings. Some experienced aestheticians have remained on staff and offer a selection of beauty services that include facials, manicures and pedicures, and de-stressing body treatments: massages, herbal wraps, body scrubs, aromatherapy, and reflexology.

Fairfield will arrange for accommodations at one of three beachfront properties within a 15-minute drive of Palm-Aire. All contain fully furnished luxury one- and two-bedroom properties.

FACILITIES
Exercise Equipment: Rowing machines, stair climbers, stationary bikes, treadmills, weight-training circuit, free weights. **Services:** Aromatherapy, deep-muscle massage, reflexology, Swedish massage; herbal wrap, loofah scrub; contrast pools (hot/cold), thalassotherapy; full beauty salon. **Swimming:** Pool. **Classes and Programs:** Fitness classes, golf and tennis clinics, personal training. **Recreation:** 5 golf courses, racquetball, squash, 35 tennis courts.

ACCOMMODATIONS
Number of accommodations available varies; all are fully furnished luxury one- and two-bedroom time-share condominiums rented for two days or more.

DINING
Though there is no spa cuisine, you can selectively order fresh fish and salads from menus at the two restaurants. For convenience, there are a few sandwich options and a fruit or chef salad available at the boutique in the spa building. **Sample Meals:** Grilled chicken sandwich with french fries and cole slaw (lunch). Veal saltimboca with prosciutto and mozzarella on a bed of spinach, served with soup or salad, potato or rice, and the vegetable of the day (dinner).

RATES
À la carte spa prices vary. Ultimate Half-Day Package ($125; includes tax and gratuity) includes massage, facial or back treatment, a fitness class, and use of all spa facilities. Deluxe Full-Day Package includes massage, facial, 2-hour aromatherapy session, fitness class, lunch, and herbal body wrap or reflexology foot treatment ($270; includes tax and gratuity). 1-night deposit required. 2-night minimum stay. AE, DC, MC, V.

DIRECTIONS
⊠ *2601 Palm-Aire Dr. N, Pompano Beach, FL 33069,* ☎ *954/972–3300 or 800/272–5624 (spa reservations),* ☎ *888–266–3287 (spa reservations or lodging),* FAX *954/968–2711.*

From Miami: I–95 north to Exit 34, west (left) on Atlantic Blvd., left on Power Line Rd., right on Palm-Aire Dr. (45 mins).

PGA NATIONAL RESORT & SPA

Luxury pampering
Nutrition and diet
Sports conditioning

This huge PGA community includes a full-service European spa, five golf courses, five croquet courts, the Health & Racquet Club, six restaurants, and varied accommodations including a deluxe inn. Though there is no organized spa program, you can plan your own comprehensive health and fitness regimen or create an action-oriented sport-and-spa package. As part of the latter, workouts with professional trainers are combined with spa services designed to enhance your sports performance. You can then hone your skills at golf, tennis, or even croquet.

More than 100 skin care and body services are offered à la carte or in spa packages at the Mediterranean-inspired spa building, which lies secluded in a gated garden just steps from your room. Designed around a central lap pool, the spa garden has shaded whirlpools where you can get a shoulder massage under cascading water. In addition, there are outdoor therapy pools, dubbed "Waters of the World," where you can enjoy herbal or thalassotherapy underwater massage, and body masks with natural plants and sea extracts. Beyond the spa are a 26-acre lake with a private beach and a championship croquet center.

At the Health & Racquet Club, instructors recommend a varied workout program to develop specific muscle groups and cardiovascular strength. Skiers might train on cross-country exercise and stair-climbing machines and alternate 20-minute sessions on Cybex, Trotter, and Nautilus equipment. Tennis players might work out on the treadmill and selected Trotter strength-training units. To set up a session with a personal trainer, call well in advance of your arrival date. Intensive workouts are held in a private training room, from 6:30 AM Monday through Saturday. Scheduled aerobics classes every morning, from step to cardio intervals and water workouts, are open to all resort guests for a small charge or as part of a spa package.

As the resort's name suggests, however, golf is the principal recreation. Courses designed by Nicklaus, Fazio, Palmer, and Litten challenge professional golfers as well as Sunday duffers. A round on the General, a course designed by Arnold Palmer, could be the goal of a regime devised by a team of golf pros and fitness instructors. Try the daily clinics, private lessons, or the advanced PGA National Golf Academy.

An on-site training center for professional spa therapists attests to the PGA Resort's dedication to the physics of wellness. The Bramham Institute provides continuing education courses and master classes. Most spa staffers take special training at the institute, and the result has been a consistently high level of guest satisfaction. Even players in the Pro/Am golf tournaments make reservations for treatments.

Adding to the resort's allure are many surrounding attractions. Atlantic beaches and the resorts of Palm Beach County are 30 minutes away. Adventurous types can sign up for an eco-tour through mangrove-lined lakes, rivers, and scenic estuaries, where you'll encounter a variety of birds and marine life. There are also sportfishing charters, narrated sightseeing tours on the Intracoastal Waterway, and casino cruises from the Port of Palm Beach.

FACILITIES
Exercise Equipment: Rowing machines, stair climbers, stationary bikes, treadmills, weight-training circuit, free weights. **Services:** Aromatherapy massage, lymphatic massage, reflexology, sports massage, Swedish massage; aromatherapy wrap, marine algae wrap, salt glow, seaweed body polish; hydrotherapy, Vichy shower; facial. **Swimming:** 3 pools. **Classes and Programs:** Golf and tennis programs. Lectures on weight management. Resort entertainment. **Recreation:** Croquet, golf, tennis, sailing; horseback riding nearby. **Children's Programs:** Daily baby-sitting.

ACCOMMODATIONS
279 rooms, 60 suites, 80 cottages.

DINING
Daily breakfast and lunch included with spa plan, dinner à la carte at 7 restaurants. Spa cuisine available. **Sample Meals:** Chesapeake Bay crab cakes, spinach-artichoke salad, yellowfin-tuna teriyaki, homemade mozzarella with fresh tomato and roasted red peppers, or grilled eggplant with

ricotta cheese (lunch); vegetarian pad thai, pan-seared ahi tuna with lump crabmeat, Siam squid salad, grilled lemon sole, broiled snapper over capellini pasta (dinner).

RATES AND PACKAGES

Daily: $119–$335 single or double, suites $195–$1,095, cottage suites $215–$425. Spa plan, per day with deluxe accommodations and meals, $509 single, $395 per person double occupancy. Full-day spa package with spa cuisine lunch (no lodging) $259, half-day escapes $99–$215. 1-night deposit required. AE, DC, MC, V.

DIRECTIONS

✉ *400 Ave. of the Champions, Palm Beach Gardens, FL 33418,* ☎ *561/ 627–2000 or 800/633–9150, spa reservations 800/843–7725,* ℻ *561/ 622–0261.*

From West Palm Beach: I–95 to Exit 57, PGA Boulevard west to resort entrance; Florida Turnpike to Exit 44, PGA Boulevard (20 mins).

PIER HOUSE CARIBBEAN SPA

Luxury pampering

As its name implies, the nautically inspired Pier House is a Caribbean–style Spa with a laissez-faire spirit in keeping with the laid-back air of Key West. A "don't worry, be happy" mentality prevails here: The biggest event of the day may well be watching the spectacular sunset with a drink in hand.

In the heart of Old Town, the spa is the perfect place to recharge and rejuvenate after exploring the historic attractions, colorful houses, and plentiful bars of a sometimes boisterous city that takes fun seriously. A short stroll brings you to the home and studio of nature illustrator John James Audubon, Ernest Hemingway's cat-dominated domain, Harry Truman's Little White House Museum, and a host of shops. You can also take a guided tour, by motorized Conch Train or by horse and carriage, both of which start at the Pier House.

The spa building has guest rooms and a boutique spa on the ground floor, where a professional trainer or aesthetician develops your personalized program. Facilities include men's and women's locker rooms with steam room and sauna, outdoor whirlpool, complete exercise circuit, and salon specializing in Prescription Plus creams and lotions formulated for your skin type. Try the Coma, a 90-minute combination of massage, reflexology, and paraffin treatment on your hands and feet

Workouts with a harbor view are a bonus when you join one of the daily aerobics classes held in the resort's waterside disco. Options include step and low-impact aerobics. All hotel guests can join the water aerobics session held in the swimming pool. More colorful is the tiny beach, set in a sandy cove, where nude sunbathers bask on the rocks.

In addition to 120 guest units in the hotel's main building, there are 22 spa rooms, some with private steam bath and sauna. White wicker furnishings, ceiling fans, and French doors opening onto private patios or balconies evoke a tropical mood, which is enhanced by the dense gardens and swaying palms outside. Dining at the waterfront restaurant is casual. It's keyed to seafood, with a few healthy selections rather than serious spa cuisine, but no one comes here to lose weight.

FACILITIES

Exercise Equipment: Stair climbers, stationary bikes, treadmills, weight-training circuit, free weights. **Services:** Aromatherapy massage, therapeutic massage; loofah scrub; deep-pore cleansing facial. **Swimming:** Pool, ocean beach. **Classes and Programs:** Aerobics, aquaerobics, one-on-one training.

ACCOMMODATIONS
130 rooms, 12 suites.

DINING
Breakfast included in spa package; other spa cuisine selections on à la carte menu. **Sample Meals:** Grilled seafood or grilled chicken salad with field greens and garden vegetables (lunch); catch of the day with mango vinaigrette and seasonal vegetables or sautéed yellowtail with key lime sauce, papaya, and avocado (dinner).

RATES AND PACKAGES
Rooms $195–$450 single or double, suites $325–$895. 2-night Stress Breaker package $659–$885 per couple. Full-day package with lunch (no lodging) $208.15, half-day $142.60. Daily facility charge for resort guests ($10–$15) waived when services are booked. 1-night advance payment (more during holidays) required. AE, DC, MC, V.

DIRECTIONS
⊠ *1 Duval St., Key West, FL 33040,* ☎ *305/296–4600 or 800/327–8340,* FAX *305/296–7568.*

From Miami: Hwy. 1 (Overseas Highway) via Seven-Mile Bridge (3 hrs).

PONTE VEDRA INN & CLUB

Luxury pampering
Sports conditioning

Upscale lodging combined with the clublike ambience of a long-established resort community make this a top choice for executive retreats as well as family vacations. You can schedule a round of golf or a tennis match along with spa services and a personalized fitness program, or settle in for a beach holiday that can include a check-up at the Mayo Clinic branch nearby. A bonus for golfers is a visit to the World Golf Hall of Fame, just a few miles down the coast at the World Golf Village, a new development with three signature golf courses.

It hasn't always been all golf, tennis, and pampering on the 300-acre stretch of northeastern Florida coastline occupied by the resort. Minerals were mined here from the turn of the century until 1928, when alumni of Princeton University developed the club facilities. The resort now includes a 36-hole golf course, 15 tennis courts, four swimming pools, miles of pristine white beaches, and even a library where you can borrow games as well as books. The full-service spa and fitness center are a recent addition, and the schedule of fitness and exercise programs is open to all guests.

The inn's main building has a clubby feel, with its formal dining room and conference center, but not to worry—guests are treated like members. Dining options include the beachfront Seafoam Dining Room atop the Surf Club, where you can pre-order from light cuisine selections, but lunch is taken on the spa patio. Lodgings are in eight two-story cottage-style buildings clustered around the golf courses. Most of the spacious rooms have private terraces or balconies with ocean views. Additional accommodations and a second health club are at a sister property, the Lodge, about a mile and a half from the main resort complex. In the area are riding stables, bowling, and a fishing pier.

Your personalized program can begin with a full evaluation of your fitness level and health needs at the Mayo facility, about 20 minutes from the resort. Using the health center's guidelines, the spa director may recommend a program that includes an energy-building regime, a customized diet, and a personal trainer for one-on-one exercise sessions. The 10,000-square-foot beachfront spa building resembles a big beach house with a distinctly Southern ambience: whitewashed and pickled-pine furnishings; muted tones of cream, blue, and taupe; and a terra-cotta tile roof topped by a lighted cupola. There are five massage rooms, five facial rooms, a wet room with whirlpool tubs and shower beds, and a salon. Services are scheduled à la carte or as part of day spa packages for men and women. The ground-floor fitness center has more than 50 pieces of exercise equipment, which can be used for a daily fee. Aerobics classes open to all resort guests are held here daily, including aquacise sessions in the outdoor lap pool. Or guests can simply relax in a Jacuzzi on the patio overlooking fairways and Lake Guana.

FACILITIES

Exercise Equipment: Cross-country ski track, ladder climber, stair climbers, stationary bikes, treadmills, free weights. **Services:** Swedish massage, Bio-Energy massage; fango wrap, glycolic peel, herbal wrap, loofah body polish; hydro-shower; facial. **Swimming:** 4 pools, ocean beach. **Recreation:** Biking, boating, golf, putting green, tennis; bowling and fishing nearby.

ACCOMMODATIONS

182 rooms, 20 suites.

DINING

Spa lunch included in full-day packages. Choices include seafood, seasonal salads, herbal tea or coffee. Light cuisine selections on à la carte menu at resort restaurants.

RATES AND PACKAGES

Daily per room (1–5 persons), $145–$260. 3 day/2 night spa package $503 for 2 persons per night. Day spa packages $85–$215.

DIRECTIONS

✉ *200 Ponte Vedra Blvd., Ponte Vedra Beach, FL 32082,* ☎ *904/285–1111 or 800/234–7842,* FAX *904/285–2111.*

From Jacksonville: I–95 to Butler Boulevard, east to Highway A1A, Ponte Vedra Boulevard (45 mins).

PRITIKIN LONGEVITY CENTER

Medical wellness
Nutrition and diet

Dieting on Miami Beach may sound like someone's idea of a joke, but the Pritikin Longevity Center takes it seriously. Like the original Pritikin center in California, this beachfront property is both a resort and a lifestyle learning center. The center's tightly structured, medically supervised residential program provides the support many people need in taking charge of their health. Doctors have found that people with angina have much less pain within two weeks of beginning the Pritikin program; people with diabetes need much less insulin. Some participants who arrive with canes leave with improved mobility; spouse and companion programs are available for those who need personal support.

At the foundation of the one- to four-week programs is the revolutionary diet introduced by the late Nathan Pritikin in 1974. Exercise, nutrition, stress management, health education, and medical services are all part of the core curriculum. Supervised by a team of doctors, nutritionists, and physiologists, the center's residents maintain a lively pace. The regimen demands discipline, so don't expect a fun-in-the-sun holiday. Along with 50 other participants, you work out in the gym or pool and walk on the beach. If you enjoy ocean swimming, it can be part of your exercise plan. The staff doctor decides what's best for you. As part of the daily schedule, there are cooking demonstrations, lectures, and three exercise sessions. A full physical examination is a major feature of the program and includes a treadmill stress test and complete blood chemistry analysis. Depending on your personal history and fitness level, you are assigned to a specialist in cardiology or internal medicine who monitors your progress on the prescribed diet and exercise program.

Guest accommodations are in a beachfront hotel. Some face traffic on Collins Avenue; others have an ocean view from the penthouse floor. Although facilities are not up to California standards, changes may be in the works.

FACILITIES
Exercise Equipment: Rowing machines, stair climbers, stationary bikes, treadmills, free weights. **Services:** Massage, acupressure appointments by request. **Swimming:** Pool. Beach access. **Classes and Programs:** Aquaerobics. Private counseling on nutrition and health, medical and physical exams. **Recreation:** Golf and tennis nearby. Nightly entertainment by local talent.

ACCOMMODATIONS
100 rooms and suites.

DINING
3 meals plus 3 snacks daily included in rates. Buffet-style breakfast and lunch; table service and menu choices at dinner. Salad bar available for lunch and dinner. **Sample Meals:** Pritikin vegetarian pizza, eggplant patties with marinara sauce (lunch); chicken teriyaki, poached salmon in dill sauce (dinner).

RATES AND PACKAGES
1-week program $3,382 single, $2,072 spouse or companion; 2-week program $6,647 single, $3,037 spouse or companion; 4 weeks $11,094 single, $5,824 companion. $500–$1,000 deposit required. AE, MC, V (for deposit only).

DIRECTIONS
⊠ *5875 Collins Ave., Miami Beach, FL 33140,* ☎ *305/866–2237 or 800/ 327–4914 (Flamingo Hotel, 305/865–8645),* ☒ *305/866–1872).*

From Miami: I–95 to Route 195 exit, Arthur Godfrey Causeway to 41st Street, left on Collins Avenue (15 mins).

SADDLEBROOK RESORT TAMPA

Luxury pampering
Sports conditioning

Shape-ups for golf and tennis are the specialty at Saddlebrook Resort. To enhance your game there are workouts at the Sports Village and clinics for a day, weekend, or extended stay. The spa provides the finishing touches: muscle-relaxing massage and underwater hydrotherapy.

The resort's Harry Hopman Tennis Program is in action daily on 47 courts. Rated ultra-intense by *Tennis Magazine,* the tennis camp has weekend-long and five-day sessions for teenagers and adults. Specialized programs are designed for recreational, junior, and professional tournament players, and personal training for five hours is available at a daily rate. All programs include unlimited access to the cardiovascular and strength-building exercise equipment at the Sports Village. The tennis complex features five different playing surfaces: Har-Tru, Laykold, Decoturf, grass, and red clay. Pros like Pete Sampras often come here to practice for tournaments.

Saddlebrook's golf facilities are equally impressive. The Arnold Palmer Golf Academy has its world headquarters here, using Saddlebrook's two 18-hole courses and a special driving range and putting green to train participants in the program. Designed to simulate all the features of a golf course, the practice area is used for group and individual instruction. From basic address positions for short game shots, you progress to putting techniques and essential drills to develop a better scoring zone. Stretching and exercises to build your golf swing are combined with hands-on training on the course. Programs are scheduled for two, three, and five days.

Camps for juniors are scheduled year-round, during school holidays and in conjunction with the Saddlebrook Academy resident program. Juniors get eight hours of rigorous training daily, three energy-building meals prepared under nutritional guidelines, and free time for recreation. Supervised by adults and trainers, the 12- to 17-year-old campers are motivated by the professionalism of the program. Budding golf pros can enroll in the college prep school course at Saddlebrook Academy, fully accredited for grades 7–12, with mornings at school and afternoons on the links.

The 480-acre resort centers around a free-form swimming pool. In addition to a country club, conference center, training facilities, and a spa, there's a main building housing the upscale dining room and bar, as well as vast ballrooms and seminar facilities. Two-story lodges linked by paved pathways and wooden bridges have easy access to the golf courses and swimming pool. Ground-floor units have a sliding door out to a terrace. Cluster 200 rooms are closest to the clubhouse. Spa cuisine is served in the Cypress Room and at the spa, and Friday evening brings a seafood buffet.

The spa, which was designed to complement the golf and tennis programs, provides all the necessary facilities but no structured program. A separate entrance leads down to spa reception and the beauty salon, with umbrella-shaded tables and fountains flanking the staircase. Elegantly tiled in light beige with green marble turquoise accents, locker rooms for men and women are equipped with steam, sauna, and whirlpool facilities and full amenities. A therapist greets you in the lounge, which leads to 12 coed treatment rooms (scheduled for expansion in 1999). There is special equipment for sports-related problems—hydromassage tub, aromatherapy soaking tub, Vichy shower, and herbal or seaweed body wrap—and a suite for couples' massage. Lunch can be pre-ordered for an al fresco break here, and you can relax in your spa robe.

A half-mile path through the clusters of guest lodges leads to the Sports Village, a resort within the resort. Here you can exercise on the latest Cybex equipment, join games, swim laps, or play tennis. Facilities include 14 tennis courts, a 1½-acre soccer and softball field, sand and grass volleyball courts, a regulation-size basketball court, and a bocce-ball court. Stretching and exercise classes are held in an open-air pavilion. Use of the facilities is included in spa and sport packages, or a daily fee will be charged to your resort account.

Children can experience the sports or enjoy the S'Kids Club. Supervised adventures include a trip to the Florida Aquarium in Tampa, where a naturalist explains local flora and fauna as well as the tanks full of fish. Nearby is Busch Gardens, a combination zoo and theme park with thrilling rides, shows for kids and adults, and an African safari. Other outings include canoeing through a nature preserve on the nearby Hillsborough River and a day at Walt Disney World.

Exercise Equipment: Stair climbers, stationary bikes, treadmills, weight-training circuit, free weights. **Services:** Aromatherapy massage, couples massage, reflexology, shiatsu, sports massage; aromatherapy salt glow, body polish, herbal wrap, seaweed wrap; balneotherapy aroma baths, micronized seaweed thalassotherapy, mood-mud balneotherapy, underwater lymphatic hydromassage, Vichy shower massage; deep-cleansing facial, eye-lifting facial, oxygenating facial. **Swimming:** 3 pools. **Classes and Programs:** Aerobics; body-composition analysis, fitness evaluation, one-on-one training. Golf and tennis clinics. **Recreation:** Basketball, biking, bocce, golf, tennis, volleyball. Poolside dancing. **Children's Programs:** S'Kids Club (ages 4–12).

ACCOMMODATIONS

790 rooms and suites.

DINING

A la carte meals at 4 restaurants. Spa menus contain information on calories and fat grams. Seasonal salad bar at Little Club Restaurant. **Sample Meals:** Gazpacho or minted strawberry soup, fruit salad, tabouli pita sandwich, vegetarian or turkey burger, grilled swordfish with vegetable salsa (lunch); summer-squash-and-roasted-corn soup, baked oysters creole with yucca chips, grouper tropicana (with vegetables, shrimp, coconut, and ginger) in a banana leaf, crisp Asian pasta with black-bean sauce, duck à l'orange (dinner).

RATES AND PACKAGES

Daily room/suite rate $110–$190 summer, $185–$325 spring/fall, $225–$380 winter, for 2 persons. 3-night Spa Escape with breakfast daily $765–$1,050 single, $651–$795 per person, double occupancy. Day Spa packages from $160. AE, D, MC, V.

DIRECTIONS

✉ *5700 Saddlebrook Way, Wesley Chapel, FL 33543,* ☎ *813/973–1111 or 800/729–8383,* FAX *813/973–4505.*

From Tampa: I-275 north to I-75 north, exit at Route 54 east to Saddlebrook entrance on right (30 mins).

SAFETY HARBOR RESORT & SPA

Luxury pampering
Mineral springs

Walking along Bayshore Drive in the morning, swimming laps under swaying palms, and soaking in mineral spring water are among the pleasures of a vacation at Safety Harbor Resort, a superspa of the 1980s fitness fad that underwent a series of management changes and facelifts while adjusting to the more relaxed fitness programs of the '90s. Meeting facilities at the 1955 hotel have been enlarged as have the dining room and café, and guest rooms, reception, and beauty salon areas have been given a fresh look.

With four mineral springs on the property, hydrotherapy has become a major feature of the spa. Modern chemical analysis shows that each spring has a different proportion of calcium, magnesium, sodium, potassium, and other minerals. This thermal water is used throughout the hotel in all Jacuzzis and swimming pools.

Aquatics is another strong feature of the health-oriented program. Private hydrotherapy tubs in the men's and women's bathhouses are enhanced with blends of herbs and marine algae for stress reduction, relief of muscular tension, and toning treatments. Exercising in the specially designed shallow indoor and outdoor pools burns calories efficiently without straining the body. Even out of the water, though, exercise instructors promote low-impact routines, and the shock-absorbing floors are specially constructed to help avoid tendonitis and shin splints. The instructors here specialize in a variety of routines, from gentle to active, to keep you from getting bored.

A member of the fitness staff will check your overall physical condition, monitor your heart rate, and analyze your body-fat-to-muscle ratio. Based on a computer analysis, a specific combination of exercise and diet will be recommended.

Bodywork appointments are made through a guest coordinator and charged on an à la carte basis or as part of seasonal packages, between two and eight days. Men's and women's locker rooms have sauna, steam room, and direct access to the exercise pool, but it's a good idea to bring footwear, even aquatic socks for water aerobics. Robe and slippers are provided daily, along with locker room amenities.

Don't expect group interaction; you're pretty much on your own until meeting kindred souls in the dining room or the nightly excursions to cultural events, movies, and shopping. Beach trips are scheduled several times a week. The spa's laid-back feeling may be just the restorative you need. For more active pursuits, there's Phil Green's Tennis Academy, where two hours of instruction daily can be combined with fitness classes. Tennis pros conduct classes at beginner, intermediate, and advanced levels. Unlimited use of the tennis courts for daytime play, a golf driving range, and transportation to a nearby golf course are other options.

Unpretentious and informal, the resort has won legions of loyal friends by providing tools for looking and feeling good. The average guest's age is 40, with a smattering of older clients (often snowbirds taking an extended vacation) and the occasional twentysomething fitness fanatic.

FACILITIES
Exercise Equipment: Ergometer, ladder stepper, rowing machines, stair climbers, stationary bikes, trampolines, treadmills, weight-training circuit, free weights. **Services:** Massage; herbal wrap, loofah body scrub, mud wrap, salt glow; facial. **Swimming:** Outdoor and indoor pools. **Classes and Programs:** Golf and tennis instruction, fitness evaluation, lectures on stress management and health-related topics. Cooking demonstrations, cultural programs. **Recreation:** Biking, tennis, volleyball. Golf and horseback riding nearby.

ACCOMMODATIONS
192 rooms.

DINING
3 meals daily with spa packages, served in main dining room or café. Spa menus with 1,100–1,200-daily-calorie meal plans available. **Sample Meals:** Vegetable quesadillas, shrimp-and-papaya salad, vegetable chili with white or brown rice (lunch); pepper-crusted salmon, lime-broiled shrimp and scallops (dinner).

RATES AND PACKAGES
Basic Spa and Fitness 3-day/2-night package, full American plan with lodging, $255–$320 single, $171–$205 double; Spa and Fitness Plans (each includes $100 in spa services per person per night and Full American Plan with lodging.) 5-day/4-night package $1,141–$1,788 single, $985–$1,340 per person double occupancy. 8-day/7-night package $1,900–$3,066 single, $1,667–$2,298 double. 3-night FILA Tennis Academy/Spa

package $508–$1,162 single, $355–$797 double. Gratuities included. 1-night deposit required. AE, D, DC, MC, V.

DIRECTIONS
✉ *105 N. Bayshore Dr., Safety Harbor, FL 34695,* ☒ *813/726–1161 or 800/237–0155,* ☒ *813/726–4268.*

From Tampa: I–275 south to Exit 20, Route 60 toward Clearwater, exit on Bayshore Boulevard (20 mins).

SANIBEL HARBOUR RESORT & SPA

Luxury pampering
Sports conditioning

Tennis-oriented workouts in the spa and at the Racquet Club make this bayside resort a great place to shape up and improve your game, but the beautiful sunset views of island-dotted San Carlos Bay from your room or your dinner table in the Victorian gazebo also make it an ideal hideaway. Lovely Sanibel Island and its excellent shelling along pristine beaches are within a short drive, or you can dance away the night at discos with the shorts and sandals set.

For tennis enthusiasts, a tennis pro and exercise physiologist team up to develop your cross-training program, which starts with a fitness evaluation and analysis of your nutritional needs. Personal trainers are on hand for exercise sessions. In addition to Cybex equipment, the spa has cardiovascular and strength-training facilities. A glass-walled gym tucked into the tennis stadium offers more than 40 aerobics classes a week, taught at variable impact levels in a plush studio with carpeted floor. Choices range from yoga fitness and line dancing to step, and there's no extra charge. The spa's indoor lap pool is used for an energizing aquafit class, and air-conditioned racquetball courts are available by the hour.

The Racquet Club schedules daylong tennis workouts at beginner, intermediate, and advanced levels as well as personal instruction and a training camp for children. By combining a two-day tennis package with a day spa package, you can enjoy the benefits of both. Play is on 12 lighted courts with clay and Spin-flex surfaces. Bring your own racket or rent equipment at the pro shop.

Set in lush tropical gardens, the spa offers a wide range of body treatments featuring FloraSpa and Repechage products—Swiss showers, aromatherapy, salt-glow body scrub, and herbal and seaweed wraps. Both men's and women's sections have sauna, steam room, five whirlpools, and hot and cold plunge pools. For a sonic massage, relax on the BETAR bed, a combination of stress-releasing musical energy impulses with your choice of music, from Bach to rock.

Rooms and suites in the resort's hotel have private balconies and Florida furniture. For more space and luxury, condominium apartments in two 12-story towers provide fully equipped kitchens, dining rooms, and washer/dryers as well as two bedrooms and baths. Among the resort's restaurants, Chez le Bear is the most refined, serving gourmet Mediterranean fare. A "Cuisine of the Sun" nightly special menu uses all natural ingredients.

As a base for exploring the gulf islands and Everglades National Park, the resort is ideally located. Just across a toll bridge on Sanibel Island is the J. N. Ding Darling Wildlife Refuge, named for a naturalist who established a walking tour of the marine habitat. Farther along the road is Captiva Island, also home to shell-covered beaches. History buffs will enjoy discovering early experiments in sound and light at the winter home and laboratory of Thomas Alva Edison in Fort Myers. Seasonal attractions include spring training camps for Major League Baseball teams and greyhound racing.

Recreation at Sanibel Harbor is family friendly, with sailboats and yacht excursions at the marina, a fishing pier, and kayaks for rent. Golfers can visit nearby country clubs, and for a romantic sunset cruise, a hundred-foot yacht sails from the resort dock. Despite all there is to do, you may be tempted to simply sit on your balcony and gaze out at the beautiful mangrove-covered islets that spread out before you.

FACILITIES
Exercise Equipment: Stair climbers, stationary bikes, treadmills, weight-training circuit. **Services:** Aromatherapy massage, reflexology, sports massage, Swedish massage; algae masque, apricot scrub, milk-and-honey body wrap, fango mud pack, herbal or seaweed wrap, salt glow; paraffin facial, seaweed facial. **Swimming:** 4 pools (1 indoor), bay beach. **Classes and Programs:** Fitness evaluation, nutritional counseling, personal training, tennis instruction. **Recreation:** Basketball, hiking, racquetball, tennis; canoeing, fishing, sailing. Golf, horseback riding nearby. **Children's Programs:** Supervised children's program (ages 5–12) daily.

ACCOMMODATIONS
240 rooms, 80 2-bedroom condominiums.

DINING
Meals included in some packages or offered à la carte. **Sample Meals:** Vegetarian terrine, whole-wheat linguini with Thai chicken breast primavera, or marinated tuna and grouper carpaccio with mixed greens (lunch); Colorado rack of lamb, whole Maine lobster, Black Angus beef medallions (dinner).

RATES AND PACKAGES
$130–$305 daily per room for 2 persons, suites $179–$329; condominium for 4 persons $179–$599. 3-day/2-night Spa Discovery package $495–$771 single in hotel, $353–$489 double in hotel, $395–$521 double in condominium; 4-day/3-night Ultimate Spa Pursuit package $719–$1,131 single in hotel, $503–$709 double in hotel, $569–$889 double in condominium; 5-day/4-night Spa Escape $981–$1,531 single in hotel, $693–$969 double, $781–$1,209 double in condominium; Spa gratuities included in packages. Day Spa packages $99–$263. Meal plans available $45–$114 per person daily (breakfast, lunch, dinner), including gratuities. Credit-card guarantee required. AE, D, DC, MC, V.

DIRECTIONS
✉ *17260 Harbour Pointe Dr., Fort Myers, FL 33908,* ☎ *941/466–2157 (spa), 941/466–4000 (resort), or 800/767–7777,* 🖷 *941/466–2198.*

From Fort Myers or Southwest Florida Regional Airport: I–75 to Exit 21 to Daniels Rd., left on Summerlin Rd. right before Sanibel Island causeway entrance, right on Harbour Pointe Dr. (20 mins).

SPA LXVI AT HYATT REGENCY PIER SIXTY-SIX RESORT

Luxury pampering

Enjoying the amenities of a day spa directly on the Intracoastal Waterway is a healthy alternative to the beach scene in Fort Lauderdale. Extensively redecorated in 1998, Spa LXVI is tucked away in the resort's 22-acre tropical gardens. A convenient place to escape from business at the nearby convention center or to relax before boarding a cruise ship, the facility is an oasis of cool luxury.

In addition to a full-service salon for body, skin, and hair treatments, the spa offers personal training, indoor and outdoor heated whirlpools, private massage rooms, exercise equipment, and locker rooms equipped with sauna, steam rooms, and Swiss showers. Aerobics classes are offered poolside, and all guests can join an exercise session in the swimming pool, but that's about the only organized activity. Everything else is à la carte or in day spa packages, which cost less than a room in the hotel.

The landmark Pier Sixty-Six rises 17 stories above the waterway. Updated recently, rooms in the circular tower feature splendid views of the Intracoastal, sea, or city. Alternately, you can take in the vistas from the revolving lounge on the top floor. Garden lanais, too, provide excellent lodgings. If you choose to leave your hideaway, there are plenty of area attractions to occupy you, starting with the redeveloped downtown area and its Arts and Science District, contemporary Museum of Art, and chic cafés and discos along the Riverwalk and Las Olas Boulevard; the vast Sawgrass Mills Outlet Mall or the upscale shops at the Galleria Mall; and entertainment that ranges from classical concerts and Broadway shows at the Broward Center for the Performing Arts to betting at the jai alai fronton. And when you want to swim in the ocean, hail the water taxi at the resort's dock for a quick trip to the beach.

FACILITIES
Exercise Equipment: Rowing machines, stair climbers, stationary bikes, weight-training equipment, treadmills, free weights. **Services:** Aromatherapy massage, sports massage, Swedish massage; seaweed wrap, salt glow; facial. **Swimming:** 2 pools. **Classes and Programs:** Aerobics, aquaerobics, fitness evaluation, personal training. **Recreation:** Tennis courts; charter-boat deep-sea fishing, parasailing, scuba, snorkeling. Golf nearby.

ACCOMMODATIONS
380 rooms, 8 suites.

DINING
On the menu at the hotel's three restaurants are low-calorie options such as fruit salads (breakfast); spinach salad (lunch); and pasta primavera (dinner).

RATES AND PACKAGES
Daily room rate $169–$409 single or double occupancy, jr. suite $259–$459. Two hours of treatments $115; The Ultimate Day at $175, includes a spa lunch poolside or in the Mariners Grille. Hotel guests pay a $10 daily fee to use the facilities, which is waived when you book a spa service. AE, DC, MC, V.

DIRECTIONS
✉ *2301 S.E. 17th St. Causeway, Fort Lauderdale, FL 33316,* ☎ *954/ 525–6666 or 800/327–3796,* ☏ *954/728–3541.*

From Fort Lauderdale International Airport: East on 17th Street Causeway to bridge (15 mins)

TURNBERRY ISLE RESORT & CLUB

Luxury pampering

If you prefer a luxurious resort that feels more like a country club than a formal destination spa, consider Turnberry Isle. The verdant 300-acre grounds, tucked away within North Miami's busy Aventura, straddle the Intracoastal Waterway. Continual van service transports guests on the flower-lined roads that lead between the main hotel at the golf and tennis club, the marina-front spa facility and hotel, and the beach club. As befits a resort operated by international hoteliers the Rafael Group, all areas are upscale and private, reserved for hotel guests and club members.

The self-contained spa facility and its adjoining 70-room boutique hotel, which overlooks yachts docked in the Intracoastal Waterway, attract dedicated spa guests and privacy seekers to their fitness facilities, spa and salon services, and casual restaurant. Rarely crowded, the spa has an outdoor exercise pool, indoor and outdoor whirlpools, two air-conditioned racquetball courts, and lounges with sundecks. Spa director Chuck McElligott, who opened spas at the Ritz-Carltons in Naples and Palm Beach, is committed to meeting guests' needs, and his solicitous staff carries out the plan, offering a robe and slippers upon arrival, smiles as they pick up wet towels, and assistance when necessary. Private trainers, top-of-the-line equipment, and a large-screen TV are available in the weight room. Aerobics classes are scheduled in the sprung-wood-floor studio, and yoga sessions are popular, too. There's a Turkish steam bath, Swedish sauna, and a new multiheaded Swiss shower. The pretty locker room lobby always has fresh-cut fruit and beverages and is well stocked with reading material. Pampering body and beauty treatments are executed by trained personnel who must have at least three years of spa experience prior to being hired and who continue to receive education and training. The range of services is extensive. For example, for the exfoliating body treatments, aestheticians use Dead Sea muds, loofah salts, and citrus products. Plans call for a new larger spa facility to be built.

The focus of Turnberry's sport facilities is golf. Designed by Robert Trent Jones, the splashy South Course, known for the 18th hole's tiny island green, has water traps on all but a handful of holes. Many a tournament pro has lost balls in all that water. By contrast, Jones's challenging North Course provides smooth, consistent greens.

For a break in the sports routine, try the beach. The Ocean Club, reached via the Lehman Causeway, is located on a sparsely populated northern strip of Miami Beach. Take a walk north along the coast past a quiet residential community with some spectacular beachfront homes. The beach club has cabanas, its own pool, and a snack bar for light lunches.

Beyond golf, spa, and beach, Turnberry's shuttle bus can deposit you at the upscale Aventura Mall, a massive celebration of the good life. There are enough restaurants, shops, and services to qualify as a small city, and in the morning, it's open early for air-conditioned walks.

Dining at any of six restaurants is yet another highlight at Turnberry Isle. The Sunset Café, on the ground floor of the spa, offers spa-style lunch choices, but dinner is eaten at the country club's dining rooms. You can opt for the relaxed checkered-tablecloth setting of the Bistro, which has an excellent selection of lighter items, or dine amid the chandeliers, silk, and battalions of servers at the formal Veranda Room, which offers a prix-fixe menu (a $40 bargain). Though the Veranda Room has fewer spa selections than the Sunset Café, there are still many healthful choices, which can be easily adapted to be lower in fat and calories. Chef Todd Weiss, formerly the spa chef at Doral, offers a number of haute spa-style selections, particularly on the luncheon menu.

Spacious accommodations are found in either the main Mediterranean-style country club complex or the smaller five-story hotel adjacent to the spa. Country club rooms are in several buildings set amid lush plantings enclosing a terrazzo-patio courtyard pool and have golf course views. With its red-tile roof and white stucco walls, the club bears a certain resemblance to its namesake, the venerable Turnberry golf resort in Scotland. But here the style is Louis XIV meets the Florida Marlins. The mixture of Versailles-wannabe furniture, gilded and stippled, with enormous café-like paintings and posters, treads a fine line between splendor and tackiness. Rooms and suites all have king-size beds, marble baths with whirlpool tubs, three phones (with two lines), and cable TV with VCR.

Future resort development appears to be following a familiar track. Luxurious new guest suites will feature a marble bathroom with sunken whirlpool tub, a separate seating area, and private balcony. A new spa building adjacent to the original hotel will include hydrotherapy facilities as well as state-of-the-art exercise equipment. The island within may be a haven of wellness, an antidote to stress in your life, but creature comforts are Turnberry's hallmark.

FACILITIES
Exercise Equipment: Ladder steppers, stair climbers, stationary bikes, weight-training circuit. **Services:** Aromatherapy massage, reflexology, shiatsu, Swedish massage; back cleansing and heat treatment, herbal wrap, loofah body scrub, mud treatments, salt glow; hydrotherapy; facial. **Swimming:** Pool. **Recreation:** Golf, racquetball, tennis, yacht charters.

ACCOMMODATIONS
340 rooms and suites, 27 1- and 2-bedroom villas.

DINING
3 à la carte meals served at 6 restaurants. Spa menu available at the Verandah. **Sample Meals:** Spicy chilled gazpacho, roll-up sandwich with vegetables and hummus, angel-hair pasta with fresh tomato and basil, seared ahi tuna with coconut–ginger sticky rice, grilled jumbo prawns (lunch); pan-seared foie gras with green-apple chutney and herbed potatoes, hearts of palm salad with fresh asparagus and beets, lavender-marinated roast rack of lamb with spinach-and-goat-cheese gratin, grilled veal chop with ragout of wild mushrooms and truffle risotto (dinner).

RATES AND PACKAGES
Daily room rates $195–$425 single or double, suites $300–$2,100. 2-night mini-spa package $899 single, $539 per person double. 1-night credit-card deposit required. AE, DC, MC, V.

DIRECTIONS
✉ *19999 W. Country Club Dr., Aventura, North Miami, FL 33180,* ☎ *305/932–6200 or 800/327–7028,* ℻ *305/933–6560.*

From Miami: I–95 to Exit 20, Ives Dairy Rd., U.S. Rte. 1, Biscayne Blvd. (25 mins).

WYNDHAM RESORT & SPA

Luxury pampering
Nutrition and diet
Sports conditioning

What was formerly the Bonaventure Spa is now a Wyndham resort, and along with the change in ownership came a change in focus. Though the Wyndham still has one of Florida's largest and best-designed spas as well as a popular spa dining room, it has updated its facilities and redesigned its spa programs and activities for shape-ups rather than stress management. There are still sybaritic pleasures galore, but the sports-oriented programs take a serious approach to fitness, motivating beginners as well as seasoned spa-goers.

You may want to stay a weekend, four days, or a full week, choosing either to enjoy unlimited exercise classes and expert bodywork and beauty treatments or to orient your visit around sports—tennis, golf, and horseback riding. Join the new Fitness Adventure series of indoor and outdoor group programs at any time and combine it with spa services à la carte or as a package. But beware adding too many extras to your spa schedule, as your bill will quickly run up.

A typical day begins with a walk or jog around the golf course before breakfast, then an hour-long aerobics class. Three levels of conditioning are offered in a dozen different classes that range from easy stretches and yoga to deep toning calisthenics and energizing routines. Workouts in the water are popular, especially for people with orthopedic problems, since joints and back are supported while in the pool. There are cardiovascular exercises for men only, as well as a thermal mineral water body scrub and massage to condition the male physique.

The range of body and skin-care treatments is enormous. Always on the cutting edge, the spa uses Kerstin Florian's European kur program, mixing thermal-water crystals from Hungary in hydrotherapy tubs. An imported line of essential oils is used in aromatherapy massage and spirulina facials. Privacy is ensured by separate wings for men and women, each with a lap pool and sundeck, newly retiled steam room and Swiss showers, wooden saunas, hot and cold plunge pools, and individual whirlpools. The coed aerobics studio has a new suspended wood floor, and there are Schwinn spinning bike sessions as well as yoga classes. Dedicated cardiovascular and strength-training rooms feature new equipment. A beauty salon offers hair styling, manicure, and pedicure.

For a personal wellness program, consultation with a sports medicine specialist is available. Dr. Bruce Fox creates a fitness regimen and diet recommendations, adding behavior modification techniques and motivational messages on cassette tapes to take home. Family-oriented activities include bike rental and airboat rides in the Everglades. Ocean beaches are 30 minutes away.

Guest rooms and suites are located in nine four-story buildings. Large rooms with balconies overlook the lake or golf course. Oversize bathrooms have a dressing area. A staff nurse interviews you on arrival and may suggest consultation on a diet plan. Thereafter you can opt for calorie-controlled meals at the spa restaurant, Horizons, or choose from among three other restaurants, some overlooking gardens and a swimming pool.

FACILITIES
Exercise Equipment: Rowing machines, stair climbers, stationary bikes, treadmills, free weights. **Services:** Aromatherapy massage, shiatsu, Swedish massage; herbal wrap, loofah body scrub, sea-kelp wrap, thermal back treatment; aromatherapy bath, Finnish sauna, hot and cold plunge baths, Turkish steam bath; facials. **Swimming:** 5 pools; ocean beach nearby. **Classes and Programs:** Aerobics, boxercise, Spinning. Private exercise, golf, and tennis lessons. Fitness and nutrition profiles, body-composition analysis. **Recreation:** Biking, golf, horseback riding, tennis.

ACCOMMODATIONS
496 rooms and suites.

DINING
3 daily meals included in some packages. Calorie-counted selections (totaling 1,200 calories) in private spa dining room. **Sample Meals:** Hummus-and-tabouli wrap, lobster-and-papaya salad (lunch); oat-bran crusted snapper with mango, or grilled raspberry-shrimp with whole-wheat pasta (dinner).

Daily rate $165–$235 single, $185–$255 for 2. Spa Classic 1-night package $118–$163 per person double; 3-night 'InSPAration' package $424–$553 per person double; 7-night Ultimate Spa Experience $882–$1,183 per person double. Perfect Day package at spa $250 (lodging not included). Additional bodywork and beauty treatments, golf and tennis packages available. 1-night deposit required 7 days after booking or credit-card confirmation. AE, D, MC, V.

✉ *250 Racquet Club Rd., Fort Lauderdale, FL 33326,* ☎ *954/389–3300 or 800/327–8090,* 𝔽𝔸𝕏 *954/384–6157.*

From Miami: I–75 north to Exit 8 (Arvida Parkway), west to Bonaventure Boulevard, Racquet Club Road (40 mins).

GEORGIA

CHATEAU ELAN

Luxury pampering

As a romantic hideaway, it would be hard to beat a spa at a winery. Chateau Elan, in the foothills of North Georgia, gives you a healthy workout along with wine tastings.

Driving through the suburbs and farmland north of Atlanta, nothing quite prepares you for the château, which resembles a 16th-century French estate set amid vineyards. The 3,400-acre gated resort community has two golf courses, an equestrian center, conference hotel, and spa. The château is, in fact, a working winery and restaurant disguised as the manor house. Directed to the spa building, you discover what looks like a southern mansion but turns out to be a Disneyesque mix of cultures and centuries.

Getting into fantasy mode takes a bit of attitude adjustment. The receptionist cheerfully provides an orientation, with Southern accent. The main floor includes a lounge where afternoon tea is served, a library with videotapes that can be borrowed for your room's VCR, and a dining room overlooking a picture-perfect lake. But it's the choice of guest rooms that is unique. Each of the 14 minisuites is themed to create a fantasy, from high-tech to Western, with matching furniture, art, and decorative items. There's a make-believe cottage room full of Georgian crafts. One has busts of Greek gods. Another re-creates the Great Gatsby era. And each room comes with matching T-shirts, presented upon your arrival. Antiques and high-tech amenities, lavish bathroom fixtures, and concierge service are standard. Two loft suites feature an upper-level bedroom with four-poster bed and two bathrooms. If you're picky about decor, specify it early. Nearby are a 274-room French-style inn and 18 small Petit Chateau villas bordering the fairways.

After discussing the spa schedule, you're left to your own devices. Recently expanded with the addition of a third floor, the spa has 30 private rooms for personal services. The range of treatments includes hydrotherapy in a tub with underwater massage jets, therapeutic massage with hot stones placed on sore muscles to ease tension, foot reflexology, body exfoliation, and herbal wraps. The in-house salon is staffed with hair stylists and specialists in skin and nail care. For stress relief, there are sessions of yoga and a cocooning alphamassage machine.

Dining options are numerous. For those not counting calories, the concierge will make dinner reservations in the winery's Le Clos, which has a classic French menu. The spa dining room provides low-fat choices in small portions designed to encourage weight loss. The menus blend European and American cuisine along with Georgia wine and water bottled by Chateau Elan. A real Irish pub was imported and re-created with a menu of traditional food and drink.

Chateau Elan guests have a princely choice of recreation: the South's largest equestrian center with three all-weather arenas, riding trails, and Grand Prix show facility; a seven-court tennis center by Stan Smith; four golf courses and country club; and indoor and outdoor swimming pools. The winery offers tours and tastings daily and houses shops and a café as well as Le Clos restaurant. During the summer, concerts and picnic dinners are held in the vineyard. For a taste of action, take the wheel of a performance car at Road Atlanta, a 2.5-mile training track with 12 turns, intense elevation changes, and high-speed straights.

Golfers are challenged by an 81-hole spread. Legendary masters Gene Sarazen, Sam Snead, and Kathy Whitworth designed the Legends, a classic course based on favorite holes of the masters. Facilities include three championship courses and a par-3 nine-hole walking course. Instruction is available in half-day clinics scheduled April through October and from the resident teaching staff. The practice facility simulates course challenges, and programs are tailored to all skill levels.

Spa-goers can mix and match activities to suit their interests. Mornings begin with easy stretches, followed by a guided hike on nature trails winding through the resort. In addition to aerobics classes, you can include horseback riding and golf along with one-on-one training and beauty salon services. All of these options come in a variety of packages; make appointments prior to your arrival to assure availability. Other options include staying at the conference hotel (which has a small health club) or budget-priced inn and scheduling spa services à la carte.

Don't expect lots of exercise equipment and group programs. In this vision of Southern comfort, there's no place for regimentation. Borrow a tape of *Gone With the Wind,* and pretend you've discovered Tara.

FACILITIES
Exercise Equipment: Stair climbers, stationary bikes, treadmills, free weights. **Services:** Aromatherapy massage, hot-stone massage, deep-tissue massage, reflexology, Swedish massage; body wrap, glycolic acid series, salt glow; hydrotherapy, mineral baths, thalassotherapy; facial. **Swimming:** 2 pools (1 indoor). **Classes and Programs:** Fitness evaluation, skin-care analysis. **Recreation:** Biking, golf, horseback riding, tennis.

ACCOMMODATIONS
288 rooms, 18 villas.

DINING
Spa plans include some meals, afternoon tea, evening snack. **Sample Meals:** Seared snapper with herbal salad, vegetarian pasta with fresh vegetables and tomato sauce (lunch); grilled tuna with wasabi pasta (dinner).

RATES AND PACKAGES
Daily rate for spa rooms $165–$250 single or double. Spa Getaway (2-night/3-day) $1,489–$1,529 per couple, $889–$929 single. Luxury week (7-night/8-day) $3,879–$3,979 per couple. Day Spa package, including lunch, services, no lodging, $175–$245. Inn rooms $79–$95 daily, single or double. Villas on request. 24-hour cancellation policy. AE, MC, V.

DIRECTIONS
⊠ *Haven Harbour Dr., Braselton, GA 30517,* ☎ *770/932–0900 or 800/ 233–9463(outside Atlanta),* ℻ *770/271–6069.*

From Atlanta: I–85 north, Exit 48, left on Old Winder Highway 211 (45 mins).

CLOISTER'S SEA ISLAND SPA

Luxury pampering

Dress up the kids, and pack your dancing shoes for a beach escape on one of the prettiest barrier islands along the Atlantic coast. Tradition and therapy meet at the Cloister's Sea Island Spa. You can join a morning beach walk and stretch class, exercise in air-conditioned comfort, and enjoy sophisticated pampering in the privacy of spa suites.

Set up a personal schedule with a spa programmer prior to your arrival, as appointments for treatments tend to fill up during peak periods. The facilities are spacious but only nine treatment rooms are available, and the aerobics studio gets full with a dozen in the class. During the winter months, special women's retreats are scheduled; otherwise group programs are limited to exercise and sports clinics. A daily facility fee ($12) is charged if you simply want to exercise, but the fee is included in spa packages by the day or longer.

Thalassotherapy by the sea is a major attraction here. Treatments include French seaweed masks and salt scrubs to nourish and cleanse the skin. In the hands of a licensed aesthetician, the facial treatment becomes a succession of cleansing and soothing experiences as four layers of aloe, seaweed, and Repechage creams are applied. While your complexion is being detoxified and moisturized to combat the ravages of time and sun, your feet are softened with paraffin wax. The final touch may be a reflexology massage, one of 18 different techniques offered by staff therapists.

Located at the resort's Beach Club, the spa is steps from swimming pools and surf, as well as restaurants offering sumptuous buffets for breakfast and lunch. Hydrotherapy is available in a specially designed tub with underwater massage jets to enhance the soothing effect of seaweed or herbal extracts added to the bath. The in-house beauty salon provides makeup consultation as well as hair styling and nail care.

Sports add a special dimension to this seaside escape. The Cloister offers 54 holes of golf at two clubs, plus an acclaimed golf learning center with indoor and outdoor training by professionals. Water sports, a tennis club with 17 courts, a cycling center with 300 bikes for rent, stables with 60 horses, a skeet and gun club, and docks for boat rental and fishing expeditions on the Intracoastal Waterway are also available.

Places to stay include lodges overlooking the beach and waterway and private cottage rental. You have a choice of twin or king beds, patio or balcony. Units are air-conditioned and have TV, sitting area, walk-in closet, phone, and desk. Despite the rather modern accommodations, tradition clings to the Cloister as attractively as the Spanish moss dangling from great old trees shading the roads. The main building, a 1928 Spanish-Mediterranean palazzo designed by Addison Mizner, is the setting for dress-up dinners with dancing and a multicourse menu. (There's also a limited selection of spa cuisine.) The family-oriented Beach Club bustles with breakfast and luncheon buffets, heavy on Southern specialties but also offering light fare. A seafood buffet and fresh fish are featured daily. Romantic carriage rides meander amid oaks along the 5-mile stretch of private beach on the Atlantic seafront.

FACILITIES

Exercise Equipment: Rowing machines, stair climbers, stationary bikes, treadmills, weight-training circuit, free weights. **Services:** Acupressure, aromatherapy massage, deep-tissue massage; body scrub, herbal or seaweed wrap. **Swimming:** 2 pools, ocean beach. **Classes and Programs:** Fitness evaluation, nutrition consultation, personal training and exercise video. **Recreation:** Biking, golf, horseback trail rides with lunch or evening cookout, skeet shooting, tennis; boating, sea kayaking, windsurfing. **Children's Programs:** Kids' fitness classes during holidays. Teenage golf clinic. Supervised program for ages 3–11 daily and evenings during spring, summer, and holidays.

ACCOMMODATIONS

262 rooms.

3 meals daily, included in spa package. Buffet meals available at Sea Island Beach Club; à la carte menu at Dining Room. **Sample Meals:** Buffet salads with accompaniments, soups, fruit salad (with cottage cheese or yogurt), sandwiches (club, grilled cheese, peanut butter and jelly), hamburgers (lunch); escargot, shrimp cocktail, caviar, seafood bisque and other soups, tossed green salad or baby romaine with crabmeat and avocado, spinach-and-basil ravioli, venison chops, grilled tournedos of veal vindaloo, pan-seared red snapper (dinner).

Spa package priced per day (minimum stay 3 nights), $418–$636 single, $326–$435 per person double. For cottage renters: 3-day spa retreat (without lodging) $480, 5-day Signature Spa Experience $800. $300 deposit required. No credit cards.

⊠ *Sea Island, GA 31561,* ☎ *912/638–3611 or 800/732–4752,* ℻ *912/638–5814.*

From Jacksonville: I–95 north, Exit 6, east on Hwy. 17 (70 mi).

KENTUCKY

FOXHOLLOW

Holistic health
Luxury pampering

Bluegrass country's only holistic health farm has everything to revitalize you except horseback riding. Set on a tranquil, rural Kentucky estate, the spa at Foxhollow has hydrotherapy in a sunlit manor house, Ayurvedic treatments, and a vast array of sophisticated, global, orthodox and complementary healing arts.

Foxhollow sprang from owner Mary Shand's personal experience as a holistic health advocate. Recognizing the need to provide a place where a full spirit can help the body and mind respond to life's challenges, Shand assembled several properties around her 1,300-acre family farm to create a wellness center and life enrichment retreat. Approached down a long lane lined by dogwood trees, the health complex now includes a modern clinic where you can consult practitioners of complementary medicine and homeopathics, exercise, and attend lectures at a learning center that is equipped with computers for health research. Housed in the airy clinic are a pediatrician, chiropractor, nutritionist, dentist, and family physician. An alliance with a Swiss center is being forged, in order to establish exchange programs and bring European specialists for workshops.

Lodged in a turn-of-the-century farmhouse (the Manor House) set in formal gardens, you enjoy modern comforts and gourmet vegetarian meals. A large living room is stocked with health magazines and adventure books to read in front of the fireplace. An adjoining library holds TV and folk art from the Shand collection of Kentucky crafts. Wander into the kitchen and the chef offers you coffee, herbal tea, and freshly baked cookies. The charming guest rooms have warm comforters on the beds, original paintings, and heirloom antiques as well as bouquets of fresh flowers. Manor House rooms have king-size or double beds and a reading chair upholstered in floral chintz, and all but one have a private bathroom. Single-story cottages a short walk from the main house have two beds and a living room with fireplace. Each unit has a phone and air-conditioning.

Overnight accommodations on a bed-and-breakfast basis are available, as are spa packages. Weekend and full-week programs include treatments and consultation. Day spa packages for men and women include a vegetarian lunch. Appointments for spa therapies are made at the Wetlands, a nearby farm converted to provide private facilities for aromatherapy massage, body wraps, and a hydrotherapy tub. An outdoor swimming pool and hot tub, organic gardening greenhouse, and demonstration kitchen are used in classes scheduled daily. Lunch is prepared and served here for day spa package guests as well as residents of the area. Complimentary transportation links the two centers, or you can hike on a woodland nature trail.

Wellness therapies are the house specialty. In addition to traditional Ayurvedic herbal treatments from India, the spa offers FloraSpa therapies incorporating lymphatic drainage and acupressure with French essential oils and seaweed extracts. Adhering to ancient Chinese medicine and holistic theories, the FloraSpa massages, body treatments, and inhalation therapies support energy balancing, relaxation, and stress relief. Staff therapists explain each step of the process and bring refreshing beverages so that you don't get dehydrated during the detoxification process.

Enhancing the experience are the rural setting and access to big-city attractions. Thoroughbreds canter outside a massage room and at Churchill Downs and its mesmerizing museum of racing. A stream runs through the woodlands, where you can pause and meditate on a hike with the resident naturalist. Evenings are convivial in the dining room, and you may wind up at a symphony concert downtown. In addition to the weekend retreats and six-night wellness programs, Foxhollow offers winter escapes on a Bahamian island. This is natural therapy at its best.

FACILITIES
Exercise Equipment: Stationary bikes, treadmills, trampolines, weight-training units, free weights. **Services:** Aromatherapy massage, reflexology, shiatsu, Swedish massage; herbal or seaweed wrap, iridology; hydrotherapy. **Swimming:** Pool. **Classes and Programs:** Aquaerobics, meditation, personal training, Pilates, yoga. Classes in vegetarian cooking, pottery, organic gardening, herbal healing, holistic health, Oriental healing. **Recreation:** Hiking, biking; golf and horseback riding nearby.

ACCOMMODATIONS
19 rooms, 6 cottages.

DINING
Single menu served at Manor House and Wetlands Spa, modified on request. Mainly vegetarian, with fish options. **Sample Meals:** Corn tortilla soup, spinach salad with goat cheese and sun-dried tomatoes, tempeh tacos with Mexican rice, berries with Devon cream (lunch); roasted garlic with Saga bleu cheese, roasted red-pepper soup, Caesar salad with salmon, red-lentil cakes, asparagus, carob-almond tart (dinner).

RATES AND PACKAGES
2-night Weekend packages from $400, Anti-aging 2-night package from $700, Medical Wellness 2-night program $800. Half-day spa package $150, full day $16–$250. MC, V.

DIRECTIONS
✉ *8909 Highway 329, Crestwood, KY 40014,* ☎ *502/241–8621 or 800/ 624–7080,* FAX *502/241–3935.*

From Louisville: I–71 to exit 14 (Crestwood), left on Highway 329 for 2.3 miles to driveway on the right (25 mins).

NORTH CAROLINA

DUKE UNIVERSITY DIET AND FITNESS CENTER

Nutrition and diet

For more than 30 years, the Duke Diet and Fitness Center (DFC) has developed a successful track record in weight and health management. People from all walks of life—young and old, beginners and returnees—come here to combat obesity and change their lives. Designed to help you address the underlying causes of your physical and weight problems, the two- to four-week medically supervised and regimented program can require stressful adjustments to assure a healthier lifestyle. One-week fitness-oriented getaways are also offered.

Housed in a former school that has an indoor exercise pool and a fully equipped gym with cardiovascular and strength-training machines, the program includes lectures, exercise sessions, and medical services as well as personal and group counseling. Starting with a physical examination Monday morning (including testing, treadmill exercise, and body-composition evaluation) and personal assessments, the specialized faculty of physicians, dieticians, and psychologists sets up a schedule based on your fitness level and personal interests. Choices range from workshops on stress management to cooking classes, fitness training to psychological counseling. The daily schedule keeps you busy from 8 AM through dinner. Massage services are available at the DFC, for an additional fee, to help you cope with stress and food obsession. Weekends and evenings provide opportunities to explore the area and take in sports events and entertainment, with group outings organized by the DFC for a modest supplement. Home-study materials are provided in a thick binder full of tips on how to continue the DFC regimen at your own pace.

Learning strategies for lifestyle change and long-term success keeps you busy in classrooms, as well as on excursions to a supermarket and restaurant. Smokers can enroll in a special program to kick the habit. Family members or close friends can accompany program participants to make the transition easier. (After receiving medical clearance, companions may participate in most of the daily activities offered at the DFC.) Despite less than ideal facilities, the program achieves impressive success rates, thanks largely to the dedicated staff under Dr. Michael A. Hamilton, DFC's long-time director.

Duke University's medical campus provides additional facilities and programs, which are slated to eventually include a hotel and new home for the Diet and Fitness Center. Until then, program participants must secure accommodations in the area; lists of apartment rentals are provided, or you can stay across the street in a suite (bedroom, living room, and kitchen) at the Duke Tower hotel. Meals, however, are strictly controlled in the DFC cafeteria, which offers bland food in small portions, served under the most basic conditions.

Downtown, the new Athletic Park sparkles, while the old Bull Durham ballfield, seen in the 1986 film of the same name, now hosts jazz concerts and soccer games. Tellingly, former tobacco warehouses have been converted to upscale condominiums and shopping arcades. Golfers can play the lush course at Washington Duke Inn on campus, and the grand old Carolina Theater houses a lively season of shows and concerts.

FACILITIES

Exercise Equipment: Rowing machines, stair climber, stationary bikes, treadmills, weight-training circuit, free weights. **Services:** Massage. **Swimming: Indoor pool. **Classes and Programs:** Body-composition testing, career counseling, personal training, psychotherapy, swimming instruction. Lectures by outside specialists, such as image consultants and dance instructors. **Recreation:** Basketball, volleyball. Golf, fishing, tennis nearby. Duke University performing arts and cultural programs.

ACCOMMODATIONS

Rooms in local inns. Duke Tower from $65 per night. Rooms in private homes $75–$110 per week.

DINING

3 low-calorie, portion-controlled meals daily at center provide 800- to 1,500-calorie diet high in complex carbohydrates, moderate in protein, low in sodium, fat, and cholesterol. Vegetarian and kosher diets accommodated. **Sample Meals:** Seafood gumbo with rice, lamb stew, or eggplant Parmesan (lunch); Italian baked fish, barbecued chicken, or black-bean tortillas (dinner).

RATES AND PACKAGES

1-week program $2,495, 2-week program $3,895, 4-week program $5,595. $500 refundable deposit required. AE, D, DC, MC, V.

DIRECTIONS

✉ *804 W. Trinity Ave., Durham, NC 27701,* ☎ *919/684–6331 or 800/ 362–8446,* ℻ *919/688–2552.*

From Raleigh-Durham Airport: I–40 to Durham Freeway (Route 147), exit at Duke Street, right on Trinity Avenue (20 mins).

STRUCTURE HOUSE

Nutrition and diet

Founded in 1977, Structure House provides an informal, residential environment for serious weight control and lifestyle change. More than 40 qualified professionals focus on behavior modification and help you to understand and overcome unhealthy lifestyles and obesity. Founder/director Gerard J. Musante, Ph.D., developed his techniques as a consulting professor at Duke University and succeeded in losing 50 pounds. Through his experience, he evolved his concept of holistic health education.

Your stay begins with a consultation about available services and programs; an individual diet and exercise regimen is planned with you. Those with diabetes, hypertension, or cardiac conditions are monitored. In order not to duplicate medical costs, and to better serve health needs, the medical staff consults with participants' home physicians.

Life at Structure House centers in a large, Georgian-style building where dining, classes, and professional services are scheduled in an atmosphere that is more college campus than resort. The spacious Life Extension Center houses classrooms and exercise facilities, where equipment and instructors equal those of many leading spa resorts. Join an aerobics class, try aquacise in the indoor and outdoor swimming pools, or set your own pace on walking trails around the wooded 21-acre campus.

Housing, in apartments in 10 two-story on-campus houses with porches, includes washer/dryer, linens, phone, TV, and weekly maid service. Participants often feel they're in a small, friendly, supportive, self-contained community. Men account for 40% of the campus residents.

A four-week program is recommended for best results. While most participants come alone, some bring a spouse or family support member, even a pet. Alumni often return for reinforcement visits, qualifying for reduced rates.

The emphasis on the psychological and emotional aspects of weight control, along with diet and exercise programs, makes the Structure House experience particularly effective.

FACILITIES
Exercise Equipment: Elliptical trainer, stair climbers, stationary bikes, treadmills, weight-training circuit, free weights. **Services:** Deep-tissue massage, Swedish massage, Trager massage; polarity therapy. **Swimming:** 2 pools (1 indoor); lakes nearby. **Classes and Programs:** Medical consultation and testing, consultation with clinical psychologist, dietary reeducation workshops. **Recreation:** Badminton, basketball, golf, Ping-Pong, tennis; golf, horseback riding nearby. Occasional parties.

ACCOMMODATIONS
76 1- and 2-bedroom apartments.

DINING
Selections from weekly menus that guests plan for themselves. Suggested 1,000-calorie menu. **Sample Meals:** 3-cheese quiche, chef's salad, bean chowder (lunch); baked chicken, filet mignon, or sea scallops in wine (dinner).

RATES AND PACKAGES
1 week $1,799 single, $1,645 per person double, for all-inclusive program and lodging. 2 weeks $3,598 single, $3,290 double; 4 weeks $7,196 single, $6,580 double. Returnee 1-week program $993 single, $839 sharing. $500-per-person deposit required. MC, V.

DIRECTIONS
✉ *3017 Pickett Rd., Durham, NC 27705,* ☎ *919/493–4205 or 800/553–0052,* ℻ *919/490–0191.*

From Raleigh-Durham Airport: I–40 west (20 mins to Structure House).

WESTGLOW SPA

Luxury pampering
Nutrition and diet

Seduced by the siren call of the Blue Ridge Mountains, you may find staying indoors difficult at this spa cum mountain mansion. The charms here go beyond body treatments, creating a healthy glow for your spirit.

Set on a 20-acre estate, Westglow was built in 1916 as a summer home by artist Elliot Dangerfield. The gracious, Colonial-style structure looks west onto Grandfather Mountain; the panoramic, breathtaking view inspired the mansion's name. Dangerfield's art studio became the spa when current owner Glynda McPheter converted Westglow into an intimate, polished country inn. Vintage furnishings, Oriental rugs, and a large library retain the mansion's classic Southern elegance, though modern bathrooms and amenities were added in 1989. Eight guest rooms and the spa's main dining facility are housed here, and the glow of Blue Ridge sunsets and gold-flecked sunrises brightens each room. Additional accommodations are found in two new guest cottages equipped with kitchenette, fireplace, air-conditioning, TV, and phone.

Bathed in light, the spa has an indoor swimming pool, men's and women's whirlpools, dry sauna, six body treatment rooms, a salon for hair and nail care, a Cybex equipment room, aerobics studio, and poolside café. Health and beauty services range from fitness and nutritional training to massage and body therapy; a daily schedule of classes is posted, though the staff will also do training and aquatics on request. The Brain Gym fosters body movements that integrate the functions of the brain, helping the body realize what the mind wants. Personal services are included in day spa packages, as well as overnight programs, and can be alternated with hiking excursions.

Don't expect a hard-core schedule of advanced classes and activities. Devise your own plan and enjoy the glory of being here. Miles of forest provide an opportunity to hike or cycle. Mountain bikes can be rented in the area, and trails abound. You can also take a rafting trip in nearby white-water rapids or go canoeing. Arrangements can be made nearby for horseback riding, golf, and in winter, downhill skiing.

Attention has been paid to a healthy diet, not easily found in Southern resorts. McPheters teaches low-fat cooking, and spa guests get to taste the results, Beautifully presented, each item is prepared to order and served on fine china. Continental cuisine also is available. At night, climb the grand staircase to your room, settle into a white linen–covered bed, and enjoy the quiet.

FACILITIES

Exercise Equipment: Stair climber, stationary bikes, weight-training circuit, free weights. **Services:** Aromatherapy massage, deep-tissue massage, Swedish massage; body scrub, cellulite/lymphatic drainage, herbal wrap, reflexology; facial. **Swimming:** Indoor pool. **Classes and Programs:** Fitness assessment, nutrition and diet consultation, personal training. **Recreation:** Biking, hiking, tennis; canoeing, golf, horseback riding, rafting, and skiing nearby.

ACCOMMODATIONS

8 rooms in main house, 2 cottages with 1–2 bedrooms.

DINING

3 meals daily included in 2- to 7-night packages. **Sample Meals:** Sweet-and-sour soup, sliced pork tenderloin on wheat bread (lunch); vegetarian platter, baked chicken, or mountain trout with couscous (dinner).

RATES AND PACKAGES

2-night package $715–$917; 7-night package $2,140–$2,772; day spa package with lunch (no lodging) $120–$250. Gratuities included. 50% deposit required. MC, V.

DIRECTIONS

✉ *Hwy. 221 S, Box 1083, Blowing Rock, NC 28605,* ☎ *704/295–4463 or 800/562–0807,* ℻ *704/295–5115.*

From Charlotte: I–77 north, I–40 west to exit 123, Highway 321 north to Blowing Rock Bypass exit for Sunset Boulevard, Main Street to Highway 221 south (2½ hrs).

SOUTH CAROLINA

HILTON HEAD HEALTH INSTITUTE

Medical wellness
Nutrition and diet

Since 1976, the concentrated courses held here have taught participants how to modify their behavior in order to achieve practical results, whether they be changing daily life and work habits, maintaining weight, stopping smoking, or managing stress. The highly structured program has a maximum of 40 participants; you can stay as many weeks as needed to gain control of problems, but the program and facilities are not designed for vacations.

Health education begins with an understanding of your body. Lectures, workshops, exercise classes, and meals designed to advance that understanding are scheduled in the institute's main building, a short walk from your living quarters. The effect of nutrition and exercise on the body's metabolism and the effect of stress on productivity and health are taught by a team of psychologists, nutritionists, and physical fitness specialists.

The delightful climate; 12 miles of white, sandy beach; and ample walking and biking trails through local nature preserves go far to enhance and renew the spirit. Other activities center on a campuslike cluster of Low Country cottages, which have traditional furniture, fine fabrics, a private porch, and color TV. Each participant has a private bedroom and bath and shares the living room and fully equipped cooking and laundry facilities with another person in the program. The structured, nutritionally balanced meal plan is based on the New Hilton Head Metabolism Diet. The medically supervised programs are suited for individuals and couples who have reached a point in their lives where change is necessary, and they need a boost to get started.

FACILITIES
Exercise Equipment: Stair climbers, stationary bikes, treadmills. **Services:** Massage, facials. **Swimming:** Pool, ocean beach. **Recreation:** Hiking, biking; tennis and golf nearby.

ACCOMMODATIONS
40 villas.

DINING
3 meals and 2 "Metabo" meals daily. **Sample Meals:** Pasta primavera with raw vegetables (lunch); chicken enchilada with salsa and brown rice (dinner).

RATES AND PACKAGES
8-day/7-night program (Sun.–Sun.) $1,705–$1,895; Discounts available for returning guests. MC, V.

DIRECTIONS
⊠ *Box 7138, Hilton Head Island, SC 29938,* ☎ *803/785–7292 or 800/ 292–2440; 800/348–2039 in Canada,* ℻ *803/686–5659.*

From Savannah: I–95 to Route 278 (50 mins).

HILTON HEAD WESTIN RESORT

Sports conditioning

Beachfront fitness clubs are hard to find in the Carolina lowlands, but the Westin Resort stands among the best on the Atlantic Coast. As a special amenity to enhance your getaway or business meeting, the resort's Spectrum Health Club provides an environment conducive to wellness.

In the health club you can cross-train for specific sports on a Cybex strength system. Equipment, classes, and personal trainers are available daily. Mornings may begin with a beach walk, led by a staff member. Invigorated by sun, sea, and air, you can join an exercise group in Reebok Step aerobics, aquacise in the pool, Resist-a-Ball toning, or muscle flexibility training. Comprehensive fitness testing is available by appointment.

Workouts in the mirrored cardiovascular training room are enhanced by sea views and, in season, passing dolphin. The oceanfront aerobics/exercise room has a patented Exerflex hardwood floor system. There are three swimming pools on the beach; one is glass-enclosed for year-round swimming and water aerobics classes. Staying in the hotel gives you full run of the club facilities for $6 per day, including a sauna misted with eucalyptus oils and three outdoor whirlpools. Although no spa package is available, appointments can be made for massage services. Located in the Port Royal Plantation, the resort also sports three PGA championship golf courses and a 16-court tennis facility.

Dining choices in the oceanview Barony Restaurant range from Low Country seafood specialties to a selection of low-cholesterol items spiced instead of salted. The Carolina Cafe buffet serves breakfast, lunch, and dinner.

Refreshed after recent renovations, the hotel's 442 guest rooms—with balconies, separate dressing areas, hair dryers, and large baths—reflect the glow of ocean light. Furnishings and architecture are reminiscent of grand Southern homes. Staying at the hotel's Royal Beach Club earns you extra amenities and access to a well-stocked lounge.

The Atlantic's warm Gulf Stream current ensures a balmy atmosphere most of the year. Casual and romantic, this is a place that makes you feel well by simply being here.

FACILITIES
Exercise Equipment: Cross-country ski track, rowing machine, stair climbers, stationary bike, weight-training circuit, free weights. **Services:** Massage. **Swimming:** 3 pools (1 indoor), ocean beach. **Classes and Programs:** Fitness testing, golf and tennis clinics, resort entertainment. **Recreation:** Croquet, golf, tennis, volleyball, water polo; horseback riding, windsurfing, sailing, and fishing nearby. **Children's Programs:** Kids Korner with arts and crafts, games, pool, and water activities morning and evening May–Sept., Nov.–Apr.

ACCOMMODATIONS
382 rooms, 30 suites.

DINING
All meals à la carte. **Sample Meals:** Charleston she-crab soup with aged sherry, Caesar salad, poached salmon with dill cream and cucumber salad (lunch); free-range chicken with black-pepper pasta and chanterelle mushroom sauce, sautéed shrimp Provençale over angel-hair pasta, broiled fish of the day (dinner).

RATES AND PACKAGES
$240–$380 for 2 in summer; Royal Beach Club $400 per couple. Suites $400–$2,000. Golf and tennis packages available. 1-night credit-card deposit required. AE, DC, MC, V.

DIRECTIONS
✉ *2 Grasslawn Ave., Hilton Head Island, SC 29928,* ☎ *803/681–4000 or 800/228–3000,* 𝔽𝔸𝕏 *803/681–1087.*

From Savannah: I–95 to Hardeeville, Route 278 (50 mins).

TENNESSEE

TENNESSEE FITNESS SPA

Nutrition and diet

Get back to nature and back in shape at this no-frills mountain camp, open mid-February–November. The Tennessee Fitness Spa organizes swimnastics, canoeing, bike rides, and walks through the scenic Great Smoky Mountains in a program designed to produce weight loss.

Regularly scheduled classes on nutrition are held in the natural stone dining hall, where the spa chef demonstrates how to cook meals that are low in fat, sodium, and sugar. Most guests are concerned with weight management, and some come for several months to develop a workable weight-loss regimen that they can continue at home.

Guests, who range in age from 20 to 70, join a group leader for a 7 AM hill walk, a 2½-mile warmup followed by stretch class and aerobics. The daily schedule rotates among step aerobics, line dancing, aquacise, floor work, and lectures. Cross-training can be followed by a volleyball game or a soak in the big hot tub. Personal services, such as massages and facials, are optional extras.

Housing choices include standard rooms (two have four beds) in six two-story wooden chalets, a penthouse, and new lake-view cottages that have four-bedroom apartments. All are simply furnished and provide a choice of a full-size bed or twins. Phones are available on request.

Casual and friendly staff members are noted for creating group support and camaraderie, which adds to the fun as you shed pounds together.

FACILITIES
Exercise Equipment: Stair climbers, stationary bikes, treadmills, free weights. **Services:** Massage, facial. **Swimming:** Pool. **Recreation:** Biking, hiking, fishing, racquetball, volleyball; horseback riding and canoe rental nearby. Pool games, movies, country line-dancing.

ACCOMMODATIONS
32 rooms, 1 4-bedroom house.

DINING
3 meals daily included in program, low in fat, sodium, and sugar. **Sample Meals:** Vegetarian pizza, stir-fry, or black beans and rice (lunch); orange roughy, chicken enchiladas, or turkey burgers (dinner).

RATES AND PACKAGES
$950 per week single including meals and program, $650 per person double; $550 per person for 4 sharing room and bath. $100 deposit required. AE, D, MC, V.

DIRECTIONS
✉ *299 Natural Bridge Park Rd., Waynesboro, TN 38485,* ☎ *931/722–5589 or 800/235–8365,* FAX *931/722–9113.*

From Nashville: I–65 south, Exit 46 west through Columbia, Highway 412 to Hohenwald, Route 20 to Highway 99 southwest (2 hrs).

VIRGINIA

HARTLAND WELLNESS CENTER

Medical wellness
Nutrition and diet

Motivation through diet, exercise, and prayer is the prescription for wellness at this Blue Ridge Mountains retreat. Hartland's long-established 10- to 18-day program teaches you how to overcome physical and emotional obstacles to a healthy lifestyle through practical nutritional instruction, private and group counseling, and physical therapy, guided by a team of physicians, dietitians, educators, chaplains, and therapists who focus on disease prevention.

Doctors and staff are all Seventh-Day Adventists, although the program is nondenominational and nonsectarian. Their specific recommendations for diet take into account your physical condition, nutritional requirements, and personal goals. (Meals at the center are vegan.) Heart disease, arthritis, cancer, diabetes, obesity, addictions, and digestive disorders are among the diseases addressed by the team of specialists.

Your personalized schedule begins with a daily check of vital signs and weight, followed by breakfast. Group exercises and lectures, aquatic therapy in the pool, individual counseling sessions, cooking class, hydrotherapy, and massage fill out the balance of the day.

The highly structured, intensive live-in program is offered in an elegant, two-story hotel-style building near Hartland College. Accommodations have antique furnishings, a cherry-wood dresser and bed, individual temperature control, and a scenic view. Ten rooms have two queen-size beds, whereas the rest have only one. Because it's situated on a 760-acre estate in the foothills of the Blue Ridge Mountains, the Hartland has extensive nature trails where you are encouraged to walk daily. There is an indoor swimming pool and limited exercise equipment for your free time. Spouses are encouraged to participate at a reduced fee.

The center's safe, self-contained environment for lodging, meals, and treatments appeals to mature dieters seeking a new start.

FACILITIES
Exercise Equipment: Stationary bikes, treadmill, weight-training circuit. **Services:** Massage, hydrotherapy. **Swimming:** Indoor pool. **Classes and Programs:** Stress-management classes, exercise counseling, smoking-cessation program, cardiac and cancer rehabilitation, medical tests, physician and nurse counseling, hands-on vegetarian cooking instruction, weight-control counseling, spiritual guidance, social events. **Recreation:** Hiking.

ACCOMMODATIONS
15 rooms.

DINING
3 vegan meals daily. **Sample Meals:** Baked tofu loaf, steamed vegetables, baked potato, and homemade bread (lunch); banana smoothie, fruit salad, ice cream (dinner).

RATES AND PACKAGES
10-day program $1,995, 18-day program $2,995. Deposit: 50% of program fee. MC, V.

DIRECTIONS

✉ *Box 1, Rapidan, VA 22733,* ☎ *540/672–3100 or 800/763–9355,* FAX *540/672–2584.*

From Washington, DC: I–66 to Lee Highway (Route 29 South to 3rd Culpeper exit, Route 15 toward Orange, to Route 614 West (about 2 hrs).

THE HOMESTEAD

Luxury pampering
Mineral springs

Step back to an era of gracious Southern hospitality, when families vacationed here and high society arrived by private train to take the waters. The mineral springs that made the Homestead famous as long ago as 1766 still gush in front of the Bath House (built in 1892 and renovated 1994–97). In the 1840s, bathing here was advertised as a panacea for just about anything that ailed you. Such claims fell out of fashion, but the Homestead endures.

Furnished with 1920s-style wicker furniture and flowered-chintz draperies, the spa still has huge marble tubs for mineral-water soaks, plus an Olympic-size indoor swimming pool, built in 1903. The pool hasn't changed since the current Homestead building opened. Light pours in from giant windows, creating an airy greenhouse effect. Hot springs continually circulate water, so the temperature hovers around 88°F. In contrast, a new fitness center upstairs offers aerobics, an array of cardiovascular and weight-resistance conditioning equipment, and a spectacular view of the grounds.

Relaxation therapy begins with a private soak in one of the marble tubs. The naturally heated thermal water, high in sulfur, magnesium, and 16 other minerals, reaches your tub at 104°F and overflows to keep the temperature constant. After a few minutes in the sauna or steam room (the men's side has a Turkish bath), you're led to a marble slab for a rubdown with coarse salt, then hosed off in the Scotch spray (hot and cold shower). After cooling down, you're treated to a massage by a real pro. The treatment, which originated here more than 100 years ago, is called Dr. Goode's Spout Bath and costs $25 . Other spa services, from aromatherapy to hairstyling, are available in the fourth-floor health and beauty salon.

Following a fire in 1901, the hotel was rebuilt in brick, with white columned verandas and the Georgian-style tower that's become a landmark in the "valley of the waters." An east wing was added just before World War I and later used to intern diplomats of countries at war with the United States. The modern south wing opened in 1973, signaling a new era of conferences and meetings. The spa building got a makeover, and new aromatherapy treatments were added, but much of the original remains. Unfortunately, nostalgia doesn't always come with a great massage, so call ahead to assure an appointment with a therapist who suits your needs.

Three golf courses and 12 tennis courts, playable most of the year, are big outdoor attractions. Sam Snead describes the Cascades Course as "America's finest mountain course," particularly for the low handicapper. Other recreation includes horseback riding, mountain trout fishing, archery, and trap shooting. Surrounded by a 15,000-acre mountain preserve, the Homestead has miles of hiking trails. In winter, snowmaking equipment prepares slopes for downhill skiing, and trails are groomed for cross-country skiing.

By day's end you may well be played out, but there's a dinner dance in the capacious old dining room as well as a multicourse menu that will put a serious dent in your diet, though the food doesn't always live up to the menu's promise. Finally, you can retreat to your room, either in the main section and tower, built 1902–1929, or in the newer, conference-oriented south wing. The choicest rooms with the best views of the surrounding mountains are in the tower. Furnishings include mahogany bedsteads, writing tables, lounge chairs, lacy white curtains, and damask draperies. Some rooms have French doors that open onto a private balcony or screened porch, fireplace, and walk-in closet. All are air-conditioned and come equipped with TV, telephone, and a large tiled bathroom.

Each season has special appeal, from blossoming spring dogwood to blazing fall foliage. Legendary for its Southern hospitality, the hotel looks like a set from *Brigadoon,* its redbrick castle with tower trimmed in white, framed by the deep green-blue colors of the Blue Ridge Mountains. Arriving in the Great Hall, flanked by 16 stately Corinthian columns, guests are treated to afternoon tea as a trio entertains with music of a quieter, gentler era. You can easily picture Thomas Jefferson rejuvenating himself in the warm springs pool, simultaneously concocting plans for a wooden covering and for the nation's independence. Even today, despite the resort's rambling size and erstwhile conventions, the Homestead makes you feel at home.

FACILITIES
Exercise Equipment: Rowing machine, treadmills, weight-training circuit, free weights. **Services:** Aromatherapy massage, Swedish massage; herbal wrap, loofah body scrub; aromatherapy bath, mineral tub, therapeutic whirlpool. **Swimming:** 3 pools (1 indoor). **Recreation:** Archery, fishing, golf, hiking, horseback riding, lawn bowling, skeet and trap shooting, tennis; cross-country and downhill skiing, ice-skating. Carriage rides, dancing, movies. **Children's Programs:** Children's lessons in swimming, tennis, and skiing; supervised playroom (summer only) and outdoor activities at spa building (fee).

ACCOMMODATIONS
432 rooms, 81 suites.

DINING
The Modified American Plan includes breakfast and dinner. **Sample Meals:** Virginia ham stuffed with greens, or roast beef with farm produce (lunch); sautéed whole trout (dinner).

RATES AND PACKAGES
MAP (2 meals daily) single $205–$410, $132–$235 double. Children with adults free through age 4, $39 age 5–12, $60 age 13–18. Packages for golf and tennis. $250 deposit required. AE, D, DC, MC, V.

DIRECTIONS
✉ *Box 2000, Hot Springs, VA 24445,* ☎ *540/839–1776 or 800/838–1776,* ℻ *540/839–7670.*

From Washington, DC: I–66 west to I–81, at Mt. Crawford Exit, Routes 257 and 42 to Goshen, Route 39 to Warm Springs, Route 220 south to Hot Springs (about 6 hrs).

THE KINGSMILL RESORT

Luxury pampering
Sports conditioning

Bring your golf clubs, your tennis racket, and your kids, because fun and fitness are on tap in equal measure at this resort. Nestled amid lush, green woodlands on the banks of the historic James River, Kingsmill makes an ideal base from which to explore Busch Gardens, Colonial Williamsburg, the scenic Tidewater area, and Atlantic beaches. Built and managed by Anheuser-Busch, the 2,900-acre resort is part of a gated residential community, complete with marina and Virginia's largest golf resort. Golfers play the Woods Course, designed by Tom Clark and Curtis Strange; the River Course, designed by Pete Dye; the Plantation Course, designed by Arnold Palmer; or a nine-hole course.

The Sports Club provides a light-filled, dedicated fitness environment. Workouts on state-of-the-art cardiovascular and weight-training equipment, one-on-one training, and indoor and outdoor swimming pools are available to all resort guests at no additional charge. There are racquetball courts, saunas, steam rooms, whirlpools, and a game room. Spa services are scheduled à la carte or in day or half-day packages. When you're ready to explore Colonial Williamsburg or Busch Gardens, the resort shuttle bus provides complimentary transportation.

Staying in one of the two-story lodges that border the river and golf courses, you gain access to a world of upscale pleasures. Villas have one–three bedrooms with king- or queen-size beds and color cable TV, and some have complete kitchens and living rooms with fireplace.

Kingsmill Resort possesses both cosmopolitan sophistication and Colonial gentility. It's big enough so corporate conferences and vacationers needn't mix. Dining ranges from formal at the river-view Bray Dining Room to casual at the Sports Club's grill and a tavern at the country club. The atmosphere is more residential than resort, and if you enjoy planning your own program, the elements are all here.

FACILITIES
Exercise Equipment: Cross-country ski machine, rowing machines, stair climbers, stationary bikes, treadmills, weigh-training circuit, free weights. **Services:** Massage, seaweed wrap, mud treatments, facial. **Swimming:** 2 pools (1 indoor). **Classes and Programs:** Aerobics, aquaerobics. **Recreation:** Billiards, golf, racquetball, shuffleboard, tennis. **Children's Programs:** Kamper summer program (ages 5–12).

ACCOMMODATIONS
400 rooms and suites.

DINING
À la carte meals in Sports Club and Bray Dining Room. **Sample Meals:** Blue crab, corn chowder, Michelob shrimp (lunch); honey-glazed salmon with corn cakes and asparagus, seafood stew in spicy wine-tomato sauce (dinner).

RATES AND PACKAGES
Seasonal pricing. $129–$176 per day single/double occupancy for guest room, $434–$571 for up to 6 adults in 3-bedroom suite in Riverview Rooms. Golf Academy package with accommodations $145–$163 per person, double; suite $163–$180. 5-day package with admission to Colonial Williamsburg and other attractions $805–$1,165 for 2 in room, $1,165–$3,811 in suite. AE, D, DC, MC, V.

✉ *1010 Kingsmill Rd., Williamsburg, VA 23185,* ☎ *757/253–1703 or 800/832–5665,* FAX *757/253–1703.*

From Washington, DC: I–95 south to I–64 east, Exit 242-A to Route 199W (3 hrs).

TAZEWELL CLUB

Luxury pampering
Sports conditioning

Trekking through Colonial America's best-known restoration will earn you a much-needed massage at the Williamsburg Lodge's Tazewell Club. And like everything in Colonial Williamsburg, it's a first-class facility programmed for family enjoyment.

Facing a golf course, the Tazewell Club is minutes from the 173-acre historic area. The workout area has views of the surrounding valley, once part of an estate belonging to a Colonial patriot. Since there wasn't much pampering in 18th-century life, the mood here is modern. Designed for newcomers as well as fitness buffs, the facilities include strength-training equipment and an aerobics studio. Low-impact aerobics classes are taught on weekdays, aquaerobics morning and night three times a week. The swimming pool, which opens onto a sundeck, is popular with families, but certain hours are reserved for lap swimmers. Pool hours are extended to 10 PM Friday and Sunday, allowing you to spend a full day touring the historic area or enjoying golf and tennis. (Nearby are two Robert Trent Jones golf courses, eight tennis courts, a croquet court, bowling green, and two outdoor swimming pools.) The spa, with separate saunas, steam rooms, and whirlpools for men and women as well as a private massage areas, is on the same floor. Try a loofah body scrub or massage and then join the revelry at the State House. Personal services, court time, and greens fees are extra.

Although there are some Tazewell Club guest rooms in the Williamsburg Lodge, admission to the club is complimentary if you stay in any of the five hotels—such as the Williamsburg Inn, a short walk away—or restored Colonial houses operated by the Colonial Williamsburg Foundation. Two deluxe suites with Jacuzzi, fireplace, wet bar, and private balcony are on the penthouse level of the club. All units are air-conditioned and have TV and phone.

FACILITIES
Exercise Equipment: Rowing machines, stationary bikes, treadmills. **Services:** Massage, loofah scrub, herbal wrap, facial. **Swimming:** 2 pools. **Classes and Programs:** Aquaerobics. **Recreation:** Badminton, biking, croquet, golf, lawn bowling, miniature golf, tennis, volleyball. 18th-century concerts, tavern entertainment, Shakespeare productions.

ACCOMMODATIONS
25 Tazewell Club rooms and 2 suites in Williamsburg Lodge, 235 rooms in Williamsburg Inn, 85 rooms in Colonial homes.

DINING
No meals at the Tazewell Club, but guests can charge meals at historic area restaurants to their rooms. Chesapeake Bay specialties are available as part of the Friday seafood buffet at the Williamsburg Lodge. Other options include the Regency Dining Room (jacket and tie required) at the Williamsburg Inn. Traditional tavern fare is served at the King's Arms, Christiana Campbell's, and Josiah Chowning's. **Sample Meals:** Peanut

In case you want to see the world.

At American Express, we're here to make your journey a smooth one. So we have over 1,700 travel service locations in over 120 countries ready to help. What else would you expect from the world's largest travel agency?

do more ®

AMERICAN EXPRESS

http://www.americanexpress.com/travel

Travel

In case you want to be welcomed there.

We're here to see that you're always welcomed at establishments everywhere. That's why millions of people carry the American Express® Card – for peace of mind, confidence, and security, around the world or just around the corner.

do more Cards

In case you're running low.

We're here to help with more than 118,000 Express Cash locations around the world. In order to enroll, just call American Express before you start your vacation.

do more

Express Cash

And just in case.

We're here with American Express® Travelers Cheques and Cheques _for Two_.® They're the safest way to carry money on your vacation and the surest way to get a refund, practically anywhere, anytime.

Another way we help you...

do more ®

Travelers Cheques

soup, stuffed trout (lunch); Chesapeake crabmeat sautéed in wine, picatta of shrimp and veal, scaloppine of lamb with garlic (dinner).

Daily rate in Tazewell wing $195–$235 single or double; regular lodge rooms $139–$189; suites $450 for 1–4. Williamsburg Inn room $265–$395, suites $525–$750 for 2. Colonial House rooms $160–$505. 1-night deposit required. AE, D, DC, MC, V.

✉ *Williamsburg Lodge, 310 South England St., Williamsburg, VA 23187,* ☎ *757/229–1000 or 800/447–8679,* FAX *757/221–8797.*

From Washington, DC: I–95 south to I–64 east (3 hrs).

YOGAVILLE

Holistic health

Its name says it all: At this spiritual community, meditation and yoga provide the central focus of daily life. A permanent community in the beautiful James River valley near Charlottesville, the ashram welcomes people of all faiths and backgrounds to study and practice the teachings of Integral yoga under the guidance of the Rev. Sri Swami Satchidananda. The body-mind connection is strengthened through in-depth workshops in three essential yoga practices: *asana* (physical postures), meditation, and *pranayama* (breathing techniques).

Guests are free to participate or observe, and special training in Hatha yoga is available for beginners. Classes begin at 6:30 AM, alternating with meals and meditation until 6 PM. Courses focus on meditation techniques and understanding karma, and guided nature walks provide an introduction to the valley's ecology. The ashram also offers a variety of two- to five-day workshops, retreats, and yoga-training programs. Chiropractic care and therapeutic massage are available at the Integral Health Center.

Guest accommodations range widely. A two-story wooden lodge, the Lotus Inn, has a health food café and private rooms, each with kitchenette, full bath, and a double bed and a sofa bed. A two-story dormitory includes classrooms as well as rooms with four–six beds sharing communal baths. Tent campsites, some with platforms, are in a wooded area near the dormitory and have shower and laundry facilities. Motor homes can also be parked on the grounds of the 750-acre retreat. The main meal is lunch, served in a communal hall. A lactovegetarian diet emphasizes whole grains, protein sources such as tofu and legumes, fresh fruit, and vegetables. Breakfast and supper buffets are light, comprising cereals, herbal tea, yogurt, and low-fat milk or the like. Those who volunteer for work in the organic garden, kitchen, or other areas of the community may earn free meals.

Services: Meditation instruction, yoga. **Swimming:** Private beach, river. **Classes and Programs:** Classes or spiritual concert. **Recreation:** Gardening, hiking.

6 private rooms; 25 dorm rooms, all with shared bath; 8 campsites.

3 meals daily included in guest rate. **Sample Meals:** Baked tofu, brown rice, steamed vegetables (lunch); miso soup, salad bar, millet, kale (dinner).

RATES AND PACKAGES

$80–$95 daily for 2 in private room, $40–$45 per person in dormitory, $60–$65 single room including meals, program. Lotus Inn rooms with private bath $85–$95 for 2. 3-day Hatha yoga program $195 dormitory, $250 in private room, $470 for 2; 4-day silent retreat $250. Campers $25–$30 daily single, $45–$50 for 2. Motor home $50 daily for 2, $300 per week. Special rates for children. Advance deposit for visits of 2 weeks or more, $100. MC, V.

DIRECTIONS

✉ *Route 604, Buckingham, VA 23921,* ☎ *804/969–3121 or 800/858–9642,* FAX *804/969–1303.*

From Washington, DC: I–66 west to Rte. 29, I–64 west (toward Lynchburg), 29 Bypass to I–64 east (toward Richmond), Rte. 20 south, Rte. 655 into Rte. 601, left on Rte. 604 (3½ hrs).

7 The Middle Atlantic States

New Jersey, Pennsylvania, West Virginia

GEORGE WASHINGTON MADE TAKING THE WATERS in West Virginia fashionable at about the same time that Europeans discovered a place called Spa in Belgium. Health resorts flourished over the years in the Poconos, the Alleghenies, and the southern Appalachians. These resorts tend to be small-scale and conservative, emphasizing service and personal attention, and oriented to golf and tennis rather than to high-energy workouts. While the renowned Greenbrier Resort in White Sulphur Springs, West Virginia, made the great leap from traditional to contemporary in its health spa, Berkeley Springs—where George Washington bathed—remains a sleepy country town with modest accommodations for spa-goers in a West Virginia state park. The Coolfont Resort, secluded in a valley near Berkeley Springs, brings together the past and present with its own blend of holistic health programs and luxury pampering. The introduction of snow-making equipment has added a new dimension to resorts throughout the area, with downhill and cross-country skiing now complementing indoor exercise.

In building the nation's first boardwalk, Atlantic City touched off a development boom along the New Jersey shore. The introduction of casino gambling in 1978 brought the town out of a long decline, and when the manufacturer of Lifecycles and other exercise equipment became a Bally company, the shore gained its first full-scale fitness center at Bally's Park Place Hotel. Like most spas in the area, it offers exercise as an amenity rather than a comprehensive health vacation program.

Diversity makes the Middle Atlantic states a rewarding destination for the fitness-oriented traveler. Choices range from charming Deerfield Spa Resort in the Poconos to the most sophisticated facilities this side of the Alleghenies at Nemacolin Woodlands in the Laurel Highlands of Pennsylvania. Affordability also distinguishes spa programs in the Mid-Atlantic region. Midweek packages offer full services at substantial savings at resorts such as the newly expanded Hilton at Short Hills, New Jersey.

NEW JERSEY

THE HILTON AT SHORT HILLS

Luxury pampering

The combination of a luxurious hotel and deluxe European health spa has made the Hilton at Short Hills a popular hideaway for Manhattanites as well as corporate executives visiting the Newark area. With full-service spa facilities—from a Roman-style pool to hydrotherapy and fango treatments—and a fitness center and calorie-conscious cuisine, this Hilton offers all the amenities of many fitness resorts. Even complimentary workout attire is provided. On the grounds are tennis courts with Har-Tru surface, lit for night action, as well as racquetball and squash courts. Just across the road is Short Hills Mall, a multi-level retail and dining complex anchored by leading brand-name shops.

Occupying two floors, the spa and fitness facilities adjoin the hotel's conference center, with direct access from parking garages. Two aerobics studios are in use daily, with scheduled classes from morning to night. Access for hotel guests staying in deluxe Towers rooms and suites is free of charge; others pay a nominal daily fee for access to exercise equipment and scheduled group-exercise classes. Secluded on the upper level is an Aveda Concept Salon, where all-natural products are used in body wraps, facials, scrubs, and massage. Spa Day packages are available.

Rooms and suites are in a seven-story glass-walled complex. For the ultimate escape, stay in a spacious Hilton Tower suite, where you'll have access to concierge services and a private lounge with complimentary breakfast, snacks, and dessert. Dinner in the elegant Dining Room is an event. For lunch, you can opt to dine on the swimming pool terrace.

FACILITIES
Exercise Equipment: Rowing machines, stationary bikes, stair climbers, treadmills, weight-training circuit, free weights. **Services:** Shiatsu, Swedish massage; body polish, herbal wrap, fango; facial. **Swimming:** Indoor and outdoor pools. **Classes and Programs:** Fitness assessment, computerized nutritional analysis, one-on-one training. **Recreation:** Racquetball, squash (fee); golf and tennis nearby.

ACCOMMODATIONS
300 rooms, 37 suites.

DINING
No meal plan. Spa cuisine served poolside or in casual Terrace Restaurant. Dinner selections also available in Dining Room (prix fixe). **Sample Meals:** Vegetable frittata, chilled poached salmon with cucumber-onion compote (lunch); crispy red snapper with lime-salsa glaze, seared tuna with ratatouille, or grilled chicken breast with pink lentils (dinner).

RATES AND PACKAGES
Rooms daily single/double per person $155–$300; Towers rooms $205–$375; suites $185–$300. Simply Spa weekend package $219 single, $140 per person double. AE, D, DC, MC, V.

DIRECTIONS
✉ 41 JFK Pkwy., Short Hills, NJ 07078, ☎ 973/379-0100 or 800/455-8667, FAX 973/379-6870.

From New York City: New Jersey Turnpike to Route 78N, or Garden State Parkway to Exit 142, Route 78 west in local traffic lane to JFK Pkwy (20 mins).

THE SPA AT BALLY'S PARK PLACE CASINO HOTEL

Luxury pampering

Escape the glitzy casinos, and indulge in a relaxing massage or vigorous workout and racquetball at the best spa on the New Jersey coast. Secluded in a beachfront tower, the Spa at Bally's is an oasis of fun and fitness. The spacious facilities and top-of-the-line equipment would be the pride of any resort, though here they serve as a complement to gambling and entertainment. It's possible not to set foot in the casino, but most of the people working out in the weights room also exercise the one-armed bandits.

The pool, saunas, and whirlpools are complimentary to hotel guests and members. Use of the cardio and strength-training equipment costs a nominal fee, which is waived if you book a spa service. In the spa complex, light streams into a domed atrium surrounded by terraced gardens. A coed, glass-walled sauna flanks the swimming pool (which often gets crowded with children and aquaerobics classes); nearby are whirlpool and showers. Upstairs are men's and women's locker rooms with Turkish bath, treatment rooms, and exercise equipment. The ultimate relaxer, favored by high rollers, is a private session in the MVP Suite, complete with its own marble whirlpool and steam shower. The best value is the $99-day-spa package, which includes lunch, salon treatments, and exercise classes such as slimnastics, low-impact aerobics, stretch and tone, and aquaerobics.

Starting your day with a walk or jog on the Boardwalk is the best antidote for an evening at the casinos. Bikes can be rented at several points. The wooden walkway, which flanks the beach for several miles, extending to residential areas of Margate and Ventnor, dates from 1870, and has been the scene of the Miss America Pageant parade since the 1920s. (During pageant week in September, many contestants are seen working out at the spa.) The beach and ocean bathing, among the finest on the East Coast, assure a healthy glow.

FACILITIES
Exercise Equipment: Cross-country ski machine, stationary bikes, stair climbers, treadmills, weight-training circuit. **Services:** Swedish massage; algae body masque, body polish, herbal wrap, loofah body scrub, seamud treatment; facial. **Swimming:** Indoor pool, ocean beach. **Classes and Programs:** Cabaret and celebrity shows. **Recreation:** Biking, racquetball; golf and tennis nearby.

ACCOMMODATIONS
1,268 rooms, 110 suites.

DINING
3 meals daily included in spa packages. Buffet lunch in Spa Café. Spa cuisine available in hotel dining rooms. **Sample Meals:** Spinach salad, lentil soup, fruits (lunch); pan-seared scallops with saffron rice, steamed salmon with onions in balsamic vinegar sauce, lobster and shrimp casserole, or scallops Newburg with lemon-dill rice (dinner).

RATES AND PACKAGES
Rooms $79–$250 per day, suites $250–$525 for 2. Spa admission $10 for hotel guests. Treatments priced individually. 1-day spa package $99, 3-day/2-night spa package $475 single, $395 per person double. (Saturday night is not included in any package plan.) AE, DC, MC, V.

DIRECTIONS

✉ *Bally's Park Place Casino Hotel & Tower, Boardwalk and Park Pl., Atlantic City, NJ 08401,* ☎ *609/340–4600, 800/772–7777, or 800/ 225–5977;* FAX *609/340–4713*

From Philadelphia and New York: Garden State Parkway to Atlantic City Expressway (1 hr).

PENNSYLVANIA

DEERFIELD SPA RESORT

Nutrition and diet

Housed in an attractive white clapboard farmhouse that dates from the 1930s, Deerfield Spa Resort is a homey, non-threatening place in which to unwind and shape up. Scheduled from April through mid-November, programs are tailored to individual needs: Participation is limited to 33 men and women, who are encouraged and instructed on exercise, diet, and nutrition, by a 30-member staff. Daily activities include yoga, tai chi, aerobics, body sculpting, step classes, aquaerobics, and naturalist-led mountain hikes in the Pocono Mountains and on parts of the Appalachian Trail.

A familylike feeling tends to develop among guests, many of whom are repeat visitors in the over-50 age bracket. Daily lectures on mind-body-spirit connections and special health concerns elicit discussion and sharing of experiences with visiting experts. An informal lounge equipped with a VCR and video library serves as an evening social center.

Workout equipment at Deerfield Spa Resort is minimal, and no activity is required. You can, however, opt for ambitious programs such as "Total Fitness," which involves selecting a menu according to your personal goals. Weekend and weeklong packages are available.

FACILITIES
Exercise Equipment: Cross-country ski track, stair climber, stationary bike, treadmill, vertical ladder climber, free weights. **Services:** Neuromuscular massage, reflexology, Reiki, shiatsu, Swedish massage; sea-salt body buff, seaweed body wrap; facial. **Swimming:** Pool. **Classes and Programs:** Guest lecturers on health-related topics, cooking demonstrations, tarot readings. **Recreation:** Golf, horseback riding, ice skating, roller skating, tennis, all nearby.

ACCOMMODATIONS
22 rooms.

DINING
3 daily meals included in rates. Fish and chicken, locally grown produce, fresh fruit. Vegetarian meals optional. **Sample Meals:** Grilled chicken, Caesar salad (lunch); baked orange roughy with herbed bread crumbs (dinner).

RATES AND PACKAGES
Weekend $404–$438 single, $330–$366 per person double. Weekly (Sun.–Sun.) $1,024–$1,125 single, $799–$935 per person double. $200-deposit required. MC, V.

DIRECTIONS
✉ *650 Resica Falls Rd., East Stroudsburg, PA 18301,* ☎ *717/223–0160 or 800/852–4494,* FAX *717/223–8270.*

From Philadelphia and New York: I–80 from New York, I–84 from New England, I–83 from the Baltimore–Washington area connect with Route 402 (Resica Falls Road).

THE HIMALAYAN INSTITUTE

Holistic health

One of the world's leading centers for the healing of mind, body, and spirit, the Himalayan Institute of Yoga Science and Philosophy of the USA was founded by Sri Swami Rama, who played a major role in bringing the teachings of yoga to the attention of physicians, psychologists, and researchers. At this 400-acre retreat, you'll learn how yoga and the science of breath, diet, and nutrition can help you develop healthy habits and overcome illness, through programs in holistic health, Hatha yoga, meditation, psychology, philosophy, and other subjects.

During his tenure as a research consultant to the Menninger Foundation Project on Voluntary Control of Internal States in 1970, the Indian-born Rama stopped his heart from pumping blood for 17 seconds, thereby revolutionizing scientists' understanding of the human ability to control the body. The Institute operates on the philosophy that individuals who learn to train the mind and body may be able to prevent and overcome illness and accelerate healing.

At the Center for Health and Healing, your counselor custom-designs an Ayurvedic rejuvenation program that addresses the whole person. Based upon a holistic health assessment, three levels of training and treatments are available, addressing problems such as low energy, high blood pressure, ulcers, arthritis, headaches, and stress-related disorders. Therapies may include one- to two-week sessions of homeopathy, detoxification, biofeedback, acupuncture, massage, yoga, and meditation. For healthy people interested in a refresher, three- to 10-day courses are offered. Cooking classes are scheduled during longer programs, focusing on organic vegetarian cuisine. Special care is provided for people returning to health after extended chronic illnesses, operations, and accidents. Also available are outpatient services that combine holistic medicine with practice yoga; and children's programs combining Eastern and Western educational concepts, Montessori methods, and yoga philosophies.

The Institute's wooded campus in the rolling foothills of the Pocono Mountains is a perfect setting in which to focus on inner awareness and calm. (To enhance this inner tranquillity, guests are asked to maintain silence from 10 PM until 8 AM, and 5 to 6 PM.) Program participants are housed in the main building or chalet apartments. The main three-story brick structure has 100 beds in spartan, shared rooms that have nothing but a sink and one or two beds (no locks, telephone, or air conditioning). Communal bathrooms are on each floor. A limited number of deluxe rooms with private bathroom are available. For extra comfort, consider upgrading to an apartment in the chalets; each two-bedroom split-level unit has a bathroom, sitting area with sofa bed, and access to a central cathedral-ceiling lounge.

FACILITIES
Exercise Equipment: Rowing machine, stationary bikes, stair climber. **Services:** Massage, Ayurvedic body therapies. **Swimming:** Pond on property, with sandy beach. **Classes and Programs:** Biofeedback training, medical and psychological consultations; classes in Hatha yoga, meditation, vegetarian cooking; lectures or practicums. **Recreation:** Basketball, cross-country skiing, handball, hiking, ice skating, tennis. **Children's Programs:** Pre-school, kindergarten, and elementary school programs (ages 3–9).

ACCOMMODATIONS
50 rooms with shared bath, 4 rooms with private bath, 4 guest houses.

DINING

3 vegetarian meals daily included in program rate, served cafeteria style. Vegetables from organic garden. **Sample Meals:** Vegetable stir-fry with basmati rice, lentil dal and homemade breads (lunch); butternut-squash soup, hummus, apple-raisin couscous, spinach-tofu bake (dinner).

RATES AND PACKAGES

Weekend seminar tuition $140–$150; shared room $100–$110 per person double. Personal retreat with meals on request. Deposit required for all programs: $50 per person for programs costing up to $300, $75 per person for programs more than $300. MC, V.

DIRECTIONS

✉ *R.R. 1, Box 400, Honesdale, PA 18431,* ☎ *717/253–5551 or 800/822–4547,* FAX *717/253–9078.*

From New York City: Lincoln Tunnel to I–80 W to Exit 34B (Route 15 N) through Milford, Route 6 W/191 N through Honesdale to Route 670 N (3 hrs).

NEMACOLIN WOODLANDS

Luxury pampering
Sports conditioning

Atop a scenic bluff in the Laurel Highlands of southwestern Pennsylvania stands the Woodlands Spa, a $6 million centerpiece of the Nemacolin Woodlands resort and conference center. The resort, once a private hunting reserve, was acquired by Joseph Hardy, founder of the nationwide 84 Lumber Co., in 1987. Since then, despite its rustic-sounding name, Nemacolin Woodlands has become a premier resort—and its four-level spa of native stone, buff brick, and glass is the best equipped this side of the Allegheny Mountains.

The range of bodywork available here is exceptional—scrubs and wraps using sea salts, oils, mud, and herbal mixtures; aromatherapy or Swedish massage; foot reflexology. After a session in the steam room or the sauna, you can relax in a glass-walled whirlpool and enjoy the view of woods and distant mountains. Downstairs is devoted to exercise: Keiser pneumatic weight training machines, bikes, treadmills, and a StairMaster with video monitors; a four-lane indoor lap pool 65 feet long, flanked by whirlpools for women and men; and a mirrored aerobics studio with spring-cushioned wood floor that can hold groups of 40 or more.

Upstairs are the beauty salon and 20 treatment rooms, spacious and airy and warmed in winter by a stone fireplace. Body care includes a detoxifying mask of moor mud, followed by a scrub and moisturizer. One room is specially designed for hydrating pedicures and manicures, a process in which your hands and feet are dipped in liquid paraffin, a coating that helps moisture penetrate outer layers of skin, leaving a smooth, soft finish. Lunch and snacks are available in the reception area, allowing you to spend the whole day indoors or at the pool.

The pace here is as relaxed or intense as you want it to be. Treatments and optional spa meals are included in packages of one to six days, or booked à la carte. Fitness classes range from high-impact aerobics to step, body sculpting, and tai chi. Personal training, as well as fitness evaluation with biofeedback analysis of body composition, can be part of your program. Nonprogram guests pay a daily fee ($15), refunded if you book a service.

As extensive as the spa-treatment options are the outdoor activities at this 1,000-acre resort. In addition to two golf courses, an indoor Equestrian Center with dressage training as well as trail rides, and outdoor tennis courts, there's championship croquet, horseshoes, biking, and trout fishing in a stocked lake. In winter, trails are groomed for cross-country skiing and snowmobiles, and the lake is filled with ice skaters. Downhill skiers can take advantage of a gentle 325-foot slope with three runs, lifts, and a snow-making system; group or individual instruction, is open to the public on a daily pass basis. Golfers are challenged by Pete Dye's par-72 6,832-yard Woodlands course, and the 6,600-yard par-70 Mystic Rock course. Instruction and video analysis of your form are offered at the Golf Academy, which has scheduled classes and private instruction year-round. Or you can drive balls indoors at a golf course simulator at the recreation center.

Your appetite sharpened by the mountain air and exercise, you can sample spa cuisine at six restaurants, including the Country Club Grill and the Caddy Shack outdoor terrace. The elegant Golden Trout dining room and the Restaurant Lautrec have low-fat, low-cholesterol menus. Afterwards, retire to an art deco English, or French-country-style room in the lodge, where tea is served daily; or settle into a spacious bedroom or terrace suite at the palace-style Chateau Lafayette. Groups desiring privacy can opt for a furnished townhouses or cottage with kitchen.

Outside the resort, there's plenty to do. Architecture by Frank Lloyd Wright is a major attraction in these hills: Fallingwater and Kentuck Knob are both a short drive away. Also nearby are the Western Maryland Scenic Railroad; Antietam Battlefield; and Fort Necessity, where George Washington lost his first battle in the French and Indian War. Back at the Woodlands Spa, an animated sculpture of Chief Nemacolin welcomes you to his tribal land.

FACILITIES
Exercise Equipment: Stationary bikes, stair climbers, treadmills, vertical ladder climbers, weight-training circuit, free weights. **Services:** Aromatherapy massage, reflexology, sports massage, Swedish massage; body wrap, loofah body polish; facial. **Swimming:** Indoor and outdoor pools. **Classes and Programs:** Fitness assessment, stress-management program, body-composition evaluation, one-on-one training. Scheduled walks and group exercise. Spa lectures and training sessions, music weekends, chess, sports bar. **Recreation:** Badminton, biking, boating, croquet, golf, horseback riding, miniature golf, shuffleboard, table tennis, tennis, trout fishing. Cross-country and downhill skiing, ice skating, snowmobiling. Racquetball nearby. **Children's Programs:** Children's playground, petting zoo, and Family Activities Center.

ACCOMMODATIONS
98 rooms in lodge, 125 rooms in hotel, 60 townhouses and cottages.

DINING
Spa packages include 2–3 meals daily. Menu on 14-day cycle. Lunch served at spa or in café. **Sample Meals:** Clam chowder and green salad (lunch); grilled chicken breast, broiled veal scallop, baked brook trout stuffed with scallops and shrimp (dinner).

RATES AND PACKAGES
Hotel rooms daily, single or double, without meals $225–$275, suites $375–$425, penthouse $375–$525. Day Spa packages without lodging $120–$294. AE, DC, MC, V.

DIRECTIONS

✉ *1001 Lafayette Dr., Farmington, PA 15437,* ☎ *412/329–8555 or 800/ 422–2736,* 🖷 *412/329–6177.*

From Washington, DC: Capital Beltway (I–495), I–270 north to Frederick, Maryland, I–70 west to I–68, Uniontown exit to Route 40 (Old National Road) to Farmington, PA (3 hrs).

WEST VIRGINIA

BERKELEY SPRINGS STATE PARK

Mineral springs

Spartan and old-fashioned by today's standards, the state-run facilities at Berkeley Springs State Park offer a down-home Blue Ridge brand of healing. Bargain prices and a sense of history are the main draws.

Ever since George and Martha Washington took the waters here, Berkeley Springs has attracted healers and promoters. A museum atop the Roman baths documents the area's development. In the last decade, the town has attracted bodyworkers and therapists, and a bottling plant exports the spring water. At the Bath House massage and health center on Fairfax Street facing the state park, you can shop for health products and spa guides, make appointments for therapeutic treatments, and take yoga and tai chi classes. Nearby is a full-service homeopathic pharmacy where medicinal tinctures are available, and educational classes and exhibits trace the development of homeopathy by a German physician, Samuel Hahnemann, 200 years ago. Tari's Premier Café on Washington Street, next door to the venerable Star Theatre, serves vegetable burgers, and Washington's Birthday is celebrated with an international waters tasting.

The West Virginia Parks and Recreation Department operates the bathhouses, which are in the center of town, just off busy Washington street. The original Roman bath building dates from 1815 and has eight 750-gallon public pools that can accommodate four people. A separate bathhouse building dating from the 1920s has separate men's and women's facilities; in the women's bath, heated mineral water spurts from enormous pipes into two three-foot-deep tiled plunge pools where patrons soak in privacy. A public swimming pool is open throughout the summer. Adding to the nostalgia of this old-fashioned spa town are a park-run spring where you can fill jugs with free, cold drinking water and summertime band concerts in a Victorian gazebo.

You can spend the night near the springs at any number of inns and hotels. The 1920s Country Inn, next to the state-run bathhouses, has a spa with mineral-water whirlpools, a beauty salon, and services such as traditional Thai massage. Appointments are open to the public, and the inn's budget-priced accommodations and restaurant offer a taste of country traditions. In addition, there are several bed-and-breakfasts in town or nearby. The Highlawn Inn (tel. 304/258–5700), a hilltop Victorian mansion, has antiques-filled rooms and a carriage house suite, some with whirlpool and fireplace, and full breakfast. Also nearby is the Coolfont Resort (*see below*), which has tent sites, RV hookups, and various accommodations, with or without spa packages. Cacapon State Park (tel. 304/258–1022 or 800/225–5982), 10 miles south of town, has cabins, lodge rooms, a restaurant, and golf course.

Berkeley Springs sits at the upper end of a three-state region, taking in parts of Pennsylvania, Maryland, and West Virginia along the Potomac River. Hikes along the C & O Canal, and tours of Harpers Ferry National Historical Park, top the list of regional attractions. Nearby Martinsburg, West Virginia, is home to the Blue Ridge Outlet Center. And in Shepherdstown, you can stroll among pre-Civil War buildings, shop for antiques, and attend a summer festival of new American theater productions.

FACILITIES
Services: Massage; hydrotherapy, Roman plunge pools. **Swimming:** Pool (open May 30–Sept. 1).

ACCOMMODATIONS
Country Inn: $39 per double, $69–$156 with private bathroom. Inn's 2-night Ultimate Spa package is $650 (Sun.–Thurs.) for 2. AE, MC, V.

RATES AND PACKAGES
Bath and massage $40 (1 hr), thermal-water bath $15 (1 hr).

DIRECTIONS
✉ *Washington St., Berkeley Springs, WV 25411,* ☎ *304/258–2711 or 800/225–5982.*

From Washington, DC: I–270 to Frederick, Maryland, I–70 west to Hancock, Maryland, cross Potomac River on Route 522 (90 mins).

COOLFONT RESORT

Holistic health
Nutrition and diet

Bring your jeans and hiking boots for an informal retreat at this 1,300-acres retreat in the foothills of the Appalachian Mountains, a favorite hideaway for stressed-out Washingtonians. Though the resort itself is more like a summer camp than a luxury spa, the services and programs at its rustic Spectrum Spa are an outstanding value. The lack of big-resort amenities is perhaps what draws so many guests back each season—though enhancements may be on the horizon, as a new management team was scheduled to take over in 1999.

The spa has 21 private rooms for a wide range of bodywork, a full-service salon, demonstration kitchen, and aerobics studio with a sprung-wood floor. In the Swim and Fitness Club are an indoor spring-fed pool, coed whirlpool and sauna, and exercise room with cardiovascular and strength-training equipment. A full range of scheduled classes is available to resort guests for a modest fee.

For those who want to immerse themselves in wellness education, members of the resident staff combine expertise in physical fitness, nutrition, massage, and holistic health in regularly scheduled programs; and guest instructors lead workshops on natural nutrition, creative problem solving, and stress reduction. Also offered regularly is a weekend of massage instruction for couples, and a weeklong Breathe-Free program for smoking cessation. For those 40 and older, Camp Rediscovery weeks, modeled after the Adult Health and Development Program at the University of Maryland, are scheduled during August and January, and Elderhostel weeks in December are conducted in cooperation with a state university. Also based here are corporate team-building programs and adventures conducted by Outward Bound. Camaraderie forms naturally among spa-goers, who share a private dining room where nutritionally balanced meals are served.

A cultural dimension adds to the appeal of Coolfont. Folk singers, chamber music ensembles, and storytelling recitals are presented on weekends; and art classes bring out amateur watercolor painters. A spring-fed lake provides family recreation and swimming in summer, and stables and golf greens are nearby. Other attractions include historic Berkeley Springs and its bargain baths (*see above*), and bargain shopping at the Blue Ridge Outlets. In winter, there's downhill skiing at the Whitetail recreation area.

Guests can choose to stay either in private chalets, a three-story lodge, or log cabins. The Manor House, listed on the National Register of Historic Places, also has several bedrooms for nonsmoking guests. Most popular are the 23 deluxe chalets, each with two bedrooms and whirlpool baths, a wood-burning stove in the living room, and a leafy deck outside. Set on a hillside, the chalets are a healthy hike from the spa and restaurant, so bring walking shoes.

FACILITIES

Exercise Equipment: Ergometer, rowing machine, stationary bike, stair climber, treadmills, weight-training unit, free weights. **Services:** Craniosacral massage, deep-tissue therapy, neuromuscular massage, sports massage; herbal wrap, loofah body scrub; facial. **Swimming:** Indoor pool; beach on private lake. **Classes and Programs:** Fitness evaluation, nutrition consultation. **Recreation:** Boating, golf, hiking, horseback riding, team sports, tennis; cross-country skiing, ice skating. Concerts, health lectures, line dancing. **Children's Programs:** Supervised camp for children (5–12) July–Aug. and seasonal weekends.

ACCOMMODATIONS

22 lodge rooms, 35 chalets, 25 log cabins, RV hookups available.

DINING

3 meals daily included in spa packages, 2 meals daily in MAP rate. Juice and fruit snacks. **Sample Meals:** Shrimp stir-fry with brown rice, grilled chicken sandwich with roasted-garlic mayonnaise (lunch); braised trout with herb crust, or lentil-and-mushroom enchilada (dinner).

RATES AND PACKAGES

Daily MAP $119–$149 single, $99–$129 per person double, including admission to Swim & Fitness Center; 2-night Spa & Fitness package $380–$400 single, $340–$360 per person double; 2-night Massage Workshop $640 per couple; 5-night Healthy Me package $730–$780 per person double. Breathe-Free program $1,395 single. Spa for a Day (no lodging) $139. 50% deposit required. AE, DC, MC, V.

DIRECTIONS

✉ *Cold Run Valley Rd., Rte. 1, Box 710, Berkeley, Springs, WV 25411,* ☎ *304/258–4500 or 800/888–8768,* FAX *304/258–5499.*

From Washington, DC: I–270/70 to Hancock, Maryland, Route 522 (2 hrs); or Pennsylvania Turnpike (I–76) at Breezewood exit.

THE GREENBRIER

Luxury pampering
Medical wellness
Mineral springs
Nutrition and diet

At this 200-year-old grande dame of spa resorts, you can savor the gilded age of Southern living while enjoying modern spa treatments and traditional mineral baths, improving your golf or tennis game, and savoring the legendary Greenbrier cuisine at one of four fine restaurants (there's an international cooking school on the premises).

The Greenbrier resort blends old-fashioned Southern comfort with high-tech spa treatments. Built around a colonnaded neoclassical hotel surrounded by formal gardens, the resort evokes another era, giving spa-goers a taste of Colonial Virginia–style grandeur. Its amenities include an international cooking school and 200-year-old thermal water therapies.

The great white neoclassical hotel has a Colonial Virginia style, with Georgian colonnades and formal gardens flanking the central structure. Parts of the resort are older, and reflect the 19th-century Southern fashion of family cottages built by plantation owners for the social season here. There are 121 guest houses and cottages on the grounds, elegantly furnished and serviced by the hotel. Frequently refurbished, guest suites are huge, with parlor and walk-in closet, traditional furniture, and Greenbrier green carpet. There is a Greenbrier look and style, an aspect of artistic rightness and service that starts at the white brick gateway.

Afternoon tea is served in one of the vast halls filled with faux Oriental decor by Dorothy Draper. The indoor 140 x 42 foot swimming pool is lavishly tiled, filled with spring water, and graced by a juice bar and wicker lounges amid potted palms. Steps from the pool, the spa, salon, exercise equipment room, and aerobics studio provide a quiet retreat. The spa staff includes both old hands and university-trained physiology specialists; they make newcomers feel comfortable about trying some of the exotic-sounding treatments. Seaweed body wraps, aromatherapy, and facials with European floral products are among the à la carte offerings.

Start with a signature treatment, the Greenbrier Bubbly bath. Step into a private tub filled with mineral water from the Alvon spring, enhanced with FloraSpa relaxing marine extracts of algae and minerals, and experience underwater jets massaging away tension. Next comes aromatherapy inhalation in the sauna or steam room. Then on to the famous Greenbrier Swiss shower or Scotch hose. Deluged and detoxed, you're ready for a body scrub or soothing buff, and the final touch, an aromatherapy massage with herbal elixirs by FloraSpa. The adjoining beauty salon takes therapy a step further with foot and hand facials using seaweed-based cleansers and masques. After a day filled with golf, tennis, and outdoor adventures, the salon aestheticians have a prescription for every need and skin type. Some use enriching spirulina, others add bee pollen to leave you glowing.

Spa director Kathryn Tuckwiller advises making appointments prior to your arrival at the resort. Each package is customized, and a spa reservationist will discuss your priorities: relaxation, recharging, new routine, pampering, tools to take home. If you're attending the LaVarenne Cooking Week, the spa will schedule you according to the class schedule, and help work off extra calories with exercise.

Cocooned in the grand manor, you'll want to dress up for dinner. The chandeliered dining room in the central section of the hotel dates from 1913, and meals are served according to time-honored tradition. Hot rolls and breads are passed constantly, and between courses you are entertained by a string ensemble. Spa cuisine options are on the menu, containing 30% fat or less, moderate in cholesterol and sodium. Presented with classic Greenbrier flair, it's a far cry from dieting.

Checkups coordinated by a team of medical doctors and personal trainers add a holistic edge. The Greenbrier Clinic, established in 1948 as a private practice, occupies a separate building that is completely equipped for diagnostic and preventive medicine. Health examinations can now be combined with spa therapy. Checking in with the resident medical staff, the participant undergoes a two-day diagnostic assessment plus advanced fitness evaluation. A doctor will confer with the spa nutritionist and physiologist to plan a personalized diet and exercise regimen. For those who desire an intensive regimen, a variety of spa packages are available, November through March.

Surrounded by 6,500 acres of Allegheny Mountain woodlands, The Greenbrier incorporates three 18-hole championship golf courses, all of which begin at a clubhouse where you can have lunch and light refreshments. Tennis is played indoors and outdoors, with five covered courts and 15 all-weather surfaces outdoors. The choice of recreation includes horseback riding, skeet and trap shooting, fly fishing, hiking, bowling, and falconry. Perhaps the most unusual attraction is underground, a bunker built to house the United States Congress if an emergency had forced evacuation during World War II. Never used, the underground capitol is perfectly preserved for escorted tours with a historian, and has been mentioned as a future site for a casino.

Even if the Vanderbilts no longer arrive by private railroad car, you can take Amtrak's Cardinal from Chicago, New York, and Washington, D.C. A hotel limo awaits at The Greenbrier's tiny train station to whisk you through the gates in grand style.

FACILITIES
Exercise Equipment: Ergometer, stationary bikes, stair climbers, treadmills, weight-training circuit, free weights. **Services:** Massage; herbal wrap, shirodhara; mineral or herbal bath; back facial, pressure-point facial. **Swimming:** Indoor and outdoor pools. **Classes and Programs:** Aerobics. One-on-one training, fitness evaluation and personal exercise program; feature films, food and wine weekends, dancing. **Recreation:** Biking, bowling, carriage rides, croquet, fishing, golf, hiking, horseback riding, platform tennis, skeet- and trap-shooting, tennis. **Children's Programs:** Sports school for children June–Labor Day.

ACCOMMODATIONS
639 lodgings, including 121 guest houses and cottages and 33 suites.

DINING
Meals included in packages. American fare plus low-calorie alternatives at breakfast and dinner in main dining room. Café service for lunch at Sam Sneed's and Draper's. **Sample Meals:** Thai shrimp salad, vegetable stir-fry with white sticky rice (lunch); seared Chilean sea bass, grilled yellowfin tuna with saffron-tomato broth (dinner).

RATES AND PACKAGES
Daily rate $183–$530 single, $160–$281 per person double, including breakfast and dinner. Suites from $303 per person, cottages and guest house $255–$384 per person. 2-day spa package $1,300 per person single or double, including 3 meals daily, 5-day spa package $2,650 per person single or double, 5-day Spa and Clinic program (Sun.–Fri.) $3,495 per person single or double. $425 room deposit required. Tax and gratuities included in spa packages. AE, DC, MC, V.

DIRECTIONS
⊠ *White Sulphur Springs, WV 24986,* ☎ *304/536–1110 or 800/624–6070,* ℻ *304/536–7854.*

From Washington, DC: I–66 west to I–81 south (to Lexington, VA), to I–64's White Sulpher Springs Exit; follow signs 1½ mi to spa.

LAKEVIEW FITNESS CENTER

Luxury pampering
Sports condititioning

Surrounded by Appalachian woodlands and skirted by a large lake in the northern panhandle of West Virginia, the Lakeview Resort has two championship courses surrounded by woodland and an excellent fitness and sports center. With a broad choice of outdoor activities, plus corporate facilities and a nursery for children, it's an affordable getaway for couples, families, and business groups.

The action is continuous at the fitness center, which has two racquetball courts, a sauna, 50-foot lap pool, climbing wall, cardiovascular and weight-training equipment, and indoor walking track (22 laps equals a mile). Nearby are two indoor and four outdoor tennis courts and an outdoor pool. Registered guests have access to all fitness facilities. Spa services, personal consultations, and exercise classes cost a small fee. Lunch and snacks are available at the spa juice bar.

Recreation options range from horseback riding to water skiing. A well-stocked lake is used for fishing and boating. For those willing to venture farther afield, extensive hiking trails wind through Cooper's Park State Forest, and there's whitewater rafting on the Cheat River. Fitness consultants lead mountain biking, hiking, and horseback forays into the nearby forests and arrange team building and communication projects for business groups and others. A nursery will watch the kids while parents work out.

FACILITIES
Exercise Equipment: Rowing machine, stationary bikes, stair climbers, treadmill, weight-training circuit, free weights. **Swimming:** 2 pools (1 indoor). **Classes and Programs:** Dancing, cabaret. **Recreation:** Boating, climbing (indoor wall), fishing, golf, horseback riding, racquetball, tennis, wallyball, waterskiing.

ACCOMMODATIONS
187 rooms at inn, 55 2-bedroom condominiums.

DINING
Light fare in lakeview restaurant, The Grille, upscale fine dining at Reflections. **Sample Meals:** Vegetable pita sandwich (lunch); pasta with vegetables, chicken salad, grilled salmon fillet (dinner).

RATES AND PACKAGES
Daily rate per room $89–$189 single, $89–$199 for 2 double. Condominium apartments (up to 6 persons) $325–$350 per day. Credit card guarantee for 1 night. AE, DC, MC, V.

DIRECTIONS
✉ 1 Lakeview Dr., Morgantown, WV 26505, ☎ 304/594–1111 or 800/624–8300, FAX 304/594–9472.

From Pittsburgh: I–79 to I–68. (90 mins).

8 New York and New England

*Connecticut, Maine,
Massachusetts, New Hampshire,
New York, Vermont*

THE 1990S saw a return to elegance throughout the northeastern states, as grand old estates were rejuvenated and hotels updated their fitness facilities and introduced European therapies. The result has been a broader range of vacation options for luxury-minded and budget-conscious travelers.

Tradition blends with the high-tech at the Norwich Inn & Spa, a Connecticut landmark. In Massachusetts, the famed Canyon Ranch in the Berkshires offers innovative health programs only minutes away from the Boston Symphony Orchestra's popular summer home at Tanglewood. Nearby, the modestly priced Kripalu Center for Yoga and Health exercises your body and mind in a sanctuary unlike traditional ashrams in its size and scope of programs. In addition, historic hotels such as The Equinox (in Vermont) and The Sagamore (in the Adirondacks) have expanded their fitness facilities.

Advancing the concept of preventive medicine, spas are teaming up with doctors, nutritionists, and psychologists in new programs that address stress control, aging, and lifestyle. At the New Age Health Spa in New York's Catskill Mountains, you can participate in a challenge course designed by experts from Outward Bound, or in a five-day program in which experts analyze your lifestyle and look for ways to improve your diet and habits. In the Hudson Valley, Omega Institute has been at the forefront of personal and professional development in holistic health since 1977.

CONNECTICUT

NORWICH INN & SPA

Holistic health
Luxury pampering

Combine a 1920s country inn with a contemporary spa set on a bluff near the Thames River, and you have a perfect escape for city dwellers. About three hours north of New York City, the imposing Georgian-style Norwich establishment blends sophisticated cuisine and state-of -the-art spa treatments with New England tradition. A major expansion in 1998 more than doubled the size of the spa facility, and a new restaurant adjoining the spa allows guests to dine in their robes before or after treatments.

You can work out at your own pace or with a personal trainer in a glass-walled room of cardio and strength training equipment, swim in a 35-foot lap pool, get an underwater massage in a hydrotherapy tub, and treat yourself to one of more than a dozen types of facials. Services and classes are offered à la carte, but daily and overnight packages provide the best value. Join the daily guided walk at 7 AM, free of charge, and get an orientation to the resort complex. For an additional fee, you can attend workshops on nutrition and cooking.

Country-chic comfort characterizes the living quarters. Public areas include a taproom with a large stone fireplace, a quiet sun room full of palms and wicker, and a lobby with a pair of pet finches. Standard guest rooms are small but homey, with antiques, four-poster beds, ceiling fans, hand-woven rugs, and lace curtains. For a splurge, stay in one of the charming villas that border a pond near the inn and golf course. Each has a fully-equipped kitchen, living room with fireplace, and ground-level or upstairs balcony. Villa guests have access to a private clubhouse, gym, swimming pool, and Jacuzzi.

Surrounded by 37 acres of woodland and the public Norwich Golf Course, the inn offers numerous diversions after workouts, including tennis on two lighted Har-tru courts and even casino gaming (the inn and nearby Foxwoods casino are owned by the Mashantucket Pequot Indian tribe). The minimum age for spa guests is 18.

FACILITIES
Exercise Equipment: Rowing machines, stair climbers, stationary bikes, treadmills, weight-training circuit, free weights. **Services:** Aromatherapy massage, Reiki, Swedish massage, sports massage; clay wrap, herbal wrap, loofah scrub, salt glow, seaweed wrap; hydrotherapy, thalassotherapy; facial. **Swimming:** Indoor and outdoor pools. **Classes and Programs:** Aerobics, one-on-one training, wellness workshops, cooking demonstrations, fitness lectures, astrology. **Recreation:** Biking, golf, hiking, tennis.

ACCOMMODATIONS
39 inn rooms, 16 suites, 75 villa suites.

DINING
Three meals daily in Escape plan; breakfast and dinner in Country Retreat package. **Sample Meals:** Grilled Talapia—a firm-flesh Atlantic whitefish—and seared Portobello mushrooms, oven-roasted eggplant with herbed feta in a pita pocket (lunch); blackened yellowfin tuna, fillet of salmon, vegetable Provençale (dinner).

RATES AND PACKAGES
Personal Escape Plan $355–$455 single, $310–$470 double per day (2-night minimum midweek, 3-night minimum weekends; deposit $250). Getaway Country Retreat with 2 meals daily, $170–$260 single, $115–$165 double. Day Spa packages $150–$300. Inn room $115–$185, single or double; villa $200–$285. Add 12% tax. AE, DC, MC, V.

DIRECTIONS
✉ 607 W. Thames (Rte. 32), Norwich, CT 06360, ☎ 860/886–2401 or 800/275–4772, ℻ 860/886–9483.

From New York City: Take Interstate–95 north to Interstate–395 north via Exit 76. From I-395's Exit 79A, take Route 2A east for ¼-mi to Exit 1 and make a left onto Route 32 north for 1½ mi (3 hrs).

MAINE

NORTHERN PINES HEALTH RESORT

Holistic health
Medical wellness
Nutrition and diet

Here's a great place to learn about lifestyle management in the great outdoors. Occupying a 68-acre lakefront preserve, the resort has holistic diet
and fitness programs designed to help you develop a positive attitude toward
weight loss and stress control. The program is unregimented; the transition is meant to be gradual.

A flexible schedule of workshops and outdoor recreation is offered year-
round. Campers range widely in age, but many are over 40. The affordable rates make it popular with singles. About 50 guests are resident in
summer (30 during the ski season), allowing for a friendly mix with lots
of personal attention from the staff. At other times, cabins are rented for
private retreats.

Each day begins with stretching exercises and a brisk walk through the
woods, followed by a choice of focus sessions or aerobics classes. Instruction
is available in transcendental meditation, art, and music. Morning and
afternoon yoga are optional. Evenings are given over to more learning
activities, from cooking classes to massage demonstrations. About 20%
of the guests opt to undertake a week-long juice fast.

The camp's lakeside log cabins date from the 1920s and provide total
seclusion for couples. New lodge rooms and cabins with two bedrooms
are on the hillside amid towering pines, spruce, and hemlock. There are
also two-person yurts (earth-covered cabins) with carpeting and modern
conveniences.

The informality and laid-back pace appeal to stressed-out professionals
who come here to rejuvenate and relax. For those who in need of a little retail therapy, the L. L. Bean headquarters are just down the road.

FACILITIES
Exercise Equipment: Cross-country ski machine, stationary bikes, weight-
training equipment, free weights. **Services:** Acupressure, aromatherapy
massage, reflexology; body wrap, herbal wrap; facials. **Swimming:** Lake.
Classes and Programs: Massage workshops, meditation, guest lectures,
storytelling, videos, yoga. **Recreation:** Canoeing, hiking, sailing.

ACCOMMODATIONS
8 cabins, 32 lodge rooms, some with shared bath.

DINING
Vegetarian diet. 3 daily buffets. Supervised fasts begin with 2 days of raw
fruit and vegetables, followed by 3 days of juices and broth. **Sample Meals:**
Lentil and vegetable soup with green salad (lunch); pasta primavera with
steamed vegetables (dinner).

RATES AND PACKAGES
1-week program (Sun.–Sun.) $731–$1,198 single, $665–$959 double.
Daily rate $115–$169 single, $95–$135 double. 50% deposit required.
AE, MC, V.

DIRECTIONS
⊠ *559 Webbs Mills Rd., Raymond, ME 04071,* ☎ *207/655–7624,* ℻
207/655–3321.

From Portland: Take Interstate–95 to Exit 8 and Route 302 northwest to Route 85 (45 mins).

POLAND SPRING HEALTH INSTITUTE

Medical wellness
Mineral springs

An extended visit to Poland Spring Health Institute is a cross between a holiday at a country B&B and a clinic at one of Europe's old-fashioned thermal spas, where mineral water is used in all manner of healing treatments. Operated for the past 20 years by a medical doctor and his wife, Poland Spring has been synonymous with healthy water for more than a century, largely due to a commercial bottling plant near the institute. The spring is the source of all the water used at the spa, from the daily 8–10 glasses that guests are asked to drink to the water used in the whirlpools and in the steam room where you receive body wraps preceding a massage. Other aspects of the program include following a vegetarian diet and participating in rigorous outdoor exercise.

Just 10 guests are accommodated in the five simple rooms of a big New England farmhouse, where the average stay is two weeks. A special program for smoking cessation (14 days) is offered, in addition to a five-day nutrition and health seminar.

Guests work closely with specialists on diabetes and stress-related ailments. Exercises and hydrotherapy treatments are prescribed individually, based on each guest's physical condition. Testing by the medical office, when needed, carries an additional charge; everything else is included in the weekly fee.

This nonprofit, private wellness center was founded in 1979 and emphasizes Christian prayer. The 260-acre property is bounded by a 2-mile-long lake, with hiking and biking trails and a parcourse, and in winter guests can cross-country ski and ice skate.

FACILITIES
Exercise Equipment: Stationary bikes. **Services:** Swedish massage. **Swimming:** Lake. **Classes and Programs:** Lectures on health-related subjects. **Recreation:** Biking, boating, canoeing, horseback riding; golf nearby.

ACCOMMODATIONS
5 rooms, most with shared bath.

DINING
Buffet-style meals rich in complex carbohydrates. No eggs, dairy products, fish, or meat. **Sample Meals:** Baked potato, green beans, salad (lunch); vegetarian lasagna with greens, corn with tossed salad and bread, vegetarian corn chowder with crackers and fruit (dinner).

RATES AND PACKAGES
Rooms with shared bath, $745 a week with meals; private room $950, tax and service charge included. $200 nonrefundable deposit required. No credit cards.

DIRECTIONS
✉ *32 Summit Spring Rd., Poland Spring, ME 04274,* ☎ *207/998–2894,* FAX *207/998–2164.*

From Boston: Take Interstate–95 north (it turns into Interstate-495 at the Maine border) to Route 26 north. Follow Route 26 for 13 mi and turn left onto Schellinger Road. Continue 1 mi and turn right (2½ hrs).

MASSACHUSETTS

CANYON RANCH IN THE BERKSHIRES

Holistic health
Luxury pampering
Medical wellness
Nutrition and diet

Driving past formal gardens and an elegant mansion, you may think you've arrived at a millionaire's mountain retreat. Once past the inn's registration desk, however, the focus on fitness and healthy living becomes quite apparent. The East Coast counterpart to the original Canyon Ranch Spa in Arizona adopts the same holistic, multi-choice approach. Counselors personalize mind-and-body programs on request, or help you select from a lengthy list of daily classes, outings, and workshops. Skiers can get in shape before tackling cross-country trails, and executives can use the latest biofeedback systems to de-stress. Attuned to the seasons in its outdoor activity, the ranch has an indoor fitness center like no other in the Northeast, complete with cardiovascular and weight training gymnasiums with advanced cross-aerobics exercise equipment, racquetball, squash, and tennis courts, running track, 75-foot swimming pool, and separate locker rooms for men and women with saunas, steam rooms, inhalation rooms, and Jacuzzis.

The main attraction for many visitors is the opportunity to rest and rejuvenate with cutting-edge treatments. The latest body treatment, a 100-minute session called Euphoria, combines an invigorating shower with an aromatherapy scalp massage using fragrant rose-geranium oil; a warm botanical body mask and gentle buffing; immersion in a hydrotub scented with grapefruit oil; and, finally, a full-body massage with warm Bindi oil. Instead of standard Swedish massage, consider the craniosacral body alignment, an osteopathic technique that releases tension in the neck, cranium, and spine. For total pampering, try the signature Parisian body polish, which uses crushed pearls to smooth and soften your skin.

The centerpiece of the 120-acre woodlands retreat is a mansion that dates from 1897—Bellefontaine—reminiscent of the Petit Trianon in Versailles. Dining at the mansion, you won't feel deprived: Though the menu is annotated with calorie counts, you can sample many items, make unlimited trips to the pasta bar, and even request butter and salt. Single guests seeking company can sit at the Captain's Table.

On either side of the elegant lobby are two floors of guest rooms. The rooms are more functional, contemporary–New England than Old World, with flowered fabric and big windows. There's space to relax in big wing chairs, watch movies (there are in-room VCRs), and write at a desk that can be adapted for computer connection. A fully-equipped computer center adjoins the guest lounge. Covered walkways connect the inn, mansion, and fitness center.

With diverse cultural attractions in the area—Tanglewood Music Festival, Jacob's Pillow Dance Festival, Williamstown Theater—summer reservations must be made well in advance. During the fall and winter, longer stays are encouraged with discounted packages and special programs on women's issues and the latest in prevention of illness. With more than 40 fitness classes daily, from yoga to line dancing, you might get frustrated if you try to fit it all in with treatments; plan accordingly. The minimum-age requirement is 14.

FACILITIES

Exercise Equipment: Cross-country skiing machines, rowing machines, stair climbers, stationary bikes, treadmills, weight-training circuit, free weights. **Services:** Reflexology, Reiki, shiatsu, sports massage, Swedish massage; acupuncture, aromatherapy wraps, herbal wraps, jin shin jyutsu, mud wraps, salt wraps, seaweed wraps; hydrotherapy. **Swimming:** Indoor and outdoor pools. **Classes and Programs:** Biofeedback training, boxercise, cooking classes, health and lifestyle lectures, holistic health counseling, line dancing, medical checkup and fitness evaluation, meditation, tai chi, yoga. **Recreation:** Aerobics, aquaerobics, basketball, biking, chi gong, cross-country skiing, hiking, tennis, racquetball, squash, canoeing, volleyball, kayaking, track.

ACCOMMODATIONS

101 rooms, 24 suites.

DINING

Menu with à la carte choices at 3 meals daily, plus salad bar and breakfast buffet (fruit, cereals, breads). **Sample Meals:** Bean and roasted eggplant couscous, kiwi-cantaloupe soup, salmon with lemon-lime yogurt dressing, pasta with lobster-fennel sauce (lunch); Cantonese tempeh stir-fry, grilled vegetable strudel with bean ragout, tuna in pepper crust with ponzu sauce, osso buco (dinner).

RATES AND PACKAGES

3-night package $1,008–$1,360 single, $1,120–$ 1,430 double. 8-day/7-night package $2,810–$3,420 single, $2,450–$2,920 double. Add 18% service charge and tax. 3-night minimum stay. 2-night deposit required. AE, D, MC, V.

DIRECTIONS

✉ *165 Kemble St. (Rte. 7A), Lenox, MA 01240,* ☎ *413/637–4100 or 800/742–9000,* ℻ *413/637–0057.*

From New York: Take Route 684 to Interstate-84 west. Exit to the Taconic State Parkway north and follow to Route 23, Hillsdale exit. Follow Route 23 east through Hillsdale to Great Barrington, and take Route 7 north through Stockbridge and Lee to Lenox. Turn left on Route 7A at Lenox Center; Canyon Ranch is ¼ mi further on the right. (about 4 hrs).

From Boston: Take the Massachusetts Turnpike to Exit 2 (Lee), and follow Route 20 west to Lenox. Turn left on Business Route 183 south and continue toward the center of town. At Trinity Church turn left onto Kemble Street; Canyon Ranch is ½ mi farther on the left.

KRIPALU CENTER FOR YOGA AND HEALTH

Holistic health
Medical wellness

Kripalu is a New Age ashram designed to help visitors achieve peace of mind and insights about healthy lifestyles based on ancient wisdom. Amrit Desai, who founded the center in 1972, developed kripalu yoga, a gentle practice that combines postures, breathing techniques, and meditation. The goal is to hold the postures for a prolonged period, so that we can turn inward and discover what is blocking us from living joyfully.

At Kripalu Center, robed residents participate in a prescribed regimen of yoga and meditation, including workshops designed to fight stress and increase well-being. Mornings begin at 5:45 with chanting by members of the resident community. A yoga session from 6:45 to 8 AM is followed by breakfast eaten in silence. Most of the guests, who can number over 300 at a time, start their day walking about the grounds, and join evening sessions of chanting. Silence is maintained during breakfast and lunch.

The center is housed in a former Jesuit seminary on a 300-acre wooded site adjacent to the Tanglewood Music Festival grounds. The four-story brick building has spartan accommodations, without daily maid service, in dormitories and private rooms, most with shared bath. Making up for the lack of creature comforts are spectacular views and gardens laid out by Frederick Law Olmsted, designer of New York's Central Park.

In addition to the daily schedule, there are week-long programs such as Men and Yoga, Life After 50, Self-Esteem, and Meditation Retreat. Other programs explore an understanding of love, work towards transforming stress, or teach the practice of gentle movements as a metaphor for taking control of one's life. Options include all-juice fasting, outdoor treks, and an intensive inner quest intended to help participants release physical and emotional blocks through integrated breathwork, dynamic yoga postures, and creative movement and play. Drawing on anatomy, psychology, and Sanskrit philosophy, these programs teach energy balancing techniques that can be used to develop a healthy lifestyle.

Each day is structured to involve you in a new awakening to your personal needs and powers. As you get oriented to the daily yoga regimen, you'll learn about optional classes such as "The Dance of Tennis"—a spiritual approach to improving performance in tennis. You can sign up for Kripalu bodywork, including soothing, meditative massage, and Phoenix Rising yoga therapy based on body posture training. Additional options include soaking in large tiled whirlpool baths or relaxing in wooden saunas. In summer, you can swim in a lake on the property. In winter, there's skiing at the nearby Butternut resort.

Supervised programs for teenagers and children encourage noncompetitive and loving friendships. Teenagers can participate in the one-week "Coming of Age" outdoor camping program, which combines yoga and sports; take leadership training; and learn communications skills. Other children's programs include a ropes course, shamanic journey, sweat lodge, and vision quest. Parents can enroll younger children on a daily fee basis in supervised sessions of yoga, dance, and sports.

FACILITIES
Services: Meditative massage, polarity therapy, shiatsu, reflexology, acupuncture, weight room. **Swimming:** Private lake. **Classes and Programs:** One-on-one yoga instruction, group yoga, communal meditation and chanting, Indian dancing. **Recreation:** Skiing, hiking, biking. **Children's Programs:** Children's programs (ages 5–12); youth programs (ages 9–19).

ACCOMMODATIONS
180 rooms, most with shared bath; 150 dormitory beds, all with shared bath.

DINING
3 buffet-style meals daily, all low-fat and vegetarian, with whole grains and vegetables, dairy products, full salad bar, fresh-baked bread. Hot or cold tea served at noon. **Sample Meals:** Vegetable quesadilla, Mexican-style rice, corn, salad (lunch); vegetable-pesto pizza with rice and beans (dinner).

RATES AND PACKAGES
Nightly rate $115–$195 single, $85–$155 double, $70–$85 dormitory. 2-night programs $285–$465 single, $255–$385 double, $235 dormitory. 6-night workshop $780–$1,320 single, $750–$1,098 double, $690 dormitory. Children's Program $40 per day; 6-day youth program $594.

25% deposit required. No refunds; deposit can be applied to future programs. MC, V.

DIRECTIONS
✉ *Box 793, Lenox, MA 01240,* ☎ *413/448–3152 or 800/741–7353,* FAX *413/448–3384.*

From Boston: Massachusetts Turnpike (I–90) to Exit B-3, Route 22 south, Route 102 east via West Stockbridge, Route 183 (2 hrs).

THE KUSHI INSTITUTE OF THE BERKSHIRES

Holistic health
Nutrition and diet

At this former Franciscan abbey set on 600 acres of woodlands and meadows, seminars focus on the art of macrobiotics—a natural-diet lifestyle often used in helping people recovering from cancer and other diseases—from food preparation and cooking to designing a balanced diet. Founded by Aveline and Michio Kushi as a year-round center for lifestyle learning, the Institute has been in the forefront of macrobiotic research and education since 1979.

Scheduled seminars vary from the week-long macrobiotic program, offered twice per month, to four- and five-day cooking intensives and spiritual retreats; a multipart spiritual training seminar is scheduled at various times of the year. The month-long macrobiotic career training program provides training for aspiring professional macrobiotic chefs, cooking teachers, lecturers, and health guides. For newcomers to macrobiotics, a week-long introductory course includes exercise and massage. Also scheduled are four or five days of instruction on preventing cancer and heart disease.

The daily activities begin with a session of *do-in,* stretching exercises that are simple and easy to learn. Periods of meditation alternate with lectures and workshops in food preparation. Individuals, couples, and families often participate together. Only 15 participants can be accommodated at any one time, so the mood is intimate and serene. Most guests stay in the main lodge (7 of the 10 plain but comfortable guest rooms share a bathroom); a dormitory building has additional rooms for participants in month-long programs. Meals are served family style.

FACILITIES
Services: Shiatsu, acupressure. **Swimming:** Lake nearby. **Classes and Programs:** Discussions and workshops on diet and nutrition, informal entertainment, massage.

ACCOMMODATIONS
10 rooms in main lodge, most with shared bath; 10 rooms in dormitory building, all with shared bath.

DINING
3 macrobiotic meals daily. **Sample Meals:** Brown rice, lentil soup with carrots and onions, steamed broccoli and cauliflower with pumpkin-seed dressing, green salad (lunch); mashed millet and cauliflower with seitan—a meatlike food made from wheat gluten—and gravy, sautéed string beans with sesame-seed dressing, steamed collard greens, and haziki salad (dinner).

RATES AND PACKAGES
6-day Way to Health seminar (Sun.–Sat.) with meals and shared bedroom, $1,495 for first participant, $1,395 accompanying person. 1-month Mac-

robiotic Career Training program $3,625 per person double. 3-day/2-night Essentials of Macrobiotics weekend $475 double. $100 deposit per person required. AE, MC, V.

DIRECTIONS
✉ *308 Leland Rd., Box 7, Becket, MA 01223,* ☎ *413/623–5742 or 800/ 975–8744,* ℻ *413/623–8827.*

From Boston: Massachusetts Turnpike (I–90), exit for Lee on Route 20 east, continue 12 miles to Route 8 north, continue 6½ miles, turn right on High Street, look for sign (2½ hrs).

MAHARISHI AYUR-VEDA HEALTH CENTER

Holistic health
Medical wellness

The meditative ambience of the Himalayas pervades what once was a millionaire's mansion. Eastern and Western medicine meet here in treatments following Ayurvedic principles. Based on an analysis of your *dosha,* or physical and emotional type, therapy includes a special diet related to body type, massage with warm oil and herbal essences, and total relaxation.

The healing process of *panchakarma* begins with a physical examination, pulse measurement, and a thorough questionnaire to determine whether you are *vata* (quick, energetic, movement prone), *pitta* (enterprising and sharp), or *kapha* (tranquil and steady). Therapy and diet are prescribed accordingly.

The medically supervised program tends to attract people with cancer and other diseases; the center's doctors and registered nurses are trained in both Eastern and Western medicine. A daily two-hour session to rid the body of impurities includes massage, heat application, and a gentle laxative. Neuromuscular training may be recommended through yoga exercises. Aromatherapy is also available, and a course in transcendental meditation is taught for an extra fee. The combination of these treatments and meditation is said to be effective in stress reduction, encouraging balance at the most fundamental level of holistic health. This is a place dedicated to rejuvenation and resolution, rather than recreation,.

Guests stay in a mansion that dates from the 1920s, once owned by a shipping magnate involved with the *Titanic.* Rooms, each with a television, VCR, telephone, and private bath, overlook either the mountains to the north or the extensive gardens that cover the Center's grounds. Meals can be taken in the dining room on the main floor, on the adjoining terrace, or in individual guest rooms—room service is provided at no extra charge.

FACILITIES
Services: Abhyanga, herbal steam bath. **Classes and Programs:** Physical examination, transcendental meditation, videotapes and lectures on health-related topics.

ACCOMMODATIONS
11 rooms, some with shared bath, 3 suites.

DINING
3 vegetarian meals daily. Simple, low-fat, dairy-free diet. **Sample Meals:** Indian rice and dal with vegetables and cooked fruit (lunch); vegetable pâté, lentil soup, green salad (dinner).

RATES AND PACKAGES
1-week Standard Rejuvenation program $3,190–$4,190 single or double. Weeklong Rasayana Program $800 per day (14-day min.). Tax included. MC, V.

DIRECTIONS
✉ *679 George Hill Rd., Lancaster, MA 01523,* ☎ *978/365–4549 or 800/290–6702,* FAX *978/368–0674.*

From Boston: Massachusetts Turnpike (I–90) west to Route 495 north, exit on Route 117 west to Route 70; entrance on George Hill Road (3 hrs).

THE OPTION INSTITUTE

Holistic health

The goal at the Option Institute, a mountain retreat, is to nurture healthy attitudes toward life rather than emphasize physical fitness. Personal attitudes, beliefs, and feelings are examined to develop a fuller understanding of how to improve one's physical and mental health. Working in group sessions and private consultations, participants are taught to be more accepting of themselves, to learn to find alternatives, and to form more loving relationships.

Founded in 1983 by Barry Neil Kaufman and Samahira Kaufman, who have written and lectured on interpersonal relationships, the Option Institute sets out to provide a stimulating environment for people from all walks of life—from young professionals to families of children with special needs. Guests come for weekends and intensive programs of up to eight weeks. The one-week Body Vital program explores the impact of attitude on body and health; the five-day Inward Bound program combines meditation with physical activity.

With a full-time staff of 60, the Kaufmans seek to teach the philosophy of their best-selling book: *Happiness Is a Choice.* The process begins with a circle of new friends sitting in a circle on the floor, discussing personal beliefs. After experiencing the process, participants say that gaining a profound sense of energy and vigor from the release of tensions has helped empower them to enjoy a happier life.

Three hours west of Boston, the 95-acre campus has simply furnished guest houses that use natural wood and lots of windows for a woodsy, rustic feeling. Some kitchen-equipped units are available. Grassy meadows, forests, and streams surround the guest houses, providing prime territory for meditation walks. Hikers have access to the Appalachian Trail, and skiers can take advantage of the nearby Butternut and Catamount ski resorts. Music and arts venues are plentiful in the surrounding Berkshire towns.

FACILITIES
Services: Swedish massage, private counseling. **Swimming:** Pond. **Classes and Programs:** Workshops and group discussions on communication, health, personal relationships. **Recreation:** Hiking, downhill and cross-country skiing.

ACCOMMODATIONS
35 rooms, most with shared bath.

DINING
3 buffet-style vegetarian meals per day. Limited eggs, cheese, milk. **Sample Meals:** Vegetarian lasagna, whole-grain casseroles (lunch); legumes, seasonal vegetables, Greek salad, pasta (dinner).

RATES AND PACKAGES
3-day weekends (Thurs.–Sun.) $595 per person double, meals included. 1-week Body Vital program $1,225 per person, double. 5-day Inward Bound $1,295. 50% deposit required. MC, V.

DIRECTIONS
✉ *2080 S. Undermountain Rd., Sheffield, MA 01257,* ☎ *413/229–2100,* FAX *413/229–8931.*

From New York City/Boston: I–95 north to Massachusetts Turnpike (I–90) west (3 hrs).

SMITH COLLEGE ADULT SPORT/FITNESS CAMP

Sports conditioning

This weeklong sports-oriented camp on the campus of Smith College is like a post-graduate course in wellness. The atmosphere is very low-key: Guests stay in student dorm rooms and share meals in the residence-hall dining room.

The three-building sports complex has first-rate facilities. Open at all times to campers are two gymnasiums, a six-lane swimming pool with two diving boards, and a strength training room; there are also indoor and outdoor tennis courts, squash courts, running tracks, and a 5,000-meter cross-country course that winds through woods and fields. A climbing wall and ropes course tempt adventurous types, and a boating house on the nearby Connecticut River provides facilities and equipment for water skiing and rowing.

Each day's program varies, encouraging you to try new sports or activities such as in-line skating, archery, yoga, and croquet. Various wake-up workouts are scheduled before breakfast: You can join a group swim, run or walk, or tai chi, for instance. Throughout the rest of the day, there are organized aerobics classes, yoga, canoeing, sculling, and group hikes and bike rides. In many events, sports psychologists test campers' physical and mental endurance.

Complementing the sports programs are fitness profiles involving flexibility and body composition tests, stress-control evaluations using biofeedback equipment, and sports medicine consultations in which you can discuss injuries with a certified athletic trainer. Evening sessions are devoted to exploring nutrition facts and fallacies and sports psychology. Swedish massage (for an extra charge) is the only spa service available. The camp takes place each year during one or two weeks in June, and is limited to 50 participants with an average age of 50 (minimum age is 20).

FACILITIES
Exercise Equipment: Weight-training circuit. **Services:** Swedish massage. **Swimming:** Lake, indoor pool. **Classes and Programs:** Cookouts, dancing, orienteering, panel discussions, tai chi, yoga. **Recreation:** Basketball, boating, squash, tennis, track.

ACCOMMODATIONS
50 dormitory beds in single and double rooms, all with shared bath.

DINING
3 buffet-style meals daily. Sample Meals: Hamburgers, cold cuts, salad bar (lunch); salmon fillet, steak, pasta primavera, baked ziti, steamed vegetables, salad bar (dinner).

RATES AND PACKAGES
$800 for 6-day program (Sun.–Sat.), includes room, meals, activities. 50% deposit required. No credit cards.

DIRECTIONS
✉ *Michelle Finley, Ainsworth Gymnasium, Smith College, Rte. 9, Northampton, MA 01063,* ☎ *413/585–3977,* ℻ *413/585–2712.*

From Boston: Massachusetts Turnpike (I–90) west to Interstate–91 north to Route 9 north (2½ hrs).

BONUS MILES MAKE GREAT SOUVENIRS.

Earn Miles With Your MCI Card.

Take the MCI Card along on this trip and start earning miles for the next one. You'll earn frequent flyer miles on all your calls and save with the low rates you've come to expect from MCI. Before you know it, you'll be on your way to some other international destination.

Sign up for MCI by calling 1-800-FLY-FREE

Is this a great time, or what? :-)

Earn Frequent Flyer Miles.

AmericanAirlines'
AAdvantage®

Continental Airlines
OnePass

△ Delta Air Lines
SkyMiles®

HAWAIIAN AIRLINES.

MIDWEST EXPRESS AIRLINES

NORTHWEST AIRLINES
WORLDPERKS®

Rapid Rewards
SOUTHWEST AIRLINES'

MILEAGE PLUS.
United Airlines

US AIRWAYS
DIVIDEND MILES

With guidebooks for every kind of travel—from weekend getaways to island hopping to adventures abroad—it's easy to understand why smart travelers go with **Fodor's**.

At bookstores everywhere.
www.fodors.com

Smart travelers go with **Fodor's**™

NEW HAMPSHIRE

WATERVILLE VALLEY RESORT

Sports conditioning

The first thing you'll notice at Waterville Valley is people on the move. There's so much to do at this 500-acre recreational mega-complex that guests never seem to stand still. In addition to downhill and cross-country skiing, hiking and horseback riding in the White Mountains, and golf at an 18-hole course, there's a year-round ice-skating rink, a mountain biking center, and a $2-million sports center with 18 clay tennis courts. Mountain peaks and forests of green fir surround the valley, which is traversed by a free shuttle bus.

Skiing gave this area its start, and it remains a major draw: 225 acres of ski terrain is crossed by more than 35 downhill trails ranked for beginner, intermediate, and advanced skiers. Snowmaking equipment assures good conditions from December to April; lessons and rentals are available. At the Cross Country Ski Center, 105 kilometers of trails lead into the heart of the White Mountain National Forest. In addition, miles of hiking trails are used for snowshoeing.

The White Mountain Athletic Club, open every day of the year, has indoor and outdoor tennis and lap swimming, an indoor running track, racquetball, squash, a strength-and-toning room, and a cardiovascular room with views of the surrounding mountains. A coed sauna and steam room are available, in addition to separate facilities. You can also sign up for aerobics classes and aquacize sessions in the pool. Massage is the only bodywork available.

Accommodations are scattered throughout the valley, ranging from chalet-style inns to condominium apartments (reservations are made through a central lodging bureau). Many units come with fully-equipped kitchens. The resort has no central dining facility, but several restaurants are easily accessible. Among the choices are Chile Peppers, which serves simple, light lunch and dinner fare, and the more upscale Valley Inn.

FACILITIES

Exercise Equipment: Rowing machines, stair climber, stationary bikes, treadmills, free weights. **Services:** Swedish massage. **Swimming:** Indoor and outdoor pools, pond. **Classes and Programs:** Aerobics, seasonal entertainment. **Recreation:** biking, hiking, ice skating, golf, racquetball, sailing, skiing, squash, tennis, track.

ACCOMMODATIONS

4,000 beds in various lodges booked through Central Reservations (☎ 800/468–2553). Leading choices: Golden Eagle Lodge, Snowy Owl Inn, Town Square, and fully equipped 2-story houses.

DINING

Restaurants nearby. No meals included in ski or spa packages.

RATES AND PACKAGES

Golden Eagle $78–$249 for 1 to 6 persons; Snowy Owl Inn $58–$229. 1-bedroom apartments at Town Square $89–$259 daily for 1 to 2 persons. Add 8% tax. 50% deposit required. AE, DC, MC, V.

DIRECTIONS
✉ *Rte. 49 (Box 349), Waterville Valley, NH 03215,* ☎ *603/236–8303 for ski and spa information, 800/468–2553 for lodging reservations,* FAX *603/236–4104.*

From Boston: Route 3 to Interstate–93, Exit 28 for Waterville, then 11 mi on Route 49 (2½ hrs).

NEW YORK

GURNEY'S INN

Luxury pampering
Nutrition and diet

Seaside seawater therapy is the specialty at this spa on the tip of Long Island, where sybarites can revel in seaweed baths, swim in a 60-foot heated seawater pool, have a seaweed facial, dine on seafood while enjoying a view of the sea, and even arrange to go deep-sea fishing from a nearby marina. Like many European spas, Gurney's uses ocean water as an integral part of advanced hydrotherapy, but unlike the medically managed thalassotherapy centers of France, Gurney's also specializes in stress management and weight management.

Among the spa's many innovative uses of seawater are underwater massages in private Roman tubs fed by filtered, heated sea water, body scrubs using salt from the Dead Sea, and body wraps that mix green Argilite mud with micronized seaweed to create a mineral-rich gel that's said to promote balance and healing in the body while relieving many symptoms of arthritis and stress.

Brisk morning walks along the shore usher in the daily program; along the way you can challenge yourself at a 14-station parcourse. After breakfast, you can join an aquatics exercise class in the pool, take a tai chi or yoga class, join a group hike along nature trails or windswept dunes, swim in the surf, or simply relax in a Roman tub. For cardiovascular and strength training, a sea-view exercise room has a full line of equipment and personal trainers on hand. Beauty treatments are available, as are programs in stress control and nutrition. The spa staff of 60 includes specialists in everything from traditional Swedish massage to craniosacral therapy, polarity, reflexology, and Trager bodywork.

Two of the inn's buildings face the beach; another three buildings are set back behind the spa, though rooms in all five have ocean views. Four luxurious oceanfront cottages provide the ideal setting for a private getaway. Guests dine either in the Cafe Monte or the more formal Sea Grill. Both restaurants have spa menus with limited-calorie options in addition to standard à la carte menus.

Though Montauk is relatively low-key compared with the nearby Hamptons, Gurney's Inn receives a fair amount of traffic, especially during the summer. The pool and classes are open to all including the convention and time-share vacation crowds that frequent Gurney's, and this puts a strain on the facilities during the peak summer season. For peace and quiet, schedule your visit when the beach crowd goes home or during the winter. Also note that this is more of a singles- or couples-oriented destination than a family resort: The minimum age at the spa is 18, and evening activity centers around the bar.

FACILITIES

Exercise Equipment: Stair climbers, stationary bikes, treadmills, weight-training circuit, free weights. **Services:** Craniosacral massage, reflexology, Reiki, shiatsu, Swedish massage; acupressure, fango, herbal wrap, loofah scrub, mud wrap, seaweed wrap; thalassotherapy; facial. **Swimming:** Indoor pool, ocean beach. **Classes and Programs:** Aerobics, aquaerobics, biofeedback, kick-boxing, personal training, tai chi, yoga; health and fitness consultation, lectures on health and nutrition; dancing and entertainment. **Recreation:** Fishing, golf, hiking, horseback riding, jogging, tennis.

ACCOMMODATIONS
105 suites, 4 cottages.

DINING
3 calorie-controlled meals (1,000–1,200 calories per day) daily, low in
salt and sugar. **Sample Meals:** Tortellini en brodo—broth with pasta
dumplings, egg-drop soup, grilled salmon, steak stir-fry, whole-wheat pasta
(lunch); paella, vegetarian lasagna, chicken breast with asparagus (dinner).

RATES AND PACKAGES
All packages include 3 meals. 3-day Escape package without room $556;
lodging $235–$280 single, $145–$180 double. Autumn-Winter 5-day
Health and Beauty Plan with lodging and meals $1,400 per person, dou-
ble. 1-day package $196.50. Daily facility fee for nonpackage visit $20.
25% deposit required. AE, DC, MC, V.

DIRECTIONS
⊠ *Old Montauk Hwy., Montauk, NY 11954,* ☎ *516/668–2345 or 800/
848–7639,* FAX *516/668–3203.*

From New York City: Long Island Expressway to Sunrise Highway
(Route 27).

MOHONK MOUNTAIN HOUSE

Luxury pampering
Sports conditioning

Nature walks have been a way of life at Mohonk Mountain House in
the Hudson River Valley since 1869. Here at the spa where "The Road
To Wellville" was filmed, hikers, runners, and cross-country skiers can
still choose from more than 100 miles of trails, paths, and carriage roads
that link scenic sites on 2,200 acres of private woodland—all in a setting
that could very well be the turn of the century.

Sprawled atop a ridge, Mohonk Mountain House looks like something
mad king Ludwig might have concocted in Bavaria: a Victorian fantasy
bristling with gables, towers, chimneys, and turrets. But while the hotel
looks like a remnant of another era, its programs explore contemporary
subjects relating to science, the arts, and health. Theme weeks have included languages, stargazing, and "Toward Self and Balance: A Woman's
Perspective." In winter, the Recreation and Renewal Package is a 5-night
midweek package that includes a complimentary massage for each day
that you participate in the program. Throughout the year there are fitness-oriented classes and outdoor activities, from skiing to snowshoeing
and ice skating.

Golfers can challenge themselves at a nine-hole par-35 course or a lighted
18-hole putting green. Equestrians can join guided trail rides (English or
Western) at the resort's stables. In winter, riding trails are groomed for
cross-country skiing. Indoors, the fitness center has a modest selection
of exercise equipment, saunas, and showers; aerobics and stretch classes
are scheduled regularly. For those who prefer a dip in cold, clear water,
Mohonk Lake is a stone's throw away.

The hotel rambles an eighth of a mile and accommodates up to 500 guests.
Choice rooms in the towers have original Victorian woodwork, working
fireplace, and balcony. The cavernous, pine-floored dining room has a
clerestory and a breathtaking view of the Catskill Mountains. Service is formal, with white tablecloths and flowers on every table; men are requested
to wear jackets to dinner. After dinner, guests attend slide shows or nature

talks, go on stargazing walks, or simply sit on the vast wooden veranda's rocking chairs, where workday pressures feel like a distant memory. On Fridays there's square dancing, and Saturdays ballroom dancing.

Exercise Equipment: Stair climber, stationary bikes, cross-country skiing machine, weight-training circuit, free weights. **Services:** Massage. **Swimming:** Lake. **Classes and Programs:** Concerts, dancing, films, speakers on health and fitness. **Recreation:** Croquet, downhill skiing, golf, ice skating, tennis. **Children's Programs:** Outdoor adventures and walks for children (ages 2–12).

261 rooms.

3 meals and afternoon tea. Buffet breakfast and lunch (with salad bar); 4-course dinner, with choice of 6 homemade desserts. Spa cuisine items available. **Sample Meals:** Manhattan clam chowder, seafood salad, green bean–rice medley, corn-crusted catfish with red-pepper sauce, chicken cutlets, carved flank steak (lunch); Hudson Valley duck terrine with tart wildberry coulis or smoked bluefish with chicory dressing, field greens with roasted-garlic vinaigrette, rosemary-roast lamb with minted couscous and grilled zucchini or salmon-stuffed sole with red rice and wilted spinach on tomato-ginger coulis (dinner).

Rooms and 3 meals daily $150–$291 single, $265–$400 for 2 persons; tower room with fireplace $400–$550 for 2. 15% service charge, taxes. Deposit, payable 1 night in advance. AE, D, DC, MC, V.

✉ *Lake Mohonk, New Paltz, NY 12561,* ☎ *914/255–1000 or 800/772–6646,* ℻ *914/256–2100.*

From New York City: New York State Thruway (I–87) to New Paltz (Exit 18), turn left onto Route 299 through New Paltz; turn right just after Walkill River Bridge. Follow Mountain Rest Road 4 miles to Mohonk Gate House.

OMEGA INSTITUTE

Holistic health
Medical wellness

Part summer camp, part holistic health center, the Omega Institute is a roving program that takes place several times throughout the year in various parts of the U.S., including the U.S. Virgin Islands. On this particular 80-acre campus in the scenic Hudson Valley, campers of all ages—families, couples, and singles—are invited to participate in more than 250 workshops scheduled from June through mid-October. Native Americans, Zen Buddhists, and Tibetan monks discuss spirituality. Other guest speakers focus on bodywork, energy healing, women and men's issues, alternative health, and psychological studies.

The core program, a five-day Wellness Week, involves working with a small group in a structured workshop where you learn how to incorporate the latest findings on health, diet, and nutrition into your lifestyle. For first-timers there are introductory weekends devoted to experiential learning, as well as workshops in self-discovery, health, and wellness. Workshops and seminars last from two to five days, and each requires a separate registration fee.

Though there is no gym on the property, groups assemble for yoga and tai chi sessions each morning and afternoon. A sauna, massage rooms, and holistic health consultation are also available—but bring your own towel and bathing suit, as facilities are coed.

Guests have a choice of accommodations that range from simple to spartan. Roommates can be matched on request in the two-room cottages, each of which share a porch. Seven dormitory rooms have two beds each; bring your own linens. Several double-occupancy tent cabins on raised platforms have electricity but little else. For those who truly want to rough it, there are campsites near the lake or up on a hill, sharing one communal bath house. Whichever option you choose, prepare to go without TV, phone, and air-conditioning.

The diverse set of participants comes together during mealtimes in the big, self-service dining room; spontaneous discussion groups often form at tables on the porch. In the evening, you can take time out for a quiet walk or jog down a country lane, or a swim in the lake. On many evenings there are performances of gospel, chanting, and dance.

Children's programs are designed to open young minds to new ideas and the traditions of people around the world. Teenagers ages 12 through 17 can enroll in all workshops with faculty approval, at full tuition, but must attend Omega with an adult. For younger children, there are programs in nature study, outdoor adventure, sports, music, movement, and game playing; some encourage family participation. During a 5-day spring retreat with monks and nuns from a Vietnamese village, children learn about mindful living and play as prayer. Family Week, in August, includes nature studies and creative games for children between the ages of 4 and 17.

FACILITIES

Services: Massage. **Swimming:** Private lake. **Classes and Programs:** Antistress counseling, concerts, films, lifestyle lectures, nutrition consultation, wellness workshops. **Recreation:** Basketball, canoeing, jogging, tennis, volleyball. **Children's Programs:** Ongoing programs (ages 4–12); scheduled kids camps (ages 12–17).

ACCOMMODATIONS

230 cabins, some with shared bath; 10 tent cabins; 56 dormitory beds. Campsites available.

DINING

3 buffet-style meals daily. Mainly vegetarian, with some fish and dairy. Locally grown fresh fruits and vegetables. Whole grains, beans, and bean products. No artificial sweeteners. **Sample Meals:** Mushroom-barley soup with focaccia, stir-fried greens with brown rice, cashew chili with cheddar (lunch); pad thai, salmon with wasabi glaze, cajun catfish, fresh ravioli (dinner).

RATES AND PACKAGES

2-day lodging $105 dormitory, $150–$185 in cabin; Introductory weekend $90. 5-day Omega Wellness Program $285–$305 plus lodging ($210 in dormitory; $295–$365 per person in double-occupancy cabins). Campsites $43 per person, per day. Meals included in lodging rates. 50% deposit required. MC, V.

DIRECTIONS

✉ *260 Lake Dr., Rhinebeck, NY 12572,* ☎ *914/266–4444 or 800/944–1001,* ℻ *914/266–4828.*

From New York City: New York State Thruway (I–87) or Saw Mill River Parkway north to the Taconic Parkway, Bull's Head Road west to Lake Drive (2 hrs).

SAGAMORE RESORT & SPA

Luxury pampering

Amid the Adirondack Mountains and set on a 70-acre private island sur-rounded by Lake George, the huge white clapboard Sagamore Resort & Spa suggests an escape to the quiet pleasures of a bygone era. The resort includes a modern health club, indoor swimming pool, and indoor ten-nis and racquetball courts. Fitness classes are scheduled throughout the day, from walks and low-impact aerobics to water exercise, at no charge.

The spa has separate sauna, whirlpool, and steam-room facilities for men and women. There is a coed fitness center, with sunlit, airy space to accommodate the equipment. Appointments are made for treatment on an à la carte basis, which includes the daily charge for club facili-ties. Flexible spa plans provide a more economical way to sample the resort's services.

In addition to massage, facials, and body treatments, the specialties here are seaweed wraps, mud therapy (using natural healing mud in body wraps), and packs for sports injuries. You can wind down your treatment with a full-body rubdown using a mixture of sea salt and massage oil that leaves your skin tingling. After the scrub with loofah sponges, the salt mixture is hosed off. Next, a coating of Adirondack herbal and floral creams leaves you with a glowing feeling. The cost: $35–$80 for each treatment; or this could be included as part of a two-day spa package. (A 17% gratu-ity is added to the cost of services.)

The classic 1930 hotel is on the site of the original Sagamore, opened in 1893. Recent additions include seven lakeside lodges. At the fitness cen-ter you can work out and enjoy an unbroken vista of Adirondack State Park. Don't miss the par-70 Donald Rose golf course, full of cross-coutry skiiers in winter, even if just for dinner at the clubhouse.

FACILITIES
Exercise Equipment: Cross-country skiing machine, rowing machines, stair climbers, stationary bikes, treadmills, weight-training circuit, free weights. **Services:** Aromatherapy massage, reflexology, Reiki, shiatsu, Swedish massage, sports massage; acupuncture, body polish, body scrub, herbal wrap, salt glow, mud wrap, seaweed wrap; hot plunge, hy-drotherapy; facial. **Swimming:** Indoor pool, lakeside docks. **Classes and Programs:** Aquaerobics, step aerobics; tai chi, guided walks, and yoga in summer. **Recreation:** Boating, cross-country skiing, downhill skiing, golf, hiking, horse-drawn sleigh rides, horseback riding, ice skating, racquet-ball, snowsledding, tennis, tobogganing, water sports.

ACCOMMODATIONS
172 rooms, 178 suites.

DINING
Meals not included in spa plan. MAP available (breakfast and dinner) for $49 per person per day. 5 restaurants and cocktail lounge on premises: steakhouse/grill, contemporary American, casual pub, dinner cruise, in-ternational buffet. All have low-calorie options, fish, and local produce.

RATES AND PACKAGES
Rooms $105–$360, suites $145–$460, condominiums $290–$520. Spa Getaway 2–3 day package $359 (accommodations not included). Pam-pering package $99–$219 (accommodations not included). 1-night de-posit required. AE, D, DC, MC, V.

DIRECTIONS
✉ *110 Sagamore Rd., Box 450, Bolton Landing, NY 12814,* ☎ *518/644–9400 or 800/358–3585,* ℻ *518/644–3033.*

From New York City: New York State Thruway (Interstate–87) to Exit 24 (Bolton Landing) (4 hrs).

SIVANANDA ASHRAM YOGA RANCH

Holistic health

When stressed-out urbanites join members of the farm community to exercise and meditate or to jog through 80 acres of woods and fields, the effect is spiritual as well as physical. Guests from diverse social and professional backgrounds around the world meet at Sivananda Ashram Yoga Ranch to share their interest in yoga.

Morning and evening, everyone participates in classes devoted to traditional yogic exercise and breathing techniques. The dozen *asana* positions range from a headstand to a spinal twist, and each has specific benefits for the body. You will be taught that proper breathing, *pranayama,* is essential for energy control.

The daily schedule includes meditation and chanting at 6 AM and 8 PM, yogic posture and breathing exercise classes at 8 AM and 4 PM, and vegetarian meals served at 10 AM and 6 PM. Participation in program activities is mandatory, including karma yoga classes and various talks on yogic practice and philosophy. A communal sweat lodge and sauna are the only spa facilities available; there is no exercise equipment, and bodywork is not offered.

Lodging is in two century-old farmhouses with simple, rustic rooms for two to four people. Tent space is also available. A large organic garden provides seasonal vegetables for the two meals served in the main house.

FACILITIES
Swimming: Pond. **Classes and Programs:** Chanting, lectures, meditation. **Recreation:** Hiking.

ACCOMMODATIONS
60 rooms, most with shared bath. Campsites available.

DINING
2 meals daily, buffet style. Lacto-vegetarian diet, including dairy products. No coffee, eggs, alcohol. **Sample Meals:** Pancakes, granola and fruit (breakfast); lentil soup, dal, basmati rice, tofu loaf (dinner).

RATES AND PACKAGES
Room $40–$55 daily, including meals; 1-month work-study program $450. $25 deposit required. MC, V.

DIRECTIONS
✉ *Budd Rd., Box 195, Woodbourne, NY 12788,* ☎ *914/436–6492 or 914/434–9242 or 800/783–9642,* ℻ *914/434–1032.*

From New York City: New York Thruway 87N to Route 17W to Exit 105B, Route 42 to Woodbourne, continue straight on Route 52 east, turn left at firehouse on Budd Road, look for signs (2 1/2 hrs).

TAI CHI FARM

Holistic health
Sports conditioning

Martial arts take on a spiritual dimension at this secluded camp, which operates only from June through September. An intensive schedule of classes and matches takes place under the direction of Master Jou Tsung Hwa, founder and director of the Tai Chi Farm, along with other experts in many specialized forms of tai chi. The mood here is strictly no-frills: The eight wooden cabins share outhouses, there's no electricity or running water, and guests are asked to bring their own bedding, linens, and cooking gear.

The spartan surroundings of the Tai Chi Farm are well-suited to the 4,000-year-old discipline. Without any distractions, you can focus on mastering the techniques of leading, sticking, neutralizing, and attacking. The emphasis here is on teaching students how to root and balance the yin of letting go with the yang of connecting and projecting energy. Specialists teach such exercises as Swimming Dragon Chi Kung, a complete muscle and organ toner that makes your body seem to flow like a swimming dragon. From the Creative Being Centre in England, a master teaches how to transform stress into self-discovery using Dragon Breath Energy.

FACILITIES
Services: Individual and group tai chi instruction. **Swimming:** Lake nearby.

ACCOMMODATIONS
8 cabins for 2–8 persons with shared outhouse. Campsites available.

DINING
No meal service. Participants prepare their own meals.

RATES AND PACKAGES
$20–$30 for weekend lodging, $85–$100 tuition (or $5 per class); $50 for 5-day workshop lodging, $180–$200 tuition. Campsites $5 per night.

DIRECTIONS
✉ *Box 828, Warwick, NY 10990,* ☎ *914/986–9233,* ℻ *914/986–9233.*

From New York City: Route 80W to Route 23 north to Interstate–94 north, 1 mi past NJ–NY state line in Warwick (1½ hrs).

VATRA MOUNTAIN VALLEY LODGE & SPA

Nutrition and diet

"Guaranteed weight loss on a 750-calorie vegetarian diet," announces the post-card with Vatra's budget package prices. A low-calorie diet and a low price tag are the main reasons guests choose Vatra. The third is serenity. Set on 23 acres at the base of Hunter Mountain in the woodsy, scenic Catskill Mountains, the resort is surrounded by trails through nearby state parklands. It's a place to walk past lonely ponds edged by cattails, rocky stream beds, rushing brooks, lovely lakes, and a waterfall; or stroll along quiet country roads. It's not a place for serious fitness buffs. Like the not-so-fancy "fat farms" of years past, Vatra strives to make everyone at home, with an unintimidating, supportive approach to shedding extra pounds.

Dieters follow a 750-calorie-per-day meal plan, though there's also a 1200-calorie-per-day alternative. No additions or variations are made without special arrangements, and no between-meal snacks are allowed. Guests on serious weight-loss programs start with a brief medical background check and orientation to determine nutritional needs and fitness level. A computerized body-composition analysis may be recommended.

The exercise program consists of two daily aquaerobics workouts, and various exercise classes led by serious fitness instructors. Spa director George Borkacki sometimes leads the 6:30 AM yoga class and occasional walking excursions. Educational lectures on food and food products are offered from time to time, usually during the high summer season and on active weekends.

The rural facility, which operates as a B&B ski lodge in winter, is 30 minutes from Woodstock and one mile from Hunter Mountain. Almost all activities take place in the main building, an expanded former farmhouse. The dining room is a large, homey, windowed room decorated with Polish collectibles. The workout room doubles as a lounge, with separate areas containing exercise equipment, mirrored exercise space, and a sofa and TV. A new, indoor, heated swimming pool is housed in a separate building. A few spa treatments are offered upstairs, in former bedrooms. Across the street from the dining room, the lodge has 25 simply furnished guest rooms and a large sundeck. Some upstairs rooms have sleeping lofts and skylights; one room has a whirlpool tub.

FACILITIES
Exercise Equipment: Stair climbers, stationary bikes, treadmills, free weights. **Services:** Aromatherapy massage, reflexology, Swedish massage; body polish, seaweed wrap; facial. **Swimming:** Indoor and outdoor pools. **Classes and Programs:** Aerobics, aquaerobics, body-composition analysis, cholesterol testing, fitness consultation, yoga. **Recreation:** Basketball, cross-country skiing, hiking, tennis, volleyball.

ACCOMMODATIONS
25 rooms.

DINING
3 vegetarian meals daily based on 750-calorie or optional 1,200-calorie weight-loss diet; optional juice fast. **Sample Meals:** Spinach fettucine primavera, carrot soup, stuffed peppers, waldorf salad (lunch); zucchini lasagna, broiled eggplant, stuffed cabbage, grilled bean curd (dinner).

RATES AND PACKAGES
Weekend packages (3 nights) $529–$640 single, $425–$495 double. 4-night midweek package $695–$850 single, $555–$695 double. Weekly (7 nights) package rates $995–$1,295 single, $795–$1,049 double. $200–$300 deposit required. AE, MC, V.

DIRECTIONS
✉ *Rte. 214, Box F, Hunter, NY 12442,* ☎ *518/263–4919 or 800/232–2772,* FAX *518/263–4994.*

From New York City: New York Thruway to Exit 19 (Kingston), Route 28 west to Phoenicia, follow signs to Exit 214 north, look for spa 15 mins farther on left (2–2½ hrs).

VERMONT

THE EQUINOX

Luxury pampering
Sports conditioning

Outdoor adventure distinguishes this Green Mountain resort. Falconry, fly-fishing, golf, tennis, cross-country skiing, snowshoeing, biking, hiking, horseback riding, and the Land Rover driving school are among the many sports options. Skiing at Mt. Equinox is another major attraction, and there's even a physiotherapy center nearby for those prone to injury.

When you first arrive, a staff member will tailor an individual exercise schedule for you, based on a computerized body-composition analysis. You will then participate in an informal discussion on exercise physiology, nutrition, and stress management. Advance planning with the spa director will help you focus on weight loss, stress management, or behavior modification.

Workout options include brisk walks or jogs on trails along the golf course, and personalized training with weights. The comprehensive fitness facilities are complimentary to all hotel guests, but several spa packages are also available. Falconry training starts at $65 per person for a 45-minute lesson, including equipment; there is also a four-day beginner's course. In this program you'll practice the handling and flying of native birds of prey in fields that have been dedicated as a nature preserve by the resort's owners, Guinness Brewing Co. Fishing enthusiasts have access to the resort's private 14-acre pond, with fly-fishing instruction and gear provided by the nearby Orvis school (separate fees apply).

After a day of sports, you can relax in luxury accommodations. The 230-year-old Equinox has hosted such notables as Mary Todd Lincoln, Ulysses S. Grant, and Theodore Roosevelt; the dining room preserves part of a 1769 tavern. Additional guest rooms are scattered throughout separate buildings embracing many different architectural styles. Rooms have a fresh but historic style, with Audubon prints and Vermont country charm.

In the heart of Vermont's arts circuit, the resort is close to major summer music and theater festivals as well as historic Hildene, home of Robert Todd Lincoln. If your idea of exercise is shopping 'til you drop, just stroll into Manchester Village.

FACILITIES
Exercise Equipment: Cross-country skiing machine, stair climber, rowing machine, stationary bikes, weight-training circuit, free weights. **Services:** Reflexology, Reiki, Swedish massage; body scrub, herbal wrap, seaweed wrap. **Swimming:** Indoor and outdoor pools. **Classes and Programs:** Live resort entertainment. **Recreation:** Biking, canoeing, golf, hiking, horse-drawn carriage rides, horseback riding, tennis; cross-country and downhill skiing nearby.

ACCOMMODATIONS
119 rooms, 36 suites, 10 3-bedroom town houses

DINING
Meals included in spa packages. **Sample Meals:** Ceviche of sole with cilantro, grilled medallion of beef with shallots, chilled asparagus with seasoned wild rice (lunch); herbed pasta with mushrooms, poached salmon, veal medallion (dinner).

Daily rate $159–$289 single, $169–$280 for 2, double. Orvis Inn suite $569–$899 for 2, 1-bedroom parlor suite for 2 $559, town house suite $369–$669 for 2. 3-night/4-day spa package $1,057 single, $833.50 per person double, $779 triple. 3-night/4-day Fun & Fitness package $919 single, $620.50 double, $541 triple. Add 7% tax, gratuity. 1-night deposit required. AE, DC, MC, V.

DIRECTIONS
✉ *Rte. 7A, Manchester Village, VT 05254,* ☎ *802/362–4700 or 800/362–4747,* ℻ *802/362–1595.*

From New York City: New England Thruway (Interstate–95) north to Interstate–91, exit at second Brattleboro turnoff for Route 9 to Route 30 (4 hrs).

GOLDEN EAGLE

Sports conditioning

Toning and body shaping are what this budget spa does best, and it draws a mixed crowd of singles and families mostly between 30 and 60. The traditional mountain lodge has winter and summer activities, and a health spa open to guests.

On 80 acres near the center of Stowe, the resort has well-developed nature trails. An brochure available at the hotel details a self-guided tour with descriptions of local flora and fauna. Staff members accompany guests on walks if requested in advance. For longer hikes and bike rides, try the Stowe Recreation Path, a 5½-mile scenic route through the valley, close to the entrance to Golden Eagle and out toward Mt. Mansfield ski area.

This is a good vacation base for families. A nature trail winds through the property, and two ponds are stocked for fishing (poles can be rented). Mountain bikes can be rented from local sporting-goods stores. The activities desk has tennis rackets available for free use on the clay tennis court. For relaxation, try the coed whirlpool and sauna.

The rooms, suites, efficiencies, apartments, and condominiums—individually decorated in a country-casual style—all have private bathrooms, air-conditioning, televisions, telephones, and at least a refrigerator and coffee maker; efficiencies, apartments, and condos have more extensive cooking facilities. Some rooms have a whirlpool or a fireplace.

FACILITIES
Exercise Equipment: Rowing machines, stair climber, stationary bikes, treadmills, weight-training equipment, free weights. **Services:** Aromatherapy massage, reflexology, Reiki, sports massage, Swedish massage. **Swimming:** Indoor and outdoor pools. **Classes and Programs:** Body sculpting. **Recreation:** Biking, fishing, tennis; golf nearby. **Children's Programs:** Supervised daily activities for ages 4–12 from June to August.

ACCOMMODATIONS
71 rooms, 18 suites, efficiencies, apartments.

DINING
No meal plan. Heart-healthy selections on breakfast and dinner menus; no lunch. **Sample Meals:** Seafood mixed grill, broiled Atlantic swordfish, Sanibel steamers, steamed vegetable and fish on bamboo (dinner).

RATES AND PACKAGES
$89–$169 daily per room for 2, single occupancy $10 less. 1-night deposit required. AE, D, DC, MC, V.

DIRECTIONS
✉ *Box 1090, Mountain Rd. (Rte. 108), Stowe, VT 05672,* ☎ *802/253–4811 or 800/626–1010,* ℻ *802/253–2561.*

From Boston and New York City: Interstate–91, Interstate–89 to Stowe exit (3½ hrs from Boston, 6½ hrs from NYC).

GREEN MOUNTAIN AT FOX RUN

Medical wellness
Nutrition and diet
Sports conditioning

On more than 20 acres of private land in the Green Mountain National Forest, overlooking the Okemo Valley and ski area, this is the country's oldest all-women program devoted to developing a self-directed plan for eating and exercise that can be integrated into your life at home. Participants range in age from 17 to over 80.

For women with a serious weight problem, coming to Green Mountain at Fox Run is a commitment to change. The difference is not just a new diet or vigorous exercise, but a new lifestyle based on healthy habits. The program provides a practical approach to eating, exercise, and stress management that can ensure long-term success.

One of the first lessons you learn here is that diets don't work. Instead of deprivation, moderation becomes the key. Three balanced meals a day are required, and you learn how to normalize your eating habits by eliminating tendencies to binge, overeat, or feel guilty about eating. This can mean giving in, ever so slightly, to an occasional yearning for sweets. Guests learn techniques to help them manage binge and emotional overeating and prevent relapses, and are shown that being more active can be as pleasant as taking a walk down a country lane. For women who have unsuccessfully attempted to manage their weight with liquid diets, there is a special program to overcome negative effects and resume a livable and enjoyable approach to eating. Professional workshops for nurses and social workers are also offered.

Working with a team of registered dietitians, exercise physiologists, and behavioral therapists with specialties in nutrition, metabolism, and stress management, you develop a personalized weight and health program that becomes part of your daily routine. A follow-up program helps you to maintain this routine at home. Tuition costs cover individual nutrition/dietary counseling and exercise prescription and modification. Massage therapy, facials, aromatherapy, body treatments, personal training, and one-on-one behavioral counseling are available at an additional expense.

Owner-operated since 1973, this is a homey place. Facilities include Cybex weight-training equipment, an outdoor heated pool, tennis courts, and some off-site indoor pools for aquacize and aquaerobics classes. Pampering services are à la carte. Daily exercise classes (aerobics and resistance- and circuit-training), walking, hiking, biking, and cross-country skiing and snowshoeing in winter fill most of the day. Aerobic dance and body-conditioning sessions teach that exercise can be fun, something that fits easily into everyday life.

Common areas include a cozy lounge with a woodstove and televisions and a high-ceiling dining room with rafters. Guest rooms have mission-style wooden furniture and Vermont-country accents.

Exercise Equipment: Cross-country skiing machine, rowing machine, stair climber, stationary bikes, treadmills, weight-training equipment, free weights. **Services:** Acupressure, reflexology, sports massage, Swedish massage; body polish, herbal wraps, salt glow, seaweed wraps; facial. **Swimming:** Indoor and outdoor pools. **Classes and Programs:** Cooking classes, cross-country skiing instruction, discussions and lectures, downhill skiing instruction, golf instruction, personal training, private counseling, tai chi, movies, yoga. **Recreation:** Cross-country skiing, downhill skiing, mountain biking, snowshoeing, tennis, track; golf, horseback riding nearby.

ACCOMMODATIONS
26 rooms.

DINING
1,400-calorie-a-day diet, low in fat and sodium, based on the USDA Food Pyramid for healthy eating. Meal plan conforms to dietary recommendations of the American Dietetic, Diabetes, Heart, and Medical Associations. Meal-plan can be modified for guests with medical conditions and vegetarians. **Sample Meals:** Sesame chicken, vegetarian roll-ups, salads, pasta, pizza (lunch); shrimp and vegetables stir-fry over basmati rice, eggplant parmesan, grilled salmon, swordfish kebabs (dinner).

RATES AND PACKAGES
1-week session $850–$2,050, 2-week $1,240–$3,900, 4-week $2,800–$6,700. Rates are seasonal and based on type of accommodation, single–triple occupancy (roommates matched on request). $500 deposit required. MC, V.

DIRECTIONS
✉ Fox La., Box 164, Ludlow, VT 05149, ☎ 802/228–8885 or 800/448–8106, FAX 802/228–8887.

From New York City: Interstate–95 north to Interstate–91, Exit 6 in Vermont (Route 103 north) to Ludlow (4½ hrs). Rates include transfers to and from select air, bus, and train stations.

NEW LIFE HIKING SPA

Holistic health
Nutrition and diet

Hiking the alpine valleys and slopes of Vermont's Green Mountains is the main attraction at New Life, though the program also involves a comprehensive shape-up including exercise programs, cooking demos, nutritional counseling, and bodywork. Developed 21 years ago by Jimmy LeSage, a former professional cook and hotel manager, New Life operates from May through October at The Inn of the Six Mountains, just outside the ski resort of Killington.

Daily group hikes are guided by New Life staff members, who divide participants into beginner, intermediate, and advanced groups. The diverse terrain of the Appalachian Trail and Vermont's Long Trail challenge you to try progressively demanding trails. The advanced hikes scale the second highest peak in Vermont, continue to neighboring Pico Peak, and end with an exuberant ride down the alpine slide. All levels are invited on an all-day hike toward the end of the session, as a climax to the program.

Exercise classes are held in a tent with specially designed floor. The afternoon program relaxes the body and works off fatigue, with Sivananda-style yoga postures and stretching. Other options, including aquacise classes, are available at the indoor complex, which includes a lap pool, steam room, and heated outdoor swimming pool and whirlpool that guests can use at any time. Nearby in Killington Village, guests can rent bikes or canoes, or sign up for racquetball.

Healthy eating complements the vigorous program of physical activity. LeSage's philosophy on nutrition and meal preparation is published in a book given to each guest; for those who want to learn more, LeSage teaches hands-on cooking classes in the hotel kitchen. Wholesome, tasty meals are served in a cheery room with mountain views. Fresh fruit, herbal teas, decaffeinated coffee, and spring water are always on hand in the hospitality lounge.

Accommodations at New Life are furnished with double beds, and have private baths, a color TV, and a telephone. The pine-paneled lobby has a lounge with fireplaces and comfy chairs.

FACILITIES
Exercise Equipment: Rowing machine, stair climber, treadmill. **Services:** Massage, facial. **Swimming:** Indoor and outdoor pools. **Classes and Programs:** Aerobics, aquaerobics, cooking demonstrations, lifestyle lectures, tai chi, yoga. **Recreation:** Tennis; golf, horseback riding, mountain biking nearby.

ACCOMMODATIONS
120 rooms.

DINING
3 meals daily. Modified Pritikin diet (1,200–1,500 calories per day) low in fats and high in complex carbohydrates. **Sample Meals:** Corn chowder with pita pizza, chicken curry salad (lunch); salmon with dill sauce and garden salad, spinach–rice casserole with string bean almondine (dinner).

RATES AND PACKAGES
3-day sampler (Thurs.–Sun.) $599 single, $540 double; 6-day/5-night program (Sun.–Fri.) $999 single, $899 double. $300 deposit required per person. MC, V.

DIRECTIONS
✉ *The Inn of the Six Mountains, Box 395, Killington, VT 05751,* ☎ *802/ 422–4302 or 800/545–9407,* ℻ *802/422–4321.*

From New York City: Interstate–95 north to Exit 24, Northway to Exit 120 (Fort Anne/Rutland), Highway 4 east via Rutland to Killington Road, Route 100 (5 hrs).

TOPNOTCH AT STOWE

Luxury pampering
Nutrition and diet
Sports conditioning

Set in Vermont's Green Mountains among the red-barn farms of Stowe, Topnotch is a classic country inn that combines pampering spa treatments with top-notch sports facilities. Among the options: Tennis at an indoor tennis center with four lighted courts; riding at the Topnotch Equestrian Center; golf at the Stowe Country Club; fishing at an Orvis school for fishermen; downhill skiing at Mount Mansfield, Vermont's highest peak; and cross-country skiing on 15 miles of groomed Nordic trails. Sport-specific fitness and conditioning classes get you in shape for tennis and skiing. Three- to seven-day programs include instruction as well as time on the courts and slopes.

For openers, the staff physiologist will put you through a "Fitness Profile" analysis based on your body composition, strength and flexibility, cardiovascular and blood tests; an exercise program is planned accordingly. Outfitted with a daily issue of shorts, T-shirt, robe and slippers, you have a choice of group sessions or one-on-one cardiovascular and strength-training sessions with a personal trainer. A skylit solarium with a coed sauna, steam room, and Jacuzzi alongside a 60-foot indoor pool are ideal for easing sore muscles. Even more sybaritic is a shoulder massage under a cascading waterfall.

The Spa at Topnotch can be enjoyed on an à la carte basis, but for best value consider one of the packages, from half-day to multi-day, which offer sports options as well as treatments and full use of the spa facilities. If you simply want to swim or exercise, hotel guests are charged a daily fee of $15, non-residents $25. The access fee is waived if you receive a treatment on the same day. Massage oils are made with Vermont wildflowers and herbs and include everything from craniosacral therapy to prenatal massage.

Though Topnotch is minutes from the bustling village center, mountain views make it feel worlds apart. A massive fireplace warms the high-ceilinged main lounge, where guests often read by the fire. Rooms are more English-antiques elegant than ski–lodgelike, and the formal dining room serves Continental fare as well as heart-healthy cuisine that attracts an international crowd.

FACILITIES
Exercise Equipment: Rowing machines, stair climbers, stationary bikes, treadmills, weight-training circuit, free weights. **Services:** Aromatherapy massage, reflexology, shiatsu, Swedish massage; acupressure, herbal wrap, loofah body scrub; hydrotherapy; facials. **Swimming:** Indoor and outdoor pools. **Classes and Programs:** Aerobics, aquacise, nutrition seminars, tennis instruction, yoga. **Recreation:** Billiards, croquet, horseback riding, mountain biking, table tennis, tennis; cross-country skiing, downhill skiing, golf nearby.

ACCOMMODATIONS
77 rooms, 20 1- to 3-bedroom town homes, 13 suites.

DINING
Breakfast included in spa packages; daily meal plans $48–$55 per person. **Sample Meals:** Mushroom-barley soup with salad of asparagus and roasted red peppers, whole-wheat pizza, chicken breast in cilantro-mint sauce (lunch); seafood pasta in three-mustard sauce, grilled chicken (dinner).

RATES AND PACKAGES
Daily without meals $150–$275 single, $75–$143 double. 4-day/3-night Tennis/Spa package $267 single, $376 for 2. AE, DC, MC, V.

DIRECTIONS
✉ *4000 Mountain Rd., Box 1458, Stowe, VT 05672,* ☎ *802/253–8585 or 800/451–8686,* ℻ *802/253–9263.*

From Boston: Interstate–93 to Concord, NH, Interstate–89 north to Exit 10 (Stowe/Waterbury), Route 100N to Stowe, left on Route 108 (Mountain Road) for 4 mi (4 hrs).

WOODSTOCK INN & RESORT

Luxury pampering
Sports conditioning

Picture the perfect New England town: the county courthouse and library facing an oval green, a covered bridge leading to immaculate farms, a cluster of fancy boutiques, and a Colonial inn. Add a full-service health and fitness center, 60 kilometers of cross-country ski trails, nearby mountains with more than 200 downhill trails, and you have the Woodstock Inn & Resort.

The current inn, the fourth on the site, spreads from the historic town green to the sports center, which includes a golf course and croquet lawn, outdoor and indoor swimming pools and tennis courts, and racquetball, squash, and volleyball courts. A little over a mile south of the inn is a health and fitness center with first-rate strength training and cardiovascular exercise equipment, an aerobics studio, and regularly scheduled classes in everything from aerobics and yoga to aquatics in the pool. Massage services, available seven days a week, include deep tissue work.

Ski resorts surround Woodstock; some of the best are Suicide Six, Killington, Ascutney Mountain, and Okemo Mountain. Cross-country skiers have their choice of scenic routes, including 20 kilometers of woodland on Mt. Peg, and 30 additional kilometers of century-old carriage roads in the midst of Vermont's first tree farm at the base of Mt. Tom, across the village green from the inn. The entire area is mapped and groomed by the Woodstock Ski Touring Center. Also available are professional instruction, equipment rental, and a heated trailside log cabin.

Time seems to stand still in this classic New England village, with its white-steeple church and red-brick county government buildings. Appropriately, there's a dress code in the inn's dining room, where hearty New England fare is a throwback to pre-health-spa days. Rooms are equally traditional, with New England antiques and patchwork quilts on the beds. The nearby Billings Farm Museum has exhibits of early New England farm life, and a prize-winning dairy barn.

FACILITIES
Exercise Equipment: Rowing machines, stationary bikes, treadmill, weight-training equipment, free weights. **Services:** Deep-tissue massage, Swedish massage. **Swimming:** Indoor and outdoor pools. **Classes and Programs:** Aerobics, aquaerobics, personal training, tennis instruction, yoga. **Recreation:** Croquet, horseshoes, nature walks, racquetball, sleigh rides, squash, tennis, volleyball; cross-country skiing, downhill skiing, horseback riding nearby.

ACCOMMODATIONS
144 rooms.

DINING
MAP (breakfast and dinner) is optional and costs $53 per person per day. Lunch is available at the restaurant. **Sample Meals:** Farm-raised Atlantic salmon with potatoes, artichokes, and lemon vinaigrette (dinner).

RATES AND PACKAGES
In summer, $159–$525 for 2 persons. Meals optional. Health & Fitness Center sports package (3 days, 2 nights) $446 single, $594 for 2 persons double, includes racquetball or tennis, massage. 2-night deposit required. AE, MC, V.

DIRECTIONS

✉ *14 The Green, Woodstock, VT 05091,* ☎ *802/457–1100 or 800/448–7900,* FAX *802/457–6699.*

From Boston: Take Interstate–93 north to Interstate–89 north (between exits 12 and 11), which you'll take into Vermont. Follow Exit 1 (Woodstock-Rutland-Route 4) to Route 4 west and continue 10 mi to the traffic rotary; the Inn will be on your right (2 hrs).

From New York: Take Interstate-95 north or the Merritt Parkway to Interstate-89 north (Exit 10N) in Vermont. Continue 2.6 mi to Exit 1 (Woodstock) and turn left at the bottom of the ramp onto Route 4 west. Follow Route 4 10 mi to the traffic rotary; the Inn will be on your right.

9 Hawaii

The Big Island, Kauai, Maui, Oahu

HAWAIIANS HAVE A WORD FOR THE pursuit of wellness: ho'oponopono. Healing is an art form here, taking from both Eastern and Western traditions—lomi-lomi massage and medicinal herbs from ancient Polynesia, shiatsu from Japan, tai chi chuan from China, and Swedish massage. Settle in at a beachfront resort, such as the Hilton Waikoloa Village on the Big Island or the nature-oriented Hyatt Regency on Kauai, and experience lomi-lomi bodywork. Drawn from hula dance, martial art (lua), and exercises developed by boaters 5,000 years ago, lomi-lomi realigns the bodies of both recipient and therapist. Love, focus, and intuition are tools employed by today's shamans, along with aromatherapy oils, tropical flower-scented lotions, and sea salts.

Polynesian culture adds an exotic dimension to the pursuit of fitness, and the ocean adds a touch of adventure. In Hawaii, there are the ancient healing therapies of the kahunas to discover and Mai Tais to sip under the tropical sun. Or you can experience the sea's roller-coaster waves aboard an outrigger canoe or its underwater color on a dive boat expedition.

Natural therapies come in many packages. On the volcanic island of Hawaii, guests at Kalani Oceanside Retreat practice yoga and attend seminars on holistic health while staying in traditional lodges made of cedar logs or camping out among the palm trees. On Maui you can indulge in the luxury of the Grand Wailea Resort and detoxify in a bath of the Hawaiian seaweed limu. Native healing traditions include sacred mud treatments at Hyatt's ANARA Spa on Kauai, herbs and plants used for body wraps at Oahu's Ihilani Resort and Spa, and exfoliating salt glows at the Grand Wailea's Spa Grande. Golfers at the Ihilani Resort rejuvenate with "Hawaiian Thalasso" seawater treatments in a unique hydrotherapy facility for muscular pain and arthritis.

Hawaii offers outdoor adventure for every taste—from horseback riding on ranches to kayaking through a wildlife refuge up Kauai's Huleia River. Polo matches abound on Oahu and the Big Island; the Hawaii Polo Club even offers five-day training programs. The waters off the Kohala coast are legendary for deep-sea fishing, and the Kona coast has spectacular sites for scuba diving—Napoopoo Beach Park and Keei Beach are favored spots. From December through May, the upper slopes of the Big Island's Mauna Kea, 13,796 feet above the sea, frequently have enough snow for sun-baked skiing. You can also try biking down a slope—Maui's 10,023-foot Mt. Haleakala. Local outfitters will drive you to the top of the extinct volcano in time to see the sunrise and provide bikes for the leisurely ride down. If you're feeling even more ambitious, you can train to compete in the strenuous Iron Man Triathlon.

Although Honolulu is said to be one of the healthiest cities to live in, Waikiki Beach hotels have some of the smallest fitness facilities. At some of the poshest hotels, the concierge may suggest a guided run on the beach or arrange admission to a well-equipped downtown club. But anyone can join the daily 8:30 AM aerobics class on the beach in front of the Pacific Beach Hotel with staffers from Gold's Gym. At Fort DeRussy, a military club, you can work out in the fully equipped health club, The Point, at Hale Koa Hotel (tel. 808/955–9155) for a daily fee, and join a beach adventure trip with locals on Thursday ($70). There's also a free clinic at the local YMCA to prepare runners for the Honolulu Marathon.

Island parks give hikers the opportunity to enjoy the real Hawaiian paradise. For information on organized treks, contact clubs such as Hawaii Ike Travel Society (tel. 808/326–5775) and the Waikiki Community Center (tel. 808/923–1808). Leeward Community College (tel. 808/

956–8946) publishes a statewide *Eco-Tourism Directory*. The comprehensive Hawaii Health and Fitness Guide is available from Aurora Productions (4400-4 Kalanianaole Hwy., Honolulu, HI 96821, tel. 808/988–7975). (Note: Before hiking alone in secluded areas check with park rangers to avoid private lands where visitors are not welcome.)

Hawaiian cuisine—combining flavors and techniques from the Pacific Rim, California, and Europe—has come a long way. Gone are the days when diners had to satisfy themselves with frozen fish flown in from the mainland and mediocre vegetables. Although there are still Brady Bunch–esque luaus with heavy pupu appetizers, terriyaki sticks, and taro root, organic farms now supply restaurants with an amazing variety of fresh produce and fruit.

THE BIG ISLAND

HILTON WAIKOLOA VILLAGE

Luxury pampering

Monorail trains and water taxis deposit guests at the Kohala Spa, secluded within the Hilton Waikoloa Village, the Big Island's largest spa resort. The spa has newly expanded facilities for workouts and wellness treatments, combining Eastern and Western therapies. Choices include thalassotherapy baths infused with limu (Hawaiian seaweed), herbal wraps, and lomi-lomi massage. Provided with a robe, guests can have lunch in the spa garden or at a new café with a healthful menu. Group exercise classes include Pilates training, tai chi chuan, yoga, water aerobics, and a sunrise power walk. Classes are covered by the spa's daily fee and can be combined in several day spa packages. There are separate quarters for men and women with saunas, steam rooms, and outdoor whirlpool. A lap pool built into lava rock is scheduled for completion in 1999.

The spa is now offering Cinema Secrets professional makeup treatments, created by Hollywood-based Maurice Stein. Developed at Universal Studios, the cosmetic line is endorsed by dermatologists for use after burns or plastic surgery. Hair, nail, and skin care is tended at a unisex salon.

A mega-resort set on 1,352 acres, Waikoloa Village offers nonstop fantasy. It has a vast swimming pool with waterfalls, hidden grotto bar, and twisting water slide. It has ancient fishponds and petroglyph fields, high-rise hotel towers, and an art collection of museum-quality Oriental and Pacific treasures. Guests sign up to swim with dolphins, take horse-drawn carriage rides into the countryside, and go surfing in catamarans. They can even indulge in a spiritual walk with guided meditation to recall the ancient kahunas.

FACILITIES
Exercise Equipment: Cross-country ski machines, rowing machine, stair climbers, stationary bikes, swimming machine, treadmills, weight-training circuit, free weights. **Services:** Aromatherapy, lomi-lomi, reflexology, shiatsu, sports, Swedish massage; body mask, loofah buff, herbal bath, herbal wrap, balneotherapy specialty bath; body facial, hydrating facial. **Swimming:** Ocean beach, seawater lagoon, 3 pools. **Recreation:** Climbing, diving, golf, horseback riding, racquetball, sailing, skiing, snorkeling, squash, tennis, windsurfing. **Children's Programs:** Children's day camp with lunch.

ACCOMMODATIONS
1,240 rooms.

DINING
Two spa-cuisine meals daily with Pleasures in Paradise package. **Sample Meals:** Chili chicken salad with marinated rice and vegetables in cilantro vinaigrette, poached salmon with cucumber and tomato on Bibb lettuce with dill couli, vegetable antipasto with tuna (lunch); grilled mahimahi; vegetarian platter (dinner).

RATES AND PACKAGES
Daily $260–$410 per room, single or double occupancy. Spa Massage sampler $92 (includes service charge and gratuity). 4-night Pleasures in Paradise package $2,154 single, $2,880 double occupancy; 7-night package $3,771 single, $5,292 double. Includes taxes and gratuities. Deposit: Confirmation by credit card. AE, D, DC, MC, V.

DIRECTIONS
✉ *69-425 Waikoloa Beach Dr., Waikoloa, 96738,* ☎ *886/885–1234 or 800/445–8667,* FAX *886/885–2901.*

From Honolulu: Interisland air services to Kona International Airport (40 mins), transfer by taxi or rental car (20 mins).

KALANI OCEANSIDE RETREAT

Holistic health
Sports conditioning

Get back to nature on a volcanic black-sand beach that steams with thermal springs. Kalani Oceanside Retreat puts you in close touch with the spectacular natural environment of the Big Island. This rough-edged budget-priced retreat offers health-oriented activities. An intercultural program, with yoga and hula, complements workshops scheduled throughout the year. Subjects covered by workshop retreats include men's health, organic gardening, and the body-mind-spirit connection. Visitors can participate or venture off to explore on their own.

Founded in 1982, the 20-acre resort attracts an interesting mix of robust, healthy men and women, families hiking the volcano trails, and professional bodyworkers attending seminars on holistic health and preventive medicine, but there is no fixed program. Of special interest are presentations on native Hawaiian cleansing rituals by islanders.

In keeping with the spirit of old Hawaii, guests are housed in hales, wood lodges made of cedar logs. Each hexagonal lodge has its own kitchen and ocean-view studio space. There is minimal furniture but many windows. The lodges have some dormitory rooms, but mostly private accommodations. They are decorated with Hawaiian art and fabrics and fresh flowers. Campers can sleep under the stars at 25 sites among the palm trees.

Therapeutic services and exercise classes are the focus of a Japanese-style spa. The wooden bathhouse has a communal hot tub, sauna heated by wood-burning stove, and private massage rooms. Four pavilions with suspended wood floors are used for yoga, aerobics, and dance performances. Nearby are a 25-foot swimming pool and a Jacuzzi, plus a fitness center.

New Agers mix easily with visitors on the Big Island—at 4,038 square miles it's the biggest island in the Hawaiian chain—and there are numerous "clothing optional" beaches as well as shops offering natural foods, crystals, tarot cards, and books. Hawaii Volcanoes National Park provides a close-up look at rivers of red-hot lava flow from Mt. Kilauea. On the Puna Coast, just south of Hilo, the resort is 5 miles from the lava flow.

FACILITIES
Exercise Equipment: Stationary bike, treadmill, weight-training circuit, free weights. **Services:** Esalen, shiatsu, Swedish massage; acupressure, acupuncture, watsu. **Swimming:** Ocean beaches, pool. **Classes and Programs:** Chiropractic services, health workshops, hula, nutrition counseling; Kripalu, Hatha, and Astanga yoga; sports conditioning. **Recreation:** Bicycle rental, hiking, horseback riding, golf, tennis, volleyball; skiing nearby. Cultural performances, traditional Hawaiian feasts.

ACCOMMODATIONS
35 rooms, some with shared bath, 8 cottages.

DINING
Primarily vegetarian. À la carte meals at Cafe Cashew. **Sample Meals:** Sautéed vegetables with tempeh and tahini sauce, broiled mahimahi,

spinach lasagna (lunch); grilled chicken, baked mahimahi with mushrooms in lemon and garlic sauce, cream of papaya–cashew soup, salad bar.

RATES AND PACKAGES

Lodge room with private bath $95–$110 per night ($145–$160 with meals) for 2 persons; 18 shared-bath lodge rooms $75–$95 ($125–$145 with meals); 3-bed rooms, $45 per person ($70–$80 with meals). 7 cottages with private baths $110–$130 ($160–$180 with meals) for 2; house with kitchen, 2 baths, $165. Tent site $20–$25. 1-night deposit required. AE, DC, MC, V.

DIRECTIONS

✉ *R.R. 2, Box 4500, Pahoa-Beach Rd., HI 96778,* ☎ *808/965–7828 or 800/800–6886,* FAX *808/965–9613.*

From Hilo: Route 11 to Keaau, Route 130 to Route 137 (45 mins).

KAUAI

HAWAIIAN WELLNESS HOLIDAY

Holistic health

Said to be attuned to the metaphysical island rhythms, Dr. Grady Deal prescribes programs to get fit and slim down. Combining a holistic approach to health and nutrition with beach condominium accommodations and therapeutic massage and chiropractic treatments, he offers a stress-free adventure in wellness.

Dr. Deal—a psychologist, licensed massage therapist, gourmet cook, and practicing chiropractor—and his wife, Roberleigh, have created a warm, homelike atmosphere for their guests. Using facilities at Poipu Beach condominiums and the nearby Hyatt Regency Hotel, the Hawaiian Wellness Holiday is tailored to individual needs and interests. By keeping the group small—an average of 10 per week—the Deals aim for a high level of success in meeting each person's goals.

The structured daily schedule involves group exercise: yoga, aerobics, and aquacise in the swimming pool. Included in the program cost are three massages or chiropractic therapy. Detoxification, weight loss, and body toning are the primary objectives. Invigorating exercise and a cleansing diet are supplemented by natural therapies.

Spending most of the day outdoors, on scenic hikes and walks as well as at aerobics classes, guests quickly discover the natural healing effect of the island. Excursions included in the basic fee take the group to such scenic places as Waimea Canyon; the NaPali coast; Lumahai beach, where South Pacific was filmed; and the Seven Sacred Pools. Kauai is said to have a rare energy vortex, a metaphysical natural beauty that relaxes the mind and body. Exploring the island with a like-minded group of health seekers adds a special quality to the fitness holiday. Each person is encouraged to search for inner energy.

Rounding out the program are lectures and cooking demonstrations. Macrobiotic and vegetarian meals are served family-style. Informal workshops on nutrition and spiritual health, meditation, and deep-breathing exercises for relaxation are offered. At the end of the day, guests can unwind in the steam room, sauna, or Jacuzzi while awaiting yet another memorable sunset.

FACILITIES
Exercise Equipment: Rowing machine, stair climbers, stationary bikes, weight-training circuit, free weights. **Services:** Deep-tissue, reflexology, shiatsu, Swedish massage. **Swimming:** Ocean beach. **Classes and Programs:** Cooking classes, chiropractic services, nutritional counseling, physical therapy, talks and slide shows on health-related topics. **Recreation:** Golf, hiking, horseback riding, tennis, water sports; biking nearby. Hawaiian cultural performances.

ACCOMMODATIONS
Condominiums at Poipu Beach.

DINING
Vegetarian, cleansing, or macrobiotic meals with whole grains, raw and cooked vegetables, fruit, juices, legumes, and fish. **Sample Meals:** Fresh vegetable salad, pasta primavera (lunch); vegetable tempeh, broiled fresh fish, free-range chicken, green salad with oil-free dressing (dinner).

RATES AND PACKAGES
All-inclusive week $2,395 single, $3,565 double, in ocean-view room; $1,995 single, $3,140 double, in garden-view room. (5% discount for 2-week program.) $500 deposit required. MC, V.

DIRECTIONS
⊠ *Box 279, Koloa, HI 96756,* ☎ *808/332–9244 or 800/338–6977,* FAX *808/332–5941.*

From Koloa: Poipu Rd. to Poipu Beach (15 mins).

HYATT REGENCY KAUAI

Luxury pampering

Secluded within the Hyatt Regency Kauai resort is the full-service ANARA Spa, which stands for "A New Age Restorative Approach." But what's new here are old Hawaiian healing treatments: a sacred red clay called alaea (Kapu Kai' Alaea is the treatment's name) used as a skin softener in a sea salt body scrub, followed by a soak in an herbal botanical bath while sipping Hawaiian hibiscus tea; lomi-lomi massage—reputed to imitate the wind-and-sea rhythms of the islands in its quick strokes—starts with chants once performed by the kahuna high priests. Skin treatments with honey-mango or papaya blossom oil and facial cleansing with gardenia-scented coconut oil are among the specialties.

An open-air courtyard encloses the lap pool and the lava-rock rinsing showers, creating a quiet place to awaken the senses. Guests can work out in an air-conditioned fitness facility, including steam room, sauna, whirlpool, and aerobics studio with impact-absorbing wood floor. Scheduled daily are aerobics classes, weight training clinics, and aqua-trim water exercise.

Services worth noting include the Ti Leaf Cool Wrap, designed to alleviate the discomfort of sunburn and elevated body temperature. Guests are spread on a bed of the cooling leaves, covered with a gel made from aloe vera and comfrey, then covered with more heat-absorbing leaves and wrapped in a sheet for 20 minutes to sweat out any toxins. Another treatment is the Sacred Bath of Hawaiian elders or kapunas: red colloidal clay from the base of Kauai's Mt. Waialeale is mixed with sea salts and spread on the body after a session in the steam room. This treatment is followed by a botanical bath with a seaweed and salt mixture, which simulates thalassotherapy in helping to stimulate blood circulation. Hair and nail care in the beauty salon can finish off the day.

Set on 50 acres of lush beachfront, the long and rambling low-rise hotel wings are designed in the style of 1930s plantations. From guest room patios and lanais there are views of a junglelike lagoon. Public areas are decorated with museum-quality Asian and Pacific art. Joggers can enjoy a two-mile course on the beach. Family-oriented programs include an introduction to island archaeology. Surrounding the grottoes, waterfalls, and swimming pools is a Robert Trent Jones, Jr.–designed golf course. Adjacent to all this is a five-acre saltwater lagoon for kayakers, snorkelers, and scuba divers. For relaxation, there's Stevenson's Library (named for island-lover Robert Louis), with its books, billiards, and cheery bar.

Nature lovers and hikers who want to explore the island can schedule a tour of Limahuli Garden, in a lush, green valley dedicated to preserving Hawaiian plants. A botanical paradise set between mountains, sky, and sea, these gardens have been cultivated since 1940, but include a Polynesian settlement believed to have been built 1,000 years ago. On the Na Pali coast near Haena, the preserve is part of the National Tropical

Botanical Garden. In the old plantation village of Waimea, where Captain Cook visited in 1778, visitors can tour the sugar mill with retired sugar growers, who share stories of bygone days.

FACILITIES

Exercise Equipment: Stationary bike, treadmill, weight-training circuit, free weights. **Services:** Esalen, lomi-lomi, shiatsu, Swedish massage; body scrub; facials. **Swimming:** Ocean beach, pool. **Classes and Programs:** Scuba classes, tennis clinics. **Recreation:** Bicycle rental, golf, hiking, tennis. **Children's Programs:** Crafts programs and Camp Hyatt day camp.

ACCOMMODATIONS

600 rooms.

DINING

No special meal plan. Low-calorie, low-fat items available daily.

RATES AND PACKAGES

$295–$435 per day for 1 or 2 persons; Regency Club $495; suites $750–$2,800. 1-day spa package $245, plus room. Credit-card confirmation. AE, D, DC, MC, V.

DIRECTIONS

✉ *1571 Poipu Rd., Koloa, Kauai, HI 96756,* ☎ *808/742–1234 or 800/228–9000,* ℻ *808/742–1557.*

From Lihue: Highway 50 to Poipu Beach Road (20 min).

MAUI

GRAND WAILEA RESORT AND SPA

Luxury pampering

Amid the splendor of waterfalls, sculpture, and tranquil pools, the 50,000-square-foot Spa Grande offers the most extensive health and fitness facilities in Hawaii. In addition to 10 individual and private Jacuzzi areas, there are Roman-style whirlpools 20 feet in diameter in the atriums of the men's and women's pavilions as well as 42 individual treatment rooms for everything from facials and loofah scrubs to mud treatments and massage.

Water sets the mood for the entire 40-acre resort. For active families, there are water slides and float trips on a 2,000-foot river circling the beach restaurant, as well as the usual water sports. For the less adventurous, there's a lap pool reserved for adults. Hydrotherapy comes with the spa's daily admission fee or as part of half-day and full-day packages. The Terme Wailea circuit begins with a choice of two treatments designed to exfoliate and cleanse the skin: a loofah scrub or Japanese goshi-goshi scrub, sitting shower, and soak in a furo tub. Next you have a choice from five specialty baths in marble and gold mosaic tubs: aromatherapy for relaxation, Maui mud to remineralize, limu (Hawaiian seaweed) for detoxification, herbal for rejuvenation, and tropical enzyme bath for toning and softening the skin. To stimulate circulation there are saunas, steam rooms, and cold-water plunges. Upstairs are private, oceanfront treatment rooms where seven types of massage and five different facials are offered. A scalp treatment combines limu, ginger, kelp, papaya, kuki nuts, and other native Hawaiian plants. The body wraps include island ti tree leaves. Ayurvedic treatments are also available.

Guests can join a morning walk for miles along a crescent of powder-soft sand, or escape the sun in the spa's air-conditioned aerobics studio, racquetball court (convertible for squash), or fitness center. The two-level beachfront facility has ocean-view suites for couples massage, as well as a relaxation room equipped with soothing mechanical massage chairs and a meditation-inducing audiovisual system. Refreshments are available from a self-service juice bar.

Two 18-hole golf courses wind through manicured grounds, and a tennis club with 14 courts offers day and night play. The day camp for kids includes group outings, special meals, and a cooking class provided by trained staffers.

Spectacular promenades lead to the open-air eateries and the Japanese and Polynesian restaurants. Set amid terrraced gardens, the eight-story hotel has a wide range of accommodations, from standard lanai rooms to concierge-level Napua Club rooms. Located on Maui's south shore, the resort is close to Kahului Airport. It's a short walk to the spa from the neighboring Four Seasons resort, whose guests are welcome here.

FACILITIES

Exercise Equipment: Rowing machines, stair climbers, stationary bikes, treadmills, weight-training circuit, free weights. **Services:** Aromatherapy, lomi-lomi, reflexology, shiatsu, sports, Swedish massage; herbal bath, loofah scrub, seaweed body pack, Ayurvedic treatment; facial. **Swimming:** Ocean beach, 2 pools. **Classes and Programs:** Consultation on health, stress management, nutrition, fitness. **Recreation:** Billiards, golf, racquetball/squash, tennis, walks; catamaran cruises, canoe rentals, snorkeling, windsurfing, scuba diving. **Children's Programs:** Keiki-land.

734 rooms, 53 suites.

DINING
All meals à la carte. Optional Italian, Japanese, and Polynesian restaurants. Organically grown island food with Italian and Provençale touches.
Sample Meals: Grilled breast of chicken with mango chili sauce, mahimahi with snap peas and roasted red peppers, black-bean salad with cilantro (lunch).

RATES AND PACKAGES
Oceanfront Grande room for 1 or 2 $495 per night; Garden $445 per night; Mountain View Terrace room $380 per night; Suites $1,100–$10,000 per night for 2; Napua Club–Ocean Front $580 per night. Day Spa packages (half- and full-day) $209–$349. AE, DC, MC, V.

DIRECTIONS
✉ *3850 Wailea Alanui Dr., Wailea, Maui, HI 96753,* ☎ *808/875–1234 or 800/888–6100,* ℻ *808/874–2442.*

From Kahului Airport on Maui: Highway 380 to Highway 350 via Kihei Highway 31.

HOTEL HANA-MAUI

Luxury pampering

Adventure begins on the hairpin curves of the narrow road that leads to the wild western side of Maui. An aura of the Old West pervades the Hotel Hana-Maui, which is set on an isolated coast in the middle of a cattle ranch. Hawaiian cowboys, called *paniolos,* lead white-face Hereford cattle in from pasture as you hike down the rocky coastal trail to catch the sunset at Red Sand Beach; a session of yoga at the Wellness Center is a nice follow-up, topped off by a shiatsu massage.

Accessible only by a dramatically winding coastal highway or by commuter aircraft, Hana is a place of soothing seclusion. Lodging is in 98 spacious one-story cottages with wood floors and walls, tropical furnishings, and private lanais. Sea Ranch cottages come with private hot tubs. In winter, it is possible to spot humpback whales while floating in the main swimming pool. A vintage Packard transports guests to the beach. During dinner in the Plantation Great House, talented members of the staff offer performances of Hawaiian music and dance in an authentic style not packaged for commercial shows.

The 66-acre complex has a small wellness center, where you can work out surrounded by panoramic views. The mirrored aerobics studio provides a varied schedule of classes: low-impact aerobics, aquacise, and yoga at $10 per class. A nature walk begins the day at 9:30 AM. The spa director's philosophy reflects an appreciation of the island's natural beauty rather than emphasizing pampering attentions. For serious hikers, there is a four-hour trek into the lush tropical forest, with a stop to swim under the cascades of a waterfall.

Secluded, almost monastic, the 50-year-old hotel is a stronghold of Hawaiian culture and nature. Hana's terrain slopes gently upward across green pastures, rising to rain forests and the Haleakala Crater. You can almost sense the magic of the fire god Pele.

FACILITIES
Exercise Equipment: Cross-country ski machine, rowing machine, stair climbers, stationary bikes, weight-training circuit. **Services:** Swedish and therapeutic massage; facial with coconut, honey, aloe vera. **Swimming:**

Ocean beaches, pool. **Classes and Programs:** Aerobics, aquacise, hiking, nature walks. **Recreation:** Breakfast cookout, baseball, hay ride, horseback riding. Folklore performances.

ACCOMMODATIONS
97 cottages.

DINING
Dining à la carte. Specializes in Asian-Pacific cuisine focusing on seafood and organic ingredients. Full-American plan $95, modified plan $75.

RATES AND PACKAGES
Daily $395–$795 per suite for 1 or 2 persons. AE, DC, MC, V.

DIRECTIONS
✉ *Box 8, Hana, Maui, HI 96713,* ☎ *808/248–8211 or 800/321–4262,* FAX *808/248–7202.*

From Kahului Airport: Transfers by van (1½ hrs) or Aloha Island Air (15 mins).

THE WESTIN MAUI

Luxury pampering

Breathtaking waterfalls, meandering streams, and a health club are among the attractions of the Westin Maui, one of Hawaii's first mega resorts. Set on 12 oceanfront acres bordered by two golf courses and a tennis complex, the Westin has a winning combination of sports and spa programs. The pool area alone features five free-form swimming pools, two water slides, and a swim-up Jacuzzi hidden away in a grotto. Swans, flamingos, and other charming characters roam freely, adding their individual personalities to the tropical atmosphere.

The coed health club offers weight-training and an exercise room where aerobics classes are held daily. Step and low-impact sessions are offered for a modest charge per class plus the daily admission fee ($15), which is waived for hotel guests. There is a steam room, sauna, and Jacuzzi for relaxing stiff, sore muscles. Massage therapy is available by appointment.

Each of the hotel's two towers has 11 floors. Rooms and suites have private lanais with views of the ocean or golf course. The exclusive Royal Beach Club rooms are especially luxurious.

While on Maui visit the new $20 million Maui Ocean Center, where you can observe cruising tiger sharks and manta rays, tiny burrowing shrimp, and waving garden eels from a transparent underwater tunnel. Set into a hillside at Maalea Harbor, the aquarium is a takeoff point for snorkelsailing and whale-watch outings as well as sunset cocktail cruises.

FACILITIES
Exercise Equipment: Stair climbers, stationary bikes, treadmill, weight-training circuit, free weights. **Services:** Acupressure, lomi-lomi, reflexology, shiatsu, Swedish massage. **Swimming:** Ocean beach, 5 pools. **Classes and Programs:** Hawaiiana demonstrations. **Recreation:** Golf, tennis, water sports. Resort entertainment. **Children's Programs:** Hawaiian arts and crafts classes and seasonal day camp (Easter, summer, Thanksgiving, Christmas).

ACCOMMODATIONS
742 rooms and suites.

DINING
All meals à la carte. 3 restaurants. Best choice: Sound of the Falls.

RATES AND PACKAGES

$265–$445 single or double occupancy, $495 Royal Beach Club rooms, $750–$2000 suites. Deposit: 2 nights' advance payment or credit-card confirmation. AE, DC, MC, V.

DIRECTIONS

✉ *2365 Kaanapali Pkwy., Lahaina, HI 96761,* ☎ *808/667–2525 or 800/228–3000,* ℻ *808/661–5764.*

From Kapalua-West Airport: Highway 30 (Honoapiilani Highway) via Lahaina (10 mins).

OAHU

IHILANI RESORT AND SPA

Luxury pampering
Mineral springs

Soak in sea water amid orchids and silk at this unique Hawaiian hydrotherapy resort. Inspired by the sea and ancient Hawaiian healing therapies, the spa program at the Ihilani Resort provides revitalization and relaxation. On Oahu's western coast, 25 minutes from Honolulu International Airport, the 640-acre resort opened in 1993. Designed for upscale travelers and members of the Ko'Olina Golf Club, the luxury hotel is set amid thousands of coconut palm trees, banyans, monkeypods, and silver buttonwood trees, as well as flowering bougainvillea, firecracker plants, and fragrant plumeria. Surrounded by four tranquil lagoons and the Waianae mountains, this property may be the ultimate Hawaiian escape.

Aerobics classes are scheduled in a coed studio on the top floor of the three-level spa, where there is also a weight room. Jacuzzi and locker rooms are on the second floor, where you enter from the hotel. An ocean environment is created with French thalassotherapy technology and salt water piped directly from the Pacific. Specially designed treatment rooms have a hydrotherapy tub by Doyer, a Vichy-style shower massage table, and a Needle Shower Pavilion with 12 shower heads for water massage. The treatments involve Hawaiian seaweed packs and wraps, salt scrubs, and facial masks with marine algae.

All four program packages offered include three spa cuisine meals daily. The Hawaiian Revitalization Program, and a Health and Vitality Program, both seven days, can begin on any day, but a Sunday welcome is suggested by the spa director, who prepares a personal program for each guest. Postural and body alignment sessions may be included, as can Swedish and shiatsu massage, or a more challenging fitness component. The four-day Energy Booster package allows you to sample therapies Tuesday through Saturday, or you can shed pounds on a four-day Getaway package for weight loss or maintenance. If you simply want a day of pampering, hotel guests can book the Ali'i For a Day package.

The spa's selection of treatments includes Hawaiian herbs and medicinal plants such as ti leaves. In addition, Essensa and Nina Ricci skin care products are used. Workout clothing is supplied daily, as are cotton robes, slippers, and personal grooming items. Complete your day with a lomi-lomi massage, where the traditional rhythmic strokes are accompanied by chanting, and perhaps a hula dancing session.

After being wrapped and steamed in herb-soaked raw linen, you can drink the same herbs in tea, or taste them in spa meals made with local seafood, seaweed, and fruits. With five restaurants, including a dedicated spa café, a splendid beach cove, golf, and tennis, this hideaway lives up to its name, "heavenly splendor."

FACILITIES
Exercise Equipment: Cross-country ski machine, rowing machines, stair climbers, stationary bikes, treadmills, weight-training circuit. **Services:** Aromatherapy, shiatsu, Swedish massage; body scrub, herbal wrap, loofah body wrap; hydrotherapy, thalassotherapy, Vichy shower; facial, marine mask. **Swimming:** Ocean beach, pools. **Classes and Programs:** Health and fitness evaluation, personal training. **Recreation:** Boccie ball, croquet, golf, snorkeling, tennis, water sports. **Children's Programs:** Supervised child-care facility available.

387 rooms, 36 suites.

DINING

3 spa-cuisine meals daily included in packages, served in the main dining room or spa café. **Sample Meals:** Vegetarian pizza, spinach lasagna (lunch); Mediterranean-style shrimp and scallops, grilled mahimahi (dinner).

RATES AND PACKAGES

7-day Revitalization program $3,646 single, $2,834 per person, double occupancy. 7-day Vitality package $3,554 single, $2,749 double. 4-day Energy Booster package $2,021 single, $1,530 double. 4-day Getaway $2,098 single, $1,618 double. Spa Day packages (no lodging) $140–$295. Daily room tariff $275–$550 for 1 or 2 persons; suites $700–$5,000. $300–$800 deposit required. AE, DC, MC, V.

DIRECTIONS

✉ *92-1001 O'lani St., Kapolei, Oahu, HI 96707, ☎ 808/679–0079 or 800/626–4446, ℻ 808/679–3387.*

From Honolulu: Highway 1 west, past Honolulu International Airport, to Ko'Olina exit (30 mins).

10 Canada

Alberta, British Columbia,
Ontario, Québec

SCENIC SPLENDOR IS AN ESSENTIAL PART of a fitness vacation in many areas of Canada, and hiking, trail rides, skiing, kayaking, and mountain biking abound. In addition, Canadian resorts offer state-of-the-art health clubs and treatment centers, as well as hot springs.

Western Canada is endowed with a wide range of health-oriented resorts, from ranches to luxury hotels, including a number of thermal springs. At the venerable Banff Springs Hotel in Alberta, sports-oriented guests visit the historic thermal springs and enjoy the most extensive selection of bodywork in Canada at the hotel's lavish Solace Spa. Outdoor adventure enthusiasts are welcome at British Columbia's caribou country Hills Health & Guest Ranch, where skiing, riding, and hiking are in order. In the lakes district, there are hot-spring soaks after hikes and fitness workouts at Mountain Trek Fitness Retreat. On the Pacific Coast, the Ocean Pointe Resort has views of Victoria's historic harbor area and museums; secluded Hollyhock and naturopathic EcoMed Wellness Spa provide holistic health programs; and skiiers at Whistler can indulge in the spa services of the newly expanded Chateau Whistler.

Ontario resort spas include the luxurious Inn at Manitou, Ste. Anne's Country Inn and Spa near Toronto, and the family-oriented Pillar & Post Inn in Shaw Theater Festival country. Thalassotherapy is the specialty of small resorts along the Gaspé Peninsula of French-speaking Québec, which also has the farmlike Centre de Santé d'Eastman. For a demanding yoga regimen, try the Sivananda Ashram, in the forrested Laurentian Mountains near Montreal. Newly upgraded, the Mont-Tremblant Park area offers a luxurious spa retreat at Club Tremblant as well as year-round sports conditioning.

Canadian spas offer more than a change of pace; since the currency exchange rate enhances the value of the U.S. dollar, there are substantial savings. (In the summer of 1998, $1 U.S. was worth $1.42 in Canadian currency.) Remember to bring identification papers for Canadian Customs: a passport will get you over the border without a hassle. Persons from outside the USA wishing to enter the States from Canada should make arrangements before leaving their home country; those planning to re-enter the States should check that they can comply with U.S. regulations. Hotel rates in Canada may include a room tax as well as GST (Goods & Services Tax). The GST on purchases is refundable to visitors upon application on departure, so save receipts from retailers.

Additional information on resorts and day spas in Québec is available from the Association des Relais de Santé du Québec (Box 971, Oka, Québec JON 1EO; ☎ 450/479–1690 or 800/788–7594).

ALBERTA

BANFF SPRINGS HOTEL

Luxury pampering
Mineral springs

After a long day of hiking or skiing, there's no better place to rejuvenate than at the Solace Spa at Banff Springs Hotel, set amid the spectacular scenery of the Canadian Rockies. Designed to mimic the historic springs, a series of mineral salt waterfalls cascade over guests in pools ranging from tepid to warm to hot. There's also a pool for swimming laps and state-of-the-art exercise equipment.

Built in the grand era of railroading at the turn of the century to accommodate visitors taking the waters, Banff Springs Hotel remains a bastion of traditional hospitality under Canadian-Pacific management. The impressive Solace Spa was added in 1995. It includes a high-tech health club and a salon, as well as private therapy rooms where you have a choice of Swedish or shiatsu massage. The hotel also has an outdoor program of golf, riding, and skiing. Visitors not staying at the hotel can use the spa for a $30 daily membership fee. Day spa packages and a four-day retreat are other options.

Opened in 1888, the turreted hotel—the largest in Canada west of Toronto—looks like a castle out of Camelot, and is equally majestic inside. Many of the 867 rooms and suites are decorated with antiques, but the entire property has been upgraded and modernized. Accommodations are in the original hotel as well as in an annex, Banff Springs Manor. There is a three-story VIP suite with private glass elevator, sauna, whirlpool, and lap pool. Instead of English lords and ladies, the baronial halls may be filled with Japanese tour groups. For maximum privacy and luxury, reserve one of four suites built into towers above the spa; views of the valley and distant mountains are priceless.

Stairs or elevator take you down from the main lobby to the three-level Solace Spa. With an aerobics studio and strength-training equipment room whose glass walls overlook the Bow River valley and majestic mountains, this is the best of the Northwest. The next level down is devoted to Kerstin Florian skin care and a beauty salon, and the pools are accessible via interior stairs from the men's and women's locker rooms. Also here are lounges with fireplace and complimentary coffee, sauna, inhalation room, steambath, and whirlpool. From the pool level, you have access to a terrace whirlpool surrounded by breathtaking mountain scenery. The minimum age in the spa is 18; in the fitness center, it's 16.

The sulfur-rich water of the natural springs has been replaced in the pools at Banff Springs Hotel with a mixture of mineral salts from the sea and other sources. Swimmers can use the huge indoor pool and interconnected heated outdoor pool for free if staying at the hotel, or with a daily membership fee. The daily admission fee to the spa is waived for hotel guests who book a minimum 25-minute spa treatment. There are 16 treatment rooms on the pool level (two specially designed for wet bodywork), and a cascade shower. Due to heavy demand for appointments, it is wise to book spa services in advance of your arrival at the resort.

Despite all the pampering activities, golf and skiing are still the main attractions here, but other summer opportunities bring cyclists and horseback riders, backpackers and river rafters. Before the railroad and hotel builders arrived in 1885, the hot springs were sacred, shrouded in clouds of steam. Rebuilt by Parks Canada, the spring-fed pools on the mountainside are open to the public, worth a hike in the morning for an inexpensive, meditative soak in misty sunlight amid the lodgepole pines. Massage and herbal body wraps are available at the Upper Springs day spa at moderate prices (☎ 403/678–0966).

Walk into town for a sampling of local history and culture. Take a guided tour at the original Cave & Basin springs; the admission fee covers entry to a museum with exhibits on the park's development (☎ 403/762–1558; admission $3.55). In the center of town, the Whyte Museum features a collection of art related to the Rockies. Banff has been called the park's Aspen because of its great collection of boutiques and shops. It also has bargain accommodations ranging from ski lodges to cozy log cabin–style hideaways. A 90-minute drive down the parkway is the site of the Calgary Stampede, and the province's biggest saloon, Wild Bill's, which draw droves of visitors from Germany and England. Four national parks converge here, embracing territory half the size of Switzerland. For a schedule of events and guided walks, visit the Banff National Park Visitor Center (☎ 403/762–1550).

The natural attractions of Banff National Park include prehistoric glaciers, alpine meadows, and cool canyons with more than 50 species of mammals, including elk, deer, bear, bighorn sheep, and mountain goats. Birdwatching and wildlife photography are among activities available in summer. The Banff Centre for the Arts—a 15-minute walk from the town center—hums with exhibits, workshops, and opera year-round, and in summer it stages spectacular concerts outdoors.

The Banff Springs Hotel is big and brawny, practically a city unto itself, and its enduring popularity is built on serving just about every interest imaginable, be it fine dining, golf, hiking, or simply enjoying a luxurious hideaway. Spa-goers may have the place to themselves during the day, when skiers and conventioneers are busy elsewhere. The hotel has 14 restaurants, from sushi bar to the formal Rob Roy dining room, plus the spa café, where healthy breakfasts and lunches are available every day.

FACILITIES
Exercise Equipment: Stair climbers, stationary bikes, treadmills, weight-training circuit, free weights. **Services**: Reflexology, shiatsu, Swedish massage, therapeutic massage; body scrub, body wraps (spirulina, moor mud, herbal, aromatherapy); hydrotherapy tub mineral and herbal baths; facials. **Swimming:** Indoor and outdoor pools. **Classes and Programs:** Fitness training, nutritional consultation. **Recreation:** Biking, bowling, golf, hiking, tennis, skiing; horseback riding and white-water rafting nearby.

ACCOMMODATIONS
770 rooms and suites.

DINING
Traditional à la carte menu in main dining room; Japanese and Italian restaurants. Spa Café open daily for breakfast and lunch.

RATES AND PACKAGES
May, $160–$280 per room (C$) daily, single or double; suites $240–$595. Summer, $180–$375 per room, suites $518–$934. Oct. 13–Dec. 22 and Jan. 2–Apr., $125–$187 per room, suites $205–$388. 1-or 2-bedroom suites (2–4 beds) $344–$579; VIP suite $1,500. 3-night/4-day Ultimate Retreat spa packages $1,551–$2,184 single, $1,236–$1,552.50 per person, double. Charlene Prickett Spa & Fitness Week (Oct.) from $1,530

per person, double. Day Spa package including lunch $145–$245 per person. Gratuities included in spa packages. AE, MC, V.

DIRECTIONS

✉ *Box 960, Banff, Alberta T0L 0C0,* ☎ *403/762–2211 or 800/268–9411, 403/762–1772 (spa),* ⅏ *403/762–5755, 403/762–1766 (spa).*

From Calgary: Trans-Canada Highway to park entrances (2 hrs), where a 1-year vehicle pass must be purchased.

MOUNTAIN ESCAPE AT LAKE LOUISE INN

Holistic health
Luxury pampering

Operated as a spring and fall retreat for women, the Mountain Escape program is a week devoted to improving body and soul. Mountain hikes don't mean roughing it, nor do you have to give up morning coffee to get fit at this alpine resort. There are scheduled walks and exercise routines in the invigorating setting of the Rocky Mountains. Lectures on healthy eating and fitness guidance from qualified staff members introduce you to the benefits of a healthy lifestyle.

Special weeks focus on holistic health, emphasizing yoga, tai chi, and self-defense. Challenge Week is a more advanced fitness program. From the sunrise eye-opener walk to an afternoon stretch-and-tone session, the emphasis is on personal development and learning how to set holistic health goals. A team of instructors works with you in small, compatible groups. Activities are geared to the general energy of the group rather than to peak performance, with one week dedicated to more challenging activities.

Breathtaking surrounding peaks come in view on walks around Lake Louise, and snow-covered Victoria Glacier is mirrored in the aqua-blue water. While one group does high-energy aerobics, another learns aquatic exercises in the pool. Two hour-long classes are scheduled each morning, and yoga is practiced before dinner. Massage and beauty services can be scheduled for an additional charge.

FACILITIES

Exercise Equipment: Free weights. **Services:** Acupressure, aromatherapy massage, reflexology, Reiki, shiatsu, sports massage, Swedish massage; body brushing; facials. **Swimming:** Indoor pool. **Classes and Programs:** Aquaerobics, Iyengar yoga, lifestyle lectures, step aerobics. **Recreation:** Bike rental, cross-country and downhill skiing, horseback riding; tennis nearby.

ACCOMMODATIONS

232 rooms.

DINING

3 meals daily plus low-fat snacks. **Sample Meals:** Pita pocket with bean soup, chicken bruschetta, pasta with tomato-basil sauce and shrimp (lunch); vegetarian lasagna, poached salmon with yogurt-dill sauce, filet mignon (dinner).

RATES AND PACKAGES

Challenge Week or Holistic Week: 6-day/6-night program $825–$998 (C$) single, $665–$745 per person, double. Condensed 4-day/4-night program $525–$708 single, $489–$525 double. $100 deposit required. AE, MC, V.

DIRECTIONS

✉ *Box 209, Lake Louise, Alberta T0L 1E0,* ☎ *403/522–3791 or 800/ 661–9237 in western Canada,* ⊠ *403/522–2018.*

From Calgary: Trans-Canada Highway west for 200 km (110 mi); take Lake Louise Drive exit west to Village Road north.

BRITISH COLUMBIA

CHATEAU WHISTLER RESORT

Luxury pampering
Sports conditioning

The serious skier or hiker will enjoy conditioning in the newly expanded fitness facility at Chateau Whistler. There's year-round skiing on the greatest vertical rise in North America, water sports in summer, and alpine hiking and horseback riding in summer, spring, and fall. Golfers can play four courses in the area, including Chateau Whistler's 18-hole course designed by Robert Trent Jones, Jr. (For information on golf packages, call 800/441–1414.)

The baronial Chateau Whistler, the largest hotel in Whistler Village, has a complete health club with a pre-ski stretch class, tennis instruction, and licensed therapists for sports massage. There are aerobics classes, a 30-foot indoor-outdoor pool, cardiovascular exercise equipment, and a coed sauna, as well as separate sets of saunas and steam rooms for men and women. Services in the 11 treatment rooms include skin care, shiatsu massage, and hydrotherapy. The 10,000 sq. ft facility makes use of natural light refracted off lead-crystal on window frames. The trendy hair salon and two massage rooms have views of Blackcomb and Whistler Mountains. Accents of slate, limestone, and richly stained wood carry the mountain motif throughout the spa.

Located at the base of two world-class ski mountains, Chateau Whistler Resort has lifts that whisk guests to alpine meadows for interpretive eco-tours, classical concerts, and stargazing. Within steps of the chateau is a pedestrian plaza, the heart of Whistler Village, with dozens of boutiques and restaurants. The 12-story Chateau was built on a grand scale in 1990, expanded in 1997 for a total of 561 rooms and rooftop garden terrace. Its cathedral-ceiling lobby offers unobstructed views of Blackcomb Mountain's famed slopes, and guest rooms feature folk art and carpets inspired by Mennonite hooked rugs. Other decorative touches include Québec armoires, birdhouses, and baskets of apples. On an outdoor deck, a Jacuzzi beckons.

FACILITIES
Exercise Equipment: Rowing machine, stair climbers, stationary bikes, treadmill, weight-training circuit, free weights. **Services:** Aromatherapy, shiatsu, sports massage; body treatments, herbal linen wrap, Ahava mud wrap, parafango; vichy shower; facials. **Swimming:** Pool. **Classes and Programs:** Tennis lessons and camps, paragliding school, sleigh rides. **Recreation:** Bike rental, canoeing, croquet, cross-country and downhill skiing, fishing, glacier skiing (summer), golf (18 holes), ice skating, tennis; horseback riding nearby. **Children's Programs:** Kids Club for ages 5–12.

ACCOMMODATIONS
561 rooms and suites.

DINING
Wildflower Restaurant has an innovative menu focusing on organic regional ingredients, with fresh seafood, wild boar, and venison in season. New Portabello tapas bar has a lounge for light meals.

RATES AND PACKAGES
$200–$319 (C$) daily in summer, single or double; $220–$359 daily in winter, suites $420–$1,199. 1-night deposit required. AE, MC, V.

DIRECTIONS

✉ *4599 Chateau Blvd., Box 100, Whistler, British Columbia V0N 1B4,*
☎ *604/938–8000 or 800/268–9411, 800/401–4018 (spa reservations),*
FAX *604/938–2055.*

From Vancouver: Highway 99 past Horseshoe Bay, Squamish, and Howe Sound (70 miles, 90 mins).

ECOMED WELLNESS SPA & CLINIC

Holistic health
Medical wellness

The naturopathic therapies at this very small bayside retreat perfectly complement outings to the parks and varied environment of Vancouver Island. Comprehensive diagnostic services and treatments include live blood cell analysis, acupuncture, oxygen therapies, stress management, nutritional counseling, and detoxification. Conditions treated include chronic fatigue syndrome, immune deficiencies, arthritis, diabetes, allergies, and cancer-related pain.

Founded and directed by Stefan Kuprowsky, M.D., the spa and clinic are at Pacific Shores Nature Resort on the forested northern end of Vancouver Island. Set on one of British Columbia's warmest swimming bays, the resort offers a fitness center with ozonated swimming pool, indoor and outdoor hot tubs, beachfront nature trail, and bird sanctuary. Spa guests stay in a cluster of contemporary beachfront homes decorated with local artwork and West Coast modern furnishings. Rooms have either a garden view or a bayfront patio. Suites have full living room with fireplace, whirlpool bath, and kitchen. Everyone gathers at the main house for meals, treatments, and consultations with Dr. Kuprowsky.

Cleansing the body of toxins is the basis of healing retreats that range from one week to a month in length. Weekends and seven-day programs are devoted to health workshops, nature walks, and inner cleansing. Spa and aesthetic services are on an à la carte basis or included in program packages. A hydrotherapy tub for herbal soaks, facials with natural products developed by Canadian skin care specialists, aromatherapy, and massage are available. Special workshops on organic gardening, natural fertility, and native spiritual traditions enhance the basic program of walks and treatments. Vegetarian meals, included in the daily program fee, feature fresh produce from nearby organic farms.

Vancouver Island provides outdoor adventure in abundance, from bathing in mountain streams to hot springs and ocean beaches, pleasant, small-town shopping, and busy ports for commercial fishing boats. Vast stands of old oaks, maple, and Douglas fir trees cover the midsection and northern tip. Hikes in a nature reserve—Rathtrevor Park—and rain forest are a major attraction. On the island's more developed southern coast is Victoria, provincial capital and cultural center. Linked to the mainland and Vancouver by ferry and airline services, the island has excellent roads and a scenic railroad for day trips.

FACILITIES
Exercise Equipment: Stair climbers, stationary bikes, treadmill, weight-training equipment, free weights. **Services:** Aromatherapy, reflexology, shiatsu, Swedish massage; mud bath, mud body wrap, seaweed body wrap; colonic irrigation; facial. **Swimming:** Indoor pool, ocean beach. **Classes and Programs:** Acupuncture, allergy testing, blood testing, nutritional consultation, psychological counseling. **Recreation:** Boccie ball, canoeing, kayaking; golf and tennis nearby.

ACCOMMODATIONS
6 rooms, 6 suites.

DINING
3 meals daily, served family-style. Vegetarian and seafood meals using local organic ingredients. Herbal tea, no coffee. **Sample Meals:** Cold kale-cucumber soup, curried pumpkin soup, smoked salmon with artichoke hearts and arugula salad, carrot-beet-ginger juice, fresh fruit crumble (lunch); fresh tropical-fruit cocktail, brown-rice sushi, shallots with roasted red pepper–tofu sauce, buckwheat noodles with shiitake mushrooms, lemon silken pie, carob-tofu mousse (dinner).

RATES AND PACKAGES
$175–$275 (C$) daily single, $150–$200 per person, double; 2-night/3-day weekend retreat $525–$725 single, $475–$575 per person, double; Inner Cleanse Weekend $1,095–$1,395 single, $1000–$1,150 double. 1-week Spa Rejuvenation $1,595–$2,295 single, $1,295–$1,650 double. 1-week Healing Intensive $3,300–$4,000 single or double, companion rate $1,750. 50% deposit required for all programs, refundable until 10 days prior to stay. MC, V.

DIRECTIONS
✉ *515-1600 Stroulger Rd., Nanoose Bay, British Columbia V9P 9B7,* ☎ *250/468–7133,* ℻ *250/468–7135.*

From Vancouver: Highway 99 to BC ferry terminal in Nanaimo, then Highway 19 (Island Highway) north to Parksville, east on Beaver Creek Wharf Road, north to Stroulger Road, left to resort gate (½ hour from ferry terminal, 3 hrs from Vancouver). Pickup available at ferry terminal.

FAIRMONT HOT SPRINGS RESORT

Mineral springs

Canada's largest hot mineral pools are one attraction of this family-oriented vacation complex in the Rocky Mountains. Surrounded by mountain forests, the privately owned Fairmont Hot Springs Resort has big swimming pools open to day visitors, who come in large numbers for sports and relaxation. There's golf, skiing, and a spacious Sports Center, where spa treatments and exercise equipment make it possible to assemble your own spa program. In addition to trail rides and guided hikes, there is an Indian village. Be forewarned: Facilities can be crowded during holiday periods, and some consider the resort touristy.

The aesthetics department provides a wide range of skin care and beauty services, à la carte. Fitness facilities and a private pool are for overnight guests, who stay in the main lodge or in one of 5 cottages. The cottages and suites have cooking facilities. Two full-size racquetball courts, one squash court, coed saunas and whirlpool, and hydra-fitness exercise equipment are available. An optional spa-cuisine menu lets you choose meals that complement your healthy regime. Breakfast buffet has fresh juices, bran muffins, yogurt, and cottage cheese.

FACILITIES
Exercise Equipment: Stationary bike, weight-training equipment. **Services:** Swedish massage; fango, herbal wrap, loofah body scrub, salt-glow scrub. **Swimming:** Indoor and outdoor pools. **Classes and Programs:** Guided hikes, yoga, aerobics, aquacise classes. **Recreation:** Downhill and cross-country skiing, fishing, golf, hiking, horseback riding, racquetball, rafting, sailing, squash, tennis, water skiing.

ACCOMMODATIONS

86 rooms, 48 suites, 5 cottages.

DINING

Breakfast included in package; other meals à la carte. **Sample Meals:** Cold cucumber soup, salad of red cabbage and apple, curried chicken with yogurt dressing, fillet of sole with braised leeks (lunch); veal cutlet with wild mushrooms, breast of chicken stuffed with lobster, fillet of red snapper with curry sauce (dinner).

RATES AND PACKAGES

$80–$200 (C$) daily per person, double occupancy. 2-night/2-day spa package, $189–$219 per person, double occupancy. Add 7% GST, 8% tax. Deposit: 1 night. AE, MC, V.

DIRECTIONS

⊠ *Box 10, Fairmont Hot Springs, British Columbia V0B 1L0,* ☎ *604/ 345–6311 or 800/663–4979,* ☎ *604/345–6616.*

From Calgary: Highway 93, north of Cranbrook (3 hrs).

HARRISON HOT SPRINGS HOTEL

Mineral springs

A lakeside resort with indoor/outdoor pools for thermal mineral water soaks, the Harrison Hot Springs Hotel is a pleasant getaway. Entered from a large pavilion (open 24 hours), the garden has an Olympic-size indoor swimming pool filled with warm spring water year-round. The sulfurous, 104°F spring water provides effective if temporary relief for aching muscles. Designed with oriental bridges and rock gardens, the large outdoor soaking pools are especially attractive.

From the main road Lake Harrison looks scruffy: The strip of rocky, gray beach is lined with parked cars and RVs, but beyond the tourist bars and souvenir stands are wilderness tracks for hiking and quiet country roads. Nearby is Minter Gardens, a showcase for Canadian horticulture, open Mar.–Oct.

The hotel, long popular with honeymooners and conventioneers, has a cozy café in the lobby, and afternoon tea is served daily in front of the lobby fireplace. While the exercise equipment looks dated, the hotel's 300 motellike rooms are well maintained. There are cottages in a private garden area and deluxe rooms in the new tower, some with lake view. Don't expect organized spa activity or low-fat cuisine; this is a place to wear jeans and boots.

FACILITIES

Exercise Equipment: Stair climber, stationary bikes, weight-training circuit. **Services:** Massage. **Swimming:** Lake, indoor and outdoor pools. **Classes and Programs:** Dinner-dances. **Recreation:** Bike rental, cross-country skiing, tennis, volleyball; horseback riding and golf nearby.

ACCOMMODATIONS

300 rooms, cottages.

RATES AND PACKAGES

$124–$180 (C$) daily, double or single occupancy; 4-day/3-night midweek package $564–$485 per person, double occupancy, $289–$493 single. AE, D, MC, V.

DIRECTIONS

⊠ *Harrison Hot Springs, British Columbia V0M 1K0,* ☎ *604/796– 2244 or 800/663–2266,* ☎ *604/796–9374.*

From Vancouver: Trans-Canada Highway (Route 1) east to exit for Route 9 at Minter Gardens; continue to Lake Harrison (2 hrs).

THE HILLS HEALTH RANCH

Luxury pampering
Medical wellness
Nutrition and diet

Saddle up for a Western-style ranch workout replete with horse rides and line dancing at The Hills Health Ranch in caribou country, in the heart of British Columbia. Informal in ambience, The Hills is distinguished for effective weight management programs and sophisticated beauty treatments. Facials, skin treatments, herbal wraps, and massages mix with hayrides and trail rides. Winter packages offer downhill and cross-country skiing, bringing together family fun and fitness.

Woodsy A-frame chalets and a two-story Ranch House fan out from the log-sided main building (non-smoking throughout), where the spa, indoor swimming pool, and dining room are located. Accommodations in the Ranch House are far from rustic, and each room has a balcony with mountain view. For families and groups, the large chalets have three bedrooms, kitchen, and living room.

During winter the ranch is busy with skiers (several teams train here). There is a new ski lodge for day visitors, who use the chairlift and downhill runs on a gentle slope equipped with a snowmaking system.

Opened in 1985, the ranch is the first Canadian Wellness Center to provide medically based programs in healthy living. Its affiliation with the University of British Columbia has led to lifestyle research and special programs for rehabilitation after injury or surgery. There is emphasis on the needs of the mature person, including maintaining a healthy heart through exercise and nutrition.

If you join the wellness program, you'll participate in exercise, nutrition, and stress management sessions, and receive bodywork treatments. After an initial fitness evaluation you'll join a small group for scheduled activities: morning power walks, daily guided hikes, aerobics and step classes, line dancing, aquaerobics in the indoor pool, circuit and weight-training, and stretching/relaxation classes. A physician will address medical concerns and a kinesiologist, aestheticians, massage therapist, and fitness instructor will work with you throughout the program.

The ranch offers an Executive Renewal Week, weekend packages, and 11-day programs year-round. With 200 kilometers (130 miles) of hiking and riding trails, there are daily outings and week-long wilderness adventure packages. A resident wrangler runs the stables, where you can join morning and afternoon horseback rides, which even novices and young riders enjoy. After a morning on the trail, lunch is served in a mountain meadow. At night, there are hayrides and a sing-along at Willy's Wigwam, an authentic tepee.

Encompassing 20,000 acres of lakes, mountains, and forest, this privately owned and operated ranch provides Western hospitality while helping you cope with weight problems and aging. Noted for heart-healthy dining, the ranch menu offers a choice of hearty fare. Some guests accomplish substantial weight loss during stays of a month or more. Adding a high level of personal attention, the resident owners Juanita and Patrick Corbett and their professional staffers cater to the whole person, helping each guest develop a healthier lifestyle.

FACILITIES
Exercise Equipment: Stair climber, stationary bikes, treadmills, weight-training circuit, free weights. **Services:** Massage, reflexology; full-body mud pack, herbal wrap, loofah scrub; facials. **Swimming:** Pool. **Classes and Programs:** Western dancing with live music, workshops on nutrition and wellness. **Recreation:** Cross-country skiing, curling, hiking, ice skating, horseback riding, tobogganing; golf, tennis, mountain-bike and canoe rental, and fishing nearby. **Children's Programs:** Riding and skiing instruction and teepee parties.

ACCOMMODATIONS
26 rooms, 20 private chalets.

DINING
3 calorie-counted spa cuisine or ranch-style meals with health packages. Personalized low-fat menu served in private dining area. **Sample Meals:** Chicken fajitas with sour cream and salsa; Mexican rice and bean casserole (lunch); salmon with honey-mustard sauce, asparagus, and seven-grain pilaf; venison in black peppercorn-maple glaze, rosti potatoes and seasonal vegetables (dinner).

RATES AND PACKAGES
Weekend: $360 single (C$), $270 per person, double. 7-day Executive Renewal package $1,727 single, $1,472 per person, double. 7-day Inches Off package $1,279 single, $999 per person, double. Successful Aging Week $1,569 single, $1,293 double. 10-night weight-loss package $2,206 single, $1,756 double. $50 or 25% deposit required 2 weeks prior to arrival. Cancellations within 2 weeks of reservation not refundable. AE, MC, V.

DIRECTIONS
✉ *C-26, 108 Mile Ranch, British Columbia V0K 2Z0,* ☎ *250/791–5225,* FAX *250/791–6384.*

Use main routes through the Rockies to the village of 100 Mile House, Highway 97.

HOLLYHOCK

Holistic health

Secluded on a Pacific coastal island, 100 miles north of Vancouver and accessible only by air or ferry, Hollyhock seems far removed from the real world. Yet from March through August the community teems with activity, with weekend getaways and more than 70 seminars and workshops offered. Subjects range from health and healing to shamanism; there's a spiritual retreat for couples and tai chi chuan training. Participants also enjoy the island retreat's guided nature walks, organic gardens, beaches, rowboats, yoga classes, stargazing, and occasional concerts. Bodywork and skin care services are available for a fee.

Since 1982, specialists in alternative therapies and spiritual health have drawn inspiration from each other in this island setting. The informal "campus," where group discussions are held, is made up of wood dormitories surrounded by forest and beach. Mornings begin at 7 o'clock with yoga, followed by meditation. Workshops run the gamut of New Age consciousness, from astrology to Vedic healing.

The beauty of Hollyhock is memorable, with gates and banisters fashioned from driftwood, seashells embedded in a hot tub overlooking the shore, and towering stands of fir trees. The organic garden, a three-quarter-acre showcase, produces flowers and veggies for the dining room.

Paths lead to Smelt Bay, a favorite place for watching the pink-rimmed sunset over Vancouver Island, and to the Bodywork Studio, where a cranial sacral massage eases tension and might release emotions. In a nearby clearing, a Zen garden surrounds a sculptured sanctuary for meditation. The healing arts program constantly changes. One day it may include the pounding percussion of African drumming, another the total silence of Metta Meditation. The idea is to get in touch with your inner self in whatever way you can.

Accommodations range from single room with bath to dormitory-style rooms with six beds. Campsites are available. The two-story main lodge has a shop and library upstairs, kitchen and dining room on the first floor, and a deck facing the Strait of Georgia. Refreshment is available at all times of the day: decaf ice tea, herbs for a tisane, perhaps an iced latte.

Arriving at Cortes Island by floatplane is a dazzling introduction to some of the most stunning natural scenery on the continent. The entire area is a glacier-carved collection of coves, capes, and fjordlike passages. Kayaking and sailing excursions are organized for visitors to experience this seascape. If you'd rather just soak in the hot tub, that's fine too.

FACILITIES
Services: Acupressure, deep-tissue, reflexology, Swedish massage; body wrap; facials. **Swimming:** Lake, ocean beaches. **Classes and Programs:** Guided bird walks, wilderness interpretation tour. **Recreation:** Kayaks, rowboat, sailboats.

ACCOMMODATIONS
21 rooms with shared bath, 2 rooms with bath, 5 dormitory rooms, 14 tent sites.

DINING
3 buffet meals daily. International cuisine, mostly vegetarian with some seafood. **Sample Meals:** Vegetarian casserole provençale with sourdough baguette, Thai fish soup with homemade bread, Greek salad (lunch); barbecue oysters, grilled salmon (dinner).

RATES AND PACKAGES
$139–$179 (C$) daily single, $109–$129 double, $89 dormitory, $59–$69 tenting. 7-night holiday package $973–$1,253 single, $763–$903 per person, double; $623 dormitory; $413–$483 camping. $32–$68 per day for children 4–12. $250 deposit required for workshop and holiday package, $125 for short stays. MC, V.

DIRECTIONS
⊠ *Box 127, Manson's Landing, Cortes Island, British Columbia V0P 1K0,* ☎ *250/935–6576 or 800/933–6339,* FAX *250/935–6424.*

From Seattle and Vancouver: By car and BC ferries (☎ 250/386–3431), via Vancouver Island.

MOUNTAIN TREK FITNESS RETREAT & HEALTH SPA

Holistic health

To get in shape, stay in shape, or significantly improve your level of fitness, head to this retreat in the beautiful Kootenay Mountains of southwestern British Columbia. Set on 34 lakeside acres of forest, it has the makings of both a health club and a spa. The 12-bedroom cedar lodge is a comfortable base from which to explore high country trails. You can picnic in pristine meadows and soak in the hot springs. There are overnight camping trips in the mountains and a program combination of fasting and internal cleansing.

Hiking and winter snowshoeing are the core activities: six treks per week, with all equipment included. Orientation is on Saturday afternoon. You'll learn the lore of the Whitewater Glacier Trail, one of the mountains' most accessible. It once attracted miners searching for gold and silver in the White Grizzly Wilderness. You may see grizzlies, deer, mountain goats, and marmots as you explore alpine slopes, expansive flower meadows, and temperate forests. The lead-and-shepherd guide system allows you to go at your own pace.

Workouts in the main lodge are scheduled before and after hikes, and exercise clothing is provided daily. Yoga sessions are held in a wood-floor studio, with views of the mountains and lake. Kripalu yoga sessions are led by Ken Scott, who has developed Dankinetics exercises based on Hatha yoga. A separate weight-training room has a selection of Cybex equipment and free weights. Within a five-minute walk are natural thermal spring baths, and there is an outdoor hot tub next to the lodge's sauna. The all-inclusive week lets you schedule three massages.

Each participant or couple has a private bedroom and bathroom in the cedar two-story lodge. There is no TV, phone, or air-conditioning. Robes and knapsacks are provided, and there's a full-service laundry room. Optional fasting weeks are structured with daily educational lectures, colonics, massage, walks, and a diet of juices. The supervised cleansing program, in cooperation with NaturesPath Center, is based on the teachings of Dr. Bernard Jensen. It includes a daily regime of cleansing drinks and enhanced intestinal cleansing. Health checkups and lectures by a naturopathic physician are included with the minimum stay of six days.

Beginner, intermediate, and advanced hikers can take advantage of more than 20 trails within an hour's drive of the lodge. Special weeks in summer are devoted to bird-watching and nature photography. Awesome scenery is matched by the serenity of Kootenay mountain country. This is a place where you can safely challenge yourself in the company of a dozen like-minded souls and a caring staff.

FACILITIES
Exercise Equipment: Weight-training circuit, free weights. **Services:** Massage; colonic irrigation. **Swimming:** Pool nearby. **Recreation:** Biking, hiking, kayaking.

ACCOMMODATIONS
10 rooms.

DINING
3 low-fat, high-carbohydrate meals daily, served buffet style, and snacks. Fresh bread baked daily. **Sample Meals:** Black bean–quinoa salad with sweet-potato muffin and fruit, millet burger; whole-wheat pita sandwich (lunch); roast-vegetable soup, cashew-carrot curry, poached salmon, tofu sukiyaki (dinner).

RATES AND PACKAGES
3- to 7-night hiking program $800–$1,750 (US$). 7-night Natural Health Fasting Program $580 and up. 7-night Yoga Tree Retreat $1,825. 3- to 7-night hiking, biking, and kayaking program $875–$1,825. 3- to 7-night snowshoeing package $800–$1,725 per person. $500 deposit required. MC, V.

DIRECTIONS
⊠ *Box 1352, Ainsworth Hot Springs, British Columbia V0G 1A0,* ☎ *250/229–5636 or 800/661–5161,* FAX *250/229–5636.*

From Vancouver and Calgary: From Vancouver, Trans-Canada Highway to Hope, Highway 3 east to Nelson, Highway 3A east, Highway 31 to Ainsworth (8 hrs).

From Calgary: Trans-Canada Highway, Highway 93 north to Highway 95 past Cranbrook, Highway 3 to Creston, Highway 3A to Kootenay Bay (ferry), Highway 31 (7 hrs).

OCEAN POINTE RESORT

Luxury pampering

With a charming harborfront location and the services of an Aveda Concept Salon, the Ocean Pointe Resort serves as both vacation retreat and day spa facility. Opened in 1992, the hotel's fitness center, free for hotel guests, is the most extensive this side of Vancouver. Its trainers have experience working with seniors as well as younger people. Scheduled classes in yoga and aquaerobics, plus a series of speakers on nutrition and lifestyle, round out the holistic program.

The hotel salon offers a wide range of beauty and facial treatments. It uses and sells Thalgo's micronized seaweed products from France and Aveda's line of natural hair-care products. You can indulge in aromatherapy baths and massages or enroll in an anticellulite program here.

Businesspeople, vacationers, and local residents are all drawn by the hotel's convenient location. Those on working holiday can take a pre-meeting morning jog along the waterfront or play a lunchtime game of squash or racquetball in the fitness center. Vacationers who have more free time can luxuriate in the glass-walled ozonated swimming pool (there's no chlorine), taking in panoramic views of the working harbor. Relaxation comes with balneotherapy—underwater massage—in a Somethy tub imported from France: air pressure jets swirl mineral salts, essential oils, or marine algae mixed for detoxification. The final touch is a full-hour massage.

Ocean Pointe also makes a convenient base from which to explore the Victorian byways of the city as well as the provincial park on the Pacific side of Vancouver Island. Take a scenic day trip on the E&N Railroad, departing from its terminal near the hotel. The mild climate enjoyed most of the year makes the island a mecca for golf, sailing, fishing, and scuba. Ocean Pointe Resort's concierge can schedule your tee-off time at the Olympic View golf course or court time on one of the hotel's two tennis courts. Seacoast Expeditions' 12-passenger Zodiacs depart from the resort dock to view marine mammal life, including whales (Apr.–Oct.).

The property is comfortable and finely decorated, with original art and antiques in all the public rooms. Many of the guest rooms are oversize and feature alcoves or dormer windows with a view of the harbor and distant Olympic Mountains. Telephones have voice mail. Spa guests can dine in The Victorian Restaurant, where the menu lists percentages of calories from fat as well as sodium content of all items. Dinner by candlelight is a bonus.

FACILITIES
Exercise Equipment: Rowing machine, stair climbers, stationary bikes, treadmill, weight-training circuit. **Services:** Aromatherapy, reflexology, Swedish and other massage; body peeling, body wrap, paraffin back treatment; thalassotherapy; facials. **Swimming:** Indoor pool. **Recreation:** Golf, racquetball, squash, tennis (2 courts).

ACCOMMODATIONS
226 rooms, 34 suites.

DINING
Lunch and dinner included in spa packages. The Victorian Restaurant
features healthy menu choices. **Sample Meals:** Dungeness crab, fennel,
and cilantro bisque, grilled chicken breast with couscous and asparagus
(lunch); medley of organic salad greens, pan-seared arctic char and lobster, tea-smoked squab on cellophane noodles (dinner).

RATES AND PACKAGES
$109–$290 (C$) daily single or double occupancy. 3-night Time-Out spa
package $1,090–$1,165 single, $883–$921 per person, double; 5-night
Rejuvenation package $1,862–$1,987 single, $1,518–$1,581 double. Day
spa packages (no lodging) $120–$300. AE, DC, MC, V.

DIRECTIONS
✉ *45 Songhee Rd., Victoria, British Columbia V9A 6T3,* ☎ *250/360–
2999 or 800/667–4677,* FAX *250/360–1041.*

From Seattle and Vancouver: By car, BC Ferries (☎ 250/386–3431) from
Seattle or Tsawwassen to Swartz Bay (3 hrs).

ONTARIO

THE INN AT MANITOU

Luxury pampering
Sports conditioning

Nestled on the shores of Lake Manitouwabing near Parry Sound, The Inn at Manitou is part summer camp, part deluxe European-style inn. Tennis clinics have been a staple here since the early 1960s, but it is also a popular retreat for guests seeking peace and seclusion. In the spring of 1990 it opened a full-service spa with fitness facility and European-style skin care treatments. Two regularly scheduled aerobics classes are held daily, either high- or low-impact, step, or stretching. The dining room serves both classic French and gourmet spa cuisine.

Open from May to October, the elegant but tiny spa is in the same building as the indoor tennis court and exercise room, with a maple hardwood "Everflex" floating floor. Among the six private treatment rooms are two designed for wet therapies (mud masks, body wraps, and loofah scrubs) and furnished with a hydrotherapy tub with 47 underwater jets and a hand-operated hose. Personal trainers are on hand to provide one-on-one sessions, and the spa director does fitness evaluations on request.

The menu of massage and mud treatments is extensive: Swedish, shiatsu, aromatherapy, reflexology, and holistic massage, body wraps, and skin care. Premassage facials and body wraps involve cleansing the skin with a Moor Mud from Austria, said to enable detoxification as the minerals and other active ingredients are absorbed by the body. Also available are mud baths in the hydrotherapy tub. Used by monks during the 14th and 15th centuries to cure everything from rheumatism to asthma and depression, the imported mud is said to contain 3,000 organic ingredients.

Fitness classes as well as a personal screening and consultation come with all spa packages. All guests are invited to join staff-led morning walks and are supplied with a pair of weighted gloves to add a little muscle toning. Consultations with the spa director assure appointments do not conflict with tennis schedules.

The inn has chalet-style rooms, most on the lakefront and each with a log-burning fireplace. Suites have a sunken living room, antique marble fireplace, dressing room, bathroom with whirlpool tub, private sauna, and sundeck. For those who need more room, there is a 3-bedroom house.

FACILITIES
Exercise Equipment: Stair climber, stationary bikes, treadmills, free weights. **Services:** Aromatherapy, reflexology, scalp massage, shiatsu, sports massage, Swedish massage, Trager massage; body mask, body polish, herbal wraps, mud wraps, seaweed or mineral bath; facials. **Swimming:** Pool. **Classes and Programs:** Fitness consultation, tennis nutrition consultation. **Recreation:** Billiards, fishing, hiking, horseback riding, lake cruises, mountain biking, tennis, water sports; golf nearby.

ACCOMMODATIONS
33 rooms, 11 suites, 3-bedroom house.

DINING
3 meals daily, choice of regular or spa-cuisine menu. Spa menu is low in sodium, fat, and cholesterol. **Sample Meals:** Seafood pasta with citrus-oregano sauce, warm white asparagus with blood-orange sabayon, pizza with marinated goat cheese (lunch); grilled breast of guinea hen with sesame

seeds, paper-baked Georgian Bay trout with peaches, roast Maine lobster with smoked-potato mousse and whiskey sauce (dinner).

RATES AND PACKAGES
$218–$370 (C$) daily per person, double; single supplement $45–$95 per day. Private house $1,100 per day. 1-day spa sampler (no lodging) $175. $500 deposit required per person. AE, DC, MC, V.

DIRECTIONS
✉ *McKellar, Ontario P0G 1C0,* ☎ *705/389–2171 or 800/571–8818,* ℻ *705/389–3818. Winter:* ✉ *77 Ingram Dr., Suite 200, Toronto, Ontario M6M 2L7,* ☎ *416/245–5606,* ℻ *416/245–2460.*

From Toronto: Highway 400 north to Parry Sound, east on Highway 124 to McKellar, south on McKellar Center Road for 5 miles (2½ hrs).

PILLAR AND POST INN

Luxury pampering

The Shaw Festival is in full swing from April through October in three theaters within walking distance of this inn, in a small village near Niagara Falls. The theatrical experience is enhanced by the inn's dramatic 100 Fountain Spa, whose treatment rooms are like sets that transport you to exotic regions of the world—China, Japan, Italy, France, Greece, Turkey, Sweden, and India. The treatments, however, are standard facials, wraps, and massages, with nothing more foreign than creams, seaweed, and mud imported from Europe.

Originally an 18th-century canning factory, the inn has wooden rafters and brick walls in the main lobby and dining room. Rooms include 32 minisuites with flowered chintz draperies, canopy bed, and fireplace. New wings include the spa and indoor swimming pool, created by the resident owner, Si Wai Lai. A warm waterfall cascades in a pine-scented rocky grotto reminiscent of Canadian hot springs. Unlike the grandeur of Niagara, the Fountain Spa is small, hushed and private. At the reception desk, visitors are supplied with robe, towel, and locker key. (Daily guest passes are available if you're not staying at the inn.) The spa is staffed by well-trained aestheticians and registered massage therapists (some qualified for medical treatments). Mornings there is an aquatic exercise class for members and guests. Otherwise you can swim laps or soak in the whirlpools. Open to all hotel guests are a fitness room and an outdoor swimming pool.

Exploring the village and nearby vineyards is the main order of the day. Founded by Americans loyal to the British crown who fled the Revolution, the town was burned to the ground by invading militiamen in 1813. Rebuilt in high Victorian style, many of the residential and commercial streets haven't changed since then. But this green and pretty town is battling to preserve its traditions even as the Shaw Festival attracts busloads of tourists. (For Shaw Festival performance schedule and ticket information, call 800/511–7429.)

Bike, jog, or drive along the Niagara Parkway to view the falls and vineyards. Winery visits allow a taste of Canadian vintages. At the Iniskillin estate, a self-guided tour explains environmental effects of the soil and cliffs forming the Niagara enscarpment, considered beneficial to production of fine wines. Continuing 15 kilometers (9 miles), Niagara Falls can be viewed from the Canadian side of the border.

FACILITIES
Exercise Equipment: Stationary bikes, treadmills, weight-training equipment, free weights. **Services:** Aromatherapy massage, reflexology, shiatsu, sports massage, Swedish massage; algae body wrap, herbal wrap, mud wrap; facials. **Swimming:** Indoor and outdoor pools. **Classes and Programs:** Aquaerobics, fitness consultation.

ACCOMMODATIONS
91 rooms, 32 suites.

DINING
Buffet-style breakfast and lunch, à la carte dinner served in the main dining room, with optional menu of lighter fare. **Sample Meals:** Assorted greens and petals with a pomegranate vinaigrette, smoked salmon sandwich with herbed goat cheese, smoked chicken and roasted pepper pizza with asiago cheese (lunch); sesame- and herb-crusted scallops with bok choy, vegatable ragout on fire-roasted onion sauce, sunflower seed- and pinenut-crusted rack of lamb with saffron-feta mashed potato (dinner).

RATES AND PACKAGES
$170 (C$)–$450 per night; 2-night Summer Escape $190–$500; 1-night 100 Fountain Spa Interlude $191–$500; 1-night Shaw Festival Package $151–$400.

DIRECTIONS
⊠ *48 John St., Box 1011, Niagara-on-the-Lake, Ontario L0S 1J0,* ☎ *905/468–2123 or 800/361–6788,* FAX *905/468–3551.*

From Toronto: Queen Elizabeth Way (QEW) to Niagara and Exit 38B to Niagara-on-the-Lake/Highway 55 on Glendale Avenue, cross over the QEW, and turn left onto York Street. At Highway 55 turn right and continue for 13 kilometers (10 miles) to Niagara-on-the-Lake. Follow signs from Main Street (2 hrs).

From New York : Interstate-190 north to the Lewiston/Queenston Bridge. Past the customs booth, turn right (east), then left (north), then right (east) again to the Niagara River Parkway. Follow the parkway to its end in Niagara-on-the-Lake and turn left (north) onto King Street (20 mins).

STE. ANNE'S COUNTRY INN & SPA

Luxury pampering

A romantic country estate, an hour's drive from Toronto, Ste. Anne's Country Inn & Spa provides a comfortable mix of luxury pampering and pure relaxation. Couples, young executives, and often a mother-daughter duo (minimum age is 16) mix in the dining room as well as in the mud bath, and at scheduled skin care treatments in the Aveda Concept Salon. Days are unstructured, allowing guests to explore the countryside, play golf, or work out in the new fitness facility.

The morning aerobics class provides a view of the 350-acre estate for a dozen early risers. The octagonal studio has a wide-plank pine floor, country-style window panes, and a fresh, invigorating feeling. Built as a farmhouse in 1857, embellished by later owners from Texas, the inn emerged from a four-year rejuvenation by the current owners in 1996 with a new 1,400-square-foot spa, spa cuisine menu, and scheduled wellness week learning programs.

Daily yoga, meditation, and aerobics classes can be combined with a soak in hot mud or herbal body scrub to soothe aching muscles and cleanse toxins from the body. In the basement, a wet treatment area and coed steam room surround the hot tub set in its own skylit cedar cubicle. Here you sink into a bath filled with a mixture of moor mud, dug from a lake formed by Canadian glaciers, and Saskatchewan clay. This treatment is followed by either a sea salt scrub or an herbal body polish, then a shower in a deluge of springwater with a high-pressure hose or the waterfall cabinet.

An expansion completed in 1998 added an 8-foot lap pool with current, a couples' hydrotherapy room, and four new treatment rooms equipped with showers. Set into a fieldstone terrace, the new hot tub provides relaxation day and night. The dining room, where all meals are prepared to order from the menu, now seats 40.

Redolent of herbs, woodsy fireplaces, and fresh flowers, the inn could be a castle in Scotland. Guest rooms in the 2-story manor house and adjoining wings are furnished with antiques; all have a fireplace and sitting area. Suites have cathedral ceiling and whirlpool tubs. Some have four-poster beds. Telephones are available on request. Carved into a stone archway at the estate entrance is Ste. Anne's coat of arms, designed for the family of Samuel Massey, who settled here to farm the rolling drumlins of the Northumberland Hills near Lake Ontario. The Latin phrase "Sol Lucet Omnibus" over the insignia translates as "Where the Sun Shines For All." But like Canadian politics in which Massey gained fame, the building has had ups and downs. The new spa built by the Corcoran family provides a sunny retreat despite the whims of weather. You can sink into a wing chair to read a book from an eclectic collection in the parlor, or repair to the Jacuzzi. The daily schedule often includes a cooking class in the kitchen.

While day spa packages offer a sampler of treatments and classes, plus lunch and tea, you have the flexibility of staying for a few days rather than following a fixed regimen. Set in rambling, stone-walled wings, guest rooms—sizes ranging from cozy to deluxe suites—are appointed with antiques, fireplace, and twin or king-size beds. Daily rates include all meals and afternoon tea. Additional accommodations nearby are available with use of the inn facilities.

Just east of Toronto and easily reached by train, the inn offers a healthful and picturesque retreat from town. Seasonal events include an introduction to massaging your partner, cooking with herbs, and painting watercolors. Also on the property are miles of trails through a cedar forest, a ranch for deer and elk, outdoor tennis courts, a spring-fed swimming pool, and an organic herb garden.

FACILITIES
Exercise Equipment: Rowing machine, stationary bike, treadmill. **Services:** Acupressure, reflexology, Reiki, Swedish massage; mud bath, seaweed body wrap. **Swimming:** Pool. **Classes and Programs:** Aerobics, Hatha yoga, tai chi. **Recreation:** Mountain biking, tennis; golf, cross-country skiing, ice skating nearby.

ACCOMMODATIONS
10 rooms, 8 suites.

DINING
3 meals daily included in room rate. Country spa fare; vegetarian meals on request. **Sample Meals:** Open-face shrimp salad and egg sandwich, warm chicken–mandarin orange salad (lunch); sole fillet wrapped with sea scallop mousse with almond-butter sautée, grilled pork tenderloin brochettes with bell peppers and onions (dinner).

RATES AND PACKAGES
Rooms $115–$265 single (C$), $70–$215 per person, double. Day spa package $184–$217 full day, $99–$130 half day. 50% deposit required. AE, D, DC, MC, V.

DIRECTIONS
✉ *R.R. 1, Grafton, Ontario KOK 2GO,* ☎ *905/349–2493 or 888/ 346–6772,* FAX *905/349–3531.*

From Toronto: Highway 401 east to Exit 487 (Grafton/Centreton), north on Aird Street for 1½ kilometers, Academy Hill Road to Massey Road (75 mins).

WHEELS COUNTRY SPA AT WHEELS INN

Luxury pampering

A family-oriented motel close to Detroit, Wheels Inn is an indoor resort with 7 acres of sports and spa facilities under one roof. Total fun and fitness is the concept. Cavort with the kids in the outdoor-indoor swimming pool and water slide, or choose from 42 revitalizing services in the European-style Wheels Health Spa.

Taking a serious approach to shape-ups, staff members have credentials for cardiovascular and muscular testing. They do basic body measurements, a wellness profile, and one-on-one training in a well-equipped fitness center.

Runners and joggers can set courses passing the town's Victorian mansions and modern marina. There are 15 routes mapped out, ranging from 1.8 to 13.5 miles, and an indoor track where 22 laps equal 1 mile.

The wide variety of revitalizing body and skin treatments offered here is unique for Canada. Services are priced on an à la carte basis or on half-day or full-day packages. In this oasis of quiet luxury, stress melts away in the hands of certified masseurs and masseuses. There is also a fully equipped beauty salon featuring Pevonia botanical skin care treatments. You can schedule a session of reflexology work on nerve centers or be cocooned in a fragrant herbal wrap. Therapeutic Swedish massage and invigorating body scrubs with a loofah sponge working sea salts and avocado oil into your skin are part of packages.

Aerobics classes, on a cushioned floor, are scheduled according to your fitness level, from beginner to high-impact for the super-advanced, and run throughout the day, from 9 AM to 7 PM. People who live nearby can join the club and use the facilities, so you'll never be at a loss for company.

All activities are coed, and you can join a group doing "aquabics" in the fitness pool, or the "renaissance" program for those with arthritis and circulatory problems. Then relax in the whirlpool and steam baths.

Meals are served in the hotel atrium and dining room, or specially prepared lunches can be served in the privacy of the spa lounge for guests who want to avoid temptation. For kids there's a supervised day-care center and "Wild Zone" amusement park on the premises.

The spa program is limited to 30 participants.

FACILITIES
Exercise Equipment: Rowing machines, stair climbers, stationary bikes, weight-training equipment, free weights. **Services:** Aromatherapy, reflexology, Swedish massage; herbal wrap, hydrotherapy, loofah body scrub, relaxation body treatment; facials. **Swimming:** Indoor and outdoor

pools. **Recreation:** Bowling, racquetball, squash, tennis, water slides. **Children's Programs:** Drop-in babysitting from newborn to 8 years. In-room child care available.

ACCOMMODATIONS
354 rooms.

DINING
3 meals totaling 1,000 calories per day for spa program participants. Low in salt and fat; choices include meat, fish, salads. **Sample Meals:** Tossed salad, poached salmon with vegetables, cold tuna plate (lunch); cold grilled chicken breast with olive-cucumber relish, brochette of shrimp and scallops on rice, fresh fruit and yogurt (dinner).

RATES AND PACKAGES
2-day/1-night pamper package $280 (C$) single, $253 double. 3-day package $771 single, $676 per person, double. Pamper Yourself package $175, $100 deposit required, refundable with 5-day notice. AE, MC, V.

DIRECTIONS
✉ *Box 637, Chatham, Ontario N7M 5K8,* ☎ *519/351–1100, 519/436–5500 (spa), 800/265–5265 or 800/265–5257 (in US),* ℻ *519/436–5541.*

From border crossing at Detroit/Windsor: Highway 401 to Exit 81 North, then turn right and left at traffic lights (1 hr).

From London, Ontario or Toronto: Highway 401.

QUÉBEC

AQUA-MER CENTER

Luxury pampering

Authentic French thalassotherapy on the Gaspé peninsula is said to enhance your immune system. The mild Atlantic climate charged with iodine and negative ions works well with the natural elements—seawater, algae, and mud. At this charming seaside inn, you can take the waters and explore the quaint towns that dot the peninsula. Primarily designed for French-speaking visitors, it's a bit of Brittany on the American coast.

The sequence of treatments prescribed for you after consultation with the professional staff involves bathing and exercising in the indoor swimming pool, which is filled with comfortably heated seawater. There are no cold plunges into the ocean, but brisk walks along the beach and a massage under alternating showers of warm and cold water are encouraged. To stimulate blood circulation and lymph drainage you are massaged in underwater-jet baths; this will enhance the effect of algae added to seawater that has been heated to a high temperature. Follow this with a toning shower that focuses high-powered jets on every muscle in your body for invigorating results.

Aqua-Mer Center has a full circuit of treatments with mud, sand, algae, and seawater. Additional complementary treatments include pressotherapy (with pressure cuffs on your legs to enhance circulation), lymphatic drainage massage, shiatsu, and negative ionization. Half of each day is reserved for personal activity, which can be guided mountain tours, excursions to area attractions, or simply relaxing in the quiet room as you enjoy the view.

There are 30 rooms in the three-story auberge and adjoining building. Program participants also stay in the nearby 15-room Thermotel. There is no TV, telephone, or air-conditioning. Day visitors are accommodated on a space-available basis.

FACILITIES
Services: Shiatsu, Swedish massage; body wraps, fango, pressotherapy; hydromassage, Swiss shower; facials. **Swimming:** Indoor pool. **Recreation:** Paddleboats, tennis; golf nearby.

ACCOMMODATIONS
45 rooms.

DINING
3 meals a day in health café at the Marine Cure Center. Approximately 1,000 calories a day, including fish, chicken, fresh seasonal vegetables. **Sample Meals:** Crab quiche with greens, spinach fettucine with grilled zucchini, pork cutlet with prunes and beets (lunch); carrot soup, mussels marinière, salmon with cucumber sauce, chocolate mousse with orange zest (dinner).

RATES AND PACKAGES
5-day marine cure includes 5 meals. $1,401–$1,521 (C$) per person; 6-day/7-night marine cure $1,195–$1,450 single, $1,045–$1,245 per person, double. 25% deposit required. Refunds with notification 30 days prior to reserved dates. MC, V.

DIRECTIONS

DIRECTIONS
✉ *868 Blvd. Perron, Carleton, Québec G0C 1J0,* ☎ *418/364–7055 or 800/463–0867,* FAX *418/364–7351; Winter:* ✉ *145 rue du Pacifique, Laval, Québec H7N 3X9,* ☎ *450/629–5591 or 800/363–2303,* FAX *450/629–5591.*

From Montréal: Highway 20 and 132 east via Mont Joli (4 hrs).

AUBERGE DU PARC INN

Luxury pampering

European-style pampering amid Victorian elegance is the order of the day at this tranquil inn perched on a hill overlooking the picturesque Baie des Chaleurs. Soft music wafts throughout as you are coddled with daily massages and cocooned in algae body wraps—a regime that drains away stress and leaves you with looks of dreamy contentment. Passive thalassotherapy treatments centered around fresh seawater from the Baie des Chaleurs and algae imported from France take about three hours a day. That leaves time to walk along the beach, play a round of tennis, curl up with a good book, or explore the scenic Gaspé coast.

While there are many opportunities to seek out exercise, there are no organized fitness classes and only a very modest exercise room with older equipment.

Owner Jeanette Lemarquand doesn't believe in imposing self-denial on her guests or in dictating to them. The gourmet cuisine is as light or as luxurious as you want, with lower calorie options available at every meal. Smoking is allowed but restricted to a separate dining room and lounge.

Accommodations are in 32 modern motel-style rooms amid landscaped gardens, a short walk from the nearly 200-year-old country manor. The inn only accepts up to 40 guests at a time and nearly half are repeat visitors. While French is most commonly spoken, staff are bilingual and welcoming.

FACILITIES
Services: Massage; algae body wrap, pressotherapy; Vichy shower; facials. **Swimming:** Indoor and outdoor pools; beaches nearby. **Recreation:** Billiards, golf, hiking; tennis; cross-country skiing, fishing, hunting nearby.

ACCOMMODATIONS
32 rooms.

DINING
3 meals daily included in package. Local seafood and produce featured. **Sample Meals:** Oven-baked fillet of sole and steamed vegetables (lunch); lamb fillet with mushrooms and green grapes (dinner).

RATES AND PACKAGES
7-day package $1,375–$1,555 (C$) single, $1,255–$1,365 per person, double. 10% deposit required. MC, V.

DIRECTIONS
✉ *C.P. 40, Paspebiac, Québec G0C 2K0,* ☎ *418/752–3355 or 800/463–0890 in Québec,* FAX *418/752–6406.*

From Québec City: On the main approach to the Gaspé Peninsula, Highway 20 to Rivière-du-Loup, then Highway 132 east via Mt-Jolie through Matapedia to Paspebiac (7 hrs).

CENTRE DE SANTÉ D'EASTMAN/ EASTMAN HEALTH CENTER

Holistic health

Settling into the Eastman Center's daily routine is like taking up residence in a health-oriented village. The group support and camaraderie of like-minded villagers means added encouragement if you are just getting started with a fitness program. Resident owner-director Jocelyna Dubuc encourages guests to learn elements of a healthy lifestyle that can be worked into their daily schedule at home. There is no obligation to follow a tightly structured regimen.

Nestled in the rolling countryside of the Eastern Townships (about an hour's drive southeast of Montréal), the Centre de Santé d'Eastman is a low-key retreat for body and mind. The bucolic setting and up-to-date facilities are a unique and necessary blend for anyone looking for a relaxing, rejuvenating getaway. Hydrotherapy is the specialty, from algae body wraps to thalasso tub.

Seven buildings house the spa facilities and up to 35 guests. The comfortably furnished country rooms have no TV or telephone. A barn is home to the kitchen and dining areas, and the stone farmhouse, complete with flared roof and jutting dormer windows, is the locale for the hospitality lounge. Exercise is optional and not strenuous. Three guided walks are held daily, and yoga and tai chi chuan sessions are scheduled. A series of treatments designed to rid the skin of impurities is also available. The spa package includes a daily massage, three meals, and a snack.

The oxygen bath is said to produce vitality and a long-lasting sense of well-being. Encased in what looks like an iron lung, you are bathed in 104°F water mixed with carbon dioxide and jets of essential oils, then you receive 10 minutes of oxygen inhalation. Another house specialty is an algae body wrap with seaweed imported from France.

FACILITIES
Services: Massage, reflexology; body scrub, body wrap, oxygen bath; hydrotherapy, thalassotherapy; facials. **Swimming:** Pond, pool. **Classes and Programs:** Cooking class, health lecture, polarity therapy, tai chi chuan, yoga. **Recreation:** Hiking, sleigh rides.

ACCOMMODATIONS
18 rooms, 1 cottage.

DINING
3 family-style meals a day. Vegetarian menu includes eggs and dairy products. **Sample Meals:** Corn and cucumber soup, salads (carrot, sprouts, lettuce), plate of raw vegetables (lunch); chinese stir-fry, eggplant parmesan, whole-wheat fettucine (dinner). At 3 PM tisanes (herbal teas) are served with fruit, cakes, and cookies.

RATES AND PACKAGES
2-day Health Stay package $330–$410 (C$) single, $290–$350 per person, double. 2-day Relaxation spa package $430–$510 single, $390–$450 double. AE, MC, V.

DIRECTIONS
✉ *895 Chemin des Diligences, Eastman, Québec J0E 1P0,* ☎ *450/297–3009 or 800/665–5272,* ☏ *450/297–3370.*

From Montréal: Autoroute 10's Exit 106 to Eastman, Route 245 to Route 112, Chemin du Lac d'Argent (1 hr).

From Vermont: Highway 55.

CLUB TREMBLANT

Luxury pampering
Sports conditioning

A happy discovery for skiers and hikers, the newly expanded and upgraded resort area of Mont-Tremblant offers a full-service spa at Club Tremblant. Overlooking the broad expanse of Lake Tremblant, the club's log lodges terrace a hillside in the Laurentian Mountains and resemble an alpine village. From the wooden deck of Spa-sur-le-Lac you can see deer grazing in the club gardens and the big new Tremblant resort village at the base of ski slopes on the opposite shore.

The woodsy ambience of the club's main lodge, dating from 1930, inspired the new spa, which is tucked below the dining room. Designed to complement the existing indoor swimming pool and exercise room, the spa has introduced skin care and stress control services to the resort. It offers massage therapies as well as the area's first hydrotherapy tub, installed in a private room. And you can experience a Sensora room, programmed with light, sound, and physical vibration. Developed by a team of Canadian psychologists, psychotherapists, and physicists, the multiple sensory system induces a trancelike effect as you are surrounded by colors and music for 25 minutes.

Skin care here can prepare you for outdoor adventure or repair damage and is popular with men. The Clarins Parisian method treatments are featured, along with Phytomer thalassotherapy products from France. Pressotherapy with air-inflated leggings enhances circulation while you relax in the lounge. At all times complimentary refreshments are served at the juice bar. While a wide range of bodywork is offered, not all therapists are on hand daily, so call ahead to discuss your personal needs.

Club Tremblant's all-inclusive packages let you combine outdoor sports, indoor fitness facilities, and full-service spa therapies. Family-oriented programs add options such as ski school instruction, aquatic sports, and supervised summer camp for kids. The club's shuttle bus provides free transportation to the mountain village, where there is a colorful assortment of shops and entertainment year-round. For those who are less athletic, a gondola ride to the mountain peak provides extraordinary views.

Mont-Tremblant climbs to 3,001 feet (914 meters), a huge, rumpled rock that since 1938 has attracted skiers. Currently, 77 named runs are on the north and south faces. Trails also are designed for cross-country skiing. At night, slopes are lit for family fun at an adventure park named *Xzone.*

Facing the mountain, Club Tremblant's private sandy beach and marina offer a full complement of summer recreation. The indoor pool and coed sauna and whirlpool stay open until 9 PM. For adventure-minded guests, the Club concierge can arrange a Formula Ford racing course at the nearby Jim Russel Racing School. During the winter season, Club Tremblant operates its own professional ski school, with equipment rentals on-site.

Guests at the Club stay in condos with a fully-equipped kitchen, dining area, living room with fireplace, balcony, and one or two bedrooms, serviced daily. Traditional Québecois wood furniture and contemporary bed coverings add ambience.

FACILITIES

Exercise Equipment: Rowing machines, stair climber, stationary bikes, treadmill, weight-training equipment, free weights. **Services:** Reflexology, shiatsu, Swedish massage; algae wrap, body exfoliation, herbal wrap, pressotherapy; hydromassage, hydrotherapy; facials. **Swimming:** Indoor and outdoor pools. **Classes and Programs:** Aquaerobics, power walks, tennis clinic. **Recreation:** Badminton, chess, croquet, hiking, horseshoes, pétanque, tennis, volleyball; biking, golf, rollerblading nearby. **Children's Programs:** Supervised activities for ages 3–14 from Memorial Day to Labor Day, including camping, fishing, hiking, minigolf, picnics, rollerblading, water games.

ACCOMMODATIONS

100 condominium apartments.

DINING

Buffet-style breakfast and dinner included. Spa cuisine and Continental fare. Choice of three dining rooms, one nonsmoking. **Sample Meals:** Ham and brie sandwich, vegetarian sandwich, soup of the day (lunch); three-shellfish mousse, cold zucchini soup with mint, roast venison with berries, loin of lamb with rosemary (dinner).

RATES AND PACKAGES

2 nights with 4 hours of spa services, $380–$750 ($C). 3 nights with 6 hours of spa services, $600–$1,175. 5 nights with 12 hours of spa services, $900–$1,900.

DIRECTIONS

✉ *121 rue Cuttle, Mont–Tremblant (Quebec), Canada J0T 1Z0,* ☎ *819/ 425–2731 or 800/567–8341,* 🖷 *819/425–5617.*

From Montréal: Interstate 15 north via Ste-Agathe, which becomes Highway 117 North, to second flashing light past St-Jovite, turn right onto Montée Ryan for 7 kilometers to lake, turn left (90 min).

GRAY ROCKS

Sports conditioning

A family-oriented lakeside resort adjoining the Mont-Tremblant provincial park, Gray Rocks has direct access to its own ski slopes and golf courses and offers a wide range of sports clinics with its all-inclusive programs. Built in 1906 as a hunting lodge, it opened the area's first Austrian-style ski school in 1938. Since 1993 the owners have focused on maintaining the lodge's old-fashioned comfort. They have also added a second golf course, hosted week-long tennis and golf camps for teenagers, and expanded the classic ski-week program.

Le Spa is a modest amenity in the main lodge, with no fitness program other than a personal trainer. Massage is available, on request, and is perhaps the best bargain at $55 ($C) per hour, taxes included. Guests aren't charged for using the exercise equipment, but selection is limited. The ozonated swimming pool is excellent for swimming laps, but it can be busy with kids during the day and evening. Also available are a coed sauna and two whirlpools.

The Gray Rocks "domain" is vast, encompassing a mountain with 20 ski trails, two golf courses (the province's oldest and newest), the largest tennis complex in Canada, a lake with beach, marina, and float-plane service, horseback riding ranch, and several guest lodges. Think of it as a university of sports. Certified instructors teach ski, golf, and tennis clinics, and in the evening, there are family activities, such as sleigh rides, and a survival course in conversational French.

Minutes from the new Mont-Tremblant village, Gray Rocks provides complimentary transportation when you sign up for a combination ski package. Rooms and suites are in the lodge and have spartan furnishings. Condos have one to three bedrooms and are fully equipped with kitchen, washer-dryer, microwave, dishwasher, TV, and fireplace. Pets are accommodated in special kennels. Seasonally priced packages included bountiful buffet meals.

FACILITIES
Exercise Equipment: Cross-country machine, rowing machine, stationary bikes, weight-training equipment, free weights. **Services:** Massage. **Swimming:** Pool, private beach. **Classes and Programs:** Dancing and theme parties, ski school (mid-Nov.–Apr.). **Recreation:** Golf, hiking, horseback riding, mountain biking, tennis.

ACCOMMODATIONS
113 rooms and suites, 56 condominiums.

RATES AND PACKAGES
Summer $99–$140 (C$) daily per person, double; winter $99–$210 daily per person, double. Summer 6-night package with 3 meals daily, $1,140–$1,690 single, $990–$1,350 per person, double. AE, DC, MC, V.

DIRECTIONS
✉ *525 Chemin Principal, Mont Tremblant, Québec J0T 1Z0,* ☎ *819/425–2771 or 800/567–6767,* 𝐅𝐀𝐗 *819/425–9156.*

From Montréal: Head north on Hwy. 20.

SIVANANDA ASHRAM

Holistic health

Joining the daily sessions of yoga held in the stunning new lodge of the Sivananda Ashram is a revitalizing experience, enhanced by pine-scented air, pure spring water, and vegetarian meals. Just an hour from Montréal, the yoga camp is an accessible oasis of peace and harmony, and there is time for skiing and family fun within the daily schedule of meditation and stretches that you are required to follow.

Campers revel in the natural beauty of 250 acres of unspoiled woodland. At dawn, you are called to meditation, followed by yogic exercise or *asanas* that stretch and invigorate the body. A first meal comes at mid-morning, peak energy time; supper follows the 4 PM *asana* session. In between, you are free to enjoy the recreational facilities, to hike, or to get a massage. Sunset meditation and a concert of Indian music and dance conclude most days.

Based on five principles for a long and healthy life prescribed by Swami Vishnu Devananda, the program teaches how to breathe and exercise and how to combine diet with positive thinking and meditation. As the headquarters of a worldwide community, including a retreat in The Bahamas and a ranch in New York State (both included in this book), the ashram is a registered charity dedicated to teaching yoga to people of all ages and backgrounds. Staffed mainly by volunteers who practice karma yoga, the ashram program is structured enough to provide discipline for newcomers, but there is enough flexibility in coaching classes and lectures for those with diverse personal goals.

Built in 1995, the main guest lodge is an ecologically sound building, constructed with straw bale insulation between earth-tone plaster walls that are supported by wooden post-and-pole beams. There are two two-story lodges with both private and dormitory rooms. Furnishings are simple, and linens are provided. Some rooms have private bath. Tent space is available on the grounds. A large hall with a heated polished floor is used for yoga and dining. Nearby is a huge, wooden pavilion used in summer for yoga classes.

Introducing children to the principles of yoga is the focus of the month-long Kids Camp held here since 1972. Designed for children 7–17, the program combines outdoor adventure, creativity, discovery, and cooperation. Living in tents with experienced counsellors, campers learn to value proper exercise, breathing, relaxation, diet, and meditation. Awakened at 7 AM for a *satsang* sesssion, they sing, chant, and listen to stories from ancient sages. After a vegetarian breakfast, campers participate in cooking class, dramatic activity, sports, and arts and crafts. Later, there's another session of yoga, with counsellors helping as the youngsters stretch and bend into the classical positions. There's even a show for parents at the end of the month.

FACILITIES
Services: Massage. **Swimming:** Pool; lake nearby. **Classes and Programs:** Yoga, bonfires, silent walks, traditional music and dancing of India. **Recreation:** Biking, cross-country and downhill skiing, hiking, volleyball. **Children's Programs:** Yoga Camp, a month-long program of yogic exercises, swimming, and other activities, for ages 4–14.

ACCOMMODATIONS
22 rooms with 62 dormitory beds, more than 100 campsites.

DINING
2 vegetarian buffets daily. No meat, fish, eggs, alcohol, or coffee. **Sample Meals:** Hot grain cereal, vegetable soup, rice and bulgar, dal, baked tofu, salad (lunch); lentil loaf, baked casserole of seasonal vegetables, rice, salad, fruit (dinner).

RATES AND PACKAGES
$58 (C$) daily per person sharing room with private bath, $45–$50 without bath. Tent space $35. $50 deposit required per person. AE, V.

DIRECTIONS
✉ *673 8th Ave., Val Morin, Québec J0T 2R0,* ☎ *819/322–3226 or 800/ 263–9642 in Canada,* 🖷 *819/322–5876.*

From Montréal: North of Montréal via the Laurentian Autoroute (Route 15), Exit 76 (1 hr).

SPA CONCEPT AT LE CHÂTEAU BROMONT

Luxury pampering
Nutrition and diet

Montréalers make up the majority of the guests at Château Bromont, located in a major ski resort near their home town and just 20 minutes from the U.S. border. Emphasizing serious shape-ups, the Château has a fully equipped gymnasium, indoor and outdoor swimming pools, and an aerobics studio. The daily schedule includes aquafitness Jazzercise, stretch and tone, and low-impact aerobics classes. The Spa Concept program gives guests the chance to enjoy European-style treatments.

Included in one- to seven-night packages are body peeling, herbal wraps, and an unusually wide choice of massages—from soothing Swedish to shiatsu, Trager, and reflexology. Special therapies include polarity, lymphatic drainage, and baths with mud, sea algae, or essential oils. There are indoor and outdoor whirlpools, and a sauna. Health programs are based on an evaluation of your lifestyle and on an energy test. The spa director may advise energy-balancing exercise and specific treatments if you are on a five-night program. Otherwise there is no minimum stay, and services can be booked à la carte. Accommodations are in a country château with rustic furnishings.

FACILITIES
Exercise equipment: Weight-training circuit, free weights, bicycles, and other cardio equipment. **Services:** Aromatherapy, reflexology, shiatsu, Swedish massage, Trager work, algotherapy, body peel, exfoliation, fango pack, herbal wrap, polarity therapy, pressotherapy; balneotherapy, colonic irrigation, lymphatic drainage; facials. **Swimming:** Indoor and outdoor pools. **Classes and Programs:** Aerobics, aquacize, jazzercize. **Recreation:** Horseshoes, mountain biking, racquetball, shuffleboard, squash, tennis, volleyball; cross-country and downhill skiing, horseback riding, water slides nearby.

ACCOMMODATIONS
154 rooms.

DINING
3 meals daily included in packages. Meals are nutritionally balanced, low in calories.

RATES AND PACKAGES
1-night package $339 single (C$), $289 per person, double; 3-night package $859 single, $729 double; 5-night package $1,209 single, $1,449 double. 1-night deposit required. MC, V.

DIRECTIONS
✉ *90 rue Stanstead, Bromont, Québec J2L 1K6,* ☎ *450/534–2717 or 800/567–7727 (in Canada),* FAX *450/534–0599.*

From Montréal: Route 10E to Exit 78, right turn on Bromont Boulevard to ski-slope area (1 hr).

11 Mexico

Baja California, Baja California Sur, Guanajuato, Jalisco, Mexico, Morelos, Nayarit, Oaxaca, Quintana Roo

THE CONCEPT OF SPAS IN MEXICO can be traced back to the ancient Aztecs, who bathed and worshipped spirits at the country's steaming hot springs. Throughout Mexico today, these *balnearios* (mineral water baths) and *baños termales* (thermal hot-spring baths) are a bargain, offering mud baths, thermal waters, and warm hospitality. The largest and most luxurious of them is in Ixtapan de la Sal, two hours' drive southeast of Mexico City, but rustic Rio Caliente Spa, secluded in a national forest near Guadalajara, provides refreshing sweats at bargain prices.

A very different experience, and a success since it opened more than 50 years ago, is the Rancho La Puerta in Baja California, founded by Deborah Szekely and her late husband. This is the action-oriented counterpart to the Golden Door in California; its holistic health program, vegetarian meals, and the stress-free environment of the Sierra Madres blend into a seamless vacation experience.

The best-equipped examples of the new resort-based spas are in Baja California at the Cabo Real golf resort, where four beach hotels opened spas in 1998. Holistic Misión del Sol in Cuernavaca and hacienda-style Hotel Cocoyoc in the state of Morelos near Mexico City add unique experiences. Notable beach resort spas are Paradise Village in Nuevo Vallarta, Nayarit state, on the Pacific coast; Melia Cancún Resort & Spa, where there are Caribbean moonlit massage cabanas; and the area's latest addition, Allegro Resorts' Royal Hideaway Playacar, featuring French thalassotherapy on the Yucatan Peninsula.

Tradition mixes with modern technology at Mexican spas. Try the *temazcal,* an Aztec sauna, at Spa Prehispanico in Oaxaca's Puerto Escondido, or at Misión del Sol in Cuernavaca. Taking the waters at Hotel Balneario San José de Purúa will be better than ever when the new Presidente Inter-Continental Hotel is completed. For a bargain-priced escape just south of the border in Tijuana, soak in thermal waters at the new Holiday Inn Agua Caliente. Near historic Santiago de Querétaro, upscale Rancho La Pitaya has a day spa with mud baths, seaweed and thermal water soaks, Reiki and shirodhara treatments, and plans for 200 villas and a 40-room hotel scheduled to open in 1999 (☎ FAX 52/42–126876).

Don't expect organized group programs; aside from Rancho La Puerta, these resort spas tailor your schedule on a personal, daily basis. Increasingly sophisticated treatments and spa cuisine appear, along with traditional food and fun, to make a healthy holiday one of Mexico's best buys.

The country code for Mexico is 52, and must be dialed before the telephone and fax numbers listed below. In Mexico, the prefix 01 is used with area codes.

All prices in this chapter are in U.S. dollars.

BAJA CALIFORNIA

HOLIDAY INN AGUA CALIENTE

Luxury pampering
Mineral springs

Discovering the hot springs at this Holiday Inn is like taking a step back to the 1930s, when Rita Hayworth, Charlie Chaplin, and Babe Ruth crossed the U.S.–Mexican border to take the waters and gamble at the casino resort that once stood on this site. Located 18 miles south of San Diego, the inn's Moorish arcades recapture the ambience of the glamorous Casino, even if the guest rooms are standard motel lodging. But treatments at the Inn's Vita Spa Agua Caliente are state-of-the-art.

The sulfur-rich thermal water fills private hydrotherapy tubs and an outdoor whirlpool. A relaxing soak is recommended when you arrive, followed by massage and body care treatments featuring a choice of marine algae (seaweed), fango mud, Dead Sea salts, and aromatherapy oils. Featured skin care products are by Guinot of Paris. Accessed by elevator on the inn's second floor, Vita Spa has 14 treatment rooms, four hydrotubs, Vichy and Swiss cascade showers, specially designed facilities for wet treatments, and a beauty salon. Couples can enjoy a massage together in a private suite.

Newcomers to these treatments will enjoy the "mothering" advice of spa director Rosa Lilla Castelianos, who trained in the U.S. Pre-schedule treatments by calling the spa's toll-free phone from the U.S. The receptionists are bilingual; therapists speak mainly Spanish. Meals with spa cuisine options can be served in the lounge, allowing guests to relax in a robe and sandals provided with their locker.

Tijuana has the advantage of combining nightlife with outings to nearby Rosarito Beach. Spectator sports include greyhound races and jai alai games. Wagering on sporting events is legal in Tijuana. Food and beverages are available at reasonable prices. Traditional bullfights are held in two rings, Plaza Monumental and Toro de Tijuana, Sunday afternoons May through September.

Many of the city's cultural activities center around "Zona Rio" a thriving new area that includes the Holiday Inn, great restaurants, and a cultural center with concert hall, IMAX theater, museum and restaurant.

FACILITIES
Services: Aromatherapy, anti-cellulite massage, reflexology, Swedish massage; aloe vera rehydration, body polish, body wrap; hydrotherapy bath, Vichy shower; facial. **Swimming:** Pool.

ACCOMMODATIONS
140 rooms.

DINING
All meals à la carte. Room-service and one restaurant. **Sample Meals:** Baked eggs Andaluza with mixture of ham and sausage, tossed green salad, or broiled chicken breast sandwich (lunch); grilled beef or chicken breast, stuffed fish fillet, fajitas with rice and roasted vegetables (dinner).

RATES AND PACKAGES
Vita Spa Sampler with 1-night accommodation, $74 per person, double occupancy; $106 single. 2-night spa retreat $158 double, $233 single. 3-night Body/Mind Renewal $285 double, $381 single. 2-night Couple's Getaway $337 for 2. AE, MC, V.

✉ *Paseo de los Heroes No. 18818, Zona Rio, Tijuana 22320, Baja California,* ☎ *66/346–925 and 346–901,* ＦＡＸ *66/346–912; spa reservations:* ✉ *Box 43288, San Diego, CA 92143,* ☎ *888/848-2928.*

From San Diego: Take Interstate-5 or Interstate-805 south to the Mexican border; cross bridge and follow yellow color-coded directions to Rio Zone (25 mins).

RANCHO LA PUERTA

Luxury pampering
Nutrition and diet

Since 1940, Rancho La Puerta has set the standard for American health resorts. Requiring a minimum stay of one week, the resort offers a multitude of activities and treatments from which to choose. Mornings begin with a hike—at a slow pace or, for the more advanced, up sacred Mount Kuchumaa. There are more than 60 daily exercise classes as well as such special programs as African dance and NIA (neuromuscular integrative action).

The original formula for fitness has expanded since the resort opened, but unchanged are the nearly perfect year-round climate, dry (an average of 341 sunny days) and pollen-free; the natural beauty of purple foothills ringed by impressive mountains; and the mostly vegetarian diet. Spiritual renewal is experienced at a new meditation labyrinth, handmade in stone mosaic, and a Native American medicine-wheel ceremony.

Still managed by members of the founding family and Mexican associates such as second-generation Rancher Jose Manuel Jasso, the ranch has a high percentage of repeat guests. Friendships form easily in classes and at big round tables in the dining hall. Briefings for newcomers set the pace on arrival day, starting with the distribution of schedules aboard the complimentary bus from the airport in San Diego. Serious bonding takes place in progressive classes, in which the intensity of exercise increases over several days.

Encouraged by instructors who use innovative techniques in workouts, and soothed by a massage or herbal wrap, guests focus on recharging their body and mind. Some classes are intense, others relaxing; counselors are on hand to help with scheduling. There is a beautiful new health center in the villas complex, as well as the original health center, where appointments can be made for bodywork and skin care at very reasonable prices. Aestheticians are well-trained, but services are basic. As gratuities are not included, you can purchase coupons (U.S. dollars or check only) to show appreciation for the staff, or leave a gratuity in envelopes at the reception center. Thoughtful touches: a self-service laundry, lounges with trays of fruit and veggies along with coffee and herbal tea, a *mercado* and well-stocked shop with exquisite jewelry as well as native handcrafts. When temperature turns cold, you'll appreciate the sweaters with Ranch logo, and colorful serapes, which make great souvenirs.

Rancho La Puerta is in the style of a Mexican village, with a central complex of swimming pools, men's and women's health centers (each with sauna, steam room, and whirlpool), library, and lounges, linked by brick-paved walkways to casitas and villas that accommodate 150 guests (there are more than 350 staff members). Gyms dot the landscape; some are open-air, others are enclosed for cool days. No sign-up is required for any of the numerous classes, including aerobic circuit training, back-care workshop, better breathing, body awareness, Hatha yoga, self-defense, and a progressive series of fitness and stretching sessions for men. Meals and socializing on shaded patios complete the daily pattern of simply doing what interests you. Advice from staffers, some of whom are old hands from The Golden Door, is always available. Sign up early for breakfast at the ranch's organic gardens, where Chef Bill Wavrin demonstrates cooking all-natural vegetarian cuisine.

This flowering oasis, set amid 575 acres of seclusion, also gives you a taste of Mexican resort life. Accommodations vary from studiolike rancheras to luxury haciendas and villas decorated with native handmade furniture and rugs. Many feature tile floors, fireplaces, and kitchenettes. There is no air-conditioning, TV, or telephones. While all guests enjoy equal access to activities, staying in a villa entitles you to have breakfast delivered, and the option of an in-room massage. Come prepared for cool evenings and sunny, dry days. There are plenty of outdoor hammocks for a siesta, and you can warm up in front of the fireplace in the lounges.

After two or three days on a low-fat, high-carbohydrate diet, without distractions from TV, newspapers, or telephone, guests usually discover that their appetite for food has decreased remarkably, while they look and feel healthier. Some do go "over the hill" into town, tempted by Tecate's shops and burrito bars. But the original concept of Deborah and Edmond Szekely endures, nurturing body and soul.

FACILITIES
Exercise Equipment: Stair climbers, stationary bikes, treadmills, weight-training circuit, free weights. **Services:** Aromatherapy massage; herbal wrap, seaweed wrap; facial. **Swimming:** 3 pools, 1 heated for aquatic exercise classes. **Classes and Programs:** Aerobics, aquaerobics, circuit training, gardening, self-defense, swimming, tai chi, yoga; guided hikes, lifestyle lectures. **Recreation:** Basketball, hiking, table tennis, tennis, volleyball. Movies.

ACCOMMODATIONS
85 cottages.

DINING
3 meals daily, mostly vegetarian; fish twice a week and wine on Friday. Breakfast and lunch are served buffet-style. **Sample Meals:** Tofu sandwiches, quesadillas of ricotta cheese and tofu, garlic herbed pizza (lunch); spinach lasagna, bean enchiladas, shrimp casserole, Thai spring roll, grilled swordfish, steamed vegetables with cilantro salsa (dinner).

RATES AND PACKAGES
7-night package (Sat.–Sat.) $1,985– $2,495 single, $1,590–$1,985 per person, double occupancy. 1-week minimum stay. $250 deposit required per person. MC, V.

DIRECTIONS
⊠ *Km 5, Carretera Federal/a Tijuana, Tecate, Baja California,* ☎ *6/654–1155; reservations in U.S.:* ⊠ *Box 463057, Escondido, CA 92046,* ☎ *760/744–4222 or 800/443–7565,* ℻ *760/744–5007.*

From San Diego airport: Complimentary transfers. Taxi, rental car available. Take Interstate-5 south to Highway 94, Tecate turnoff to Route 188, south to border crossing, right at 2nd light, onto Highway 2, 3 mi on right (1½ hrs).

ROSARITO BEACH HOTEL & CASA PLAYA SPA

Luxury pampering

Opened in 1926, this hotel once attracted Hollywood celebrities but now caters to tour groups intent on partying by the pool. When the owners converted their beachfront mansion into Casa Playa Spa, the resort gained a new lease on life. Secluded and quiet, the spa offers customized programs only; there are no group programs or exercise classes.

Entering a whitewashed, red-tiled archway, you'll discover an aging lobby tiled and decorated with murals by Matias Santoyo. The ocean-front rooms and suites have either a balcony or patio. An eight-story addition was completed in 1994.

In the spa adjoining the hotel, you are offered an extensive list of body-work and beauty-salon services. Sandals, a robe, towels, and a personal locker are issued daily. The coed whirlpool, sauna, steam room, and fitness gym are open to all hotel guests. A daily membership fee ($10) is charged for use of the facilities, exercise classes cost $5 each. Seaweed and fango treatments are the specialty here. Given the advantageous exchange rate of dollars for pesos, the aromatherapy facials and massages are a bargain.

Rosarito Beach stretches 20 miles from the U.S. border and is easily reached by a new toll road bypassing Tijuana. Baja's newest municipality, it has garish hotels and upscale condominiums mixed with cheap beach restaurants and shops selling tourist stuff. There are handmade pottery, silver jewelry, and wrought iron furniture. On the beach, horseback rides cost $5. And about a mile south is the Fox Studio Baja, where "Titanic" was filmed, now offering an hour-long tour when movies aren't in production.

FACILITIES
Exercise Equipment: Stair climber, stationary bikes, treadmills, weight-training equipment, free weights. **Services:** Aromatherapy, reflexology, Swedish massage; body polish, body wrap, parafango heat pack, salt-glow scrub; facial. **Swimming:** 2 pools, children's pool. **Classes and Programs:** Cholesterol test, fitness profile, personal training. **Recreation:** Golf, racquetball, surfing, tennis, volleyball; horseback riding nearby.

ACCOMMODATIONS
240 rooms, 40 suites.

DINING
All meals à la carte. **Sample Meals:** Steamed halibut, skinless roasted chicken with steamed vegetable and rice, spinach salad (lunch); tequila-sautéed salmon with mushrooms, spinach pasta with tomato sauce, green gazpacho (dinner).

RATES AND PACKAGES
$79–$199 per night, double. AE, MC, V.

DIRECTIONS
✉ *Blvd. Benito Juarez #31, Plaza Rosarito, Baja California Norte 22710,* ☎ *661/20–144 or 800/343–8582,* 🖷 *661/21–176.*

From San Diego: Interstate-5 or Interstate-805 to the U.S./Mexico border at Tijuana; follow signs to Highway 1-D "Rosarito-Ensenada Cuota" (toll road), south to 3rd Rosarito Beach exit (45 mins).

BAJA CALIFORNIA SUR

CABO REAL RESORT

Luxury pampering

Luxury comes in many packages at this megaresort near the tip of Baja California. New and remarkable for having four resort spas in four distinctive beach hotels and two 18-hole championship golf courses, the Cabo Real Resort complex stretches for several miles along the Sea of Cortez as it meets the Pacific Ocean. Staying at one hotel gives you access to the others. Not that you'll want to leave; each is a world unto itself.

There are differing levels of service and facilities at the spas of Los Cabos (*see* the individual hotel descriptions, *below*). No exercise classes are scheduled, but yoga is offered on flower-bedecked terraces and in air-conditioned studios.

Rising dramatically from ocean surf to mountain slopes, emerald green fairways contrast with the desert landscape. Golfers at all skill levels are challenged by the par 72 course designed by Robert Trent Jones II, and they can look forward to playing Jack Nicklaus's El Dorado course, scheduled for completion in 1999. The most unique hole, the 15th on Jones's layout, sits right on the beach between the Melia Cabo Real Beach and Golf Resort and Rosewood's Las Ventanas al Paraiso, allowing you to watch the action while dining or lounging at the swimming pools. Steps away, Casa Del Mar Golf Resort & Spa presents a low-key alternative, with suites clustered around its grand hacienda. Next in line is the Melia Los Cabos Beach and Golf Resort, an all-suites hotel offering the largest indoor spa on the coast.

Nature lovers head for craggy desert trails, best explored in company with a naturalist like Jim Elfers (☎ 114/31–706). The dusty, sun-scorched landscape reveals cactus of every variety: chain-link cholla, cardon cactus with arms held high, and fat barrel cactus. Amid vegetation such as prickly pear and yellow morning glory, birders spot white-winged doves, hermit warblers, plovers, and yellow and vermillion flycatchers. For something more adventurous, take the wheel of a Honda ATV on a guided tour of the Cabo Real nature preserve. But the most impressive sight is the annual migration of California gray whales close to the beaches, every January to March. Organized whale-watching tours are easily arranged at the hotels. The breeding grounds are primarily on the Pacific side, but some whales make their way around the cape to the Sea of Cortez.

The sea is integral to Los Cabos life. Pounding surf along the beach at Cabo Real deters swimmers, yet there is a protected cove at one of the hotels. Fishermen marvel at the size of marlin here. Canoeing and kayaking excursions are organized by tour operators; windsurfers and small boats can be rented on the beach. You can also explore underwater with scuba equipment or snorkels.

Visitors can come for a day with prior arrangement of spa reservations or tee time. Each of the hotels takes pride in its restaurants, allowing guests to enjoy everything from spa cuisine to New York steaks and traditional Mexican fare.

Casa del Mar Golf Resort & Spa

In a grand hacienda, the Avanti Spa here makes you feel like family. Airy and air-conditioned, it offers a full range of Pevonia Botanica skin care, bodywork, hydrotherapy, and a salon for hair and nail care.

Suites have showers and hot tubs, marble floors, a screened balcony or terrace, and minimal furniture.

FACILITIES

Exercise Equipment: Stationary bikes, treadmills, weight-training equipment, free weights. **Services:** Aromatherapy, sports massage; moor mud body wrap, seaweed body wrap, salt glow exfoliation; underwater lymphatic hydromassage, Vichy shower; facial. **Swimming:** 7 pools. **Classes and Programs:** Horseback riding instruction. **Recreation:** Golf, horseback riding, paddle tennis, tennis.

ACCOMMODATIONS

56 suites.

DINING

Meals served at The Dining Room terrace or indoors. **Sample Meals:** Buffet with yogurt, fresh fruit, cereals, Mexican-style eggs (breakfast); seafood cocktail, choice of 7 salads, ceviche of marinated sea bass and shrimp, chicken with fine herbs, chilies *rellenos,* grilled beef fillet with rice and beans (lunch); shrimp Caesar salad, Xochitl broth and pasta, seafood *relleno,* sea bass in cilantro sauce, lobster (dinner).

RATES AND PACKAGES

In season, $250–$450 daily. Credit-card guarantee required. AE, MC, V.

DIRECTIONS

✉ *Km 19.5 Carretera Transpeninsular, Los Cabos, B.C.S. CP 23410,* ☎ *114/40–030 or 800/221–8808, 800/393–0400 for golf-course reservations,* 𝖥𝖠𝖷 *114/40–034.*

Las Ventanas al Paraiso

Tucked away in the gardens, the two-level spa at Las Ventanas has indoor and outdoor facilities for massage and relaxation. In-suite treatments are also offered.

The resort terraces from a dramatic loggia to hideaway casitas on the beach. One- to three-bedroom suites are lavishly appointed with Mexican ceramics, carvings, and fabrics. All have marble showers, traditional Conchuela limestone floors, rattan seating, a fireplace, and a terrace. Rooftop suites open to a latticed terrace with a soaking pool and a whirlpool. All suites have a telescope.

FACILITIES

Exercise Equipment: Stair climber, stationary bikes, treadmills, weight-training equipment, free weights. **Services:** Aromatherapy, reflexology, sports, Swedish massage, trigger point therapy; algae body wrap, moor mud wrap; facial. **Classes and Programs:** Personal training.

ACCOMMODATIONS

61 suites.

DINING

Meals included in some packages. Californian and contemporary Mexican cuisine are served at poolside restaurant and beachfront seafood grill. Prepared to order and served with flair, meals include low-fat selections. **Sample Meals:** Seafood enchilada, black bean soup (lunch); seafood chowder, salad of organic greens, grilled Sonoran beef and chicken, poached sea bass (dinner).

RATES AND PACKAGES

In season, $475–$3,000 daily for 2; summer, $275–$2,500. There is a 3-night minimum on weekends. Pure Romance Package for two $3,500–$8,900 per week, including spa services, meals, golf. Day Spa packages

$150–$325, plus 12% tax, 15% gratuity. Credit-card guarantee required. AE, MC, V.

DIRECTIONS
✉ *Km. 19.5 Carretera Transpeninsular, CP 23410, Baja California Sur, 23400,* ☎ *114/40–300 or 888/525–0483,* FAX *114/40–301.*

Melia Cabo Real Beach & Golf Resort

Mayan carvings adorn the walls in the rooms, which all have landscaped terraces.

FACILITIES
Exercise Equipment: Stair climber, stationary bikes, weight-training circuit, free weights. **Services:** Massage, reflexology; herbal wrap, mineral salt wrap. **Swimming:** Beach, 2 pools. **Classes and Programs:** Personal training. **Recreation:** Beach volleyball, scuba, table tennis, tennis, water sports; boat tours, golf, horseback riding nearby.

ACCOMMODATIONS
286 rooms, 14 suites.

DINING
All meals à la carte buffets. **Sample Meals:** Minestrone soup, steamed broccoli and cauliflower, broiled chicken breast, tossed salad, zucchini and tomato (lunch); broiled beef, broiled fish, vegetarian plate with cottage cheese, spinach salad (dinner).

RATES AND PACKAGES
$202–$250 daily, single or double occupancy; suites $247–$640. Credit-card guarantee required. AE, MC, V.

DIRECTIONS
✉ *Carretera Cabo San Lucas, Sector 5, Km 19.5, Los Cabos, Baja California Sur 23400,* ☎ *114/40–000 or 800/336–3542,* FAX *114/40–101.*

From Cabo San Lucas International Airport: Take Highway 1 southwest (25 km); the resort entrance is at Kilometer 19 (30 mins).

Melia Los Cabos Beach & Golf Resort

This all-suites hotel opened a spa in late 1998 (too late for review). A free shuttle service operates to its sister hotel.

The suites are in a contemporary high-rise complex and consist of spacious rooms with marble floors and wood furniture.

FACILITIES
Exercise Equipment: Not available at press time. **Services:** Aromatherapy, Swedish massage; body scrub, body wrap; facial. **Swimming:** Pool. **Classes and Programs:** Aerobics, personal training, step aerobics, yoga. **Recreation:** Horseback riding, tennis, water sports.

ACCOMMODATIONS
150 suites.

DINING
No meal plan. Meals are served in two restaurants. **Sample Meals:** Fresh fruit, carrot/orange juice, fritatta with ratatouille (breakfast); shrimp cocktail, grilled vegetables with goat cheese, grilled fish (lunch); Napoleon of spinach and smoked salmon with citrus and caviar dressing, spinach pasta tagliatelle with sautéed shrimp, charcoal-grilled beef in fresh rosemary sauce, sea bass fillet, Viennese pastry (dinner).

RATES AND PACKAGES
$280–$500 per night, single or double, in-season. AE, D, MC, V.

DIRECTIONS
⊠ *Km. 18.5 Transpeninsular Hwy. 1, Los Cabos, B.C.S. CP 23400,* ☎ *114/40–202 or 800/336- -3542,* FAX *114/40–058.*

GUANAJUATO

HOTEL BALNEARIO COMANJILLA

Mineral springs

Providing limited spa services, this bargain-priced hotel has thermal water piped into some bathrooms as well as two swimming pools. A convenient base from which to explore some of Mexico's most interesting colonial towns, it is restful and quiet. Shaded pathways covered by canopies of pine trees lead to an Olympic-size pool filled with thermal water, ideal for a relaxing soak or swimming laps. Another smaller pool is warmer, said to be fed by 48 springs. Gardens surround the pools and two-story hotel wings, one of which houses an aerobics studio and conference facilities. In the main building, the restaurant is elegantly old-fashioned, serving traditional Mexican food.

Exercise programs are organized on request only, and massage ($25) appointments must be made well in advance. Medical and nutritional consultation is available to guests in Spanish only. The well-appointed guest rooms, tennis courts, and stables make the trip worthwhile regardless of language barriers. Many honeymooners and Texas snowbirds take advantage. Rooms, in Spanish-colonial buildings, have a balcony or patio, with a view of the forest or pool. Four suites have step-down Roman bath with thermal water.

Located on the new Pan-Am Highway, the hotel is minutes from the Bajio regional airport of León, an industrial center noted for leather products. This is the place to shop for shoes and clothing. Nearby is historic Guanajuato, a university town of great culture built on Spanish silver mine fortunes. Another colonial treasure, San Miguel de Allende, is 52 miles to the east of León.

FACILITIES
Exercise Equipment: Stationary bikes, free weights. **Services:** Massage; facial. **Swimming:** 2 pools. **Classes and Programs:** Medical evaluation. **Recreation:** Biking, billiards, horseback riding, table tennis, tennis.

ACCOMMODATIONS
120 rooms.

DINING
3 meals daily. An à la carte menu is offered in the hotel dining room.

RATES AND PACKAGES
$47 for two persons in standard double room; $63 for two persons in suite.

DIRECTIONS
✉ *Carretera Panamericana 45, Km. 385, Apt. Postal 111, 37000 León, Gto.,* ☎ *47/12–0091,* FAX *47/12–0949.*

From León: Highway 45 to Silao, Km 385; follow rural road signs to hotel (40 mins). Taxi, rental car available at Bajio Regional Airport (20 mins).

JALISCO

QUALTON CLUB & SPA VALLARTA

Luxury pampering

Fitness evaluations, medical consultations, and some of the best body-work this side of the Sierra Madres can be had at the Qualton Club Spa. And at this all-inclusive hotel, your meals, drinks, and admission to the fitness facilities are included in the daily rate.

Located in a seaside complex of high-rise hotels near the international airport, this budget-priced property has the area's largest fitness center. The daily schedule of free classes includes yoga, step aerobics, and water aerobics. A full circuit of strength-training equipment is in use day and night. (A daily $10 spa pass is available to nonresidents.)

In the air-conditioned aerobics studio, certified aerobics instructors conduct group exercise sessions from 7AM to 7:30 PM daily. At 7AM a tennis clinic starts the day, followed by low-impact aerobics, cross-training workout sessions, and yoga. There are also bodywork and beauty-salon services available daily, in special packages or à la carte. Fitness evaluations are conducted in specially equipped testing rooms. Staff members test your aerobic capacity, strength, flexibility, and blood pressure prior to starting you on a schedule of exercise.

A wide range of relaxing massages, herbal wraps, and facials are available, too, and guests are pampered with body and beauty treatments using natural extracts and herbs. Even the thermal clay in fango treatments has a history: It comes from a volcanic source in Michoacán, where it is purified for exclusive use here.

Set in beautiful gardens, the hotel's main 14-story tower is flanked by two 5-story buildings, creating a quiet, self-contained complex. At no extra charge, you can use non-motorized water sports equipment, take an introductory scuba lesson, and dine at the beach restaurant. Puerto Vallarta discos invite club members to accept complimentary admission passes, but the club's nightly entertainment and theme shows are hard to beat.

FACILITIES
Exercise Equipment: Stair climbers, stationary bikes, treadmills, weight-training circuit, free weights. **Services:** Acupressure, aromatherapy massage, reflexology, Swedish massage; fango, herbal wrap, loofah body scrub; facial. **Swimming:** Pool, ocean beach. **Classes and Programs:** Meditation, scuba lesson, step aerobics, tennis clinic, water aerobics, yoga. **Recreation:** Golf, horseback riding, tennis, water sports.

ACCOMMODATIONS
214 rooms, 4 suites.

DINING
3 meals daily, buffet or à la carte, plus afternoon snacks and beverages. 3 restaurants on the premises with international menus (cuisine changes daily). **Sample Meals:** Vegetarian chili, grilled fish, sautéed vegetables (lunch); chicken fajitas, pasta primavera, baked snapper, broiled chicken Florentine with steamed vegetables (dinner).

RATES AND PACKAGES
$75 daily per person, double occupancy, with 3 meals; $90 single, $60 per person, triple. 1-night deposit required. AE, DC, MC, V.

DIRECTIONS
✉ *Km 2.5 Av. Las Palmas, Puerto Vallarta, Jalisco, 48300,* ☎ *322/43–216 or 322/43–308,* FAX *322/44–447.*

From Puerta Vallarta airport: Take Blvd. F. M. Ascensio south (8 min). Taxi, rental car available.

RÍO CALIENTE SPA

Holistic health
Mineral springs
Nutrition and diet

This rustic retreat attracts an eclectic mix of people seeking stress relief. Clothing is optional, nudity the norm for soaking in the thermal water pools. The prices are affordable, and devotees return year after year.

For thousands of years, Huichol Indians used the meandering river of hot mineral water for curative purposes. Now the fertile valley around the tiny village of La Primavera is a national forest. And the Río Caliente Spa offers nature-oriented holidays, including three vegetarian meals daily, unlimited use of the pools and steam room, hikes, and classes. While there are optional outings, including a shopping trip to Guadalajara's famed crafts market, the resort accepts no credit cards and has no telephone on site.

The synthesis of therapies, diet, sun, and bathing puts everyone in a mellow mood. As you enter the bathhouse you'll encounter a 20-foot wall of volcanic rock, in front of which are wooden benches where guests relax while enjoying a sweat. A stream of hot thermal water snakes through the room, emitting puffs of steam. Welcome to the Aztec steam room. Open 24 hours every day, the pools and steam room are a place to commune with nature. Try soaking under the stars as clouds of steam rise off the pool; the water is hot, heavy with lithium said to have a therapeutic effect for depression and stress.

Classes in yoga, tai chi, and aquatics are scheduled for all guests who want to participate. Lectures can cover birdwatching, weaving, or Alanon principles for recovering alcoholics, depending on who's visiting. Spontaneous scheduling appears daily on the blackboard in the dining room.

Spa services are provided by a well-trained staff, at á la carte prices starting at $25 for massage, $7 for mud wraps. Packages are offered for anti-aging in the clinic, with homeopathic remedies such as human growth hormone injections. It's not luxury pampering, but the regulars don't seem to notice or care.

The main building houses small and simple cabanas and rooms, with hand-crafted beds and chairs, and colorful fabrics by local artisans. There are no phones, TV, or air-conditioning. All rooms have a fireplace.

FACILITIES
Services: Anti-cellulite, reflexology, Reiki, Swedish massage; acupuncture, fango; facial. **Swimming:** Outdoor swimming pool, separate walled plunge pools for men and women, waterfall for nude bathing. **Recreation:** Hiking.

ACCOMMODATIONS
50 rooms.

DINING
3 vegetarian meals daily, served buffet-style. Tropical foods in season include guavas, jícama, zapote, and guanabana. **Sample Meals:** Organic raw

greens, raw and cooked vegetables, soups (lunch); salads, home-baked grain casseroles, tropical fruits (dinner).

RATES AND PACKAGES
$85–$97 daily per person, double occupancy, with 3 meals; $101–$116 single. 7-night program $615 per person, sharing, $740 single. 10-night stress-buster package $880 per person, double, $1,060 single. $250 deposit required. No credit cards.

DIRECTIONS
⊠ *Apdo. Postal 5-67 Colonia Chapalita, Guadalajara 43042, Jalisco,* ☎ *no phone at spa; Reservations:* ⊠ *Box 897, Millbrae, CA 94030,* ☎ *650/ 615–9543 or 800/200–2927,* ℻ *650/615–0601.*

From Guadalajara: Highway 80 to La Primavera (1 hr). Taxi, rental car available.

MEXICO

AVANDARO GOLF & SPA RESORT

Luxury pampering

An upscale escape from Mexico City, this family-oriented resort is a well-kept secret. The spa complements a pine-scented golf course. Workouts in the aerobics studio come with a view of golfers surrounded by an alpine forest. Villas and *casitas* cluster on a hillside amid manicured lawns that slope down to the clubhouse. As a weekend escape, it provides plenty of services but no structured programs.

The Avandaro Hotel, secluded and gated, sits well above the town of Valle de Bravo, 90 miles west of Mexico City. Settled by the Nahuatl Indians, this valley in the Sierra Madre mountains was named Temascaltepec from the words *temazcali* ("House of Baths") and *tepac* ("hill"] for its curative waters and mud. Orchids and hibiscus grow wild at waterfalls in the hills. The cooler temperatures can be attributed to the area's high altitude, 6,000 feet above sea level. The lake is man-made and changed the town into an artist colony, named for local patriot Nicolas Bravo. While the heart of town remains true to its 16th-century roots, French and Italian restaurants crowd the narrow, cobbled streets, where discos elbow chic crafts boutiques and shops selling imported athletic equipment.

Checking in at the spa building of the Avandaro, you'll find multi-lingual personnel ready to arrange treatments for stress reduction as well as anticellulite programs. Among options are a nonsurgical facelift and *Electros Suenòs* ("Electric Dreams"), an electronic relaxer said to simulate sleep. In the sunlit atrium, water gushes into a coed whirlpool surrounded by sauna, steam room, lockers, and relaxation lounge, where you await a therapist. An aerobics studio is equipped with exercise videos, but instructors and yoga classes are mainly scheduled weekends. Request a personal trainer, who can also arrange biking trips with a local outfitter. Divided into men's and women's sections, the spa focuses on highly personalized service. There are three facial rooms, three rooms equipped for herbal wraps and loofah scrubs, six massage areas, and a complete salon section. Exercise shorts and T-shirts are provided along with bathrobes in the locker rooms.

Carved out of the pine forest, velvety-green lawns of Avandaro's 18-hole, par 72, Percy Cliff–designed championship golf course spread beyond the spa building. A river flows through it, and there are great views of the mountains. Also on the resort's 300 acres are a pool, seven tennis courts, and two restaurants.

Accommodations are in Spanish colonial–style adobe villas and in standard rooms in motel-style cabins near the reception center. All have a wood-burning fireplace. Suites have a sitting area, dining table, and balcony or terrace. Expect nights to be cool, perfect for having the fireplace aglow when you return from dinner.

Meals can be on the heavy side, so talk to the spa director in advance of your arrival if you prefer light cuisine or a special diet. The chefs here have learned to reduce fat and calories, while enhancing natural flavors of farm-fresh produce. Vegetarian meals can be arranged. A nutritional/health analysis is available in Spanish and English.

Valle de Bravo's most unique attraction is the Monarch butterfly migration. November through March, billions of Monarchs flock here from Canada and the northern U.S. Guided hikes of the butterfly sanctuaries provide a closeup of endless showers of color during the mating season. Hikers are cautioned to tread carefully on the wooded trails, so as not to disturb the delicate Monarchs. Driving in the area can involve dodging cows and the butterflies, fluttering in and along roads as they return to Canada in March.

For a change of pace, plan an excursion to the nearby Loto Azul Hotel, a meditation retreat complete with Japanese-style hot tub and *temazcal* Indian-style steam bath. Shop in the lakeside village for arts and crafts, join the locals at sidewalk cafés around the *zocalo,* the bustling main square typical of Mexican towns. Boats can be chartered on the lake for fishing, and windsurfing and waterskiing rentals are available. Other sights include La Gavia, a 16th-century working hacienda; the Navarro de Toluca volcano; and the waterfalls at Velo de Novia. The air is clear and cool—average daytime temperatures range from 72°F to 80°F in the winter and spring, slightly higher during dry summer months. It's hard to believe that congested Mexico City is two hours from this peaceful colonial village.

FACILITIES

Exercise Equipment: Rowing machine, stair climbers, stationary bikes, treadmills, weight- training equipment, free weights. **Services:** Aromatherapy, reflexology, shiatsu, sports, Swedish massage; herbal wrap, loofah salt glow, pressotherapy; facials. **Swimming:** Pool. **Classes and Programs:** Antistress biofeedback, nutritional analysis. **Recreation:** Golf (18 holes), hiking, table tennis, tennis; hang gliding, horseback riding, water sports nearby.

ACCOMMODATIONS

20 rooms, 41 suites.

DINING

3 meals daily from spa cuisine à la carte menu in Las Terrazas Restaurant included with spa packages. Weekend rate for suites includes breakfast only. **Sample Meals:** Crabmeat salad, couscous with vegetables (lunch); grilled mountain trout, chicken tostada (dinner).

RATES AND PACKAGES

8-day/7-night Slim & Trim package $1,745–$2,187 for 2 persons, double occupancy, $1,120–$1,340 single. Daily rate without spa for 2 persons, double occupancy, in standard room $86, in suite $180. 50% deposit required. AE, MC, V.

DIRECTIONS

✉ *Vega del Rio S/N-Fraccionamiento Avandaro, Valle de Bravo 51200,* ☎ *726/60–366, 800/223–6510 (in the U.S.),* FAX *726/60–905; Mexico City:* ✉ *Anatole France 139, Polanco C. P. 11560,* ☎ *528/01–532,* FAX *528/20–578.*

From Mexico City: Complimentary transfers from airport and Zona Rosa hotels is included in spa packages. Rental car available at airport and in town. Constituyendes Avenida to Autopista (toll road) Route 15 via Toluca, Highway 134 through national forest, Highway 86, Highway 8 to Valle de Bravo (3 hrs).

BALNEARIOS

Mineral springs

A central belt cutting all the way to the Gulf of Mexico as well as the Pacific coast of Mexico comprises a vast volcanic zone. Hundreds of hot springs dot the region, and one entire state— Aguascalientes—has been named for the hot waters.

Offering little more than a relaxing soak in public pools and rustic accommodations, the *balnearios* are a time-honored tradition. While most of the springs are not developed, some are popular with Mexican families, and within this volcanic area is Mexico's most beautiful mountain scenery. Here are some of the places where "taking the waters" can be enjoyed year-round. (Special thanks to Mike Nelson, author of *Spas & Hot Springs of Mexico,* for assistance in updating these listings.)

Agua Blanca Hotel, Jungapeo, Michoacán

✉ *Carretera Zitacuaro, Cd. Hidalgo,* ☎ *725/70–056 or 725/70–067.*

Set deep in a canyon is the 18-room Agua Blanca hotel, with three thermal pools fed by radioactive waters that flow over cascades at 30°C. Considered beneficial for drinking, the water has a purgative effect. Rooms cost about $30; No credit cards are accepted. Silence, manicured lawns, and luxuriant flower beds enhance this serene escape. Nearby are San Jose Purua and the sanctuary of Monarch butterflies.

Agua Hedionda Hotel Villasenor

✉ *Av. Progreso s/n, Cuautla, Morelos,* ☎ *735/26–521,* FAX *735/26–562.*

Sulfuric waters fill two public pools, wading pools, and eight private pools here. Facilities include showers and dressing rooms, and the resort houses a restaurant with dancing on weekends. Across the road, Hotel Villasenor offers 60 rooms, 3 suites, and a restaurant with vegetarian selections. Rooms are $20–$25. This one is located close to Cuernavaca.

El Almeal

✉ *Prolongacion Virginia Hernandez s/n. Cuautla, Morelos,* ☎ *735/ 50–820.*

Two spring-fed pools, wading pools, playing fields, and a restaurant enhance this public spa. Dressing rooms and lockers are provided for daily admission fee. Scenic railroad excursion Thursday, Saturday, and Sunday. There are hiking trails nearby to Popacatepti and Ixtaccihuatl.

Hotel Balneario Atzimba

✉ *Av. Lazaro Cardenas, 58930 Zinapecuaro, Michoacán,* ☎ *455/50–042,* FAX *455/50–050.*

Adjacent to a popular water park, this rustic 12-cabin resort with thermal water baths is about 30 minutes from Morelia, capital of the state. There is a small restaurant and lots of space for unwinding. Nearby butterfly sanctuaries make this a good base for hikes during Monarch mating season, from November to March.

Hotel Balneario La Caldera

✉ *Km. 29 Libramiento, Carretera Abosolo, Abasolo, Michoacacàn 36970,* ☎ FAX *469/30–020 and 469/30–021.*

Private baths fed with 169°F thermal mineral water, an outdoor whirlpool, two swimming pools, two basketball courts, squash court, two tennis courts, soccer field, and extensive gardens are features of the 116-room La Caldera. All rooms have private bath, TV, and air-conditioning. Rates are about $40 double (MC and V accepted). There is a good restaurant, popular on weekends. The hotel is located on Highway 110, just west of Irapuato, Mexico's strawberry center.

Hotel Balneario Lourdes

Reservation office: ✉ *Francisco Zarco 389, San Luis Potosi, S.L.P.,* ☎ *481/70–554,* FAX *482/51–434.*

An old hacienda converted as spa and meeting center, Lourdes offers 34 double rooms, a heated pool fed by mineral waters, whirlpool, horseback riding, and squash and tennis courts. Five private rooms have step-down Roman baths. The restaurant prepares vegetarian meals on request. The waters are recommended for drinking, and a bottling plant adjoins the property. Located on Highway 57, 59 kilometers (33 miles) south of the picturesque colonial city of San Luis Potosi. Overnight accommodations average $30 double.

Hotel Baños Termales de Chignahuapan

✉ *Km. 5 Carretera de Chignahuapan, Puebla,* ☎ *777/10–599.*

Dramatically situated at the edge of a canyon into which a cold-water stream plunges hundreds of feet and mixes with hot sulfur springs, this hotel has 12 double rooms and 24 singles, all with private bath and a small balcony. There are a dozen tiled pools outdoors, some covered, with water temperatures varying from hot to warm. Beds in the hotel are referred to as "matrimonials," possibly because the water is believed to help women who have difficulty in conception. Nearby are Tiaxcala, a colonial town noted for the Sanctuary of the Virgin of Ocotlan, and pre-Hispanic murals at the Cacaxtla archaeological site.

Hotel Taninul

✉ *Km. 15 Carretera Cd., Valles-Tampico, Cd. Valles; Mailing Address:* ✉ *Box 87, Cd. Valles, S.L.P.,* ☎ *138/20–000,* FAX *138/24–414.*

Time seems to stand still in this once-glamorous tropical hideaway near the Texas border. Located 15 minutes from Ciudad Valles and 100 kilometers (62 miles) from Tampico, the three-star Hotel Taninul has 130 air-conditioned rooms and 14 suites. Overnight accommodations cost about $35. The thermal-water pool, fed by sulfur springs with globs of organic matter, and a freshwater swimming pool are part of the spa complex. Services include facial, massage, manicure, and pedicure. There are a restaurant and tennis courts for hotel guests.

Las Estacas Nature Park

✉ *Tlaltizapán, Morelos,* ☎ *734/50–077,* FAX *731/24–412; Mailing Address:* ✉ *C.P. 62000, Cuernavaca, Mor.*

Towering stands of bamboo, amate, and royal palm trees shade swift-flowing streams from a volcanic spring that pours 8,000 liters of water per second into the park's one-kilometer waterway. Clear and refreshingly cool, the river is popular with families who float in tubes, swim, and dive. Overnight accommodations ($11) are in 10 nicely maintained cabins, with private bathroom, twin beds, porch. Visitors come for a day ($3), relax in the *palapas* for lunch, and join volleyball, basketball, and soccer games. Children's wading pools adjoin a concrete swimming pool. There's a campground, trailer park, and miniature golf. Located near Cuernavaca, the park is developing educational programs about the ecology of the area, once a major sugar-growing center. *Tarzan* was filmed here.

Oaxtepec Vacation Center

⊠ *Cuautla, Morelos,* ☏ *735/60–101. Reservation Center in Mexico City: Heriberto Frias 241, Col. Navarte or C.P. 03020, Mexico, D.F.,* ☏ *563/94–200 or 563/90–071.*

A 40-room hotel and a dozen cottages provide overnight accommodations around vast spring-fed swimming pools. Located 56 kilometers (35 miles) east of Cuernavaca, near Cuautla in the state of Morelos, the thermal springs here were a favorite retreat of Móctezuma. Built as a retreat for government workers, the recreation complex has athletic fields and restaurants run by the Mexican Social Security Institute. Hotel rooms, open to the public, cost about $40.

Spa Pre-Hispanico at Hotel Aldea del Bazar

⊠ *Av. Benito Juarez Lote No. 7, Puerto Escondido, Oaxaca 71980,* ☏ *958/20–508.*

Surfers congregate on the Pacific beaches, but you can retreat to a tropical garden secluded in the upscale Bacocho residential area, where Moorish-themed Hotel Aldea del Bazar features the *temazcal* bath, a 500-year-old sweat lodge for cleansing toxins from the body and attaining a spiritual state. Start with a body scrub and massage under the palm trees, then sit in the marble-walled temazcals (one for groups, one solo) as herbal water is poured on hot rocks. Try a facial with mud from volcanic ash. Therapists speak little or no English, and their technique is more vigorous than expert, but a cool alternative to the sun-soaked beach. Connected to the beach by a long walkway, the white-walled hotel's 47 deluxe rooms and two suites create a Moorish fantasy, commanding top dollar for the area, about $70 per room. Spa services and meals can be charged to your room; credit cards accepted are MC, V. A modest restaurant adjoins the huge swimming pool, but the hotel's private beach club has a restaurant serving chilled avocado soup, grilled fish, and chicken. Located off coastal Highway 200, which connects to Huatulco, this laid-back town centers on a seafront strip of bars, restaurants, and colorful Hotel Santa Fe for open-air dining. About 35 miles down the coast is a marine ecology center dedicated to protection of sea turtles, Centro Mexicano de la Tortuga, open daily. On market days, visit the old Mercado Benito Juarez. The nearby regional airport has scheduled flights to Mexico City (50 min) on Aeromexico and Continental Airlines.

HOTEL IXTAPAN

Luxury pampering
Mineral springs

Hotel Ixtapan, the largest and most luxurious thermal springs health resort in Mexico, is in Ixtapan de la Sal, which has been a popular center for cures since the 16th-century Aztec emperor Móctezuma came to bathe. Recently rejuvenated by the resident owners, the hotel's health and beauty programs feature fresh-fruit facials, a calorie-controlled meal option, and bathing in thermal waters. Aquacise classes are held in an outdoor, plankton-laden thermal-water pool, 20 meters by 8 meters, open to all guests. Also in the gardens is a shaded whirlpool filled with filtered fresh water.

Don't expect much in the way of organized programs. The main reason to come here is relaxation and affordable spa treatments. An easy escape southwest of Mexico City by car (119 km/65 mi), the resort is near a new superhighway to Acapulco and close enough to historic Taxco for day trips.

Opened in 1942, the hotel combines a late Art Deco look with laid-back Mexican hospitality. Want traditional food or vegetarian meals instead of the weight-loss plan? No problem. Interested in romantic seclusion? Try the Roman Baths just for two. Simply ask at the front desk, because many staff members do not speak English. Privately owned and operated, the 35-acre resort includes a 9-hole golf course and lush gardens that lead to a public pool and bathhouse. This can also lead to crowds and noise on weekends, so it's wise to let the hotel know of your needs well in advance of your arrival.

Set your own schedule. Rent mountain bikes to explore the area on a guided trail ride to Taxco, where silver craftsmen and cold beer welcome you. Or go hiking in the high desert just outside town. Most of the spa guests, however, are middle-aged and simply want to relax.

Separate floors in the hotel provide spa facilities for men and women. Therapists may not be consistent in technique, but make up for any lapses with great gusto. The exercise equipment is minimal, but there's a sun-drenched deck for stretching. Guest rooms have been refurbished, although the carpeting and colors are drab. A water treatment plant and a power plant maintain the hotel's safety. The spa has a marble whirlpool centerpiece where you can relax while awaiting a facial or massage in private cubicles.

The thermal waters originate from an extinct volcano. Piped into a huge lake in the Parque Acuatico adjoining the hotel grounds, the thermal springs also fill the exclusive Roman Baths that function as a day spa. You can have a private soak in one of 20 marble-walled Roman baths, which come with two beds where you rest and cool down. The sunken whirlpools, large enough to hold six adults or a family, are filled with warm mineral water, ideal for a late-afternoon soak or a Sunday indulgence when hotel masseurs have the day off.

Packages are an excellent value, including daily massage and treatments in four- and seven-day programs. Treatments are gentle and relaxing, and exercise classes are not strenuous. The facialists mix fresh fruit into creams for skin care. Optional diet plan and medical supervision are available with the spa packages.

Family-oriented, the hotel has a disco, bars, train rides, horse-drawn carriages, water slides, and a bowling alley. There are 48 private villas adjoining the hotel, with accommodations for families. If budgetary constraints are your prime concern, this may be a good choice for combining fun and fitness.

FACILITIES
Exercise Equipment: Cross-country skiing machine, rowing machine, stair climber, stationary bike, treadmill, weight-training circuit, free weights. **Services:** Massage, reflexology; acupuncture, mud pack; facial. **Swimming:** Indoor and outdoor pools. **Recreation:** Badminton, golf, horseback riding, tennis, volleyball. Folkloric ballet.

ACCOMMODATIONS
168 rooms, 48 villas.

DINING
3 meals daily. Choice of full menu in main dining room or spa room. 900-calorie spa menu available. **Sample Meals:** Chicken with mushrooms, tuna fish platter (lunch); fresh rainbow trout, omelet, cheese plate (dinner).

RATES AND PACKAGES
$135–$210 daily for 2. 7-day/6-night spa program (Sun.–Sat.) $784–
$825 per person, double occupancy, $945–$995 single. 4-day/4-night pro-
gram (Sun.–Thurs. or Wed.–Sun.) $404–$425 per person, double,
$565–$650 single. 50% deposit required. AE, MC, V.

DIRECTIONS
✉ *Ixtapan de la Sal, 51900 Mexico,* ☎ *714/30–021, 800/638–7950 (U.S.
reservations),* FAX *714/30–856; in Mexico City:* ✉ *Tonala 177, Col. Roma,
C.P. 06700, Mexico City, D.F.,* ☎ *556/45–860,* FAX *526/42–613.*

From Mexico City: Take toll road (cuota) Highway 95D south, past Cuernavaca to the Taxco exit, Highway 55 north 20 mi (2 hrs). Transfers available through hotel, $95.

MORELOS

HOSTERIA LAS QUINTAS

Luxury pampering

This in-city inn provides a sense of history and a look at ecology, along with sophisticated pampering. Lots of personal attention from staffers makes up for the lack of organized exercise programs, and you can join guided excursions to nearby archaeological sites and thermal springs.

Adventure travelers and environmentalists might not be excited about the these outings, but spa-goers may enjoy the challenge of climbing a pyramid instead of a StairMaster. Promoting the concept of ecotourism, the spa encourages guests to explore the rugged mountains that surround the city. Scheduled for an additional fee, and available only on request, these outings include a visit to Tepoztlan, considered an "energy center" by New Agers. On market days, old ladies sell fruit and dried chilies next to tie-dyed expatriates hawking crystals. A steep, rocky trail leads from the town to a mountaintop Olmec pyramid and spectacular view. How about an "aerobic shopping tour" to Taxco, where silver sellers outnumber the tourists? Or a trip to the lagoons of Zempoala, where you hike in a pine forest or go horseback riding? A spa staffer escorts you if other guests don't sign up.

Among four noteworthy spas in the area, the spa at Hosteria Las Quintas provides first-class pampering. The facilities, however, are hardly European in style. The ambience is more like a beauty salon. Treatments range from hair styling and manicure to massage and body wraps with Dead Sea mud or French marine algae. Open to the public as well as hotel guests, the facilities face a garden and restaurant, often busy with meetings of local groups.

Accommodations are suites in a walled garden complex. Some have a terrace; most are in two-story units. Glazed-tile floors open to a screened balcony. Some have a fireplace, whirlpool bath, and sitting area.

In a residential area, close to the colonial and commercial centers of the city, Las Quintas makes a good base for shopping and sightseeing excursions. It also offers a golf package that allows guests to play at the area's five courses.

FACILITIES
Exercise Equipment: Cross-country skiing machines, stair climber, stationary bikes, treadmills, weight-training equipment, free weights. **Services:** Reflexology, shiatsu, Swedish massage; body scrub, herbal wrap, mud wrap, seaweed wrap; facial. **Swimming:** 2 pools. **Classes and Programs:** Conversational Spanish, crafts, fitness evaluation, garden bonsai tour, medical examination, yoga.

ACCOMMODATIONS
60 suites.

DINING
3 meals included in spa packages. Without package, 3-meal plan $58 per person per day. **Sample Meals:** Fresh juices, fruits, cereals, omelet (breakfast); vegetarian burrito, pasta, grilled fish (lunch); baked chicken with black beans and rice, fillet of fish sautéed in wine, roasted vegetables, pasta primavera (dinner).

RATES AND PACKAGES
Suites: $120–$170 per night. 2-night Stress Relief package $509 per person, double occupancy, $606 single. 4-night Pampering Program $952

per person, double, $1,146 single. 4-night Golf/Spa Getaway $1,019 per person, double, $1,215 single. AE, MC, V.

DIRECTIONS

✉ *Blvd. Diaz Ordaz 9, Cuernavaca 62440, Morelos,* ☎ *731/83–949 or 888/772–7639,* ℻ *731/83–895.*

From Mexico City: Hotel supplies coupon for complimentary round-trip transportation on bus with scheduled service throughout the day. Taxi, car rental available. Take toll road Highway 95D to IMSS exit, calle Diaz Ordaz for about 2 km (2 hr).

HOTEL HACIENDA COCOYOC

Luxury pampering

Discovering a former sugar plantation, complete with aqueduct and modern spa, comes as a surprise when you enter the ancient walls of Hacienda Cocoyoc. Set amid lush lawns and vast swimming pools, the spa building is a separate, sybaritic enclave. There are separate wings for men and women with steam bath, sauna, showers (Swiss multijet), wet-treatment room, and private massage rooms. Sunlight streams into the lounges where you await treatments, or relax in a big whirlpool under a pyramid-shaped skylight. Locker room attendants hand you lime water refreshers (water comes from a well on the property) and provide robe and sandals. Amenities include hair dryer and grooming items. The daily facility fee added to your bill is $8.

Spa services can be combined with golf at the resort's sister club in a nearby residential development, or the 9-hole course adjoining the spa. And there are personal trainers for tennis and golf, as well as for workouts and water aerobics. The exercise room is small, but Nautilus equipment is available without charge.

With a wide range of treatments à la carte, the spa concentrates on relaxation techniques, detoxifying, and revitalizing. Slip into the alpha jet capsule and see if you can generate relaxing alpha waves. The spa environment itself, all polished stone and wood in golden tones, is conducive to a stress-free escape. Shaded walkways lined by ancient banyan trees lead to the main part of the hotel. Meals can be at the spa café or in the main dining room, where informality is the rule, and calories aren't counted on the menu.

Accommodations are in several buildings, in high-ceiling suites and private casitas, with no air-conditioning. Staying in one of the casitas that border the gardens adds a romantic touch. Each unit comes with a walled garden where a pool big enough for two provides a refreshing dip in the morning and evening. In the bathroom, hand-painted tiles cover the walls and step-down shower. The main hacienda houses regal guest rooms as well as two restaurants and conference facilities.

Family owned and operated, Cocoyoc's 22-acre complex includes a 16th-century chapel restored by the current director's father. Heirlooms enhance public rooms in the family mansion. Secluded from the outside world of noisy truck traffic and sugar cane farming, this is quintessential, old-fashioned Mexico.

FACILITIES

Exercise Equipment: Stair climbers, stationary bikes, weight-training equipment. **Services:** Anti-stress, reflexology, sports, Swedish massage; glycolic peel, loofah scrub, mineral mud wrap, pressotherapy; thalasso wrap, hydromassage; facial. **Swimming:** 4 pools. **Classes and Programs:**

Computerized body-composition analysis. **Recreation:** Golf, jogging, tennis.

ACCOMMODATIONS
263 rooms, 24 suites.

DINING
All meals à la carte. Two restaurants serve Mexican and Continental spa selections. **Sample Meals:** Spinach crepe, stuffed baby squid (lunch); grilled fish fillet with steamed vegetables, chicken breast stuffed with *huichole* corn mushroom (dinner).

RATES AND PACKAGES
$365–$595 daily per room for 2, suite with pool $650– $1,100. AE, MC, V.

DIRECTIONS
✉ *Box 300, Cuautla 622736, Morelos,* ☎ *735/62–211 or 735/61–211, 550–7331 (in Mexico City),* FAX *52/735–612–12.*

From Mexico City: Highway 95 to Autopista Acapulco, exit at Cualtla di Teopoztlian, Highway 115 (2 hrs). Van service offered by hotel, $100 round-trip. Taxi, rental car available.

MISIÓN DEL SOL

Holistic health
Luxury pampering

Serenity envelops you at the gate. No cars are allowed in this urban Shangri-La. Escorted by golf cart to the reception lounge, you are greeted at a massive mandala created by Tibetan monks. Crystals stud the grounds, absorbing bad and imparting good energy. People speak softly and dress in soft cotton clothing straight out of a New Age natural fiber catalog. More retreat than resort, the Misión offers programs that blend many philosophies and religions, seeking universal truth.

The spirit here may be New Age but creature comforts are deluxe. Designed as a Santa Fe–style village, Misión del Sol comprises two-story lodges and family-size villas surrounded by a 5-acre ecological park. Entering your room, you are calmed by the sounds and smells of nature after the long drive from Mexico City. Tall screened windows open on an herb garden and flowering hedges that border waterways. The rooms, paved entirely in polished stone and decorated with natural fibers and wood, are a symphony of earth tones. All that's missing are TV, air-conditioning, and a minibar.

Aerobics and aquaerobics top the daily schedule, posted only in Spanish. There is also an hour-long *caminata acumulativa,* a guided run through the neighborhood villas of wealthy weekenders who once included Woolworth heiress Barbara Hutton. Choices include tennis, tai chi, ceramics, lectures, and every morning at 10, an hour of yoga. You're asked to check in with the program director to learn if the group is meeting on the lawn or in the lecture hall over the dining room.

Bilingual staff members make newcomers comfortable. The guests are an interesting mix: Europeans on a study tour, stressed-out Mexico City professionals, and mothers bonding with daughters at a special retreat. Smoking is common in the dining room, prohibited in other areas. Excursions are planned to a nearby town said to be a center for New Agers, Tepoztlan, where there is an Aztec pyramid and 16th-century chapel adorned in Indian motifs. Also on the list, for a fee, are whitewater rafting and bicycling.

Secluded on the grounds are a meditation pavilion built around a Zen sand garden, the spa complex with soaking pool tiled in Zodiac signs, coed whirlpool and swimming pool, and a domed *temazcal* sweat lodge big enough for 20 meditators. If your visit coincides with the new moon, an ancient ceremony for cleansing body and mind will be held in the *temazcal*. Otherwise, appointments for massage, facials, and seaweed wrap are made at the spa complex.

Orchestrating the program and planned expansion of the domed guest lodges is German-born Renate von Dorren and a team of Mexican architects. They devoted two years to conserving the site's ecology before construction began, installing solar energy and water recycling systems, finding craftsmen to make adobe brick of sun-dried clay, which allows the walls to "breathe." Nutritionists planned the menu for a broad variety of diets, mainly vegetarian but allowing for meat and fish to be served.

Cuernavaca's colonial center, noisy and congested, is about 20 minutes by taxi from the Misión.

Located 53 mi (83 km) from Mexico City, the city enjoys a year-round springlike climate. With the fast new toll road to Acapulco nearby, the Misión van makes the trip from Mexico City's airport in about an hour.

FACILITIES
Exercise Equipment: Stair climbers, weight-training equipment, free weights. **Services:** Anti-cellulite, aromatherapy, craniosacral, reflexology, Reiki, shiatsu, Swedish massage; acupuncture, body scrub, mud body wrap, seaweed body wrap; facial. **Swimming:** Pool. **Classes and Programs:** Aerobics, aquaerobics, daily run; workshops on science, Buddhism, nutrition, ecology, self-awareness; classes in ceramics, painting, conversational English, Spanish. **Recreation:** Biking, hiking, paddle tennis, tennis, volleyball; golf nearby.

ACCOMMODATIONS
90 rooms, 10 villas.

DINING
Generously-portioned organic dishes served in open-air dining room. Choices are made from à la carte daily menu. **Sample Meals:** Egg-white omelet, fresh fruit, yogurt, cereals (breakfast); beet soup, salad, vegetarian burrito (lunch); vegetarian lasagna, grilled lamb chops, poached chicken with seasonal vegetables, tamales (dinner).

RATES AND PACKAGES
$170 daily, room and breakfast for 2, $118 single, suites in villas $237–$356; spa day package (no lodging) $120; 2-night health package $530 single, $430 per person, double; 3-night Energy Interlude $807 single, $633 per person, double; 4-night Harmony Interlude $1,011 single, $778 per person, double; 7-night Sol Interlude $2,250 single, $1,842 per person, double. MC, V.

DIRECTIONS
✉ *Av. Gral. Diego Diaz González 31, Cuernavaca, Morelos 62550,* ☎ *732/10–999 or 800/999–9100,* FAX *732/11–195.*

From Mexico City: Take toll road Highway 95D toward Acapulco, exit marked Cuatula Civac to Paseo Cuahunahuac under freeway to Avenida 10 de Abril; follow signs to Hotel Camino Real Sumiya, turn right (south) and continue through residential section and Zocalo Parres, right on Avenida General Diego Diaz Gonzalez (1 hr).

NAYARIT

PARADISE VILLAGE BEACH RESORT

Luxury pampering

Bring the family for a beach vacation while you luxuriate at one of the fanciest spa structures in Mexico. Set on a peninsula between the beach and marina, the spa at Paradise Village Beach Resort is a modern Mayan temple of glass and marble devoted to health, fitness, and beauty. Inside this cool oasis are separate wings for men and women, equipped with private hydrotherapy tubs, Vichy shower, whirlpool, sauna, and steam room. The coed cardiovascular and weight training rooms have state-of-the-art equipment and views of the water and TV. Aerobics classes are scheduled throughout the day in a mirrored studio, and there's an indoor lap pool, so you can escape the sun and kids at the resort pool. A snack bar offers refreshment.

Spa director Diana Mestre, an old hand in these parts, brings together ancient healing arts and the latest electronic equipment. Start with a computerized diagnosis of your fitness level, or iris diagnosis, then set up a personalized program of preventive and rejuvenation treatments. Workouts with a personal trainer can help you get started on an exercise program. Therapy selections are extensive, from sea fango for tired and swollen feet to a Mayan milk bath that rehydrates your entire body. You are then escorted to private marble-walled rooms for massage, facials, and wraps. Energy balancing therapies are a specialty here, administered by a specialist trained in Oriental massage techniques such as Anma shiatsu and acupressure. Day packages with spa lunch start at $45, and several multiday spa vacation packages are available.

Completely self-contained, the resort provides lots of recreation and lodging options, plus comforting security. Accommodations in the eight-story beachfront tower are in condominium apartments, with two or three bedrooms, full kitchen, and living room, plus private terrace. There is daily maid service. The hotel features a lagoon-size swimming pool, complete with rocky grottoes, flowing waterfalls, and a Mayan-style temple. There is an 18-hole golf course at the resort, plus another nearby.

Outdoor adventures begin steps from the spa building. Sailing courses, speedboat excursions, and deep sea fishing are offered at the marina. Bike tours are organized for basic and advanced bikers. Kayaking is a new way to explore Banderas Bay and its marine estuaries.

Located 8 miles north of the old cobbled streets of Puerto Vallarta, the new beach resorts around Paradise Village stretch for 2.9 miles. Numerous tennis clubs and a shopping center complement the golf course and marina. For privacy, head north to the town of Bucerias, then follow the bend of Banderas Bay past several small and pristine beaches. Nightlife and action downtown put P.V. on the tourist map, and its artisans lend glamour to the gallery scene. You can go to bullfights (Nov.–Apr.) Wednesday at 5 PM at a modest Plaza de Toros on the airport road.

FACILITIES
Exercise Equipment: Stationary bikes, treadmills, weight-training circuit, free weights. **Services:** Aromatherapy, reflexology, shiatsu massage; herbal wrap, loofah body scrub, paraffin body treatment; thalassotherapy, Vichy shower; facial. **Swimming:** Indoor and outdoor pools, ocean beach. **Classes and Programs:** Aerobics, fitness evaluation. **Recreation:** Fishing, golf, horseback riding, kayaking, tennis, windsurfing.

ACCOMMODATIONS
265 apartments with one or two bedrooms.

DINING
3 meals daily included in spa packages. Choice of spa menu or regular restaurant, with beverage credit.

RATES AND PACKAGES
3-night Renewal package $628–$754 single, $430–$493 per person, double occupancy; 7-night Stress Reducer $1,538–$1,832 single, $1,081–$1,228 per person, double. Day Spa packages $74–$196. AE, MC, V.

DIRECTIONS
✉ *Av. de los Cocoteros 001, Nueva Vallarta, Nayarit 63731,* ☎ *322/66–770 or 800/995–5714,* ℻ *322/66–713.*

From Puerto Vallarta: Take coastal highway north (20 mins). Taxi, rental car available.

OAXACA

CLUB MED-HUATULCO

Sports conditioning

Not your typical Club Med, this megaresort, set between green hills and emerald waters, features a fitness center and lessons in trapeze flying. Located on the Pacific coast, 525 kilometers (325 miles) south of Acapulco, Club Med Huatulco resembles a colonial village and is part of a masterplanned tourism community.

Choose between sports and exercise to help work off the éclairs or chocolate mousse from last night's dinner. Sessions of low- and high-impact aerobics and stretching (45–60 minutes) are offered throughout the day. You have unlimited 24-hour access to three air-conditioned squash courts, tennis on 12 courts, and a practice golf course. Water-sports activities are popular, but the challenge of flying on a circus trapeze is the big attraction. Instructors strap you to safety cables and demonstrate proper form between 4 and 6 every afternoon. Those who survive stage a show Friday evening.

Opened in 1988, Huatuclco is the largest Club Med in North America. It has its own water purification system, using reverse osmosis. On twin coves, casita-style lodgings are terraced on the hillsides. Decorated with local crafts and bedspreads, each has rattan furniture and a private sea-view terrace with hammock. Children over 6 can be accommodated with their parents. There are three large freshwater swimming pools (one is Olympic-size) and a choice of four ocean beaches with gentle surf. Meals are served in five specialty dining rooms. The all-inclusive package, which is a Club Med tradition, takes the stress out of a week devoted to well-being.

FACILITIES
Exercise Equipment: Stair climbers, stationary bikes, weight-training circuit, free weights. **Services:** Massage. **Swimming:** Beaches, pools. **Classes and Programs:** Aerobics, aquaerobics, circus workshops (among them, trapeze and juggling classes), step aerobics. **Recreation:** Archery, basketball, billiards, kayaking, table tennis, sailing, snorkeling, softball, squash, tennis, volleyball, windsurfing; fishing, golf, horseback riding, scuba diving nearby. **Children's Programs:** Teen club with supervised sports for ages 12–17.

ACCOMMODATIONS
500 rooms.

DINING
3 meals, served buffet-style. Choice of 4 restaurants serving Italian, Argentine, Moroccan, seafood, Club Med salads, grilled chicken, and tropical fruits. Milk, coffee, tea, and wine (at dinner) included.

RATES AND PACKAGES
$999–$1,199 per person per week, double occupancy; includes airfare from gateway city. Add 20% for single. 25% deposit required. AE, MC, V.

DIRECTIONS
✉ *Bahia de Tangolunda, Santa Cruz, 70989, Oaxaca,* ☎ *958/10–076, 212/977–2100 or 800/258–2633 (reservations in U.S.),* FAX *958/10–101.*

From airport: Free transfers to resort. Taxi available.

QUINTANA ROO

MELIA CANCÚN RESORT & SPA

Luxury pampering

When you want it all—luxury accommodations, sybaritic spa, archaeological sites to explore, and nightlife to celebrate—this is the place to fulfill fantasies of Mexico. Set amid the strip of high-rise hotels for which Cancún is renowned, the Melia is perched on a spectacular white sand beach overlooking the turquoise waters of the Caribbean. Enjoying massages poolside is the prescription for relaxation, and outdoor treatment cabanas let you enjoy the sea air without the sun. At night, torches illuminate the cabanas, contributing to the romantic mood.

Secluded in an atrium garden, the spa provides a cool respite from the beach. Compact and coed, the 10,000 sq. ft. facility is operated by Florida-based MCM International and staffed by Mexican therapists. In addition to a well-equipped, air-conditioned fitness center, it has 11 treatment rooms; this includes one suite where couples can be massaged together. The spa also offers plenty of skin care options, with Pevonia Swiss-formula botanical products.

Open to outsiders as well as hotel guests, the spa charges a daily fee for use of the facilities; the fee is waived when you book a treatment. Because it lacks an aerobics studio, exercise classes are held on the pool terrace and in the swimming pool. At day's end try the spa's aloe spritzer—a soothing tonic, involving a body shampoo followed by a cooling aloe body gel. Other specialties are the Mayan clay mask, sea-salt loofah scrub, and aromatherapy massage.

Rising 9 stories above the spa, the hotel reflects Mayan temple design. Guest rooms are modern, however, and most have a balcony facing the sea. An attentive, bilingual staff provide information on local events and attractions. New is an underwater ride aboard a scuba vehicle named BOB (Breathing Observation Bubble), which you can try without diving certification (☎ 83–44–40). Tours to Mayan sites by boat and bus are scheduled daily.

A slender, 14-mile-long island linked by roadways to the mainland, Cancún is a Caribbean playground with few rivals. Since its founding in 1971, the town and resort have been synonymous with hedonistic holidays.

FACILITIES
Exercise Equipment: Stair climbers, stationary bikes, treadmills, weight-training equipment, free weights. **Services:** Aromatherapy massage; aloe body wrap, loofah body scrub; hydrating facial. **Swimming:** 3 pools, ocean beach. **Classes and Programs:** Exercise classes. **Recreation:** Golf, tennis, water sports. Ballet Folklorico.

ACCOMMODATIONS
413 rooms, 37 suites.

DINING
Meal plan is optional. 5 restaurants have international menus; meal plan permits special requests. Spa meals served in the Spa Caribe room. Buffet-style breakfast; poolside service for lunch. **Sample Meals:** Grilled grouper, vegetarian burrito, salads (lunch); fresh pasta, grilled chicken, vegetarian plate (dinner).

RATES AND PACKAGES
$200–$290 daily per room (single or double occupancy), suites $370–$412. Spa packages from $297 per night. 3-night/4-day package $926–$1,132 per person, double occupancy. AE, MC, V.

DIRECTIONS
✉ *Blvd. Kukulkan, Km. 16.5, Zona Hotelera, 77500 Cancún, Quintana Roo,* ☎ *988/51–114 or 800/336–3542,* FAX *988/51–263.*

From Cancún International Airport: Main road to Zona Hotelera, turn left on Boulevard Kukulkan (15 mins). Taxi service and rental cars are available.

ROYAL HIDEAWAY PLAYACAR

Luxury pampering

New on the Yucatan Peninsula, 40 miles south of Cancún, this is the first Mexican resort to feature French thalassotherapy treatments. Scheduled to open early in 1999, the Royal Hideaway beach complex includes 11 villa-type buildings, with rooms and suites on three floors. All meals, drinks, and use of sports equipment are included in the rates, however spa treatments involve an extra charge.

Designed in the style of a Spanish colonial village, the resort features four restaurants, supper club, beach club, and cigar bar. Food is available 24 hours, from room service as well as all-day service at the beach grill. For dinner, you can make reservations for Italian, Caribbean/Mexican, and Californian cuisine, or go with the nightly theme at the main restaurant.

The spa building, unavailable for a visit as this edition went to press, was designed by Florida- based consultants and the French firm Thalgo, producers of marine cosmetics used in skin and body care treatments. Their original patented concentrates of seaweed extracts come from the Atlantic waters off Brittany. Facing the Caribbean beach, Mexican therapists will administer facials, body wraps, and relaxing hydrotherapy treatments.

Recreation at the resort is nonstop, and guests have unlimited use of equipment such as kayaks and snorkeling gear. Organized activities include basketball, boccie, and croquet. Special fees apply for golf, horseback riding, scuba diving, and deep-sea fishing.

Developed and operated by Allegro Resorts, this upscale hideaway is surrounded by hotels and shopping complexes. Ferries to Cozumel dock nearby, and cruise-ship passengers come ashore here, adding traffic and crowds at certain times.

FACILITIES
Exercise Equipment: Stair climbers, stationary bikes, treadmills, weight-training circuit, free weights. **Services:** Aromatherapy massage; body wrap; hydrotherapy, Vichy shower; facial. **Swimming:** 2 outdoor pools, ocean beach. **Recreation:** Bikes, billiards, board games, chess, golf, horseback riding, shuffleboard, table tennis, tennis, water sports.

ACCOMMODATIONS
200 rooms, junior suites, presidential suites, and villas.

DINING
3 meals daily, plus drinks, at four restaurants and at the beach club. **Sample Meals:** Omelet, cold buffet with fresh fruit, cereals, yogurt, *huevos rancheros* (breakfast); grilled fish or chicken, vegetarian burger, vegetarian pizza, seafood salad (lunch); pasta, vegetarian lasagna, grilled salmon or swordfish, Ceasar salad (dinner).

RATES AND PACKAGES

3-night Royal Hideaway package $764–$1,699 per person, double occupancy; add $150 for single. 5-night package $1,147–$2,763 per person, double; add $250 for single.

DIRECTIONS

✉ *Desarollo Playacar, Lote Hotelero No. 6, 77710 Playa del Carmen, Quintana Roo,* ☎ *Reservations in U.S.: 800/858–2258 or 305/460–8961,* FAX *305/460–8964.*

From Cancún: Free transfers to and from the airport. Highway 307 south (30 min).

12 The Caribbean, the Bahamas, Bermuda

Aruba, The Bahamas, Belize, Bermuda, Bonaire, Dominican Republic, Grenada, Guadeloupe, Jamaica, Martinique, Nevis, Puerto Rico, St. Lucia, St. Martin/St. Maarten, U.S. Virgin Islands

THE CURRENT TREND in the Caribbean is to import European thalassotherapy and American fitness programs. On French St. Martin, Privilege Resort and Spa has sailing and tennis options. Spas on St. Lucia hark back to the time of King Louis XIV, who built baths in the 17th century for his troops at the hot springs. Today you can relax at the tony Jalousie Plantation or get seawater treatments at Le Sport, the fitness buff's counterpart to Club Med. For a structured course of treatments, Martinique has a dedicated thalassotherapy center.

Jamaica offers the widest range of options, from all-inclusive resorts like The Enchanted Garden and luxurious Grand Lido Sans Souci, to the rustic Milk River Bath Hotel. Negril's sports-oriented Swept Away expands the range of opportunities for combining a Caribbean holiday with a health regimen.

Bermuda vacations may include French facials and bodywork at the Sonesta Beach Resort or Cambridge Beaches, both with well-appointed spas operated by the Bersalon group. Cruise ship passengers are welcome to use the spa facilities. Hiking along the Railway Trail can complete your fitness regimen on the island.

Holistic island retreats are good healthy alternatives to resorts. The Bahamas have no-frills Sivananda Ashram on Paradise Beach in Nassau, as well as upscale Sandals Royal Bahamian Resort & Spa. St. John in the U.S. Virgin Islands is the winter outpost for the New York–based Omega Institute's programs. And in Puerto Rico, the rain forest and the ocean provide backdrops for bodywork at La Casa de Vida Natural.

Today the Caribbean spa experience is a mixture of fun and fitness. Don't expect a self-contained spa with structured programs; instead look for a resort within your budget that offers many options. You can go scuba diving at a Bonaire resort spa, take the waters on Guadeloupe at Ravine Chaude, or play golf at the Four Seasons Resort on Nevis or Hyatt Regency casino resort on Aruba.

All prices in this chapter are in U.S. dollars.

ARUBA

HYATT REGENCY ARUBA

Luxury pampering

There's action around the clock at this resort on Dutch Aruba, 15 miles off the northern coast of Venezuela. With a dry warmth cooled by the constant trade winds, the 70-square-mile island is an autonomous state within the Netherlands fold and one of the most stable, secure, and prosperous islands in the Caribbean. It has colorful Dutch colonial villages such as San Nicholas and caves with hieroglyphics, as well as glitzy casino hotels clustered on Palm Beach.

Set on a 12-acre strip of beach, two miles from the island's pastel-colored capital of Oranjestad, the Hyatt Regency Aruba resort focuses on water sports. Opened in 1990, the resort has an 8,000-square-foot three-level swimming pool with cascading waterfalls and tropical lagoons facing a powdery white sand beach. Guests can take advantage of canoe rentals, sailboats, and a 50-foot luxury catamaran for sunset cruises. There are also two dive boats that ferry guests to coral reefs and sunken shipwrecks.

The health and fitness facilities—including exercise room, coed sauna, steam room, outdoor whirlpool, and sundeck for aerobics classes—overlook the sea and are open to hotel guests without charge. For those who don't want to get wet or sweat, the gardens feature a 5,000-square-foot saltwater lagoon replete with native fish and wildlife; a poolside restaurant fashioned out of native coral stone is good for lounging.

Hike from the natural bridge (carved by the sea), on the rugged coast near Boca Prins, to Andicouri for a romantic picnic on a secluded beach surrounded by a coconut plantation. Aruba's volcanic origins are revealed at Casi Bari, a rock garden of giants, and at tall, unusual rock formations called Ayo. Hikers can enjoy panoramic, breezy views from paths cut into the rock. Arikok National Park is home to iguanas, hares, wild goats, and the rare wayacca tree.

Golfers gain a new perspective on the island's desert landscape of cacti, wind-shaped divi divi trees, and rock formations at the Tierra Del Sol Golf & Country Club. Managed by Hyatt, the 18-hole, par-71 course designed by the Trent Jones group is open to the public.

Rooms and suites are in a nine-story tower and two wings of four and five stories. The Regency Club has 27 deluxe rooms, with lounge and concierge service. All rooms have a balcony. Children under 12 stay free with parents.

Four restaurants offer heart-healthy menu options, including vegetarian dishes, fruit salad, and grilled fish. The snack bar in the health spa sells herbal teas, protein drinks, and fruit.

FACILITIES

Exercise Equipment: Rowing machine, stair climber, stationary bikes, treadmill, weight-training circuit, free weights. **Services:** Acupressure, reflexology, shiatsu, Swedish massage. **Swimming:** Ocean beach, pool. **Classes and Programs:** Carnival costume show and barbecue, casino. **Recreation:** Biking, tennis, water sports. **Children's Programs:** Camp Hyatt for ages 3–12 schedules activities including nature walks.

ACCOMMODATIONS

342 rooms, 18 suites.

DINING
All meals à la carte. Meal plan is available for an additional fee.

RATES AND PACKAGES
$205–$430 per room daily, single or double occupancy; suite $430–$1,805; Regency Club $360–$495. 1- to 3-night deposit required. AE, DC, MC, V.

DIRECTIONS
⊠ *85 Juan E. Irausquin Blvd., Aruba,* ☎ *297/86–1234 or 800/233–1234,* FAX *297/86–1682.*

From Aruba International Airport: L. G. Smith Boulevard to Palm Beach (20 mins).

THE BAHAMAS

SANDALS ROYAL BAHAMIAN RESORT AND SPA

Luxury pampering

At the newly expanded Sandals Royal Bahamian Resort there's never a bill for meals and drinks. This all-inclusive couples-only resort is a private oasis of luxury with the best little spa in the Bahamas. You can work out on a Cybex circuit in an air-conditioned penthouse with ocean views or get your feet wet trying one of the numerous water sports. Although most activities are included with the daily rate, spa services and personal trainers come at an additional cost.

Created as part of a major renovation in 1996, the spa facilities include a Vichy shower, hydrotherapy tub, coed whirlpool, sauna and steam rooms, lockers, and five treatment rooms. Among the sophisticated therapies are Kerstin Florian's kräuter herbal bath and a face masque with spirulina algae. There is a beauty salon for hair and nail care. Beachside aerobics classes are scheduled daily at no charge, but there are no indoor facilities for group exercise. Reached by elevator from the manor, the spa is steps from the beach and swimming pool. Guests from other hotels and cruise ships are accommodated on a space-available basis.

Spread over 23 acres of landscaped gardens and beach, the resort includes a sports complex with tennis, volleyball, croquet, and indoor game room. Sun worshipers can retreat to a private offshore island and enjoy nature in the buff, then cover up for lunch at a breezy bar or a dip in a freshwater pool and whirlpool. Golfers get complimentary greens fees and transportation to nearby Cable Beach Golf Club. Water sports equipment is complimentary at a dockside pavilion. Scuba trips for certified divers are included, with equipment at no charge.

Guests stay in the beachfront towers or deluxe garden cottages. Beachfront suites provide private balcony with sweeping ocean views. Honeymooners gain added privacy in garden villa suites, which have their own swimming pool. Opened in 1948 as the Balmoral Club, a private reserve for the rich and titled, the 6-story Windsor wing was joined in 1998 by a 210-room complex of luxury suites and concierge services. Facing a powdery sand beach, the twin towers frame a vast swimming pool, where waterfalls massage your shoulders, a water-mist sprays cooling vapors, and the open-air bar has swim-up service. The eight restaurants offer heart-healthy options. There is Asian-Pacific and Italian fare as well as Bahamian fare in the Cafe Goombay and gourmet cuisine in the Crystal Room, where white-glove dinner service must be reserved in advance.

FACILITIES
Exercise Equipment: Stair climbers, stationary bikes, treadmills, weight-training circuit, free weights. **Services:** Aromatherapy, reflexology, Swedish massage; anti-cellulite treatment, herbal wrap, mud bath; facial. **Swimming:** Ocean beach, pools. **Recreation:** Billiards, boating, canoeing, croquet, karaoke, kayaking, lawn chess, shuffleboard, snorkeling, tennis, volleyball, windsurfing; Bicycle rental and golf nearby. Casino and theater nearby.

ACCOMMODATIONS
196 rooms, 27 suites.

DINING

3 meals daily in 6 restaurants, plus unlimited snacks, fruit and juice, and alcoholic beverages. **Sample Meals:** Conch fritters, seafood salad, grilled grouper (lunch); mousse of Bahamian conch and scallops baked in saffron sauce, grouper in pastry with sabayon sauce, roasted rack of lamb with herbs (dinner).

RATES AND PACKAGES

$418–$2,250 daily per person, double occupancy. 7-night package $2,740–$3,050 per person, double. 2-night minimum stay. $400 deposit required. AE, DC, MC, V.

DIRECTIONS

✉ Box C.B. 13005, Cable Beach, Nassau, Bahamas, ☎ 242/327–6400 or 800/726–3257, ℻ 242/327–1894.

From Nassau International Airport: Coastal road (10 mins).

SIVANANDA ASHRAM YOGA RETREAT

Holistic health

Before long, even those out of shape are doing shoulder stands at this ashram on one of the best-known beaches in the Bahamas. Secluded in a grove of pines and palm trees, the Sivananda Ashram attracts an eclectic group of yoga devotees. Equal parts spiritual retreat and tropical holiday, the ashram operates educational programs that are practical and affordable. Based on the teachings of Swami Vishnu Devananda, the yogic discipline and vegetarian diet here are identical to Sivananda ashrams in Canada, New York, and California. But the sunny climate and beach make this one of the best bargains anywhere. People come here to recuperate from job burnout or to heal after surgery.

The regimen is intensive, and attendance at classes and meditations is mandatory for all guests. Mornings begin at 6 with a session of yogic exercises, or asanas, to stretch and invigorate the body. Chanting sessions are held twice daily, at 8 AM and 4 PM, although attendance is not strictly enforced. Brunch is served at 10, then you are free to enjoy the beach or a relaxing massage.

Located on the northern tip of a public beach, the retreat is shaded by casuarina trees and palms, which lend privacy from neighbors at Club Med. Although there are big luxury hotels and casinos a short walk away, the environment here is suffused with a mystical quality. The main house, once the retreat of a wealthy family and leased since 1967 to the Sivananda group in appreciation for healing services, might have sunk into the sand long ago without the volunteer labor of the retreat members.

Lodging is in dormitories and cabins furnished with bare essentials. Each room has 1–4 beds; linens and towels are provided. There are communal shower, toilet, and laundry facilities. Many guests prefer to bring their own tent and camp among the tropical shrubbery. You may arrive any day; average stay is two weeks. Transportation to city docks is provided by the ashram's boat.

Meals are a communal affair, with buffets of steamed vegetables, lentils, and salads—many of which are bland, because no spices, onion, or garlic are used. There is an organic herb and vegetable garden. Coconuts come gratis from the palm trees that shelter the 4½-acre compound. For snacks and sweets, a canteen is tucked into a building near the communal laundry and shower facilities. After meals, guests wash their own plates and utensils and dry them on open-air racks. There's no air-conditioning at this retreat, but a water filtration system provides plenty of cool, chemical-free drinking water.

FACILITIES

Services: Reflexology, shiatsu massage. **Swimming:** Ocean beach. **Classes and Programs:** Concerts, personal counseling, workshops in Vedata culture and philosophy. **Recreation:** Tennis, volleyball, walking trails. **Children's Programs:** Yoga instruction for children.

ACCOMMODATIONS

103 beds in dormitory rooms and cabins with shared baths, 50 campsites.

DINING

2 lacto-vegetarian buffet meals daily. No fish, meat, fowl, eggs, or coffee served. **Sample Meals:** Lentil loaf, spinach, wheat bread (lunch); tofu stir-fry with rice, steamed vegetables, green salad, dal, basmati rice, greens (dinner).

RATES AND PACKAGES

$55–$70 daily per person in dormitory rooms shared by 2–6 persons. Single cabin $85–$110, semi-private room $60–$90 per person. Tent space $50–$64 daily per person. 1-night deposit required. MC, V.

DIRECTIONS

✉ *Box N7550, Paradise Island, Nassau, Bahamas,* ☎ *242/363–2902 or 800/783–9642,* FAX *242/363–3783.*

From Nassau International Airport: Shared taxi van to Mermaid Marina at Bay and Deveaux streets. Shuttle service by Ashram boat operates on schedule.

BELIZE

MARUBA RESORT & JUNGLE SPA

Holistic health
Luxury pampering

Set amid 4,000 acres of rain forest, gardens, and orchards, the Maruba Resort & Jungle Spa provides a relaxing, romantic, natural environment. Unscheduled activities depend on the weather and what guests want to do. Discuss your interests with a resort representative before you book to be sure that this resort can fullfill your ideas of a jungle adventure.

Picking ingredients right off the trees, owner Franziska Nicholson and her brother Nicky brew medicinal tea and blend cream for skin care. That includes an anti-itch lotion, a mix of antiseptic allspice and bark from the gumbolimbo tree, to alleviate the pain of sunburn and insect bites. Sand scrubs, sea sulfur clay body packs, and a Mayan herbal wrap reduce stress and muscle fatigue while improving circulation and cleansing the skin.

Mornings are devoted to jungle safaris, by boat, bike, on horseback, or on foot. For the already fit, there is a 24-mile trek to Altun Ha, a Mayan archaeological site. Divers can take an excursion that includes use of scuba equipment at a nearby beach. Hiking with an experienced herbalist introduces you to medicinal uses of local indigenous plants. In the jungle you may encounter howler monkeys, crocodile, jabiru stork, and perhaps a rare keel billed toucan. Another tour takes you by boat to spectacular ruins at Lamnai, inhabited over 3,000 years ago.

A pre-breakfast walk and stretch pumps up your metabolism and gets the kinks out. Included in the daily program are scheduled exercise sessions set to jungle rhythms, a punta rock low-impact cardiovascular workout, and aquaerobics to hip-hop and rock. One-on-one training is available for an additional fee. Be aware that services are not always available as advertised.

The fusion of Mayan, Creole, and African designs in the architecture and decor is dramatic. Most rooms have thatched roofs, with palms or other plants growing inside, and vines winding around fixtures. Hammocks swing lazily amid the cabanas, and you can watch the birds without disturbing their activities. From the Jungle Suite, set high above the trees, the view takes in pineapple fields and coconut palms surrounding the compound.

With temperatures between 80°F and 90°F, it is easy to work up a sweat. The open-air spa provides a variety of one- to five-night packages; some include fishing and bird-watching, others focus on weight control and rejuvenation. Rooms and suites are in cabanas constructed of indigenous materials; each has a ceiling fan, but air-conditioning is available for a $10 daily charge in most rooms. There are no TVs or telephones. Meal plans include breakfast only, breakfast and dinner, or three meals daily. Notable are the five-course dinners, with fresh seafood ranging from conch to lobster, as well as game and vegetables raised right on the property.

After a day trekking in the rain forest, a soak in the rock-walled waterfall swimming pool is the preferred cool-down. At night, a Japanese hot tub makes stargazing an unforgettable experience. The forest comes alive with animal sounds—the rasp and hoot of howler monkeys, the endless percussion of insects—as you dine by candlelight.

FACILITIES

Exercise Equipment: Free weights. **Services:** Aromatherapy, therapeutic massage; body scrub, clay pack, herbal wrap, mineral bath, moor mud pack, sea sulfur pack, seaweed wrap; bee-honey facial treatment, facial. **Swimming:** Outdoor pool. **Classes and Programs:** Personal training. **Recreation:** Biking, bird watching, boating, canoeing, fishing, hiking, horseback riding; snorkling and scuba diving nearby..

ACCOMMODATIONS

8 rooms, 9 suites.

DINING

3 meals daily included in spa packages. **Sample Meals:** Tostada with grilled chicken, smoked-fish salad, venison sandwich, lobster salad (lunch); red snapper, pasta with tomato-papaya sauce, grilled shrimp with anise-seed rice (dinner).

RATES AND PACKAGES

$110–$157 daily single, $130–$223 for 2 persons, double occupancy; suites $150–$280 per person, single or double. 1-night spa package $310 single, $280 per person, double; 2-night Rejuvenation package $470 single, $410 double; 5-night package $1,300 single, $1,153 double; 26-day weight control program $4,147 single or double. Day Spa package with lunch $125–$135. 1-night deposit required. AE, MC, V.

DIRECTIONS

⊠ *40½ Old Northern Hwy., Maskall Village,* ☎ *501/3–22199; Reservations:* ⊠ *Box 300703, Houston, TX 77230,* ☎ *713/799–2031 or 800/627–8227,* FAX *713/795–8573.*

From Godson International Airport: Old Northern Highway to Maskall Village (45 mins). The resort provides transfers three times daily for arriving and departing guests ($50 round-trip).

BERMUDA

CAMBRIDGE BEACHES

Luxury pampering

The island's only cottage colony with a full-service spa, Cambridge Beaches offers European treatments not usually found at American spas. Programs range from a one-day Spa Retreat to week-long packages that focus on weight management, body toning, and anti-stress treatments. Nutrition and fitness consultations are included in some packages, and all include spa gratuities.

Cathiodermie facials by Guinot of Paris incorporate gentle stimulation of skin tissue with electronic rollers that cause a tingling sensation. Using a thermal clay mask, the licensed aesthetician dissolves impurities and toxins, leaving the tissue rehydrated and rejuvenated. Ionithermie treatments firm and tone slack skin and help rid the body of cellulite. Using galvanic current, the Ionithermie machine is attached to face, body, or bust. Treatments over a period of several days are said to shed inches. This can be combined with bodywraps using seaweed, plant extracts, and other natural ingredients.

Sunlight dapples the indoor swimming pools at the Ocean Spa, which resembles a traditional Bermudian cottage, with pink stucco walls and a whitewashed roof, ridged to collect rainwater. The spa building has a beauty salon and juice bar, as well as a lap pool. There is also a hydrotherapy pool equipped with underwater jets that create a current to enhance the benefits of swimming. Guests relax on the pool terrace, where refreshments can be served. The glass dome that covers the pools is open during warm months.

Accommodations are in cottage rooms and suites with traditional furnishings. Most have a whirlpool bath. TV is not included, but sets can be rented. A 200-year-old house serves as social center, restaurant, and pub. Guests gather here for tea and formal dining (which means jacket and tie for men). A social hostess introduces newcomers to managing director Michael J. Winfield, who is the very picture of a proper Bermudian in gray flannel shorts and blue blazer.

A Cambridge Beaches "Classic Spa Day" might start with a consultation and computerized body-fat analysis, followed by exercise, sauna, and massage. A half-day program for men includes massage, Cathiodermie facial for rough skin, and Redken hair treatment. The locker room has a coed sauna, steam bath, and whirlpool; robes and toiletries are provided. Both full-day and half-day packages include lunch on a bayside terrace.

The four-day winter escape package (mid-Nov.–Apr.) can be customized to meet your needs. Included are accommodations with water views, afternoon tea, and full breakfast and dinner daily, with the option of having spa cuisine cooked to order. Evenings are dress-up occasions, with music and often dancing outdoors on a terrace that overlooks Cambridge's private marina on Somerset Long Bay. Casual elegance sets the style here, with an international mix of guests, many of whom return every year.

Set on a 25-acre peninsula, with five private coves on the ocean side and a bayside marina, Cambridge Beaches is in Somerset, a tiny parish of shady lanes and old homes, ideal for walks, jogging, and hikes. A moped can be rented and taken aboard a ferry to St. George's, at the eastern end of the island, via Hamilton, where the best shops and pubs are located. A short hike from Cambridge Beaches brings you to Scaur Hill Fort, built in the 1870s to protect the Royal Naval Dockyard. Now it's a 22-acre park with breathtaking views of the Great Sound and its armada of sailboats. Spend a day at the restored Dockyard complex, a maritime museum and crafts center, with several pleasant places to dine. Hikers and bikers can use the Railway Trail, a secluded 18-mile track that runs toward Southampton along the route of the old Bermuda Railway, past beautiful estates, the Lantana Cottages (where you can dine on an exchange plan with Cambridge Beaches), and the Somerset Squire pub.

The 21-square-mile island is divided into nine geographical divisions, called parishes, served by public bus. With nearly 150 islands, Bermuda has numerous bridges, as well as ferry services. The town of St. George, founded in 1612 on the eastern tip of the island, retains many quaint features of 17th-century community life. The city of Hamilton, capital of Bermuda since 1815, offers the new Underwater Exploration Institute, where visitors do a simulated dive, tour displays of exotic seashells, and dine on seafood at an upscale waterside restaurant. You can charter a sailboat or go snorkeling at the Royal Naval Dockyard, which has an underwater trail for novice snorkelers.

Learn about the island ecology at Bermuda Botanical Gardens, 36 acres of subtropical groves and formal gardens, including an orchid house and the remarkable Garden for the Blind, where all the plants are aromatic. Traversing the island from east to west is a swath of green parks, 79 nature preserves linked to beaches of dazzling pink sand created by wind and surf grinding tiny particles of coral from the surrounding reefs.

Passionate about cricket, Bermudians gather for matches every Sunday during the summer. Kite-flying matches are held at Easter time. There are eight British-style golf courses. Driving is British-style, too, with traffic staying on the left side of the road.

FACILITIES
Exercise Equipment: Stair climbers, stationary bikes, treadmill, weight-training circuit, free weights. **Services:** Aromatherapy, reflexology, Reiki, sports, Swedish massage; G5 toning, paraffin body wraps, salt-glow polish, seaweed wrap; facials. **Swimming:** Indoor and outdoor pools, 5 beaches. **Classes and Programs:** Computerized body-fat analysis, fitness consultation, nutrition consultation. **Recreation:** Bike rental, boating, canoeing, croquet, kayaking, moped rental, snorkeling, tennis, windsurfing; golf nearby. Cruises, dancing, live entertainment.

ACCOMMODATIONS
69 rooms, 19 suites.

DINING
Breakfast, dinner, and tea included in daily rate. Breakfast is served buffet-style. **Sample Meals:** Pesto pasta with shrimp and lemon, fish chowder, chicken–macadamia nut salad (lunch); seafood jambalaya, chicken breast with couscous, linguini with shrimp (dinner).

RATES AND PACKAGES
Lodging $365–$595 daily for 2 persons, double occupancy. 2-night deposit required. At press time new package rates were not available. No credit cards.

DIRECTIONS
✉ *30 Kings Point Rd., Sandys MA 02, Bermuda,* ☎ *441/234–0331 or 800/468–7300,* ℻ *441/234–3352.*

From Hamilton: Complimentary ferry 3 times per week, with scheduled service to Watford Bridge (20 mins). Taxi available; no rental cars.

SONESTA BEACH RESORT

Luxury pampering

You can bring the kids to this big beach resort and give yourself a spa break. While youngsters enjoy complimentary activities at the Kids Corner summer program (June 15–Labor Day), adults can work out at the Bersalon Spa.

Packing an impressive array of treatments and exercise equipment in minimal space, this spa is more an amenity than a full-service facility. Still, you can drop in between business meetings or after a round of golf or plan a comprehensive schedule of treatments and exercise classes for three to seven days. The spa has 12 treatment rooms, an aerobics studio, strength-training and cardiovascular room, and well-equipped lounges for men and women. Minimum age in the spa is 18.

Aerobics classes are either moderate or vigorous, plotted over 30- or 40-minute periods, alternating active and passive exercise with relaxing stretches. You can select from early morning walks (moderate), circuit training (vigorous), workouts in the water, and yoga. Morning yoga sessions are held on the lawn overlooking the sea. One of the special features of the resort's spa packages is a low rate for three persons sharing one of the big oceanfront bedrooms.

If you simply want to be pampered and left alone to swim or shop, there are four-day spa sampler packages. Services are similar to Cambridge Beaches, and you may want to schedule some treatments at that sister spa. Scheduled throughout the day, group exercise routines and one-on-one sessions with a personal trainer can be included in a program tailored to your interests and fitness level. Daily walks on the beach and stretch classes are open to all guests at the resort for a fee of $10 per session. Or you can pay a daily facility charge ($12) to use the whirlpool baths, Finnish sauna, Turkish steam bath, and exercise equipment.

Set on a 25-acre peninsula, the resort has three beaches with gentle surf, tennis courts, and water sports. For swimmers, the freshwater swimming pool has an all-weather glass dome enclosure.

Sea, sky, flowering bougainvillea, and the pinkest sand you've ever seen: that's what makes a Bermuda vacation. The Sonesta Resort is located right in the middle of the South Shore beaches, a privileged area close to island attractions yet secluded and peaceful. The guest rooms and Bay Wing suites are in a six-story hotel, with ocean and bay views. Rooms have a balcony or patio. Spacious split-level units have a sitting area and dressing room, modern rattan furniture, and floor-to-ceiling windows. Guest rooms facing the sea underwent a major makeover in 1996.

While it is a foreign destination, 650 miles east of North Carolina, Bermuda enjoys a balmy, subtropical climate. Britain's oldest and only self-governing colony has law courts and museums in Hamilton, the island capital. Shopping along Bay Street, where the big cruise ships dock, is pegged to the U.S. dollar, but Bermudian tradition is everywhere.

FACILITIES
Exercise Equipment: Stair climbers, stationary bikes, treadmills, weight-training circuit, free weights. **Services:** Aromatherapy, G5 mechanical, reflexology, sports, Swedish massage; herbal wrap, loofah body scrub; facial. **Swimming:** Indoor and outdoor pools, ocean beaches. **Classes and Programs:** Aerobics and stretch class, personal training, snorkeling instruction, tennis lessons. **Recreation:** Badminton, croquet, horse-and-buggy rides, scuba diving, shuffleboard, table tennis, tennis, volleyball,

windsurfing; bicycle rental, golf, horseback riding nearby. Live entertainment. **Children's Programs:** Just Us Kids activities for ages 3–12.

ACCOMMODATIONS
403 rooms, suites, split-level units.

DINING
Breakfast and dinner daily included in some packages. 2 juice breaks are included in the daily program. Lunch served à la carte at the SeaGrape and Boat Bay Club. **Sample Meals:** Vegetarian quesadillas, avocado sandwich with tomato and cheese (lunch); grilled swordfish, vegetarian lasagna, vegetables skewers with sea scallops (dinner).

RATES AND PACKAGES
$240–$390 daily per room, $350–$1,050 suites. 4-day/3-night Spa Sampler package $810–$1,950 single or double occupancy. 5-day/4-night Eurospa Classic package $1,450–$2,295 per person, double, $2,390–$3,270 single. 2-night deposit required. AE, DC, MC, V.

DIRECTIONS
✉ *Box HM 1070, Shore Rd., Southampton, Bermuda SN02,* ☎ *441/238–8122 or 800/766–3782,* ℻ *441/238–8463.*

From Bermuda International Airport: Take North Shore Road to South Road (45 min). Moped available, no rental cars.

BONAIRE

HARBOUR VILLAGE BEACH RESORT

Luxury pampering

Designed to complement an active diving and snorkeling program, the spa at Harbour Village Resort is a cool and calm retreat from the beach scene. This is the best place to experience treatments with Bonaire sea salts, used for body polishing and baths. Water attractions include an outdoor Roman-style step-down pool for aerobics and toning classes, as well as a tranquil lounging pool into which cascades refreshing desalinated water. Finishing touches at the beauty salon include haircut, manicure, and pedicure.

Bonairian fitness programs begin with exercise on the beach and in the water. After a day of diving, you can retreat to the spa for a sports massage, body exfoliation, and the calming effects of breathing class. Relaxation techniques are taught by spa staff members, who also conduct sessions of tai chi. Mornings they lead nature hikes or a 4-mile bike ride along the island's rugged but beautiful coastline to cliffs called 1,000 steps. Welcome to Bonaire's natural StairMaster.

The two-story spa building has an aerobics studio with specially designed sprung floor, workout room with cardiovascular and weight-training equipment, and café. Minimum age in the spa is 14. Treatments are in nine air-conditioned and windowed rooms, or outdoors in massage cabanas. Try the sea-accented La Mer products from France, used in facials and aromatherapy massage. Signature treatments include a seaweed masque, body wrap, and botanical soak.

Opened in 1995, the red-tile-roofed facility fits into the Dutch-Caribbean style of the resort villas. On a quarter-mile stretch of white sand beach, Harbour Village has a 60-slip marina, tennis courts with night lighting, and a full-service dive shop.

While the landscape is arid, underwater spectacle is the big draw. The coral reef, marine life, and more than 200 species of fish visible beneath the water's surface are endlessly fascinating. A structured snorkeling program introduced by the island government in cooperation with *Skin Diver* magazine provides in-depth looks at prime sites. Established in 1979 to safeguard these treasures, Bonaire National Park is much like a museum, with guides and information to round-out the experience as you float peacefully or explore with scuba equipment. The trails start right at the resort beach, and dive boat trips are scheduled daily.

The spa café sells fruit juices, shakes, and grilled seafood, and a spa menu is available in the resort's restaurant. Rooms and suites are in two-story villas clustered around courtyards and on a private beach. Ground-floor lanai suites have a veranda facing the beach. Furnished with rattan seating, all rooms have ceiling fans as well as air-conditioning.

FACILITIES
Exercise Equipment: Rowing machines, stair climbers, stationary bikes, treadmills, weight-training circuit. **Services:** Aromatherapy, reflexology, shiatsu, sports massage; body polish, sea salt exfoliation; hydrotherapy bath; facial. **Swimming:** Pool, ocean beach. **Recreation:** Deep-sea fishing, diving, sailing, snorkeling, tennis; bike rental, horseback riding nearby.

ACCOMMODATIONS
60 rooms, 18 suites.

DINING

All meals à la carte. 4 restaurants serve spa items. **Sample Meals:** Smoked turkey sandwich, charbroiled catch of the day (lunch); cannelloni, poached wahoo fish, braised chicken (dinner).

RATES AND PACKAGES

$275–$405 daily per room for one or two persons, suites $445–$705. 7-night spa package program $2,078–$2,401 single, $1,398–$1,568 double. Half-day spa program package $132, including facility fee. AE, D, MC, V.

DIRECTIONS

✉ *Box 312, Kralendijk, Bonaire, Netherlands Antilles,* ☎ *5997–7500,* FAX *5997–7507. Reservations:* ☎ *305/567–9509 or 800/424–0004,* FAX *305/567–9659.*

From airport: Follow road east out of airport (to the right) to its end at the stadium in Kralendijk. Turn north (left) at the stadium and continue about 3 mi, following "Hotels" signs. Free transfers are provided to and from the airport; taxis and rental cars are available at the airport (10 min).

DOMINICAN REPUBLIC

RENAISSANCE JARAGUA HOTEL

Luxury pampering

The new and the old meet on Santo Domingo's Avenida George Washington, a lively strip of hotels, restaurants, and shops known as the Malecon. There is no beach here, but guests at Renaissance Jaragua Hotel & Casino hardly notice; with an oversize swimming pool surrounded by tropical gardens, Scandinavian saunas, Turkish steam bath, Roman whirlpool, and cold plunge, the hotel's Wellness Place spa is an ideal escape from the sun.

At the freestanding fitness facility, all marble and glass, you can work out on exercise equipment, join a class in the aerobics studio, or try a scheduled aquacize class in the Olympic-size swimming pool.

Pampering services come in several packages or à la carte. You can get an herbal wrap, a body scrub, a facial, or a massage. The daily entrance fee of $10 is waived when you book a massage. With this come robe, slippers, and snacks of fresh fruit and juices throughout the day.

Secluded on 14½ palm-fringed acres, the hotel has a tennis stadium with four clay courts and spectator seating. During the day this facility can be used by spa guests free of charge. From your room it's a pleasant walk or jog through the garden and alongside the lagoon to the spa. Not for a serious spa buff, this is a place to relax and join the merengue beat.

The 10-story hotel and 2-story wing underwent a recent facelift, and all rooms have the standard modern look of Renaissance resorts by Marriott. Dining options range from a New York deli to Italian pizzeria, with a formal dining room that features seafood with a Latin accent. The closest beaches are about an hour up the coast, at Boca Chica. Upscale accommodations and golf at the Casa de Campo resort are worth an overnight visit.

The hemisphere's oldest city, Santo Domingo combines Spanish culture with African rhythms and has a spirit that's pure Caribbean. Stroll the hemisphere's oldest street, Calle las Damas, and visit the cathedral where Columbus is said to have been buried. Nearby, the Alcazar de Colon regally re-creates the 16th-century palace built for the discoverer's son, Diego Columbus.

FACILITIES
Exercise Equipment: Rowing machine, stationary bikes, treadmills, weight-training circuit, free weights. **Services:** Reflexology, Swedish massage; herbal wrap, salt-glow body scrub; facial. **Swimming:** Outdoor pool. **Classes and Programs:** Aerobics, aquacize. **Recreation:** Tennis (4 courts). Casino theater, concerts and opera at National Theater.

ACCOMMODATIONS
292 rooms, 6 suites.

DINING
All meals à la carte. Choice of heart-healthy options at 3 international restaurants. **Sample Meals:** Rice and beans, fruit plate, spinach salad (lunch); char-broiled or grilled steak on a spit, stir-fry of chinese vegetables, fresh homemade pasta and shrimp (dinner).

RATES AND PACKAGES
$115–$145 daily for 2 persons; 1- and 2-bedroom suites $225–$700 for 2 persons. 1-night deposit required. AE, DC, MC, V.

DIRECTIONS
✉ *367 George Washington Ave., Santo Domingo, Dominican Republic,* ☎ *809/221–2222 or 800/468–3571,* 𝔽𝔸𝕏 *809/686–0528.*

From Las Americas Airport: By taxi (35 mins). Public bus, rental car available.

GRENADA

LASOURCE

Luxury pampering

Daily treatments come with the all-inclusive package at LaSource, but don't expect a structured program. You can set your own schedule for group exercise. Aerobics classes (one hour) include step, stretch and tone, and floor exercise with reggae music. There are daily sessions of yoga, meditation, and tai chi, and a group jog takes place on the beach each morning. Join the optional daily hike at 7 AM to explore the island, then relax in the coed sauna and outdoor whirlpool.

Like its sister resort on St. Lucia (LeSport), LaSource offers a "Body Holiday" package, with accommodations, spa cuisine, and a private nine-hole golf course to enjoy on an unlimited basis. Once you arrive you can forget about money matters; even wine and bottled waters are included in the package, and tipping is not permitted.

Getting appointments for spa services is another matter. Sign up at the tiny fitness facility as soon as you arrive, as demand sometimes exceeds capacity. Treatment rooms in The Oasis Spa are steps from the beach, but thalassotherapy seaweed body wraps and aromatherapy massage with essential oils of herbs and flowers involve products imported from France. After an examination by the resort's nurse, you are given complimentary treatments. Only one session per day comes with your package, but additional services may be charged to your account, based on availability. Minimum age in the spa is 15.

Secluded amid 40 acres of lush gardens on Grenada's southwestern coast, the resort's accommodations evoke the style of a Victorian-era West Indian village. The elegant colonial architecture features handcrafted wooden trellises and high-ceiling rooms, some of them beamed. Marble floors, Bokhara rugs, and chenille bedspreads add to the charm, as do custom-carved four-poster beds, doors, and shutters. Some rooms have terra-cotta tile balconies. Suites come with a bay window and pullout sofa bed. There are no TVs here. Wood, including mahogany and teak imported from Venezuela, is used extensively in several four-story buildings on the grounds.

Plantations on the 120-square-mile island produce spices that season your meals and drinks. The aroma of nutmeg, cinnamon, and cocoa fills the air as you hike or drive along the coast. The main port, airport, and administrative center are at St. George's, a vibrant town that can be toured on foot in several hours. At the west end of the Carenage docks, the Grenada National Museum offers a look at past and recent history. Traces of the military intervention by the U.S. in 1983 remain, but the island today is stable and independent.

FACILITIES

Exercise Equipment: Rowing machines, stair climber, stationary bikes, weight-training circuit, free weights. **Services:** Aromatherapy, reflexology massage; thalassotherapy seaweed body wrap, loofah salt rub; facial. **Swimming:** Ocean beaches, pools. **Classes and Programs:** Classes in couples massage, jazz warm-up, floor exercise with reggae, stress management. Yoga, aerobics, meditatio, stretch and tone, tai chi. **Recreation:** Archery, fencing, golf (9 holes), scuba diving, snorkeling, table tennis, tennis, volleyball, water sports. Dancing with live music.

ACCOMMODATIONS
91 rooms, 9 suites.

DINING
3 meals and tea daily. Breakfast is served buffet-style. Lunch and dinner are offered at the Terrace Restaurant, and a light dinner menu is served at the Great House. **Sample Meals:** Cabbage roll of risotto, local vegetables in callaloo puree (lunch); spicy crab cakes, cassoulet of duck and sausage with white haricot beans, char-grilled marlin with eggplant caviar (dinner).

RATES AND PACKAGES
Daily package $210–$315 per person, double occupancy. Single supplement $65 per night. AE, MC, V.

DIRECTIONS
✉ *Box 852, St. George's, Grenada, West Indies,* ☎ *473/444–2556 or 800/544–2883,* FAX *473/444–2561.*

From Point Salines International Airport: Transfers provided (5 mins). Taxi, rental car available.

GUADELOUPE

CENTRE DE THALASSOTHÉRAPIE MANIOUKANI

Medical wellness
Mineral springs

Set on a hillside overlooking the sea, Centre de Thalassothérapie Manioukani uses fresh seawater in its baths and in an exercise pool where physical fitness classes are held every morning. The heated seawater is said to improve circulation in your legs, and to help persons suffering from rheumatism. Also offered are postnatal and slimming programs.

Opened in 1995, this attractive building is owned and operated by medical specialists Drs. Pierre and Cordinne Saint-Luce. Consultation with a physiologist, chiropractor, and dietitian can be included in a program tailored to your needs. Facilities include hydromassage tubs, nasal spray, and a hammam (steam room).

Aches and pains are soaked away in a huge pool filled daily with fresh seawater. Exercise sessions in the water are provided by a personal trainer. Stressed-out visitors can simply come for a massage, then relax in the solarium overlooking sailboats in the marina. Serious muscular problems are treated in a hydromassage tub of seawater and with a body masque of Phytomer seaweed products imported from France.

Guadeloupe moves to a creole beat, part French, part African. Spend mornings swimming in the sea off black sand beaches, or hike to hot thermal springs left by once active volcanoes. The trails on La Soufrière bear witness to the island's still puffing volcanic forces.

Lodging is not available at Manioukani, but there are excellent accommodations nearby. Free transportation is provided for guests booking an overnight package at Hotel Saint-Georges in the nearby town of Saint-Claude. The 40-room Saint-Georges has a restaurant and bar, as well as its own pool and fitness center. Also within walking distance of the Manioukani are the elegant cottages of Le Jardin Malanga set in tropical gardens at L'Hermitage.

Flexible scheduling is a big advantage at Manioukani. Book a one-day package or multi-day program, with or without meals and accommodations. Options include dietetic meals, physical fitness training, and simply relaxation. Concentrated programs (*cures*) for six days address rheumatism, arthritis, circulatory problems, skin care, and slimming.

FACILITIES
Services: Algae wrap, herbal bath, hydromassage, thalassotherapy, Vichy shower. **Swimming:** Pools. **Classes and Programs:** Aquaerobics, personal training.

ACCOMMODATIONS
Nearby hotels include:

Hotel Saint-Georges, Rue Gratien Parize, 97120 Saint-Claude, Guadeloupe, ☎ 590/80–10–10, ℻ 590/80–30–50.

Le Jardin Malanga, L'Hermitage, 97114 Trois-Rivières, Guadeloupe, ☎ 590/92–67–57, ℻ 590/92–67–58.

DINING
No meal plan.

RATES AND PACKAGES
About $27 per spa treatment, $46 for 2 treatments. 2-day weekend package $133 without lodging. 6-day dietetic program $487 per person, plus $816–$1684 per person, double accommodations with meals. 12-day fitness program $912 per person, plus $1492–$3368 per person, double accommodations with meals. $199 deposit required. No credit cards.

DIRECTIONS
✉ *Marina Rivière-Sens, 97113 Gourbeyre, Guadeloupe,* ☎ *590/99–02–02,* FAX *590/81–65–23.*

From Pôle Caraïbes International Airport: The Centre Manioukani is about 50 min from the airport. Free transfers are offered at most area hotels. Taxis and rental cars are available at the airport.

ESPACE SANTÉ DE RAVINE CHAUDE

Mineral springs

Christopher Columbus saw the volcano La Soufrière erupting when he stepped ashore November 4, 1493, at Sainte-Marie, a fishing village along the road to Guadeloupe's principal city, Pointe-à-Pitre. Although La Soufrière is no longer active, the volcanic waters are now tapped for therapeutic use.

Today Pointe-à-Pitre bustles with its port, shopping centers, and marinas. On market days the stalls are filled with herb sellers hawking natural seasonings and medicines: *matriquin, Marie-Perrine, zhébe-gras, fleupapillon, bois-de-l'homme, bonnet-carré,* and the like. All the tastes and stimulations of the Creole flavorings and remedies are on sale alongside modern pharmacies and boutiques laden with Parisian fashions. In August it all comes together in honor of St. Laurent, patron saint of cooks, in La Fête de Cuisinières.

As an overseas department of France (not a colony or an independent country), Guadeloupe offers its citizens all the benefits of the mother country, including health insurance coverage for the cost of spa therapy. The spa complex at Ravine Chaude, which opened in 1992, provides a wide range of treatments and pools. You can receive both thalassotherapy and thermal water therapies on a par with those available at resorts in Brittany and the French Riviera.

The facilities at Ravine Chaude include baths and two swimming pools filled with thermal water, three restaurants, and a solarium. A medical doctor is on staff to consult with visitors on treatments. Therapies for rheumatism and stress relief are structured as a "cure" over several days. Postnatal care also is provided through underwater massage, aromatherapy, and pressotherapy. Open daily from 10 AM to 11 PM, the spa charges an admission fee, and treatments are priced individually or in a package. Though a weekend spa package including lodging and meals is available, there are no hotel facilities on the premises. Visitors generally arrange for nearby lodging, which ranges from deluxe to inexpensive.

FACILITIES
Services: Deep-tissue massage; algae wrap, aromatherapy bath, hydromassage, mud wrap, pressotherapy; thalassotherapy, underwater massage, Vichy shower. **Swimming:** Pools. **Classes and Programs:** Medical consultation. **Recreation:** Hiking nearby.

ACCOMMODATIONS

Available nearby at Auberge de la Distillerie (☎ 590/94–25–91), Créol'inn Hotel (☎ 590/94–19–28), Les Gîtes La Roseraie (☎ 590/25–61–31), and Le Relais des Sources (☎ 590/25–61–04).

DINING

No meal plan. Le Bain Bleu restaurant on the premises; others minutes from the Espace Santé. Most area restaurants serve menus of creole cuisine based on fresh native fish and produce.

RATES AND PACKAGES

Daily pool fee: about $4. Costs of treatments range from $25 for a mud wrap to $47 for a complete facial treatment. Treatment packages are available for $42 for a mud wrap and thermal bath to $83 for your choice of 4 treatments plus lunch. A weekend spa package including meals, 4 treatments, and 1 night of lodging costs $233.

DIRECTIONS

✉ *Centre Thermale René Toribio, Ravine Chaude, 97129 Le Lamentin, Guadeloupe,* ☎ *590/25–75–92;* FAX *590/25–76–28.*

From Pôle Caraïbes International Airport: Espace Santé de Ravine Chaude is about 20 from the airport. Taxis and rental cars are available.

JAMAICA

BATH FOUNTAIN HOTEL

Mineral springs

You have to get off the beaten track to explore some of the most scenic areas of the hilly island of Jamaica. In addition to breathtaking vistas there are botanical gardens, a bird sanctuary, and mineral springs that have been attracting cure seekers for nearly two centuries.

Legend holds that an African slave, wounded in an uprising, was healed by bathing in pools of water fed by hot springs located high in the lush valleys between Kingston and Port Antonio. English plantation owners seeking respite from the coastal heat spread the word. By the beginning of the 18th century there was a spa hotel, church, and botanical garden for cultivation of medicinal herbs in the town of Bath. What remains today is primitive, nothing like its Georgian namesake in England. The waters, however, still gush forth in a setting of tropical splendor enjoyed by hill people and visitors.

From the town, a narrow road cuts through fern gullies alongside the Sulphur River to reach Bath Fountain Hotel. Cut into rocks beneath the hotel are private chambers where you can soak in the sulfurous warm water.

The hotel's 17 guest rooms are airy and simply furnished; none has air-conditioning. Two rooms have a balcony. Meals are prepared to order in the public dining room (no credit cards).

RATES AND PACKAGES
$30 daily with shared bath, $40 with private bath, for 2 persons.

DIRECTIONS
✉ *Bath Post Office, St. Thomas Parish, Jamaica,* ☎ FAX *876/982–8410.*

From Norman Manley International Airport, Kingston: Take St. Thomas Road from the left side of the roundabout near the Airport exit. Follow this road east through Kingston for about 48 mi to the gas station at Port Morant. Turn left at the the gas station and follow signs to Bath and the hotel.

THE ENCHANTED GARDEN

Luxury pampering

Designed as an alternative to beach resorts, The Enchanted Garden comprises 20 acres of rain forest, botanical gardens, waterfalls, and rolling lawns. Here you can take a class in couples massage, float in a natural pool beneath a cascade, or bliss out in one of the private garden nooks where a masseur or masseuse awaits with aromatherapy.

The spa is a cheerful, air-conditioned hideaway. Emphasis is on all things natural, from facials with fresh-cut aloe plants to aromatherapy with jasmine oils straight from the garden. More than 50 essential oils are available, custom-mixed to suit your mood. The menu of services includes treatments with vegetable mud, rich in trace elements from the sea, and micronized seaweed.

A typical day may begin with a power walk through the exquisite botanical gardens on the hillside, climbing to the top of the falls. Lunch can be a beach picnic outing, or selected from the pasta bar at the pools. The all-inclusive package plan allows you to dine at several specialty restaurants in the gardens, selecting spa cuisine options that are low in fat, sodium, and calories.

Strolling to the spa, you can stop at the Seaquarium building to plan excursions, take tea, and learn about the island's flora and fauna. A soaring aviary provides a walk-through tour and some close-up bird-watching. The botanical gardens and aviary are open to visitors who come for lunch or dinner ($45–$55) or just for a tour ($10). Combined with a half-day package in the spa, this is a bargain escape for cruise ship passengers and guests at hotels in Ocho Rios.

The spa's scheduled group exercise sessions in the aerobics studio are stretch and tone, body sculpting, dancercise, and yoga. The limited selection of exercise equipment may be a disappointment for fitness buffs, though the facilities do include a Turkish steam bath, Finnish sauna, outdoor whirlpools, and a Swiss shower with multiple heads. Robe and sandals are provided. Minimum age in the spa is 16.

Accommodations are in rooms and suites terraced into the hillside gardens. There are also a number of townhouses with sunken living room, private patio with plunge pool, and kitchen.

Daily excursions with lunch at a small beach club down the hill are an option, without charge. For more active adventures, you may want to rent a car and drive along the coastal route to Dunn's River waterfalls (a slippery challenge to climbers) and visit Port Antonio, a Victorian town made famous by movie star Errol Flynn and the banana boats (sing "hey Mr. Talleyman"). Shop for island produce and crafts at Musgrave Market; naseberry (known also as sapodilla), cho-cho, star apple, pimiento, and the tiny fig banana are heaped on stands. Nearby, Boston Beach is lined with smoky shacks selling jerk pork and chicken barbecued over a pimiento wood fire. If this brings out the naturalist in you, head inland through Fern Gulley to the town of Bath for a look at Jamaica's original spa gardens and mineral springs.

FACILITIES
Exercise Equipment: Cross-country skiing machine, rowing machines, stationary bikes, treadmill, free weights. **Services:** Aromatherapy, reflexology, shiatsu, Swedish massage; body wraps, collagen body polish, salt-glow body scrub; hydrotherapy bath with essential oils. **Swimming:** Pools; ocean beach nearby. **Classes and Programs:** Aerobics, tai chi, yoga, and meditation classes. **Recreation:** Scuba diving, tennis, water volleyball; golf and horseback riding nearby. Jamaican show and buffet dinner on Friday.

ACCOMMODATIONS
60 rooms, 53 suites.

DINING
3 meals daily, plus snacks, afternoon tea, and an open bar. Restaurants serve pasta, Middle Eastern, Far Eastern, and New American cuisine. **Sample Meals:** Warm curried crab and papaya salad, cold poached scallops with tomato vinaigrette (lunch); grilled marlin, fillet of mahimahi with papaya relish, pepper-crusted beef with white beans (dinner).

RATES AND PACKAGES
Half-day spa package $90–$190, full-day $100–$210. All-inclusive package $165–$215 daily single, $140–$170 per person, double occupancy; 1-bedroom suite with living room $215–$250 single, $190–$225 per person, double. AE, MC, V.

DIRECTIONS
✉ *Box 284, Ocho Rios, St. Ann, Jamaica, West Indies,* ☎ *809/974–1400 or 800/847–2535,* ☎ *809/974–5823.*

From Montego Bay airport: Complimentary transfers. Taxi, rental car available.

THE GRAND LIDO SANS SOUCI

Luxury pampering
Mineral springs

Charlie's Spa at the Grand Lido Sans Souci resort takes a fresh approach to island holidays. It's more hedonistic than health-oriented, and the pampering atmosphere up on the hill, where treatments are given, complements vigorous workouts on the beach. This is a pleasant place to tone up or slim down.

With the sea on one side and a cascade of mineral water on the other, the spa provides instant stress reduction. The waters, however, are not used for therapy or beauty treatments. You can soak or swim at leisure, or join an exercise session in the pool. You can also head for the air-conditioned, beach-level exercise equipment room. Above it is an open-air pavilion where group exercise sessions are scheduled several times a day. Minimum age at the spa is 16.

Managed by SuperClubs, Sans Souci is an upscale all-inclusive Grand Lido resort, with spa services, meals, drinks, golf, tennis, and water sports included in the daily tariff. Begin with a fast-paced walk through the terraced gardens and along the curve of beach, where tennis courts and water sports await your pleasure. The sound of a violin or flute may draw you to the beach restaurant, where a band of roving musicians entertains. Buffet breakfast and lunch here is a sampler of island fare, plus Continental and Japanese favorites.

Bodywork and facials at the spa require appointments. Check in early at the tiny spa office alongside a pool that's home to mascot Charlie, a huge sea turtle who thrives in the mineral water. Spa director Margaret Spencer has turned the spa terrace into a quiet place for al fresco reflexology treatments, and there's a juice bar serving free smoothies. Treatments are limited to 25 minutes.

The Hideaway is a charming gazebo on the rocks, just big enough for a private massage. Facials and other treatments are given inside tiny wooden cottages clinging to the rocks. Higher up is "The Ridge," where seaweed and mud wraps are scheduled in rock-walled wet-treatment rooms with an alfresco shower. At the top is a beauty salon, where a complimentary manicure and pedicure are offered.

A beach-level grotto conceals a dry sauna and treatment area for skin exfoliation with sea salt, followed by a rubdown with cleansing oil and then a walk into the sea. The shallow water here is a mix of saltiness and refreshingly cool mineral water from the springs. It's ideal for washing off oils and salts used for body scrubs (depending on your skin type, the scrub will include aloe, peppermint, or coconut, plus cornmeal).

Sybarites can enjoy a secluded soak in a whirlpool tucked into the garden. A special treat is hidden in a beach grotto where the spring water seeps into a sand-bottom pool. For extra privacy, request an upper-level suite, or one of the penthouses, where you can sunbathe among the treetops.

All guest rooms are in villa-style buildings overlooking gardens and the sea. All have marble bathrooms, many of them with whirlpool tubs. Suites in the beach wing are smaller and can be noisy at night because of the 24-hour bar below. All have private balcony and air-conditioning but no window screens. The minibar is stocked with complimentary wine, waters, and beer. There's a three-night minimum stay during high season.

The all-inclusive program attracts a younger guest than previously encountered here—many honeymooners, some families with adult children, and single spa goers. About half the guests in recent years have been Japanese couples, many taking marriage vows in a beach pavilion. Afternoon tea in the Great House is an opportunity to mix with guests and make plans for the gala beach party or tennis. Hostesses introduce single newcomers to one another. Be sure to make dinner reservations in the Great House dining room or on the terrace under the stars at the Beach Grille. In addition to gala evenings on the lawn, there is nonstop food and beverage service at the beach bar.

FACILITIES
Exercise Equipment: Rowing machine, stair climber, stationary bikes, treadmill, weight-training circuit, free weights. **Services:** Aromatherapy, reflexology massage; body scrub, fango, mud wrap, seaweed wrap; facial. **Swimming:** Beaches, pools. **Classes and Programs:** Aerobics, aquacise. **Recreation:** Basketball, bikes, croquet, kayaking, scuba diving, snorkeling, volleyball, water-sports; golf, horseback riding, polo nearby. Dancing, live music on terrace; shopping excursions.

ACCOMMODATIONS
186 rooms, 24 suites.

DINING
3 meals daily, plus snacks and 24-hour room service. **Sample Meals:** Grilled tuna sandwich, shrimp ceviche, pasta primavera, spinach and ricotta cannelloni (lunch); seafood fettuccine, smoked marlin, broiled lobster, vegetarian lasagna (dinner).

RATES AND PACKAGES
3-night package $880–$1,130 per person, double occupancy; suite $1,130–$1,480; penthouse $1,390–$1,830. 7-night package $1,760–$2,200 per person, double; suite $2,440–$2,870; penthouse $3,000–$3,560. Single supplement: $150 per day. AE, D, DC, MC, V.

DIRECTIONS
✉ *Box 103, Ocho Rios, St. Ann, Jamaica,* ☎ *876/994–1353 or 800/859–7873,* ℻ *876/994–1544.*

From Montego Bay Airport: Transfers (about 2 hrs) are included in packages. Taxi or limousine available at all times.

MILK RIVER BATH AND HOTEL

Mineral springs

West of Kingston's high-rise government center, past agricultural and industrial developments, is the former capital city, Spanish Town, and from there you can reach the Milk River mineral baths in about two hours. Stop to admire the main square, surrounded by Georgian buildings that date from 1762. One now houses the Jamaican People's Museum of Craft and Technology. A classical statue of Admiral George Rodney commemorates his 1792 naval victory over the French that saved the British colony.

Continuing westward on Route B12 past the market town of May Pen, you reach the Milk River, near a crossroads called Toll Gate. Built on a hillside, the spa hotel here has private cubicles hewn from stone that are filled directly from the springs. As at Bath, an analysis of the water (in 1952) confirmed a high degree of beneficial radioactivity and minerals, similar to that of the best European spa waters.

Although there are no special treatments or exercise equipment, the hotel has a large outdoor swimming pool filled with the cool mineral water. Ocean beaches and citrus groves are a few miles away. Trout Hall, which grows ugli fruit, can be visited on request.

Most of the guests at Milk River come to soak three times a day, reserving cubicles with the receptionist. Massage is available on request. Bottles of mineral water are on the tables in the dining room.

The hotel has seen better days, but the 20 guest rooms are simple and clean, and nine have private bathrooms. The mineral-water swimming pool is open to day-only visitors for a small fee.

Breakfast and dinner are included in the daily rate. Lunch choices might include curried goat or fried chicken; dinner, roasted chicken, grilled pepper steak, or broiled lobster and shrimp.

RATES AND PACKAGES
$48–$93 daily, single or double occupancy. A meal plan is $42 daily. AE, MC, V.

DIRECTIONS
✉ *Milk River Post Office, Clarendon, Jamaica,* ☎ *876/987–6544,* FAX *876/986–4962.*

From Norman Manley International Airport, Kingston: Follow Route A1 west to May Pen, then take Route B3 south to Clarendon. There will be signs for Milk River and the hotel (1½ hrs).

SWEPT AWAY

Sports conditioning

As a counterpoint to the laid-back pace of life on the beach at Negril, the secluded, couples-only Swept Away resort offers a gym full of exercise equipment and a studio with resilient flooring for group exercise and aerobics. Set amid lush gardens in a 20-acre complex are 10 tennis courts lit for night play, air-conditioned racquetball and squash courts, a professional basketball court, and a 25-meter swimming pool. The all-inclusive rates cover unlimited use of the facilities, tennis lessons with resident professionals, and a fully equipped dive shop, as well as round-trip transportation from the international airport at Montego Bay. There is a three-night minimum stay.

The couples-only policy extends to friends of the same sex sharing a suite, all of which have king-size beds. From the open-air reception area, paths lead to 26 two-story villas set rather close together in beachside gardens. The standard villa has four minisuites arranged on two levels around a plant-filled atrium. Each unit has a private veranda, minimalist furnishings, island prints and ceramics, and a large step-in shower enclosure in the bathroom. It is a quiet environment, far removed from the frenetic pace of most vacation villages, but plenty of action vibrates at the tennis complex and around the beach bar and pool. Most guests are young couples, some are honeymooners.

The sports center is set apart from the villas by the island's main road. At the reception desk you can book courts and massages, and check on scheduled classes in the aerobics pavilion. Among more than 12 group exercise sessions are body sculpting, boxercise, aquacise, step aerobics, and low- to high-impact aerobics. Sports complex director Nancy Machado and instructors certified by the Aerobics and Fitness Association of America provide personal consultations. Joggers can check out a nine-station parcourse on the half-mile running track. Cool-down options include yoga, stress management class, saunas, steam rooms, and an outdoor Jacuzzi.

Tennis buffs get workouts with pros at three daily clinics. There is a ball machine and racket-stringing equipment. If you haven't brought a racket, you can borrow one. Tournaments are held throughout the week. Visiting tennis pros on the United States Professional Tennis Registry are often in residence and offer clinics at no additional charge.

Massage therapy is in thatch-roofed pavilions at the center of the sports complex. Get into an island mood with hydrotherapy in a rock-walled tub filled with marine water or herbal oils to relax and soothe tired muscles. Facials and bodywork, such as wraps, scrubs, and waxing, are available, and so is nail and hair care. (Oasis Spa services are not part of the all-inclusive package; charges go on your account.)

The weight room here is an open-air pavilion with high-tech German equipment. Instructors are on hand throughout the day to coach you on proper use of the equipment, including Cybex and Matrix units. The adjoining aerobics studio pulses with sessions of Reebok step, abs and gluts, body sculpting, and stretch. A power-lifting competition is scheduled every Wednesday evening; the gym stays open till 11 PM.

Golfers get unlimited play at the nearby Negril Hills Golf Club, an 18 hole, par 72 course set on 6,600 yards of rolling hills. Round-trip transportation also is complimentary for Swept Away guests. The resort offers unlimited use of water-sports equipment for windsurfing, kayaking, sunfish sailing, paddle-boating, and waterskiing. Snorkeling gear is also provided, as are outings in a glass-bottom boat. For certified divers, trips to nearby reefs depart three times daily in the resort's own dive boat. A certification course is available for an extra fee.

Special weeks devoted to sports and wellness, and certification courses for personal trainers are scheduled throughout the year. Meals are served in three locations: the big, open-air social pavilion has sumptuous buffets for breakfast, lunch, and dinner; a beach grill serves snack, salads, and dinner entrées broiled to order; and there's a formal restaurant with Continental fare for dinner, served in an open-air garden pavilion at the sports complex. Alcoholic beverages are included. Dieters can follow a spa menu plan on the buffet, with selections that total 1,800 calories per day. Choices include fresh island fruits and produce, fish, and veggie bar.

With the ambience of a private club, Swept Away allows you to set your own pace. Bicycles are available when you want to explore the area's more lively beaches. The resort activities desk can arrange outings (for an extra fee), such as a guided trail ride on horseback through the tropical back country, and a sunset catamaran cruise to caves near Rick's Cafe. Local outfitters take hikers to scenic waterfalls and a natural whirlpool, and for a walk through the bush.

FACILITIES

Exercise Equipment: Cross-country skiing machine, rowing machine, stair climbers, stationary bikes, weight-training circuit, free weights. **Services:** Reflexology, sports, Swedish massage; body scrub, herbal and mineral bath, seaweed wrap; facial. **Swimming:** Ocean beach, pools. **Classes and**

Programs: Tennis instruction, scuba lessons, personal consultation. **Recreation:** Basketball, diving, jogging, kayaking, racquetball, squash, tennis, windsurfing. Live music, nightly dancing.

ACCOMMODATIONS
134 suites.

DINING
3 meals daily. Spa-cuisine and Jamaican specialties available in four restaurants. **Sample meals:** Steamed vegetables, grilled-chicken Caesar salad, plum tomatoes with goat cheese and olive oil (lunch); fettuccine with baby shrimp and okra in vermouth sauce, pan-fried snapper with red wine-caper sauce, goat chops in phyllo dough, curried-goat stew (dinner).

RATES AND PACKAGES
4-day/3-night package $1,350–$2,080 per couple; 8-days/7-night package $2,700–$4,410 per couple. 1-night deposit required. AE, DC, MC, V.

DIRECTIONS
✉ *Box 77, Norman Manley Blvd., Negril, Jamaica* ☎ *876/957–4061 or 800/545–7937* FAX *876/957–4060.*

From Montego Bay: Round-trip transfers provided (1½ hrs). Rental car, taxi available.

MARTINIQUE

CENTRE DE THALASSOTHÉRAPIE DU CARBET

Medical wellness

Seawater and kinesitherapy are the basis of an aquatic workout at the indoor pools of the Centre de Thalassothérapie near Fort-de-France, capital city of Martinique. Considered effective in the treatment of rheumatism, the four-step procedure takes about 2½ hours and costs about $50.

Beginning with a plunge into heated seawater (33°C), you may participate in group exercise or simply relax. The pool has built-in underwater jets to massage sore muscles. A more intense underwater massage is next, in a private tub with jets designed to effect lymphatic drainage. The third step is a *douche à affusion*, a full body massage under a continuous shower of seawater.

The massage therapist devotes special attention to relieving tension in the vertebrae of your spine. The water pressure helps relax muscles. The final douche is in a shower stall lined with high-pressure jets aimed at cellulite points, the abdomen, and the vertebrae.

Supplementary services available include electrotherapy to recondition muscles after injury, an algae body mask, and antiarthritis and antiaging treatments for the skin. Inhalation of seawater mist is advised for asthma sufferers, and negative ions are introduced to relieve nervous tension.

Located on the island's northeastern coast, near the old capital of St-Pierre, the thalassotherapy center is about a 30-minute drive from Fort-de-France. Although the 64-km (40-mi) roundtrip can be done in an afternoon, plan to stay at a nearby hotel and visit the lush island interior as well as the ruins of St-Pierre, destroyed in 1902 by an eruption of Mont Pelée. Take the coastal road N2 to Le Carbet for a swim at the beach, then past the Musée Volcanologique on N3 to hike trails up Mt. Pelée at Le Morne Rouge. The center is open to the public every day with the exception of Sunday. The beach here, Grand'Anse, is one of the islanders' favorites. There are no public facilities, so change at the center.

FACILITIES
Services: Massage; seawater thalassotherapy, pressotherapy, seaweed treatments, gel application, kinesitherapy, electrotherapy, algae body mask, antiarthritis and antiaging treatments for skin, seawater mist inhalation.

ACCOMMODATIONS
Nearby hotels include:

Hotel Marouba (tel. 596/78–12–88; fax 596/78–05–65), which has single rooms at $73–$103 daily and double rooms at $113–$158 for two persons, including Continental breakfast.

Hotel Christophe Colomb (tel. 596/78–05–38) with 10 single and double rooms at $41–$50 daily.

DIRECTIONS
✉ *Grand'Anse, 97221 Carbet, Martinique,* ☎ *596/78–08–78,* FAX *596/78–09–80.*

From Fort-de-France: Take the coastal road toward St. Pierre, 16 mi (25 mins). Taxi, rental car available.

NEVIS

FOUR SEASONS RESORT NEVIS

Luxury pampering
Sports conditioning

Pristine beaches, aquamarine seas, and tropical rain forests set the scene for the Four Seasons Resort on tiny Nevis, and guests set their own pace, choosing among a number of sports options, including golf and tennis. There is no organized fitness program here, and spa services are limited to massage, but the exercise equipment is first rate.

Visitors arrive aboard a private launch at the resort's dock after a VIP greeting in St. Kitts, Nevis's sister island, 2 miles and 30 minutes across the channel. Or private planes can land at the tiny Nevis airstrip.

A sports-vacation package, available year-round, is an excellent value, with unlimited tennis and golf. The tennis complex has 10 courts supervised by Peter Burwash professionals, who provide clinics and one-on-one training. The 18-hole golf course was designed by Robert Trent Jones, Sr. You play on the slopes of cloud-capped Nevis Peak, which inspired Columbus to call the island "Las Nieves," or "snow." Joggers and walkers can circuit the links on a paved path that goes through lush forest and up into the foothills.

Swimmers enjoy a U-shaped freshwater pool with dedicated lap lanes that connect to a spacious, free-form swimming area. The entire beach complex is designed to provide easy access to free water sports equipment, from sailboards to kayaks to snorkeling gear. The Pool Cabana restaurant serves lunch—a full menu with Four Seasons "Alternative Cuisine" options. Pool attendants spritz sunbathers with Evian.

The best place for serious workouts is the air-conditioned Health Club. Few island resorts offer such an extensive selection of equipment: 4 Stair-Masters (PT4000), 4 Quinton treadmills, Schwinn airdyne bikes, and a Concept II rowing machine. Located in the Sports Pavilion, the fitness facilities include an aerobics studio equipped with 10 Reebok Step units, 15 Airboards, assorted free weights, and a Body Masters training unit with chest press. There are men's and ladies' saunas, a unisex hair salon, and three massage rooms. Group exercise sessions, including step, stretch-and-tone, and aquaerobics, and early morning walks and beach jogs are open to all guests, free of charge. Croquet, volleyball, and shuffleboard are also offered.

Details make the difference: iced facecloths and pitchers of fresh fruit juices in the exercise room; morning coffee and muffins laid out at the health club; a library of feature films for your VCR viewing; and in-room massage at your convenience.

The Dining Room is reminiscent of a plantation great house, with a plank floor, a high ceiling with rafters, a cut-stone fireplace, ceiling fans, and a small dance floor. The "Alternative Cuisine" found at all Four Seasons hotels is low in sodium and fat, easy on calorie count, and full of fresh herbs and vegetables. Seafood is the main attraction, but other island fare also can be sampled.

The 12 plantation-style guest lodges have screened porches on the second floor and private patios with screened doors for ground-floor rooms. Each building has about a dozen rooms and suites, provided with robes and slippers, TV and VCR, and minibar. The staid interiors have an austere feeling, traditional Ethan Allen furniture that whispers "class" rather than luxury. Bathrooms are extra-large, with separate stall shower and toilet room. Also available are fully furnished and serviced private villas and estate homes. There is a complimentary self-service laundry facility in each lodge.

The legacy of 300 years of British rule is still evident on the 36-square-mile island. Thanks to its sulfur bath and health spa, its 82 sugar estates, and the slave trade, the island once was known as the "Queen of the Caribbees." British naval hero Admiral Lord Horatio Nelson came for the restorative baths and stayed to marry Lady Nesbit at her family's plantation in 1787. Visits to their home and church highlight island tours.

Nevis delights bird watchers, star gazers, and eco-travelers. Much of the island remains pastoral and undeveloped, providing opportunities for hiking and walking tours. The Four Seasons "Natural Nevis" package features outings to fresh water ponds, the ruins of a sugar mill, and to a coconut plantation. A perfect way to end the day is on Nevis Peak, where the sunset is spectacular and you might catch a glimpse of wild monkeys with 6-foot-long tails.

History buffs can join a walking tour of the island's tiny capital, Charlestown, founded in 1660, where thermal soaks are offered at a wooden bathhouse adjoining the once-exclusive Bath Hotel (circa 1778), now in disrepair and used as a police building. The 18th-century buildings in town house law courts full of wigged barristers, and the offices of island officials seeking independence from their federation with St. Kitts. Nevis could become the world's newest republic and smallest nation but for one (Vatican City), complete with traffic jams and offshore banking.

FACILITIES
Exercise Equipment: Rowing machine, stair climbers, stationary bikes, treadmills, weight-training equipment, free weights. **Services:** Aromatherapy, sports, Swedish massage. **Swimming:** Ocean beach, pools. **Classes and Programs:** Step, stretch-and-tone, aquaerobics, walks, beach jogs. **Recreation:** Billiards, croquet, darts, fishing, golf (18 holes), kayaking, sailboarding, scuba diving, shuffleboard, snorkeling, tennis (10 courts), volleyball, water sports; horseback riding nearby. Dancing, folklore show, movies (Mon. and Fri.). **Children's Programs:** Day-long activities for children ages 3–10.

ACCOMMODATIONS
179 rooms, 17 suites, 20 private villas.

DINING
All meals are à la carte unless Modified American Plan is purchased: $85 for breakfast and dinner daily (included in some packages). **Sample Meals:** Herbed smoked chicken with mixed seasonal greens; salad with sweet peppers and marinated Spanish onions, Caesar salad (lunch); grilled Caribbean fish, seafood gumbo, local hen and lamb, blackened local red snapper with sautéed spaghetti squash, seared salmon with warm bean-sprout salad, local yellow tomato with Maui onion and roasted-pepper vinaigrette, spinach salad with jerk chicken (dinner).

RATES AND PACKAGES
$275–$685 daily per room, single and double; suites $475–$2,525 for 1-bedroom, $1,010–$3,210 for 2-bedroom; villas and homes $750–$4,000 daily. 7-night Romance in Paradise package, $4,298–$7,274 for 2 persons, including breakfast and dinner. Sporting Spree package $614–$1,124 for 2 persons, with breakfast and dinner. 3-night deposit required. AE, DC, MC, V.

DIRECTIONS

✉ *Box 565, Charlestown, Nevis, West Indies,* ☎ *869/469–1111 or 800/ 332–3442 reservations in U.S., 800/268–6282 reservations in Canada,* FAX *869/469–1112.*

From St. Kitts: Resort shuttle to 40-passenger launch ($65 round-trip).

PUERTO RICO

LA CASA DE VIDA NATURAL

Holistic health
Medical wellness

Secluded in the foothills of the Caribbean National Forest, with panoramic views of the ocean and mountains, the 10-acre La Casa de Vida Natural has carved out a rustic center for natural health, offering vegetarian meals; mud, herbal, and seaweed treatments; and psychological counseling.

Located 30 minutes from the fleshpots of San Juan, this low-key, informal getaway hosts holistic health weeks, weekend workshops, and special seminars with healers from many parts of the world. One of the island's best ocean beaches is just down the hill at Luquillo, and hiking trails lead into the lush rain forest of El Yunque. Accommodations are in a renovated farmhouse and guest house, with space for a dozen guests and staff. There is no air-conditioning, and some rooms share a bath.

The health center offers nonintrusive diagnostic procedures as well as kinesiology and massage. Workshops on physical and mental health are scheduled periodically, and individual counseling is available by appointment with owner-director Jane G. Goldberg, Ph.D., a New York–based psychologist. Programs may focus on building a psychological immune system, love and hate in health, or organic farming. Specialists on staff include a naturopathic doctor and a certified acupuncturist.

The center aims to serve a wide range of needs with its integrated biological and psychological approach to prevention and cure of disease. Therapies such as cleansing the body with burial in sand and immersion in mud can be combined with colonics and urine analysis. La Casa uses the island's natural resources and draws from the treatments of several healing cultures. There's a sea glow massage to stimulate the lymphatic system with a sea-salt exfoliation, an abianga oil massage using principles of Ayurvedic medicine, and a Reiki energy-balancing massage. Body wraps are done using fresh plants and herbs grown on the grounds—eucalyptus, ylang-ylang, mango, papaya, and banana—formulated to be either calming, energizing, or detoxifying. Mud for wraps comes from clay deposits in the forest and serves as a powerful detoxifier. In addition, aerobics classes and jazzercise are organized in an open-air pavilion.

Excursions organized for La Casa guests include hikes to pre-Columbian petroglyphs in the rain forest and to a barrier reef at Luquillo Beach. Once home to a thriving coconut plantation, the crescent-shape, white-sand beach is perfect for swimming and picnics. Commonly known as El Yunque, the Caribbean National Forest is the only tropical rain forest managed by the U.S. Forest Service. It encompasses 28,000 acres, at elevations up to 3,526 feet. The public trails reveal 240 different tree species, as well as orchids and wildflowers. Brief tropical showers keep things lush, moist, and cool.

Warm sulfur springs known to the earliest Taino Indians are a 90-minute drive from La Casa, at the Parador Baños de Coamo. A modest mountain inn, the Parador offers Puerto Rican meals as well as overnight lodging (Hwy 152 south to Rt. 14; tel. 809/825–2186).

FACILITIES
Services: Aromatherapy, Reiki massage, sea glow massage, abiango oil massage, acupuncture, colonic irrigation, herbal wrap, mud pack, polarity therapy, sand burial, seaweed wrap; facial. **Swimming:** River nearby,

ocean beaches nearby. **Classes and Programs:** Aerobics, Jazzercise, Holistic medical counseling, meditation, nutritional and psychological consultation, yoga instruction. **Recreation:** Hiking, river boating.

ACCOMMODATIONS
7 rooms, some with shared bath.

DINING
3 meals daily. Vegetarian diet emphasizes raw fruits and vegetables grown on the property, whole-grain home-baked bread. **Sample Meals:** Miso soup, organic salad, falafel (lunch); organic Chinese stir-fry, home-made chutney, freshly sprouted green salad (dinner).

RATES AND PACKAGES
Weekdays $75 daily single with breakfast only, $45 per person, double; weekends $175 single, $100 per person, double. 5-day workshop $595 single, $535 per person, double occupancy. $125 deposit for workshops or 2 nights' lodging. Nonprogram lodging $125, single $100 per couple, including meals. MC, V.

DIRECTIONS
✉ Box 1916, Rio Grande, Luquillo, Puerto Rico 00745, ☎ 787/887–4359 or 212/260–5823, ⛶ 787/887–4359.

From San Juan: Complimentary airport transfers (1 hr). Rental car, taxi, public car (*publico*) available. Highway 3 east to Luquillo Beach, Route 186 to Route 9960, El Verde.

THE RITZ-CARLTON SAN JUAN HOTEL & CASINO

Luxury pampering

The Caribbean's newest and most luxurious spa is set amid beachside gardens, tennis courts, and the swimming pool at the Ritz-Carlton San Juan. Here you are cocooned in posh treatment rooms where you receive the latest in skin care and bodywork. An airy gym full of state-of-the-art exercise equipment is at your disposal for serious workouts, and you can sample the spa cuisine menu at an alfresco café.

Elegantly housed in a 12,000-square-foot hacienda, the spa gleams with marble floors, pale stone walls, and crystal chandeliers. Sunlight brightens the reception area, where you check in. Ustairs are the ladies and gentlemen's locker rooms, with all the amenities. The coed whirlpool and sauna are tucked into the ladies' area. Located on the ground floor, the fitness center has a full Cybex circuit, 11 Spinning bikes, and aerobics studio. Water aerobics, alfresco massage, and a whirlpool pavilion complement the outdoor swimming pool.

This is a full-service day spa that primarily serves the hotel's guests; however, cruise ship passengers, convention-goers, and others can use the facility by paying the daily fee. Call the spa early for reservations. The daily facility fee is waived when you book spa services, and there are half-day and full-day packages. Gratuities are not included.

The spa has hydrotherapy equipment for therapeutic baths with moor mud, sea salts, or aromatherapy oils. It also has a unique private suite for a couple or family, where treatments can be performed simultaneously. A salon for hair and nail care is in the building.

Try something new from the à la carte menu of spa treatments: Ayurvedic scalp massage, smoothing mud masque for your hands and feet using Dead Sea salts and mud, Reiki energy balancing, Thai massage to release energy blockages, or sports massage. CranioSacral therapy, effective for sufferers of migraine headaches and sinus problems, is practiced here by certified therapists using a light touch to align the skull and pelvis, relieving areas of tension. The goal of spa director Katherine Calzada is to link healing arts from the East and West with those of her native island. Holistic health and spiritual energy merge in the registered Sonomatherapy program, scheduled over three to four days.

Kids, too, can learn about skin care and the relaxing benefits of massage. Designed to teach the importance of self-care and prevention of illness, the Ritz Kids spa services cover nails, facial cleansing, and massage. Each treatment takes 25 minutes and requires the presence of a parent or guardian. Appointments are scheduled for children 4 to 17 years of age. The program includes cooking classes, educational games, and arts and crafts, and there's a children's menu served in a supervised facility.

Located in the Isla Verde suburb of San Juan, minutes from the airport and historic sites, the Ritz-Carlton is a world apart from the hustle and bustle of beach resorts. Entered from a broad porte cochere, the lobby has a romantic Mediterranean look reminiscent of the 1940s. Plush draperies on tall windows, potted palms, and a pianist playing in the lounge add to the glamorous ambience. Full afternoon tea is served here, as are drinks. Nearby are a cigar bar and a 24-hour casino, the largest on the island. The club-floor concierge lounge serves food and beverages throughout the day.

The hotel has more than 400 rooms and suites, with traditional furniture and bright tropical fabrics. Corner rooms have a wall-to-wall window and private balcony.

FACILITIES
Exercise Equipment: Stair climbers, stationary bikes, treadmills, weight-training equipment, free weights. **Services:** Ayurvedic scalp, aromatherapy, deep-tissue, Reiki, reflexology, Shirodhara, Sports, Swedish, Thai massage; Bindi, body wrap, mud masque; CranioSacral therapy, hydrotherapy, Sonomatherapy; facial. **Swimming:** Ocean beach, pool. **Classes and Programs:** Aerobics, aquacise, Latin dance aerobics, Spinning, yoga. **Recreation:** Casino, tennis, water sports; golf nearby. **Children's Program:** Ritz Kids (ages 4-17).

ACCOMMODATIONS
403 rooms, 11 suites.

DINING
All meals à la carte. **Sample Meals:** Gazpacho, seafood salad, turkey burger (lunch); grilled salmon, skinless chicken breast, pasta (dinner).

RATES AND PACKAGES
$300–$475 per room, single or double occupancy; suites $825–$1,300. Day Spa packages $175–$480. 3-day San Juan Getaway $720. AE, MC, V.

DIRECTIONS
✉ *6961 State Rd. No. 187, Isla Verde, Carolina, Puerto Rico 00979,* ☎ *787/253–1700 or 800/241–3333,* 🖷 *787/253–0700.*

From Luis Muñoz Marin International Airport: Take the access road to State Road 187 (5 min).

ST. LUCIA

THE JALOUSIE HILTON RESORT AND SPA

Luxury pampering
Mineral springs

Arriving at the Jalousie Hilton Resort and Spa by helicopter or yacht is like arriving on "Fantasy Island." Framed by deep-green sugarloaf-shaped peaks called the Pitons, the resort terraces up from the sea in a 325-acre nature preserve. The private villas and suites are set in a lush rain forest above a picture-perfect crescent beach. At the top of the hill, overlooking both the Atlantic and Caribbean, sits a full-service spa and fitness center.

Hiking to the hilltop spa beats a StairMaster workout. For the faint-hearted, a van provides transportation. Windswept cottages have private treatment rooms and air-conditioned racquetball/squash courts. An airy wood-roofed gym has an aerobics studio and LifeFitness exercise equipment. Here you can join exercise groups every morning, doing step and low-impact aerobics. Sheltered from the wind, four tennis courts are lit for night play.

Treatments at the spa feature cosmetics made from organic and marine elements. FloraSpa facials include deep cleaning the skin with a seaweed masque followed by an herbal balancing lotion. Hydrotherapy comes with algae-infused water bubbling from 47 underwater jets. There are body wraps, manicures, and pedicures. A salon provides haircuts and styling. The ultimate luxury here is a massage combined with a soak in the whirlpool on a hilltop pavilion open to the sea view.

Dotting the hillside are individual villas cantilevered off the sloping grounds. Each has a high beamed ceiling, fan, sitting area, and a private plunge pool on the veranda, with views of the sea and the Pitons. The outdoor wet bar by the pool has refreshments for sunset gazing. The resort was once a sugar plantation, and the 17th-century sugar mill now houses a chic restaurant and deluxe suites. Native fruit trees, flowering shrubs, palms, and tall coconut trees abound. A call to the transportation desk brings a van to take you to the beach club, where you can enjoy a sumptuous buffet lunch.

The Great House, inspired by the elegant central gathering rooms of 18th-century colonial estates, provides a quiet place for reading, afternoon tea, billiards, or chess. You can relax over cocktails prior to The Plantation Restaurant's gourmet dinner. For more informal dining, The Pier House serves seafood and Creole specialties (dinner only) enlivened by local musicians.

The Learning Center at Jalousie (pronounced ja-LUCY) provides ecology programs for kids, ages 5 to 17, supervised by islanders. There are nature walks, an exploration of the beaches, and games to instill an appreciation of the natural beauty and volcanic springs surrounding the resort. Tennis and golf lessons are included, and there are biology courses on Mondays, Wednesdays, and Fridays. Activities at the resort are complimentary; outings require modest fees.

Situated at the southern end of the Windward Islands, in the Lesser Antilles, St. Lucia has constant trade winds and balmy weather. Jalousie is near the village of Soufrière, about an hour's drive from the airport. The whole area is a marine park and major snorkeling destination.

About five minutes by car from the hotel are the free mud baths at Sulpher Springs. Take an old bathing suit and smear the smelly mud on whatever muscular aches or skin problems need attention, then wash off in the brownish stream that cascades from the springs. There are also thermal baths at Mt. Soufrière and Diamond Falls. A dormant volcano, with pits and open craters of boiling, sulfurous mud, Soufrière has spring-fed pools of cool mineral water that have been used since French forces occupied the island during the 17th century.

Nature lovers revel in the island's numerous preserves. Symbolized by the Jacquot, an indigenous parrot prized for its brilliant plummage, St. Lucian wildlife is protected by wardens of the Forestry Department, who welcome visitors at their aviary and small zoo in Union.

FACILITIES
Exercise Equipment: Rowing machine, stationary bikes, treadmills, weight-training equipment, free weights. **Services:** Massage; body polish, body scrub, sea salt-glow, seaweed wrap; hydrotherapy; facials. **Swimming:** Beach, pool. **Classes and Programs:** Step and low-impact aerobics. **Recreation:** Basketball, golf, horseback riding, racquetball, scuba diving, snorkeling, squash, tennis (4 lighted courts), water sports, windsurfing. **Children's Program:** Tennis and golf lessons, ecology program at Learning Center for ages 5–17.

ACCOMMODATIONS
49 suites, 65 villas.

DINING
2-meal plan (breakfast and dinner) $75 per person, per day. Breakfast-only plan $19 per person, per day. Formal dining room and 3 casual restaurants serve Continental and Caribbean fare. **Sample Meals:** On-beach buffet of seafood, fresh salads, stew, and island vegetables (lunch); grilled grouper, lobster, chicken, and pasta (dinner).

RATES AND PACKAGES
Day spa packages available. Rooms, suites, and villas $425–$1,050 daily in-season. Daily spa fee for nonguests $75. AE, MC, V.

DIRECTIONS
⊠ *Box 251, Soufrière, St. Lucia, West Indies,* ☎ *758/459–7666 or 800/445–8667,* 𝔽𝔸𝕏 *758/459–7667.*

From Hewanorra International Airport in Vieux Fort: Take coastal road to Soufrière (45 min). A free shuttle to and from the airport is provided by the resort. Helicopter transfer ($60–$75 each way, minimum 2 persons) arranged by resort on request.

LE SPORT

Luxury pampering
Sports conditioning

French-style thalassotherapy and skin care are part of the "Body Holiday" package at the all-inclusive Le Sport, St. Lucia's answer to Club Med. Guests on a "Body Holiday" get two daily treatments at the elegant Oasis, a hillside spa with sophisticated European equipment, including a hydrotherapy tub and Swiss needle shower.

There's a swimming pool and whirlpool, and guests can indulge in a massage, bathe in algae, and relax with a seaweed wrap. Also available for an additional fee are exclusive beauty treatments at Institut Clarins, featuring Parisian products for facials, hair and nail care, and a jet-lag restorative program.

The food segment of the Body Holiday program is called "cuisine legère," which simply means that calories don't count. Emulating the renowned Michel Guerard, the chefs provide meals balanced in complex carbohydrates and low in sodium and sugar. You can also choose from interesting options on the regular menu. Wine is included with lunch and dinner, and an open bar is stocked with premium brand liquors, fresh fruit juices, and mineral waters.

A checkup with the staff nurse precedes any treatment. Stress-linked fatigue and muscle tension, poor circulation, and lymphatic drainage are noted, and measurements are taken for blood pressure, heart rate, and weight. A prescribed course of treatments can include the "hydrator," a bubbling bath with herbs and sea algae, in which underwater jets needle away at the fatty tissue found on the upper arms, thighs, and calves. Another pool fitted with underwater jets is for exercise in seawater, which is denser than fresh water and thus gives greater support for the body. And the therapeutic nutrients of seaweed act as catalysts to create changes in the skin as you are wrapped, cocoonlike, in a coating of algae and sea mud. The seawater spray with a jet hose, said to improve circulation, intimidates some guests. The scheduled treatments are included in the price of your holiday package; salon services can be booked à la carte.

Meditation, exercise sessions, and outings are scheduled daily at the Oasis. In the air-conditioned aerobics studio you can join yoga, tone and stretch, and step aerobics, or work with a personal trainer at no charge. Scheduled group exercise sessions are ranked according to intensity. All guests can join morning walks and hikes, archery sessions, guided bike trips, and water aerobics.

This is a laissez-faire spa, not for those who want a regimented program. The eat-and-drink-all-you-want policy suits honeymooners and young couples, many from Europe (minimum age in the spa is 15). The wide range of options, from water sports to massage classes for couples to tai chi and tennis lessons, makes this an excellent sampler of spa life. Visitors not staying at the resort can purchase a one-day pass and schedule treatments à la carte.

Accommodations are in plantation-style buildings with four levels of rooms (no elevators). Each has a balcony or patio, with oceanfront or garden view. Cool, contemporary interiors are accented by marble floors, rattan furniture, and floral-print fabrics. Secluded on a private cove, the club-like facilities open to a large swimming pool where the social scene is nonstop.

Le Sport is not far from the Diamond Falls, where sulfurous water flows into natural pools near a seven-acre crater of boiling yellow-gray mud and hissing steam vents. Bathing here is said to cure whatever ails you.

FACILITIES
Exercise Equipment: Rowing machine, stair climber, stationary bike, treadmills, weight-training circuit, free weights. **Services:** Aromatherapy, reflexology massage; body wrap, loofah scrub; hydrotherapy, Scotch douche; facial. **Swimming:** Ocean beach, pools. **Classes and Programs:** Golf instruction. Tennis lessons, yoga, tone and stretch, step aerobics, water aerobics, meditation, personal trainer, guided walks and hikes, bike trips, tai chi. **Recreation:** Archery, biking, croquet, fencing, golf, scuba diving, tennis, volleyball, waterskiing, windsurfing. Disco, live music nightly.

ACCOMMODATIONS
102 rooms.

DINING

3 meals daily. Breakfast and lunch buffets. **Sample Meals:** Stuffed chicken legs in leek-and-cream sauce with wild rice, julienne of carrots and zucchini (lunch); steamed kingfish with carrot and pimiento sauce, scallop of veal with champagne sabayon, fresh asparagus, sea scallops with a julienne of carrots and snow peas in raspberry vinaigrette (dinner).

RATES AND PACKAGES

$250–$345 daily per person, double or triple occupancy; single supplement $75 daily. 3-bedroom Plantation House, $500 daily, single supplement $300. Credit-card guarantee for 3 nights. AE, D, MC, V.

DIRECTIONS

✉ *Box 437, Castries, St. Lucia,* ☎ *758/450–8551 or 800/544–2883,* ℻ *758/450–0368.*

From airport: Complimentary transfers on arrival/departure at Hewanora Airport (90 mins) and George Charles Airport (20 min.). Taxi, rental car available.

From Castries: Take the coastal road to Gros Ilet (10 mins).

ST. MARTIN/ST. MAARTEN

PRIVILEGE RESORT AND SPA

Luxury pampering
Sports conditioning

Panoramic views come with workouts at the Privilege Resort and Spa, which is perched on hills overlooking the beach and marina at Anse Marcel, on the French side of this bi-national island. This unique hideaway provides European treatments to rejuvenate sun-damaged skin and aching muscles, as well as six-day "cures"—courses for slimming, anti-stress, or simply relaxing.

For a sampler of French balneotherapy, try an underwater massage in the high-tech Doyer tub, or the Swiss shower temple, a multijet cabinet equipped with a control panel for cascades of varying intensity. The sea-oriented treatments make use of Phytomer purified marine algae and seaweed from Brittany.

Sailing and sports training can be combined with the spa program or arranged to fit your own schedule. Aerobics classes are held in the late afternoon or at 8:30 AM. One of the most popular sessions, open to all resort guests without charge, is "aquagym" in the outdoor swimming pool cantilevered between the spa and restaurant. Close by the pool is the sports complex with tennis, squash, and racquetball courts, and an open-air pavilion with exercise equipment. A trainer is available for body-building and a few rounds of boxing-bag technique.

Opened in 1992, both the hotel and spa at Privilege Resort provide privacy and Old World service not found in neighboring resorts. Most of the guest rooms are in Creole-style cottages with terra-cotta tile floor and separate seating area with sofabed. Some visitors are housed in ultra-privacy at the residence of the resort owner. Suites have two marble-walled bathrooms in addition to a large living room and private balcony. While all lodging is air-conditioned, there is no screening to protect against mosquitoes if you prefer fresh air at night.

Programs for four to seven nights offer a wide variety of sports and spa options, plus a shopping excursion. On Sunday, when the spa is closed, guests sail to neighboring islands, with lunch on board, at no extra charge. A three-day sailing package is available for those desiring an extended cruise. Other seasonal packages take advantage of low summer rates. If you want to do it all, the eight-day Spa Trek package is a VIP adventure, complete with sightseeing and airport transfers by helicopter.

FACILITIES
Exercise Equipment: Stationary bikes, weight-training equipment, free weights. **Services:** Shiatsu, Swedish, underwater massage; mud wrap, seaweed wrap; hydrotherapy. **Swimming:** Ocean beach, pools. **Classes and Programs:** Aerobics, aquagym. **Recreation:** Racquetball, sailing, squash, tennis, water sports; golf, horseback riding nearby.

ACCOMMODATIONS
20 rooms, 4 suites.

DINING
Breakfast and dinner daily at 2 restaurants are included in spa packages. No spa menu. **Sample Meals:** Caribbean fish soup and green salad, grilled tuna steak with steamed vegetables (lunch); salmon escallope in a Creole sauce, carpaccio of fish Tahitian style, snails in pastry with white wine

and mushrooms, shrimp in a basil sauce, scallop ravioli with leeks, duck breast with mango compote (dinner).

RATES AND PACKAGES
Daily rate with Continental breakfast $255–$367 for 2 persons in double room, $255–$294 single, suites $440–$556. 7-night Spa Trek Program $1,795–$2,040 per person, double occupancy, $2,225–$2,850 single. 5-night Health Spa package $1,240–$1,478 double, $1,550–$2,056 single, suite $1,475–$1,720. AE, MC, V.

DIRECTIONS
✉ *Anse Marcel, 97150 St. Martin, French West Indies,* ☎ *590/87–3838, reservations* ☎ *800/874–8541,* FAX *590/87–4412.*

From Princess Julianna Airport: Complimentary transfers included in packages (30 mins). Taxi available; rental car available at resort.

U.S. VIRGIN ISLANDS

OMEGA JOURNEYS AT MAHO BAY

Holistic health

Workshops in health, music, movement, and personal growth are mixed with fun in the sun during four weeklong programs planned in January by the New York–based Omega Institute. The annual migration to the sunny beaches of St. John is joined by faculty members who lead explorations into the body, mind, and spirit. Living close to nature in a tent village, the workshop participants experience many dimensions of natural healing.

Early birds can start the day with sunrise meditation, tai chi, or yoga. Workshops run two hours each morning and afternoon, allowing participants to cover several subjects. Informal and experiential, the group sessions are devoted to bringing health, mindfulness, and peace into the many dimensions of contemporary life.

Drawn from a variety of professions, ages, and backgrounds, the participants find common ground in the open-minded, natural atmosphere, which is a hallmark of summers at Omega Institute's campus in New York's Hudson River valley. Vegetarian meals prepared by Institute chefs are part of the daily program. During a typical week you will meet international experts in holistic health, stress management, and lifestyle change. Spiritual awareness comes naturally, thanks to the pristine beauty of the island, mainly managed by the U.S. National Park Service.

On 14 acres overlooking white-sand beach, Maho Bay Camp Resort is a unique tent-cottage community dedicated to the concept of simple comforts and life in harmony with nature. Perched in thickly wooded hillsides, the canvas-walled cottages are set on plank decks that cantilever over the forest. The 16-by-16-foot units blend in so naturally that they seem to be part of the environment. Each has two beds, a living/dining area with two-burner propane stove, lounge chairs, and sofa. Linens and bedding are supplied, but there is no maid service. Boardwalks connect to the toilets, showers, dining pavilion, and commissary.

Within the Virgin Islands National Park, the campground has unrestricted access to miles of pristine beaches and well-marked hiking trails. The National Park Service conducts free tours and lectures on island flora, fauna, and marine biology, as well as on St. John's colorful history and culture.

FACILITIES
Swimming: Ocean beaches. **Classes and Programs:** energy training, nutritional consultation, meditation, tai chi, yoga instruction. **Recreation:** Hiking, tennis, snorkeling, volleyball. Concerts.

ACCOMMODATIONS
96 tents and cottages.

DINING
3 vegetarian meals daily, buffet-style. Some fish and dairy products are available. **Sample Meals:** Green salad with sprouts and nuts, home-baked whole wheat bread, vegetable soup, lentil loaf (lunch); vegetarian lasagna, baked eggplant Parmesan, tofu casserole (dinner).

RATES AND PACKAGES
1-week package: $1,025 per person, double occupancy 50% deposit required. MC, V.

DIRECTIONS

✉ *Box 310, Maho Bay, St. John,* ☎ *809/776–6240. Reservations:* ✉ *Omega Institute, 260 Lake Dr., Rhinebeck, NY 12572,* ☎ *914/266–4444 or 800/944–1001,* FAX *914/266–4828.*

From Cruz Bay: Bus or shuttle service from ferry landing run along Northshore Rd. (15 mins). Car rental, taxi, minimoke, bicycle rental available.

13 Health & Fitness Cruises

STAYING FIT AT SEA is no longer a matter of doing 10 laps around the promenade deck. Today's luxury liners feature fitness facilities and programs that are the equal of anything ashore.

Your ship has come in, but selecting a cruise from the new wave of superliners, sail ships, and all-suite luxury liners will require a bit of research. Start by checking itineraries and costs (see *Fodor's The Best Cruises*) and contacting a knowledgeable travel agent accredited by the Cruise Lines International Association (CLIA, ☎ 212/921–0066).

Since water is the basic ingredient in many spa cures, it was argued, a spa on the high seas should only make the experience more enjoyable. With abundant fresh air and sunshine, pools filled with filtered seawater, and aerobics classes on deck, the cruise would be an invigorating escape from health club routines at home. For cruise connoisseurs, however, diet was a dirty word. And the gourmet meals and lavish buffets aboard ship have been the downfall of many calorie counters. Then came the American Heart Association's "Eating Away From Home" program adapted for shipboard dining by most cruise lines. Outstanding examples are Michel Roux's vegetarian menu for Celebrity Cruises' liners, the menu of spa cuisine aboard Cunard's *Queen Elizabeth 2*, the Holland America Line's "Light and Healthy" cuisine, and Carnival Cruises' Spa Nautica menu.

Advance planning is important for those on a special diet. Specific foods and general preferences should be discussed with a travel agent, who can then secure a confirmation of your meal plan from the cruise line. All the leading lines offer such services at no extra charge.

Smoke-free cruising is now an option on Norwegian Cruise Lines, and no-smoking cabins and dining rooms are available on most ships.

Norwegian Cruise Line has annual Fitness and Beauty cruises in October. Guest lecturers on nutrition, sports medicine, hairstyling, and makeup make the trip along with football, golf, and tennis stars. Basketball cruises, baseball cruises, and football cruises allow passengers to team up for fun and fitness aboard the *Seaward* and its sister ship the *Norway*. Taking spas to sea, Sheila Cluff (The Oaks at Ojai, Palms at Palm Springs, CA) leads programs aboard Caribbean, Alaska, and Mexican Riviera cruises (☎ 800/892–4995).

Shore excursions on these cruises offer more than shopping and sightseeing. Several lines provide entrée to local racquet clubs, golf courses, and fitness centers. Some ships have access to private ports of call, islands where passengers may swim, snorkel, and sunbathe on their own "deserted island." Princess Cruises' *Grand Princess,* and the Disney Cruise Line's new ships have scheduled nature walks and bicycle tours. For water sports, it's hard to beat Wind Sail Cruises' dive-in marina on the *Wind Spirit, Wind Star,* and the new *Wind Surf.*

While the Caribbean and the Bahamas account for 60% of all cruise destinations, a steadily growing fleet of ships sails from California and Canadian ports. Alaska, the Mexican Riviera, and the Hawaiian islands offer exciting variations on the cruise theme. The rates quoted here are published, and may be discounted at certain times of the year. In addition, some cruise lines offer discounts for early bookings, and for repeat passengers.

As a new wave of luxury liners comes on line, look for more adventure cruises exploring less-traveled ports and nature preserves. Small, specially designed expedition vessels sailing to Alaska and along the Pacific coast for Clipper Adventure Cruises and Windstar Cruises lead this trend combining fun and fitness.

This chapter highlights the best spas at sea in North American waters. Cruise fares are given as a basis for planning, as of mid-1998, and options include cruise-only fares, without an airline flight to your port of embarkation, or an air/sea fare combination. Also, there are port taxes added to fares. For newcomers to fitness programs, the cruise may be a good way to inaugurate a personal fitness routine that can then be continued effectively at home. Staff instructors offer one-on-one workouts—perhaps the best bargain in fitness education. And there's a healthy bonus from mother nature: The bracing effect of the fresh air generated by sea water and sun may be just what the doctor ordered for our high-pressure society.

CARNIVAL CRUISE LINES

The 2,040-passenger megaships *Sensation, Ecstasy, Fascination, Fantasy, Inspiration,* and *Imagination* give Carnival Cruise Lines passengers access to spas that are bigger than the on-board casinos. Carnival's Fantasy-class ships pushed the envelope with their 12,000-square-ft Nautica spas where you can exercise with a view of the sea on a Keiser progressive-resistance system, Nautilus equipment, rowing and stair-climbing machines, free weights, and stationary bicycles. On the two uppermost decks, with floor-to-ceiling windows, the spa has six whirlpools (also with a sea view), men's and women's saunas, steam rooms, showers, and locker rooms. The large glass-and-mirror-enclosed aerobics studio is busy all day. Classes include "Cardio-Funk" and "Cardio-Pump," step, and an hour-long advanced high-energy workout. You can join aquaerobics in the swimming pool or organized walks on the ships' upper decks. A ⅛-mi jogging track encircles the deck. Familiarizations with the equipment and talks by the spa staff are offered regularly throughout each cruise. On deck are swimming pools, and the Carnival *Destiny* has an impressive water slide.

A beauty salon and private massage rooms complete the facilities. Services offered by Steiner spa professionals include a range of facials, massages, and beauty treatments in a spacious two-level spa. Among the "European-style" treatments are Ionithermie slimming through use of a cleansing algae concentrate, and "La Therapie" facial with essential oils and low-level electrical stimulation. Several rooms designed for seaweed treatments and herbal wraps have private showers, and one has a hydrotherapy bath. Appointments can be made immediately after embarkation, and services are available on days when the ship is in port.

Calorie-conscious passengers can take advantage of a Nautica Spa Selection on the menu at each meal. In addition, a circular salad bar in the grill area is open for lunch and dinner, and there is a pasta station with made-to-order selections.

While the spa has separate saunas for men and women, the coed whirlpools made of red-and-black ceramic tile allow passengers to bask in bubbling water while gazing up to the heavens through a skylight.

Carnival Cruise Lines. ⊠ *3655 NW 87th Ave., Miami, FL 33178,* ☎ *305/ 599–2600 or 800/227–6482.* Commissioned in 1990–1996. Liberian registry, Italian officers, international staff. Ports: Caribbean, Mexico.

Exercise Equipment: 35 weight-training units, Precor 825L bikes, StairMaster PT4000, Precor steppers, rower, free weights (2–25 lbs), Roman chairs, benches. **Services:** Massage, reflexology, loofah scrub, facial, cathiodermie facial, herbal pack, aromatherapy, pressotherapy, G5 weight-loss massage, eucalyptus steam inhalation. Beauty salon for hair, nail and make-up consultation. **Swimming:** 1–2 outdoor pools. **Recreation:** Trap-shooting, table tennis, shuffleboard. **Children's Programs:** Children's play room on all ships.

Fares include airfare from major cities: $709–$1,339 for 4-day cruise to the Bahamas; $1,574–$2,439 for 7-day cruise.

CELEBRITY CRUISES

With the largest thalassotherapy pools afloat, the *Century, Galaxy,* and *Mercury* feature sea-oriented treatments.

The top-deck AquaSpa[SM] has an indoor exercise pool with underwater jets. Workouts in the warm seawater enhance circulation, leaving you relaxed and refreshed. Nearby are a coed steam room and separate locker rooms with shower/sauna for men and women.

The 10,000-square-ft spas are operated by Steiner Transocean. Each has a window-walled weights room, providing panoramic views as you exercise. Classes are scheduled in a cushion-floored aerobics studio, and passengers relax in six outdoor whirlpools. For an Asian de-stressor, try Rasul, based on a cleansing ceremony that includes a seaweed-soap shower, medicinal mud pack, herbal steam bath, and massage. The Aquameditation bath, new to the *Century* and the *Galaxy,* includes rotating shower heads in a pre-massage soak. The extensive selection of beauty services is provided by a professional staff, who also schedule fitness classes that range from cardio-funk low-impact aerobics to designer body conditioning and a 30-minute session of aquaerobics in the outdoor swimming pool. In addition to a dozen pieces of exercise equipment, there are ¼-mi outdoor jogging tracks.

Dieters choose between a full vegetarian menu designed by London restaurateur Michel Roux and the regular menu with highlighted items that are low in sodium and cholesterol.

The 52 Sky Suites with marble-tiled baths and butler service are top of the line; there are also 61 cabins with balconies.

Celebrity Cruises. ⊠ *5201 Blue Lagoon Dr., Miami, FL 33126,* ☎ *305/262–8322 or 800/437–3111.* Deluxe staterooms and outside cabins; most cabins are compact, all have private shower and toilet. Liberian registry, Greek officers, and European staff. Ports: Caribbean, Alaska, Bermuda.

Exercise Equipment: Weight-training equipment, treadmills, NordicTrack cross-country ski machine, Aerobicycles, virtual-reality bikes, rowing machines, free weights. **Services:** Massage, reflexology, seaweed treatments, cathiodermie revitalizing facial, ionithermie slimming treatment, body brushing, personal fitness analysis, body-fat analysis, personal training; salon for hair, nail, and skin care. **Swimming:** 2 outdoor swimming pools. **Classes and Programs:** Aerobics. **Children's Programs:** Supervised daily programs for ages 3–17.

Fares for 7-day cruise from $1,625–$3,425 per person, double occupancy, not including airfare. Sails from Miami on Saturday and Sunday.

COSTA CRUISE LINES

Italian-accented cruising with the Costa fleet reached a peak in 1996 with the debut of the 1,950-passenger flagship MV *CostaVictoria.* Featuring spa treatments with the exclusive Terme di Saturnia cosmetics developed at one of Italy's leading spa resorts, the Pompeii Spa offers a variety of "ahh la carte"[SM] body therapies, including seaweed or algae, and moor mud. Workouts come with great views of the sea in a window-walled fitness center, which has weight-training equipment, stationary bicycles, and stairsteppers. The spa is staffed with well-trained Steiner professionals who can develop a personalized exercise program for you. Services can be selected in packages from half-day to six days, pre-booked by your travel agent.

At the center of the Pompeii Spa is an indoor swimming pool surrounded by columns; certain lanes are dedicated to lap swimmers. The room itself has a large Italian mosaic covering the walls and the ceiling. Separate dressing rooms for men and women include Turkish bath, Finnish sauna, and showers. From the center of the spa, a 500-meter jogging track connects to the gymnasium and an aerobics studio on Traviata Deck (#6).

Built in Italy, this glamorous liner recalls the golden era of transatlantic ships. Mealtime resembles a Roman festival, but heart-healthy options are on the menu. And for exercise, there's a pizza dough throwing contest, tarantella dancing, and boccie ball games.

Costa Cruise Lines. ⊠ *Brickell Bayview Centre, 80 S.W. 8th St., Miami, FL 33130,* ☎ *305/358–7325 or 800/462–6782.* Deluxe outside staterooms and suites with whirlpool bath; standard cabins, with 2 lower beds that convert to a queen-size bed, shower and toilet. 20 staterooms equipped for persons with disabilities. Italian registry, Italian officers and dining room staff, European stewardesses.

Exercise Equipment: Strength-training equipment, cardiovascular equipment including treadmills, step machine, rower. **Services:** Massage, reflexology, body wrap, body scrub, thalassotherapy, hydrotherapy bath, deep-cleansing facial, rehydrating facial, personal training.

Cruises to the Eastern and Western Caribbean. Fares for a 7-day cruise from Ft. Lauderdale without airfare, reserved 90 days or more in advance, $599–$3,039 per person, double occupancy.

CRYSTAL HARMONY

This 960-passenger liner has a 3,000-square-ft ocean-view spa and fitness center that offers aerobic and Jazzercise instruction and treatments that include thalassotherapy, moortherapy, and aromatherapy. Passengers relax in men's and women's saunas and steam rooms, tee-off at a golf simulator, jog on a full promenade deck, play on paddle tennis or volleyball courts, swim in a lap pool, soak in Jacuzzis, or socialize in an indoor/outdoor swimming pool with built-in bar. A fitness trainer is aboard, and there are special slimming programs using the DeCleor program. Operated by Steiner, the pampering program includes facials, body wrap, and a French hand treatment. The spa also offers a salon for hair, nail, and skin care, and a men's barbershop.

All staterooms have bathroom with tub and shower, double vanity. Dinner is served at your choice of time in Italian or Chinese restaurants.

Crystal Cruises. ⊠ *2121 Avenue of the Stars, Suite 200, Los Angeles, CA 90067,* ☎ *310/785–9300 or 800/446–6620.* 8 passenger decks with 480 deluxe staterooms, including 62 penthouse suites. All outside accommodations except 19 inside cabins; many have private verandas; all have king- or queen-size beds. Bahamian registry, Norwegian and Japanese officers, Italian dining staff, international crew.

Exercise Equipment: Treadmills, Lifecycles, StairMasters, rowing machines, Lifecircuit weight training machines, free weights. **Services:** Massage, facials, body scrub, herbal wrap; foot, hand, and eye treatments; personal trainer; beauty salon.

Cruises from Acapulco, New Orleans, San Juan, Fort Lauderdale. Fares including airfare for 11-day trans-Canal cruise $1,980–$16,450 per person, double occupancy.

DISNEY CRUISE LINE

Offering more entertainment options than any ship afloat, Disney Cruise Line provides an oasis of rejuvenation and relaxation for adults. Aboard the *Disney Magic,* the Vista Spa & Salon occupies one of the ship's highest points, overlooking the captain's bridge. Guests can work out while enjoying sea views. Featuring treatments from around the world, including hydrotherapy and unique thermal-bath rooms, the Vista Spa has 11 treatment rooms in addition to a common area devoted to a tropical rain shower and aromatic mists. You can indulge in seaweed and mud treatments, or get an underwater massage. Fitness enthusiasts enjoy the latest Cybex equipment, including the Cybex VR2 line for strength training, and the first onboard Cybex Reactor. There are stationary bikes, Tectrix virtual-reality stair climbers, and free weights with a Smith press unit.

The Disney Cruise vacation comes in 3-, 4-, and 7-day packages and includes a visit to the Walt Disney World Resort.

On-board accommodations range from standard inside staterooms, which sleep two, to royal two-bedroom suites with private verandahs, which sleep five. Each room has a private bathroom, individual climate control, a color television, private voice mail, and a hair dryer.

Disney Cruise Line. ✉ *Box 22804, Lake Buena Vista, FL 32830,* ☎ *407/ 566–7000 or 800/511–1333.* Bahamian registry, international officers and staff.

Exercise Equipment: Cybex strength-training equipment, Cybex Reactor, cross-country skiing machine, rowing machines, Smith press, stair climbers, stationary bikes, treadmills, free weights. **Services:** Massage, hydrotherapy, facials, manicure, pedicure, hairstyling, makeup consultation. **Swimming:** 4 pools. **Classes and Programs:** Aerobics, aquacise, personal training. **Recreation:** Badminton, basketball, biking, boating, guided walks, hiking, paddle tennis, shuffleboard, soccer, snorkeling, table tennis, volleyball. Broadway-style musical theater, dance club, first-run movie theater, comedy club, piano bar, sports bar. **Children's Programs:** Age-appropriate daily activities for ages 3–17.

Fares for the 3-day cruise to the Bahamas range from $799–$2,789 per person (including economy airfare, transfers, meals) based on double occupancy and class of accommodations. Fares for the 4-day cruise to the Bahamas range from $909–$2,999 (same inclusions as above). Fares for the 7-day Resort-and-Cruise package range from $1,295–$4,225 (same inclusions as above, plus admission to Walt Disney World).

HOLLAND AMERICA LINE

With a Passport to Fitness program aboard every ship in its fleet, Holland America Line offers one of the best values in health and fitness cruises year-round. Passengers pick up a passport aboard the ship to earn stamps for fitness classes, team sports, and beauty treatments. Even ordering lunch and dinner from the Light and Healthy menu in the dining room earns a stamp (the menu includes such items as grilled seabass with warm tomato salad, or chicken breast salad). Prizes are awarded for 20–40 stamps. Aerobics classes and aquatic workouts are available to all passengers. Tennis and golf programs and a scuba certification course are offered on shore excursions. The Ocean Spa has a gymnasium with exercise equipment and a small area for aerobics classes. Large windows provide ocean views while you're working out. In fair weather, exercise classes are held on the teak deck. There are locker rooms for men and women, with steam rooms and saunas, plus four massage rooms.

Immaculately maintained and decorated with an extensive collection of art and antiques, the Dutch fleet has a new flagship, the 1,320-passenger *Rotterdam VI*. These are true ocean liners, with services and amenities in the grand tradition of transatlantic travel.

The Ocean Spas aboard the 1,266-passenger sister ships *Maasdam, Statendam, Veendam,* and *Ryndam* have 4,126 square ft for an aerobics studio, strength training equipment, stationary bicycles, treadmills, stairclimbers, rowing machines, and free weights. Refresh at the juice bar, sets of saunas and steam rooms, and two outdoor whirlpools. The spa is operated by Steiner, and offers aromatherapy, body wraps, and massage, as well as hair salon services.

Holland America Line. ✉ *300 Elliott Ave. W, Seattle, WA 98119,* ☎ *206/ 281–3535 or 800/426–0327.* Netherlands Antilles registry, Dutch and British officers, Indonesian and Filipino staff.

Exercise Equipment: 10-unit Hydra-Fitness circuit, Lifecycles, StairMasters, rowing machines, free and pulley weights, slant boards, treadmills. **Services:** Massage, facials, manicure, pedicure, hairstyling, makeup consultation. **Swimming:** 2 outdoor swimming pools (1 has whirlpool jets). **Recreation:** Tennis courts, shuffleboard, scuba instruction, volleyball.

Caribbean cruise fares start at $1,006, with 40%–45% savings possible through advance-booking program. Fares for 7-day Alaska cruise from $1,100, with 25% savings for early bookings. Winter cruises from Ft. Lauderdale, Tampa, and New Orleans. Other cruises: New England and Eastern Canada, Panama Canal, Mexico, Hawaii.

SS NORWAY

The 14-room, 6,000-square-ft Roman Spa, which opened in 1990, aboard the *SS Norway* launched a new era of spa luxury at sea. Featuring the first hydrotherapy baths on a cruise ship, the spa employs European-trained specialists in thalassotherapy, shiatsu, reflexology, aromatherapy, thermal body wraps, and a wide range of beauty services. Services can be booked à la carte; five package programs are available for a complete spa vacation, ranging from a half-day introductory sampler for $124.50 to 10 hours of treatments for $493. The daily fee for use of the spa facility is waived if you book a treatment such as the $66 massage, plus 12% gratuity.

On Dolphin Deck, the new Roman Spa is a sybaritic enclave of 16 private treatment rooms (each equipped with shower), men's and women's saunas and steam rooms, a seawater aquacise pool and Jacuzzi, juice bar, and an exercise room with computerized cardiovascular equipment. The *Norway*'s spa treatments incorporate ancient Roman philosophy and a sea theme with Phytomer marine algae and moor mud products by Remé

Laure. For relaxation, try 30 minutes in the Alpha capsule, an egg-shaped device that stimulates the body with motion and sound. Advance appointments prior to sailing can be made by calling the spa operators, Steiner Group (☎ 800/275–5293 or 305/358–9002). The spa is open every day, 8–8 during the cruise.

For more active passengers there is a "In Motion on the Ocean" fitness program that awards prizes for participating in the various physical activities scheduled every day. The ship's Olympic Deck is dedicated to fitness: a glass-walled gymnasium with state-of-the-art exercise equipment, and a 360-degree jogging/walking track. Team games are organized in the "Norway Olympics," and snorkeling is offered at a beach party on NCL's private uninhabited island in the Bahamas. Added features during the Fitness and Beauty Cruise at the end of October include workshops on nutrition, sports medicine, and skin care; running clinics; and workouts with sports personalities. During the rest of the year, golf and tennis Pro-Am cruises have professionals aboard to help improve your game, and opportunities for play abound on shore. Fitness walks are organized in each port.

Norwegian Cruise Line. ⊠ *7665 Corporate Center Dr., Miami, FL 33126,* ☎ *305/436–4000 or 800/327–7030.* Entered service as the *France,* in 1962, refitted as the *Norway* in 1979, renovated and expanded in 1990, refurbished 1996. 2,032 passengers. Bahamian registry and officers, international staff.

Exercise Equipment: Gymnasium with Cybex weight-training equipment, Concept 2 rower, Liferowers, Lifecycles, Lifesteps, free weights, Ivanko dumbells; Roman spa with Bally cardiovascular equipment. **Services:** Massage, facials, hydrotherapy bath, bodywrap, makeup cleansing; hair, nail, and skin care. **Swimming:** 2 outdoor swimming pools. **Recreation:** Outdoor jogging track, racquetball, basketball, volleyball courts, golf putting and driving areas, skeet shooting.

Cruise-only fares $649–$3,299, not including airfare and transfers. Year-round 7-night cruises departing from Miami on Saturday.

THE NORWEGIAN MAJESTY

The *Norwegian Majesty* debuted in 1992 as the first ship to ban smoking in the dining room. 132 of the cabins are also smoke-free.

A well-equipped sea-view spa managed by Steiner is situated high atop the ship, and healthful Regal Bodies spa cuisine is available in the dining room. The spa has an aerobics studio with wooden floor where aerobics and tai chi classes are scheduled daily. There are massage rooms, 2 saunas, a smallish outdoor swimming pool, and a pair of whirlpools.

Norwegian Cruise Line. ⊠ *7665 Corporate Center Dr., Miami, FL 33126,* ☎ *305/436–4000 or 800/327–7030.* Commissioned in 1992. 1,056 passengers. Panamanian registry, Norwegian officers, international crew.

Exercise Equipment: StairMasters, Lifecycle, Fly, recumbent bike, weight training machines, free weights, NordicTrack cross-country machine, rowing machine. **Services:** Massage, personal training; hair, nail, and skin salon.

Cruises from Miami. Fares for 3-night Bahamas cruise, including airfare, $359–$959 per person, double occupancy; 4-night cruise to Nassau, Key West, and private island, $409–$1,049 per person. Summer cruises to Bermuda from Boston, $1,199–$2,099.

PRINCESS CRUISES

After 30 years of "Love Boat" fame, Princess Cruise Lines introduced Grand Class℠ ships and the world's largest cruise ship, *Grand Princess*.

Fourteen stories high and nearly three football fields in length, with five swimming pools, two restaurants tiered on three decks, and a computerized golf center, these floating resorts feature both intimate spaces and grand vistas. With over a dozen pieces of exercise equipment in the 3,250-square-ft fitness center, plus an outdoor ⅙-mi jogging track, the fitness facilities are part of the Cruisercise® program that awards prizes for participation in exercise activity. The fleetwide program was designed by Kathy Smith, fitness trainer for the Stars & Stripes U.S. sailing team. On all ships a daily schedule of classes includes walk-a-mile, stretch and tone, high- or low-impact aerobics, and aquacise.

High on the ship, with views overlooking the bow, The Riviera Spa wraps around a swimming pool and Jacuzzi on the Lido deck. The spacious beauty salon has 10 stations for hairstyling and eight treatment rooms, one with a hydrotherapy tub. Sign up for facials, massage, body wraps, and a hydrotherapy soak in seaweed or herbs.

The dining room menu offers heart-healthy items that are low in sodium and cholesterol, prepared according to American Heart Association guidelines. Dining options include a 24-hour food court in the Lido Cafe, and a pizzeria.

Recalling the days of the great ocean liners, the teak decks and decorative accents in brass, warm woods, and marble enhance spacious staterooms. More than 70% of the cabins have a private balcony.

Princess Cruises. ⊠ *10100 Santa Monica Blvd., Los Angeles, CA 90067,* ☎ *310/553–1770 or 800/421–0522.* British registry and officers, Italian dining room staff, British stewards.

Exercise Equipment: Hydra-fitness 11-station multipurpose weights unit, rowing machines, treadmill, Paramount Uniflex sports trainer, Lifecycles, slant boards, free weights. **Services:** Massage, facials, moortherapy facial mask, leg and back treatment, throat and décolleté treatment, foot and hand treatment, body wrap, eye treatment. Salon for hair, nail, and skin care. **Swimming:** 5 outdoor swimming pools (with a 33' pool for laps). **Classes and Programs:** Aerobics.

Cruises include Alaska, Trans-Panama Canal, Caribbean. Cruise-only fares for 7 days from Ft. Lauderdale, $991–$2,461 per person, double occupancy. 7-day Alaska cruise from Vancouver $1,514–$4,229 double, cruise only.

QUEEN ELIZABETH 2

The Steiner spa aboard Cunard's majestic *Queen Elizabeth 2* is a treat for body, mind, and spirit. Steiner, after all, holds royal warrants as hairdresser to the queen. But here the accent is on thalassotherapy, a French concept of seawater-based bodywork and exercise in fresh seawater. An indoor swimming pool is part of the fitness center (open to all passengers free of charge), which has a full line of Cybex equipment and computerized exercise bikes, as well as an aerobics studio. The spa is a separate enclave on the ship's lowest deck (7) with a unique hydrotherapy pool in which you follow a circuit of underwater jets. The effect is like getting your muscles massaged while you exercise or relax amid bubbling geysers. The London-trained therapists usher you into a private treatment room (there are

10) for a seaweed body mask, enveloping you in a mixture of Phytomer algae, followed by a full-hour massage to sounds of the sea. Other treatments on the spa's list provide the energizing and remineralizing effect of a hydrotub bath with freeze-dried seaweed, inhalations to clear your sinus problems, or a water blitz massage in which concentrated jets play across your body. Spacious and accented by teak and silver, the white-tile spa pool, coed steam room, and locker rooms with saunas can be used for a daily fee or as part of packages. The Steiner salon is on an upper deck (1) with four private rooms for ionithermie anti-cellulite body-slimming treatments and cathiodermie deep-cleansing facials.

Newly created spa cuisine is on the menu in all dining rooms, made to order in the Grill rooms. The benefits of British Airways' "Well-Being in the Air" program are an added bonus, as your QE2 ticket includes one-way air transportation with the option of following a scientifically designed fitness and food plan during the flight.

On all voyages, including Caribbean and Bermuda cruises, passengers can participate in the fitness center's scheduled classes. One-on-one training is offered for a fee, as well as a nutritional assessment and fitness evaluation. Open from 7AM to 7PM, the indoor saltwater swimming pool can be reached by elevator. Additional swimming pools are on deck.

Following a major face-lift in 1994, the superliner reflects a distinctive lifestyle as well as the heritage and tradition of great ocean liners. Transformation of the Lido into an informal buffet-style restaurant for breakfast and lunch, new bathrooms in all cabins, an Observation Lounge with panoramic vistas, and a pub with dart board are among recent enhancements.

Cunard Line. ✉ *6100 Blue Lagoon D., Miami, FL 33126,* ☎ *305/463-3000 or 800/223-0764.* Launched in 1967, re-entered service 1987; major refurbishment 1994. 1,756 passengers. British registry, British and European officers.

Exercise Equipment: 7-unit Cybex weight-training circuit, StairMasters, Lifecycles, treadmills, free weights, personal trainer. **Services:** Massage, ionithermie, cathiodermie facial, Phytomer seaweed body mask, Elemis aromatherapy facial, thalassotherapy body scrub, Oligomer hydrotherapeutic bath. Salon for hair, nail, and skin care. **Classes and Programs:** Aerobics.

Cruises from New York to New England, Bermuda, Caribbean. 6-day cruise-only fares $1,620–$5,270, suites $10,520–$18,290 per person, double occupancy. Transatlantic air/sea fares $2,860–$9,330, suites $22,290–$39,080 per person, double.

SSC RADISSON DIAMOND

The entire top deck of the *SSC Radisson Diamond* is devoted to a spa and jogging track, and there is a marina that descends into the sea. The twin-hull design accommodates 177 staterooms. SSC (Semi-Submersible Craft) technology minimizes engine and propeller noise and maximizes deck space. From the five-story atrium, you are whisked up a glass elevator to three decks of suites (there are 12 decks total) and a glass-walled dining room. All cabins are suite-size with private balcony, queen-size bed, TV, VCR, stereo, and a full bath with shower.

The Diamond Spa, on Deck 11, offers a selection of services by Steiner. Past the reception area are two skin-care rooms, four rooms for body-work. There are separate saunas and steam rooms for men and women, and exercise equipment. Exercise classes, scheduled twice each morning and afternoon, are held in the main lounge or on deck. You can join stretch/walk at 7:30 AM, then a step class, water aerobics, or line dancing. The open-air swimming pool and Jacuzzi are tiny, but in port you can swim in a floating marina equipped for snorkeling, windsurfing, and water jet boats.

With an open-seating policy in the main dining room, you can order off the menu, request a special diet, or select from the "Simplicity" menu. Evening entertainment is limited to the casino and TV. The ship's rates do not cover personal services in the spa and salon.

Radisson Seven Seas Cruises. ✉ *600 Corporate Dr., Suite 410, Fort Lauderdale, FL 33334,* ☎ *800/477–7500,* reservations *800/285–1835.* Launched in 1992. 350 passengers. Bahamian registry, European officers, Filipino and Scandinavian crew.

Exercise Equipment: 7-unit Cybex weight-training circuit, StairMasters, Lifecycles, treadmills, free weights, personal trainer. **Services**: Massage, ionithermie, cathiodermie facial, Phytomer seaweed body mask, Elemis aromatherapy facial, thalassotherapy body scrub, Oligomer hydrotherapeutic bath. Salon for hair, nail, and skin care. **Classes and Programs:** Aerobics.

Cruises from New York to New England, Bermuda, Caribbean. 6-day cruise-only fares $1,620–$5,270, suites $10,520–$18,290 per person, double occupancy. Transatlantic air/sea fares $2,860–$9,330, suites $22,290–$39,080 per person, double.

ROYAL CARIBBEAN INTERNATIONAL

The 1995 introduction of Royal Caribbean International's 70,000-ton, 1,804- passenger *Legend of the Seas* marked the company's first design of a ship for destinations outside the Caribbean and Bahamas. Known for its *Song of Norway* (which has no spa/exercise facility), and 2,354-passenger *Monarch of the Seas,* RCI now cruises to Hawaii and Alaska, as well as offering Panama Canal, transatlantic, and European programs. With the arrival of sister ship *Splendour of the Seas* in 1996, the fleet gained a second megaship, and four more arrived through 1998.

From the Centrum, a dramatic, glass-walled atrium on these new liners, elevators whisk you to the Steiner spa high atop the ship. There is a fitness program called ShipShape, an 18-hole miniature golf course with real links, and heart-healthy cuisine in the restaurants.

On these French-built megaships, the spa is on Sun Deck just aft of the Solarium, an indoor/outdoor dining and entertainment area with swimming pool under a retractable glass canopy. Decorated with green plants, Roman columns, statues and artworks, it's a convenient place to unwind after exercise sessions. Reached from the central lobby, the spa contains a unisex hair salon with seven stations, two treatment rooms for facials and manicure/pedicure, five massage rooms, and changing rooms with saunas and steam baths. There is an aerobics area large enough for 35 participants during scheduled classes, and exercise equipment facing the glass-walled view of the sea.

Steiner offers a variety of packages during the cruise, and the spa remains open for treatments during port days.

Royal Caribbean International. ✉ *1050 Caribbean Way, Miami, FL 33132,* ☎ *305/539–6000 or 800/327–6700.* Norwegian registry and officers, international staff.

Exercise Equipment: 10-unit strength-training system, recumbent bicycles, step machines, treadmills, incline benches, free weights. **Services:** Massage, reflexology, herbal wrap; salon for hair, nail, and skin care.

Cruises from Miami, Honolulu, Vancouver, Los Angeles, San Juan, New York, Boston, Barcelona, Harwick. Fares with early booking discount for 10- and 11-night Panama Canal cruise from $1,763 per person, double occupancy; 7-night Alaska or Caribbean cruise from $1,049.

SEAWARD

The *Seaward*, a Finnish-built addition to the Norwegian Cruise Line fleet, is a 42,000-ton beauty complete with cascading waterfall, cushioned running track, and basketball court. Although smaller than her big sister the *Norway*, she has a ¼-mi promenade deck that encircles the ship—a detail missing on many new liners. The top-deck spa/salon, operated by Steiner of London, all glass and gleaming chrome, affords panoramic views of the sea to those working out. Separate saunas and showers are provided for men and women, and massage is available. The accent is on sports: The ship's two swimming pools and adjacent whirlpools have splash areas surrounded by Astroturf, where a "dive-in" center offers snorkeling equipment and instruction. Excursions in port take in some of the finest golf courses and tennis courts in the islands. Pro-Am cruises team passengers with golf and tennis pros on designated weeks throughout the year. Racquet Club cruises and Tee-Up golf cruises offer clinics and workshops at sea and special games and matches ashore.

Dining alternatives include a choice of lighter meals at an informal café and an à la carte restaurant where meals are prepared to order.

Norwegian Cruise Line. ⊠ *7665 Corporate Center Dr., Miami, FL 33126,* ☎ *305/436–4000 or 800/327–7030.* Inaugurated in 1988. 1,504 passengers. Bahamian registry, Norwegian officers, international crew.

Exercise Equipment: Cybex strength-training equipment, Lifecycles , Lifefitness cardiovascular exercise equipment, rowing machines, Ivanko free weight dumbbells. **Services:** Massage, facials, moortherapy facial mask, throat and decolleté treatment; eye, foot, and hand treatments; exfoliation; herbal or thermal body wrap; salon for hair, nail, and skin care. **Swimming:** 2 outdoor pools. **Recreation:** Volleyball, snorkeling, skeet shooting, golf driving.

Cruises from San Juan. Cruise-only fare $749–$2,149 per person, double occupancy.

SEAWIND CROWN

Sailing from Aruba, the classic *Seawind Crown* offers features not found on larger ships, such as squash and volleyball courts, as well as a fitness center. In addition to the coed sauna and cold plunge pool, there are two outdoor swimming pools (one heated) and a jogging track for deck exercise.

Premier Cruises. ⊠ *901 S. America Way, Miami, FL 33132,* ☎ *305/285–9494 or 800/990–7770.* Commissioned as TSS *Vasco da Gama*, rebuilt 1989. Panamanian registry. International dining room staff and cabin service. 764 passengers. Cabins have color TV, terry cloth robes, bathroom with hair dryer.

Exercise Equipment: StairMaster, 4-station Universal strength training machine, AerobiCycle, Universal free weights, benches. **Services:** Massage; salon for hair, nail, and skin-care.

Cruises from Aruba every Sunday. Fares $1,198–$2,398 per person, double occupancy, including airfare and early booking discount from U.S. cities. Accommodations for people with disabilities in 2 cabins.

WINDSTAR CRUISES

A blend of modern technology and the romance of cruising under sail, the yachtlike *Wind Surf* brought new excitement to the seagoing spa concept in 1998. Offering an intensive fitness program patterned after land spas, the ship's 10,000-square-ft spa is remarkably large for a ship that carries only 312 passengers. There are two restaurants serving coastal cuisine. While the line's three ships have spas operated by Steiner, Wind Surf may sail away with top honors for spagoers.

Wind Spirit and *Wind Star* offer a tiny fitness center and a full program of water sports. While under sail, a computerized system raises the six sails automatically in less than two minutes. While anchored in secluded coves, away from the routes of the large cruise ships, the vessel's crew members organize waterskiing and snorkeling expeditions. There is scuba equipment aboard for certified divers. Shore excursions to golf and tennis resorts can be arranged through the ship's purser.

Windstar Cruises. ⊠ *300 Elliott Ave. W., Seattle, WA 98119,* ☎ *206/281–3535 or 800/258–7245.* Commissioned in 1988. 148 passengers. Bahamian registry, international crew.

Exercise Equipment: 2 rowing machines, stationary bikes, outdoor swimming pool, sauna. **Services:** Massage, facial, hand, and foot treatment. **Recreation:** Water sports, shore excursions for golf and tennis.

Cruises the Windward and Leeward islands. Fares for 7-day cruise $3,466 per person, double occupancy, with advance reservation discount, $5,938 single. Suite $4,455–$8,570. Airfare not included.

Glossary

A

Abhyanga. Rhythmic herbal-oil massage performed by two therapists, followed by hot towel treatment.

Acupressure. Finger massage intended to release muscle tension by applying pressure to the nerves.

Aikido. Japanese martial art.

Alexander Technique. A massage system created in the 1890s by the Australian actor F. M. Alexander to correct physical habits that cause stress and help improve posture.

Algotherapy. Seaweed bath. See *Thalassotherapy*.

Aquaerobics. Aerobics workouts in a swimming pool; stretch, strength, and stamina exercises that combine water resistance and body movements. Also *aquafit* and *aquacise*.

Aromabath. See *herbal wrap*.

Aromatherapy. Massage with oils from essences of plants and flowers intended to relax the skin's connective tissues and stimulate the natural flow of lymph.

Asana. A posture used in the practice of yoga.

Ayurvedic. 4,000-year-old Indian treatments, based on teachings from the Vedic scriptures, using oils, massage, and herbs.

B

Bach Cures. Healing with floral essences and oils.

Balneology. Traditional study and practice of water-based treatments using geothermal hot springs, mineral water, or seawater.

Balneotherapy. *See Balneology.*

Barre. Balance bar or rail used during exercise.

Bindi. Bodywork combining exfoliation, herbal treatment, and light massage.

Bioenergetics. Exchange of energy between persons giving and receiving massage.

Body brushing. Exfoliating treatment involving the dry brushing of skin to remove dead cells and stimulate circulation, then the application of hydrating oils to soften the skin.

Body composition test. Evaluation of lean body mass and percentage of body fat. A computerized system compares personal data with standard percentages to determine whether an individual is overweight.

Body polish. Use of large sea sponges to gently cleanse, exfoliate, and hydrate the body.

Body sugaring. Hair-removal process said to date from the time of Cleopatra.

Boxaerobics. High-energy aerobics incorporating boxing movements and kicks.

C

Cardio theater. System for plugging TV or radio headphones into exercise equipment.

Chi Kung. Chinese energy exercise; breathing and body movements recharge energy.

Circuit training. The combination of aerobics and high-energy workout with weight-resistance equipment.

Circuit weight work. See *Circuit training*.

Clay wrap. See *mud wrap*.

Cold plunge. Deep pool for the rapid contraction of the capillaries; stimulates circulation after sauna.

Colonic irrigation. Enema to cleanse high into the colon with water.

Complementary medicine. Complements to traditional Western medicine incorporating the ancient arts of acupuncture and Chinese herbal medicine. Also *complementary healing arts*.

Contour. Calisthenics for deep toning of muscle groups.

Craniosacral therapy. Massage therapy focusing on the head and neck.

Crystal healing. Healing energy believed to be generated by quartz and other minerals.

Cures. Course of treatments. Also *kur*.

Cybex. Patented equipment for isokinetic strength testing and training.

D

David System. Pneumatic weight training units in which air is pumped. See *Circuit training*.

Drinking cure. Medically prescribed regimen of mineral water consumption.

E

Ergometer. Exercise machine designed for muscular contraction.

F

Fango. A mud pack or body coating intended to promote the release of toxins and relieve muscular and arthritic pain.

Fast. Supervised diet of water, juice, nuts, seeds; intended to produce significant weight loss.

Feldenkrais Method. Developed by Israeli physicist Moshe Feldenkrais in the 1940s to reprogram the nervous system through movement augmented by physical pressure and manipulation.

Free weights. Hand-held dumbbells or barbells.

G

Gestalt. Sensory awareness; the inner experience of being.

Glycolic exfoliation. A treatment that breaks down the glue bond that holds dry skin on the face; softens lines and smooths skin.

Gommage. A cleansing and moisturizing theatment that makes use of creams applied with movements similar to those of an extensive massage.

Guided imagery. Visualization to stimulate the body's immune system.

G5. Percussive hand massage to relax tense muscles.

H

Hatha yoga. System of yoga that focuses on bodily control through use of asanas. Also *asana*.

Haysack wrap. Kneipp treatment with steamed hay intended to detoxify the body.

Hellerwork. A system of deep tissue bodywork, stress reduction, and movement reeducation developed by Joseph Heller.

Herbal wrap. A treatment in which moisture, heat, and herbal essences penetrate the skin while the body is wrapped in hot linens, plastic sheets, and blankets; it is intended to promote muscle relaxation and the elimination of toxins. Also *aromabath, herbal bath*.

Herbology. The therapeutic use of herbs in treatments and diet.

Hot plunge. Deep pool for the rapid dilation of the capillaries.

Hydromassage. See *hydrotub*.

Hydrotherapy. Underwater massage; alternating hot and cold showers; and other water-oriented treatments.

Hydrotub. Underwater massage in deep tubs equipped with high-pressure jets and hand-manipulated hose. Also *hydromassage*.

I

Inhalations. Hot vapors, or steam mixed with eucalyptus oil, inhaled to decongest the respiratory system; breathed through inhalation equipment or in a special steam room.

Interval training. A combination of high-energy exercise followed by a period of low-intensity activity.

Iridology. A theory that links markings in the iris of the eye to the condition of organs of the body.

Iyengar yoga. Exercise system developed in India by B.K.S. Iyengar.

J

Jin shin do. Ancient art of harmonizing life energy within the body; practiced by placing fingertips over clothing on designated body parts.

Jin shin jyutsu. Ancient Japanese form of body balancing.

K

Keiser. A patented system of pneumatic weight-training units.

Kick boxing. A form of self-defense that involves punching kicking, and blocking.

Kneipp kur. Treatments combining hydrotherapy, herbology, and a diet of natural foods, developed in Germany in the mid-1800s by Pastor Sebastian Kneipp.

Kripalu. Literally, "the compassionate union of body, mind, and spirit," a form of yoga that combines physical postures (asanas) with meditation.

Kur. Course of treatments, as in Kneipp kur, usually associated with baths or drinking mineral water under medical supervision at European thermal spring spas.

L

Lap pool. A pool with swimming lanes for working out; lap length varies.

Lifecycle. A computer-programmed exercise bike, made by Bally.

Lomi-Lomi. Hawaiian rhythmical rocking massage.

M

Maharishi. A Hindu teacher of mystical knowledge.

Maximal heart rate. An individual's highest attainable heart rate (the number of heartbeats per minute). It is best determined by means of a graded maximal exercise test, but an estimate can be made by subtracting one's age from 220. See *target heart rate.*

Mud wrap. Body treatment using warm mud to cleanse pores and lift impurities.

N

Naturopathy. Natural healing prescriptions that use plants and flowers.

Nautilus. Patented strength training equipment designed to isolate one muscle group for each exercise movement that contracts and lengthens against gravity.

O

Ovo-lacto diet. A regimen that includes eggs and dairy products.

P

Panchakarma. A type of massage therapy that uses warm, herbalized oils and aims to restore balance to the body.

Parafango. Combination of mud and paraffin wax. See *fango.*

Paraffin wrap. Process of removing dead skin cells with hot oil and Japanese dry-brushing techniques, then applying a hydrating wax treatment to entire body.

Parcourse. A trail, usually outdoors, equipped with exercise stations. Also *parcours, vitacourse.*

Pilates Method. Strength training movements developed in Germany by Dr. Joseph Pilates during the 1920s.

Pizichilli. Purifying experience in which a continuous stream of warm, herbalized oil is poured over the body as two therapists perform a gentle massage.

Plyometrics. Jumps and push steps to strengthen leg muscles. See *Step aerobics.*

Polarity therapy. Balancing the energy within the body through a combination of massage, meditation, exercise, and diet; created by Dr. Randolph Stone.

Pressotherapy. Pressure cuffs used to improve circulation on feet.

Pressure-point massage. Massage and body work which uses pressure on designated body parts that connect to major nerves, to relieve stress.

Q

Qi-gong. See *Chi Kung*.

R

Radiance technique. See *Reiki*.

Rebirthing. A yoga breathing technique combined with guided meditation to relax and clear the mind. Also *reliving the experience of birth*.

Reflexology. Massage of the pressure points on the feet, hands, and ears; intended to relax the parts of the body.

Reiki. An ancient healing method that teaches universal life energy through the laying on of hands and mental and spiritual balancing. Intended to relieve acute emotional and physical conditions. Also *radiance technique*.

Rolfing. A bodywork system developed by Ida Rolf that improves balance and flexibility through manipulation of rigid muscles, bones, and joints. It is intended to improve energy flow and relieve stress (often related to emotional trauma).

Roman pool. A step-down whirlpool bath, for one or two persons.

Rubenfeld Synergy. A method of integrating body and mind through verbal expression and gentle touch, developed by Ilana Rubenfeld.

Russian bath. Steam bath to flush toxins from the body.

S

Salt glow. A cleansing treatment, using coarse salt to remove dead skin, similar to the loofah body scrub. Also *salt rub*.

Salt rub. See *salt glow*.

Scotch douche. A showerlike treatment with high-pressure hoses that alternate hot and cold water, intended to improve circulation through rapid contraction and dilation of the capillaries.

Seaweed wrap. A wrap using concentrated seawater and nutrient-packed seaweed; minerals, proteins, rare trace elements, and vitamins are absorbed into the bloodstream to revitalize the skin and body.

Shamanism. Spiritual and natural healing performed by medicine men and women.

Shiroabhyanganasya. Head, face, and neck massage followed by herbal steam treatment, heat packs, and herbal drops for nasal passages, to remove impurities and congestion.

Shirodhara. Ayurvedic massage in which warm herbal oil is dropped on the forehead ("the third eye"), and rubbed gently into the hair and scalp.

Shiatsu. A massage technique developed by Tokujiro Namikoshi that uses finger (*shi*) pressure (*atsu*) to stimulate the body's inner powers of balance and healing.

Sitz bath. Immersion of the hips and lower body in herbal hot water, followed by cold water, to stimulate the immune system. Also a Kneipp treatment for constipation, hemorrhoids, prostate problems, menstrual problems, and digestive upsets.

Spa cuisine. Fresh, natural foods low in saturated fats and cholesterol, with an emphasis on whole grains, low-fat dairy products, lean protein, fresh fruit, fish, and vegetables and an avoidance of added salt and products containing sodium and artificial colorings, flavorings, and preservatives.

Spinning. Group exercise class on Schwinn stationary bicycles, intended to provide aerobic conditioning by pedaling quickly at varied resistance levels.

Step aerobics. Rhythmic stepping on and off a small platform.

Stress management. A program of meditation and deep relaxation intended to reduce the ill effects of stress on the system.

Sweat lodge. Native American body-purification ceremony.

Swedana. Herbal steam treatment to reduce tension and release impurities through the skin.

Sweat lodge. A Native American–inspired purifying ritual that takes place in a natural sauna made of rocks.

Swedish massage. A treatment that duplicates gymnastics movements with stroking, kneading, friction, vibration, and tapping to relax muscles gently; devised at the University of Stockholm early in the 19th century by Per Heinrik Ling.

Swiss shower. A multijet bath that alternates hot and cold water, often used after mud wraps and other body treatments.

T

Tai chi. (Sometimes called tai chi chuan.) Movements intended to unite body and mind; an ancient Oriental discipline for exercise and meditation.

Target heart rate. The number of heartbeats per minute an individual tries to attain during exercise; the figure is 60% to 90% of one's maximal heart rate. The American College of Sports Medicine recommends maintaining this rate for 20–30 minutes during exercise three to five days a week. See *maximal heart rate.*

Thalassotherapy. Water-based treatments that use seawater, seaweed, algae, and sea air; an ancient Greek therapy.

Trager massage. A technique developed by Milton Trager that employs a gentle, rhythmic shaking of the body to release tension from the joints.

V

Vichy shower. Hydrotherapy treatment; spa guest lies on a cushioned, waterproof mat and is showered by jets.

Vishesh. Deep-tissue friction massage given by two therapists, followed by hot towel treatment.

Vodder massage. Manual lymph drainage technique developed by Danish-born Emile Vodder in the 1950s.

W

Wallyball. Game similar to volleyball, using four walls of an indoor court.

Watsu. An underwater treatment that blends the techniques of deep-tissue massage, acupressure, shiatsu, and yoga.

Y

Yoga. A discipline of stretching and toning the body through movements or asana postures, controlled deep breathing, relaxation techniques, and diet. A school of Hindu philosophy that advocates physical and mental discipline for the unity of mind, body, and spirit. Also *asana*.

Z

Zen shiatsu. A Japanese acupressure art intended to relieve tension and balance the body.

The United States

CANADA

BRITISH COLUMBIA
ALBERTA
SASKATCHEWAN
MANITOBA

Vancouver
Victoria
Calgary
Regina
Winnipeg

Seattle
Olympia
WASHINGTON
Spokane
Columbia R.
Trans-Canada Hwy.

Portland
Salem
Great Falls
Missouri R.

OREGON
IDAHO
MONTANA
Helena
Billings

NORTH DAKOTA
Fargo
Bismarck

Boise
Snake R.

SOUTH DAKOTA
Pierre
Missouri R.

WYOMING

Carson City
Sacramento
San Francisco
NEVADA
Salt Lake City
UTAH
Cheyenne
Denver
NEBRASKA
Lincoln

Fresno
101

Las Vegas
Colorado R.
Colorado Springs
COLORADO
KANSAS

CALIFORNIA
Santa Barbara
Los Angeles
San Diego
Flagstaff
ARIZONA
Phoenix
Tucson

Taos
Albuquerque
Santa Fe
NEW MEXICO
OKLAHOMA
Oklahoma City
Amarillo

PACIFIC OCEAN
BAJA CALIFORNIA
SONORA
El Paso
CHIHUAHUA
Rio Grande
TEXAS
Dallas
Austin
San Antonio

RUSSIA
ARCTIC OCEAN

Bering Sea
Bering Strait
Nome
ALASKA
Fairbanks
CANADA
MEXICO
COAHUILA
NUEVO LEON
TAMAULIPAS

Anchorage

ALEUTIAN ISLANDS
Juneau

PACIFIC OCEAN

Honolulu
Oahu
Maui
HAWAII
Hawaii
PACIFIC OCEAN

0   400 miles
0   400 km

N

ONTARIO
CANADA
QUÉBEC
NEW BRUNSWICK
Québec
Fredericton
MAINE
95
Montréal
Augusta
Lake Superior
Ottawa
Montpelier
91
95
MINNESOTA
Duluth
35
VT
Concord
89
N.H.
Boston
WISCONSIN
MICHIGAN
Lake Huron
Toronto
Lake Ontario
Albany
MASS.
94
St. Paul
Green Bay
Buffalo
90
88
Hartford
R.I.
Providence
Minneapolis
Milwaukee
Lansing
NEW YORK
Lake Erie
87
CONN.
Madison
Detroit
Cleveland
New York
90
94
N.J.
IOWA
Chicago
94
90
80
PENNSYLVANIA
Trenton
Omaha
80
Des Moines
74
39
55
Pittsburgh
Harrisburg
76
Philadelphia
65
69
75
OHIO
77
70
MD
Dover
35
INDIANA
Columbus
Baltimore
DEL.
ILLINOIS
Springfield
Indianapolis
WEST VIRGINIA
Annapolis
Washington, D.C.
opeka
70
Cincinnati
Charleston
95
Richmond
55
Louisville
Frankfort
81
64
Norfolk
Kansas City
St. Louis
VIRGINIA
Jefferson City
KENTUCKY
65
75
95
Raleigh
MISSOURI
44
81
85
NORTH CAROLINA
Tulsa
Nashville
40
77
40
40
ARKANSAS
TENNESSEE
75
Memphis
65
85
Columbia
Little Rock
40
Tennessee
59
75
SOUTH CAROLINA
55
30
Birmingham
Atlanta
GEORGIA
26
MISSISSIPPI
20
85
16
Savannah
Jackson
20
Montgomery
95
Jacksonville
49
ALABAMA
65
75
45
55
Baton Rouge
Mobile
10
Tallahassee
10
12
10
FLORIDA
Orlando
Houston
New Orleans
LOUISIANA
4

ATLANTIC OCEAN

Mississippi R.
Ohio R.
Savannah R.
Mississippi R.

Bahama Islands
75
95
141
Miami
Nassau

Gulf of Mexico

N   0   500 miles
     0   800 km

CUBA

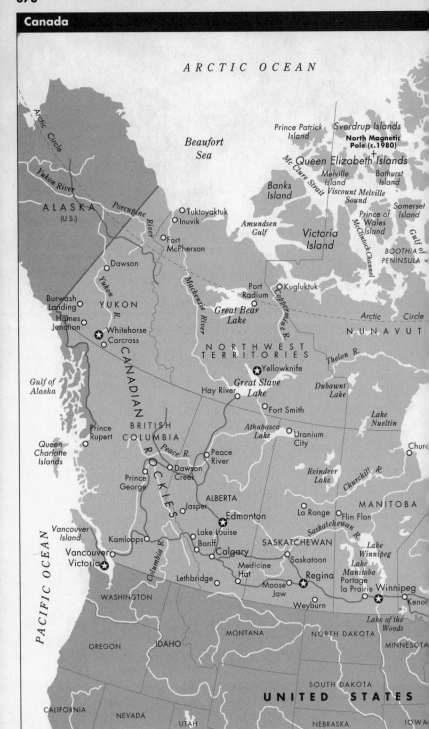

ARCTIC OCEAN

Beaufort
Sea

Prince Patrick
Island

Sverdrup Islands

**North Magnetic
Pole (c.1980)**
+

Queen Elizabeth Islands

McClure Strait

Melville
Island

Bathurst
Island

Viscount Melville
Sound

Banks
Island

Prince of
Wales
Island

Somerset
Island

McClintock Channel

BOOTHIA
PENINSULA

Gulf

ALASKA
(U.S.)

Arctic Circle

Yukon River

Porcupine River

○Tuktoyaktuk
○Inuvik

○Fort
McPherson

Amundsen
Gulf

Victoria
Island

Dawson

Yukon R.

YUKON

Burwash
Landing ○
Haines
Junction ○

✪Whitehorse
○Carcross

Mackenzie River

Port
Radium

Great Bear
Lake

○Kugluktuk

Coppermine R.

Arctic   Circle

N U N A V U T

Gulf of
Alaska

CANADIAN

N O R T H W E S T
T E R R I T O R I E S

Thelon R.

✪Yellowknife

Great Slave
Lake

Hay River

Dubawnt
Lake

Lake
Nueltin

Prince
Rupert

BRITISH
COLUMBIA

Fort Smith

Athabasca
Lake

○Uranium
City

Queen
Charlotte
Islands

Peace R.

Peace
River

Reindeer
Lake

Churchill R.

Chur

Dawson
Creek

Prince
George

ROCKIES

ALBERTA

○Jasper

La Ronge○ ○Flin Flon

M A N I T O B A

Saskatchewan R.

Vancouver
Island

Kamloops○

Columbia R.

✪Edmonton

Lake Louise○
○Banff

Calgary✪

SASKATCHEWAN

○Saskatoon

Lake
Winnipeg

Vancouver○
Victoria○✪

Lethbridge
○

Medicine
Hat○

Moose○
Jaw

Regina✪

Lake
Manitoba

Portage
la Prairie Winnipeg
✪

WASHINGTON

○Weyburn

Kenor

Lake of the
Woods

PACIFIC OCEAN

OREGON

IDAHO

MONTANA

NORTH DAKOTA

MINNESOTA

CALIFORNIA

NEVADA

UTAH

SOUTH DAKOTA

U N I T E D   S T A T E S

NEBRASKA

IOWA

Ellesmere Island

Devon Island

Lancaster Sound

GREENLAND
(Denmark)

Baffin Bay

Baffin Island

Davis Strait

Denmark Strait

ICELAND

Prince Charles Island

Foxe Basin

Lake Amadjuak

Iqaluit ✪

Lake Harbour

Hudson Strait

Southampton Island

Coats Island

Mansel Island

Ivujivik ○

Cape Chidley

Labrador Sea

Ungava Bay

Nain ○

Hudson Bay

Belcher Islands

Fort Severn ○

Severn R.

James Bay

Fort George ○

Moosonee ○

Schefferville ○

LABRADOR

Goose Bay ○

Labrador City ○

Battle Harbour

N E W F O U N D L A N D

Gander ✪

St. John's ✪

Q U E B E C

Sept-Iles ○

Anticosti Island

Lake Mistassini

GASPÉ PENINSULA

St. Lawrence River

ST. PIERRE AND MIQUELON (France)

O N T A R I O

Rimouski ○

Chicoutimi ○

Lake Nipigon

Cochrane ○

Ste.-Agathe-Des-Monts ○

Québec City ✪

Trois-Rivières ○

NEW BRUNSWICK

PRINCE EDWARD ISLAND

Sydney ○

Charlottetown ✪

Thunder Bay ○

Timmins ○

North Bay ○

Montréal ✪

Fredericton ✪

NOVA SCOTIA

Saint John ○

Halifax ✪

Lake Superior

Sudbury ○

Ottawa ✪

Bay of Fundy

Sault Ste. Marie ○

Lake Huron

Toronto ✪

Lake Ontario

MAINE

N

ATLANTIC OCEAN

WISCONSIN

Lake Michigan

MICHIGAN

Niagara Falls ○

Lake Erie

NEW YORK

VT

N.H.

MASSACHUSETTS

R.I.

CONN.

ILLINOIS

INDIANA

OHIO

PENNSYLVANIA

N.J.

0 — 400 miles

0 — 600 km

The Caribbean

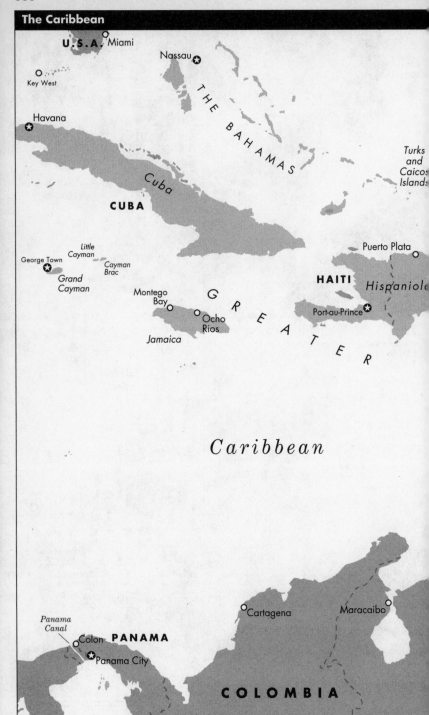

U.S.A. Miami

Key West

Nassau

THE BAHAMAS

Havana

Cuba

CUBA

Turks
and
Caicos
Islands

Little
Cayman

George Town

Cayman
Brac

Grand
Cayman

Puerto Plata

HAITI   *Hispaniola*

Montego
Bay

G R E A T E R

Ocho
Rios

Port-au-Prince

Jamaica

Caribbean

*Panama
Canal*

Colon   PANAMA

Cartagena

Maracaibo

Panama City

COLOMBIA

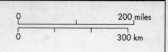

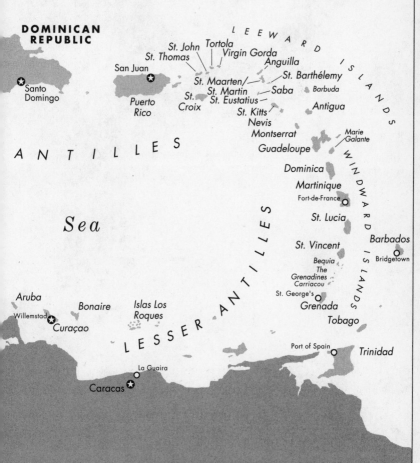

ATLANTIC OCEAN

N

**DOMINICAN
REPUBLIC**

L E E W A R D

St. John *Tortola*

St. Thomas *Virgin Gorda*

San Juan *Anguilla*

*Santo
Domingo*

St. Barthélemy

St. Maarten/

*Puerto
Rico*

St. Martin *Saba* *Barbuda*

St. *St. Eustatius*

Croix *St. Kitts* *Antigua*

Nevis

I S L A N D S

Montserrat

*Marie
Galante*

A N T I L L E S

Guadeloupe

Dominica

W I N D W A R D

Martinique

Sea

Fort-de-France

St. Lucia

I S L A N D S

St. Vincent *Barbados*

Bridgetown

Bequia

The

Grenadines

Carriacou

St. George's

Aruba

Bonaire

*Islas Los
Roques*

Grenada

Tobago

Willemstad

Curaçao

L E S S E R   A N T I L L E S

Port of Spain

Trinidad

La Guaira

Caracas

V E N E Z U E L A

0   200 miles

0   300 km

Tijuana
CA.
Ensenada
Mexicali
ARIZONA
NEW MEXICO
Tucson

BAJA
Nogales
Ciudad
Juárez

Golfo
Nuevo
Casas Grandes
Hermosillo
Chihuahua

de
Guaymas

Ciudad
Obregón
SIERRA

California
Los Mochis
MADRE

La Paz
Culiacán
Gómez
Palacio
Torreón

San José del Cabo
Durango
Fresnillo

Cabo
San Lucas
Mazatlán
OCCIDENTAL
Zacatecas

Túxpan
San Luis Potosí

Tepic
León

Puerto Vallarta
Guadalajara
Guanajuato

Colima
Morelia

Manzanillo
Pátzcuaro
SIERRA

PACIFIC
Ixtapa/
Zihuatanejo

OCEAN
Acapulco

N

0   200 miles

0   300 km

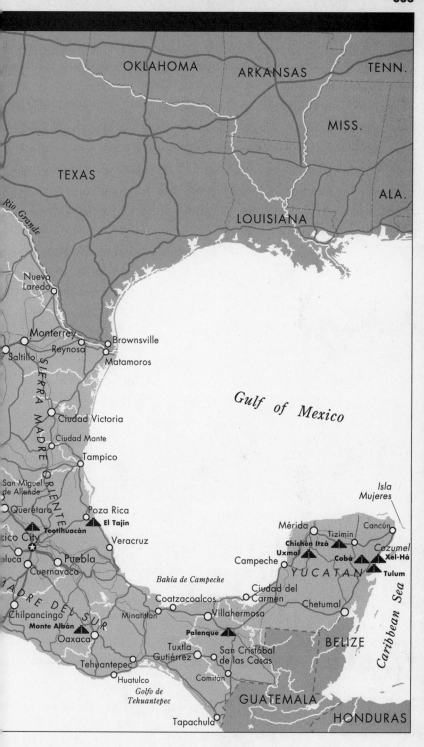

OKLAHOMA

ARKANSAS

TENN.

MISS.

TEXAS

LOUISIANA

ALA.

Rio Grande

Nueva
Laredo

Monterrey
Reynosa

Brownsville

Saltillo

Matamoros

SIERRA MADRE ORIENTAL

Ciudad Victoria

Ciudad Mante

Tampico

Gulf of Mexico

San Miguel
de Allende

Querétaro

Poza Rica

El Tajín

ico City

Teotihuacán

Veracruz

Mérida

*Isla
Mujeres*

Cancún

Chichén Itzá

Tizimín

Cozumel

oluca

Puebla

Uxmal

Campeche

Cobá

Xel-Há

Cuernavaca

YUCATAN

Tulum

MADRE DEL SUR

Bahía de Campeche

Chilpancingo

Monte Albán

Coatzacoalcos

Ciudad del
Carmen

Chetumal

Minatitlán

Villahermosa

Caribbean Sea

Oaxaca

Palenque

Tehuantepec

Tuxtla
Gutiérrez

San Cristóbal
de las Casas

BELIZE

Huatulco

Comitán

*Golfo de
Tehuantepec*

GUATEMALA

HONDURAS

Tapachula

Directory 1: Alphabetical Listing of Resorts

Directory 2:
Listing of
Resorts
by Program

Holistic Health

Luxury Pampering

Medical Wellness

Mineral Springs

Nutrition and Diet

Hilton Head Health Institute *172*
Hippocrates Health Institute *143*
The Kerr House *122*
The Kushi Institute of the Berkshires *208*
La Costa Resort & Spa *29*
Lake Austin Spa Resort *106*
The Last Resort *77*
Lido Spa Hotel *144*
New Life Hiking Spa *226*
Northern Pines Health Resort *203*
The Oaks at Ojai *31*
The Palms *34*
The Peaks Resort & Golden Door Spa *57*
The Phoenician Centre for Well-Being *47*
Preventive Medicine Research Institute *14*
Pritikin Longevity Center (California) *35*
Pritikin Longevity Center (Florida) *150*
PGA National Resort & Spa *146*
Rancho La Puerta *280*
Río Caliente Spa *289*
St. Helena Hospital Health Center *15*
Spa Concept at Le Château Bromont *275*
Structure House *169*
Tassajara Zen Monastery *19*
Tennessee Fitness Spa *175*
Topnotch at Stowe *227*
Uchee Pines Lifestyle Center *131*
Vatra Mountain Valley Lodge & Spa *221*
Westglow Spa *170*
Wyndham Resort & Spa *159*

Sports Conditioning

The Aspen Club *50*
Chateau Whistler Resort *253*
Cliff Lodge at Snowbird *73*
Club Med-Huatulco *304*
Club Tremblant *272*
Disney Institute *135*
The Doral Golf Resort and Spa *137*
Eden Roc Resort & Spa *139*
The Equinox *223*
Four Seasons Resort and Club *104*
Four Seasons Resort Nevis *339*
Gold Lake Mountain Resort & Spa *54*
Golden Eagle *224*
Global Fitness Adventures *53*
Gray Rocks *273*
Green Mountain at Fox Run *225*
Hilton Head Westin Resort *173*
The Inn at Manitou *263*
Kalani Oceanside Retreat *235*
The Kingsmill Resort *179*
Lakeview Fitness Center *198*
Le Sport *346*
The Lodge & Spa at Cordillera *56*
Lodge at Potosi Hot Springs *86*
McKinley Chalet Resort *82*
Mohonk Mountain House *216*

NOTES

NOTES

NOTES

NOTES

Looking for a different kind of vacation?

Fodors makes it easy with a full line of guidebooks to suit a variety of interests—from sports and adventure to romance to family fun.

At bookstores everywhere.
www.fodors.com

WHEREVER YOU TRAVEL, *H*ELP IS NEVER FAR AWAY.

From planning your trip to

providing travel assistance along

the way, American Express®

Travel Service Offices are

always there to help

you do more.